FUTURE OF REGIONAL COOPERATION IN ASIA AND THE PACIFIC

Book Endorsements

Armida Salsiah Alisjahbana
Under-Secretary-General of the United Nations and Executive Secretary of ESCAP

The regional integration framework can promote smooth translation of sustainable development strategies and policies into meaningful action. Such framework has been benefiting countries over the decades to raise their living standard; and mitigating adverse impacts of new and emerging socio-economic challenges.

However, regional integration and coordination of trade and investment policies are not high on the agenda of regional and global fora. Recently, countries are undertaking unilateral policies that threaten the basic principles of the rule-based economic cooperation and practices. In view of this uncertain economic environment, "Future of Regional Cooperation in Asia and the Pacific", co-edited by Bambang Susantono and Cyn-Young Park, brings to the forefront the importance of regional integration in Asia and the Pacific. By detailing the policy implications of deepening integrative processes, the book analytically clarifies the selected areas of priority such as technology, infrastructure, and trade and investment; and identifies the opportunities for a successful regional integration.

The authors have also elaborated on a broader context of the regional engagements that can highlight various interrelated processes, which could unleash the spirit of regional cooperation. The diverse perspectives of these chapters could also provide essential lessons for countries to learn from each other in the region. To this end, this book underscores the importance of regional cooperation as an important tool to address the challenges to advancing the 2030 Agenda for Sustainable Development in our region.

I am confident that this book will be used by academics and policy makers in Asia and Pacific and beyond.

Peter A. Petri
Carl J. Shapiro Professor of International Finance, Brandeis University

Although many essays in this book were written before the coronavirus pandemic, their themes resonate even more directly in the wake of the crisis. The joint provision of Asian public goods will advance Asian interests not just in health but also in many other fields. Moreover, "strengthening the bond within Asia will enable the region to contribute to solving global issues." Asian cooperation has never been more important than today, given global uncertainty and wavering leadership. The book addresses this challenge with a sophisticated analytical framework and state-of-the-art econometric studies of regional public goods arising in infrastructure, investments, trade and finance. But it does not stop there, it also offers recommendations for institutional change. For example, it shows that financial integration has lagged trade and investment cooperation, with frequent adverse effects on regional financial stability, and then offers practical suggestions for work in those areas. The book will be an excellent resource for scholars of regional economic connections, policy makers committed to better regional institutions, and indeed all serious students of Asian integration.

Michael G. Plummer
Director, SAIS Europe and Eni Professor of International Economics
The Johns Hopkins University

The momentum behind international economic integration slowed significantly after the Great Recession of 2008-09, weighed down by rising protectionism, stasis at the multilateral level, and the US-China trade conflict, which has had a particularly deleterious effect on Asia-Pacific trade and investment. The COVID-19 pandemic has posed a new set of challenges. But economic cooperation can overcome conflict and crisis; it just takes the right approach and bold leadership. This excellent book, *Future of Regional Cooperation in Asia and the Pacific*, is remarkable in its scope and depth in identifying and evaluating salient modalities of cooperation and integration in Asia and the Pacific, from trade and finance to technology and public goods, using a variety of cutting-edge empirical techniques and interesting conceptual frameworks. Drs. Susantono and Park should be commended on this very important contribution, and their outstanding job in bringing together such an interesting set of issues and a great team of researchers to tackle them.

Hal Hill
H.W. Arndt Professor Emeritus of Southeast Asian Economies
College of Asia and the Pacific, Australian National University

The editors and contributors are to be congratulated for these 14 stimulating, analytical and policy-relevant papers examining various aspects of regional cooperation in the Asia-Pacific region. The scope is commendably broad and eclectic, from theoretical foundations and empirical analysis to 'new' challenges such as managing the COVID-19 crisis and carbon market cooperation. Highly recommended.

Mari Pangestu
Managing Director of Development Policy and Partnerships
The World Bank

For the past five decades, regional cooperation and integration has served this region well in boosting shared prosperity and reducing poverty. The COVID-19 pandemic has caused a historic setback to decades of development progress, and also exposed gaps in regional cooperation. This is a moment for reflection for policy makers across Asia and the Pacific and, as COVID-19 reshapes the world, we need to think innovatively on how future regional cooperation could be strengthened and be more agile in addressing the development challenges of our time. This publication is an important contribution towards that endeavor.

Kunio Mikuriya
Secretary General
World Customs Organization

This book focuses on broad themes that support the goal of building a more inclusive, resilient, and sustainable future for the Asia and the Pacific region. Undoubtedly, regional cooperation and integration is one of the key ingredients to achieve this rather ambitious goal and customs administrations play an important role in it. A role which has become even more crucial during a global crisis of the magnitude of the COVID-19 pandemic. Additionally, e-commerce is rapidly advancing, while digitalization is creating new trade opportunities that will further contribute to the economic development and integration of the region. From a customs perspective, this book provides insights on how customs and other border agencies could work together with the trade and transport sectors, and effectively contribute to reaching the common goals of greater regional cooperation and integration.

FUTURE OF REGIONAL COOPERATION IN ASIA AND THE PACIFIC

Edited by Bambang Susantono and Cyn-Young Park

NOVEMBER 2020

ADB

ASIAN DEVELOPMENT BANK

Corrigenda to ADB publications may be found at http://www.adb.org/publications/corrigenda.

Notes:
In this publication, "$" refers to United States dollars.
ADB recognizes "Hong Kong" as Hong Kong, China; "China" as the People's Republic of China; "Korea" as the Republic of Korea; and "Great Britain" as the United Kingdom.

Cover design by Achilleus De Mesa Coronel.

Contents

Tables, Figures, and Boxes

TABLES

FIGURES

BOXES

Foreword

Regional cooperation has been a powerful force for economic development and inclusive growth in Asia and the Pacific.[1] This has been accomplished through trade and investment agreements, technology cooperation, cross-border infrastructure projects, and the creation of regional institutions. The region has made significant progress toward economic integration over the past half century because of increased trade and investment, infrastructure connectivity, and mobility among its populations. The economies of Asia have also benefited from policy coordination that builds on shared goals and common political will.

In spite of these important gains, the region is now facing considerable challenges, with notable disruptions to global trade, supply chains, and travel due to the coronavirus disease (COVID-19) pandemic. Addressing these challenges will require stronger and more coordinated actions to reconnect economies, rebuild trade and transport links, and safely restore free movement for people by making the best use of digitalization and innovation. The COVID-19 pandemic is also revealing the need to strengthen communities and enhance social equity through regional cooperation and integration, in order to ensure a recovery that is robust, inclusive, and sustainable. Increased investments in regional health cooperation, promotion of disaster and climate resilience, and protection of ocean health are clear cases for urgent coordinated action.

I am pleased to introduce this edited collection of peer-reviewed research on regional integration and cooperation in Asia. It is critically important at this moment to examine the extent to which various forms of regional cooperation have contributed to the achievement of development goals. Such

---

[1] Asia and the Pacific, hereinafter referred to as Asia, refers to the 46 developing member economies of the Asian Development Bank (ADB) plus Australia, Japan, and New Zealand.

analysis will provide insights on how future regional cooperation initiatives can be strengthened and reimagined for a world reshaped by the COVID-19 pandemic, so that economies across the region can quickly and effectively tackle issues such as widening inequality, regional and global health crises, and climate change. It is clear that addressing each of these challenges requires strong coordination, shared resources, and effective cross-border institutions.

This book contains detailed studies that are useful for policy makers, researchers, and others with an interest in the Asia region and beyond. The studies critically examine regional cooperation initiatives through the lens of addressing the development challenges for neighboring economies through collective dialogue, commitment, and action. These works capture the experience and lessons gained from pursuing the goals of sustainable development and high and inclusive growth through increased economic cooperation and integration.

To maintain this growth while also rebuilding for sustainability, resilience, and inclusive development in the face of large-scale shocks brought about by events such as natural disasters and global pandemics, the region must continue to rethink its regional cooperation and integration strategies. This reexamination should include strategies to bolster solidarity, network connectivity, and sustainability across economies. Asia needs to accelerate its efforts to build regional infrastructure, remove barriers, and manage transboundary water and environmental issues.

While some have suggested that recent border closures and travel restrictions are signs that globalization has ground irreversibly to a halt, I believe that globalization will return, but in a different shape. To prepare wisely for this renewed globalization, the economies of Asia and the Pacific need to usher in a strengthened and open regionalism for the post-pandemic era—so that the Asia region can continue to be the engine of global economic growth and make solid progress toward achieving the Sustainable Development Goals. I hope this collection of knowledge work will contribute to regaining this momentum.

I am grateful to the authors, researchers, and editors of the studies contained here for their contributions to this important discussion.

Masatsugu Asakawa
President
Asian Development Bank

Preface

Open trade and investment is critical to the region's prosperity and development. By creating new jobs and business opportunities, transferring technology, and promoting innovation, open trade and investment has cultivated a vibrant middle class in many countries. Over the past 50 years, regional cooperation and integration (RCI) in Asia and the Pacific has accelerated, spurring robust economic growth and a sharp reduction in poverty. Regional institutions have been created, nurtured, and empowered with the political will and necessary structures to address common challenges and achieve shared ambitions, such as the United Nations Sustainable Development Goals. Various regional institutions and subregional economic cooperation initiatives with support of the Asian Development Bank (ADB) have also laid the foundation for deeper and more effective RCI.

However, the COVID-19 crisis threatens to reverse economic, social, and development gains made over the past few decades and widen the gap between the haves and have nots. Unprecedented disruptions to global trade and a synchronized fall in global demand brought by the pandemic may reinforce the trend of deglobalization that began some time ago. In these conditions, it is crucial to reassess development pathways by seizing new opportunities through deeper regional cooperation and integration. Robust intraregional trade and investment linkages can drive inclusive, resilient, and sustainable growth. Further, reducing remaining barriers to trade and investment is essential, especially for smaller countries eager to compete in international markets and become the region's next economic tigers. Deeper regional cooperation is also needed to tackle development challenges that have transnational—or even transcontinental—implications. These challenges include cross-border infrastructure and connectivity, regional health security and infectious disease control, climate change, disaster risk, and other potential crisis management issues.

This book is a compilation of research papers on the RCI development agenda prepared over the past several years for ADB's annual *Asian Economic Integration Report*. It explores how to strengthen and better leverage RCI to help attain the Sustainable Development Goals.

The four pillars of ADB's RCI strategy promote (i) infrastructure connectivity, (ii) regional public goods, (iii) regional trade and investment, and (iv) financial cooperation. The papers in this book demonstrate that stronger regional cooperation can deliver solutions to development challenges in Asia and the Pacific by building regional infrastructure, boosting intraregional trade and investment, and strengthening regional institutions. The papers also show the value of increased financial cooperation. Since the 1997/98 Asian financial crisis, the region's policy makers have made great strides in reducing financial vulnerabilities and creating a regional financial safety net to protect economies from new shocks. As we look to the future, they should also strive to enhance regional health security, increase resilience in public health systems, step up carbon market cooperation for a low-carbon economy, and protect ocean health.

Bambang Susantono
Vice-President for Knowledge Management and Sustainable Development
Asian Development Bank

Cyn-Young Park
Director, Regional Cooperation and Integration Division
Economic Research and Regional Cooperation Department
Asian Development Bank

Acknowledgments

This book contains a collection of scholarly papers on regional cooperation and integration.

Bambang Susantono, Vice-President, Knowledge Management and Sustainable Development, Asian Development Bank (ADB), and **Cyn-Young Park**, Director of the Regional Cooperation and Integration Division, Economic Research and Regional Cooperation Department, ADB, edited this book, comprising 14 chapters in four parts.

The editors would like to thank the following contributors whose insights and research made this collection possible:

Manuel Leonard Albis—Assistant Professor, School of Statistics, University of the Philippines.

Ricardo Ang III—PhD economics student and graduate research assistant, Andrew Young School of Policy Studies, Georgia State University.

Douglas Arner—Kerry Holdings Professor in Law, University of Hong Kong; Senior Fellow of Melbourne Law School, University of Melbourne; and Non-Executive Director of Aptorum Group [NASDAQ: APM].

Emilios Avgouleas—Chair of International Banking Law and Finance, University of Edinburgh.

Scott Barrett—Vice Dean, School of International and Public Affairs & Earth Institute, Columbia University.

Steven Beck—Advisor (Trade and Supply Chain Finance), Private Sector Operations Department, ADB.

Ross Buckley—Scientia Professor, and King & Wood Mallesons Chair of International Finance Law, University of South Wales.

Stijn Claessens—Head of Financial Stability Policy and Deputy Head of the Monetary and Economic Department, Bank for International Settlements.

Megan Counahan—former Health Specialist, Central and West Asia Department, ADB.

Virender Kumar Duggal—Principal Climate Change Specialist, Sustainable Development and Climate Change Department, ADB.

Michael Griffin—Technical Officer, Strategic Development and Partnerships, World Health Organization.

Jong Woo Kang—Principal Economist, Regional Cooperation and Integration Division, Economic Research and Regional Cooperation Department, ADB.

Fahad Khan—Economist at Economic Analysis and Operational Support Division, Economic Research and Regional Cooperation Department, ADB.

Sonalini Khetrapal—Health Specialist, Health Sector Group, Sector Advisory Service Cluster, Sustainable Development and Climate Change Department, ADB.

Kijin Kim—Economist at Regional Cooperation and Integration Division, Economic Research and Regional Cooperation Department, ADB.

Chang-Soo Lee—Professor at College of International Studies, Kyung Hee University.

Hyun-Hoon Lee—Professor, Department of International Trade and Business, Kangwon National University

Junkyu Lee—Chief of Finance Sector Group, Sustainable Development and Climate Change Department, ADB.

Eva McGovern—consultant, Sustainable Development and Climate Change Department, ADB.

Anna Oposa—consultant, Sustainable Development and Climate Change Department, ADB.

Lisa Kircher Pagkalinawan—consultant, Sustainable Development and Climate Change Department, ADB.

Jane Parry—independent consultant and communications expert.

Natalia Ramondo—Associate Professor of Economics, School of Global Policy & Strategy.

Peter Rosenkranz—Economist at Regional Cooperation and Integration Division, Economic Research and Regional Cooperation Department, ADB.

Susann Roth—Principal Knowledge Sharing and Services Specialist, Knowledge Advisory Service Center, Sustainable Development and Climate Change Department, ADB

Todd Sandler—Chair Emeritus Vibhooti Shukla Professor of Economics and Political Economy, University of Texas at Dallas.

Gerard Servais—Unit Head, Project Administration, Southeast Asia Department, ADB.

Mara Claire Tayag—Senior Economics Officer at Regional Cooperation and Integration Division, Economic Research and Regional Cooperation Department, ADB.

Bambang Susantono and Cyn-Young Park led the editorial team with production and editorial support from Paulo Rodelio Halili, Mara Claire Tayag, and Carol Ongchangco. James Unwin assisted in editing work. Joseph Manglicmot typeset and produced the layout, Joe Mark Ganaban assisted in typesetting, and Achilleus De Mesa Coronel created the cover design. Lawrence Casiraya proofread the report with assistance from Paulo Rodelio Halili and Carol Ongchangco, while Marjorie Celis handled the page proof checking. Support for printing and publishing was provided by the Printing Services Unit of ADB's Office of Administrative Services and by the Department of Communications. Karen Lane, Duncan Mcleod, Rolando Avendano, Kijin Kim, and Maria Criselda Aherrera coordinated the launch and dissemination of the book.

Executive Summary and Overview

Asia and the Pacific[1] as a region has emerged as a new growth pole that helped pull the global economy out of the recession associated with the global financial crisis of 2008–2009 and contributed to a more balanced and resilient global economic expansion. At the end of 2019, Asia accounted for 34.5% of world gross domestic product (GDP) up from 16.3% in 1970. Excluding the advanced economies of Australia, Japan, and New Zealand, the share likewise increased to 26.9% from 7.5% over the same period. But the coronavirus disease (COVID-19) outbreak that began in Wuhan, People's Republic of China (PRC) in December 2019 and spread globally, presents unprecedented challenges to Asia and beyond. As of 5 October 2020, there are more than 35 million confirmed cases, including more than a million deaths globally. Most countries and territories around the world have imposed lockdowns of varying degrees, pushing the global economy into its worst recession in recent history.

Nearly 10 months into the pandemic, there is no clear end in sight. While a small number of countries are slowly reopening with great caution, the global economy is still in a fragile state. However, the global trade environment has turned cloudy in recent months, with heightened geopolitical uncertainties including the United States (US)-PRC trade tensions and the continued disruptions in supply chains and logistics, adding concerns to the growth prospect of the global economy. The precarious global situation in turn calls for renewed regional efforts to maintain economic openness and use regional cooperation and integration as a platform to further advance achievement of development goals.

Asia is a region of vast socioeconomic diversity. Given the region's huge diversity, near-term goals and strategies will mean different things to

---

[1]   Asia and the Pacific, hereinafter referred to as Asia, refers to the 46 developing member economies of the Asian Development Bank (ADB) plus Australia, Japan, and New Zealand.

different economies. Nevertheless, the region's economies share the important objectives of sustaining high growth and making that growth inclusive. For the vast potential of developing Asia to be realized, the power of regional cooperation needs to be strengthened and leveraged, paying greater attention to making the impacts more inclusive while ensuring them to be more socially and environmentally sustainable.

Despite Asia's impressive growth over the past half a century, the region remains home to almost half of the world's poor, while large development gaps persist. Sustained high growth is essential. But growth alone has proven insufficient for poverty reduction and at times has even exacerbated worrying trends toward greater inequality and environmental degradation that destabilize economies, destroy local communities, and undermine social cohesion. Given uncertainties over global economic strength, inclusive and sustainable growth in Asia is imperative for the region's own prosperity and for a balanced and resilient global economy.

Greater regional cooperation holds a key to unlock the potential of Asia's regional dynamism to achieve more balanced, inclusive, and sustainable growth. Recognizing its enormous potential, ADB has adopted regional cooperation and integration (RCI) as one of the seven operational priorities of its Strategy 2030.[2] With its vision to achieve a prosperous, inclusive, resilient, and sustainable Asia and the Pacific, ADB aims to increase support for connectivity, provision of regional public goods and collective actions to mitigate cross-border risks such as climate change, pollution, energy and water security, and communicable and infectious diseases, while enhancing financial sector cooperation and subregional initiatives for greater market integration.

Efforts toward reaching the Sustainable Development Goals (SDGs) can also create important synergy for the region's pursuit of environmentally and socially sustainable growth by minimizing environmental degradation and strengthening the public provision of social protections and services. Regional cooperation should be also leveraged to encourage regional economies to

---

[2] In 2018, ADB launched a renewed corporate strategy, Strategy 2030, which recognizes regional cooperation and integration (RCI) as a strategic operational priority. RCI is the seventh operational priority under Strategy 2030 which will be executed through the following strategic directions. https://www.adb.org/sites/default/files/institutional-document/435391/strategy-2030-main-document.pdf; https://www.adb.org/documents/strategy-2030-op7-regional-cooperation-integration.

exert positive influence on each other in design and implementation of public policies and provision of regional public goods.

More forceful collaboration on regional public goods will maximize opportunities arising from strong regional dynamics to achieve the SDGs. More importantly, stronger regional cooperation is a must to deal with transboundary vulnerabilities and risks such as the spread of infectious diseases like COVID-19 and climate hazards. With growing economic and policy interdependence, the regional economies face many development challenges that have increasingly transnational impacts. Regional cooperation can help tackle critical economic, social, and environmental issues commonly facing the regional economies more efficiently and effectively. More importantly, it can create peer pressure to mobilize support for significant causes and produce collective actions for common objectives—such as tackling key social issues, controlling regional health risks, and achieving environmental sustainability. Strong policy coordination through sharing knowledge and experience could promote best practices and maximize policy impacts by creating synergy and reducing duplication.

The strengthening of regional economic ties needs to go on to be leveraged to bring poor countries together in regional trade and production networks. Increasing regional business activity will naturally lead to further economic integration. The building of physical and communication infrastructure to facilitate trade needs to be focused on connecting the poor, remote, and disadvantaged to regional centers. Connectivity, both physical and human, can allow the poor to take advantage of the regional economic and social network, and so improve job opportunities and welfare. Adequate supply of quality infrastructure is fundamental for all of the above by facilitating cross-border mobility of labor and capital in the drive to allocate the region's resources more efficiently—enhancing productivity and reducing development gaps along the way.

Policies should also promote regional cooperation with aim to reinvigorate growth that supports broader economic participation and generate socially equitable results. For example, boosting intraregional trade and investments can strengthen resilient trade and supply chains at the time of waning support for globalization, while contributing to productive employment and economic opportunities for all participants. It is also important to understand how the rise of global and regional value chains and the digital economy, and the transformation of many economies toward services sectors present opportunities for developing economies to engage in international trade. In doing so, however, open trade may also worsen widening inequalities unless proper policy attention is paid to improving the distribution of growth benefits and reducing barriers to economic participation of socially disadvantaged groups through domestic structural reforms. A significant part of the answer to achieving socially equitable results through trade is to provide targeted support to sectors that are highly likely to benefit the socially excluded and underrepresented groups, such as small and medium-sized enterprises and female-owned firms that struggle to reach international markets.

Beyond the active trade of manufacturing goods, policy efforts should aim to accelerate the liberalization of financial services and ease impediments to cross-border financial flows and capital market developments. Financial development eventually leading to market integration is an essential part of economic integration and will improve allocative efficiency of financial resources, therefore enhancing competitiveness of regional economies. Yet risks of financial contagion are real, calling for effective cross-border policy coordination to prevent and manage crisis risks. Regional financial cooperation should focus on increasing regulatory oversight to avoid a buildup of systemic risks and strengthening financial safety nets to effectively respond to financial crisis that may derail growth.

In this context, this book focuses on areas within four broad themes for spurring policy efforts toward creating more inclusive, resilient, and sustainable future for Asia-Pacific economies by: (1) promoting regional public goods that are supplied by states in geographic proximity and that primarily benefit the states in the region; (2) leveraging trade and investment for inclusive growth, particularly through boosting intraregional trade and foreign direct investment to raise participation in global value chains; (3) strengthening financial cooperation with special policy attention to crisis prevention and management; and (4) building resilience in preparing for the post-COVID-19.

Overview of the Book

This book is divided into four parts. Part I, *Regional Public Goods* (Chapters 1–4), looks at the conceptual foundations of regional public goods, their spillovers, and cross-border effects. Investments in regional infrastructure, health, and the environment help tackle common development challenges facing regional economies more effectively and efficiently. But spillovers, cross-border effects, and other factors leading to missing markets and market failures make investment in regional public goods very difficult. The value of matching investments in regional public goods to meet specific needs—one that takes full account of efficiencies in sharing knowledge and building institutional capacity—is explained and how to resolve these issues through collective actions is explored.

Part II, *Trade and Investment* (Chapters 5–7) discusses trade facilitation, global value chains, and foreign direct investment in the region. Trade has played an essential role in economic growth and poverty reduction in Asia and the Pacific by opening up markets to investment and contributing to job creation. Yet even as total trade volume has grown an average 12% a year between 1960 and 2018 in Asia, the gains have been uneven. Recognition of the forces at play and how opportunities afforded by cross-border infrastructure and technology, alongside the evolution of online platforms for trade and finance, can help the benefits of trade to be shared more broadly. This part also considers how foreign direct investment by multinational firms can spur the region's involvement in global value chains and productivity growth.

Part III, *Financial Cooperation* (Chapters 8–10), reviews the lessons the policy makers have learned from past financial crises, including the Asian financial crisis 1997/1998 and the global financial crisis of 2008/2009. It demonstrates the finance sector and its growing global network as a channel for increased volatility and duration in financial cycles, although empirical research should go deeper and wider to increase clarity about the links between macroeconomic conditions and finance. In line with globalized finance and increased prominence of financial cycles, building effective institutions for systemic crisis prevention and management is important. The region's financial authorities should be vigilant to take every opportunity to identify potential sources of instability. Part III ends with an analysis of financial conditions in Asia, which concludes that greater regional financial cooperation is essential for safeguarding regional financial stability and should be elevated in the regional policy agenda.

Part IV, *Building Resilience* (Chapters 11–14), takes a renewed look at growing concerns about regional health issues triggered by the COVID-19 as well as how to pave paths to a resilient future in Asia through stronger regional cooperation on health, carbon markets, and ocean health. Asia has been at high risk for emerging and re-emerging infectious diseases, including those with pandemic potential. Adding to a complex set of emerging threats to human health facing the region, frequency and severity of natural hazards and adverse climate events have increased. Sustaining high growth without doing irreversible damage to the environment has been a big challenge for most developing countries. Given the complexity of the dynamic relations between health, climate change, and development, the region needs to rethink its development strategies to build resilience in national and regional health systems against infectious disease outbreaks, reduce greenhouse gas emissions, and generate new opportunities and jobs from the green and blue economy.

Regional Public Goods

In **Chapter 1**, *Scott Barrett* explains that regional public goods often cannot be supplied unless enough states first possess the capacity to supply national public goods. Regional disease elimination, for example, depends on each state in the region being able to control the disease domestically. Similarly, the supply of global public goods often demands minimal state and regional capacity. Although sovereignty causes countries to adopt policies and to make investments that are of a local and national nature, once the most attractive of these opportunities has been exploited, it needs to look for other ways to advance the well-being of its citizens. Regional cooperation is one such way. The chapter finds that, in most case, the supply of regional public goods can be a more sensible response than pursuit only of national goals. Examples of how this holds true focus on climate change mitigation, such as how integrated electricity grids can boost the economics of renewable energy, or how technologies like electric vehicles are more likely to be adopted if investment is coordinated at the regional level.

The role of particular Asian institutions in providing subregional, regional, and transregional public goods is considered in **Chapter 2**, where *Todd Sandler* presents in-depth analysis of regional public goods with a focus on their technologies of aggregation. Seven essential aggregator technologies are related to the prognosis for efficient provision of regional public goods. The chapter finds that while little policy intervention is required for aggregator technologies that provide some types of regional public goods, but in other situations, Asian institutions at subregional and regional levels are needed to pool efforts, build capacity, or shore up weakest-link contributors. At times, low-income countries often with low capacity would go to international communities or multilateral institutions to enable their efforts. The chapter also relates connectivity, natural resources and environment, and peace and security as among the predominant gaps in regional public goods that can be enhanced by policy intervention.

Regionally coordinated infrastructure, access to the internet, and advancements in human capital are making positive contributions to economic growth in Asia. *Kijin Kim, Junkyu Lee, Manuel Leonard Albis, and Ricardo B. Ang III* explore this in detail in **Chapter 3**, with analysis of the effects of road and rail transportation, energy sector investments and the provision of information and communication technology (telephone, mobile, and broadband) on GDP growth rates in domestic economies that have developed these infrastructures, and on the spillovers to neighboring countries. Spatial panel regression models on broadband infrastructure and human capital indicate statistically robust positive externalities. Such spillover effects suggest that the quantity and quality of a nation's infrastructure can have a key role on economic growth in its neighboring countries.

Part I ends with an examination of infrastructure shocks in developing Asia in **Chapter 4**, where *Chang-Soo Lee, Junkyu Lee, and Kijin Kim* measure the economic impacts of cross-border infrastructure and technology using computable general equilibrium models. The findings suggest that large-scale infrastructure in the economies in Asia and the Pacific stimulates the region's economic growth, although the effects on individual economies are not significant across the board. Moreover, trading partners of the infrastructure-stimulating region, such as Japan, the Republic of Korea, other developed Asian countries, and countries like the US and European Union members, benefit from the region's infrastructure projects through their inputs in building the infrastructure. The chapter concludes that foreign beneficiaries' participation in the region's infrastructure projects is recommended.

Trade and Investment

In **Chapter 5**, *Fahad Khan and Kijin Kim* discuss how relatively high trade costs and restricted access to international trade, including due to both tariffs and nontariff barriers, need to be reduced to promote trade and share the benefits of trade more broadly and evenly. They show the importance of reducing trade costs through improved domestic and cross-border connectivity, why institutional reform is needed, and how global initiatives such as Aid for Trade and the Trade Facilitation Agreement can help developing economies improve trading conditions where resource and capacity constraints are major impediments.

In **Chapter 6**, *Natalia Ramondo* highlights new evidence on the determinants of the activity of affiliates of multinational firms in Asia and their participation in global value chains, presenting unique data from all countries in the region which allows affiliates to be classified as serving host markets or as trade-oriented. The key finding is that a country's engagement in global value chain trade is positively related to the presence of trade-oriented foreign plants. The chapter finds that trade-oriented foreign affiliates are more likely found among large plants in poorer countries with exports in downstream sectors, weaker rule of law, relatively more labor than capital, and low cost to export. Also, the more that affiliates have strong input–output links with their parent, the more likely they are to engage in international trade—the effect appears strongest for the PRC. Finally, stronger input–output links among domestic firms in an industry seems to attract foreign firms, regardless of their activity.

Many studies have found that foreign direct investment (FDI) can play a positive role in spurring economic growth and income of host countries. *Hyun-Hoon Lee* ends Part II by looking further into the role of foreign cooperation in host economies, with **Chapter 7** taking a broad view of policy factors that influence FDI decisions. Taking data on bilateral greenfield investments and mergers and acquisitions involving foreign investors across 26 countries, the chapter finds that FDI flows from high-income to developing countries are significantly influenced by the quality of local governance in services sectors; more so than for the primary sector. A favorable business environment in developing countries may help overcome poor local governance because it encourages high-income countries to make greenfield investments, whereas multinationals from emerging economies appear to be less concerned with local business environments.

Financial Cooperation

The global financial crisis of 2008 spurred a major rethink about the role of the banking and finance sector in the volatility in economic fluctuations and how it should be reflected in policymaking. *Stijn Claessens* in **Chapter 8** contends that the intricacies of the global finance sector have emerged as a source and transmission channel of shocks in tandem with financial cycles that are longer and deeper than business cycles. This chapter reviews current thinking on why and how financial cycles arise, with emphasis on their domestic and cross-border implications in emerging Asia. Lastly, it draws the lessons of financial crises, reviewing their causes and consequences of crises. It finds that good crisis management and prevention policies would be essential to ensure financial and economic stability amid recurring financial crises.

Fragility that periodically erupts into a full-blown financial crisis is an integral and increasingly common feature of market-based financial systems. This belies perceptions that financial systems are normally stable. In **Chapter 9**, *Ross P. Buckley, Emilios Avgouleas, and Douglas W. Arner* set out the case for arguing that when the timing of the next major crisis remains elusive to expert eyes, the best preparation is to build defenses, including effective institutions, while trying to identify potential sources of instability. The chapter compares and contrasts the three major crises of the past three decades, both to distill the lessons to be learned from them and to identify what more can be done to strengthen financial systems throughout the world. The chapter concludes that the region's policy makers should take every opportunity to learn and work to build stronger and more effective financial systems.

The succeeding chapter shows in detail how financial integration is an important part of the policy agenda for Asia. In **Chapter 10**, *Cyn-Young Park, Peter Rosenkranz, and Mara Claire Tayag* explain that potential benefits of financial integration are significant because it offers opportunities for better consumption smoothing and risk sharing across borders. However, they also demonstrate that financial integration can be an important transmission channel for global shocks and financial contagion. The chapter presents an analysis of Asia's financial integration using measures based on quantity and price of international financial assets. It assesses the risks of financial contagion associated with financial integration by estimating the impact of global and regional shocks on local equity and bond markets in Asia. After discussing the need for policy reforms aimed at enhancing financial efficiency, inclusivity, and stability, in the region, the chapter concludes that episodes of financial crisis prove that regional financial cooperation is essential in responding to systemic risks and for safeguarding regional financial stability.

Building Resilience

During the COVID-19 pandemic, the global market for personal protective equipment (PPE) has not properly functioned due to a surge in demand and constraints in supply and logistics, including export bans for PPE and key materials. In **Chapter 11**, *Cyn-Young Park, Kijin Kim, Susann Roth, Steven Beck, Jong Woo Kang, Mara Claire Tayag, and Michael Griffin* argued concerted efforts both within and across borders should be made to boost production and open up exports while mobilizing available supplies more efficiently, mapping manufacturing facilities and their capacities, and closely monitoring the evolution of the supply and demand. Multilateral development banks including ADB can help support PPE producers with funding and logistics capacity; strengthen supply chain and trade finance programs; and target aid to support vulnerable groups such as women, children, and the elderly.

Regional cooperation is essential to protect health security across Asia and the Pacific. In **Chapter 12**, *Megan Counahan, Sonalini Khetrapal, Jane Parry, Gerard Servais, and Susann Roth* highlight the region's vulnerabilities to infectious diseases. As the coronavirus disease (COVID-19) pandemic has starkly illustrated, many countries in the region have been hot spots for emerging and re-emerging diseases, due to a confluence of factors including close proximity of human and domestic husbandry, climate, poverty, high population density, and insufficient disease surveillance, diagnostic capacity, and outbreak reporting. Strengthening national regional health systems is an important building block for regional health security. They also emphasize the fundamental need for cross-border and multilateral support and cooperation in protecting health security.

In **Chapter 13**, *Virender Kumar Duggal* discusses how carbon markets provide an opportunity to reduce carbon emissions in a cost-effective manner and incentivize revenue transfers and technology diffusion. This chapter aims to improve understanding of the economics of carbon markets based on an overview of existing carbon markets, notably the Emissions Trading Systems (ETSs). It discusses potential of carbon markets in the post 2020 era under Article 6 of the Paris Agreement. In designing the strategies for increased use of carbon markets, the chapter not only highlights the effectiveness of carbon markets as a climate policy tool moving forward but also its potential in guiding countries toward a cost effective and low-carbon path. While barriers remain, carbon markets can help the region reduce greenhouse gas emissions and carve a pathway to a low-carbon economy.

The Asia and Pacific region faces a unique connection and dependence on the oceans, but transboundary threats such as climate change, pollution, overfishing and unsustainable development, as well as weak enforcement of regulations, have pushed the region's ocean ecosystems to the brink of collapse. In **Chapter 14,** *Lisa Kircher Pagkalinawan, Anna Oposa, and Eva McGovern* argue that regional cooperation can help address these issues through coordinated implementation of best practices, good governance, and enforcement of international agreements among country governments, international and local organizations. This chapter discusses the region's progress and prospects for a resilient future by improving ocean health and stimulating the blue economy.

PART 1
REGIONAL PUBLIC GOODS

"International cooperation is vital to keeping our globe safe, commerce flowing, and our planet habitable."

Angus Deaton, 2015 Nobel Laureate in Economics

Regional Public Goods: Conceptual Foundations

1

Scott Barrett

Throughout history, humanity has endeavored to improve the human condition. Over the last several decades, almost every conceivable measure of well-being has improved, including life expectancy at birth, infant mortality, literacy, civil and political freedoms, and the material standard of living. These have not always improved steadily. Reversals have happened; for example, civil and political freedoms have recently fallen in some countries (Freedom House 2018). Improvements have not been uniformly distributed (per capita incomes have not converged, either domestically or internationally) and some countries have advanced much more than others. Overall, however, the improvements achieved in recent decades have been remarkable.

Another remarkable observation is that data on these key constituents of human well-being are prepared and presented at the country rather than at the local or regional levels. The reason, of course, is that national institutions are primarily responsible for these outcomes. Institutions like property rights systems, the rule of law, and contract enforcement—all established at the national level—play a fundamental role in making markets efficient and, therefore, in raising the material standard of living. National governments also impose taxes, a necessary arrangement for the supply of national public goods. Perhaps the first responsibility of a state is to provide national security—a national public good—and income taxes historically have been introduced to finance wars. Today, of course, taxes finance many other national public goods that contribute to human well-being. These range from crime control to systems of sanitation and from a road network to clean drinking water.

Taxation is a constraint on individual freedoms, but one that the citizens of every free country willingly accept. In the absence of taxation, national public goods would need to be financed voluntarily, but it is the nature of public goods that everyone obtains the benefits of provision whether they contribute to its provision or not. Under a pure voluntary system, individuals have an incentive not to contribute, or to contribute very little—the "free rider" problem. Compulsion allows the state to provide what individuals on their own cannot provide.

Regulation is another means by which governments supply national public goods. The public good of clean air, for example, is typically supplied by pollution regulation, not public financing. And while taxation is needed to finance national defense, in many countries, especially in times of war, this is supplemented by conscription. Similarly, during a public health emergency, individuals suspected of being infected, and of posing a danger to others, can be placed under quarantine. Even without an epidemic, governments routinely require that children be vaccinated. This is not just to protect these children. It is to prevent the conditions that would allow an epidemic to emerge and threaten others: a public good.

Coercion—whether for the purposes of taxation or regulation—can also be used for malevolent purposes. It can be used to subjugate and exploit a population, to reap windfalls for an elite, and to build militaries that threaten a state's neighbors. The purposes to which government powers can be put depend on the sources from which a government derives its authority—whether from the gun or the ballot box. This is one reason democratic institutions are important; the threat of losing an election creates an incentive for governments to serve the interests of citizens. Other government institutions, such as a constitution and independent judiciary, further restrain abuses of power and help prevent a majority from stepping on the rights of individuals and minorities. Although the focus of this chapter is on regional cooperation, it is important to recognize from the outset the importance of national institutions, not least for the way they shape the behavior of the main players in the international arena and determine their ability to act. National institutions help to determine a state's interests (whether it is representative of a broad swathe of the population, say, or beholden to a particular group). They affect the ability of an executive to negotiate agreements with regional neighbors. National institutions also determine whether a state can deliver on its promises. A state that is unable to supply national public goods is also unlikely to be able to contribute to the supply of regional public goods, at least where external assistance is not provided.

National public goods may be paramount to improving human well-being, but every person's well-being is also shaped by the actions of governments other than their own. The need for national defense, for example, depends on the nature of external threats. A country's defense requirements depend on the weapons systems possessed by its potential enemies. Arms control can thus be mutually beneficial. A country's security also depends on whether it can rely on friendly states to come to its aid in the event of an attack: the international public good of collective security. Even better, the promise of assistance, if credible, can deter an attack, and so reduce the need for a buildup in armaments. This is important to individuals not only because security contributes directly to well-being but also because savings in defense spending can be shifted to supply other public goods.

The focus in this chapter is on regional public goods—public goods that are supplied by states situated in geographic proximity to one another and that primarily benefit the states belonging to this region. However, it is as well to note the connections among the different levels of public good. Regional public goods often cannot be supplied unless (at least enough) states within the region also possess the capacity to supply national public goods. Indeed, the provision of regional public goods is often built upon the foundations laid by states within the region supplying national public goods (regional disease elimination, for example, depends on each state within the region being able to control the disease domestically). Similarly, the supply of global public goods often demands minimal state and regional capacity. For example, the effort to eradicate polio globally was initiated only after the disease had been eliminated from large regions of the world, such as the Americas. Regional polio elimination served as a stepping-stone to global eradication.

The powers vested in national governments are not available at the regional and global levels. Action at the international level must be voluntary. Of course, volunteerism also operates at the national level; intervention by government is not the only means by which public goods are provided. However, states exist and have taken on larger roles because state provision of public goods often succeeds better than volunteerism. These same powers do not exist at the regional level. The most advanced regional institution is the European Union (EU), but the EU lacks the authority to tax EU citizens directly. Some decisions within Europe can be made by qualified majority, but some, such as fiscal measures, require unanimity. Why are regional bodies constrained in this way? The reason is that the values of the citizens of different states vary, and the citizens of few if any states would be willing to have their fates determined directly by others. This is not to say that sovereignty is immutable. Examples of restraints on sovereignty include qualified majority voting in the EU (every member state is bound by the decision of a qualified majority, whether the state voted with the majority or against it) and decisions by the United Nations (UN) Security Council in the area of peace and security. Such examples, however, are exceptions. And even these arrangements only persist because they are self-enforcing. A state exercises its sovereignty in deciding to join an organization like the EU. Even after joining, a state retains the right subsequently to withdraw from the arrangement—a right the United Kingdom has exercised.

The consequence of sovereignty is that the supply of regional public goods depends on the willingness of states in the region to contribute to their supply voluntarily.

It should not be assumed that unilateralism will fail to supply critical public goods. The United States (US), for example, developed the world's two polio vaccines on its own and for its own self-interests, and because these vaccines were never patented, they have been available to the whole world to produce (the knowledge of how to make the vaccine is the public good; once made, a vaccine is a private good).

It also should not be assumed that multilateralism is destined to fail. As explained later, the incentive for states to cooperate varies from situation to situation. In some cases, success requires nothing more than coordination.

In other cases, however, true cooperation, supported by enforcement, is needed. Even in these cases, cooperation can succeed, provided certain prerequisites are satisfied. First, it must be possible for each party to observe whether others have fulfilled their promises. Monitoring is essential. Second, parties must interact so that any observed violations of an agreement can be punished. Reciprocity is essential. Third, punishments must be credible, meaning that it must be in the interests of the parties harmed by a violation to impose the punishments they had promised to impose, should the agreement be violated. Finally, the magnitude of these punishments must be large enough to deter any party from violating the agreement in the first place.

The first two of these prerequisites are the easiest to fulfill. The main constraint imposed by monitoring is that countries must negotiate obligations that are easily observed. For example, it is easy to observe whether countries have undertaken an aboveground nuclear test. Belowground testing is more difficult to observe. The second requirement is almost automatically satisfied.

Not only do countries interact , but international law ensures that each new government is bound by the obligations agreed by its predecessors. Of course, a new government is free to withdraw from any of these agreements, but only as allowed by the terms of these agreements. As an example, President Donald Trump has indicated his desire to withdraw the US from the Paris Agreement on climate change, which was signed by former President Barack Obama; but because of the treaty's withdrawal process, the US remains bound by the requirements of this agreement until 4 November 2020 (a day after the next presidential election).

The latter two prerequisites are the hardest to satisfy. Large punishments may be needed to deter free riding, but large punishments tend to be less credible. The folk theorems of repeated games say that, provided the players meet indefinitely and are sufficiently patient, full cooperation can be sustained by noncooperative behavior. However, these theorems apply to subgame-perfect Nash equilibria. A more compelling concept for regional public goods is a renegotiation proof equilibrium (Barrett 2003). This is because the provision of a public good is a cooperative effort, and if a player punishes another player who deviated from an agreement to cooperate, the punishment will harm all other players who had cooperated previously. International trade agreements are easy to enforce because they rely on direct reciprocity (if one player is harmed by a deviation, it can target its punishment to the player that deviated). Agreements to supply public goods are very difficult to enforce because they must rely on diffused reciprocity.

Against these barriers to cooperation, there are aspects of regional public goods that may facilitate their provision. First, the number of countries needing to cooperate on a regional issue may be relatively small, and cooperation generally becomes more difficult as the number of countries involved increases. Second, regional hegemons may have strong incentives to play a big role in contributing to a regional public good. Third, tighter integration among countries may create more situations favoring coordination. Fourth, some portion of the benefits of provision may be national in nature, reducing the incentive to free ride. Finally, because countries interact in different spheres simultaneously, there may be opportunities for them to leverage cooperation in one area with cooperation in other areas.

Two forces combine to explain why regional public goods are particularly important today. First, sovereignty naturally causes countries to adopt policies and to make investments that are of a local and national nature; but once a country has exploited the most attractive of these opportunities, it needs to look for other ways to advance the well-being of its citizens, and regional cooperation is one such way. For example, a country may act to limit its own sources of air pollution, but if a substantial portion of its pollution is "imported" from its neighbors, then there will come a point where the returns to improving air quality locally will favor a regional approach. Second, efforts to supply certain vital global public goods have failed or succeeded only partially, and the supply of regional public goods can be a more sensible response than pursuit only of national goals. As an example, the Paris Agreement on climate change, a voluntary agreement lacking any meaningful enforcement powers, asks nation states to pledge to reduce their emissions, when the best means for reducing emissions can involve regional efforts. For example, an integrated, regional electricity grid would allow power to be transmitted over long distances, giving a boost to the economics of renewable energy.

Similarly, road networks and the need to match the hardware of an automobile with the software of its fuel mean that technologies like electric vehicles are more likely to be adopted if investment is coordinated at the regional level. Electricity grids and a network of charging stations are not public goods, but they are an indirect means for supplying the public good of reductions in greenhouse gas emissions.

Examples of Regional Public Goods

Table 1.1 lists examples of regional public goods. As noted previously, the distinction between national, regional, and global public goods can be blurred. The table emphasizes the regional aspects of public goods.

Classifications

Generically, a *public good* has two features. First, *non-exclusivity*: if the good is available for one person (or state) to consume, it is available for others to consume as well, and these other persons (or states) cannot be excluded from consuming the good. Second, *nonrivalry*: one person's (or state's) consumption of the good does not reduce the amount of the good available to other persons (states). An example is a lighthouse, an aid for navigation by maritime pilots. If a lighthouse is erected and operated for one boater, it is available to all boaters in the area, and each boater's use of the lighthouse does not impinge on the ability of others to use it.

Table 1.1: Selected Regional Public Goods

	Problem	Regional Public Good	External Benefits
Peace and Security	Nonproliferation of nuclear weapons	As regards regional conflicts, yes; but even in these cases there are global spillovers.	Provides a level of security to all countries in the region and beyond.
	Taboo on use of nuclear weapons	Yes; also a global public good.	Provides a level of security to all countries in the region and beyond.
	Prohibition on nuclear testing	Yes; also a global public good.	Limits development of new weapons, and thus a technological arms race.
	Prevention of terrorism	Yes, in some cases; also a global public good.	Measures that destroy terrorist capacity are a regional public good; measures that defend a country from attack are a national public good. These measures may have negative spillovers for other target countries in the region and globally.
	Peacekeeping and conflict prevention	Yes; in some cases also a global public good.	Benefits are greatest for countries that neighbor a conflict.
	Preventing state failure	Yes; also a global public good.	Failed states can prevent weakest-link global public goods from being supplied.
Communicable Diseases	Surveillance for emerging infectious diseases	Yes, if reported; also a global public good.	Countries that know about a new outbreak can take steps to limit imports. In Asia, particularly important for avian influenza.
	Response to outbreaks of emerging and re-emerging diseases	Yes; also a global public good.	Actions taken to suppress new outbreaks prevent communicable diseases from spreading.
	Elimination of communicable diseases	Yes.	Breaks chain of transmission within region. Particularly valuable if risk of imports from outside of region is low. May serve as stepping-stone to global elimination and even eradication.
	Disease eradication	Yes, for tropical diseases confined to the region.	Yields every country a dividend of avoiding both future infections and the need to control.

continued on next page

Table 1.1: *continued*

	Problem	Regional Public Good	External Benefits
Regional Commons	Preventing emergence of resistance	Yes.	No risk of importing resistant pathogens; current treatments remain effective.
	Climate change	Emission reductions are a global public good; adaptation is a local public good and may, in some cases, be a regional public good.	Emission reductions lower the risk of climate change to every country; adaptation reduces the damages from climate change to particular countries.
	Air pollution control	Yes, when the pollution is transboundary in nature.	Main benefits to human health; also, acid rain.
	River basin management	Yes, especially as regards riparian states.	Water sharing, flood control, water quality benefits to all riparian states.
	Control of marine pollution	Protection of regional seas a regional public good.	Protects marine life; is especially beneficial to coastal states.
	Control of persistent pollutants	Yes, since these can be transported long distances.	Protects human health and the environment.
	Control of hazardous waste transport	Yes; reduces the risk associated with transport, and ensures that trade in waste is non-exploitative.	Especially beneficial to countries with weak governance that import wastes.
	Marine fisheries management	High-seas fisheries and migratory stocks are open access resources.	Controls on harvests increase sustainable yields; may prevent collapse of stocks.
	Biodiversity and nature conservation	Values related to existence and carbon sequestration are global public goods; otherwise, a regional or national public good.	Conservation of ecosystem function usually a regional or national public good.
	Invasive species	Yes, as regards prevention of exports; defense against imports a national public good, but also helps prevent spread.	Prevention of exports of invasive species benefits all countries.
Knowledge	Research and development	Yes, if access to knowledge is unrestricted, and research and development (R&D) particularly beneficial to the region.	Benefits countries that can use the knowledge directly, which may be of special value to countries in the region.
	Harmonization of intellectual property rules	Yes, indirectly, to the extent that it increases R&D spending.	Extension of property rights should increase knowledge production at the margin; it would also redistribute rents to past R&D.

continued on next page

Table 1.1: *continued*

	Problem	Regional Public Good	External Benefits
	Big science	Yes, if access to knowledge were unrestricted within the region; otherwise a club good.	Knowledge obtained may be of direct or indirect benefit to every country.
	Controls on dangerous scientific experiments	Yes, particularly if impacts would be regional.	Controls can reduce risks that, in some cases, threaten every country.
Trade and Finance	International trade	Bilateral and especially regional trade agreements may supply regional public goods indirectly.	Creation and maintenance of a generalized environment conducive to free trade helps to discourage discriminatory trade restrictions and may help promote peace and security.
	International financial stability	Prevention of contagion a regional public good.	Primarily benefits states with weak financial governance.
Other	Technical standards	Yes, provided they are not proprietary.	Some standards are better than others and so it can be important for countries to agree on setting the right standards.
	Tsunami warning system	Yes.	Here the region would be all countries in an ocean area.

Source: Compiled by author.

Table 1.2 shows how public goods are to be distinguished from other kinds of goods.

Private goods are consumed exclusively and involve rivalry. If I purchase a bag of rice, the rice belongs to me, and my possession of the good means that others cannot consume it. The fundamental theorems of welfare economics assume that all goods have these properties.

Two other kinds of good are a mixture of these extremes:

Club goods involve some exclusivity but do not involve rivalry among the group of users. An example is a toll road that is not subject to congestion (congestion implies rivalry).

Common property resources involve rivalry but not exclusivity. An example is a fishery, access to which has been restricted to a community.

Table 1.2: Classification of Goods

Item	Rivalry	Nonrivalry
Exclusivity	Private good	Club good
Non-exclusivity	Common property	Public good

Source: Author.

All members of the community have access (non-members are excluded; if there is truly no exclusion, the resource is subject to open access), but each member's harvest reduces the stock of fish available to others.

One important point about these goods is the role that government plays in determining their properties. A book is a private good, but the words contained in the book are only private if protected by copyright laws. Knowledge is a public good but inventions are private so long as they are under patent. Given that a book has been written and an invention invented, efficiency requires that access be based on marginal cost, which ignores the sunk cost incurred in creating these goods. However, if the writer and inventor could not hope to recover their costs, they probably would not have written the book or invented the innovative item in the first place. Copyright and patent laws exist to provide these incentives.

Property rights to pharmaceuticals are a particularly sensitive issue. A patent is needed to encourage investment in new drug development, but high prices create a "deadweight loss" for welfare. This can become a political issue in times of crisis. Following the 2001 anthrax attacks in the US, local politicians proposed that the antibiotic Cipro be subject to compulsory licensing, a move that would ensure supply at low price by making the knowledge of how to produce the drug a public good but that would also reduce the value of the patent to its owner, Bayer. Perhaps because of this threat, the company "donated" certain volumes of the drug to the US government and offered other amounts at a discount.[1] This example illustrates a fact that is often overlooked: property rights are human inventions, determined in a political context.

Public goods are jurisdictional in nature. They may be local, national, international, regional, or global. The lighthouse mentioned previously is an example of a *local public good*. The quintessential *national public good*

---

[1] R. Fletcher. 2001. Bitter pill. *The Telegraph.* 28 October. https://www.telegraph.co.uk/finance/2739515/Bitter-pill.html.

is national defense. *International or transnational public goods* are enjoyed simultaneously by a multiple of countries, irrespective of their geography. *Regional public goods* are enjoyed by a multiple of countries situated close to one another. An example is flood protection within a river basin. *Global public goods* are available to be consumed by people everywhere. An example is protection of the ozone layer.

Regional and global public goods are both international public goods, but not all international public goods are either regional or global in nature. For example, the eradication of yaws, a disease confined to tropical countries in Africa, Latin America, and the Asia and Pacific region (in 2016, the reported cases in Asia and Pacific were in Indonesia, Papua New Guinea, Solomon Islands, Timor-Leste, and Vanuatu) is international in nature. It would benefit rich countries little if at all, and so is not truly a global public good. At the same time, its supply would require efforts from a multiple of regions rather than just one. The World Health Organization is leading an effort to eradicate yaws worldwide. Elimination of yaws in the Asia and the Pacific region would be a necessary step toward global eradication, but it may also bring substantial benefits to the region even if global eradication fails, so long as the risk of the disease being imported and re-established is low.

Determinants of Provision

What determines whether a regional public good is provided? This depends on the incentives countries in the region must provide the good, both individually and collectively. Is a country better off when providing the good than when not providing it? If the answer is "yes," then the country has an incentive to provide it; if "no," then the country does not have an incentive to supply the public good. Sometimes, as we shall see, the incentive each country must supply the good depends on whether others supply it.

Are all countries better off when every country supplies the public good? If so, then all countries collectively have an incentive to supply it.

Of course, what is of particular interest are situations in which national and collective interests clash—when countries have little individual incentive to supply the good unilaterally but all countries together have a strong collective incentive to supply it. This gap between the incentives to supply a public good unilaterally and multilaterally widens as the number of countries benefiting from provision increases.

To examine the kinds of incentive that can exist, it will help to provide an abstract representation of states' interests. In this section, I show how variations in the expression of states' interests change the incentives for countries to supply regional public good.

Before proceeding, I should explain and justify the approach I shall take here. The approach is to formalize the incentive problem using noncooperative game theory. The essential assumptions of this approach are: (i) that states are monolithic actors; (ii) that information is perfect and complete, meaning that each "player" knows the preferences of all the other players and can observe their actions; and (iii) that states cannot appeal to a third party to enforce any agreements they may choose to enter.

The assumption that states are monoliths is obviously an enormous simplification. The executive of every country has the power and authority to engage in relations with other states, but agreements among states, particularly when they are of a multinational nature, typically require ratification by a state's legislature, which may itself be subject to lobbying pressure from various interest groups. From this perspective, treaty negotiation is a multistage game (Putnam 1988). Knowing that ratification is required, and that it may be subject to lobbying pressures, an executive may need to modify its own preferences to secure a legislative majority vote. But this is only to say that a state's preferences in negotiations must reflect the "swing" voter in the country's legislature (this would be the median voter under a simple majority voting rule). The assumption that states negotiate as monoliths is a simplification, but it is a transparent way of understanding how a state's national interests, broadly defined, affect its relations with other states.

The assumption of complete information means that every state can discern the national interests of every other state. Put more crudely, it means that every state can tell whether other states are lying or bluffing in their negotiations. The assumption of perfect information means that every state can observe the actions taken by others. For example, if a state pledges to reduce its fishing, this assumption implies that other states can observe whether this state has in fact reduced its fishing. These assumptions are again simplistic, but not unreasonable. A state's interests are usually easy for others to discern—and technical and economic analyses of regional public good supply can reveal these interests for all to see. Moreover, because cooperation presumes the ability to observe whether others behave as they promised, states typically choose to negotiate behaviors that are readily observable. For example, compliance with an agreement to ban the use of big drift nets is easily monitored from the air. Catch limits would be more difficult to monitor.

The final assumption about states not being able to appeal to a third party to enforce agreements is simply a reflection of sovereignty. Sovereignty means that states are free to join or not to join an international agreement as they please. Under international law, states are expected to comply with the agreements they sign up to (this requirement being expressed in "customary law"), but this is a very weak obligation: if a state wants not to comply with an agreement, it may simply withdraw from the agreement and so cease to be legally bound by its obligations.

This approach is to be contrasted with others that might be considered. Cooperative game theory, for example, assumes that agreements among players are binding. This approach is clearly irrelevant to relations among sovereign countries. The theory of mechanism design can be employed to overcome information problems in the supply of public goods, but it presumes that a central authority can impose a mechanism on others and that the central problem is incomplete information. In the international arena, there is no central authority, and information problems are secondary to sovereignty problems. For example, the parties to the Framework Convention on Climate Change negotiated the Kyoto Protocol to impose binding emission limits on certain countries, but this agreement fell apart. The problem was not that countries failed to come to an agreement about what to do. The problem was that they were unable to enforce the limits they had negotiated. In mechanism design, the incentive to free ride is expressed in players misrepresenting their true preferences. In the supply of regional public goods, the incentive to free ride is expressed in countries failing to undertake the provision levels that they and all other players know should be undertaken for their collective benefit. Overcoming this free riding problem requires not "mechanism design" but "treaty design."

Linear Public Goods Game

Assume that every state acts independently (meaning, unilaterally) with the objective of maximizing its own welfare (national self-interest). It will help to assume as well that all countries are symmetric, meaning that they have identical payoff functions. Later, I shall relax both assumptions.

To begin, suppose that there are N countries, and that each country must decide whether to contribute to the public good (that is, the decision to contribute is binary). Country i ($i = 1,...,N$) chooses to provide the good ($q_i = 1$) or not to provide it ($q_i = 0$) with the objective of maximizing its payoff, denoted π_i, taking as given the provision choices of all other states in the region. The simplest representation of payoffs is for a linear public good:

$$\pi_i = bQ - cq_i, \text{ where } Q = q_i + Q_{-i} = q_i + \sum_{j=1, j\neq i}^{N} q_j. \tag{0.1}$$

Here, Q represents the aggregate provision by all countries, qi the amount provided by country i, and Q-i the amount supplied by all countries except i. These are variables in the equation. The letters b and c, by contrast, represent parameters, with b being the benefit each country gets from one more unit of provision and c the cost to any country of supplying one more unit of the public good. The payoff to country i, π_i is measured in currency units. The variables q, Q-i, and Q may be measured in physical units (for example, representing tons of pollution controlled). The parameters b and c are measured in monetary units (for example, b may represent the benefit, measured in currency units, of a ton of pollution abatement, and c the cost of undertaking that unit of abatement).

Eq. (0.1) models provision of a regional (linear) public good as a "game" in the sense that the outcome any state i can realize depends not only on what i does but also on what the other states do. The public good described in (0.1) is supplied depending on the "aggregate effort."

Intuitively (and this can be confirmed using simple calculus), every country i will want to supply the good unilaterally if $b > c$, whereas if $c > b$ every country will want not to supply the good unilaterally (if $b = c$, countries will be indifferent between supplying and not supplying the public good unilaterally). The solutions as regards each country acting unilaterally, taking as given how the other countries act, is the *Nash equilibrium* of this game. In a Nash equilibrium, no state can gain by changing what it is doing, given what all the other states are doing (or are expected to do).

The best that all states in the region can do collectively is to choose provision levels $q_1, q_2, ..., q_N$ so as to maximize

$$\Pi = \sum_{j=1}^{N} \pi_j = bQN - cQ, \tag{0.2}$$

which requires that every state contribute to the public good if $bN > c$ and not to supply it if $c > bN$ (if $c = bN$, the region will be indifferent between supplying and not supplying the public good). This solution describes the *full cooperative outcome* of the linear public goods game.

Table 1.3 describes all possible situations within this linear model. The first row shows the conditions under which countries have neither unilateral nor collective incentives to supply the regional public good. Here, there is no conflict between individual self-interest and the interests of all states in a region; there is no need for regional cooperation. The third row shows the conditions under which countries have unilateral incentives to supply the public good, and this outcome is the best possible outcome for the entire region. Here again, there is no need for regional cooperation. Finally, the middle row shows the conditions under which the region does best when every country supplies the public good, but no country within the region has an incentive to supply the public good unilaterally. This middle case is the one that is relevant for regional public policy. It describes provision of the public good as a *"prisoner's dilemma game."*

Table 1.3: Linear Public Goods Game

Condition	Nash Equilibrium	Full Cooperative Outcome	In Words	Game
$c > bN$	$q_i^{NE} = 0$	$q_i^{FC} = 0$	The good is not provided, and should not be provided.	–
$bN > c > b$	$q_i^{NE} = 0$	$q_i^{FC} = 1$	The good is not provided, but should be provided.	Prisoner's dilemma
$b > c$	$q_i^{NE} = 1$	$q_i^{FC} = 1$	The good is provided, and should be provided.	–

Source: Author.

How to know if a region faces a prisoner's dilemma? In such cases, countries in the region are likely to declare an interest in cooperating for mutual gain. They may complain that other countries are not doing enough and excuse their own inaction by saying that they would do more if only they could be sure that others would do more. Climate negotiations fit this description perfectly on the global scale. Countries agreed in Paris that mean global temperature change must stay well below 2°C, but act to ensure that temperature change will exceed this amount.

Asymmetry

It is very easy to extend the analysis presented thus far to the case where countries are asymmetric. For example, suppose that the cost parameter is the same for every country but that the benefit parameter varies by country. Then the analysis will be essentially unchanged. There will be a prisoner's dilemma provided $\sum_{i=1}^{N} b_i > c > b_j$ holds for all $j = 1,..., N$.

Asymmetry can create some interesting situations. Suppose $b_j > c$ for some j but not every j. Then, in the Nash equilibrium, some countries will supply the good and some will not supply it.

It is also easy to explore differences in the cost parameter among the N countries. Country j will supply the public good so long as $b_j > c_j$, whereas if $b_j < c_j$, country j will not supply it. Supply by country j is efficient if $\sum_i b_i > c_j$ whether $b_j > c_j$ or $b_j < c_j$. The fact that some countries supply the public good does not mean that the public good is being supplied efficiently.

Nonlinear Public Goods Games

We can also modify the assumption that payoffs are linear in provision.

Suppose, for example, that costs are quadratic rather than linear:

$$\pi_i = bQ - c\frac{q_i^2}{2}.$$

In this case, in a Nash equilibrium, every country supplies b/c units of the public good. However, full cooperation requires that every country supply bN/c units of the public good. Every state supplies $1/N$th as much as it should supply in the full cooperative outcome.

Suppose instead that eq (0.1) is replaced by

$$\pi_i = b\left(Q - \frac{\alpha Q^2}{2}\right) - cq_i\left(1 - \frac{\beta Q_{-i}}{(N-1)}\right), \qquad (0.3)$$

where $Q_{-i} = \sum_{j=1,j\neq i}^{N} q_j$. Then it is clear that (0.3) is identical to (0.1) for $\alpha = \beta = 0$. Now, benefits are quadratic and the costs of supply for each country depend on what other countries in the region are doing.

There are two interesting cases:

Case 1: $\alpha > 0$ and $b = 0$. In this case, the marginal benefit to a country of supplying the public good decreases in the number of others that supply it. An example is pollution abatement. When pollution levels are high, because few if any countries are abating their emissions, the damages avoided by abatement can be very high, creating an incentive for some countries to reduce their emissions. As more countries do so, however, the marginal benefit to reducing emissions further falls, causing the remaining countries not to reduce their emissions.

Case 2: $\alpha = 0$ and $\beta > 0$. In this case, the cost to country i of supplying the public good decreases in the number of other countries that supply it. This could occur if the technology for supplying the public good exhibited strong economies of scale or network externalities.

As shown in Table 1.4, for Case 1 there is a unique Nash equilibrium, which can be "interior," meaning that, in this equilibrium, some countries supply the public good and some do not, even though all countries would be better off if all supplied it. This is a *"chicken game."*

Earlier, we saw that for the linear game, asymmetry may mean that in equilibrium, some countries supply the public good and some do not. This outcome is like the one described above for the chicken game, but the reasons are different. In the chicken game, all countries are symmetric (they have identical payoff functions). They just behave differently, and therefore obtain a different payoff, in equilibrium. With asymmetry, we know which countries will supply the public good and which will not supply it. With the chicken game, we know the number of countries that will supply the public good in equilibrium, but we do not know their identities.

For Case 2, there are two Nash equilibria (in pure strategies), one in which no country supplies the public good and one in which every country supplies it (and in which it is in the collective interests of all states in the region that everyone supplies it). This is a *"coordination game."*

Table 1.4: Two Nonlinear Public Goods Games

Condition	Nash Equilibrium	Full Cooperative Outcome	In Words	Game
$\beta = 0$, $\alpha N >$ $1 - c/b >$ $\alpha > 0$	z^{NE} contribute, where z^{NE} is the smallest integer greater than $\frac{1}{\alpha}\left(1 - \frac{c}{b}\right) - 1$; $N - z^{NE}$ do not contribute	$q_i^{FC} = 1$ for all i provided $\left(1 - \frac{c}{bN}\right) > \alpha N$	Some, but not all, countries provide the public good, when all countries should provide it.	Chicken
$\alpha = 0$, $1 > \frac{b}{c} >$ $1 - \beta$	$q_i^{NE} = 0$ and $q_i^{NE} = 1$, with a tipping point at $Q_{-i} = \left(1 - \frac{b}{c}\right)\frac{(N-1)}{\beta}$	$q_i^{FC} = 1$, provided $bN - c + 2c\beta > 0$.	Either all countries provide the public good or none does, when it is best that all provide it.	Coordination

Source: Author.

Discrete Public Goods

The public goods described thus far are of the "aggregate effort" variety. The total amount supplied is the sum of the amounts supplied by different countries. A *discrete public good* is different; an aggregate effort is needed, but supply is binary: the good is either supplied or it is not supplied.[2]

An example is "big science," an input into the supply of knowledge, a public good. Discovery of the Higgs boson, a major breakthrough, confirmed

---

[2] This concept is similar to but also very different from a "best shot" public good (see Hirshleifer 1983, Arce, Daniel, and Sandler 2002). With a best-shot public good, the amount supplied is the amount supplied by the player who supplies the most. The similarity is that it is possible, as explained later in this section, that only one player will supply the discrete public good. However, in this case the outcome is efficient, and efficiency is not guaranteed or even to be expected in the case of best-shot public goods. Development of a vaccine is sometimes mentioned as an example of a best-shot public good. But it is really more akin to a discrete public good in that enough money must be spent in order to develop a vaccine; spending more than this amount does not increase supply; and vaccine development can be financed by and even undertaken by a consortium of players rather than by individual players acting independently.

the Standard Model of physics.[3] The discovery was made by experiments performed using the largest and most complex machine ever made, the Large Hadron Collider at CERN, a machine that collides protons and lead ions at energies approaching the speed of light, a machine that, to fulfill experimental needs, had to be produced according to exacting specifications. Half a collider would not have supplied any knowledge, and two colliders wouldn't have supplied any additional knowledge.

Associated with the design specifications for the Large Hadron Collider was a budget for its construction. To see how the public good was supplied, denote the total cost of construction by C, and suppose that there is an aggregate benefit to the world of supplying this public good, denoted B. Obviously, for provision of the public good to be "efficient," we must have $B > C$.

Will the good be supplied? Suppose that country i derives a benefit Bi from provision, and suppose further that countries are labeled such that Country 1 derives the greatest benefit, Country 2 the next greatest benefit, and so on down to Country N, which derives the least benefit; that is $B_1 > B_2 > ... > B_{N-1} > B_N > 0$ with $B = B_1 + B_2 + ... + B_N$. Then we obtain the following two insights:

First, if, $B_1 > C$, then full provision is a Nash equilibrium, meaning that we can be sure that the public good will be provided. The reason for this is that, even if all the other countries do not contribute to the public good, Country 1 has an incentive to supply it. Of course, it may also be the case that $B_2 > C > B_3$, in which case Country 2 also has an incentive to supply the good unilaterally if no other country supplies it. Clearly, what we cannot say here is which country will supply the good. We can only say that it will be supplied.

Second, if $B > C > B_1$, then we cannot be sure that the public good will be supplied, even though all countries would be better off if the good were supplied. Suppose, however, that $B_1 + B_2 > C$. Then these two countries together have a strong collective incentive to supply the public good. Suppose that a third party asks each country i ($i = 1, 2$) to contribute an amount of money Mi, such that $B_i > M_i$ and $M_1 + M_2 = C$. It seems natural in this situation for the third party to ask each country to contribute an amount that is

---

3   CERN is financed by 22 member states, all of them European; India and Pakistan are associate members. Other big science endeavors have more representation by Asian economies. For example, ITER, a project to conduct experiments in nuclear fusion, is funded by six economies plus the European Union, including Taipei,China; India; Japan; and the Republic of Korea.

proportional to its share of the total benefit. That is, $\bar{M}_i = C \times B_i/(B_1 + B_2)$. Then it is obvious that if country i contributes Mi, country j ($j \neq i$) can do no better than to contribute Mj, a Nash equilibrium. Here, we thus have another coordination game. Contributing zero is a Nash equilibrium, but contributing $\bar{M}_j$ is also a Nash equilibrium.

In my example, if the third party offers the countries a take it or leave it offer, both would take it provided each was sure that the other country would also take it. Could the parties reach agreement on their own, without the aid of this third party? The answer is yes. They would simply have to negotiate a burden-sharing arrangement. Although the financing game has many Nash equilibria, negotiations typically converge around *focal points* (Schelling 1960). Indeed, the proposal to set contributions proportional to each country's share of the total benefit is a clear focal point.

I have so far considered only a bilateral negotiation. Are multilateral negotiations much more difficult? Not necessarily. As numbers increase, so do the transactions costs of negotiation. But countries also have an incentive to reduce transactions costs, and they can do this by looking for a simple way to arrive at an acceptable outcome. An example is how countries agree on a burden-sharing rule for financing the UN budget. Every 3 years, a Contributions Committee makes a proposal for how the costs should be shared, and the General Assembly votes to accept or reject it (almost always this vote is by consensus). The committee uses a formula. There is a minimum amount every member must pay. There is also a maximum payment (which applies only to the US). Otherwise, payments reflect countries' ability and to some extent their willingness to pay (Barrett 2007).

If all countries can agree on how to finance the UN, then surely a subset of countries can agree on how to finance the supply of other public goods. Indeed, the UN scale of assessments is the obvious focal point for related negotiations—an example being the financing of compliance by developing countries with the Montreal Protocol. In other cases, there will be incentives to deviate from the UN scale. An example is peacekeeping operations. Peacekeeping is to a large extent a regional public good, because the countries in the immediate neighborhood of a conflict are most at risk from spillovers, such as the exodus of refugees. For this reason, the countries more at risk tend to finance the larger share of the cost of peacekeeping operations. Similarly, when the UN supports a peacekeeping mission, the countries that must decide whether to act are expected to pay a higher share than other countries, all else equal. The main point is not that burden sharing is a trivial exercise. The main point is that countries are able to agree on how to share costs when they have a strong incentive to supply the public good.

In summary, discrete public goods are very likely to be provided, as they merely require coordination.

Threshold Public Goods

Provision of a public good sometimes involves a threshold. An example is the critical immunization needed to achieve elimination. Below this level, the disease continues to circulate within a territory. Above this level, the disease dies out locally. Control short of elimination is an aggregate effort; control to the point of elimination is a threshold public good. What happens at the elimination point is that all the people without personal immunity acquire "herd immunity," thanks to the protection given to them by the people with personal immunity.

The budget for building a project like the Large Hadron Collider is also like a threshold. If funding falls short of the target, the project cannot be completed. And there is nothing to gain by raising more money than needed to construct the project—these monies should be spent on other worthwhile activities or investments.

What is significant about *threshold public goods* is that a very large change in payoffs occurs in the vicinity of the threshold, a change that creates a strong incentive for countries to supply the good. Supply of threshold public goods is a coordination game.

But this is only true if the threshold is certain, as it is in the UN operating budget, or at least very small. As uncertainty about the threshold increases, the collective action problem flips from being a coordination game to being a prisoner's dilemma (Barrett 2013).

Another consideration is the impact of crossing the threshold relative to the cost (that is, the aggregate net benefit of crossing the threshold). The larger is this value, the greater is the incentive for countries to coordinate. This value can also be uncertain, but uncertainty about this value does not affect collective action. The expected value affects collective action, but not the uncertainty (Barrett 2013). This is because countries' behavior determines whether the threshold is met, but it cannot determine the impact that is realized given that the threshold is crossed.

Note also that thresholds may be "good" or "bad." The threshold of disease control that achieves elimination is "good." The threshold of greenhouse gas concentrations that triggers "dangerous" climate change is "bad."

Threshold uncertainty varies from one public good to another. For disease elimination, the threshold is normally certain. A country seeking to eliminate a disease can observe from experience the immunization level needed to achieve elimination in other countries. At least as important, elimination really requires zero cases, so as an elimination effort advances, the goal can shift from achieving mass immunization to specific interventions that target groups of people among whom the disease continues to circulate. In other words, as the program to supply the public good advances, uncertainty about the threshold shrinks. This is why the effort to eradicate polio continues year after year. If the global public good of polio eradication fails, the reason will not be because the world did not try hard to supply it.

For other threshold public goods, uncertainty about the threshold is not only large but substantially irreducible. This is true for novel situations such as avoiding "dangerous" climate change. It is simply impossible to know for sure where such a threshold may lie, because the situation we face at any time is unprecedented. There has been recent scientific effort to detect "early warning signals" of an impending threshold (see, for example, Scheffer et al. 2012), but these approaches are prone to error (a threshold is detected when it does not exist or it is not detected when it does exist) and in any event such signals may appear too late for countries to change course.

Weakest-Link Public Goods

The supply of a *weakest-link regional public good* depends on the size of the smallest contribution. As an example, the ability of a system of dikes to hold back the sea depends on the weakest-link in the entire system: the polder that is the most vulnerable to failure.

At the international level, an important regional public good is disease elimination. This is an interesting example, as it combines features of a discrete public good and a weakest-link public good. A disease is eliminated if there cease to be any indigenous cases. That is, the disease may be imported from outside the region; these imports might even cause secondary infections among locals; but no cases originate from within the region.

To eliminate a disease within a region, the disease must be eliminated from within every state in the region. Elimination at the national level is like a discrete public good. Normally, it is not necessary to protect every resident of the state directly. Instead, once enough people are protected directly, all others will be protected indirectly by "herd immunity." For the vaccine-preventable diseases, epidemiologists can estimate a critical immunization such that, for a smaller immunization, the disease will continue to spread, whereas for a higher immunization, the disease will disappear. For example, for polio, the critical immunization is about 80%. If at least this fraction of a population is protected from polio, and a case of polio is imported into the community, it is very unlikely that the disease will spread. There may be secondary cases. In all likelihood, however, an epidemic will not break out; the disease will disappear.

Let q_c denote the critical immunization for a disease and let q_i denote the fraction of the population within country i, that is immune. If there are N countries in the region, the regional public good of disease elimination will be achieved provided

$$\min\left(q_1, q_2, \ldots, q_N\right) \geq q^c. \qquad (0.4)$$

Achieving such a level can be relatively easy for some countries, but impossibly difficult for others, especially countries that are torn by conflict; in 2017, there were just 22 confirmed cases of wild poliovirus worldwide, all in Afghanistan and Pakistan. These states are the disease's last strongholds in an effort that has been on the verge of success every year since 2000.

Elimination by a state is worth pursuing provided the marginal social benefit of avoiding the last case at the threshold exceeds the corresponding marginal cost (Barrett 2013). Elimination is not normally considered to be an investment, because it requires ongoing interventions. For example, polio has been eliminated almost everywhere, but for elimination to persist, countries must continue to vaccinate to a high level. Should they let their guard down, the disease could be imported, sparking a fresh epidemic.

What, then, is special about regional elimination? Probably the main difference is that states within a region tend to be tightly integrated. Transport linkages and trade mean that interactions between states within the region far exceed those between each state and the rest of the world. In such a situation, it may not pay or even be feasible for a single country to eliminate a disease, if the country's neighbors do not also eliminate a disease, but it may pay all states within a region to eliminate a disease collectively. In these situations, regional elimination will be a coordination game.

Institutions for Provision

So far, two kinds of outcome have been considered. In one, every country acts independently (the Nash equilibrium). In the other, all countries act collectively (full cooperation). In some cases, these outcomes coincide. In other cases, they diverge. The later situations are the ones that should concern us most and are the focus here.

Before proceeding, it will help to distinguish "institutions" from "organizations," as the two words are often used interchangeably. International institutions establish the rules for how states are expected to interact, whereas international organizations are assemblages of states empowered to act by and subject to these rules. The UN is an organization, comprised at any one time of a membership, represented by particular governments. However, this organization must operate within the framework established by the UN Charter, an institution. Similarly, the Asian Development Bank (ADB), an organization, acts in accordance with the wishes of its members, subject to the rules expressed in the Agreement Establishing the ADB, an institution. Organizations matter; they can do great things or sit on their hands; they may even cause some damage. Ultimately, however, organizations are constrained by the institution that determines what they must and must not do, and what they can and cannot do.

These constraints are not fixed. They change in response to states' changing power relations and their changing interests, including as regards transnational public goods and commons problems. Before the UN, there was the League of Nations, and before the League of Nations, there was no overarching organization responsible for world peace, a global public good. It took two world wars for countries to be willing to create the UN. Similarly, before around 1970, the seas belonged to every state beyond a 3-mile territorial limit, whereas during the 1970s customary law extended this limit to 12 miles and, even more significantly, created a new property right for coastal states, the Exclusive Economic Zone (EEZ). Creation of the EEZ had both efficiency and distributional consequences. By nationalizing the resources of the seas, the EEZ closed a part of the commons, enabling many fisheries to be managed more efficiently, even as the move also transferred wealth from all states (a wealth that had been appropriated mainly by a few, powerful, distant water fishing nations) to the coastal states.

The UN and the property rights arrangements for the oceans supply public goods and overcome commons problems with a very broad brush. It is more common for regional and global public goods to be supplied by agreements that are aimed at supplying a public good or to address a particular commons problem. For example, the world's regional fisheries are managed by regional fisheries management organizations, each established by a separate treaty.

This piecemeal approach works best because transnational public goods vary enormously, and there cannot be a one-size-fits-all remedy. Some transnational public goods can only be supplied with the active engagement of all countries, others are regional in nature; some have a high ratio of benefits to costs, others have a low ratio; some involve thresholds, others do not, and so on. Partly because of such differences, the best means for supplying a public good will vary from issue to issue. Protection of the stratospheric ozone layer and limits to climate change are both global public goods involving the atmosphere, but our attempts to supply these global public goods have differed. The Montreal Protocol on the ozone layer incorporates a trade restriction between parties and non-parties, whereas the Paris Agreement on climate change makes no linkage to trade.

My earlier analysis revealed different kinds of public goods problems. First, there are situations in which full supply of a public good is Nash equilibrium. A particularly interesting example is for a discrete public good where the benefit Country 1 gets from the good being supplied exceeds the cost of supply: $B_1 > C$. In this case we can be confident that the good will be supplied.

As noted, it may also be the case that one or more other countries may be willing to supply the public good unilaterally if Country 1 should fail to supply it. Or it may be the case that a group of countries will choose to supply it together. In other words, Nash equilibria—that is, different configurations of supply—may exist. The main point is that, for this kind of public good, non-supply is not a Nash equilibrium. We can be confident that the public good will be supplied. Government funding of R&D is an example of this kind of situation. Many governments fund R&D, yielding knowledge that is available worldwide: a positive spillover.

Second, there are situations in which there exist at least two Nash equilibria, one of which is inefficient and involves non-supply of a public good and at least one of which is efficient, involving full supply. This is a coordination game: countries must somehow ensure that they end up in an efficient equilibrium and not in the inefficient one. In this situation, an international institution for the supply of this public good is almost sure to be effective, because the efficient outcome can be sustained as a Nash equilibrium. The agreement only needs to "select" a Nash equilibrium that is efficient. The funding of big science, like the CERN project, is a prime example of this kind of situation.

Another example of this kind of situation is a weakest-link regional or global public good. According to the Constitution of the World Health Organization (WHO), the World Health Assembly—the decision-making body of the organization comprising all members, each having one vote—may adopt "regulations," which are legally binding on all members except for countries that specifically reject the regulation or issue reservations about it. This institution is unique in that it resets the default for participation. On other issues, the default rule in international law is that countries are "out" of an agreement unless they specifically choose to be "in." As regards regulations adopted by WHO, by contrast, member states are "in" unless they specifically declare that they wish to be "out." In all cases, countries ultimately have the sovereign right to decide, but the default rule may still affect behavior.

A situation favoring this approach concerns the emergence and spread of new diseases. Actions to limit emergence and spread is a weakest link game because infectious agents can emerge anywhere and, having done so, pose a threat to people everywhere. Any country that chooses to be "out" of an agreement to prevent emergence, to carry out surveillance for the detection of emergence, to report outbreaks, and to limit spread, poses a risk to all other countries. Therefore, obligations in all these areas are spelled out in the International Health Regulations, a set of rules binding on all countries. These rules used to apply to only a handful of diseases, but they were revised in 2005 in the wake of the SARS outbreak. SARS originated in the People's Republic of China (PRC), which did not report the outbreak to WHO. Under the rules that existed at that time, the PRC was under no legal obligation to report. However, the delay in reporting put all other countries at risk. Today, thanks to the 2005 revisions to the International Health Regulations, all countries are obligated to report outbreaks "that may constitute a public health emergency of international concern."

As noted, disease eradication is also a weakest link transnational public good. But rather than be addressed through regulations, disease eradication programs have been launched through resolutions adopted by the World Health Assembly. Essentially, the world has relied on a voluntary approach to supplying this public good. This approach seems to have been good enough, for the effort to eradicate smallpox succeeded, and though the ongoing efforts to eradicate polio and Guinea worm disease have faltered, the reason is not for lack of resources.

Regional public health initiatives are pursued using a similar approach. For example, the goal of eliminating measles and rubella from Southeast Asia by 2020 was adopted by a resolution (specifically, SEA/RC66/R5) approved by WHO Regional Committee for South-East Asia in 2013.[4] Similarly, in 2005, WHO Regional Committee for the Western Pacific adopted a resolution (WPR/RC56.R8) to eliminate measles by 2012; and, when that goal was missed, reaffirmed the goal of elimination in subsequent resolutions.[5] However, in the documents on these initiatives, no mention—let alone emphasis—is placed on the advantages to pursuing elimination as a regional goal in a coordinated fashion.[6] The key benefit of elimination to a country is herd immunity and the key benefit to coordinated elimination is a reduction in the risk of imports of the disease from neighboring countries.

As noted, countries find it particularly difficult to supply aggregate effort public goods that, lacking an identifiable threshold, resemble a prisoner's dilemma. Institutions can help in supplying these public goods, by changing the rules of the game to align countries' self-interests with their collective interests (Barrett 2003, 2007, and 2016). Supply is normally facilitated by international agreements. Examples in the Asia region include the ASEAN Agreement on Transboundary Haze Pollution, adopted in 2002; the Convention to Ban the Importation into Forum Island Countries of

---

[4] This region comprises 11 countries: Bangladesh, Bhutan, the Democratic People's Republic of Korea, India, Indonesia, Maldives, Myanmar, Nepal, Sri Lanka, Thailand, and Timor-Leste.

[5] This region comprises 28 countries and nine territories. The 28 countries are: Australia, Brunei Darussalam, Cambodia, the People's Republic of China, Cook Islands, Fiji, Japan, Kiribati, the Lao People's Democratic Republic, Malaysia, the Marshall Islands, the Federated States of Micronesia, Mongolia, Nauru, New Zealand, Niue, Palau, Papua New Guinea, the Philippines, the Republic of Korea, Samoa, Singapore, Solomon Islands, Tokelau, Tonga, Tuvalu, Vanuatu, and Viet Nam.

[6] For example, the Strategic Plan for Measles Elimination in the Southeast Asia Region lists seven benefits to measles elimination, from the benefits to individuals who are vaccinated to the benefits to the health systems of individual countries; see http://www.searo.who. int/immunization/documents/sear_mr_strategic_plan_2014_2020.pdf, especially p. 22. No mention is made to the benefits of regional coordination of measles elimination.

Hazardous and Radioactive Wastes and to Control the Transboundary Movement and Management of Hazardous Wastes within the South Pacific Region, adopted in 1995; and the regional fisheries agreements discussed in the companion paper on case studies. There are also several bilateral agreements on bird migration involving Australia. The first, with Japan, was adopted in 1974; the second, with the PRC, was adopted in 1986; and the third, with the Republic of Korea, was adopted in 2006.

The central problem for agreements like these is enforcement; the need to prevent (deter) free riding. Enforcement is often assumed to relate exclusively to compliance. In domestic situations, enforcement is about compliance. In international situations, however, free riding can be expressed in three different ways. First, countries may choose not to participate in an agreement. Second, they may choose to participate but not comply. Third, countries may both participate and comply but only because the agreement only asks its parties to do what they would have done anyway.

There are two ways in which enforcement can be incorporated into an agreement. The first is direct and the second is strategic.

The direct approach involves countries agreeing to supply some amount of a public good, with these obligations being enforced by reciprocity. That is, if one country chooses not to cooperate, then other countries must "punish" this country by choosing not to cooperate. The idea is that, if this punishment hurts the first country enough, then the first country will be deterred from not cooperating. A famous strategy of this kind is known as "Tit for Tat" (especially Axelrod 1984). This involves responding to kindness with kindness and to meanness with meanness. The strategy is intuitively appealing, but it also has many problems. Fortunately, similar strategies can be shown to be very effective.[7] The big problem with reciprocity is that it works well in symmetric, bilateral relations, but not well for supplying a public good when the number of countries is relatively large. This is why trade agreements tend to be effective and agreements to supply a global public good, when enforced directly, tend not to be effective. Trade is bilateral. If country A imposes a tariff on country B, country B can reciprocate by imposing a tariff on country A—without affecting its trade relations with other countries. By contrast, if country A should fail to supply a global public

---

[7] In general, the Tit for Tat strategy lacks credibility. A similar strategy that avoids this problem is "Getting Even" (Barret 2003).

good, and country B were to punish country A by not supplying the public good, country B would harm all the other countries that benefit from this public good.

The experience with the Kyoto Protocol on climate change illustrates the nature of the problem. Countries considered a proposal whereby, should a party to the agreement fail to limit its emissions as promised, this country would undertake even greater emission reductions in a subsequent period, to make up for the violation and then some. The additional abatement required by this mechanism was meant to serve as a punishment. However, this approach required that the country punish itself. Other countries were not asked to behave in a reciprocal fashion—almost certainly because doing so would not have been credible. In the end, this mechanism was never adopted, meaning that the agreement lacked any means to enforce its emission reduction obligations. The reason Kyoto ran into problems was not only that it lacked a compliance mechanism but also that it asked some countries to do more than they would have done without the agreement. In other words, the agreement did not simply codify the Nash equilibrium but required that some parties do more than was probably in their self-interests to do. Canada was in a particularly tight spot, as it had ratified the agreement but was wildly off course for complying with it. Rather than not comply, Canada took the easiest way out. It simply withdrew from the agreement. In doing so, Canada fulfilled its obligations under international law—but, of course, it also failed to supply the global public good. Previously, of course, the US opted not to participate in the Kyoto Protocol. Once again, the reason was that there were no negative consequences to this decision. The Kyoto Protocol failed to enforce participation.

The new Paris Agreement on climate change also takes a direct approach to supplying the global public good of climate change mitigation. However, the obligations in the Paris Agreement are declared unilaterally and are voluntary. This design improves on the Kyoto Protocol in that it encourages participation. However, it also contains a major weakness: countries are only willing to participate in the agreement because they can simply pledge to meet the emission level they would have met even if the agreement had not existed. The Paris Agreement would not fall apart (despite the decision by President Trump to withdraw, a symbolic move given that the agreement lacks an enforcement mechanism) nor will it achieve much.

As I said, the direct approach to enforcement works fine when relations are bilateral and nearly symmetric. By extension, the approach can be effective if imperfect when very few countries need to cooperate to supply a public good. Fortunately, although ADB has many member countries, as regards the provision of a regional public good, only a handful of countries may be of central importance. For example, the Mekong River Basin is shared by just six countries, a much smaller number than the membership of ADB let alone of the UN. Having said this, the ability to enforce an agreement by direct reciprocity can drop sharply as the number of countries needing to cooperate increases. This is why the second approach to enforcement—the strategic approach—is important, even for the Asia and Pacific region.

The direct approach involves asking countries to supply the public good, and then figuring out how these obligations to supply can be enforced. The strategic approach involves identifying opportunities for enforcement and then structuring the agreement to exploit these opportunities. The main insight is that countries are very good at coordinating and very bad at enforcing voluntary cooperation. Hence, the strategic approach involves thinking through how a public goods problem can be converted into a coordination game.

One version of this approach incorporates a trade measure related to the obligations. For example, the Montreal Protocol to protect the ozone layer not only requires that parties contribute to the public good by reducing their consumption and production of chlorofluorocarbons (CFCs). It also requires that the parties to the agreement not trade in CFCs or products containing CFCs with non-parties. Essentially, the Montreal Protocol manipulates the incentives to participate. If very few countries are in the agreement, the gain to free riding will exceed the cost of being shut out of markets. However, as more countries participate in the agreement, the cost of being shut out of markets increases. If enough countries are in, it will pay all the others to join. The way to design this agreement is thus not only to incorporate the trade measure but also to ensure that the agreement only enters into force once "enough" countries have opted to participate. This way, a country cannot lose by ratifying the agreement (if the agreement does not come into force, the country would be under no legal obligation to comply), and it will gain by ratifying it (so long as the gain from having access to markets exceeds the loss to not being able to free ride). It is by this mechanism that, despite ozone layer protection being a global public good, the Montreal Protocol has been able to sustain full cooperation (Barrett 2003).

A similar outcome may be sustained by linking different issues. In the companion paper on case studies, I cite a paper that showed that it may help to link cooperation on river basin development to cooperation on trade among the countries that share the Mekong River. I do not want to be misunderstood. Linking provision of a regional public good to trade cooperation would not always work, and it may be a risky strategy (the consequence could be that provision of the public good fails and that trade is restricted).[8] The important point is that the individuals involved in negotiating agreements for provision of regional public goods should be alert to opportunities to structure their agreements so as to create a coordination situation.

Another example is the international agreement on controlling marine pollution by releases of crude oil. Rather than ask countries to reduce their releases directly, the agreement known as MARPOL asks parties to do so indirectly, by adopting a technology standard that separates ballast water from the oil cargo sections of a tanker. This helped because tanker transport is a network, subject to substantial network externalities. As more coastal states joined the agreement, more tanker owners wanted to comply with the standard; and as more tankers complied with the standard, more coastal states wanted to participate in the agreement and enforce the standard (Barrett 2003). Like the Montreal Protocol, participation and compliance with this agreement is virtually perfect.

However, there is one difference. The Montreal approach can sustain a first-best outcome because, so long as the threat to restrict trade is credible, provision of the public good can be full without trade ever being restricted. By contrast, technology standards are typically inefficient. In the case of tankers, it is inefficient not to use space on a tanker to carry cargo when making a delivery. However, this design element is crucial to the success of the agreement in limiting pollution. In short, though MARPOL has full participation and compliance, and improves on the noncooperative outcome, it falls short of the full cooperative outcome. MARPOL is a second-best treaty.

The last point I wish to make about institutions is that it may be a mistake for countries, ADB, and negotiators to look only for first-best solutions. It is an instinct to want to achieve the ideal outcome. However, if such an outcome

---

[8] Nordhaus (2015), in an analysis of linking cooperation on climate change to cooperation on international trade, shows that linkage would not always work, even with his assumption that countries cannot retaliate against a club of countries that decide to link.

cannot be enforced, an agreement aiming to achieve the ideal may ultimately fail to improve on the status quo ante. The strategic approach involves not only reconsideration of the means of cooperation, but also reconsideration of the goals of international cooperation. In some situations, more may be achieved by aiming "low" than by aiming "high."[9]

---

[9] For a demonstration of this phenomenon in the experimental lab, see Barrett and Dannenberg (2017).

References

Arce, M., G. Daniel, and T. Sandler. 2002. *Regional Public Goods: Typologies, Provision, Financing, and Development Assistance*. Stockholm: Almkvist & Wiksell International.

Axelrod, R. 1984. *The Evolution of Cooperation*. New York: Basic Books.

Barrett, S. 2003, *Environment and Statecraft: The Strategy of Environmental Treaty-Making*. Oxford: Oxford University Press.

———. 2007. *Why Cooperate? The Incentive to Supply Global Public Goods*. Oxford: Oxford University Press.

———. 2013. Economic Considerations for the Eradication Endgame. *Philosophical Transactions of the Royal Society B*. 368 (1,623). 20120149.

———. 2013. Climate Treaties and Approaching Catastrophes. *Journal of Environmental Economics and Management*. 66 (2). pp. 235–50.

———. 2016. Coordination vs Voluntarism and Enforcement in Sustaining International Environmental Cooperation, *Proceedings of the National Academy of Sciences*. 113 (51). pp. 14, 515–22.

Barrett, S., and A. Dannenberg. 2017. Tipping versus Cooperating to Supply a Public Good. *Journal of the European Economic Association*. 15 (4). pp. 910–41.

Freedom House. 2018. *Freedom in the World 2018*. Washington, DC.

Hirshleifer, J. 1983. From Weakest-Link to Best-Shot: The Voluntary Provision of Public Goods. *Public Choice*. 41 (3). pp. 371–386.

Nordhaus, W. 2015. Climate Clubs: Overcoming Free Riding in International Climate Policy. *American Economic Review*. 105 (4). pp. 1,339–70.

Putnam, R. D. 1988. Diplomacy and Domestic Politics: The Logic of Two-Level Games. *International Organization*. 42 (3). pp. 427–60.

Scheffer, M., S. R. Carpenter, T. M. Lenton, and J. Bascompete. 2012. Anticipating Critical Transitions. *Science.* 388 (6105). pp. 344–8.

Schelling, T. C. 1960. *The Strategy of Conflict.* Cambridge, MA: Harvard University Press.

Regional Public Goods and Their Technologies of Aggregation

2

Todd Sandler

Public goods display three properties of publicness, to varying extent, thereby complicating the need for policy intervention. In particular, these goods' benefits may be wholly or partly nonrival in consumption, while their benefits may be completely or partly nonexcludable among recipients.[1] For example, reducing air pollution, which is a pure public good, yields nonrival benefits that are nonexcludable for individuals within the polluted area. A third property of publicness is the technology of aggregation (or aggregator technology), which indicates how individual provision or contributions determine the overall quantity available for consumption by benefit recipients (Cornes 1993; Cornes and Sandler 1986; Hirshleifer 1983; Sandler 1992, 1997).

In addition to these properties, public goods display diverse ranges of benefit spillovers within a nation or region, or more broadly across regions or the entire globe. Alternative spillover ranges influence the jurisdiction or institutional arrangement to best serve recipients. This follows because allocative efficiency requires the aggregate marginal benefits derived by recipients to match the marginal cost of provision.[2] Ideally, this match can be fostered through *subsidiarity*, where the providing or assisting jurisdiction precisely matches the benefit range of the public good (Olson 1969; Sandler 2004, 2006). As such, global public goods should be provided or assisted by multilateral institutions, such as the World Health Organization (WHO) in, say, curbing the spread of influenza, while regional public goods (RPGs) should be provided or

---

[1] Benefits are nonrival when the consumption by one agent does not detract, in the slightest, from the consumption opportunities that remain for others from the same unit of the good. Nonexcludability of benefits means that, once provided, the good's benefits can be received by payers and nonpayers alike within the good's spillover range.

[2] For national public goods, the recipients are in the country, while for transnational public goods, the recipients are in the benefit-receiving countries.

assisted by regional institutions, such as the Asian Development Bank (ADB) in, say, supplying region-based infrastructure. Blind adherence to subsidiarity is not always advisable, because this may result in a proliferation of subregional jurisdictions and large transaction costs.

The three properties of public goods help determine their prognosis for efficient provision and, therefore, any need for corrective action at national, subregional, regional, transregional, or global levels. For example, a regional club good with partly rival benefits that are excludable can be provided by member countries with little policy intervention (Buchanan 1965; Sandler 2013a). At the regional level, this can apply to an interregional highway network (e.g., the Western Regional Road Corridor or the East–West Corridor Project), where loans from ADB can help fund the initial investment and later can be repaid through tolls.[3] In contrast, curbing acid rain is a regional or transregional public good that requires policy coordination and monitoring if this environmental concern is to be properly addressed (Chung 2007; Kahn 2004; Murdoch, Sandler, and Sargent 1997). The technology of aggregation can help in ascertaining the need for policy intervention at the regional level (Arce and Sandler 2002, 2003; Berg and Horrall 2008; Sandler 2006; Tres and Barbieri 2017). Consider the promotion of regional financial stability, in which poor financial practices in one country can weaken the financial integrity of the entire region (Kawai 2017). Maintaining financial stability is the quintessential weakest- or weaker-link public good, whose level is disproportionately determined by the country or countries with the most vulnerable financial institutions and the poorest financial practices. To deal with this issue, ADB established the Regional Economic Monitoring Unit in 1999 (Rana 2004). The Asian financial crisis indicated the need to develop long-term currency bond markets to enhance local capital markets, to promote crisis-triggered liquidity, and to encourage sound regulatory practices and supervision (ADB 2017, Kawai 2017).

This chapter takes a new in-depth look at the role of aggregator technologies on the provision of RPGs in Asia. An essential task in accomplishing this is to relate the seven primary aggregators to their prognosis for efficient provision and the concomitant need for policy intervention. The chapter also relates functional areas (e.g., natural resources and the environment, connectivity, and economic cooperation and integration) to aggregator

---

[3] Another club good is the Turkmenistan–Uzbekistan–Tajikistan–Afghanistan–Pakistan Power Interconnection Framework, which received a $240 million loan from the Asian Development Bank for its fifth phase in December 2016 (ADB 2017).

technologies and select Asian institutions. Asia is a huge geographical area with many distinct subregions, so that jurisdictional boundaries must be addressed in subregional public goods, RPGs, and transregional public goods. In response, a diverse set of subregional, regional, and interregional institutions have developed. For some public goods, these institutions are assisted by multilateral institutions and other participants (e.g., partnerships, nongovernment organizations [NGOs], and charitable foundations). The chapter also re-examines the application of subsidiarity in light of diverse spillover ranges of Asian public goods.

At the outset, it should be emphasized that the configuration of the three properties of public goods only partly indicates the need for remedial action, owing to intervening considerations. For instance, the inherent incentive to contribute efficiently to a weakest-link public good hinges on all participants (say, countries in a region) possessing the same tastes and income (Sandler 1992). Under these circumstances, every country matches the other countries' ideal contributions and there is no gain from free riding (Hirshleifer 1983). In fact, the allocative outcome is optimal. If income, but not tastes, differ, then some countries may not be able to afford the efficient level of the good that all countries desire. In this situation, the poorest or "weakest-link" country needs its provision level subsidized or shored up by others. Shoring up weakest-link countries presents a free-rider problem of its own as countries wait for others to lend a hand (Sandler 2006, 2016). In such circumstances, ADB may have to do the shoring up or provide guidance for others to do so. The one-to-one link between the three properties of publicness and the required institutional arrangement may also fail because the institutional arrangement may endogenously affect one or more of the goods' properties. For example, WHO may make its gathered information freely available, thereby making the good nonexcludable. Similarly, a club arrangement may withhold benefits from nonpayers through an institution-imposed exclusion device.

The rest of the chapter presents preliminaries, investigates aggregator technologies and three alternative types of public goods, and relates aggregator technologies to the need for policy intervention. The chapter then focuses on functional areas, their predominant aggregator technologies, and associated Asian institutions. It examines subsidiarity followed by the role of Asian and other institutions in providing subregional public goods, RPGs, and transregional public goods.

Even though the analysis is on Asian public goods and institutions, this analysis can also be applied to the same in European and Latin American regions. The issues and insights addressed here apply to all regions.

Preliminaries

The notion of a region must be addressed. Its basis may be founded on alternative grounds (Arce and Sandler 2002). Most commonly, a region is a territorial subsystem based on geographical location such as sub-Saharan Africa, Europe, Latin America and the Caribbean, or Asia (Sandler 2006). For large regions such as Asia and the Pacific, subregions are often defined— i.e., Central Asia, East Asia, Southeast Asia, South Asia, Pacific, and Oceania (ADB 2017).[4] Alternatively, a region could be a geological (based on earth formations such as mountains, plains, or coastlines), political (e.g., countries in a military alliance), cultural, historical (e.g., past colonial ties), or geoclimatic in nature. For RPGs, a region corresponds to the *basis that gives rise to countries receiving the good's benefits*. If the public good is agricultural best practices, then shared geoclimatic conditions are germane; if, however, the public good is a transportation network, the geographic location is relevant. Throughout this study, the regional basis is geographical. Asia has geographical subregions that correspond to the relevant benefit spillover range for some public goods. When the public good benefits reach beyond the entire region, a transregional entity, which may consist of a network between regions, must be considered. For example, acid rain stemming from sulfur emissions in Asia may impact parts of California, making for a transregional basis for actions to reduce these Asia emissions.

RPGs provide benefit spillovers for much of a region, while subregional public goods offer benefit spillovers for some subregion. Thus, an Asian intraregional highway network is an Asian RPG, as are sound financial practice rules and governance for Asia to avert future financial crises. River navigation agreements and border development projects in the Greater Mekong Subregion (GMS) represent subregional public goods (Westcott 2004). Often, subregional public goods must be linked to achieve a regionwide public good, so that subregional highways, railways, communication systems, and power grids may be the initial steps to achieving the sought-after regional infrastructure. In so doing,

---

[4] These are the subregions designated by ADB and consist in total of 48 countries with varying degrees of regional cooperation and integration (ADB 2017), where Southeast Asia is the most integrated and Central Asia is the least integrated.

connectivity—a public good in its own right—must be pursued so that these subregional units can be joined (Acharya 2017; Estevadeordal and Goodman 2017; Jordana 2017; Prasad 2017). Thus, railways must use the same gauged tracks, while communication networks must be conformable (Sakai and Nguyen 2004). Subregional institutions should supply and coordinate member countries' actions for subregional public goods if relevant spillover recipients' marginal gains are to be matched with the goods' marginal provision costs. Of course, no coordinating actions are required in those rare circumstances when the properties of the subregional public goods motivate countries to take the proper actions. Regional institutions, such as ADB and Asia-Pacific Economic Cooperation, should foster the provision of RPGs and the transforming of joined subregional public goods into an RPG when coordination is necessary.

The new regionalism gave rise to the interest in RPGs (Stålgren 2000). This regionalism arose from increased regional exchanges of goods, services, people, financial capital, pollution, diseases, virtual transmissions, externalities, and public good spillovers. In many ways, regionalism was a more local representation of globalization, which arose from increased global flows. Regionalism is a powerful motivator of RPG provision to manage some of these cross-regional flows, such as pollution, refugees, conflict, financial flows, and trade exchanges. In so doing, regional and subregional institutions grew in number and included free trade agreements, custom unions, regulatory agencies, and regional development banks. At the regional level, RPGs experienced supporting (e.g., spatial and cultural propinquity, past and ongoing interactions, and common concerns) and inhibiting factors (e.g., regional rivalries, past conflicts, leadership concerns) (Sandler 2006). Unlike global public goods, the absence of donor countries' spillovers also inhibited outside assistance for some RPGs, thereby bolstering the need for regional development banks, regional institutions, and subregional institutions as a sources of other assistance.

A final preliminary involves functional areas for public goods. In the case of global public goods, the International Task Force on Global Public Goods (2004) delineated six areas—global commons, financial stability, trade regimes, peace and security, communicable diseases, and knowledge—and commissioned studies on each. More recently, Estevadeordal and Goodman (2017) indicated six functional areas for RPGs that include natural resources and environment, economic cooperation and integration, human and social development, governance and institutions, peace and security, and connectivity. Only peace and security is the same in the two lists.

Obviously, the global commons is not appropriate for RPGs and has been replaced by natural resources and environment, which includes addressing water pollution, curbing acid rain, managing the regional commons, and ameliorating regional environmental issues. At the regional level, economic cooperation and integration involves promoting free trade agreements, fostering foreign direct investment, maintaining financial stability, and bolstering economic growth. Human and social development concern education, health, knowledge creation, and culture, while governance and institutions involve regulatory practices, rule of law, policy harmonization, and other region-based governance needs. Peace and security addresses conflict resolution, refugee flows, drug trafficking, terrorism, and corruption. Finally, connectivity is associated with transportation and other regional infrastructure networks. These functional areas are much more inclusive and multiplex in nature than the earlier list for global public goods. As such, many aggregator technologies apply to each functional area, as explored in on the section *Functional Areas, Aggregator Technologies, and Associated Regional Institutions.*

Taxonomies: Select Aggregator Technologies and Regional Public Goods

In this chapter, seven common technologies of aggregation are considered and related to three types of public goods—pure public, impure public, and club goods. Traditionally, the summation aggregator was assumed for all forms of public goods, where the overall level of the public good equals the sum of the contributors' provision (Samuelson 1954, 1955). At the regional level, accumulated pollutants in an interstate lake abide by a summation aggregator. This aggregator makes each contributor's supply or provision effort a perfect substitute for that of other contributors, thereby encouraging free riding and underprovision. For a weighted-sum aggregator, each contributor's provision is assigned an empirically determined weight before being summed to determine the overall level of the public good. A weighted sum aggregator limits substitutability and applies to the reduction of acid rain or river pollution, for which a country's relative location affects its ability to ameliorate the pollutant. Upstream countries can do more to reduce river pollution than downstream countries. In Asia, the Long-Range Transboundary Air Pollution (LRTAP) program in Northeast Asia and the Acid Deposition Monitoring Network in East Asia are intended to ascertain these weights based on the monitored dispersion of pollutants from the source to the recipient countries (Chung 2017).

The smallest contribution fixes the aggregate level for a weakest-link public good. Weakest-link aggregation is associated with actions to curb the spread of an infectious disease or the surveillance of regional financial crises (e.g., Economic Review and Policy Dialogue in Asia). A less extreme form of weakest link is weaker link, where the smallest contribution has the greatest influence on the good's aggregate level, followed by the second-smallest contribution, and so on (Cornes 1993; Cornes and Sandler 1986; Sandler 1992). Actions to impede the spread of financial instability abide by the weaker-link aggregator.

The threshold aggregator requires the provision of the public good to meet or exceed some level before benefits are generated. Preparation to avert flooding along a riverbank requires some level of sandbagging or levying if flooding is to be addressed at all. Sandbagging beyond this threshold does more to curtail flooding. For best-shot public goods, the largest contribution determines the goods' aggregate level. Examples include ending regional conflicts, developing financial best practices, or setting up a regional internet system.[5] Finally, better-shot public goods are a softer version of best shot, for which the largest contribution has the greatest marginal influence on the good's overall level, followed by the second-largest contribution, and so on. Other aggregator technologies may combine these basic forms; for example, once a threshold is reached, the good's level beyond the threshold may hinge on the smallest contribution. Joint products allow an activity to provide two or more public goods, each of which may correspond to different aggregator technologies.

Each of these basic aggregators may be related to alternative types of public goods that display different degrees of nonrivalry and nonexcludability of benefits. In Table 2.1, three types of public goods are associated with seven aggregators. Pure public goods offer nonrival benefits that are nonexcludable and include curbing an ecosystem's pollution or ending a regional conflict. Impure public goods are associated with nonrival or partly rival benefits that may or may not be excludable. Examples include accommodating refugees from a regional conflict, where such action can be ended or excluded by a recipient country. Curbing the spread of regional terrorist campaigns is subject to rivalry as actions in one area may limit actions elsewhere. Club goods consist of a public good whose benefits are partly rival but excludable at a negligible cost, e.g., interregional highway network, air traffic control system, or interregional railway network.

---

[5] On advancing internet systems in Asia and the Pacific, see Suominen (2017).

Table 2.1: Regional Public Goods: Aggregate Technologies and Three Public Good Types

Aggregation Technology	Pure Public Good	Impure Public Good	Club
Summation: Overall level of public good equals the sum of the region's contributions	Limiting region-specific air pollution	Providing public health infrastructure or accommodating refugees from a nearby conflict	Interregional highway network or interregional parks
Weighted sum: Overall level of public good equals a weighted sum of the region's contributions	Controlling the spread of an infectious outbreak at the regional level	Reducing acid rain or volatile organic substances	Regional electric grid or monitoring system
Weakest link: Smallest contribution of the region's countries determines the good's aggregate level	Maintaining the functionality or operation of a regional network	Surveillance of regional financial crisis or a pest	Air traffic control system or air traffic corridors
Weaker link: Smallest contribution in the region has the greatest influence on the good's aggregate level, followed by the second-smallest contribution, and so on	Forestalling the spread of political instability or maintaining sterilization	Inhibiting regional pest or crop disease diffusion	Interregional railway network
Threshold: Benefits from the regional public good only arise once the cumulative contributed quantity surpasses a threshold amount	Establishing an early warning system for tsunamis	Suppressing regional forest fires or curbing flooding	Crisis-management teams or conflict-curtailment force
Best shot: Largest contribution in the region determines the good's aggregate level	Curtailing or ending regional conflict or ending insurrections	Developing financial best practices or uncovering agricultural best practices	Providing region-based internet system
Better shot: Largest contribution in the region has the greatest influence on the good's aggregate level, followed by the second-largest contribution, and so on	Uncovering best practices, including treatment regimens for a region-based disease	Limiting the diffusion of regional instability or drug trafficking	Hazard-testing facility

Source: Author.

If aggregators are ignored, then pure public goods have the poorest prognosis for supply efficiency owing to free riding and contributors not accounting for the benefits that they conferred on others. Even if exclusion could be practiced, nonrivalry means that it is inadvisable to do so, because the incremental cost of extending consumption to others is costless (Sandler 2004). Hence, social welfare declines when exclusion is practiced with a pure public good. Impure public goods are generally undersupplied or overused because of limited exclusion and partial rivalry (Sandler 2013b). The inefficiency associated with impure public goods is less extreme than that of pure public goods if some exclusion is practiced to account for consumption-related incremental costs. If no crowding- or rivalry-internalizing tolls are charged, then impure public goods are overused. Club goods offer the best prognosis for efficiency as tolls internalize crowding externalities. Ideally, regional clubs can charge their members or user countries for their revealed utilization, where the collected tolls are used to cover provision cost over time. ADB or subregional institutions (Central Asia Regional Economic Cooperation [CAREC] program, GMS program, South Asia Subregional Economic Cooperation [SASEC]) can offer loans or grants to initially pay for regional club goods, such as highway, power, communication, or railway networks. The proceeds from the tolls can later repay these loans.

Next, the efficiency prognosis and policy recommendations are considered for the seven aggregators. The strongest free-riding incentive characterizes summation, given the associated substitutability of contributors' provision. From a game-theoretic vantage, this substitutability gives rise to a prisoner's dilemma, for which the dominant action is not to contribute. As such, remedial policy is needed by regional and subregional institutions. These actions can take the form of loans or grants to fund the regional pure public goods. Multilateral institutions and others (e.g., charitable foundations, partnerships, or NGOs) can bolster efforts to fund these pure public goods.

For RPGs, repeated interactions among potential providers may overcome prisoner's dilemma concerns as countries employ tit for tat strategies that reward cooperation and punish noncooperation. Weighted-sum aggregators have less free-riding incentives as countries become informed about how they impact provision. In an acid rain scenario, downwind countries are the main recipients of depositions and are, thus, motivated to come to an understanding with other countries to control sulfur and nitrogen emissions. Thus, there is a need to monitor and make the information available. When remedial policy is carried out by regional and subregional institutions to bolster countries' actions, this information on weights allows these institutions to distribute their resources among countries, where these resources have the greatest effect based on spatial and other factors. The gathering and provision of information facilitate the supply of weighted-sum RPGs and subregional public goods. In Europe, significant and lasting progress has been made in addressing a host of transboundary air pollution problems once the spatial weight matrices were uncovered through UN-supported monitoring (Murdoch, Sandler, and Sargent 1997).

If all countries in a region have identical endowments and tastes, then weakest-link pure public goods present no efficiency concerns as each country *matches* one another's ideal provision level.[6] There are no free-rider incentives because to contribute less brings down everyone's consumption level to the smallest contribution. Problems occur when endowments differ because poorer countries cannot afford the optimal level and must be assisted or shored up (Sandler 1997). The necessary assistance can come from ADB in the form of grants since loans may unduly burden such poor countries. For weakest-link RPGs, capability building is the key consideration. Such shoring-up efforts can also come from global organizations, subregional institutions (e.g., CAREC or GMS), NGOs, or a dominant country such as the People's Republic of China (PRC). Without some coordination in shoring up weakest-link countries, a prisoners' dilemma arises because countries prefer others to do the assisting. Consequently, regional and subregional institutions play an important shoring-up role in regions plagued by inequality and weakest-link RPGs. Weaker-link RPGs have a somewhat more favorable prognosis, even when endowments differ insofar as complete matching behavior is not needed but some shoring-up efforts are still required. Once again, regional, subregional, and other aid-giving institutions have a capability-building role so that all regional countries can contribute toward the public good.

Compared to summation RPGs, threshold RPGs offer greater incentive to act until the threshold is obtained. Once reached, a free-riding incentive exists for countries that do not contribute to the threshold. Unless the threshold requires every country to contribute, provision is inefficient as contributors do not account for benefits derived by noncontributors. A larger threshold pushes the provision outcome toward efficient provision. ADB and subregional institutions can influence (or design) the threshold to be large so that more efficient provision results.[7] Threshold RPGs present

---

[6]   Impure public goods still confront underprovision and overuse concerns given partial rivalry.

[7]   Other design principles that promote optimal supply for a threshold RPG is to allow for cost sharing or refundability (if the threshold is not reached) (Sandler 2004).

a coordination problem for countries that can be orchestrated by ADB and other institutions by rewarding or subsidizing countries for contributing toward reaching the threshold. In other instances, these institutions can pool efforts by contributing funds of their own or reaching out to charitable foundations or partnerships for funds. The underlying game form is that of assurance, where leadership can achieve the desired outcome among alternative equilibriums (Arce 2001; Sandler and Sargent 1995).

For best-shot RPGs, inequality among regional countries is conducive to provision, because it becomes more likely that one country has the means to support the necessary provision.[8] A key concern for best-shot subregional public goods is the potential absence of a really well-endowed country. For Asian subregions, only the Pacific may be a concern. Central Asia has Kazakhstan; East Asia has the PRC; South Asia has India; Southeast Asia has Indonesia, the Philippines, Singapore, and Viet Nam; and Oceania has Australia. At the regional level, the issue becomes a coordination issue when there are potential best-shooter countries, because only a single capable country needs to provide the best-shot RPGs or subregional public goods. ADB and the Association of Southeast Asian Nations (ASEAN) can serve to coordinate action, where countries take turns at providing best-shot RPGs and subregional public goods. If the required best-shooter country is not available, then regional institutions can pool actions or coordinate action among the subregions. In many instances, ADB loans can assist the best-shooter country to supply the good. Loans are appropriate because such best shooters are motivated to supply the good for the gains that they receive. For expensive best-shot RPGs, ADB can solicit funds from the World Bank, WHO, the United Nations (UN), or other multilateral institutions. Hegemony is conducive to best-shot RPG and subregional public good provision; hence, the economic rise of the PRC and India greatly serves the provision of these best-shot goods. Better-shot RPGs and subregional public goods are even easier to provide efficiently than their best-shot counterparts. Since more than one country can act, there is less need to coordinate or concentrate provision activity. Moreover, more than one provision level is permitted. For example, for polio, both the Salk and Sabine vaccines provided protection, but Salk was preferred because it did not employ a live virus to induce immunity. Better-shot public goods require less need for hegemony, pooling of actions, and outside intervention.

---

[8] Inequality is favorable for best-shot RPGs but is unfavorable for weakest-link RPGs. This was first indicated by Sandler (1997).

Functional Areas, Aggregator Technologies, and Associated Regional Institutions

The chapter now turns to the six functional areas, previously introduced, to relate each to their predominant aggregator technology and some relevant Asian regional institutions. In the left column of Table 2.2, each of the functional areas is listed along with representative RPGs and subregional public goods. The middle column indicates the predominant aggregators and the right-hand column contains some associated Asian institutions.

A host of regional commons issues concerning air and water transport of pollution is addressed by natural resources and environment. Summation and weighted sum are the primary aggregators for this area. For weighted sum, monitoring is essential to ascertain the transport matrices from emission source to recipient country, giving rise to such entities as the Acid Deposition Monitoring Network in East Asia and the Long-Range Transboundary Air Pollution in Northeast Asia. Similar monitoring systems are needed throughout Asia's subregions, so that an overall emission-recipient matrix can be constructed for the entire Asia and Pacific region. Renewable energy is also an important concern throughout the region, especially if greenhouse gases are to be controlled (Chung 2017; Kahn 2004; Sandler 2004). Many Asian economies are large generators of greenhouse gases, so that multilateral institutions (e.g., UN Environment Programme and World Bank) and networks (the Global Environment Facility) must bolster regional actions to address global public goods and transregional public goods, such as climate change, species preservation, and very long-range transboundary pollutants. This functional area contains summation aggregators that are difficult to address and weighted-sum aggregators that are much easier to deal with.

Economic cooperation and integration is heavily influenced by weakest-link aggregators, which call for actions to shore up or support poorer countries in subregions. This is particularly true for maintaining financial and macroeconomic stability (Berrettoni and Lucángeli 2012, Kawai 2017, Rana 2004; Westcott 2004). Relevant institutions include GMS, South Asian Association for Regional Cooperation (SAARC), ASEAN, and CAREC. Free trade agreements also play a role by promoting trade, furthering economic integration, and fostering foreign direct investment within and among subregions. In some instances (e.g., regional economic growth and promoting trade), summation is a relevant aggregator.

Table 2.2: Functional Areas—Predominant Aggregator Technologies and Select Asian Regional Institutions

Functional Areas (Public Goods)	Aggregator	Asian Regional Institutions
Natural Resources and Environment: (e.g., maintaining biodiversity, curbing acid rain, engaging in reforestation, managing commons, reducing ambient air pollution)	Summation, Weighted sum	Acid Deposition Monitoring Network in East Asia; Long-Range Transboundary Air Pollution in Northeast Asia; Pacific Island Renewable Energy Investment Program
Economic Cooperation and Integration: (e.g., creating free trade agreements, fostering foreign and portfolio investments, maintaining financial stability, establishing good policies, maintaining macroeconomic stability, fostering regional growth)	Summation, Weakest link Better shot	Greater Mekong Subregion (GMS) Program; South Asian Association for Regional Cooperation; Association of Southeast Asian Nations (ASEAN); Central Asia Regional Economic Cooperation; Free Trade Area of the Asia-Pacific; South Asian Free Trade Area
Human and Social Development: (e.g., promoting education, bolstering health, creating knowledge creation, maintaining culture, furthering science)	Weakest link, Weaker link, Best shot Better shot	GMS Health Security Project
Governance and Institutions: (e.g., regulatory practices, regional collectives, rule of law, banking practices, benchmarking data, capacity building, policy harmonization, surveillance, institution building)	Best shot, Better shot, Threshold, Weakest link	Economic Review and Policy Dialogue; South Asian Telecommunication Regulators Council; Chiang Mai Initiative Multilateralization; ASEAN+3 Macroeconomic Research Office
Peace and Security: (e.g., peacekeeping, crisis management, limiting weapon proliferation, managing refugee flows, territorial dispute resolution, alliance, curbing drug trafficking, controlling terrorism, limiting corruption)	Best shot, Better shot, Threshold, Weakest link	No region-wide Asia-Pacific alliance. Some non-aggression pacts (e.g., India and Pakistan, and the People's Republic of China and Pakistan). Alliances with the United States, ASEAN
Connectivity: (e.g., transportation and communications networks, interregional infrastructure, customs control and harmonization, interregional power grids, air traffic control and corridors)	Weakest link, Weaker link Threshold	Border economic zone development; East Asia and Pacific Infrastructure Regulatory Forum; South Asia Forum for Infrastructure Regulation; Turkmenistan–Uzbekistan–Tajikistan–Afghanistan–Pakistan Power Interconnection Framework; GMS Cross-Border Transport Facilitation Agreement

Source: Author.

By encompassing both health and knowledge, human and social development includes two of the International Task Force on Global Public Goods (2004) functional areas. Health is affected by both weakest-link and best-shot aggregators (Arce and Sandler 2002). Forestalling the spread of infectious diseases is a weaker- or weakest-link public good, while discovering new vaccines or treatment regiments are better- or best-shot public goods. The GMS Health Security Project is a relevant Asian subregional institution. Knowledge creation and culture preservation are better- and best-shot public goods. Asia needs more subregional institutions to champion health and knowledge public goods specific to Asia. Without these Asian-based institutions, NGOs, charitable foundations (e.g., the Gates Foundation), WHO, and global institutions address health and knowledge in Asia. This functional area is difficult to address since it contains both extreme aggregators, one of which calls for greater income equality and the other of which calls for greater income inequality (Sandler 1997).

Governance and institutions often involve developing best practices, which is a quintessential better- or best-shot RPG. Examples include regulatory practices, banking practices, and benchmarking data (Berg and Horrall 2008). Relevant Asian institutions include the Economic Review and Policy Dialogue, the South Asian Telecommunication Regulator Council, the Chiang Mai Initiative Multilateralization, and the ASEAN+3 Macroeconomic Research Office. In institution building, RPGs and subregional public goods include rule of law, capacity building, policy harmonization, and surveillance, all of which abide by threshold or weakest-link aggregators. Vastly different aggregators are involved, since governance and institution formation require different activities. Fortunately, threshold and weakest-link aggregators can be addressed in many circumstances, especially when ADB and global institutions lend a hand.

Peace and security also encompass many diverse activities that include peacekeeping, managing crises, limiting weapon proliferation, managing refugee flows, and resolving territorial disputes. Such activities are better- and best-shot RPGs that could be handled by subregional or regional military alliances; however, no such alliance exists in the Asia and Pacific region. There are some bilateral non-aggression pacts and bilateral alliances with the United States. Consequently, Asia has relied on UN peacekeeping missions to deal with conflicts. In contrast, drug trafficking and terrorism represent weakest-link RPGs that have plagued Afghanistan, India, Pakistan, and Uzbekistan, with some negative spillovers to the rest of the world—e.g., the hijackings on 9/11. This is a functional area for Asia that needs much more attention. Asia has endured many intrastate conflicts that could, if unchecked, contaminate neighboring states (George, Hou, and Sandler 2019). The same contamination can stem from terrorist groups, guerrillas, and drug gangs (Mendelson-Forman 2017).

The final functional area concerns connectivity, where subregions' infrastructure must be linked in a seamless fashion to tie together the region's transportation, communication, digital, air traffic control, and power networks (Prasad 2017; Sakai and Nguyen 2004; Suominen 2017). Connectivity also concerns customs control, where similar procedures are followed that facilitate commerce, while protecting national interests. For connectivity, weaker- and weakest-link aggregators are predominant. Failure of even a single country's infrastructure to be joined properly with that of its neighbors can seriously reduce the functionality of the network throughout Asia. To forestall such consequences, oversight and support at the regional level must come from ADB in the form of grants to eliminate choke points or linkage failures. Such failures will generally characterize the poorest countries, which may gain the least from network integrity. Thus, there is the need for grants, not loans, to shore up these weakest-link-challenged countries. As the network gets started, the threshold aggregator applies as network milestones must be surpassed in establishing a multicountry network. For Asia, Table 2.2 indicates a few representative institutions that foster connectivities. These include the East Asia and Pacific Infrastructure Regulatory Forum, the South Asia Forum for Infrastructure Regulation, the Turkmenistan–Uzbekistan–Tajikistan–Afghanistan–Pakistan Power Interconnection Framework, and the GMS Cross-Border Transport Facilitation Agreement. Connectivity action should first be at the subregional level, followed by efforts at the regional level to link the subregions. If the subsequent regional linkages are to be successful, then subregional grids must be compatible.

On Subsidiarity

With subsidiarity, the jurisdictional range of the political institution, charged with providing the public good, matches the corresponding benefit range of the public good. Accordingly, subregional public goods are supplied by subregional institutions; RPGs are supplied by regional institutions; and transregional public goods are supplied by interregional networks (e.g., the Consultative Group for International Agricultural Research). Subsidiarity aims to equate the good's benefit recipients' summed marginal benefits to the good's marginal provision costs, thereby achieving efficient supply. If the public good's spillover range exceeds that of the institution's jurisdiction, then provision decisions will fail to account for some benefit recipients, thereby resulting in undersupply. If, however, the institution's jurisdiction exceeds that of the public good's spillover range, then overprovision is anticipated as nonrecipients cover some of the good's provision cost.

In its pristine form, the application of subsidiarity ignores factors that can limit its desirability. The top half of Table 2.3 indicates supporting factors, the first two having just been addressed. Subsidiarity can curtail some transaction costs through repeated interactions that allow benefit recipients to understand one another. This adherence to the same jurisdictional arrangement can promote institutional evolution and innovation. Subsidiarity focuses on the benefit recipients, who are those with a stake in the provision of the public good. If subsidiarity means supplying the public goods at the subregional or regional levels, then the mission creep of global institutions is avoided unless weakest-link and best-shot considerations require capacity building at these lower levels by such institutions.

Other factors detract from strict adherence to subsidiarity, as displayed in Table 2.3. Economies of scale may justify an RPG-providing jurisdiction, whose domain exceeds that of a good's spillover range if the reduced unit costs offset any inefficiency losses. For peacekeeping missions, the UN can achieve scale economies not achievable at the regional or subregional levels. Economies of scope refer to cost savings when two or more subregional public goods or RPGs are supplied by the same institution even though the goods' benefit recipients are not precisely the same. Oversized jurisdictions are warranted when economies of learning occur as larger cumulative provision of one or more RPG takes place.[9] Another obstacle to subsidiarity may derive from the absence of the requisite regional institution or jurisdiction, so that the next nearest (smaller or larger) jurisdiction must be used. A plethora of subregional public goods contain their own spillover range. Tailoring jurisdictions to these spillover ranges would result in a proliferation of jurisdictions that is costly to support, especially considering commonly shared inputs for administration. Thus, CAREC, SAARC, and GMS must oversee a range of subregional public goods, some of which possess quite diverse benefit recipients. Transregional public goods require interregional cooperation so that links must be forged, as in ADB–Inter-American

---

[9]   Economies of learning result in a shift down in the unit cost curve as the total output levels surpass set levels.

Table 2.3: Supporting and Detracting Factors on Regional Subsidiarity

Supporting Factors

- Bolsters efficiency by matching recipients' marginal gains with marginal provision costs
- Curtails tax spillovers to non-beneficiaries, thereby fostering efficiency
- Limits transaction costs by augmenting repeated interactions, reducing asymmetric information, and curtailing the number of participants
- Promotes the evolution of regional institutions based on shared culture, experiences, challenges, norms, and values
- Fosters intraregional institutional innovations
- Focuses on participants with the most at stake
- Ends "mission creep" of global institutions

Detracting Factors

- Economies of scale favor larger jurisdictions than spillover range of regional public goods (RPGs)
- Economies of scope endorse providing two or more RPGs whose spillover ranges do not coincide
- Economies of learning may require oversized jurisdictions to augment the cumulative level of RPG provision
- Requisite subsidiarity-based institution (jurisdiction) may not exist
- Too expensive to tailor jurisdictions to each subregional public good owing to the proliferation of jurisdictions
- Transregional public goods may require interregional cooperation or linkage
- Aggregator technologies (e.g., best shot, better shot, and threshold) may favor pooling efforts beyond requisite jurisdiction
- Aggregator technologies (e.g., weakest link and weaker link) may necessitate bolstering capacity by participants beyond the spillover range of the public good
- Requisite financing may require a jurisdiction beyond the good's range of benefit spillovers

Source: Author.

Development Bank, to support such goods that influence portions of both regions. For some best-shot, better-shot, and threshold public goods, the requisite effort may require the pooling of resources beyond the subsidiarity-identified institution. This may be true for medical research, where actions need to draw expertise from the world's premier facilities. Similarly, weakest- and weaker-link RPGs may require bolstering the capability of the region by drawing funds from beyond the goods' spillover ranges to subsidize financially challenged countries. Addressing some subregional public goods may be beyond the financial assets of some subregions, so that outside assistance is needed.

Some policy conclusions follow. First, strict adherence to subsidiarity is generally inadvisable given so many subregional public goods and RPGs with diverse spillover ranges. Second, regional and subregional institutions need to supply multiple public goods even when their spillover ranges do not overlap. Third, regional institutions must coordinate actions among subregional institutions, while transregional institutions must coordinate actions among regional institutions. These actions can address the failure to adhere strictly to subsidiarity. Fourth, a host of other institutions (see the next section) can assist with respect to weakest-link, threshold, and best-shot RPGs, when shoring-up and capability-building concerns are relevant.

Role of Institutions in Providing Subregional Public Goods, Regional Public Goods, and Transregional Public Goods

Myriad institutions play an essential role in providing subregional public goods, RPGs, and transregional public goods in Asia. Table 2.4 lists six sets of essential institutions and the roles they assume, some of which were mentioned earlier.

ADB and ASEAN are sources for funding and coordinating action to provide these public goods. Subregional institutions focus their actions for subregional public goods and can reach out to partnerships, charitable foundations, NGOs, and dominant countries for additional funding in pooling efforts for best-shot and threshold subregional public goods or in shoring up weakest-link contributors. Free trade agreements not only promote regional trade, but also promote connectivity, governance, and institution building. These collectives can also provide collateral for loans for large-scale public goods. Global institutions generate knowledge and best practices, while also supplying global public goods and transregional public goods. These multilateral institutions not only coordinate actions with regional development banks, but also offer additional funds. The UN has specialized agencies to assist essential functional areas, such as peace and security (peacekeeping operations), and programs for natural resources and environment and human and social development. Partnerships, charitable foundations, and other institutions provide capacity for best-shot and threshold regional public goods and shore up weakest-link contributors. Networks foster interregional connectivity and address some key functional areas.

Table 2.4: Role of Institutions in Subregional, Regional, and Transregional Public Goods in Asia

Institutions	Purposes
ADB, ASEAN	Support subregional, regional, and transregional public goods. Grants are useful to shore up weakest- and weaker-link countries; loans are more suited to other aggregation technologies. ADB and ASEAN can coordinate efforts for threshold public goods and pool efforts for best- and better-shot public goods. Provide monitoring and information to motivate countries actions, especially for weighted-sum regional public goods. Subsidize membership fees and tolls for poor countries in clubs.
Subregional Cooperation • CAREC • SAARC • GMS • SASEC	Support national, subregional, and regional public goods through grants and loans. Coordinate and sequence subregional and regional public good provision in the subregion. Seek funding from partnerships, charitable foundations, and ADB. Motivate a dominant country to provide best-shot subregional public goods or to shore up weaker and weakest links. Promote capability building and institutional strengthening.
Free Trade Areas • SAFTA • FTAAP	Promote regional trade. Foster connectivity, governance, and institution building within the region. Provide collateral for loans, especially for threshold, best-shot and better-shot subregional and regional public goods.
World Bank, United Nations, UNEP, UNDP, IMF, and World Health Organization	Support transregional and global public goods. Provide information and develop best practices for public good provision. Coordinate efforts with ADB, IDB, and other regional development banks. Address functional areas such as natural resources and environment, peace and security, governance and institution, human and social development, and economic cooperation and development.
Partnerships, Charitable Foundations, Nongovernment Organizations, Dominant Country	Shore up weakest-link, weaker-link, and threshold subregional and regional public goods. Bolster funding for best-shot and better-shot regional public goods. Partnerships can draw on components' comparative advantage.
Networks • CGIAR • GEF • ADB-IDB linkage	Provide transregional public goods and promote interregional connectivity. For example, GEF addresses regional and global commons issues and CGIAR focuses on disseminating knowledge.

ADB = Asian Development Bank, ASEAN = Association of Southeast Asian Nations, CAREC = Central Asia Regional Economic Cooperation, CGIAR = Consultative Group for International Agricultural Research, FTAAP = Free Trade Area of the Asia-Pacific, GEF = Global Environment Facility, GMS = Greater Mekong Subregion, IDB = Inter-American Development Bank, IMF = International Monetary Fund, SAARC = South Asian Association for Regional Cooperation, SAFTA = South Asian Free Trade Area, SASEC = South Asia Subregional Economic Cooperation, UNDP = United Nations Development Programme, UNEP = United Nations Environment Programme.

Source: Author.

Some Policy Recommendations

There are many policy recommendations to highlight. First, blind adherence to subsidiarity is not advisable, especially given that benefit spillover ranges for many subregional public goods do not match.

Second, if benefit-receiving countries possess different spending capabilities for weakest-link RPGs and subregional public goods, then grants are preferable to loans when shoring up income-challenged contributors. Loans are more appropriate for supporting best-shot and threshold RPGs, however, because the likely providers tend to have enough endowments and a high stake in the good's provision to want to assume the loans.

Third, monitoring and information gathering are crucial when providing weighted-sum RPGs, so that each country's impact on the overall quantity of the RPG is known.

Fourth, ADB and other regional institutions must coordinate efforts for threshold RPGs, especially when the required threshold number of countries is less than potential contributors.

Fifth, because functional areas are affected differently by aggregator technologies, policies must account for these areas' predominant aggregators. That is, for connectivity, policy to shore up weakest-links is essential, while for peace and security, policy to attain the necessary best-shot response is key.

Sixth, a club arrangement can achieve efficiency for many infrastructure and connectivity RPGs.

Seventh, loans should be used to fund the club RPGs; the proceeds from congestion-internalizing tolls can later repay the loans.

Eighth, policy intervention regarding RPGs must pay heed to the underlying aggregator technology. Such intervention may be essential for summation RPGs, but unnecessary for weakest-link RPGs when the region contains similarly endowed countries. Policy intervention may be unnecessary for some best-shot RPGs if a dominant, rich country has the means to supply the good.

Ninth, partnerships, charitable foundations, and NGOs serve important capability-enhancing and shoring-up roles for best-shot and weakest-link RPGs, respectively.

Lastly, networks and multilateral institutions are suited to supplying transregional public goods.

References

Acharya, A. 2017. Regionalism in the Evolving World Order: Power, Leadership, and the Provision of Public Goods. In Antoni Estevadeordal and Louis W. Goodman, eds. *21ˢᵗ Century Cooperation: Regional Public Goods, Global Governance, and Sustainable Development*. London: Routledge.

Arce, D.G. 2001. Leadership and the Aggregation of International Collective Action. *Oxford Economic Papers*. 53 (2). pp. 114–37.

Arce, D.G. and T. Sandler. 2002. *Regional Public Goods: Typologies, Provision, Financing, and Development Assistance*. Stockholm: Almquist and Wiksell for International Expert Group on Development Issues, Swedish Ministry for Foreign Affairs.

———. 2003. Health-Promoting Alliances. *European Journal of Political Economy*. 19 (3). pp. 355–75.

Asian Development Bank. 2017. *Asian Economic Integration Report 2017: The Era of Financial Interconnectedness, How Can Asia Strengthen Financial Resilience?* Manila.

Berg, S.V. and J. Horrall. 2008. Networks of Regulatory Agencies as Regional Public Goods: Improving Infrastructure Performance. *Review of International Organizations*. 3 (2). pp. 179–200.

Berrettoni, D. and J. Lucángeli (2012. MERCOSUR: Asymmetries and the MERCOSUR Structural Fund (FOCEM). *Integration & Trade Journal*. 16 (1). pp. 33–43.

Buchanan, J. M. 1965. An Economic Theory of Clubs. *Economica*. 32 (1). pp. 1–14.

Chung, S. 2017. Building Regional Environmental Governance: Northeast Asia's Unique Path to Sustainable Development. In Antoni Estevadeordal and Louis W. Goodman, eds. *21ˢᵗ Century Cooperation: Regional Public Goods, Global Governance, and Sustainable Development*. London: Routledge.

Cornes, R. 1993. Dyke Maintenance and Other Stories: Some Neglected Types of Public Goods. *Quarterly Journal of Economics*. 108 (1). pp. 259–71.

Cornes, R. and T. Sandler. 1986. *The Theory of Externalities, Public Goods, and Club Goods*. Cambridge: Cambridge University Press.

Estevadeordal, A. and L.W. Goodman. 2017. 21st Century Cooperation, Regional Public Goods, and Sustainable Development. in Antoni Estevadeordal and Louis W. Goodman, eds. *21st Century Cooperation: Regional Public Goods, Global Governance, and Sustainable Development*. London: Routledge.

George, J., D. Hou, and T. Sandler. 2019. Asia-Pacific Demand for Military Expenditure: Spatial Panel and SUR Estimates. *Defence and Peace Economics*. 30 (4). pp. 381–401.

Hirshleifer, J. 1983. From Weakest-Link to Best-Shot: The Voluntary Provision of Public Goods. *Public Choice*. 41 (3). pp. 371–86.

International Task Force on Global Public Goods. 2004. *Meeting Global Challenges: International Cooperation in the National Interest*. Stockholm: Erlanders Infologists Väst AB.

Jordana, J. 2017. Transnational Policy Networks and Regional Public Goods in Latin America. In Antoni Estevadeordal and Louis W. Goodman, eds. *21st Century Cooperation: Regional Public Goods, Global Governance, and Sustainable Development. London*: Routledge.

Kahn, M.E. 2004. Environmental Regional Public Goods in Asia and Latin America. In Antoni Estevadeordal, Brian Frantz, and Tam Robert Nguyen, eds. *Regional Public Goods: From Theory to Practice*. Washington, DC: Inter-American Development Bank and Asian Development Bank.

Kawai, M. 2017. Asia's Financial Stability as a Regional and Global Public Good. In Antoni Estevadeordal and Louis W. Goodman, eds. *21st Century Cooperation: Regional Public Goods, Global Governance, and Sustainable Development*. London: Routledge.

Mendelson-Forman, J. 2017. Open Borders: A Regional Public Good. In Antoni Estevadeordal and Louis W. Goodman, eds. *21st Century Cooperation: Regional Public Goods, Global Governance, and Sustainable Development*. London: Routledge.

Murdoch, J. C., T. Sandler, and K. Sargent. 1997. A Tale of Two Collectives: Sulfur versus Nitrogen Oxides Emission Reduction in Europe. *Economica*. 64 (2). pp. 281–301.

Olson, M. 1969. The Principle of 'Fiscal Equivalence': The Division of Responsibilities among Different Levels of Government. *American Economic Review*. 59 (2). pp. 478–87.

Prasad, J. 2017. Connectivity and Infrastructure as 21st Century Regional Public Goods. In Antoni Estevadeordal and Louis W. Goodman, eds. *21st Century Cooperation: Regional Public Goods, Global Governance, and Sustainable Development*. London: Routledge.

Rana, P. B. 2004. Monetary and Financial Cooperation in Asia. In Antoni Estevadeordal, Brian Frantz, and Tam Robert Nguyen, eds. *Regional Public Goods: From Theory to Practice*. Washington, DC: Inter-American Development Bank and Asian Development Bank.

Sakai, K. and T. R. Nguyen. 2004. Coordinating the Supply of Regional Public Goods: The Greater Mekong Subregional Program. in Antoni Estevadeordal, Brian Frantz, and Tam Robert Nguyen, eds. *Regional Public Goods: From Theory to Practice*. Washington, DC: Inter-American Development Bank and Asian Development Bank.

Samuelson, P. A. 1954. The Pure Theory of Public Expenditure. *Review of Economics and Statistics*. 36 (4). pp. 387–89.

——. 1955. A Diagrammatic Exposition of a Theory of Public Expenditure. *Review of Economics and Statistics*. 37 (3). pp. 350–56.

Sandler, T. 1992. *Collective Action: Theory and Applications*. Ann Arbor, MI: University of Michigan Press.

——. 1997. *Global Challenges*. Cambridge: Cambridge University Press.

——. 2004. *Global Collective Action*. Cambridge: Cambridge University Press.

———. 2006. Regional Public Goods and International Organizations. *Review of International Organizations*. 1 (1). pp. 5–25.

———. 2013a. Buchanan Clubs. *Constitutional Political Economy*. 24 (4): 265–85.

———. 2013b. Public Goods and Regional Cooperation for Development: A New Look. *Integration & Trade Journal*. 17 (1): 13–24.

———. 2016. Strategic Aspects of Difficult Global Challenges. *Global Policy*. 7 (Supplement). pp. 33–44.

Sandler, T. and K. Sargent. 1995. Management of Transnational Commons: Coordination, Publicness, and Treaty Formation. *Land Economics*. 71 (2). pp. 145–162.

Stålgren, P. 2000. Regional Public Goods and the Future of International Development Cooperation: A Review of the Literature. *Working Paper 2000:2*, Expert Group on Development Issues, Swedish Ministry for Foreign Affairs, Stockholm.

Suominen, K. 2017. Advancing Digitization as a Regional Public Good. In Antoni Estevadeordal and Louis W. Goodman, eds. *21ˢᵗ Century Cooperation: Regional Public Goods, Global Governance, and Sustainable Development*. London: Routledge.

Tres, J. and P. Barbieri. 2017. Can Regional Standards Be Above the National Norm? Impact Evaluation Issues for Regional Public Goods. In Antoni Estevadeordal and Louis W. Goodman, eds. *21st Century Cooperation: Regional Public Goods, Global Governance, and Sustainable Development*. London: Routledge.

Westcott, C. C. 2004. Promoting the Provision of Regional Public Goods in Asia. In Antoni Estevadeordal, Brian Frantz, and Tam Robert Nguyen, eds. *Regional Public Goods: From Theory to Practice*. Washington, DC: Inter-American Development Bank and Asian Development Bank.

Benefits and Spillover Effects of Infrastructure: A Spatial Econometric Approach

3

Kijin Kim, Junkyu Lee, Manuel Leonard Albis, and Ricardo Ang III

The positive contribution of infrastructure on economic growth has long been found in a large body of the literature, although the magnitude of the impact is the subject of considerable uncertainty. As one of the major production factors, higher infrastructure capital is strongly associated with higher income (Figure 3.1). Combined with financially interconnected markets, infrastructure allows people and capital to move more freely not just within own countries but to other countries in the neighborhood (defined by geographical or economic proximity), creating spillover effects across borders.

For instance, intra- and inter-country externalities from building and improving a transport network, are made possible through redistribution of production resources and productivity gains due to agglomeration (Tong et al. 2013). The transport network enables the impact of the global value chains—a formal source of spillover effects—to more easily extend across multiple economies. At the same time, the use of information and communication technology (ICT) increases productivity internally by raising the quality and productivity of other inputs, and externally by facilitating dissemination of knowledge from one firm, industry, or country to another (Moshiri 2016). Rising interconnectedness through infrastructure and its externalities suggests that investigating the economic benefits of infrastructure should account for not only direct impacts within a country, but also indirect impacts over neighboring countries.

This chapter estimates the economic benefits of infrastructure on output. Two broad categories of infrastructure are examined: (i) transport (roads and rails) and energy, and (ii) the ICT infrastructure that covers telephone, mobile, and fixed broadband subscriptions. A spatial econometric analysis is employed separately to estimate the direct and indirect or cross-border benefits of infrastructure.

Figure 3.1: National Income versus Infrastructure by Type, (average 2010–2014)

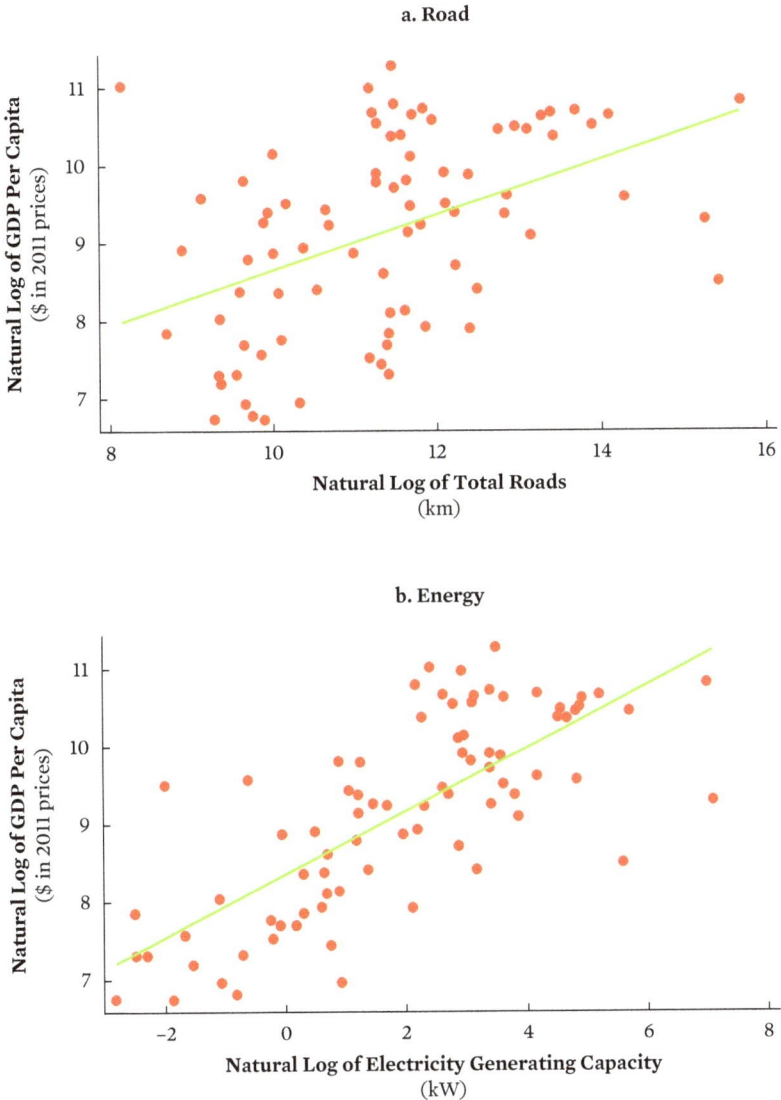

a. Road

b. Energy

continued on next page

Figure 3.1 continued

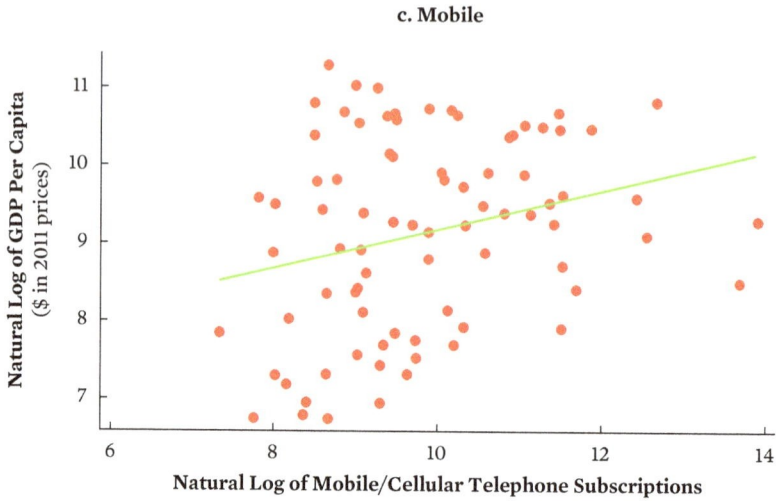

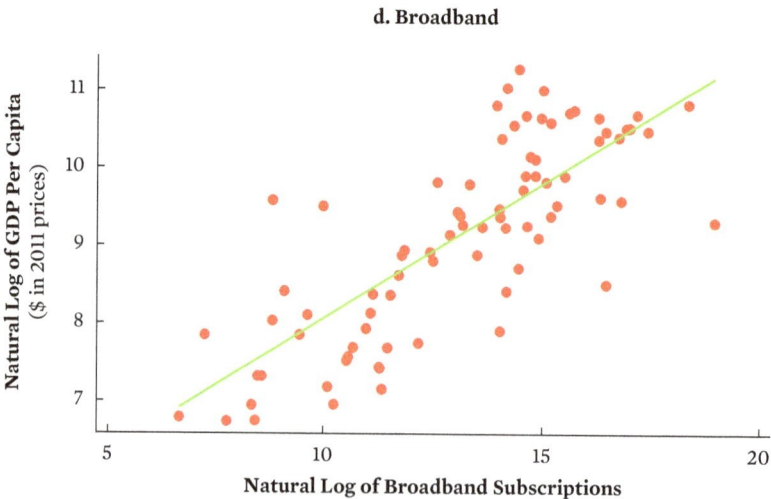

c. Mobile

d. Broadband

GDP = gross domestic product, km = kilometer, kW = kilowatt.

Note: Each dot represents a country in the sample; values are averages for 2010–2014.

Source: Penn World Table 9.0; International Road Federation; United States Energy Information Administration; International Telecommunication Union.

In our preferred spatial panels models, significant and positive cross-border spillover effects of the broadband infrastructure and human capital are found under the assumption that economic connectivity is represented by physical proximity. These results are robust to the choice of a spatial weight matrix. Our results also indicate that rail infrastructure shows positive and significant output impacts on neighboring countries and on own countries.

Although most studies have employed this method to the analysis of subnational economy spillovers, this chapter describes one of the few studies that explicitly apply the spatial econometric approach to cross-county infrastructure panel data. The results highlight the need to distinguish the non-infrastructure variable from the total capital stock variable, which are commonly used in the empirical models together with the infrastructure stock variables already included in the estimates of total capital. The study also attempts to shed light on the literature on regional public goods (RPGs), as explored in detail in Chapter 2. A transportation network is a good example of an RPG. Most literature in this area is theoretical or qualitative, while attempts to measure RPGs are usually limited to the input side or investments in RPGs. Therefore, another value of this chapter is the attempt to measure the output side of RPGs by estimating the direct benefits and spillover effects of infrastructure as an RPG.[1]

The next section of the chapter is a brief survey of the literature discussing the benefits and spillover effects of infrastructure and the motivations for the use of the spatial econometric models in achieving the chapter's objectives. This is followed by explanation of the structure of the spatial and non-spatial panel models to be estimated, discussion of the data, and the results of spatial and non-spatial models.

---

[1] It might be more reasonable to limit our focus to cross-border infrastructure given its intended influence on multiple countries targeted. However, cross-country data on cross-border infrastructure are rarely available. Instead, this study uses national-level infrastructure data which conceptually covers the infrastructure that connects to other countries. Our approach can be viewed from the perspective that being connected locally is a necessary condition for being connected across borders; therefore local infrastructure ultimately contributes to higher cross-border connectivity. For the percentage of cross-border (or regional) infrastructure of total infrastructure projects, an indicative measure for Asia is about 4%, which is comparable to Europe (Bhattacharyay 2010).

Literature Review

Benefits and Spillover Effects of Infrastructure

The key role of physical infrastructure is often highlighted in empirical studies as facilitating trade and reducing trade costs, with variants of the gravity models commonly used. Most of the infrastructure variables in those studies are perception-based indicators collected from surveys, which makes it difficult to interpret the degrees of their changes by nature.

Several studies confirm the spillover effects of ICT and transport infrastructure on output. These are mostly based on subnational studies such as in the People's Republic of China (PRC). For recent examples, Hu and Luo (2017), exploring cities in Hunan province, find that road infrastructure has significant positive direct and indirect effects on economic growth, with the indirect effect greater than the direct effect. Yu et al. (2013) find the existence of both positive and negative spatial spillovers of infrastructure across regions of the PRC. Looking at the United States (US), Tong et al. (2013) find that road disbursement has a significant positive direct effect on a state's agricultural output, while also beneficial to agricultural development in other states.

For ICT infrastructure, Moshiri (2016) shows that ICT can have a positive impact on labor productivity, but with differences across regions, industries, and time.[2] The results show that the impact of ICT investment in the US on Canada, a major trading partner, has spilled over to some Canadian provinces and industries, while the overall ICT effects are concentrated in those ICT-intensive provinces and industries. ICT capital is also found to be an important source of total factor productivity growth (van Leeuwen and van der Wiel 2003). More recently, Lin et al. (2017) explore the evidence of the spillover effect of the internet, highlighting its effects on growth as a conduit for new technology flows to neighboring regions to generate new knowledge and facilitate the exchange of knowledge.

---

[2] Unlike transport infrastructure generally measured by the lengths of total roads and rails, the proxies for ICT infrastructure come in various forms due to its wider scope of coverage (OECD, 2002): for example, telephone and mobile/cellular phone subscriptions; access to the internet; the number of computers, software, and communications; and electrical and electronic equipment (O'Mahony and Vecchi 2005; Skorupinska and Torrent-Sellens 2015; Calderón, Moral-Benito, and Serven 2015; Shahiduzzaman, Layton, and Alam 2015; Wamboye, Adekola, and Sergi 2016; and Lin et al. 2017).

Spillover effects of infrastructure can also be negative, as found in the literature. An increase in infrastructure in neighboring countries may harm the own region's economy. While intraregional effects of infrastructure are generally positive, the negative interregional spillover effects can be explained by a competing economic relationship between own and neighboring regions in acquiring resources for production (while a positive interregional spillover means a complementary relationship) or that products from the regions may compete for markets. Subnational-level studies find that infrastructure investment in one region may draw mobile production factors away from other regions (for examples from the US, see Boarnet 1998; Cohen and Manaco 2007; Sloboda and Yao 2008). Regional competition takes various forms, depending on horizontal/vertical competitive relations and the type of competition and competitors (Batey and Friedrich 2000). In the case of cross-country spillover effects, one can expect smaller degrees of negative (or positive) externalities, if any, given the higher restrictions imposed on factor movements across countries.

Motivation for the Use of Spatial Econometric Models

To provide a basis for the spatial econometric methods to achieve the objectives of the chapter, the following are reviewed: (i) an omitted variables motivation, (ii) spatial heterogeneity motivation, and (iii) externalities-based motivation (LeSage and Pace 2009).

In spatial samples, an omitted variable bias easily arises when unobservable factors (e.g., locational advantages) that are likely to be spatially correlated have an influence on the dependent variable (e.g., national income). A spatial autoregressive (SAR) model can address this omitted variable bias with a spatial lag (i.e., a linear combination of neighbors' y's).

$$\text{SAR model in a matrix form: } y = \rho W y + X\beta + \varepsilon \qquad (1)$$

where y is the $n \times 1$ vector of a dependent variable, W is the $n \times n$ spatial weight matrix representing the neighboring structure between n observational units, ρ is the spatial AR coefficient (a scalar), X is the $n \times p$ matrix of explanatory variables, and β is the $p \times 1$ coefficient vector.

Unlike a panel regression model with the coefficients assumed to be identical for all observational units, a spatial panel model allows each spatial unit to react differently mainly because each unit has different set of neighbors and is affected by them. This is easy to show in the reduced-form of the SAR model with $\text{abs}(\rho) < 1$:

$$\text{Reduced form SAR model: } y = (I - \rho W)^{-1}X\beta + (I - \rho W)^{-1}\varepsilon \quad (2)$$

where $(I - \rho W)^{-1} = I + \rho W + \rho^2 W^2 + \rho^3 W^3 + \cdots$. The W represents immediate (first-order) neighbors, W^2 neighbors to the first-order neighbors, and so on. Note that ρ is zero in non-spatial panel models.

As the impact of a shock dissipates over time through a temporal lag in the AR model, the SAR model allows us to model a spatial dependence where a shock in the error at any location is transmitted to other regions, with its impact dissipating over physical or economic distance (Anselin 2003). Moreover, externalities from neighbors' characteristics (WX) can be reflected together with the spatial term in the spatial Durbin Model (SDM):

$$SDM \text{ in a matrix form: } y = \rho W y + X\beta + WX\gamma + \varepsilon \quad (3).$$

Models

Non-Spatial Panel Regression Model

For the non-spatial panel models, the Cobb-Douglas production function is used, following Calderón, Moral-Benito, and Serven (2015).

$$Y_{it} = A_{it} K_{it}^{\alpha} Z_{it}^{\gamma} \left(e^{\phi H_{it}} P_{it}\right)^{1-\alpha-\gamma} \quad (4)$$

Y denotes real output, A total factor productivity, K and Z physical and infrastructure capital, respectively, H human capital, and P total population. i is the index corresponding to country $i = \{1, \ldots, n\}$, while t is the index corresponding to time $t = \{1, \ldots, T\}$. Constant returns to scale is assumed following prior studies. Dividing by the population and taking natural logarithms, we estimate the panel regression model by:

$$y_{it} = \beta_0 + \beta_1 k_{it} + \beta_2 h_{it} + \mathbf{z}_{it}\boldsymbol{\eta} + \mu_i + \gamma_t + \varepsilon_{it} \quad (5)$$

where k_{it} is the per capita capital stock, h_{it} is human capital, $\mathbf{z}_{it}$ is a vector of infrastructure variables, μ_{it} is the unobserved country effect, γ_{it} is the time fixed effect, ε_{it} is a random fluctuation, and β_0, β_1, β_2, and $\boldsymbol{\eta}$ are elasticities. The μ_i captures any idiosyncratic effect in the ith country that may affect its output. On one hand, the idiosyncratic effect could be economic in nature, which may be correlated with the capital and human capital stock. On the other hand, the idiosyncratic effect could be cultural in such a way that it is unique to the country and is independent of the economy.

Spatial Panel Regression Model

Spatial Weight Matrix[3]

The economic growth of a country is affected by the characteristics of its neighbors when spatial spillover effects are present. The definition of a neighborhood depends on a symmetric weight matrix, denoted by $\mathbf{W}_{n \times n} = \{w_{ij}\}$, where $w_{ij} > w_{ik}$ implies that country i is closer to country j than with country k. The weight matrix is often measured in terms of geographic distance, e.g., $w_{ij} = 1/d_{ij}$ where d_{ij} is the geographic distance between country i and j. The neighborhood can also be defined in terms of economic distance, e.g., the total trade flows between the two countries. The $\mathbf{W}_{n \times n}$ is often row-standardized to aid interpretation. Three weight matrices are used: (i) exponential decay $\mathbf{W}_1 = \{\exp(-0.01*1/d_{ij})\}$, (ii) inverse of distance $\mathbf{W}_2 = \{1/d_{ij}\}$, and (iii) inverse of square of distance $\mathbf{W}_3 = \{1/d_{ij}^2\}$, all with a 25th percentile cutoff, i.e., the neighbors of a particular country are only the closest 25% of all countries in terms of distance. Countries with distance beyond the cutoff have a weight of zero. The use of a percentile cutoff instead of an absolute distance cutoff reduces the effect of country area size.

Spatial Durbin Model

The spatial Durbin model (SDM) is implemented to account for the spatial spillover effect in the production function of country in the form of the weighted average of the regressors, in addition to the weighted average of the of the output of neighbors, given by the equation:

$$y_{it} = \beta_0 + \beta_1 k_{it} + \beta_2 h_{it} + z_{it}\eta + \sum_{j=1}^{n} w_{ij}x_j'\theta + \rho \sum_{j=1}^{n} w_{ij}y_{jt}\,\mu_i + \gamma_t + \varepsilon_{it} \quad (6)$$

[3] In a spatial weight matrix, the extent to which a location is interconnected with all other locations is imposed a *priori*. Thus, the spatial weight matrix should not be treated as something to be estimated, but as exogenous. As such, geography-based (e.g., contiguity- and distance-based) weights that are free of the endogeneity issue have been widely used. This paper also follows this traditional concept of a spatial weight matrix that requires to be exogenous. However, interconnectedness can be represented by economic distance such as trade flows and there have been many attempts to address an endogenous spatial weight matrix in the recent spatial econometric literature. We leave these issues to future research.

where **x** is a pool of regressor variables deemed as a source of spatial spillover effects with its corresponding coefficient vector **θ**.

Average Direct and Indirect Impacts

The expected values of y's in the SDM can be written in a matrix form:

$$E(\mathbf{Y}_t) = (\mathbf{I} - \rho\mathbf{W})^{-1}[\mathbf{X}_t\boldsymbol{\beta} + \mathbf{W}\mathbf{X}_t\boldsymbol{\theta}] \quad (7)$$

where $\mathbf{Y}_t$ is a $n \times 1$ vector of response variable of each cross-section unit, $\mathbf{X}_t$ is an $n \times p$ matrix of regressor variables with an $p \times 1$ coefficient vector $\boldsymbol{\beta}$, $\mathbf{X}_t = [\mathbf{x}_{1t} \quad \mathbf{x}_{2t} \quad \cdots \quad \mathbf{x}_{pt}]$, $\mathbf{X}_t\boldsymbol{\beta} = \sum_{k=1}^{p}\beta_k\mathbf{x}_{kt}$, $\boldsymbol{\theta}$, is an $p \times 1$ spatial coefficient vector of the regressors, and $\mathbf{X}_t\boldsymbol{\theta} = \sum_{k=1}^{p}\theta_k\mathbf{x}_{kt}$.

The average direct effect is given by:[4]

$$\overline{Direct} = \frac{1}{n}\sum_{i=1}^{n}\frac{\partial E(y_{it})}{\partial x_{ki,t}} = n^{-1}tr\big((\mathbf{I} - \rho\mathbf{W})^{-1}(\beta_k\mathbf{I}_n + \theta_k\mathbf{W})\big) \quad (8)$$

The average total effect is given by:

$$\overline{Total} = \frac{1}{n}\sum_{i=1}^{n}\sum_{j=1}^{n}\frac{\partial E(y_{jt})}{\partial x_{ki,t}} = n^{-1}\mathbf{1}_n'(\mathbf{I} - \rho\mathbf{W})^{-1}(\beta_k\mathbf{I}_n + \theta_k\mathbf{W})\mathbf{1}_n$$

The average indirect effect is estimated from the difference of the average total effect and the average direct effect.

Data

The variables were primarily taken from the data set in Calderón, Moral-Benito, and Serven (2015) which spans only from 1960 to 2000 and we

---

[4] Step-by-step derivations of the direct and indirect effects in the SDM can be found in Appendix A3.1.

extended it up to 2014.[5] Two new ICT infrastructure variables, mobile and fixed broadband subscriptions, were added. In the final data set, we have a panel data for 78 countries covering years 1960 to 2014 except for mobile and broadband subscriptions that are available from 1995 to 2014.[6]

The dependent variable, per capita income, is computed by dividing the output-side real GDP at chained purchasing power parity (in $ million 2011) by the population. Both variables are from the Penn World Table 9.0 (PWT). The data for capital stock at constant 2011 national prices (in $ million 2011) is also from the PWT.

Six types of infrastructure variables are used separately under two broader categories for analysis:

- Transport and energy (TRE) infrastructure variables: length of total roads (in km), length of rails (in route-km), and electricity generating capacity (in million Kw);
- ICT infrastructure variables: fixed-telephone subscriptions, mobile/cellular telephone subscriptions, and fixed broadband subscriptions.[7]

Roads and rails data are from the World Road Statistics of the International Road Federation, and electricity generating capacity from the United States Energy Information Administration. Data for telephone and mobile subscriptions are from the International Telecommunication Union, and fixed broadband subscriptions from the World Development Indicators.

For the variable for human capital, we use average years of secondary schooling by country obtained from Barro and Lee (2013). The Barro and Lee data set only provides average years of secondary schooling every 5 years from 1950 to 2010. To have complete annual data from 1960 to 2014, the

---

[5] More details on the data and variable are presented in Appendix A3.2.

[6] The final data set includes 15 countries in Asia and the Pacific: (East Asia) People's Republic of China, Japan, Republic of Korea; (South Asia) Bangladesh, India, Nepal, Sri Lanka; (Southeast Asia) Indonesia, Malaysia, Philippines, Singapore, Thailand; (Central and West Asia) Pakistan; (Pacific) Australia, New Zealand.

[7] The exact definitions of each ICT infrastructure variable are as follows: (i) fixed-telephone subscriptions: the sum of active number of analogue fixed-telephone lines, (ii) mobile/cellular telephone subscriptions: the number of subscriptions to a public mobile-telephone service that provide access to the public switched telephone network using cellular technology, and (iii) fixed broadband subscriptions: fixed subscriptions to high-speed access to the public internet.

available data for year *i* was used from year *i* to year *i* + 4 (i.e., 1960 data was used until year 1964; 1965 data used until 1969; and so on).

It is important to note that the capital stock variable commonly used in the literature, including our study, is comprehensive in coverage. In other words, total capital includes all asset classes of gross fixed capital formation (GFCF) in the public and private industrial sectors of the National Accounts: residential and non-residential buildings, machinery and equipment, and civil engineering works.[8] A few papers have raised this issue of double counting when total capital is used together with infrastructure as explanatory variables in the regression model. Berndt and Hansson (1991) and Canning and Bennathan (1999) made a note of caution in the interpretation of the coefficients. As a robustness check, Égert, Kozluk, and Sutherland (2009) use *private* investment instead of *total* investment as an explanatory variable together with infrastructure to show the double counting issue is less of a serious problem.

However, considering that the large shares of infrastructure stock contained in the total capital stock are highly varying by country, it is important to address potential biases from the double counting issue.[9] Therefore, we attempt to extract non-infrastructure capital stock from the total capital stock variable using a statistical method; i.e., regressing total capital stock on infrastructure variables, and using the residuals as a proxy for non-infrastructure variable (see Appendix A3.3 for more details).

It should be also noted that the original data sources include many missing values for less developed countries; these omissions prevent us from running the spatial panel model due to missing information on neighbors. Thus, the data are collapsed from an annual frequency to a 5-year frequency by

[8] To our inquiry about whether the capital stock in the latest PWT data set includes both private and public infrastructure, one of the co-authors in Feenstra, Inklaar, and Timmer (2015) confirmed that: "Total investment across all assets adds up to gross fixed capital formation from the National Accounts, so anything included in that concept (according to the System of National Accounts each country adhered to two years ago) will be covered in PWT data. That certainly covers civil engineering works and these are economy-wide figures, so cover both private and public investments."

[9] ADB (2017 Box 3.4) suggests that infrastructure as a percentage of general government GFCF widely vary by country, from 40% (Pakistan) to 70% (Fiji). In general, national account statistics are not disaggregated enough to identify infrastructure investments (ADB 2017). Costs for even collecting disaggregated information publicly available from central and local governments (e.g., budget data) at the national level may be prohibitive. Moreover, infrastructure investments in the private sectors and public–private partnership projects will require other data sources.

averaging non-missing values only. As a result, the missing value problem is significantly reduced by taking non-overlapping 5-year moving averages. For the missing cells even after taking averages, the midpoint of the preceding and succeeding years are taken instead as estimates of the missing values. For cases where missing data occurs at the beginning (or at the end) of each series, the values at the succeeding (or preceding) years were used as estimates instead. As a robustness check, we provide, in the next section, the estimation results when original yearly data with missing values are used for non-spatial models.

Results

Exploratory Analysis: Spatial Autocorrelation

Moran's I, a measure of spatial autocorrelation at a point in time, for the dependent variable suggest that national income is positively correlated with neighboring countries' incomes.[10] Furthermore, the statistics trending upward indicate that national economies have increasingly been interconnected over the 4 decades (Figure 3.2). Positive and significant spatial dependence indicates that countries with similar income levels are clustered and this spatial correlation of income is known to be very persistent over time (Acemoglu and Robinson 2012). Positive spatial autocorrelations increasing over time are found in all other variables. These findings are consistent regardless of the choice of the spatial weight matrix.

Estimation Results: Average Direct and Indirect Impacts[11]

Along with the non-spatial panel models, the spatial Durbin models are estimated using a various combination of infrastructure variables and spatial weight matrices. By infrastructure type, the two main models are identified:

---

[10] Moran's I is defined by $I = \frac{\sum_{i=1}^{N}\sum_{j=1}^{N} w_{ij}(y_i-\bar{y})(y_j-y)}{N^{-1}\sum_{i=1}^{N}(y_i-\bar{y})^2 \sum_{i=1}^{N}\sum_{j=1}^{N} w_{ij}}$ where N is the number of observational units; $W = \{w_{ij}\}$.

[11] Statistical tests point to no spurious relationship among the variables in the model. The unit root tests for our panel data suggest that all variables are non-stationary, and the panel cointegration tests indicate that the variables are cointegrated. This implies that national income, total capital, human capital, and infrastructure variables in levels (logged) are in a stable long-run relationship. Estimations results for spatial and non-spatial panel models are presented in Appendix 3.4. It is worth noting that there is little effect when taking 5-year averages and performing imputation when compared to yearly raw values especially for the TRE cases.

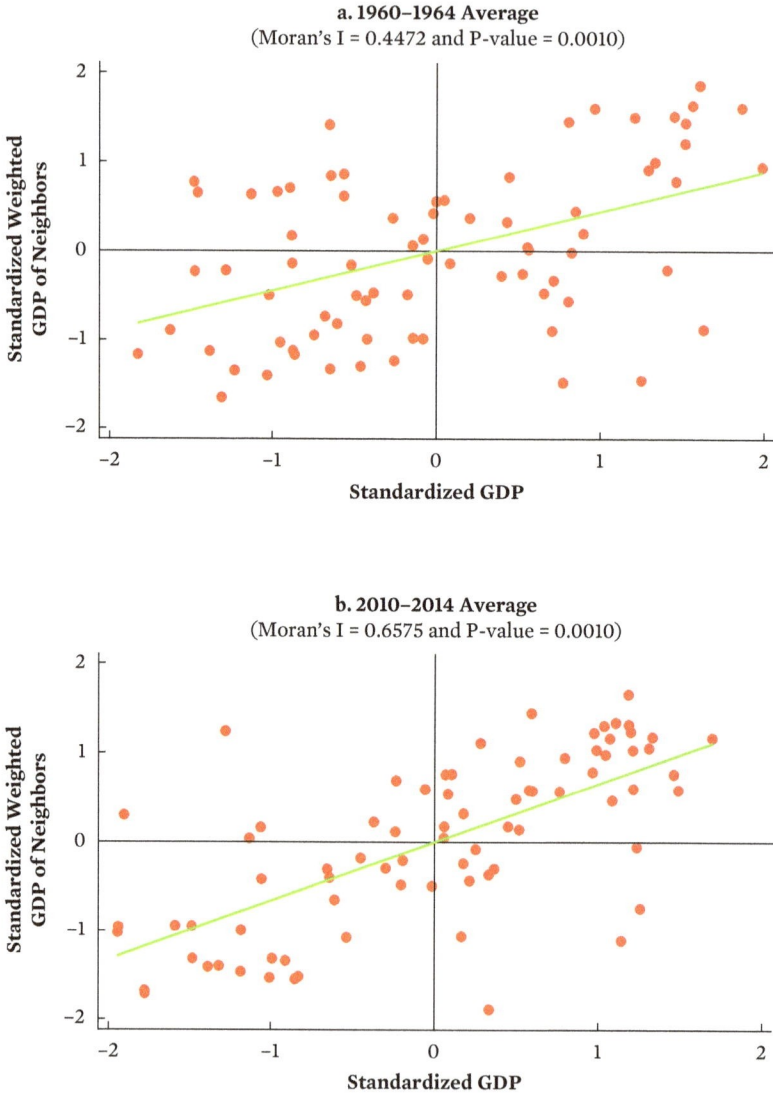

Figure 3.2: Moran's Scatter Plot for y

a. 1960–1964 Average
(Moran's I = 0.4472 and P-value = 0.0010)

b. 2010–2014 Average
(Moran's I = 0.6575 and P-value = 0.0010)

GDP = gross domestic product .

Note: W_1 = {exp(-0.01*d)} is used; x-axis is log (capita GDP); y-axis is weighted average of neighboring countries log (per cap GDP).

Source: Penn World Table 9.0; Authors' calculations.

(i) transport and energy infrastructure including roads, rails, and electricity generating capacity (TRE); and (ii) ICT infrastructure, including telephone, mobile, and broadband. In addition, models using either total capital (TC) stock or non-infrastructure capital (NIC) stock are also estimated. For the spatial models, three types of weight matrices are used, namely, exponential decay (**W1**), inverse distance (**W2**), and square of inverse distance with a cutoff (**W3**), all with a 25th percentile cutoff. All in all, a total of 16 spatial and non-spatial models are estimated, with direct and indirect effects presented in Tables 3.2 to 3.3. The main findings are summarized in Table 3.1.

Table 3.1: Summary of Average Direct and Indirect Impacts on Output: Output Elasticity

1% increase in: (+1 year for Human capital)	%ΔOutput in		1% increase in: (+1 year for Human capital)	%ΔOutput in	
	Own Country	Neighbors		Own Country	Neighbors
Non-TRE infra	(0.03)	–	Non-ICT infra	(0.03)	–
Human capital	(0.09–0.14)	(0.13–0.26)	Human capital	(0.10–0.13)	–
TRE: Roads	(0.10–0.11)	–	ICT: Telephone	–	–
TRE: Rails	(0.15–0.17)	(0.46)[1]	ICT: Mobile	–	–
TRE: Energy	(0.20–0.22)	–	ICT: Broadband	(0.02–0.03)[2]	(0.03–0.11)

ICT = information and communication technology, TRE = transport and energy.
[1] For **W2** only; [2] For **W1** and **W3** only.
Source: Authors' calculations.

One of the major highlights between the models with the non-infrastructure capital variable (NIC; columns 1–4) and those with the total capital stock variable (TC; columns 5–8) is that all direct effects under the transport and energy (TRE) model are positive and significant, while only total capital and human capital have positive and significant direct effects under the TRE–TC (Table 3.2). This suggests that the total capital stock variable already including all asset types of capital stock absorbs the effects of infrastructure stock, hence leading to insignificant results in the TRE–TC model. It is also worth highlighting the role of human capital whose direct impact on economic growth is highly robust across the board. In the NIC models, human capital has an estimated direct output effect of 0.09-0.14 per a 1-year increase in years of schooling, while the effect is 0.06-0.09 in the TC model (Table 3.2).

Table 3.2 further indicates that the direct output elasticity of roads, rails and energy infrastructure in the TRE–NIC spatial models are 0.10-0.11, 0.15-0.17, and 0.20-0.22 (whose results slightly vary by the spatial weight matrix), respectively, while these elasticities are insignificant under the TRE–TC spatial models. Furthermore, the non-TRE infrastructure also shows significant, but smaller output impact compared to the TRE infrastructure. When it comes to indirect impacts of the TRE infrastructure, only the rails variable under the TRE–NIC model using **W2** show significant indirect effects. Our direct output elasticity estimates of transport and energy infrastructure are mostly within the range of those found in the literature although they widely vary by infrastructure variable, geographical unit, and methodology (Guild 1998).

Among the three types in the ICT infrastructure, broadband shows not only positive direct impact, but also indirect impact on output in the ICT–NIC model (Table 3.3). The spillover effect of access to the internet on neighboring countries' output (0.03-0.11) is estimated to be much larger than that the direct effect in the own countries (0.02-0.03). The positive spillover of broadband is robust to the choice of the spatial weight matrix.

An Illustration of Cross-Border Spillover of Infrastructure

To illustrate how a positive shock in access of the internet propagates across space, we assume a 1% increase in broadband subscription in the PRC under the ICT–NIC model using the **W3** weight matrix. Note that the total effects differ by the choice of country from which a shock originates because every country has different neighbors. There are direct and spillover effects on income from a 1% increase in access to the internet in the PRC in the long term. The simulation shows that a 10% positive shock in broadband in the PRC leads to an increase in its own income by 0.17% in the long term. Potential knowledge spillover through higher access to the internet in the PRC also have positive income shock on its neighboring countries (a total of 0.24%), whose magnitude decreases with distance as assumed in the spatial weight matrix.

Table 3.2: Direct and Indirect Effects for Transportation and Energy

On Per Capita GDP	Models with Non-Infrastructure Capital				Models with Total Capital			
	Non-Spatial (1)	Spatial; W1 (2)	Spatial; W2 (3)	Spatial; W3 (4)	Non-Spatial (5)	Spatial; W1 (6)	Spatial; W2 (7)	Spatial; W3 (8)
(Direct Effect)								
Total capital	–	–	–	–	0.5661***	0.5240***	0.4875***	0.4939***
					(0.0696)	(0.0727)	(0.0849)	(0.0810)
Non-TRE infra	0.0318**	0.0327**	0.0276*	0.0285*	–	–	–	–
	(0.0155)	(0.0155)	(0.0158)	(0.0160)				
Human capital	0.1919***	0.1436***	0.0902**	0.1058**	0.0671**	0.0887***	0.0426	0.0611**
	(0.0452)	(0.0343)	(0.0435)	(0.0414)	(0.0312)	(0.0301)	(0.0312)	(0.0301)
TRE: Roads	0.1034*	0.1004**	0.1097**	0.1023**	-0.0192	-0.0015	0.0121	0.0088
	(0.0554)	(0.0486)	(0.0513)	(0.0493)	(0.0362)	(0.0347)	(0.0341)	(0.0331)
TRE: Rails	0.1815***	0.1670***	0.1468**	0.1578***	0.0605	0.0467	0.0456	0.0475
	(0.0623)	(0.0563)	(0.0652)	(0.0585)	(0.0466)	(0.0436)	(0.0476)	(0.0457)
TRE: Energy	0.2509***	0.2177***	0.1978***	0.2036***	0.0739	0.0750	0.0751	0.0782
	(0.0603)	(0.0587)	(0.0509)	(0.0583)	(0.0618)	(0.0567)	(0.0572)	(0.0568)
(Indirect Effect)								
Total capital	–	–	–	–	–	0.1054	0.3057	0.2499
						(0.0883)	(0.2516)	(0.1698)
Non-TRE infra	–	0.0175	0.0415	0.0229	–	–	–	–
		(0.0147)	(0.0409)	(0.0241)				
Human capital	–	0.1293***	0.2555***	0.2084***	–	0.0194	0.0706	0.0432
		(0.0361)	(0.0852)	(0.0563)		(0.0353)	(0.0798)	(0.0543)
TRE: Roads	–	0.0174	-0.1303	-0.0635	–	-0.0358	-0.1569	-0.1444
		(0.0581)	(0.2567)	(0.1325)		(0.0464)	(0.2000)	(0.1058)
TRE: Rails	–	0.0377	0.4608**	0.1654	–	-0.0671	-0.0676	-0.1414

continued on next page

Table 3.2 continued

On Per Capita GDP	Models with Non-Infrastructure Capital				Models with Total Capital			
	Non-Spatial (1)	Spatial; W1 (2)	Spatial; W2 (3)	Spatial; W3 (4)	Non-Spatial (5)	Spatial; W1 (6)	Spatial; W2 (7)	Spatial; W3 (8)
		(0.0722)	(0.1796)	(0.1277)		(0.0616)	(0.1717)	(0.1347)
TRE: Energy	—	0.0339 (0.0450)	0.2321 (0.1880)	0.0984 (0.0881)	—	-0.0204 (0.0476)	-0.0691 (0.1607)	-0.0737 (0.0931)
(Total Effect)								
Total capital	—	—	—	—	0.5661*** (0.0696)	0.6294*** (0.1086)	0.7931*** (0.2505)	0.7438*** (0.1722)
Non-TRE infra	0.0318** (0.0155)	0.0502 (0.0234)	0.0690 (0.0424)	0.0514* (0.0292)	—	—	—	—
Human capital	0.1919*** (0.0452)	0.2729*** (0.0358)	0.3457*** (0.0795)	0.3143*** (0.0511)	0.0671** (0.0312)	0.1081*** (0.0406)	0.1132 (0.0893)	0.1043* (0.0618)
TRE: Roads	0.1034* (0.0554)	0.1177 (0.0850)	-0.0206 (0.2756)	0.0388 (0.1580)	-0.0192 (0.0362)	-0.0373 (0.0648)	-0.1448 (0.2122)	-0.1356 (0.1192)
TRE: Rails	0.1815*** (0.0623)	0.2047** (0.0804)	0.6077*** (0.1817)	0.3232** (0.1305)	0.0605 (0.0466)	-0.0204 (0.0578)	-0.0220 (0.1586)	-0.0939 (0.1242)
TRE: Energy	0.2509*** (0.0603)	0.2515*** (0.0652)	0.4298** (0.2053)	0.3020*** (0.1026)	0.0739 (0.0618)	0.0546 (0.0576)	0.0060 (0.1662)	0.0045 (0.0888)

ICT = information and communication technology; TRE = transport and energy.

Notes: Figures in parenthesis are robust standard errors; W1 = {exp(−0.01*d)}; W2 = {1/d}; W3 = {1/d²} with, all a 25th percentile cutoff; * $p < 0.1$, ** $p < 0.05$, and *** $p < 0.01$.

Source: Authors' calculations.

Table 3.3: Average Direct and Indirect Effects for Information and Communication Technology

On Per capita GDP	Models with Non-Infrastructure Capital				Models with Total Capital			
	Non-Spatial (1)	Spatial; W1 (2)	Spatial; W2 (3)	Spatial; W3 (4)	Non-Spatial (5)	Spatial; W1 (6)	Spatial; W2 (7)	Spatial; W3 (8)
(Direct Effect)								
Total capital	—	—	—	—	0.4722***	0.5182***	0.4559***	0.5015***
					(0.1316)	(0.1337)	(0.1172)	(0.1253)
Non-ICT infra	0.0262	0.0291*	0.0291*	0.0291*	—	—	—	—
	(0.0162)	(0.0171)	(0.0158)	(0.0167)				
Human capital	0.0883	0.1289**	0.0986**	0.1125**	0.0807	0.0940**	0.0876*	0.0924**
	(0.0597)	(0.0516)	(0.0496)	(0.0520)	(0.0525)	(0.0439)	(0.0457)	(0.0454)
ICT: Telephone	0.0325	-0.0004	0.0123	0.0049	-0.0360	-0.0528	-0.0507	-0.0561
	(0.0560)	(0.0475)	(0.0486)	(0.0493)	(0.0495)	(0.0448)	(0.0434)	(0.0454)
ICT: Mobile	0.0150	0.0073	0.0173	0.0069	0.0262*	0.0161	0.0194	0.0121
	(0.0163)	(0.0241)	(0.0256)	(0.0305)	(0.0157)	(0.0227)	(0.0259)	(0.0309)
ICT: Broadband	0.0171	0.0299***	0.0155	0.0236**	0.0152	0.0215**	0.0132	0.0202*
	(0.0109)	(0.0112)	(0.0107)	(0.0112)	(0.0105)	(0.0105)	(0.0096)	(0.0103)
(Indirect Effect)								
Total capital	—	—	—	—	—	0.0085	0.3441*	0.123
						(0.0953)	(0.1927)	(0.1301)
Non-ICT infra	—	0.0027	0.0730*	0.0116	—	—	—	—
		(0.0188)	(0.0409)	(0.0354)				
Human capital	—	0.0429	-0.0872	0.0278	—	-0.0052	-0.2162**	-0.0666
		(0.0405)	(0.1144)	(0.0798)		(0.0338)	(0.1067)	(0.0691)
ICT: Telephone	—	0.0663	0.2643	0.1343	—	0.0193	0.0192	0.0380

continued on next page

Table 3.3 continued

On Per capita GDP	Models with Non-Infrastructure Capital				Models with Total Capital			
	Non-Spatial (1)	Spatial; W1 (2)	Spatial; W2 (3)	Spatial; W3 (4)	Non-Spatial (5)	Spatial; W1 (6)	Spatial; W2 (7)	Spatial; W3 (8)
		(0.0697)	(0.2459)	(0.1522)		(0.0629)	(0.2232)	(0.1365)
ICT: Mobile	—	0.0223	-0.0268	0.0114	—	0.0134	0.0042	0.0172
		(0.0355)	(0.0575)	(0.0523)		(0.0343)	(0.0526)	(0.0491)
ICT: Broadband	—	0.0292**	0.1121***	0.0512***	—	0.0150	0.0520**	0.0200
		(0.0141)	(0.0213)	(0.0192)		(0.0142)	(0.0235)	(0.0190)
(Total Effect)								
Total capital	—	—	—	—	0.4722***	0.5267***	0.8000***	0.6245***
					(0.1316)	(0.1395)	(0.2044)	(0.1607)
Non-ICT infra	0.0262	0.0317	0.1022***	0.0407	—	—	—	—
	(0.0162)	(0.021)	(0.0371)	(0.0322)				
Human capital	0.0883	0.1718**	0.0114	0.1403	0.0807	0.0887	-0.1286	0.0258
	(0.0597)	(0.0692)	(0.1357)	(0.1075)	(0.0525)	(0.0568)	(0.1186)	(0.0850)
ICT: Telephone	0.0325	0.0659	0.2766	0.1392	-0.0360	-0.0335	-0.0316	-0.0181
	(0.0560)	(0.0802)	(0.2552)	(0.1602)	(0.0495)	(0.0629)	(0.2206)	(0.1314)
ICT: Mobile	0.0150	0.0296	-0.0095	0.0184	0.0262*	0.0295*	0.0236	0.0294
	(0.0163)	(0.0189)	(0.0442)	(0.0317)	(0.0157)	(0.0179)	(0.0377)	(0.0269)
ICT: Broadband	0.0171	0.0591***	0.1276***	0.0748***	0.0152	0.0365***	0.0652***	0.0402**
	(0.0109)	(0.0113)	(0.0199)	(0.0172)	(0.0105)	(0.0127)	(0.0205)	(0.0170)

ICT = information and communication technology, TRE = transport and energy.

Notes: Figures in parenthesis are robust standard errors; $W1 = \{exp(-0.01*d)\}$; $W2 = \{1/d\}$; $W3 = \{1/d^3\}$, all with a 25th percentile cutoff; * $p < 0.1$, ** $p < 0.05$, and *** $p < 0.01$.

Source: Authors' calculations.

Conclusions

This paper estimates direct benefits and cross-border spillover effects of transport (road and rail) and energy and ICT infrastructure (telephone, mobile, and broadband). Using the spatial panel regression models, there is a highly positive and significant impact of infrastructure, particularly transport and energy, on own countries. Furthermore, the positive externalities of rail, broadband, and human capital are found, and these results are robust for broadband and human capital regardless of the choice of spatial weight matrices.

Our finding on spillover effects of rail infrastructure provides support for the key role of other countries' transport infrastructure on own country's economies. The quality of infrastructure of trading partners is often highlighted as one of the major determinants that facilitate bilateral trade. For example, using the gravity model, Grigoriou (2007) finds that the infrastructure of neighboring countries is essential because of the transit effect in landlocked Central Asian countries whose main modes of transportation to trade are road and rail.

The cross-border spillover effect of broadband infrastructure is estimated to be larger than its within-country effect. This implies that increased access to the internet can benefit not only own country's economic growth, but neighboring economies to a larger extent. A positive link between higher internet access and economic growth is easily found in the literature (for example, Choi and Yi 2005; Pradhan et al. 2014).

Human capital also shows positive cross-border spillover effects on growth. Human capital activities involve not only transmission of available knowledge, but also the production of new knowledge that is the source of innovation and technical change (Mincer 1981). Human capital positively affects productivity, and so educated labor has a much higher marginal product (Fleisher, Li, and Zhao 2008).

In sum, the empirical results of this chapter confirm positive *direct* contributions of infrastructure, access to technology, and human capital on economic growth. More importantly, their impacts are going beyond more than one country. When combined with their characteristics as public (or club) goods, the border-crossing benefits suggest there are regional public goods aspects of transport network, access to internet, and education. And it should be also noted that ICT, including the internet, has enormous potential in Asia to raise the equity, quality, and efficiency of education through ICT-enabled teaching and learning (ADB 2017b).

References

Acemoglu, D. and J. Robinson. 2012. *Why Nations Fail: The Origins of Power, Prosperity and Poverty.* New York, NY: Crown.

Asian Development Bank (ADB). 2017a. *Meeting Asia's Infrastructure Needs.* Manila. Retrieved from https://www.adb.org/publications/asia-infrastructure-needs.

ADB. 2017b. *Innovative Strategies for Accelerated Human Resource Development in South Asia: Information and Communication Technology for Education—Special Focus on Bangladesh, Nepal, and Sri Lanka.* Manila. Retrieved from https://www.adb.org/publications/innovative-strategies-ict-education-bangladesh-nepal-sri-lanka.

Anselin, L. 2003. Spatial Externalities, Spatial Multipliers and Spatial Econometrics. *International Regional Science Review. 26* (2). pp. 153-166. doi:10.1177/0160017602250972.

Barro, R. J. and J. W. Lee. 2013. A New Data Set of Educational Attainment in the World, 1950–2010. *Journal of Development Economics.* 104 (C). pp. 184-198. doi:10.1016/j.jdeveco.2012.10.001.

Batey, P. W. and P. Friedrich. 2000. Regional Competition. Berlin: Springer.

Berndt, E. R. and B. Hansson. 1991. Measuring the Contribution of Public Infrastructure Capital in Sweden. *NBER Working Paper Series.* No. 3842. Retrieved from https://www.nber.org/papers/w3842.

Bhattacharyay, B. 2010. Estimating Demand for Infrastructure in Energy, Transport, Telecommunications, Water and Sanitation in Asia and the Pacific: 2010-2020. *ADBI Working Paper Series.* No. 248. Retrieved from https://www.adb.org/publications/estimating-demand-infrastructure-energy-transport-telecommunications-water-sanitation.

Boarnet, M.G. 1998. Spillovers and the Locational Effects of Public Infrastructure. *Journal of Regional Science.* 38 (3). pp. 381–400. doi:10.1111/0022-4146.00099.

Calderón, C., E. Moral-Benito, and L. Servén. 2015. Is Infrastructure Capital Productive? A Dynamic Heterogeneous Approach. *Journal of Applied Econometrics*. 30 (2). pp. 177–98. doi:10.1002/jae.2373.

Canning, D. and E. Bennathan. 1999. *The Social Rate of Return on Infrastructure Investments*. World Bank Policy Research Working Paper Series. No. 2390. Retrieved from http://documents.worldbank.org/curated/en/261281468766808543/The-social-rate-of-return-on-infrastructure-investments.

Choi, C. and M. H. Yi. 2009. The Effect of the Internet on Economic Growth: Evidence from Cross-country Panel Data. *Economics Letters*. 105 (1). pp. 39–41. doi:10.1016/j.econlet.2009.03.028.

Cohen, J. and K. Monaco. 2007. Ports and Highways Infrastructure: An Analysis of Intra- and Inter-state Spillovers. *International Regional Science Review*. 31 (3). pp. 257–74. doi:10.1177/0160017608318946.

Égert, B., T. Kozluk, and D. Sutherland. 2009. *Infrastructure and Growth: Empirical Evidence*. OECD Economics Department Working Paper Series. No. 685. Retrieved from https://www.oecd-ilibrary.org/economics/infrastructure-and-growth_225682848268.

Feenstra, R. C., R. Inklaar, and M. P. Timmer. 2015. The Next Generation of the Penn World Table. *American Economic Review*. 105 (10). pp. 3150-182. doi:10.1257/aer.20130954.

Fleisher, B.M., H. Li, and M. Q. Zhao. 2008. Human Capital, Economic Growth, and Regional Inequality in China. *IZA Discussion Paper Series*. No. 3576. Retrieved from https://www.econstor.eu/bitstream/10419/34981/1/573334765.pdf.

Grigoriou, C. 2007. Landlockedness, Infrastructure and Trade: New Estimates for Central Asian Countries. *World Bank Policy Research Working Paper Series*. No. 4335. Retrieved from https://openknowledge.worldbank.org/handle/10986/7294.

Guild, R. L. 1998. Infrastructure Investment and Regional Development: Theory and Evidence. *Department of Planning Working Paper Series*. No. 98-3. Auckland: University of Auckland.

Hu, Z. and S. Luo. 2017. Road Infrastructure, Spatial Spillover and County Economic Growth. *IOP Conference Series: Materials Science and Engineering*. 231 (1). 012028. doi: 10.1088/1757-899X/231/1/012028.

LeSage, J. and P. Pace. 2009. *Introduction to Spatial Econometrics*. Retrieved from https://www.crcpress.com/Introduction-to-Spatial-Econometrics/LeSage-Pace/p/book/9781420064247.

Lin, J., Z. Yu, Y. D. Wei, and M. Wang. 2017. Internet Access, Spillover and Regional Development in China. *Sustainability*. 9 (12). 946. doi:10.3390/su9060946.

Mincer, J. 1981. Human Capital and Economic Growth. *NBER Working Paper Series*. No. 803. Retrieved from https://www.nber.org/papers/w0803.pdf.

Moshiri, S. 2016. ICT Spillovers and Productivity in Canada: Provincial and Industry Analysis. *Economics of Innovation and New Technology*. 25 (8). pp. 801-20. doi:10.1080/10438599.2016.1159864.

O'Mahony, M. and M. Vecchi. 2005. Quantifying the Impact of ICT Capital on Output Growth: A Heterogeneous Dynamic Panel Approach. *Economica*. 72 (288). pp. 615–33. doi: 10.1111/j.1468-0335.2005.0435.x.

Organisation for Economic Co-operation and Development (OECD). 2002. *Measuring the Information Economy*. Retrieved from https://www.oecd.org/sti/ieconomy/1835738.pdf.

Pradhan, R. P., M. B. Arvin, N. R. Norman, and S. K. Bele. 2014. Economic Growth and the Development of Telecommunications Infrastructure in the G-20 Countries: A Panel-VAR Approach. *Telecommunications Policy*. 38 (7). pp. 634–49. doi:10.1016/j.telpol.2014.03.001.

Sandler, T. 2006. Regional Public Goods and International Organizations *The Review of International Organizations*. 1 (1). pp. 5–25. doi:10.1007/s11558-006-6604-2.

Shahiduzzaman, M., A. Layton, and K. Alam. 2015. On the Contribution of Information and Communication Technology to Productivity Growth in Australia. *Economic Change and Restructuring*. 48 (3–4). pp 281–304. doi:10.1007/s10644-015-9171-9.

Skorupinska, A. and J. Torrent-Sellens. 2015. The Role of ICT in the Productivity of Central and Eastern European Countries: Cross-country Comparison. *Revista de Economía Mundial.* 39 (1). pp. 201–22.

Sloboda, B. and V. Yao. 2008. Interstate Spillovers of Private Capital and Public Spending. *The Annals of Regional Science.* 42 (3). pp. 505–18. doi:10.1007/s00168-007-0181-z.

Tong, T., T. H. E. Yu, S. H. Cho, K. Jensen, and D. D. Ugarte. 2013. Evaluating the Spatial Spillover Effects of Transportation Infrastructure on Agricultural Output Across the United States. *Journal of Transport Geography.* 30 (June). pp. 47–55. doi:10.1016/j.jtrangeo.2013.03.001.

van Leeuwen, G. and H. van der Wiel. 2003. *Spillover Effects of ICT.* cpb Report No. 2003/3. Retrieved from https://pdfs.semanticscholar. org/8e50/d4245c1b1d241d04f135e5ece2235ec51ab5.pdf.

Wamboye, E., A. Adekola, and B. Sergi. 2016. ICTs and Labour Productivity Growth in Sub-Saharan Africa. *International Labour Review.* 155 (2). pp. 231–52. doi:10.1111/j.1564-913X.2014.00021.x.

Yu, N., M. De Jong, S. Storm, and J. Mi. 2013. Spatial Spillover Effects of Transport Infrastructure: Evidence from Chinese Regions. *Journal of Transport Geography.* 28 (C). pp. 56–66. doi: 10.1016/j. jtrangeo.2012.10.009.

APPENDIX A3.1

Derivation of Direct and Indirect Effects in the Spatial Durbin Model

The spatial Durbin model (SDM) can be written in matrix form:

$$Y_t = \rho WY_t + X_t\beta + WX_t\theta + \mu + \epsilon_t \text{ (A1)}$$

where Y_t is a $n \times 1$ vector of response variable of each cross-section unit, X_t is an $n \times p$ matrix of regressor variables with an $p \times 1$ coefficient vector β, Θ is an $p \times 1$ spatial coefficient vector of the regressors, μ is the $n \times 1$ vector of unobserved heterogeneities, and ϵ_t is the vector of random fluctuations. The fixed time effects are discarded in the presence of variable cointegration. The reduced-form of the equation can be derived by subtracting both sides of the equation by ρWY_t and solving for Y_t:

$$Y_t - \rho WY_t = X_t\beta + WX_t\theta + \mu + \epsilon_t$$

$$\rightarrow (I - \rho W)Y_t = X_t\beta + WX_t\theta + \mu + \epsilon_t$$

$$\rightarrow Y_t = (I - \rho W)^{-1}[X_t\beta + WX_t\theta + \mu + \epsilon_t] \text{ (A2)}$$

The reduced-form of the SDM model requires the invertibility of $(I - \rho W)$. Getting the expected value of Y_t yields:

$$E(Y_t) = (I - \rho W)^{-1}[X_t\beta + WX_t\theta] \text{(A3)}$$

The X_t matrix can be partitioned column-wise such that $X_t = [X_{1t} \ X_{2t} \ \cdots \ X_{pt}]$, so that $X_t\beta = \sum_{k=1}^{p} \beta_k x_{kt}$, and $X_t\theta - \sum_{k=1}^{p} \theta_k x_{kt}$. $E(Y_t)$ becomes:

$$E(Y_t) = (I - \rho W)^{-1}\left\{\sum_{k=1}^{p} \beta_k x_{kt} + \sum_{k=1}^{p} \theta_k Wx_{kt}\right\} = \sum_{k=1}^{p}(I - \rho W)^{-1}(\beta_k I_n + \theta_k W)x_{kt} \text{ (A4)}$$

Hence, getting the partial derivative of $E(Y_t)$ with respect to x_{kt} yields:

$$\frac{\partial E(Y_t)}{\partial x_{kt}} = \begin{bmatrix} \frac{\partial E(y_{1t})}{\partial x_{k1,t}} & \frac{\partial E(y_{2t})}{\partial x_{k1,t}} & \cdots & \frac{\partial E(y_{nt})}{\partial x_{k1,t}} \\ \frac{\partial E(y_{1t})}{\partial x_{k2,t}} & \frac{\partial E(y_{2t})}{\partial x_{k2,t}} & \cdots & \frac{\partial E(y_{nt})}{\partial x_{k2,t}} \\ \vdots & \vdots & \ddots & \vdots \\ \frac{\partial E(y_{1t})}{\partial x_{kn,t}} & \frac{\partial E(y_{2t})}{\partial x_{kn,t}} & \cdots & \frac{\partial E(y_{nt})}{\partial x_{kn,t}} \end{bmatrix} = (I - \rho W)^{-1}(\beta_k I_n + \theta_k W) \text{ (A5)}$$

The direct effect of $x_{ik,t}$ on y_{it} is on the diagonal elements of $\frac{\partial E(Y_t)}{\partial x_{kt}}$. The average direct effect is the average of $\frac{\partial E(y_{1t})}{\partial x_{k1,t}}$ is given by:

$$Direct = \frac{1}{n}\sum_{i=1}^{n}\frac{\partial E(y_{it})}{\partial x_{ki,t}} = n^{-1}tr\big((I - \rho W)^{-1}(\beta_k I_n + \theta_k W)\big) \text{ (A6)}$$

The total effect of $x_{ik,t}$ on all y_{jt} is $\sum_{j=1}^{n}\frac{\partial E(y_{jt})}{\partial x_{ki,t}}$, which is the sum of the ith row of $\frac{\partial E(Y_t)}{\partial x_{kt}}$. The average total effect is the mean of the row totals of $\frac{\partial E(Y_t)}{\partial x_{kt}}$, given by the form:

$$Total = \frac{1}{n}\sum_{i=1}^{n}\sum_{j=1}^{n}\frac{\partial E(y_{jt})}{\partial x_{ki,t}} = n^{-1}1'_n(I - \rho W)^{-1}(\beta_k I_n + \theta_k W)1_n \text{ (A7)}$$

where 1_n is a summing vector of dimension n. The average indirect effect of a particular regressor is estimated from the difference of the average total effect and the average direct effect:

$$Indirect = \frac{1}{n}\sum_{i=1}^{n}\sum_{j=1}^{n}\frac{\partial E(y_{jt})}{\partial x_{ki,t}} - \frac{1}{n}\sum_{i=1}^{n}\frac{\partial E(y_{it})}{\partial x_{ki,t}} \text{ (A8)}$$

APPENDIX A3.2

Data Description

Variable	Description	Source
y_output	Output-side real GDP at chained PPPs (in $ million 2011)	Penn World Table 9.0
pop	Population (in million)	Penn World Table 9.0
secondary	Average years of secondary schooling	Barro & Lee (2013) data set
rkna	Capital stock at constant 2011 national prices (in $ million 2011)	Penn World Table 9.0
troads	Total roads (in km)	International Road Federation
rails	Total rail lines (in route-km)	World Bank's World Development Indicators
tlines	Fixed-telephone subscriptions (thousands)	International Telecommunication Union
mobile	Mobile/cellular telephone subscriptions (thousands)	International Telecommunication Union
broadband	Fixed broadband subscriptions from the World Bank's World Development Indicators	World Bank's World Development Indicators
egc	Electricity generating capacity (million kW)	US Energy Information Administration

GDP = gross domestic product, km = kilometer, kW = kilowatt, PPP = purchasing power parity.

List of Countries (78)

Africa (25)

Algeria	Kenya	Morocco	Tanzania
Benin	Lesotho	Mozambique	Togo
Cameroon	Liberia	Niger	Tunisia
Congo, Rep. of	Malawi	Rwanda	Uganda
Egypt, Arab Rep. of	Mali	Senegal	Zambia
Gabon	Mauritania	South Africa	Zimbabwe
Ghana			

Asia and the Pacific (15)

Australia	Korea, Rep. of	Pakistan	Philippines
New Zealand	Bangladesh	Sri Lanka	Singapore
China, People's Rep. of	India	Indonesia	Thailand
Japan	Nepal	Malaysia	

Europe (17)

Austria	Germany	Netherlands	Spain
Belgium	Greece	Norway	Sweden
Denmark	Ireland	Portugal	Switzerland
Finland	Italy	Romania	United Kingdom
France			

South America (19)

Argentina	Costa Rica	Honduras	Paraguay
Bolivia	Dominican Republic	Jamaica	Peru
Brazil	Ecuador	Mexico	Uruguay
Chile	El Salvador	Nicaragua	Venezuela
Colombia	Guatemala	Panama	

North America (2)

Canada	United States

APPENDIX A3.3

Construction of Non-Infrastructure Capital Stock

Conceptually, the total capital stock K^{lt} (in constant dollars; **observed**) of country l at time t can be written as:

$$K^{lt} = K_{inf}^{lt} + K_{noninf}^{lt} = \sum_{i=1}^{m} p_{inf,i}^{l} q_{inf,i}^{lt} + \sum_{j=1}^{n} p_{noninf,j}^{l} q_{noninf,j}^{lt} \quad (A9)$$

where

- K_{inf}^{lt} = total infrastructure capital stock (in constant dollars; unobserved); K_{noninf}^{lt} = total non-infrastructure capital stock (in constant dollars; unobserved)
- $q_{inf,i}^{lt}$ = infrastructure capital stock for type i (**observed**); $p_{inf,i}^{l}$ = price of $q_{inf,i}^{lt}$ in the base year (unobserved)
- $q_{noninf,j}^{lt}$ = non-infrastructure capital stock for type j (unobserved); $p_{noninf,j}^{l}$ = price of $q_{noninf,j}^{lt}$ in the base year (unobserved).

For simplicity, we assume that the p's already reflect the depreciation of each capital item.

For each country, we regress the total capital stock on infrastructure capital stock for type i $q_{inf,i}^{lt}$ *without a constant*:

$$K^{lt} = \beta_1^l q_{inf,1}^{lt} + \beta_2^l q_{inf,2}^{lt} + \cdots + \beta_m^l q_{inf,m}^{lt} + \varepsilon^{lt} \quad (A10)$$

where the β's can be seen as the prices of each infrastructure type. From the estimated equation, we can write:

$$\hat{\varepsilon}_{lt} = K^{lt} - \sum_{i=1}^{m} \hat{p}_{inf,i}^{l} q_{inf,i}^{lt} = K^{lt} - \hat{K}_{inf}^{lt} = \hat{K}_{noninf}^{lt} \quad (A11)$$

where $\hat{p}_{inf,i}^{l} = \hat{\beta}_i^l$.

Therefore,

$$\hat{K}_{noninf}^{lt} = \hat{\varepsilon}^{lt} \quad (A12)$$

which leads us to express non-infrastructure capital as the residual of the models.

APPENDIX A3.4

Estimation Results for Spatial and Non–Spatial Models

Table A3.4.1: Estimation Results (Transportation and Energy)

y=Per cap GDP	Models with Non-Infrastructure Capital					Models with Total Capital				
	Non-Spatial (1)	Non-Spatial¹ (2)	Spatial; W1 (3)	Spatial; W2 (4)	Spatial; W3 (5)	Non-Spatial (6)	Non-Spatial¹ (7)	Spatial; W1 (8)	Spatial; W2 (9)	Spatial; W3 (10)
X										
Total capital	–	–	–	–	–	0.5661***	0.5797***	0.5175***	0.4781***	0.4833***
						(0.0696)	(0.0797)	(0.0705)	(0.0833)	(0.0794)
Non-TRE Infra	0.0318**	0.0201**	0.0304**	0.0259*	0.0267*	–	–	–	–	–
	(0.0155)	(0.0083)	(0.0148)	(0.0155)	(0.0156)					
Human capital	0.1919***	0.2413***	0.1320***	0.0848**	0.0958**	0.0671**	0.0840*	0.0894***	0.0426	0.0612*
	(0.0452)	(0.0597)	(0.0376)	(0.0462)	(0.0447)	(0.0312)	(0.0431)	(0.0315)	(0.0322)	(0.0313)
TRE: Roads	0.1034*	0.0940*	0.0944*	0.1090**	0.1020**	-0.0192	-0.0210	-0.0034	0.0129	0.0106
	(0.0554)	(0.0546)	(0.0496)	(0.0521)	(0.0492)	(0.0362)	(0.0356)	(0.0357)	(0.0344)	(0.0336)
TRE: Rails	0.1815***	0.1288*	0.1647***	0.1363**	0.1505***	0.0605	-0.0379	0.0494	0.0464	0.0518
	(0.0623)	(0.0771)	(0.0595)	(0.0679)	(0.0612)	(0.0466)	(0.0658)	(0.0456)	(0.0493)	(0.048)
TRE: Energy	0.2509***	0.2742***	0.2177***	0.1928***	0.2011***	0.0739	0.0634	0.0802	0.0785	0.0836
	(0.0603)	(0.0660)	(0.0643)	(0.0537)	(0.0624)	(0.0618)	(0.0513)	(0.0623)	(0.0618)	(0.0624)
Wx										
Total capital	–	–	–	–	–	–	–	0.0561	0.0517	0.1211
								(0.0899)	(0.1895)	(0.1559)

continued on next page

Table A3.4.1 continued

y=Per cap GDP	Models with Non-Infrastructure Capital					Models with Total Capital				
	Non-Spatial (1)	Non-Spatial[1] (2)	Spatial; W1 (3)	Spatial; W2 (4)	Spatial; W3 (5)	Non-Spatial (6)	Non-Spatial[1] (7)	Spatial; W1 (8)	Spatial; W2 (9)	Spatial; W3 (10)
Non-TRE Infra	–	–	0.0077 (0.0129)	0.0126 (0.0275)	0.0062 (0.0187)	–	–	–	–	–
Human capital	–	–	0.0824** (0.0387)	0.1139* (0.0644)	0.1108** (0.054)	–	–	0.0117 (0.0355)	0.0419 (0.0563)	0.0281 (0.0477)
TRE: Roads	–	–	-0.0036 (0.0491)	-0.1077 (0.1366)	-0.0732 (0.0847)	–	–	-0.0335 (0.0436)	-0.1039 (0.1264)	-0.1213 (0.0834)
TRE: Rails	–	–	-0.0072 (0.0696)	0.2072* (0.1227)	0.0616 (0.1037)	–	–	-0.0711 (0.0605)	-0.0541 (0.1242)	-0.1269 (0.1141)
TRE: Energy	–	–	-0.0224 (0.0517)	0.0431 (0.1038)	-0.007 (0.0759)	–	–	-0.0276 (0.0527)	-0.0720 (0.1185)	-0.0764 (0.0895)
Wy	–	–	0.2179*** (0.0407)	0.4300*** (0.0814)	0.3478*** (0.0663)	–	–	0.0781** (0.0364)	0.3091*** (0.0841)	0.1733*** (0.0572)
Country FE	Yes	Yes	Yes	Yes	Yes	Yes	Yes	Yes	Yes	Yes
Time FE	Yes	Yes	No	No	No	Yes	Yes	No	No	No
Obs	858	1653	858	858	858	858	3369	858	858	858
#Years	11	55	11	11	11	11	55	11	11	11
#Country	78	78	78	78	78	78	78	78	78	78
R2	0.8267	0.8613	0.8324	0.7955	0.8217	0.9082		0.9121	0.9103	0.9004

FE = fixed effects, GDP = gross domestic product, TRE = transport and energy.

Notes: (1) Original annual data with missing values for 1960–2014 are used; the other columns are when all variables are taken 5-year averages and missing values are imputed; (2) All variables are in logs; figures in parenthesis are robust standard errors; (3) W1 = {exp(-0.01*d)}; W2 = {1/d}; W3 = {1/d³}, all with a 25th percentile cutoff; (4) * p < 0.1, ** p < 0.05, and *** p < 0.01.

Source: Authors' calculations.

Table A3.4.2: Estimation Results for Information and Communication Technology

y=Per cap GDP	Models with Non-Infrastructure Capital					Models with Total Capital				
	Non-Spatial (1)	Non-Spatial[1] (2)	Spatial; W1 (3)	Spatial; W2 (4)	Spatial; W3 (5)	Non-Spatial (6)	Non-Spatial[1] (7)	Spatial; W1 (8)	Spatial; W2 (9)	Spatial; W3 (10)
X										
Total capital	–	–	–	–	–	0.4722***	0.6019***	0.5128***	0.4543***	0.4974***
						(0.1316)	(0.1213)	(0.1290)	(0.1128)	(0.1214)
Non-TRE Infra	0.0262	0.0096	0.0284*	0.0282*	0.0282*	–	–	–	–	–
	(0.0162)	(0.0064)	(0.0166)	(0.0157)	(0.0166)					
Human capital	0.0883	0.0504	0.1311**	0.1001**	0.1135**	0.0807	0.0684**	0.0954**	0.0876*	0.0939**
	(0.0597)	(0.0524)	(0.0538)	(0.0507)	(0.0535)	(0.0525)	(0.0327)	(0.0454)	(0.0462)	(0.0465)
TRE: Roads	0.0325	0.0593	-0.0030	0.0080	-0.0005	-0.0360	0.0249	-0.0564	-0.0548	-0.0605
	(0.0560)	(0.0518)	(0.0488)	(0.0490)	(0.0502)	(0.0495)	(0.0409)	(0.0458)	(0.0447)	(0.0469)
TRE: Rails	0.0150	0.0877**	0.0074	0.0172	0.0063	0.0262*	0.0830***	0.0168	0.0203	0.0129
	(0.0163)	(0.0367)	(0.0248)	(0.0267)	(0.0324)	(0.0157)	(0.0277)	(0.0232)	(0.0274)	(0.0330)
TRE: Energy	0.0171	0.0041	0.0299***	0.0149	0.0225**	0.0152	0.0023	0.0220**	0.0138	0.0204*
	(0.0109)	(0.0152)	(0.0113)	(0.0108)	(0.0114)	(0.0105)	(0.0104)	(0.0107)	(0.0101)	(0.0108)
Wx										
Total capital	–	–	–	–	–	–	–	0.0276	0.3986	0.1118
								(0.0926)	(0.2644)	(0.1575)
Non-TRE Infra	–	–	0.0034	0.0654*	0.0074	–	–	–	–	–
			(0.0191)	(0.0388)	(0.0337)					
Human capital	–	–	0.0471	-0.0855	0.0178	–	–	-0.0001	-0.2214*	-0.0651
			(0.0397)	(0.1000)	(0.0706)			(0.0328)	(0.1131)	(0.0649)

continued on next page

Table A3.4.2 continued

y=Per cap GDP	Models with Non-Infrastructure Capital					Models with Total Capital				
	Non-Spatial (1)	Non-Spatial[1] (2)	Spatial; W1 (3)	Spatial; W2 (4)	Spatial; W3 (5)	Non-Spatial (6)	Non-Spatial[1] (7)	Spatial; W1 (8)	Spatial; W2 (9)	Spatial; W3 (10)
TRE: Roads	–	–	0.0691	0.2566	0.1315	–	–	0.0219	0.0339	0.0484
			(0.0699)	(0.2337)	(0.1410)			(0.0636)	(0.2232)	(0.1295)
TRE: Rails	–	–	0.0228	-0.0277	0.0095	–	–	0.0140	0.0022	0.0146
			(0.0359)	(0.0560)	(0.0522)			(0.0352)	(0.0550)	(0.0509)
TRE: Energy	–	–	0.0305**	0.1046***	0.0457**	–	–	0.0172	0.0594**	0.0208
			(0.0139)	(0.0289)	(0.0193)			(0.0136)	(0.0275)	(0.0181)
Wy	–	–	-0.0277	0.0648	0.0857	–	–	-0.0497	-0.0847	0.0099
			(0.0619)	(0.1495)	(0.0901)			(0.0669)	(0.1823)	(0.1049)
Country FE	Yes	Yes	Yes	Yes	Yes	Yes	Yes	Yes	Yes	Yes
Time FE	Yes	Yes	No	No	No	Yes	Yes	No	No	No
Obs	312	523	312	312	312	312	1021	312	312	312
#Years	4	17	4	4	4	4	17	4	4	4
#Country	78	78	78	78	78	78	78	78	78	78
R2	0.7209	0.6926	0.8229	0.7708	0.8187	0.9431	0.9548	0.9460	0.9243	0.9387

FE = fixed effects, GDP = gross domestic product, TRE = transport and energy.

Notes: (1) Original annual data with missing values for 1995–2014 are used; the other columns are when all variables are taken 5 year averages and missing values are imputed; For ICT-TC annual raw data, there are no broadband values for years 1995–1997; (2) All variables are in logs; figures in parenthesis are robust standard errors; (3) $W1 = \{\exp(-0.01*d)\}$; $W2 = \{1/d\}$; $W3 = \{1/d^2\}$, all with a 25th percentile cutoff; (4) $* \, p < 0.1$, $** \, p < 0.05$, and $*** \, p < 0.01$.

Source: Authors' calculations.

Measuring the Economic Impacts of Cross-Border Infrastructure and Technology: CGE Analysis

4

Chang-Soo Lee, Junkyu Lee, and Kijin Kim

Introduction

Large-scale infrastructure shocks in Asia and the Pacific are expected to stimulate the region's economic growth significantly by increasing productivity growth in infrastructure industries and through domestic spillovers across other industries. Cross-border spillovers across other regions are also at play.

Among the data on needed infrastructure in the region, during 2016–2030, 45 countries will need $22.55 trillion (baseline) in infrastructure investment, according to the Asian Development Bank (ADB).[1] Of the total baseline need, $13.12 trillion will be for the People's Republic of China (PRC), or about 70% of the total and about 49.6% of that country's gross domestic product (GDP). The analysis covered 10 categories of infrastructure; including transport (road, rail, seaport, airport), power (electricity); telecommunications (mobile, telephone, broadband); and water supply; and sanitation. Of the total baseline investment need, $11.69 trillion (51.8% in total) will be for electricity, $7.4 trillion (32.8%) for road and rail, and $1.95 trillion (14.8%) for mobile networks.

The needs of the analysis in this chapter are slightly narrower, however. The data above are not suitable for the infrastructure shocks of Global Trade Analysis Project (GTAP) analysis, which calls for data that include stimulations in infrastructure in accordance with structural changes/ stimulation in other industries and other policy stimulation in infrastructure (gap data). Because the baseline of the following GTAP analysis does not

---

[1] As per Table A4.1, the estimated total was $22,551 billion (2015 constant dollar) in baseline and $26,166 billion climate-adjusted during 2016–2030 (ADB 2017). Please see the Table A4.1 for a complete list of the economies.

consider structural changes of all industries—transformations of input–output linkages across industries of all regions over time—gap data are accurate for the infrastructure shocks of the GTAP analysis. As such, and according to ADB (2018), gap data cover 25 instead of 45 countries and 2016–2020 instead of 2016–2030 for the needs data.[2] The estimated total needs in 2016–2020 was $1.12 trillion (2015 constant dollar) and the gap was 27% of the needs in the baseline (Table 4.1). When PRC data are excluded, the gap was 57% of the need.

Table 4.1: Estimation of Infrastructure Needs and Gap, 25 Developing Asia and Pacific Countries, 2016–2020 ($ billion, 2015 prices)

Subregion	Current Investment $ Billion	Baseline Estimates (2016–2020)			Including Climate Change Costs (2016–2020)		
		Annual Infrastructure Need		Gap as % of Average Annual Projected GDP	Annual Infrastructure Need		Gap as % of Average Annual Projected GDP
		$ Billion in 2015 Prices	as % of GDP		$ Billion in 2015 Prices	as % of GDP	
Central Asia	5.84	10.80	5.1	2.3	12.44	5.9	3.1
East Asia	686.04	756.50	5.8	0.5	840.23	6.4	1.2
South Asia	133.55	293.88	8.6	4.7	328.57	9.6	5.7
Southeast Asia	54.95	147.37	6.0	3.8	156.81	6.4	4.1
The Pacific	0.56	1.98	8.7	6.2	2.13	9.4	6.9
Totals	880.94	1,210.54	6.3	1.7	1,340.18	7.0	2.4

GDP = gross domestic product.
Source: ADB (2018).

Discussions in the literature of regional public goods are ample, but quantitative measurement on the impacts of stimulating infrastructure are rare. This chapter aims to fill this gap by estimating the macroeconomic

---

[2]   The 25 include two countries in East Asia (the PRC and Mongolia), 7 countries of Southeast Asia (Indonesia, Cambodia, Myanmar, Malaysia, the Philippines, Thailand, and Viet Nam); 6 countries of South Asia (Bangladesh, Bhutan, India, Sri Lanka, Maldives, and Nepal); 5 countries of Central and West Asia (Afghanistan, Armenia, Kazakhstan, the Kyrgyz Republic, and Pakistan); and 5 countries of the Pacific (Fiji, the Federated States of Micronesia, Kiribati, the Marshall Islands, and Papua New Guinea).

impact of such investment using the GTAP model, which is able to clarify the channels of the impacts.

The chapter measures the economic impact of the infrastructure gap on ADB member and non-member countries using the standardized computable general equilibrium (CGE) framework, the GTAP model, as estimated by ADB (2018).

Simply put, the GTAP model—a system of simultaneous equations—is a standardized international trade model comprising a set of equilibrium equations of microeconomics, macroeconomics, and international trade. For example, each sector's output (supply) and consumption (demand) are decided respectively by a sectoral profit maximization condition and utility maximization condition (price version), and price of that good is decided by the sectoral market-clearing conditions. And the GTAP model (simultaneous equations) is solved using the GTAP database and exogenous policy shocks. This analysis uses a recent version of the GTAP database (preliminary version 10), a sort of world input–output table of the year 2014, which has 141 regions and 57 sectors.

Among the GTAP model's strengths is that it is a widely used standardized trade model and its results and processes are therefore clear and transparent. It is also suitable for multiregional, large-scale-shock analysis because the model functions like a platform implementing many types of shocks together, and because access to a sort of world input–output data is very easy. Among its weaknesses, most technical changes are purely exogenous variables, whereas the GTAP automatically calculates many parameters of variables. External sources or studies are therefore necessary to implement hypothetical policy shocks under reasonable assumptions.

Considering the purpose of the analysis, three types of channel of impact triggered by three types of corresponding policy shocks are implemented in the standard GTAP model. The first channel is "direct impacts in infrastructure industries" consisting of the increase in production and productivity growth in the infrastructure industries (i). The second channel is the "intermediate-input-i-augmenting technical change in other industries of the same region" to measure within-the-region spillover effects. The third is the "import-i-from-r-augmenting technical change in other region, s," to measure cross-border spillover effects. This measures imported-intermediate-input augmenting technical change, when the imported i is the non-transportation sector, and trade facilitation effects, when the imported i is the transportation sector.

The chapter does not intend to measure impacts accurately because different CGE models have different solutions. Instead, it focuses more on (i) constructing the analytical framework measuring the impacts of the large-scale infrastructure shocks with clarified channels of impact, and (ii) finding policy implications from the various simulation results.

Notably, the chapter underestimates the real impacts of infrastructure shocks, for several reasons. First, the analytical framework in the chapter, as noted, is the standardized GTAP model focusing on static gains while ignoring dynamic gains. Second, the infrastructure shocks of the chapter do not include stimulating infrastructure in Asian developed economies (Hong Kong, China; the Republic of Korea; Singapore; and Taipei,China) and, because of this, cross-border impacts are underestimated. Third is the limitation of the GTAP analysis in assuming the input–output linkages across industries of regions of the base year, 2014, being the same as those of 2015 to 2020.

The next section of the chapter reviews the literature on CGE studies on measurement of infrastructure-boosting impacts. The chapter then explains the GTAP model and how to implement three channels of infrastructure shocks in the same model. More specifically, the key variables and equations of the model, which shocked in the CGE simulations later, are introduced. It explains the accommodation of the GTAP base data and ADB's policy shock data, then introduces three analytical scenarios with assumptions on comprising components.

Literature Review: Three Channels

Experimenting on the huge amount of infrastructure shocks using the GTAP model raises two fundamental considerations. The first is whether CGE studies exist that similarly experiment with huge shocks like this. The second is whether benchmark studies exist for this chapter. Zhai (2012) is the answer in both cases. In the first consideration, studies do exist, but usually for policy purposes (as in Zhai 2012) and rarely as serious academic studies.

The CGE literature has ample topic-specific and small-scale studies, rather than general ones. Specific CGE studies measuring the economic impacts of overseas development assistance on a recipient country include Clausen and Schurenberg-Frosch (2012); Wiebelt et al. (2011); Agenor, Bayraktar, and El Aynaoui (2008); Adam and Bevan (2006); Vos (1998); Bandara (1995); and Lee and Song (2013). This literature usually focuses on the importance of infrastructure investment and the impact of quality upgrading or productivity growth in infrastructure.

Following this idea, this chapter implements a "quality-upgrading channel of infrastructure-stimulating" experiment. According to economic growth theory, improvements in the quality of infrastructure, particularly in developing countries, is *the* long-term factor of economic growth boosting the GDP growth rate or GDP per capita. Accumulation of physical or human capital, by contrast, changes only the value level of GDP or of GDP per capita. More simply, the change in quality of infrastructure functions in the same way as technological change, or decrease in trade cost in the price version, in the development stage (Jones and Vollrath 2013).

Another type of topic-specific CGE study in the literature focuses on trade facilitation. This measures the impact on cross-border trade facilitation of stimulating infrastructure (Fugazza and Maur 2008; Ando 2009; Zaki 2014; Walmsley and Minor 2016; Suh et al. 2013). The main concern in these studies is reductions in trade costs and measurement of the cross-border impacts of those reductions. These studies are also classified into two groups by the type of shock they implement in CGE simulations. One uses "imported-intermediate input technical change" or "shipping-cost technical-change" shock (Kim, Park, and Park 2006; Ando 2009; Zhai 2012). The other uses "reduction in tariff equivalents" shocks (Suh et al. 2013).

Zhai (2012) could be a benchmark CGE study experimenting with large-scale as well as international-level infrastructure shocks, like this chapter. Zhai estimates the benefits of the infrastructure investment ($8.22 trillion in total) of 2010–2012, and this focuses only on one channel of impacts—trade facilitation across borders. The basic idea is that stimulating infrastructure reduces transportation costs across borders. This chapter develops this idea further, in that it takes the idea further to mean stimulating infrastructure reduces trade costs of intermediate (infrastructure) inputs across industries within the border (domestic spillovers) as well as across borders (cross-border spillovers).

Notably, Lee and Kim (2017) emphasize cross-border spillovers and their macroeconomic feedback effects. The general equilibrium framework can fully capture both.

Other countries also benefit from one country's efforts to stimulate infrastructure: provision of infrastructure directly facilitates cross-border trade-increasing connectivity between countries and this increases specialization in production toward more competitive sectors, again indirectly improving efficiency in factor allocations.

This chapter defines three types of channels through which policy shocks, as per the infrastructure gap of ADB (2018), can work in the model. The first is "direct increase in production and productivity growth in infrastructure industries (i)". The second is the "intermediate-input-i-augmenting technical change in other industries of the same region" to measure within-the-region spillover effects. The third is "import-i-from-r-augmenting technical change in other region, s" to measure the cross-border effects of r's investment in infrastructure. The first channel of direct impact is the focus of the overseas development assistance-related policy and academic studies (Clausen and Schurenberg-Frosch 2012; Wiebelt et al. 2011; Agenor, Bayraktar, and El Aynaoui 2008; Adam and Bevan 2006; Vos 1998; Bandara 1995; and Lee and Song 2013).[3]

Calculation of the second channel domestic spillovers across industries of the same region can be validated when the purpose of investment in infrastructure is considered, overcoming bottlenecks from low-quality infrastructure. This is along the same line as the Hirschman 1969 argument of "unbalanced growth" emphasizing domestic forward and backward linkages, complementarity, and investment in infrastructure (transportation and electricity). In short, in developing countries characterized by scarce resources and inadequate infrastructure, a production increase in one industry can induce production in other industries sequentially and repeatedly.

The third type of channel, cross-border spillovers, is also employed in the literature reviewed earlier. Coe and Helpman (1995), Sjoholm (1996, 1999),

---

[3] A reminder that the calculation of the impact of an increase in production in the CGE model is equivalent to calculation of the multiplier effects in production and value-added in that industry of input–output table analysis.

and van Meijl and van Tongeren (1999) model technical change mediated by imported intermediate goods, while Ando (2009), Kim, Park, and Park (2006), and Suh et al. (2013) apply this in trade facilitation studies. In sum, this third channel measures imported-intermediate-input-i-augmenting technical change when the imported i is the non-transportation sector and trade facilitation effects when the imported i is the transportation sector.

GTAP Model and Shock Variables

GTAP Model and Infrastructure Shocks

As noted, the CGE model is a system of simultaneous equations, which comprises a set of equilibrium equations of microeconomics, macroeconomics, and international trade. For example, each sector's output (supply) and consumption (demand) are decided respectively by the sectoral profit maximization condition and utility maximization condition (in price versions in the GTAP model), and the price of that good is decided by the sectoral market-clearing conditions.

The GTAP model is a static CGE model of the world economy. It is based on the assumptions of perfect competitive markets and constant returns to scale. It is a static model in the sense that factors (unskilled and skilled labor, capital, land, and natural resources) are fixed in quantity terms after policy shocks. It is also characterized by the constant elasticity of substitution and constant elasticity of transformation function structure of demand and supply, allowing very simple estimation and calibration, introduction of global bank structuring, international shipping and tracing transport margins, use of price versions of equilibrium conditions instead of quantity versions, assumptions on the mobility of factors, and so on. This standardized model is composed of eight modules: (i) government consumption; (ii) private consumption; (iii) firms; (iv) investment, global bank, and savings; (v) international trade; (vi) international transport services; (vii) regional household; and (viii) equilibrium conditions.

Let us think of the nesting structure of sectoral production of a region. For example, Figure 4.1 shows the constant elasticity of transformation structure of production in the "firms" bloc.

Gross output (*qo*) of an industry (*j*) of a region (*r*) is a composite of value-added (*qva*) and intermediate input (*qf*). Value-added (*qva*) of an industry (*j*) of a region (*r*) is a composite of land, labor, and capital. Similarly, intermediate input (*qf*) of an industry (*j*) of a region (*r*) is a composite of domestic intermediate nest (*qfd*), which is sourced from domestic (*r*) industries (*i*), and imported intermediate nest (*qfm*), which is sourced from foreign (*s*) industries (*i*). If we investigate further, despite the lack of mention in the figure, *qfm* (*i*,*j*,*r*) is a composite of *qfm* (*i*,*j*,*r*) from region 1, that from region 2, and so on. This complicated composite nest can easily and fully be calibrated just from the information on constant elasticities of transformation of all nests.

Also notable about this nest structure is that quantity variables in the figure, for instance, *qo*, are endogenous, while corresponding technical changes, for instance, *ao*, are exogenous. In this way, all types of technical changes are defined exogenous variables in the GTAP model and, because of this, implementing technical-change-type policy shocks are very straightforward. It is also noteworthy that technical changes in the GTAP model involve direct reduction in prices or costs, because equilibrium conditions in the model are usually represented by price versions instead of quantity versions.

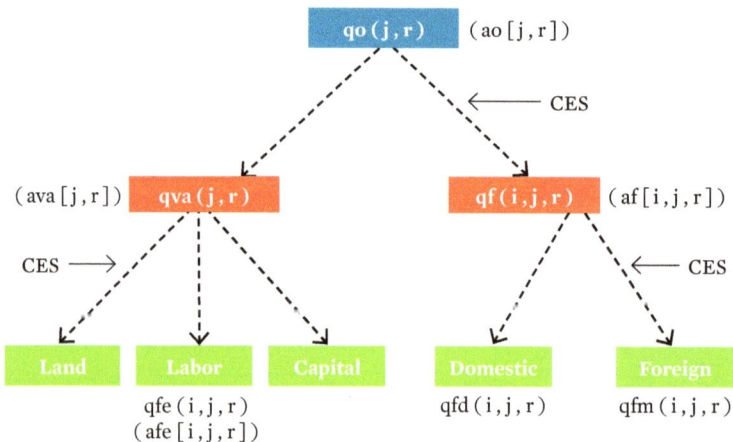

Figure 4.1: Production Structure of the GTAP Model

GTAP = Global Trade Analysis Project.
Source: Authors.

How to Implement Infrastructure Shocks?

Like any other CGE model, zero-profit and market-clearing conditions decide equilibrium price and production of an industry j of region r.

$$ps(j,r) + ao(j,r) \qquad\qquad (1)$$
$$= \text{sum}(i, ENDW\_COMM, STC(i,j,r) * [pfe(i,j,r) - afe(i,j,r) - ava(j,r)])$$
$$+ \text{sum}(i, TRAD\_COMM, STC(i,j,r) * [pf(i,j,r) - af(i,j,r)])$$
$$+ profitslack(j,r).$$

$$qo(i,r) \qquad\qquad (2)$$
$$= SHRDM(i,r) * qds(i,r)$$
$$+ \text{sum}(s, REG, SHRXMD(i,r,s) * qxs(i,r,s))$$
$$+ tradslack(i,r).$$

Equation 1: profit max. condition
$ps(j,r)$: supply price of commodity i in region r,
$pfe(i,j,r)$: firms' price for endowment commodity i in industry j, region r,
$pf(i,j,r)$: firms' price for commodity i for use by j in r,
$STC(i,j,r)$: share of i in total costs of j in r,
$ao(j,r)$: output augmenting technical change in sector j of r,
$ava(i,r)$: value-added augmenting technical change in sector i of r,
$af(i,j,r)$: composite intermediate input i augmenting tech change by j of r,
$afe(i,j,r)$: primary factor i augmenting technical change by j of r,
$profitslack(j,r)$: slack variable in the zero-profit equation,
$ams(i,r,s)$: import i from region r augmenting technical change in region s.

Equation 2: market clearing condition
$qo(i,r)$: industry output of commodity i in region r,
$qds(i,r)$: domestic sales of commodity i in r,
$qxs(i,r,s)$: export sales of commodity i from r to region s,
$SHRDM(i,r)$: share of domestic sales of i in r,
$SHRXMD(i,r,s)$: share of export sales of i to s in r,
$tradslack(i,r)$: slack variable in tradeable market clearing condition.

As a design strategy of policy simulations, this chapter makes policy shocks as well as channels of impacts of shocks very clear and easily interpretable without modifying the GTAP model structure. In this regard, the basic simulation scheme is concentrating on direct impact, treating the infrastructure gap estimated by ADB (2018) as a policy shock increasing production and the overall productivity of those infrastructure industries. Inclusion of technical change can be validated when considering the long-term purpose of investments in those industries. In the GTAP language, these policy shocks are coded by percentage changes in production and technical change [$qo(i, r)$ and $ao(i, r)$], respectively. In the GTAP model, an exogenous increase in production causes dis-equilibriums in infrastructure and non-infrastructure industries first, then restores general equilibrium again by the worldwide readjustment process initiated by changes in price and *profitslack* of region r.

The other positive expected consequences resulting from infrastructure shocks in one region should be domestic spillovers across other industries and cross-border spillover effects. The direct channel through which the infrastructure shock affects other domestic industries is technical infrastructure-intermediate-input-i-augmenting technical change in other industries js, $af(i,j,r)$ in equation (1). Simply put, domestic industries can benefit from saving infrastructure-intermediate inputs in the production process. These types of backward linkages start first from the shocked infrastructure industry and then move to others. They then move from benefited industries to others, this process repeating infinitely like multiplier effects in the input–output table. But this chapter focuses only on the first direct effect.

Similarly, the direct channel through which the infrastructure shock causes positive cross-border consequences is import-i-from-region-r augmenting technical change in other regions, $ams(i,r,s)$, and technical change shipping from region r, $ats(r)$, or technical change in m's shipping of i from region r to s, $atmfsd(m,i,r,s)$. That is, foreign s benefits from infrastructure shock of i in r by saving imported intermediate-inputs in the production process [$ams(i,r,s)$] and/or by reduction in transportation cost [$ats(r)$ or $atmfsd(m,i,r,s)$]. Regarding these international spillovers, this chapter includes only import-i-from-region-r augmenting technical change in other regions, $ams(i,r,s)$, and this is also limited only in infrastructure industry i in policy simulations. This cross-border spillover effect can be magnified in a way that the range of industry i of region r expanded to benefited industries of infrastructure investment in $ams(i,r,s)$ shock and trade facilitation is considered by $ats(r)$ or $atmfsd(m,i,r,s)$.

Data and Scenarios

Aggregation Scheme: Region and Industry

GTAP's (Version 10) 141 regions are aggregated into the 10 regions outlined in Table 4.2, while GTAP's 57 sectors are aggregated into the 20 industries, as in Table 4.3.

Table 4.2: Aggregation of Regions, 10 Regions

Region/Economy	Group Name		Economies Included
PRC	CHNN		PRC
Japan	JPNN		Japan
Korea	KORR		The Republic of Korea
ASEAN–4	ASN4		Indonesia, Malaysia, Philippines, Thailand
CLMV	CLMV		Cambodia, Lao PDR, Myanmar, Viet Nam
		ASEAN developed	Brunei Darussalam, Singapore
Asian developed	ADED	East Asia Others	Hong Kong, China; Taipei,China
			Australia, New Zealand
		Central and West Asia	Armenia, Azerbaijan, Georgia, Kazakhstan, Kyrgyz Republic, Tajikistan, Turkmenistan, Uzbekistan
Other member countries	MEMB	South Asia	Afghanistan, Bangladesh, Bhutan, India, Maldives, Nepal, Pakistan, Sri Lanka
		Pacific	Cook Islands, Fiji, Kiribati, Marshall Islands, Federated States of Micronesia, Nauru, Papua New Guinea, Samoa, Solomon Islands, Timor-Leste, Tonga, Palau, Tuvalu, Vanuatu
		East Asia	Mongolia
US	USAA		US
EU	EU27		Excluding United Kingdom
ROW	ROWW		

ASEAN = Association of Southeast Asian Nations, EU = European Union, Lao PDR = Lao People's Democratic Republic, PRC = People's Republic of China, ROW = rest of the world, US = United States.
Source: Authors' description.

Policy Shocks

As noted, ADB (2018) estimates the infrastructure gap in 25 countries in Asia and the Pacific during 2016–2020. It covers 10 categories of infrastructure need, including transport, road, rail, seaport, airport, power (electricity), mobile, telephone, broadband, and water supply and sanitation.

Table 4.3: Aggregation of Industries, 20 Sectors

Item	Sector in this Study	Infrastructure Sector in ADB
1	Agriculture (including food)	
2	Mining	
3	Textile and clothing	
4	Chemical	
5	Metal	
6	Vehicles	
7	Electronic products	Mobile
8	Other manufacturing	
9	Electricity and gas	Electricity
10	Water and sewage	Water
11	Construction	
12	Trade	
13	Transport–land	Rail, road
14	Transport–sea	Seaport
15	Transport–air	Airport
16	Communications	Broadband, telephone
17	Financial services	
18	Other business services	
19	Public services	Sanitation
20	Other services	

Source: Authors' description.

Country-level data are aggregated based on the regional aggregation scheme in Table 4.2.[4] ADB country-level data are aggregated into those of the corresponding regions in Table 4.2: those in the PRC, Republic of Korea, ASEAN–4, CLMV, Asian developed, and other ADB member countries (MEMB). Ten categories of infrastructure need are aggregated into the

---

[4] The share of a member country's GDP in the region's total GDP are weights aggregating member countries into a region. Country- and category-level data are aggregated to construct the gap value ($ billion) in the table.

eight: electricity (Eity), water supply (Wate), land transport (Land = rail + road), sea transport (Seap), air transport (Airp), telecommunications (Tele = telephone + broadband), sanitation (Sani), and mobile (Mobi). And these eight categories are connected to the aggregated industries of Table 4.3 (see the last column of the table).[5]

These aggregated values (2015 $) in the third column of the table are then transformed into growth rates in gap values, which is a required format for policy simulations. To convert integrated categories of values (infrastructure gap) to equivalent growth rates, each industry's gross output data is required. This chapter employs the value of sectoral outputs of GTAP data (reference year 2014) and sectoral gross outputs of 2015 MRIO (Multi-Regional Input–Output Table). Higher output values from the two sources are used when converting the level data to growth rates. The fourth column of Table 4.4 reports results.

These cannot be used as policy shocks directly because of the difference between the infrastructure-gap sectors (ADB Data: the first column of Table 4.4) and GTAP aggregated industry (the second column of Table 4.3). In other words, the share of infrastructure-shock sector (the first column of Table 4.4) in aggregated industry (the second column of Table 4.3) should be adjusted. For example, the road and rail sector's output share in related aggregated industry (transport) are close to 100%, whereas the mobile sector's output share in related aggregated industry (electronic products) should be less than 30%. This output share (fifth column of Table 4.4) should be multiplied to get the final growth rates in the sixth column as output (qo) shock.

The final column of the table is productivity shocks (ao shocks). The chapter assumes that the productivity shock is 30% of "qo" shocks.[6] As noted earlier, the basic purpose of stimulation of infrastructure is quality upgrading or productivity growth, rather than more production of output in infrastructure industries. But there is no clear-cut answer to what extent productivity grows when the infrastructure sector is stimulated. This chapter assumes that productivity growth is about 30% of the growth in infrastructure output, which can be calculated from the gap data. In other words, the chapter calculates the output growth shock just for deriving the productivity growth shock in the infrastructure industry.

---

[5] A reminder: the "mobile" category of ADB is classified as "electronics" while "sanitation" is classified as "public service," including health services instead of "water, sewage and disposal of wastes" in the GTAP database.

[6] While it might be worthwhile looking for evidence in past literature, the authors know of no relevant studies.

Table 4.4: Policy Shocks to Measure Direct Impacts
(%)

Infrastructure Sector	Region	qo (Sum of 2016–20; Output) shock				ao (Sum of 2016–20; Productivity) shock
		Infrastructure Gap (billion $)	Gap Growth Rate (%) (a)	Sector Share (%) (b)	Gap Growth Rate (%) - Adjusted (c) = (a*b/100)	Assumption: 30% of Output Shock (d) = c*0.3
Mobile	PRC	26.85	3.96	20	0.79	0.24
	ASEAN–4	19.47	17.23	25	4.31	1.29
	CLMV	6.27	101.09	30	30.33	9.10
	Other members	36.30	57.89	30	17.37	5.21
Electricity	PRC	193.77	35.59	90	32.04	9.61
	ASEAN–4	51.43	77.01	90	69.31	20.79
	CLMV	9.74	49.68	90	44.71	13.41
	Other members	92.77	146.52	90	131.87	39.56
Water	PRC	4.55	14.03	80	11.22	3.37
	ASEAN–4	2.76	32.27	80	25.81	7.74
	CLMV	1.22	166.94	70	116.85	35.06
	Other members	11.80	56.65	70	39.65	11.90
Road and rail	PRC	82.04	9.34	100	9.34	2.80
	ASEAN–4	59.52	54.51	100	54.51	16.35
	CLMV	7.92	87.47	100	87.47	26.24
	Other members	169.37	47.20	100	47.20	14.16
Seaport	PRC	5.64	5.22	100	5.22	1.57
	ASEAN–4	1.72	3.86	100	3.86	1.16
	CLMV	0.17	5.09	100	5.09	1.53
	Other members	0.76	1.06	100	1.06	0.32
Airport	PRC	0.46	0.63	100	0.63	0.19
	ASEAN–4	0.29	0.61	100	0.61	0.18
	CLMV	0.05	0.83	100	0.83	0.25
	Other members	0.15	0.19	100	0.19	0.06
Communication	PRC	6.14	1.91	100	1.91	0.57
	ASEAN–4	1.59	2.06	100	2.06	0.62
	CLMV	0.49	9.30	100	9.30	2.79
	Other members	1.19	1.28	100	1.28	0.38
Sanitation	PRC	5.29	0.28	10	0.03	0.01
	ASEAN–4	3.83	1.39	10	0.14	0.04
	CLMV	1.18	3.70	10	0.37	0.11
	Other members	5.67	0.94	10	0.09	0.03

ASEAN–4 = Indonesia, Malaysia, the Philippines, and Thailand; CLMV = Cambodia, Lao People's Democratic Republic, Myanmar, and Viet Nam; PRC = People's Republic of China.

Notes: Number in the cell is summation of annual growth rates in the specified period except cells of the sixth column. Gross domestic product growth rates calculated from CEPII (2016).

Source: Authors' calculation.

This chapter uses two shocks to measure direct impacts in the stimulated industries of a stimulating region: production shock $[qo(i, r)]$ and productivity shock $[ao(i, r)]$ in the observed infrastructure industries. Direct impacts are converging to productivity growth, or reduction in price or cost of the output of infrastructure industries when considering the long-term purpose of investments in those industries.[7]

As noted, other policy shocks in this chapter are infrastructure-input-i-augmenting technical change in other industries of the same region $[af(i, j, r)]$ to measure domestic spillovers and import-i-from-region-r augmenting technical change in region foreign s $[ams(i, r, s)]$ to measure cross-border spillovers. The analysis assumes that $af(i, j, r)$ and $ams(i, r, s)$ is 15% and 10%, respectively, during 2016–2020. This implies that the $af(i, j, r)$ and $ams(i, r, s)$ shock is 3% and 2%, respectively, a year.

The infrastructure-input-i-augmenting technical change in other industries of the same region $[af(i, j, r)]$ can be validated from stimulating the region's economic activity by overcoming the bottleneck of low-quality infrastructure, another of the long-term reasons for investment in infrastructure. The basic intuition is that domestic industries can benefit from saving infrastructure inputs in the production process or from improved backward linkages between infrastructure and other industries. The assumption in this analysis is that $af(i, j, r)$ is 15% for 5 years, or 3% a year.

Similarly, import-i-from-region-r augmenting technical change in other region $[ams(i, r, s)]$ can be validated from strengthening economic ties and facilitating trade with lowering shipping costs in Asia and the Pacific by upgrading low-quality infrastructure in potential high growth developing countries, another of the long-term reasons for investment in infrastructure. This chapter's assumption is that $ams(i, r, s)$ is 10% for 5 years, or 2% a year.

Scenarios

The analysis measures (i) direct impacts on infrastructure industry (i) of the region (r); (ii) domestic spillovers, impacts on other industries (j) of the region (r), which use stimulated infrastructure output as intermediate input; and (iii) cross-border spillovers, impacts on industries (j) of the foreign (s), which import stimulated infrastructure output of region r and

---

[7]   This implies that the output expansion effect in the short run would be limited in the long term.

use as intermediate input. Direct impacts are decomposed into output growth effect and productivity growth effect, but this analysis focuses only on the productivity effect. To measure these three channels of impact, the corresponding three types of policy shock are necessary: (i) productivity (and output) shock to measure direct impacts, (ii) infrastructure-input-i-augmenting technical change in other industries of the same region $[af(i, j, r)]$ to measure domestic spillovers, and (iii) import-i-from-region-r augmenting technical change in region foreign s $[ams(i, r, s)]$ to measure cross-border spillovers. The policy shock values are explained in the succeeding section.

Table 4.5: Simulation Scheme

Scenario	Direct Impacts		Domestic Spillovers	Cross-border Spillovers
	Output Shock	Productivity Shock		
SC_0	qo (i, r) in Table 4.4	ao (i, r) = 30% of qo (i, r)	none	none
SC_1	none	ao (i, r) = 30% of qo (i, r)	none	none
SC_2	none	ao (i, r) = 30% of qo (i, r)	af (i, j, r) = 15% for 5 years	same
SC_3	none	ao (i, r) = 30% of qo (i, r)	af (i, j, r) = 15% for 5 years	ams (i, m, s) = 10% for 5 years

Notes:
(i) r is infrastructure-stimulating region: People's Republic of China (PRC), ASEAN–4, Cambodia, Lao People's Democratic Republic, Myanmar, and Viet Nam (CLMV), and other member countries (MEMB) in Table 4.2.
(ii) s is a country not equaling to r. For example, if r is the PRC, then s is each trading partner of the PRC: all regions in Table 4.2 except the PRC.
(iii) i is stimulated infrastructure industry: electricity and gas, water and sewage, land transport, sea transport, air transport, communications, electronic products, and public services in Table 4.3.
(iv) j is other domestic industry including i using/purchasing i as intermediate input of production.
(v) m is an industry of a foreign trading partner (s) which imports i from r and uses as intermediate input of production.
Source: Authors.

Table 4.5 summarizes the simulation scheme of the analysis here. SC_1 is a policy scenario to measure productivity growth effects in stimulated infrastructure industries of a region. SC_2 is a policy scenario to measure domestic spillover effects as well as productivity growth effects in a stimulating region. The difference between the results of SC_2 and of SC_1 could lead us to valuable insights on the significance and transmission mechanism of domestic spillover effects. Finally, SC_3 is a policy scenario to measure cross-border spillover effects in non-stimulating regions as well as domestic spillover and productivity growth effects in a stimulating region. We expect valuable insights on the significance of and structural understanding on the cross-border spillover effects from the difference between the results of SC_3 and of SC_2.

Results

Overall Effects

Panel A of Table 4.6 reports overall macroeconomic impacts of the three infrastructure-stimulating scenarios. Let us focus on the percentage change in constant GDP. Productivity shocks of SC_1 have positive and significant impact on rates of growth in GDP of infrastructure-stimulating regions: 0.72% in PRC, 1.86% in ASEAN–4, 4.65% in CLMV, and 4.68% in MEMB, whereas productivity shocks have negative impacts on other regions except Japan. The impact on GDP growth rates are intensified in SC_2 of domestic spillovers as well as productivity shocks. On one hand, GDP growth rates of infrastructure-stimulating regions are much higher than those of SC_1: 4.70% in the PRC, 4.76% in ASEAN 4, 9.61% in CLMV, and 7.28% in MEMB. On the other, negative GDP growth of non-stimulating regions except Japan are much higher than those of SC_1: –0.14% in the Republic of Korea, –0.05% in Asian developed (ADED), –0.03% in the United States (US), and –0.07% in the European Union.

Now let us check the changes in GDP growth rates when moving to SC_3 adding cross-border spillover shocks from SC_2. First, the growth rates in infrastructure-stimulating regions are higher than those in SC_2, but the gaps between the two pairs of a region are small. The GDP growth rates in SC_3 are 4.92% in the PRC, 5.33% in ASEAN–4, 11.98% in CLMV, and 7.39% in MEMB. Second, the growth rates in infrastructure-stimulating regions, showing negative numbers in SC_1 and SC_2, positive in SC_3: 0.30% in the Republic of Korea, 0.38% in ADED, 0.10% in the US, and 0.07% in the European Union.

These results lead us to the following conclusions and policy implications. First, large-scale infrastructure shocks in Asia and the Pacific are expected to stimulate the region's and other region's economic growth significantly by (i) increasing productivity growth in infrastructure industries, (ii) boosting domestic spillovers across industries within each stimulating region, and (iii) cross-border spillovers across regions.

Table 4.6: Overall Impacts

Panel A: Macroeconomic Impacts

Region	% Change in Constant GDP (qgdp, %)			Change in Constant GDP (million $, 2014)			Equivalent Variation (change in welfare, EV, million $, 2014)			% Change in Output of Capital Goods Industry (qcgds, %)		
	SC_1	SC_2	SC_3	SC_1	SC_2	SC_3	SC_1	SC_2	SC_3	SC_1	SC_2	SC_3
PRC	0.72	4.60	4.92	74,368	475,807	509,601	76,345	476,255	528,030	1.26	9.49	10.08
Japan	0.00	0.02	0.25	195	1,013	11,304	-677	-5,965	-1,734	-0.68	-2.36	-1.81
Korea, Rep. of	-0.01	-0.14	0.30	-98	-1,913	4,184	53	-6,997	-6,415	-0.47	-3.21	-3.77
ASEAN-4	1.86	4.76	5.33	35,670	91,233	102,247	35,332	90,797	111,430	2.84	9.25	12.05
CLMV	4.65	9.61	11.98	13,133	27,165	33,858	11,637	23,593	32,405	7.81	16.62	22.76
Asian developed	-0.01	-0.05	0.38	-209	-1,295	10,743	-111	-928	6,755	-0.42	-1.92	-1.84
Other members	4.68	7.28	7.39	145,244	225,633	229,055	154,701	241,129	247,178	7.32	12.32	12.44
US	-0.01	-0.03	0.10	-1,198	-5,896	17,232	-4,593	-17,303	-5,684	-0.62	-1.98	-1.66
EU	-0.02	-0.07	0.07	-2,663	-10,788	10,354	-2,660	-14,431	-2,748	-0.65	-2.36	-2.55
ROW	-0.02	-0.06	0.07	-3,756	-13,560	13,714	-9,352	574	32,045	-0.55	-1.80	-1.84

Panel B: Impacts on Trade

Region	% Change in Volume of Exports by Region (qxwreg, %)			% Change in Volume of Imports by Region (qiwreg, %)			% Change in Price of Merchandise Exports by Region (pxwreg, %)			% Change in Price of Merchandise Imports by Region (piwreg, %)		
	SC_1	SC_2	SC_3	SC_1	SC_2	SC_3	SC_1	SC_2	SC_3	SC_1	SC_2	SC_3
PRC	-0.68	-4.61	-1.17	0.36	3.47	8.81	-0.45	-1.71	-1.37	-0.65	-2.17	-2.75
Japan	0.53	2.23	2.48	-0.29	-1.08	-1.03	-0.64	-2.45	-3.12	-0.55	-1.68	-1.71

continued on next page

Table 4.6 continued

Panel B: Impacts on Trade

Region	% Change in Volume of Exports by Region (qxwreg, %)			% Change in Volume of Imports by Region (qiwreg, %)			% Change in Price of Merchandise Exports by Region (pxwreg, %)			% Change in Price of Merchandise Imports by Region (piwreg, %)		
	SC.1	SC.2	SC.3	SC.1	SC.2	SC.3	SC.1	SC.2	SC.3	SC.1	SC.2	SC.3
Korea, Rep. of	0.22	1.22	1.99	-0.06	-1.46	-1.96	-0.58	-2.79	-3.84	-0.62	-1.92	-2.07
ASEAN-4	0.29	-0.52	3.19	1.26	2.53	8.62	-0.57	-1.81	-0.91	-0.55	-1.73	-1.95
CLMV	10.94	15.27	25.26	11.00	16.02	27.24	-1.33	-3.37	-2.95	-0.33	-1.32	-1.39
Asian developed	0.11	-0.65	-1.16	-0.18	-2.14	-3.28	-0.59	-2.10	-2.74	-0.61	-2.08	-2.28
Other members	-3.41	-6.37	-5.50	3.28	4.44	5.31	0.32	0.36	0.54	-0.54	-1.40	-1.48
US	0.73	2.40	2.30	-0.40	-1.29	-1.43	-0.69	-2.25	-2.84	-0.56	-1.87	-2.09
EU	0.25	0.72	0.52	-0.08	-0.56	-1.08	-0.63	-1.97	-2.53	-0.64	-1.89	-2.29
ROW	0.32	0.73	0.65	-0.18	-0.50	-0.69	-0.70	-1.66	-1.94	-0.61	-1.85	-2.17

Panel C: Impacts on Global Margins

Transport Sector	% Change in Global Margin Usage (qtm, %)			% Change in Price of Global Margin Services (pt, %)		
	SC.1	SC.2	SC.3	SC.1	SC.2	SC.3
Land transport	0.28	-0.08	0.11	-0.98	-2.34	-2.80
Sea transport	-0.05	0.06	0.38	-0.62	-1.70	-2.05
Air transport	0.13	0.21	0.87	-0.57	-1.76	-2.04

ASEAN-4 = Indonesia, Malaysia, the Philippines, and Thailand; CLMV = Cambodia, Lao People's Democratic Republic, Myanmar, and Viet Nam; EU = European Union; PRC = People's Republic of China; ROW = rest of the world; SC = policy scenario; US = United States.
Source: Authors' calculation.

Second, all regions of Asia and the Pacific and the others benefit from stimulating infrastructure in the PRC, ASEAN–4, CLMV, and MEMB in real GDP growth. Clearly, the four infrastructure-boosting regions benefit most, followed by non-boosting regions in Asia and the Pacific, and then non-Asia and Pacific regions (SC_3).

Third, for each infrastructure-stimulating region, domestic spillovers—strengthening the forward linkages of infrastructure industries of a region to other domestic industries—are most significant and crucial in three types of channel to enhance the potential benefits of the provision of regional public goods. Thus, each region's capability to design infrastructure-stimulating policy consistent with evolutions of input–output relations is very important.

Fourth, for a non-stimulating region, cross-border spillovers, strengthening the forward linkages of infrastructure industries of stimulating regions to foreign industries, are most significant and crucial in three types of channel to enhance the potential benefits of the provision of regional public goods.

Fifth, for each infrastructure-stimulating region, the cross-border spillovers are a significant and positive contributor to real GDP growth, but that influence is not so large compared with that of domestic spillovers.

Panel C of Table 4.6 reports three scenario effects on margins of three types of global transport: land, sea, and air. Prices (transport costs) of three types of global margin services decrease in all the cases. This implies that cross-border and domestic transportation costs decrease greatly, or domestic and international trade facilitation progresses greatly, as a result of infrastructure-boosting policy in the four regions. As noted earlier, quality upgrading of infrastructure leading to decreases in trade and/or transportation costs is one of the long-term reasons for boosting infrastructure industries, and the reductions in transport margins of panel C are evidence of that achievement. Also notable, domestic spillover shocks are most significant and a strong booster of reductions in prices of global margin services for three types of transportation. On the other hand, reductions in trade costs due to infrastructure-boosting shocks result in a decrease in regional prices of merchandise exports and imports.

Cross-Border Spillovers: Impacts on Import Prices of Non-Stimulating Regions

The impacts of cross-border spillovers could be captured by the difference between the effects of SC_3 and of SC_2, as proposed earlier. In other words, they are impacts triggered by cross-border intermediate trades with lower trade costs or prices than before. Sometimes, however, third factors cause reductions in trade costs or prices and, then, create cross-border spillovers. To conceptualize this indirect cross-border spillover, in sum, cross-border spillovers result not only from reductions in trade costs or prices directly, but also from productivity growth or domestic spillovers indirectly activating reductions in trade costs or prices.

The last three columns of panel B report that import prices of a region decrease greatly after infrastructure-boosting shocks in seven sectors of the four regions. This would be direct and indirect cross-border spillover effects. Here again, domestic spillovers, strengthening the forward linkages of infrastructure industries of a region to other domestic industries, are most significant and crucial in reductions in import prices of the other regions. Domestic spillovers result in the expansion of domestic input–output linkages with lower costs than before and this expansion then stimulates domestic–foreign (import) IO linkages across border automatically with lower trade costs.

The market prices of imports (PIM in the GTAP notation) is the transmission variable of direct and indirect cross-border spillovers and the reduction in this (% change in PIM, pim in GTAP notation) is a crucial indicator of the existence of direct and indirect cross-border spillovers. Table 4.7 reports the percentage change in composite imports. Panel A is percentage change in market price of imports resulting from productivity shocks, panel B is that resulting from productivity and domestic spillover shocks, and panel C is that resulting from productivity shock and domestic as well as cross-border spillover shocks.

The following findings are evident from Table 4.7. First, contrary to the expectation that reductions in import prices are concentrated on infrastructure-boosting regions, the reductions in non-boosting regions are basically the same level. This leads to the conclusion that overall cross-border spillovers exist and regional public goods is working, and that non-boosting regions benefit a lot via cross-border transactions of intermediate goods, including transport services.

Table 4.7: Impacts on Import Prices
(% change in market price of composite import, pim, %)

Panel A: SC_1

Region / Sector	PRC	Japan	Korea, Rep. of	ASEAN-4	CLMV	Asian Developed	Other Members	US	EU	ROW
Agriculture	-0.12	-0.09	-0.13	0.22	0.64	-0.05	0.70	-0.13	-0.45	-0.24
Mining	-0.77	-0.77	-0.78	-0.74	-0.85	-0.77	-0.78	-0.79	-0.78	-0.78
Textile and clothing	0.10	0.11	0.29	-0.06	-0.15	0.04	0.06	0.29	-0.11	-0.04
Chemical	-0.62	-0.60	-0.63	-0.57	-0.49	-0.62	-0.62	-0.66	-0.68	-0.68
Metal	-0.68	-0.64	-0.69	-0.64	-0.63	-0.68	-0.69	-0.68	-0.67	-0.71
Vehicles	-0.62	-0.41	-0.57	-0.33	-0.26	-0.50	-0.40	-0.59	-0.60	-0.55
Electronic product	-1.06	-0.85	-0.83	-1.15	-0.74	-0.92	-1.11	-0.91	-0.96	-1.02
Other manufacturing	-0.41	-0.25	-0.43	-0.36	-0.29	-0.38	-0.42	-0.41	-0.55	-0.50
Electricity and gas	-6.57	-10.60	-9.07	-5.55	-8.58	-7.86	10.40	-6.27	-3.57	-5.32
Water and sewage	-1.59	-1.91	-1.88	-1.49	-1.63	-1.86	-1.58	-1.97	-1.56	-1.61
Construction	-0.51	-0.48	-0.50	-0.50	-0.50	-0.43	-0.49	-0.42	-0.46	-0.48
Trade	-0.43	-0.29	-0.27	-0.40	-0.39	-0.35	-0.37	-0.36	-0.42	-0.39
Transport–land	-2.36	-2.26	-2.21	-1.79	-1.87	-2.34	-1.66	-2.10	-1.66	-2.01
Transport–sea	-0.58	-0.62	-0.39	-0.56	-0.56	-0.49	-0.65	-0.66	-0.59	-0.58
Transport–air	-0.54	-0.58	-0.55	-0.60	-0.60	-0.56	-0.60	-0.57	-0.60	-0.60
Communications	-0.23	-0.45	-0.23	-0.41	-0.40	-0.28	-0.48	-0.21	-0.46	-0.40

continued on next page

Table 4.7 continued

Panel A: SC.1

Region / Sector	PRC	Japan	Korea, Rep. of	ASEAN-4	CLMV	Asian Developed	Other Members	US	EU	ROW
Financial services	-0.15	-0.53	-0.33	-0.45	-0.49	-0.22	-0.52	-0.46	-0.52	-0.45
Business services	0.06	-0.43	-0.18	-0.30	-0.11	-0.22	-0.47	0.45	-0.35	-0.26
Public services	-0.35	-0.44	-0.39	-0.42	-0.35	-0.32	-0.46	-0.09	-0.42	-0.39
Other services	-0.41	-0.39	-0.32	-0.41	-0.38	-0.31	-0.45	-0.31	-0.39	-0.40

Panel B: SC.2

Region / Sector	PRC	Japan	Korea, Rep. of	ASEAN-4	CLMV	Asian Developed	Other Members	US	EU	ROW
Agriculture	-0.92	-0.33	-0.43	0.19	1.00	-0.31	0.97	-0.70	-1.53	-1.11
Mining	-1.29	-1.26	-1.28	-1.19	-1.15	-1.24	-1.29	-1.31	-1.30	-1.31
Textile and clothing	-0.55	2.18	2.03	1.18	1.26	1.39	1.74	1.43	-0.22	0.62
Chemical	-1.56	-1.19	-1.26	-1.12	-0.67	-1.24	-1.09	-1.37	-1.64	-1.51
Metal	-1.97	-1.23	-1.25	-1.31	-0.79	-1.29	-1.53	-1.54	-1.81	-1.69
Vehicles	-2.15	-1.18	-1.77	-1.23	-0.76	-1.76	-1.59	-1.93	-1.95	-1.86
Electronic product	-4.87	-6.99	-6.44	-6.29	-6.34	-6.32	-7.05	-6.68	-5.24	-6.17
Other manufacturing	-1.73	-0.18	-0.98	-0.75	-0.45	-0.92	-0.85	-0.82	-1.59	-1.32
Electricity and gas	-7.42	11.18	-9.75	-6.23	-8.33	-7.89	10.96	-7.02	-4.58	-6.17
Water and sewage	-2.87	-2.94	-2.91	-2.67	-2.76	-2.85	-2.76	-2.96	-2.70	-2.76
Construction	-2.01	-1.97	-1.68	-1.79	-1.77	-1.56	-1.76	-1.59	-1.64	-1.67

continued on next page

Table 4.7 continued

Panel B: SC_2

Sector	PRC	Japan	Korea, Rep. of	ASEAN-4	CLMV	Asian Developed	Other Members	US	EU	ROW
Trade	-1.90	-0.68	-0.76	-1.39	-1.33	-1.26	-1.10	-1.53	-1.40	-1.40
Transport-land	-3.34	-2.89	-2.97	-2.74	-2.83	-3.02	-2.69	-2.90	-2.69	-2.92
Transport-sea	-1.80	-1.85	-1.54	-1.74	-1.74	-1.64	-1.87	-1.78	-1.77	-1.76
Transport-air	-1.83	-1.83	-1.80	-1.81	-1.83	-1.76	-1.81	-1.77	-1.81	-1.80
Communications	-1.73	-1.67	-1.47	-1.81	-1.78	-1.55	-1.84	-1.47	-1.84	-1.75
Financial services	-1.39	-1.98	-1.50	-1.79	-1.90	-1.27	-1.95	-1.79	-1.92	-1.79
Business services	-1.10	-1.79	-1.34	-1.60	-1.29	-1.42	-1.80	-0.36	-1.64	-1.50
Public services	-1.74	-1.60	-1.50	-1.64	-1.65	-1.22	-1.78	-1.07	-1.63	-1.66
Other services	-1.79	-1.37	-1.21	-1.58	-1.51	-1.11	-1.66	-1.11	-1.53	-1.54

Panel C: SC_3

Sector	PRC	Japan	Korea, Rep. of	ASEAN-4	CLMV	Asian Developed	Other Members	US	EU	ROW
Agriculture	-1.02	-0.26	-0.44	0.40	1.38	-0.22	1.43	-0.78	-1.89	-1.35
Mining	-1.26	-1.20	-1.24	-1.08	-1.01	-1.18	-1.26	-1.28	-1.27	-1.29
Textile and clothing	-0.51	3.31	3.19	1.87	1.95	2.13	2.54	2.22	-0.17	0.98
Chemical	-1.66	-1.14	-1.26	-0.99	-0.27	-1.22	-1.02	-1.47	-1.90	-1.68
Metal	-2.30	-1.11	-1.22	-1.26	-0.40	-1.22	-1.69	-1.73	-2.20	-1.94
Vehicles	-2.74	-1.29	-2.21	-1.23	-0.57	-2.10	-1.95	-2.45	-2.49	-2.33

continued on next page

Table 4.7 continued

Panel C: SC.3

Region / Sector	PRC	Japan	Korea, Rep. of	ASEAN-4	CLMV	Asian Developed	Other Members	US	EU	ROW
Electronic product	-9.17	-14.34	-13.26	-12.55	-13.07	-12.90	-14.22	-13.73	-10.66	-12.59
Other manufacturing	-2.05	0.27	-0.99	-0.60	-0.13	-0.86	-0.84	-0.80	-1.99	-1.55
Electricity and gas	-10.56	-15.53	-13.71	-9.07	-13.99	-12.91	-15.34	-10.05	-6.52	-8.89
Water and sewage	-4.26	-5.13	-5.01	-4.15	-4.37	-4.97	-4.29	-4.97	-4.15	-4.32
Construction	-2.48	-2.44	-2.02	-2.20	-2.17	-1.83	-2.14	-1.87	-1.99	-2.02
Trade	-2.37	-0.83	-0.93	-1.74	-1.66	-1.54	-1.34	-1.89	-1.74	-1.73
Transport–land	-5.20	-5.32	-5.21	-4.31	-4.43	-5.40	-4.07	-4.87	-3.98	-4.57
Transport–sea	-3.64	-2.93	-3.12	-2.99	-3.06	-3.27	-2.93	-4.06	-3.01	-3.12
Transport–air	-2.96	-3.13	-2.93	-2.83	-2.91	-3.04	-2.87	-3.14	-2.91	-2.92
Communications	-3.36	-3.48	-3.65	-3.18	-3.20	-3.54	-3.19	-3.44	-3.05	-3.22
Financial services	-1.80	-2.45	-1.86	-2.25	-2.38	-1.61	-2.41	-2.24	-2.40	-2.24
Business services	-1.50	-2.28	-1.73	-2.06	-1.70	-1.81	-2.26	-0.61	-2.10	-1.92
Public services	-2.68	-2.97	-2.89	-2.75	-2.72	-2.86	-2.78	-2.58	-2.66	-2.73
Other services	-2.18	-1.69	-1.47	-1.98	-1.87	-1.35	-2.04	-1.33	-1.88	-1.89

ASEAN–4 = Indonesia, Malaysia, the Philippines, and Thailand; CMLV = Cambodia, Myanmar, Lao People's Democratic Republic, and Viet Nam; EU = European Union; pim = market price of imports; PRC = People's Republic of China; ROW = rest of the world; SC = policy scenario; US = United States.

Source: Authors' calculation.

Second, reductions in import prices are higher in infrastructure-stimulating industries than non-stimulating industries. More specifically they are highest in electricity and gas (electricity), electronic products (mobile), water and sewage (water), and land transport (rail and road). In metal and vehicles, which use considerable infrastructure outputs, reductions in import prices are higher than in other non-stimulating industries. Third, the main driver of the reductions in import prices differs across infrastructure industries. Cross-border spillover shock (*ams*) is the top contributor to those reductions in electronic products (mobile), sea transport, air transport, water and sewage, and communications, while productivity shock is the main contributor in electricity and gas (electricity) and land transport (rail and road).

Impacts on a Region's Sectoral Production

Infrastructure-boosting policy in region r is modeled by three separate shocks. Productivity shock [$ao(i, r)$] and domestic spillover shock [intermediate-input-i-augmenting technical change in industry j, $af(i, j, r)$] result in reductions in prices and expansion of all sectoral outputs in region r through domestic input–output linkages on the one hand. The (direct) cross-border spillover shock [import-i-from-region-r augmenting technical change in other region s, $ams(i, r, s)$], triggered by infrastructure-boosting policy in region r, results in reductions in the import price of i from r in region s's industry j, through international input–output linkages, leading to reductions in output j's price as well as increases in output j. These two processes occur simultaneously. Moreover, sometimes, region s is also an infrastructure-boosting region, and then infrastructure-boosting shocks in the four regions might result in cumulative impacts, reductions in prices of industrial outputs, and increases in industrial outputs of all regions, when ignoring fixed supply of factors and domestic as well as world market-clearing conditions.

In this framework, we can check price changes from Table 4.8 and quantity changes from Table 4.9 as the final results of infrastructure-stimulating experiments. Table 4.8 reports percentage changes in the supply price of commodities (*ps* in GTAP notation) for all regions. First, non-stimulating regions such as Japan, the Republic of Korea, Asian developed, the United States, and the EU all show reductions in all sectoral prices, as per expectations. However, in infrastructure-stimulating regions, some infrastructure industries show price decreases but others, increases. The reason for this is higher factor costs due to the fixed supply of factors (labor, capital, land, and so on). If an industry heavily employs intermediate goods in the production process, the price of gross output is not likely to increase. If another industry heavily employs factors, the supply price of that factor is likely to increase.

Table 4.9 reports the percentage change in the industrial output of commodities (qo in GTAP notation) for all regions. First, an infrastructure-stimulating region, such as the PRC, is likely to produce more sectoral output when the price of that output declines, as in Table 4.8, and vice versa. This was true in electronic products, land, sea, and air transport, and communications when only focusing on infrastructure industries. But this is not the case for electricity (and gas) and water (and sewage) (Table 4.9, Panel C). The reason for this is differences in profitability, including different shares of factors in total costs, across industries after infrastructure shocks; increases in production in the industries of relatively higher profitability; and decreases in production at the relatively lower profitability industries.

Now, consider non-stimulating regions, a region's industrial production decreases (increases) when an infrastructure-stimulating region's production increases (decreases)—or profitability of sectoral production (competitiveness) across regions matter. In addition, the sectoral market-clearing condition in the world market is also working, therefore, sometimes, one region's production of output, competitive at the country level, can decrease.

At any rate, a region's sectoral production changes (qo_i) are the sum of sectoral value-added changes (qva_i) and sectoral intermediate-composite changes (qf_i). When a region's sectoral value-added (factors) changes are aggregated over all sectors, this is equal to changes in constant GDP ($qgdp$) of panel A of Table 4.6. In sum, $qgdp$, qo, and qva are interrelated in this way.

Summary and Policy Implications

Large-scale infrastructure shocks in Asia and the Pacific are expected to stimulate the region's economic growth significantly (i) by increasing productivity growth in infrastructure industries, (ii) through domestic spillovers triggered by the infrastructure-input augmenting technical changes in other industries of the same region, and (iii) cross-border spillovers due to the imported-infrastructure-input augmenting technical changes in foreign industries (trade partners).

Table 4.8: Impacts on Supply Prices
(% change in supply price of commodities, ps, %)

Panel A: SC_1

Region / Sector	PRC	Japan	Korea, Rep. of	ASEAN–4	CLMV	Asian Developed	Other Members	US	EU	ROW
Land	1.14	-0.22	0.22	1.38	-1.23	1.70	10.33	0.24	0.29	0.28
Unskilled labor	0.82	-0.65	-0.52	2.69	8.84	-0.49	7.31	-0.72	-0.59	-0.61
Skilled labor	1.01	-0.63	-0.51	2.73	9.22	-0.44	6.29	-0.67	-0.58	-0.62
Capital	0.68	-0.61	-0.52	2.36	9.03	-0.50	7.16	-0.68	-0.62	-0.64
Natural resources	-2.94	-0.51	-0.31	-6.35	-10.93	-2.04	-10.98	-1.06	-1.29	-1.23
Agriculture	0.32	-0.55	-0.36	1.22	3.66	-0.36	4.11	-0.62	-0.57	-0.55
Mining	-0.96	-0.72	-0.67	-0.68	-0.53	-0.79	-0.71	-0.78	-0.81	-0.80
Textile and clothing	-0.10	-0.51	-0.38	0.49	2.03	-0.48	1.95	-0.63	-0.52	-0.56
Chemical	-0.55	-0.67	-0.65	-0.21	1.85	-0.62	-0.69	-0.72	-0.67	-0.71
Metal	-0.70	-0.65	-0.59	-0.38	0.38	-0.59	-1.75	-0.69	-0.64	-0.68
Vehicles	-0.27	-0.62	-0.56	0.40	2.36	-0.52	0.74	-0.68	-0.62	-0.63
Electronic product	-0.63	-0.66	-0.61	-1.58	-8.19	-0.64	-4.46	-0.72	-0.69	-0.71
Other manufacturing	-0.30	-0.61	-0.54	0.26	2.15	-0.52	0.72	-0.68	-0.62	-0.64
Electricity and gas	-9.65	-0.66	-0.66	19.46	-8.32	-0.61	-28.71	-0.70	-0.68	-0.70
Water and sewage	-4.20	-0.62	-0.54	-7.94	-22.47	-0.51	-11.40	-0.72	-0.62	-0.73
Construction	-0.14	-0.63	-0.55	0.71	3.44	-0.51	2.30	-0.69	-0.61	-0.64
Trade	0.34	-0.62	-0.52	1.30	5.66	-0.50	4.65	-0.68	-0.61	-0.63

continued on next page

Table 4.8 continued

Panel A: SC_1

Region / Sector	PRC	Japan	Korea, Rep. of	ASEAN-4	CLMV	Asian Developed	Other Members	US	EU	ROW
Transport–land	-2.90	-0.63	-0.56	13.88	-17.71	-0.55	-9.81	-0.74	-0.65	-0.66
Transport–sea	-1.84	-0.65	-0.56	-0.81	-0.05	-0.70	3.50	-0.68	-0.72	-0.69
Transport–air	-0.27	-0.68	-0.56	-0.48	1.67	-0.57	2.38	-0.70	-0.68	-0.68
Communications	-0.40	-0.61	-0.52	0.87	3.04	-0.51	3.52	-0.68	-0.62	-0.64
Financial services	0.44	-0.62	-0.52	1.72	5.86	-0.47	5.07	-0.67	-0.60	-0.63
Business services	0.17	-0.62	-0.53	1.19	5.69	-0.50	3.96	-0.68	-0.60	-0.63
Public services	0.36	-0.62	-0.53	1.44	5.62	-0.48	4.92	-0.68	-0.60	-0.63
Other services	0.41	-0.61	-0.52	1.86	7.17	-0.50	5.95	-0.67	-0.61	-0.63
Capital goods commodities	-0.21	-0.62	-0.54	0.28	2.06	-0.52	1.23	-0.68	-0.62	-0.63

Panel B: SC_2

	PRC	Japan	Korea, Rep. of	ASEAN-4	CLMV	Asian Developed	Other Members	US	EU	ROW
Land	5.92	-1.20	0.12	2.00	-1.95	5.73	16.57	0.56	0.30	0.20
Unskilled labor	7.93	-2.78	-3.23	7.35	18.00	-2.35	11.25	-2.49	-2.04	-1.95
Skilled labor	8.62	-2.76	-3.28	7.27	18.79	-2.06	9.83	-2.41	-2.02	-1.97
Capital	7.02	-2.59	-3.50	6.49	18.26	-2.35	10.90	-2.37	-2.13	-1.95
Natural resources	11.44	0.84	3.96	-14.93	-19.46	3.57	-12.76	1.89	1.87	0.65

continued on next page

Table 4.8 continued

Panel B: SC_2

	PRC	Japan	Korea, Rep. of	ASEAN–4	CLMV	Asian Developed	Other Members	US	EU	ROW
Agriculture	4.47	-2.20	-1.93	3.18	7.32	-1.60	6.01	-2.13	-1.87	-1.71
Mining	-1.06	-1.53	-1.41	-0.88	-0.63	-1.30	-1.14	-1.34	-1.35	-1.29
Textile and clothing	2.81	-1.69	-1.83	2.19	4.61	-1.85	2.41	-2.08	-1.65	-1.60
Chemical	0.94	-1.89	-1.99	0.29	3.75	-1.63	-1.28	-1.88	-1.75	-1.61
Metal	0.66	-2.27	-2.53	0.05	0.25	-1.87	-2.67	-2.26	-1.94	-1.81
Vehicles	1.31	-2.46	-2.83	0.74	4.13	-2.04	0.28	-2.30	-2.00	-1.91
Electronic products	-8.19	-3.16	-3.63	-9.10	-16.00	-3.43	-9.29	-3.11	-2.76	-2.69
Other manufacturing	1.19	2.44	-2.81	1.12	3.87	-2.03	0.27	-2.33	-2.03	-1.87
Electricity and gas	-8.51	-2.15	-2.14	-20.05	-5.77	-1.90	-28.83	-2.16	-1.96	-1.76
Water and sewage	-3.05	-2.56	-3.11	-7.12	-18.98	-2.18	-12.89	-2.37	-2.05	-1.98
Construction	1.77	-2.50	-2.95	2.30	5.46	-2.10	2.35	-2.35	-2.02	-1.89
Trade	4.73	-2.56	-3.00	3.40	11.05	-2.20	6.69	-2.40	-2.03	-1.92
Transport–land	-0.87	-2.46	-2.92	-13.05	-14.59	-2.11	-9.11	-2.25	-1.99	-1.85
Transport–sea	-1.16	-2.34	-2.31	-2.11	0.86	-2.05	3.61	-2.28	-1.94	-1.86
Transport–air	0.83	-2.35	-2.39	-2.27	3.65	-1.97	1.81	-2.13	-1.86	-1.82
Communications	1.42	-2.60	-3.24	1.97	6.51	-2.33	2.25	-2.46	-2.16	-2.05
Financial services	4.83	-2.61	-3.24	4.33	10.92	-2.19	7.18	-2.41	-2.05	-1.94
Business services	2.46	-2.59	-3.27	2.91	10.87	-2.22	5.02	-2.46	-2.07	-1.95
Public services	4.04	-2.57	-3.13	3.77	10.53	-2.13	7.05	-2.38	-2.03	-1.95

continued on next page

Table 4.8 continued

Panel B: SC.2

	PRC	Japan	Korea, Rep. of	ASEAN–4	CLMV	Asian Developed	Other Members	US	EU	ROW
Other services	5.00	-2.58	-3.27	5.01	14.30	-2.25	8.71	-2.32	-2.08	-1.93
Capital goods commodities	0.85	-2.63	-2.90	-0.54	2.21	-2.22	0.17	-2.42	-2.11	-2.00

Panel C: SC.3

	PRC	Japan	Korea, Rep. of	ASEAN–4	CLMV	Asian Developed	Other Members	US	EU	ROW
Land	6.49	-1.25	0.54	0.71	-4.42	7.81	17.12	0.98	0.67	0.45
Unskilled labor	9.70	-3.37	-4.04	11.18	27.68	-2.76	11.95	-3.04	-2.54	-2.41
Skilled labor	10.65	-3.43	-4.11	11.50	29.48	-2.39	10.65	-2.98	-2.53	-2.44
Capital	8.68	-3.13	-4.57	10.45	28.54	-2.85	11.49	-2.92	-2.69	-2.40
Natural resources	-15.06	2.21	6.75	23.30	-30.26	6.44	-13.64	3.59	4.31	2.20
Agriculture	5.77	-2.65	-2.39	5.38	11.45	-1.87	6.54	-2.62	-2.34	-2.10
Mining	-0.87	-1.45	-1.34	-0.60	-0.03	-1.23	-1.03	-1.35	-1.35	-1.25
Textile and clothing	4.06	-1.94	-2.22	4.61	7.93	-2.20	2.90	-2.53	-2.06	-1.95
Chemical	1.86	-2.15	-2.34	1.98	7.45	-1.81	-1.07	-2.18	-2.09	-1.83
Metal	1.61	-2.69	-3.16	1.97	3.46	-2.15	-2.38	-2.77	-2.44	-2.20
Vehicles	2.30	-3.09	-3.80	2.76	7.79	-2.48	0.56	-2.92	-2.59	-2.43
Electronic products	-8.24	-4.87	-5.92	-9.17	-16.43	-5.90	-9.95	-5.02	-4.50	-4.33
Other manufacturing	2.23	-3.05	-3.70	3.35	7.75	-2.50	0.58	-2.93	-2.66	-2.35
Electricity and gas	-7.65	-2.52	-2.58	18.42	-0.07	-2.22	-28.54	-2.61	-2.44	-2.10

continued on next page

Table 4.8 continued

Panel C: SC_3

	PRC	Japan	Korea, Rep. of	ASEAN-4	CLMV	Asian Developed	Other Members	US	EU	ROW
Water and sewage	-1.70	-3.10	-4.00	-4.17	-13.45	-2.66	-12.48	-2.95	-2.61	-2.48
Construction	2.97	-3.05	-3.86	4.86	10.01	-2.56	2.79	-2.90	-2.58	-2.36
Trade	6.24	-3.12	-3.89	6.56	18.08	-2.74	7.24	-3.00	-2.59	-2.41
Transport–land	0.43	-2.99	-3.75	10.73	-10.39	-2.59	-8.72	-2.79	-2.51	-2.27
Transport–sea	0.08	-2.96	-3.25	0.01	3.98	-2.79	4.00	-2.82	-2.53	-2.34
Transport–air	1.98	-2.90	-3.14	-0.28	7.19	-2.44	2.18	-2.58	-2.31	-2.24
Communications	2.74	-3.21	-4.41	5.35	13.23	-3.09	2.31	-3.18	-2.90	-2.71
Financial services	6.37	-3.19	-4.21	7.97	18.74	-2.63	7.74	-2.99	-2.61	-2.42
Business services	3.73	-3.21	-4.32	6.22	18.15	-2.79	5.52	-3.16	-2.65	-2.44
Public services	5.55	-3.14	-4.02	7.20	17.84	-2.59	7.69	-2.96	-2.58	-2.45
Other services	6.51	-3.13	-4.25	8.62	22.71	-2.76	9.28	-2.90	-2.64	-2.40
Capital goods commodities	1.86	-3.54	-3.96	1.04	5.23	-2.99	0.32	-3.23	-2.85	-2.70

ASEAN-4 = Indonesia, Malaysia, the Philippines, and Thailand; CMLV = Cambodia, Myanmar, Lao People's Democratic Republic, and Viet Nam; EU = European Union; ps = supply price of commodities; PRC = People's Republic of China; ROW = rest of the world; SC = policy scenario; US = United States.
Source: Authors' calculation.

Table 4.9: Impacts on Regions' Industrial Production
(% change in industry's output, constant, %)

Panel A: SC_1

Sector / Region	PRC	Japan	Korea, Rep. of	ASEAN-4	CLMV	Asian Developed	Other Members	US	EU	ROW
Land	0	0	0	0	0	0	0	0	0	0
Unskilled labor	0	0	0	0	0	0	0	0	0	0
Skilled labor	0	0	0	0	0	0	0	0	0	0
Capital	0	0	0	0	0	0	0	0	0	0
Natural resources	0	0	0	0	0	0	0	0	0	0
Agriculture	0.16	0.22	0.3	-0.49	-3.71	1.14	1.18	0.5	0.49	0.48
Mining	0.77	-0.18	-0.25	-1.59	-4.07	-0.27	-3.25	-0.06	-0.17	-0.09
Textile and clothing	0.40	1.50	1.18	-1.64	-13.38	1.43	-4.4	1.35	2.31	1.56
Chemical	0.09	0.14	0.16	-1.14	-3.63	0.15	-0.38	0.11	0	0.06
Metal	0.59	0.19	0.15	0.61	-2.93	-0.06	6.02	-0.08	-0.15	-0.05
Vehicles	0.37	0.47	0.52	-1.11	-4.18	0.04	0.75	0.10	0.22	0.10
Electronic product	1.67	-1.25	-1.13	5.45	92.2	-2.15	18.58	-1.09	-2.42	-1.54
Other manufacturing	0.25	0.69	0.54	-1.62	-10.33	0.55	1.61	0.19	0.33	0.31
Electricity and gas	0.42	0.04	0.05	4.87	0.29	-0.42	9.28	-0.34	-1.36	-0.86
Water and sewage	1.27	-0.02	0.01	4.33	3.71	-0.1	8.32	-0.02	-0.12	-0.14
Construction	1.20	-0.53	-0.37	2.42	7.17	-0.35	6.02	-0.46	-0.44	-0.46
Trade	0.19	-0.03	0.03	1.06	5.05	0.11	2.51	-0.06	0.04	-0.01

continued on next page

Table 4.9 continued

Panel A: SC_1

Sector \ Region	PRC	Japan	Korea, Rep. of	ASEAN–4	CLMV	Asian Developed	Other Members	US	EU	ROW
Transport–land	0.38	-0.11	-0.39	12.36	17.53	-0.62	5.09	-0.34	-0.54	-0.47
Transport–sea	0.51	0.05	-0.06	0.59	0.89	0.20	-2.98	-0.03	0.23	0.10
Transport–air	0.09	0.22	0.07	0.69	-0.38	0.11	-2.08	0.09	0.36	0.20
Communications	0.46	-0.01	0.05	0.25	0.88	0.08	0.70	0.02	0.10	0.04
Financial services	0.12	0.04	0.04	0.26	-5.66	0.13	-0.83	0.01	0.11	0.08
Business services	0.31	-0.04	0.10	-0.86	-2.23	0.17	-4.03	0.12	0.08	0.12
Public services	0.52	-0.01	-0.03	1.12	1.82	0.01	3.14	0.01	0.00	-0.02
Other services	0.43	-0.01	0.02	1.29	2.75	0.06	4.68	0	0.04	-0.01
Capital goods commodities	1.26	-0.68	-0.47	2.84	7.81	-0.42	7.32	-0.62	-0.65	-0.55

Panel B: SC_2

Sector	PRC	Japan	Korea, Rep. of	ASEAN–4	CLMV	Asian Developed	Other Members	US	EU	ROW
Land	0	0	0	0	0	0	0	0	0	0
Unskilled labor	0	0	0	0	0	0	0	0	0	0
Skilled labor	0	0	0	0	0	0	0	0	0	0
Capital	0	0	0	0	0	0	0	0	0	0
Natural resources	0	0	0	0	0	0	0	0	0	0
Agriculture	-0.77	0.83	1.44	-2.03	-6.98	4.19	2.01	1.63	1.32	1.16

continued on next page

Table 4.9 continued

Panel B: SC_2

Sector	PRC	Japan	Korea, Rep. of	ASEAN-4	CLMV	Asian Developed	Other Members	US	EU	ROW
Mining	-3.93	1.86	3.15	-4.01	-8.13	0.87	-4.34	0.58	0.64	0.36
Textile and clothing	-6.08	8.55	10.45	-4.66	-23.98	9.75	-3.03	5.47	9.18	6.15
Chemical	-2.60	1.37	3.12	-4.12	-7.09	2.07	-0.93	0.76	0.86	0.29
Metal	0.81	2.99	4.56	0.03	-2.34	2.76	8.47	0.72	0.87	0.57
Vehicles	0.97	3.5	5.59	-2.91	-7.18	1.15	1.19	0.81	0.89	-0.25
Electronic product	10.3	-16.05	-16.93	21.78	152.79	-23.15	6.75	-13.74	-22.58	-17.96
Other manufacturing	-0.50	5.25	6.46	-4.95	-17.39	3.95	3.62	1.42	1.90	1.09
Electricity and gas	-11.45	0.36	0.89	-5.83	-9.16	-0.14	-0.56	-0.38	-0.99	-0.75
Water and sewage	-4.33	-0.06	0.86	-1.1	-7.78	0.26	4.45	-0.03	-0.04	-0.32
Construction	9.04	-1.81	-2.52	7.79	15.36	-1.54	10.24	-1.50	-1.64	-1.52
Trade	0.99	-0.09	0.09	3.42	9.53	0.73	3.96	-0.46	0.07	-0.06
Transport–land	-10.74	-0.03	0.63	4.00	5.59	-0.23	-2.38	-0.16	-0.37	-0.50
Transport–sea	-8.12	0.91	0.91	-6.66	-7.46	0.50	-7.21	-0.14	0.30	0.02
Transport–air	-11.19	0.54	0.83	-2.53	-8.50	0.12	-8.71	-0.14	-0.07	-0.20
Communications	-6.54	-0.08	0.16	-7.31	-6.45	0.26	-7.05	-0.05	0.12	-0.03
Financial services	0.02	0.23	0.33	0.16	-10.44	0.35	-1.09	-0.07	0.23	0.13
Business services	2.37	-0.25	0.48	-3	-4.72	0.38	-5.77	0.06	-0.04	-0.03
Public services	1.79	-0.26	-0.6	2.48	3.75	0.03	4.41	0.03	-0.02	0.06

continued on next page

Table 4.9 continued

Panel B: SC_2

Sector	PRC	Japan	Korea, Rep. of	ASEAN-4	CLMV	Asian Developed	Other Members	US	EU	ROW
Other services	2.42	-0.05	-0.10	2.91	5.65	0.38	7.01	-0.04	0.08	0.07
Capital goods commodities	9.49	-2.36	-3.21	9.25	16.62	-1.92	12.32	-1.98	-2.36	-1.80

Panel C: SC_3

	PRC	Japan	Korea, Rep. of	ASEAN-4	CLMV	Asian Developed	Other Members	US	EU	ROW
Land	0	0	0	0	0	0	0	0	0	0
Unskilled labor	0	0	0	0	0	0	0	0	0	0
Skilled labor	0	0	0	0	0	0	0	0	0	0
Capital	0	0	0	0	0	0	0	0	0	0
Natural resources	0	0	0	0	0	0	0	0	0	0
Agriculture	-1.27	1.13	2.01	-4.07	-10.82	5.50	1.96	2.18	1.83	1.54
Mining	-5.13	2.97	4.78	-6.50	-13.86	1.36	-4.62	0.88	1.15	0.63
Textile and clothing	-8.53	11.43	14.31	-11.19	-36.8	12.96	-3.33	7.46	12.58	8.34
Chemical	-3.52	1.89	4.78	-7.42	-12.33	3.46	-1.23	0.97	1.43	0.47
Metal	-0.32	4.41	7.07	-4.07	-15.14	4.34	6.99	0.90	1.76	1.06
Vehicles	-0.38	5.10	8.71	-7.20	-13.04	1.74	-0.06	1.50	1.80	0.04
Electronic product	22.5	-28.49	-27.72	50.08	234.37	-35.63	-2.50	-28.31	-44.2	-36.01

continued on next page

Table 4.9 continued

Panel C: SC_3

	PRC	Japan	Korea, Rep. of	ASEAN–4	CLMV	Asian Developed	Other Members	US	EU	ROW
Other manufacturing	-2.04	7.95	9.89	-11.3	-28.95	6.06	2.89	2.32	3.24	1.80
Electricity and gas	-11.77	0.47	1.28	-4.26	-11.36	-0.27	2.10	-0.67	-1.43	-1.09
Water and sewage	-4.06	-0.12	1.35	0.17	-7.61	0.42	4.99	-0.07	-0.04	-0.29
Construction	9.59	-1.32	-2.85	10.02	20.85	-1.43	10.31	-1.32	-1.72	-1.54
Trade	1.04	-0.01	0.20	5.30	13.34	1.08	3.93	-0.76	0.13	-0.04
Transport–land	-10.64	-0.02	0.78	6.86	5.05	-0.48	-1.53	-0.37	-0.64	-0.81
Transport–sea	-8.45	1.34	1.75	-4.81	-6.88	0.58	-5.29	-0.43	0.09	-0.37
Transport–air	-9.72	0.05	1.12	3.23	-6.53	-0.44	-4.54	-0.74	-1.08	-0.95
Communications	-6.13	-0.09	0.27	-6.02	-6.39	0.18	-5.85	-0.10	0.02	-0.13
Financial services	0.18	0.34	0.60	-0.10	-16.39	0.40	-1.37	-0.10	0.38	0.21
Business services	2.5	-0.31	0.79	-5.41	-7.81	0.56	-6.81	-0.06	0.03	-0.03
Public services	2.16	-0.43	-0.7	2.95	4.85	0.10	4.79	0.07	0.01	0.16
Other services	2.69	0.01	0.06	3.15	7.56	0.68	7.11	0.02	0.20	0.20
Capital goods commodities	10.08	-1.81	-3.77	12.05	22.76	-1.84	12.44	-1.66	-2.55	-1.84

ASEAN–4 = Indonesia, Malaysia, the Philippines, and Thailand; CMLV = Cambodia, Myanmar, Lao People's Democratic Republic, and Viet Nam; EU = European Union; PRC = People's Republic of China; ROW = rest of the world; SC = policy scenario; US = United States.

Source: Authors' calculation.

All subregions of Asia and the Pacific and others benefit from stimulating infrastructure in the PRC, ASEAN–4, CLMV, and MEMB in growth in real GDP. Clearly, boosting infrastructure benefits the four regions most, followed by non-boosting regions in Asia and the Pacific, then non-Asia and Pacific regions (SC_3).

However, the size of the impacts estimated by this analysis is not larger than what is expected to happen in the future. First, this is because the analysis focused on static instead of dynamic gains. Second, infrastructure shocks in this analysis do not include stimulating infrastructure in Asian developed economies (Hong Kong, China; the Republic of Korea; Singapore; and Taipei,China) and, because of this, cross-border impacts are underestimated. Third, is the limitation of the GTAP analysis, assuming the input–output linkages across industries of regions of the base year, 2014, being the same as those of 2015 to 2020.

Findings and Policy Implications

First, as noted, the impacts on the infrastructure-stimulating region—CLMV, ASEAN–4, other ADB member countries, and the PRC—benefit most from infrastructure shocks.

Second, for each infrastructure-stimulating region, domestic spillovers— strengthening the forward linkages of infrastructure industries of a region to other domestic industries—are most significant and crucial in three types of channel to enhance the potential benefits of the provision of regional public goods. Thus, each region's capability to design infrastructure-stimulating policy consistent with evolutions of input–output relations is very important.[8]

Third, for a non-stimulating region, cross-border spillovers, strengthening the forward linkages of infrastructure industries of stimulating regions to foreign industries, are most significant and crucial in three types of channel to enhance the potential benefits of the provision of regional public goods. In other words, trading partners of infrastructure-stimulating regions— Japan, the Republic of Korea, other developed Asian countries, as well as non-ADB regions like the European Union and the United States—benefit from the region's infrastructure projects. These benefits are channeled by

---

[8]   This is the main argument of Hirschman (1969) characterized by forward and backward linkages, complementarity across industries, and induced investment.

the importation of infrastructure-intermediate-input with cheaper price or cost (imported-infrastructure-augmenting technical change from the perspective of the importing regions).

Fourth, infrastructure-stimulating regions also benefit from the cross-border spillover linkages. This channel is a significant and positive contributor to real GDP growth, but this influence is not so large as that of domestic spillovers.

Fifth, final and total cross-border spillovers result not only from reductions in trade costs directly (direct cross-border spillovers), but also from productivity growth or domestic spillovers triggering reductions in trade costs sequentially (indirect cross-border spillovers). As far as final and total cross-border spillover impacts are concerned, the domestic spillover channel (infrastructure-input augmenting technical changes in other domestic industries) is the most significant and crucial in terms of reductions in import prices of other regions (trading partners).

The sixth finding is an extension of the abovementioned second and fifth findings. Strengthening the forward linkages of infrastructure industries of a region to domestic and foreign industries, which use infrastructure inputs, is very crucial to enhance the potential benefits of the provision of regional public goods. Also, very important is a region's capability to design infrastructure investment consistent with the evolution of dynamic competitiveness of other domestic industries of the region. This could help reduce the possible risk of excessive concentration of resources in infrastructure industries without strengthening input–output and interregional trade linkages. In short, a region can enhance the effectiveness of the linkages between infrastructure and non-infrastructure industries across border by deliberately harmonizing policy design.

The last finding is an extension of the third, fourth, and fifth findings. To minimize a sort-of-free-riding problem, foreign beneficiary countries' participation in a region's infrastructure projects is recommended and emphasized. One can consider a strategy to finance regional infrastructure projects from external (international) sources, preventing possible free-riding problems. Minimum benefits to other region (s) from a region (r)'s policy shock in infrastructure (i) can be measured by import i from r augmenting a technical change in s, as introduced in the earlier CGE simulations. These measured benefits to other countries are likely to be minimal in the sense that the measured benefit here has only direct cross-border benefits, ignoring the indirect benefits already mentioned.

References

Adam, C. S. and D. L. Bevan. 2006. Aid and the Supply Side: Public Investment, Export Performance, and Dutch Disease in Low-Income Countries. *The World Bank Economic Review*. 20 (2). pp. 2671–90.

Agenor, P. R., N. Bayraktar, and K. El Aynaoui. 2008. Roads Out of Poverty? Assessing the Links between Aid, Public Investment, Growth, and Poverty Reduction. *Journal of Development Economics*. 86 (2). pp. 277–95.

Ando, M. 2009. Impacts of FTAs in East Asia: CGE Simulation Analysis. *Research Institute of Economy, Trade, and Industry Discussion Papers*. No. 09037.

Asian Development Bank (ADB). 2017. *Meeting Asia's Infrastructure Needs*. Manila.

——. 2018. Key Indicators Database. https://kidb.adb.org/kidb/ (accessed July 2018).

Bandara, J. 1995. Dutch Disease in a Developing Country: The Case of Foreign Capital Inflows to Sri Lanka. *Seoul Journal of Economics*. 8 (3). pp. 311–29.

Clausen, V. and H. Schurenberg-Frosch. 2012. Aid, Spending Strategies and Productivity Effects: A Multi-Sectoral CGE Analysis for Zambia. *Economic Modelling*. 29 (6). pp. 2254–268.

CEPII. 2016. EconMap Database V2.4_3. http://www.cepii.fr/CEPII/ en/ bdd_modele /presentation.asp?id=13.

Coe, D. T. and E. Helpman. 1995. International R&D Spillovers. *European Economic Review*. 39 (5). pp. 859–887.

Fugazza, M. and J. Maur. 2008. Non-Tariff Barriers in Computable General Equilibrium Modelling. *Policy Issues in International Trade and Commodities Study Series*. No. 38.

Hirschman, A. O. 1969. The Strategy of Economic Development. In A. N. Agawal and S. P. Singh, eds. *Accelerating Investment in Developing Economies*. London: Oxford Press.

Jones, C. I. and D. Vollrath. 2013. *Introduction to Economic Growth.* New York: W. W. Norton.

Kim, S., S. Park, and I. Park. 2006. *Trade Facilitation in APEC: Economic Impacts and Policy Options.* Seoul: Korea Institute for International Economic Policy.

Lee, C. S. and B. Song. 2013. *Mongolian Economy Development Strategy: CGE Analysis and Case Study.* Seoul: Korea Institute for International Economic Policy.

Lee, J. and K. Kim. 2017. Optimal Provision of RPGs in Asia and the Pacific. Report presented at AEIR 2018 Inception Workshop on Regional Public Goods. 14 December.

Sjoholm, F. 1996. International Transfer of Knowledge: The Role of International Trade and Geographic Proximity. *Weltwirtschaftliches* 132 (1). pp. 97–115.

———. 1999. Exports, Imports and Productivity: Results from Indonesian Establishment Data. *World Development.* 27 (4). pp. 705–15.

Suh, J. K, S. Oh, J. Park, M. Kim, and C-S Lee. 2013. *Economic Impact of the Bali Packages of the Doha Round.* Seoul: Korea Institute for International Economic Policy.

van Meijl, H. and F. van Tongeren. 1999. Endogenous International Technology Spillovers and Biased Technical Change in the GTAP Model. *GTAP Technical Paper* No. 15.

Vos, R. 1998. Aid Flows and 'Dutch Disease' in a General Equilibrium Framework for Pakistan. *Journal of Policy Modeling.* 20 (1). pp. 77–109.

Walmsley, T. and P. Minor. 2016. Willingness to Pay in CGE Models: Estimating the Benefits of Improved Customs Efficiencies within the WTO Trade Facilitation Agreement. *ImpactEcon Working Paper Series.* No. 002 Rev 2.

Wiebelt, M., R. Schweickert, C. Breisinger, and M. Böhme. 2011. Oil Revenues for Public Investment in Africa: Targeting Urban or Rural Areas? *Review of World Economics.* 147 (4). pp. 745–70.

Zaki, C. 2010. Towards an Explicit Modeling of Trade Facilitation in CGE Models: Evidence from Egypt. *MPRA Paper Series*. No. 23353. https://mpra.ub.uni-muenchen.de/23353/.

——. 2014. An Empirical Assessment of the Trade Facilitation Initiative: Econometric Evidence and Global Economic Effects. *World Trade Review*. 13 (1). pp. 103–30.

Zhai, F. 2012. Benefits of Infrastructure Investment: An Empirical Analysis. In B. N. Bhattacharyay, M. Kawai, and R. M. Nag, eds. *Infrastructure for Asian Connectivity*. Cheltenham: Edward Elgar.

APPENDIX A4

Table A4.1: Estimation of Infrastructure Needs by Region, 45 Developing Asian Economies, 2016–2030
($ billion, 2015 prices)

Region/Subregion	Projected Annual GDP Growth	2030 UN Population Projection (billion)	2030 Projected GDP per Capita (2015 $)	Baseline Estimates			Climate-Adjusted Estimates**		
				Investment Needs	Annual Average	Investment Needs as % of GDP	Investment Needs	Annual Average	Investment Needs as % of GDP
Central Asia	3.1	0.096	6,202	492	33	6.8	565	38	7.8
East Asia	5.1	1.503	18,602	13,781	919	4.5	16,062	1,071	5.2
South Asia*	6.5	2.059	3,446	5,477	365	7.6	6,347	423	8.8
Southeast Asia	5.1	0.723	7,040	2,759	184	5	3,147	210	5.7
Pacific	3.1	0.014	2,889	42	2.8	8.2	46	3.1	9.1
Asia and the Pacific	5.3	4.396	9,277	22,551	1,503	5.1	26,166	1,744	5.9

GDP = gross domestic product, UN = United Nations.
Note: The 45 economies are Afghanistan; Armenia; Azerbaijan; Bangladesh; Bhutan; Brunei Darussalam; Cambodia; Cook Islands; Fiji; Georgia; Hong Kong, China; India; Indonesia; Kazakhstan; Kiribati; Rep. of Korea; Kyrgyz Republic; Lao People's Democratic Republic (PDR); Malaysia; Maldives; Marshall Islands; Fed. States of Micronesia; Mongolia; Myanmar; Nauru; Nepal; Pakistan; Palau; Papua New Guinea; the Philippines; PRC; Samoa; Singapore; Solomon Islands; Sri Lanka; Taipei,China; Tajikistan; Thailand; Timor-Leste; Tonga; Turkmenistan; Tuvalu; Uzbekistan; Vanuatu; and Viet Nam.
* Pakistan and Afghanistan are included in South Asia. ** Climate change adjusted figures include climate mitigation and climate proofing costs, but do not include other adaptation costs, especially those associated with sea level rise.
Source: ADB (2017).

Table A4.2: Impacts on World Trade by Commodities

Sector	%Change in Volume of Exports by Commodity (qxwcom, %)			%Change in Volume of Imports by Commodity (qiwcom, %)			%Change in Merchandise Exports by Commodity (pxwcom, %)			%Change in Merchandise Imports by Commodity (piwcom, %)		
	SC.1	SC.2	SC.3	SC.1	SC.2	SC.3	SC.1	SC.2	SC.3	SC.1	SC.2	SC.3
Agriculture	0.38	1.32	1.68	0.39	1.34	1.71	-0.16	-0.87	-1.02	-0.20	-0.93	-1.10
Mining	-0.26	0.22	0.42	-0.26	0.21	0.41	-0.79	-1.26	-1.21	-0.78	-1.29	-1.25
Textile and clothing	-0.75	-2.92	-4.00	-0.75	-2.95	-4.04	0.04	0.70	1.13	0.01	0.61	1.00
Chemical products	0.04	0.36	0.62	0.03	0.35	0.60	-0.65	-1.46	-1.58	-0.66	-1.47	-1.60
Metal products	0.46	1.31	1.84	0.46	1.29	1.80	-0.68	-1.64	-1.85	-0.69	-1.65	-1.87
Vehicles	0.19	0.96	1.57	0.19	0.95	1.56	-0.56	-1.87	-2.36	-0.56	-1.88	-2.36
Electronic products	0.78	-1.87	1.87	0.78	-1.81	1.99	-0.98	-6.01	-7.30	-0.98	-5.95	-7.23
Other manufacturing	0.05	-0.19	-0.24	0.04	-0.23	-0.31	-0.46	-1.24	-1.42	-0.47	-1.26	-1.45
Electricity and gas	8.37	7.46	12.33	8.37	7.46	12.33	-4.70	-5.59	-6.45	-4.70	-5.59	-6.45
Water and sewage	1.25	0.23	2.59	1.25	0.23	2.59	-1.66	-2.78	-3.01	-1.66	-2.78	-3.01
Construction	0.56	1.14	1.71	0.56	1.14	1.71	-0.48	-1.72	-2.09	-0.48	-1.72	-2.09
Trade	0.48	1.96	2.41	0.48	1.96	2.41	-0.39	-1.42	-1.76	-0.39	-1.42	-1.76
Transport–land	0.81	-0.05	0.58	1.06	-0.04	0.80	-1.63	-2.69	-3.02	-1.93	-2.86	-3.12
Transport–sea	0.02	-0.06	0.21	0.22	-0.41	-0.29	-0.61	-1.72	-2.06	-0.57	-1.75	-2.10
Transport–air	0.23	-0.25	0.13	0.26	-0.38	-0.07	-0.58	-1.79	-2.04	-0.59	-1.80	-2.04
Communications	0.03	-0.69	0.02	0.03	-0.69	0.02	-0.39	-1.75	-2.16	-0.39	-1.75	-2.16
Financial services	0.43	1.13	1.47	0.43	1.13	1.47	-0.45	-1.80	-2.26	-0.45	-1.80	-2.26
Other business services	-0.12	-0.22	-0.28	-0.12	-0.22	-0.28	-0.23	-1.45	-1.88	-0.23	-1.45	-1.88
Public services	0.21	0.53	1.08	0.21	0.53	1.08	-0.34	-1.53	-1.82	-0.34	-1.53	-1.82
Other services	0.35	0.95	1.28	0.35	0.95	1.28	-0.39	-1.48	-1.81	-0.39	-1.48	-1.81

Source: Authors' calculation.

Table A4.3: Impacts on Regions' Industrial Exports
(% change in country's industrial exports, FOB, %)

Panel A: SC_1

Sector	PRC	Japan	Korea, Rep. of	ASEAN-4	CLMV	Asian Developed	Other Members	United States	European Union	Rest of World
Agriculture	-0.79	3.11	2.29	-3.53	-14.27	2.76	-14.92	2.59	1.09	2.22
Mining	1.40	-1.44	-2.01	-1.53	-3.88	-0.42	-1.15	-0.31	-0.06	-0.11
Textile and clothing	0.35	3.43	1.45	-3.67	-13.55	2.61	-13.15	3.87	3.03	3.60
Chemical products	-0.43	0.33	0.32	-1.94	-12.18	0.32	0.19	0.30	0.03	0.29
Metal products	1.43	0.78	0.76	-0.45	-4.65	0.22	8.27	0.07	-0.20	0.15
Vehicles	-0.94	0.85	0.90	-4.34	-15.02	0.36	-6.36	0.88	0.33	0.31
Electronic products	-1.73	-2.14	-1.35	6.13	92.46	-2.22	37.07	-2.02	-2.64	-2.01
Other manufacturing	-0.83	1.90	1.58	-4.30	-16.68	1.56	-8.16	1.50	0.77	1.22
Electricity and gas	30.80	-26.24	-21.20	179.79	26.95	-22.92	419.69	-15.66	-11.46	-14.82
Water and sewage	17.78	-5.78	-5.94	46.74	283.89	-6.58	80.99	-4.39	-3.93	-4.08
Construction	-0.76	1.54	0.92	-4.08	-13.21	0.63	-9.64	1.14	1.11	1.06
Trade	-2.11	1.69	1.33	-5.96	-19.76	1.25	-16.79	1.74	1.13	1.21
Transport–land	4.89	-4.48	-0.94	62.08	77.38	-2.60	32.77	-3.16	-2.15	-2.97
Transport–sea	1.33	0.02	-0.09	0.60	-1.18	0.25	-6.30	0.14	0.28	0.23
Transport–air	-0.61	0.45	0.10	-0.18	-7.23	0.16	-8.96	0.52	0.58	0.54
Communications	0.21	1.26	0.76	-4.69	-12.11	0.69	-13.62	1.39	0.79	0.97
Financial services	-2.90	1.09	0.63	-7.58	-20.56	1.18	-18.12	1.38	0.76	1.07
Other business services	-1.38	1.61	1.34	-5.40	-19.79	1.30	-14.50	1.49	1.18	1.43
Public services	-2.58	1.46	1.01	-6.42	-19.72	1.03	-17.60	1.63	0.99	1.33
Other services	-2.81	1.47	0.91	-7.95	-24.09	1.16	-20.61	1.79	1.02	1.25

continued on next page

Table A4.3 continued

Panel B: SC_2

Sector	PRC	Japan	Korea, Rep. of	ASEAN-4	CLMV	Asian Developed	Other Members	United States	European Union	Rest of World
Agriculture	-18.69	11.10	9.77	-11.26	-26.85	9.77	-21.65	8.80	2.90	5.42
Mining	-1.33	2.65	0.88	-3.60	-8.49	0.49	-1.47	1.21	1.20	0.53
Textile and clothing	-14.94	17.88	17.80	-11.04	-25.04	18.77	-14.27	18.41	12.31	13.09
Chemical products	-11.96	4.29	5.68	-6.96	-22.73	3.69	-0.76	2.42	1.31	0.99
Metal products	-12.37	9.93	11.58	-6.97	-5.72	6.10	9.19	5.07	1.70	2.08
Vehicles	-16.36	5.81	8.61	-11.55	-27.57	3.32	-10.13	4.32	1.31	0.12
Electronic products	20.56	-25.76	-21.21	29.18	157.59	-24.64	34.92	-24.83	-24.95	-26.57
Other manufacturing	-16.09	13.28	17.10	-13.29	-28.64	10.52	-10.58	8.02	4.06	3.94
Electricity and gas	17.78	-24.89	-19.49	174.68	1.81	-22.87	392.54	-13.59	-10.46	-14.93
Water and sewage	2.55	-3.05	0.34	29.63	178.60	-5.68	84.55	-2.52	-2.90	-4.45
Construction	-12.05	6.02	6.39	-13.59	-22.74	2.06	-13.87	2.56	2.33	1.65
Trade	-19.99	8.23	10.19	-15.79	-35.39	7.44	-24.26	5.21	3.75	3.06
Transport–land	-6.81	-2.90	0.31	49.64	50.66	-2.39	23.66	-2.32	-1.87	-3.21
Transport–sea	-0.55	0.81	0.77	0.61	-5.94	0.48	-8.12	0.84	0.34	0.12
Transport–air	-5.04	1.32	1.14	1.34	-17.12	-0.04	-11.48	0.80	0.07	-0.26
Communications	-11.92	2.76	5.27	-13.75	-26.97	1.61	-14.68	2.17	0.89	0.48
Financial services	-21.65	4.77	6.74	-19.76	-36.42	4.11	-26.44	3.67	1.63	1.69
Other business services	-13.93	4.56	7.74	-15.51	-36.28	3.55	-21.36	3.53	1.96	1.74
Public services	-19.26	4.82	6.80	-17.76	-35.46	4.46	-26.96	4.12	2.10	2.16
Other services	-21.53	7.13	9.07	-21.11	-42.71	6.16	-30.50	4.83	2.69	2.82

continued on next page

Table A4.3 continued

Panel C: SC.3

Sector	PRC	Japan	Korea, Rep. of	ASEAN-4	CLMV	Asian Developed	Other Members	United States	European Union	Rest of World
Agriculture	-22.65	14.62	13.37	-18.60	-38.08	12.56	-22.69	11.51	3.92	6.95
Mining	-2.47	2.57	0.64	-5.55	-14.48	0.71	-2.02	2.31	1.99	0.91
Textile and clothing	-20.00	23.28	23.61	-22.63	-38.24	24.59	-15.59	24.77	16.89	17.85
Chemical products	-16.25	6.36	8.86	-14.12	-35.37	6.30	-2.42	3.42	2.20	1.64
Metal products	-17.70	14.74	17.83	-17.59	-22.31	9.05	5.73	7.45	3.17	3.40
Vehicles	-22.67	8.02	13.10	-22.21	-41.76	4.45	-13.45	6.05	2.43	0.61
Electronic products	45.88	-40.70	-31.61	75.81	255.23	-35.96	78.63	-45.58	-48.20	-50.28
Other manufacturing	-22.80	19.10	26.04	-25.77	-45.27	15.44	-13.71	11.40	6.56	5.92
Electricity and gas	55.04	-30.64	-25.55	248.42	4.30	-27.97	581.99	-19.29	-14.95	-20.69
Water and sewage	37.89	-5.17	-0.17	59.17	181.60	-7.93	163.22	-4.82	-5.32	-7.14
Construction	-16.78	7.70	9.52	-22.13	-34.83	3.02	-16.08	3.75	3.64	2.56
Trade	-25.20	10.16	13.74	-25.79	-49.36	9.58	-26.26	6.55	4.85	3.81
Transport–land	9.40	-4.96	0.56	68.10	54.37	-3.43	47.09	-4.06	-2.99	-5.10
Transport–sea	-1.12	1.26	1.63	8.50	-2.60	0.71	-4.09	0.87	0.18	-0.31
Transport–air	2.96	0.89	1.72	15.87	-9.55	-0.80	6.00	0.12	-1.10	-1.59
Communications	4.74	1.05	6.00	-4.36	-27.35	0.64	6.78	1.18	-0.06	-0.83
Financial services	-27.11	5.83	9.28	-30.57	-51.65	4.67	-28.53	4.58	2.29	2.12
Other business services	-19.31	5.38	10.62	-26.40	-50.85	4.31	-23.97	4.57	2.48	1.95
Public services	-3.90	3.17	6.22	-8.10	-36.27	3.44	-10.05	3.67	1.06	0.65
Other services	-26.61	8.83	12.65	-31.41	-56.72	7.80	-32.47	6.16	3.81	3.72

ASEAN-4 = Indonesia, Malaysia, the Philippines, Thailand; CMLV = Cambodia, Myanmar, Lao People's Democratic Republic, and Viet Nam; FOB = free on board; SC = policy scenario; PRC = People's Republic of China.

Source: Authors' calculation.

Table A4.4: Impacts on the Regions' Industrial Imports
(% change in region's industrial imports, CIF, %)

Panel A: SC_1

Sector	PRC	Japan	Korea, Rep. of	ASEAN–4	CLMV	Asian Developed	Other Members	United States	European Union	Rest of World
Agriculture	1.17	-0.93	-0.53	2.29	5.55	-0.41	10.63	-0.95	-0.02	-0.50
Mining	-0.78	0.13	0.15	-2.44	-3.41	0.03	-0.75	0.12	-0.13	-0.17
Textile and clothing	-0.53	-1.02	-1.27	1.20	-7.17	-1.12	6.38	-2.16	-0.21	-0.97
Chemical products	0.19	-0.02	-0.04	0.36	3.64	-0.06	-0.56	-0.09	0.04	-0.07
Metal products	0.35	-0.05	0.34	1.04	18.57	0.13	1.94	-0.13	-0.01	-0.04
Vehicles	1.56	-0.51	0.06	2.40	5.48	-0.25	6.46	-0.40	-0.07	-0.24
Electronic products	0.31	-0.15	-0.13	2.52	41.61	-0.57	-0.83	0.09	-0.44	0.13
Other manufacturing	0.74	-1.03	-0.39	2.20	5.88	-0.42	7.01	-0.92	-0.27	-0.45
Electricity and gas	-8.02	34.24	27.87	-39.85	2.96	23.15	-46.15	17.21	7.73	13.53
Water and sewage	-7.10	3.70	3.81	-12.91	-48.56	3.91	-14.89	3.60	2.51	2.47
Construction	1.91	-0.96	-0.35	3.48	11.23	-0.40	9.58	-1.13	-0.67	-0.77
Trade	1.72	-0.62	-0.42	5.33	15.43	-0.25	13.72	-0.65	-0.37	-0.48
Transport–land	-0.86	3.01	2.68	-16.67	-20.98	2.69	-10.95	2.06	1.56	2.35
Transport–sea	-2.26	0.03	-0.08	-0.13	1.08	-0.11	6.43	-0.08	-0.02	-0.15
Transport–air	0.52	-0.10	0.02	1.91	5.90	0.05	7.38	-0.18	-0.12	-0.11
Communications	0.11	-0.31	-0.43	2.72	9.27	-0.32	9.72	-0.86	-0.26	-0.43
Financial services	1.15	-0.13	-0.32	5.20	12.08	-0.48	11.21	-0.49	-0.09	-0.35
Other business services	0.53	-0.41	-0.62	3.42	13.43	-0.53	7.17	-2.03	-0.52	-0.71
Public services	1.88	-0.45	-0.49	5.25	13.75	-0.30	13.88	-0.77	-0.31	-0.47
Other services	1.89	-0.42	-0.34	6.25	16.28	-0.24	14.87	-0.73	-0.38	-0.46

continued on next page

Table A4.4 continued

Panel B: SC.2

Sector	PRC	Japan	Korea, Rep. of	ASEAN-4	CLMV	Asian Developed	Other Members	United States	European Union	Rest of World
Agriculture	11.81	-3.60	-2.45	6.30	11.77	-1.71	16.77	-2.74	-0.08	-0.83
Mining	-1.35	1.27	2.82	-5.38	-5.70	1.65	-0.96	0.67	0.60	0.14
Textile and clothing	8.55	-5.74	-4.94	1.40	-13.33	-6.63	4.55	-8.13	-0.29	-3.76
Chemical products	5.63	-0.77	-1.56	1.33	5.68	-0.96	-0.96		0.21	-0.15
Metal products	10.87	-3.27	-1.54	4.49	32.67	-1.07	4.22	-2.17	0.08	-0.67
Vehicles	14.02	-2.63	-1.66	7.14	10.72	-1.33	10.55	-1.42	-0.21	-0.55
Electronic products	-14.33	4.20	-3.53	-4.52	49.54	-6.24	-8.67	6.04	-3.58	2.63
Other manufacturing	13.44	-5.67	-5.14	7.11	11.66	-3.07	9.52	-4.73	-1.55	-1.61
Electricity and gas	-13.40	30.52	23.63	-49.81	4.66	19.46	-50.82	14.99	7.38	13.06
Water and sewage	-12.97	1.10	-0.95	-10.73	-51.62	3.61	-15.32	1.73	1.82	2.31
Construction	17.24	-3.34	-4.16	11.96	23.68	-1.93	15.62	-3.41	-2.09	-1.96
Trade	14.94	-3.56	-4.06	14.69	33.18	-1.63	21.79	-1.85	-1.61	-1.06
Transport–land	-7.23	0.86	-0.01	-18.38	-18.73	1.42	-13.31	0.97	1.22	1.82
Transport–sea	-10.79	0.58	0.82	-11.99	-6.90	0.05	0.11	-1.03	0.00	-0.16
Transport–air	-7.95	-0.96	-0.79	-0.89	6.04	-0.20	5.06	-0.58	-0.25	-0.08
Communications	-1.25	-1.76	-2.67	-2.47	12.87	-1.03	2.75	-1.87	-0.57	-0.58
Financial services	12.84	-0.89	-3.06	14.58	24.64	-2.72	18.99	-1.52	-0.14	-0.34
Other business services	9.71	-1.67	-3.70	10.12	28.14	-2.44	11.37	-3.98	-1.38	-1.13
Public services	13.54	-4.10	-5.44	14.72	28.77	-1.77	20.66	-2.75	-0.12	-0.49
Other services	15.62	-2.33	-3.75	17.90	36.05	-1.53	24.89	-2.85	-0.97	-0.85

continued on next page

Table A4.4 continued

Panel C: SC.3

Sector	PRC	Japan	Korea, Rep. of	ASEAN-4	CLMV	Asian Developed	Other Members	United States	European Union	Rest of World
Agriculture	14.48	-4.48	-3.14	9.59	18.09	-2.05	17.45	-3.45	-0.04	-0.93
Mining	-1.84	1.77	4.33	-7.67	-11.07	2.79	-1.05	0.79	1.05	0.30
Textile and clothing	11.15	-7.74	-7.06	2.71	-20.82	-8.66	3.57	-10.74	-0.22	-4.84
Chemical products	7.93	-1.20	-2.55	4.51	10.14	-1.40	-0.55	-1.54	0.24	-0.27
Metal products	15.02	-5.35	-2.37	7.87	49.76	-1.56	4.68	-3.29	0.28	-1.09
Vehicles	18.71	-3.34	-1.96	10.42	16.00	-1.40	12.20	-1.38	0.12	-0.49
Electronic products	1.62	8.88	-4.84	17.58	90.57	-11.60	-3.45	10.25	-9.57	2.18
Other manufacturing	18.34	-7.70	-7.36	11.20	18.05	-4.11	10.34	-6.31	-2.31	-2.05
Electricity and gas	-4.77	43.08	33.25	-43.03	36.75	31.15	-44.88	21.49	10.60	18.90
Water and sewage	-7.11	3.85	0.40	0.32	-46.80	6.83	-11.40	4.03	3.14	4.20
Construction	21.61	-2.93	-5.52	18.34	37.96	-2.07	17.47	-3.60	-2.51	-2.20
Trade	19.40	-4.28	-5.26	23.16	53.11	-1.99	23.60	-2.48	-2.58	-1.33
Transport–land	-3.14	1.88	0.25	-12.56	-9.51	2.01	-11.22	1.44	1.39	2.56
Transport–sea	-7.22	0.64	0.41	-6.62	-2.29	-0.11	2.01	-1.34	-0.48	0.02
Transport–air	-4.61	-1.12	-1.48	4.57	13.91	-0.02	5.90	-0.41	-0.46	0.02
Communications	3.45	-1.13	-2.85	5.47	28.87	-0.66	4.28	-1.25	-0.58	-0.13
Financial services	17.10		-4.01	23.79	39.26	-3.54	20.90	-1.84	-0.21	-0.37
Other business services	13.44	-1.90	-5.09	16.77	45.37	-3.32	12.57	-4.97	-2.02	-1.34
Public services	18.50	-6.03	-7.12	24.16	48.17	-1.09	23.69	-4.30	0.38	-0.10
Other services	19.99	-2.73	-4.87	27.47	57.30	-1.75	26.97	-4.03	-1.25	-1.06

ASEAN-4 = Indonesia, Malaysia, the Philippines, Thailand; CMLV = Cambodia, Myanmar, Lao People's Democratic Republic, and Viet Nam; CLMV = Cambodia, Myanmar, Lao People's Democratic Republic, and Viet Nam; CIF = cost, insurance, and freight; SC = policy scenario; PRC = People's Republic of China.

Source: Authors' calculation.

PART 2
TRADE AND INVESTMENT

"We need to remember that trade is a great peacemaker that enriches people and increases international understanding and ties between nations."

Dan Quayle, former Vice President of the United States

Trade Facilitation and Aid for Trade for Inclusive Trade in Asia and the Pacific

5

Kijin Kim and Fahad Khan

Trade is essential to economic growth and poverty reduction in Asia and the Pacific. It enhances access to new markets, promotes new investment, and contributes to productivity growth and job creation. The region's total trade has grown an average 20% annually over the past 5 decades, while the ratio of trade to gross domestic product (GDP) rose from 17% in 1960 to 52% in 2016. Extreme poverty fell to 9% in 2016, from 68% in 1981.

Despite impressive progress in economic growth and transformation, gains from trade have been uneven. Average output per capita has risen significantly across the region, but low-income and geographically isolated landlocked and sea-locked economies, smaller firms, and vulnerable groups, including women, have benefited much less from international trade. A major reason is relatively high trade costs and limited access to international markets, in part due to capacity constraints. Better trade facilitation is crucial to reducing trade costs further, improving trade efficiency, and expanding global value chains. Although lower tariffs have reduced trade costs substantially since 2000, nontariff barriers remain significant. These arise largely from inefficient transport infrastructure and logistics services, and cumbersome regulatory procedures and documentation. Trade facilitation initiatives can help lower these costs and raise opportunities for participation in global value chains.

Many studies have noted the positive impact of trade facilitation on trade flows and economic growth, where even modest reductions in trade transaction costs can significantly increase trade flows. Customs modernization also helps to raise efficiency at border crossings and to reduce smuggling and corruption, and it could raise government revenues if gains are effectively transferred to increased tax revenues. Moreover, trade facilitation measures can attract foreign direct investment. Efficient border procedures improve the business environment by minimizing delays in production and delivery.

Trade facilitation measures can also have greater impact in developing countries than in developed countries, based on the higher marginal impact of simplified customs procedures in less-developed trade systems.

In the last several years, the global trade landscape has changed significantly. Changes include the rise of global value chains and the digital economy and the transformation of many economies toward services. These developments will continue to present opportunities for developing economies to engage in international trade, but may also worsen widening inequalities. Moreover, the recent stagnation of Asia's trade and the rise of protectionist tendencies challenge economic integration and inclusive development. Developing countries must continue to improve productive capacity and connectivity through economic infrastructure and to enact trade and regulatory reforms. Such efforts should leverage sectors highly likely to boost inclusive trade and growth, such as small and medium-sized enterprises (SMEs) and female-owned firms, so that the benefits of trade can be shared more equally. Where resource and institutional constraints are prevalent, global initiatives such as Aid for Trade (AfT) and the Trade Facilitation Agreement can help developing economies make needed reforms.

This chapter briefly reviews latest updates on trade costs and the status of implementing trade facilitation measures in Asia and the Pacific. It looks at the status and role of domestic and cross-border infrastructure in enhancing connectivity to reduce trade costs in the region. The discussion considers the implications for inclusivity of enhancing the participation of small and medium-sized firms and female-owned enterprises, and policy considerations for improving trade outcomes.

Trade Costs and Trade Facilitation Implementation

Generally, trade costs in Asia and the Pacific have gradually declined, with wide disparities across subregions. For trading goods, the East Asia-3 economies have the lowest trade costs, although trade costs declined more sharply in the Russian Federation and the Central Asia-3 economies in recent years (Figure 5.1). Trade costs also remained highest in regions facing significant geographical obstacles, particularly the Russian Federation, the Central Asia-3, and the Pacific-2. Since 2014, trade costs have increased in all subregions. This may be due in part to increasingly inward-oriented policies and geopolitical tensions in recent years, and natural disasters in the Pacific.

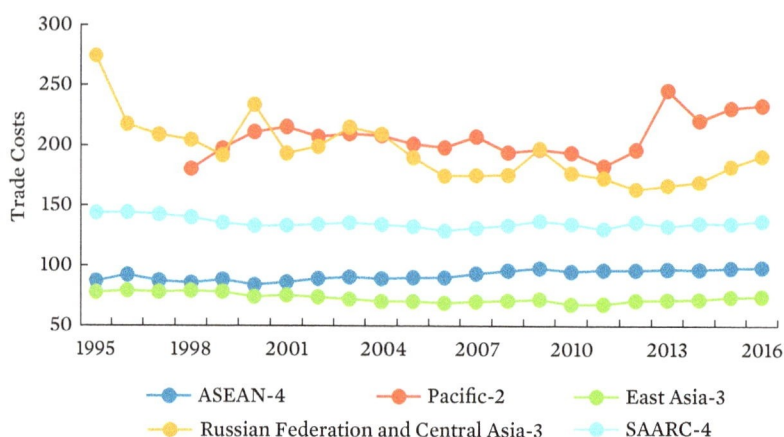

Figure 5.1: Trade Costs of Asia and the Pacific Subregions with Large Developed Economies in the Goods Sector, 1995–2016 (% of goods' value)

ASEAN–4 = Indonesia, Malaysia, the Philippines, Thailand; Central Asia-3 = Georgia, Kazakhstan, and Kyrgyz Republic; East Asia-3 = the People's Republic of China, Japan, the Republic of Korea; Pacific-2 = Fiji and Papua New Guinea; SAARC-4 = Bangladesh, India, Pakistan, Sri Lanka; and SAARC = South Asian Association for Regional Cooperation.

Note: Trade costs shown are trade-weighted average costs of countries in each subregion with the three largest developed economies (Germany, Japan, United States) and may be interpreted as tariff equivalents.

Source: ADB calculations using data from ESCAP-World Bank Trade Cost Database. www.unescap.org/resources/escap-world-bank-trade-cost-database (accessed November 2019).

The growing number of nontariff measures may have also contributed to this phenomenon, with trade costs valued at more than twice that of tariffs and estimated to cost as much as 1.6% of global GDP (ESCAP 2019).[1]

Recent trade facilitation initiatives are among the main avenues for reducing trade costs. The World Trade Organization (WTO) Trade Facilitation Agreement (TFA)[2]—ratified by 33 economies in Asia and the Pacific as of

---

[1] Nontariff measures "are policy measures other than ordinary customs tariffs that can potentially have an economic effect on international trade in goods, changing quantities traded, or prices or both" (ESCAP 2019).

[2] The agreement came into force on 22 February 2017 upon ratification by two-thirds of WTO members.

November 2019 (Table 5.1)—with only three WTO members in the region left to ratify: Solomon Islands, Tonga, and Vanuatu. Maldives most recently presented its instrument of ratification on 1 October 2019. Economies in Asia and the Pacific have also made significant progress in implementing the agreement, as seen in official notifications. As of August 2019, 65% of the WTO TFA had been implemented in the region, a 6-percentage-point rise from 2017. Based on the date of implementation countries provide in their notifications, an additional 11.1% of measures are expected be implemented by 22 February 2024, bringing the regional TFA implementation average above 76%.

Table 5.1: WTO TFA Ratification by Asia and Pacific WTO Members, as of November 2019

Subregion	Member	Subregion	Member
East Asia	Mongolia (Nov 2016) PRC (Sept 2015) Taipei,China (Aug 2015) Korea, Republic of (July 2015) Japan (June 2015) Hong Kong, China (Dec 2014)	**South Asia**	Maldives (Oct 2019) Nepal (Jan 2017) Bangladesh (Sept 2016) Afghanistan (July 2016) Sri Lanka (May 2016) India (Apr 2016) Pakistan (Oct 2015)
Southeast Asia	Indonesia (Dec 2017) Philippines (Oct 2016) Cambodia (Feb 2016) Myanmar (Dec 2015) Brunei Darussalam (Dec 2015) Viet Nam (Dec 2015) Thailand (Oct 2015) Lao PDR (Sept 2015) Malaysia (May 2015) Singapore (Jan 2015)	**Central Asia**	Tajikistan (July 2019) Armenia (Mar 2017) Kyrgyz Republic (Dec 2016) Kazakhstan (May 2016) Georgia (Jan 2016)
		Pacific	Papua New Guinea (March 2018) Fiji (May 2017) Samoa (Apr 2016) New Zealand (Sept 2015) Australia (June 2015)

PRC = People's Republic of China, Lao PDR = Lao People's Democratic Republic, TFA = Trade Facilitation Agreement, WTO = World Trade Organization.
Note: Dates in parentheses indicate dates of ratification.
Source: WTO TFA Database (accessed November 2019).

Figure 5.2 presents trade facilitation implementation rates measured through the United Nations (UN) Global Survey on Digital and Sustainable Trade Facilitation by subregion and groups of countries with special needs, which include least-developed countries, landlocked developing countries, and small island developing states. After Australia and New Zealand, the highest average rates were in East Asia (79.3%); Southeast Asia and Timor-Leste (70.3%); the Russian Federation and Central Asia (65.6%); and South Asia, Iran, and Turkey (55.4%). The Pacific lags at 35.5%.

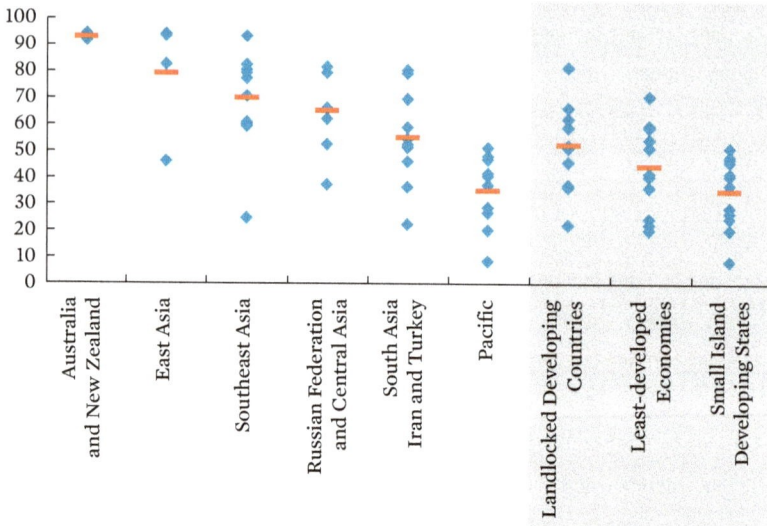

Figure 5.2: Trade Facilitation Implementation across Asia and Pacific Subregions and Countries with Special Needs, 2019 (%)

Notes:

1. East Asia includes the People's Republic of China, Japan, the Republic of Korea, and Mongolia; Central Asia includes Armenia, Azerbaijan, Georgia, Kazakhstan, the Kyrgyz Republic, Tajikistan, and Uzbekistan; the Pacific includes Fiji, Kiribati, the Federated States of Micronesia, Nauru, Palau, Papua New Guinea, Samoa, Solomon Islands, Tonga, Tuvalu, and Vanuatu; South Asia includes Afghanistan, Bangladesh, Bhutan, India, Maldives, Nepal, Pakistan, and Sri Lanka; Southeast Asia includes Brunei Darussalam, Cambodia, Indonesia, the Lao People's Democratic Republic (Lao PDR), Malaysia, Myanmar, the Philippines, Singapore, Thailand, Timor-Leste, and Viet Nam; landlocked developing countries include Afghanistan, Armenia, Azerbaijan, Bhutan, Kazakhstan, the Kyrgyz Republic, the Lao PDR, Mongolia, Nepal, Tajikistan, and Uzbekistan; least-developed countries include Afghanistan, Bangladesh, Bhutan, Cambodia, Kiribati, the Lao PDR, Myanmar, Nepal, Solomon Islands, Timor-Leste, Tuvalu, and Vanuatu; small island developing states include Fiji, Kiribati, Maldives, the Federated States of Micronesia, Nauru, Palau, Papua New Guinea, Samoa, Solomon Islands, Timor-Leste, Tonga, Tuvalu, and Vanuatu.

2. Blue diamonds represent country scores; red lines are group averages.

Source: ESCAP (2019).

Trade facilitation implementation rates vary widely within each subregional group, with differences most pronounced in Southeast Asia because it includes Timor-Leste, a country that is not yet a member of the Association of Southeast Asian Nations (ASEAN). Otherwise, the progress of ASEAN regional integration seems to have played a positive role in trade facilitation implementation. Differences in trade facilitation implementation are less pronounced among the small Pacific islands, attributed to their relative isolation as island economies and similar implementation constraints.

Countries with special needs also face difficulties in implementing measures on trade facilitation. The average implementation level of these countries varies between 8.6% (Nauru) and 81.7% (Azerbaijan), depending on the group considered. Interestingly, landlocked developing countries as a group have higher implementation than least-developed countries and small island developing states. This may be attributed to the importance of trade (and transit) facilitation by these countries, as reflected in the Vienna Programme of Action. The program falls under the auspices of the UN Office of the High Representative for the Least Developed Countries, Landlocked Developing Countries, and Small Island Developing States. The office promotes expansion of efficient transit systems and transport development, enhancement of trade and competitiveness, structural transformation, and regional cooperation in support of inclusive and sustainable development.[3]

Figure 5.3 shows trade facilitation implementation by different types of measures. General trade facilitation measures included in the WTO TFA are widely implemented: measures related to "transparency" have the highest implementation rates (regional average implementation at 77%). Implementation of measures to streamline trade "formalities" and for "transit facilitation" also exceed 70%. Regional average implementation exceeds 60% for measures related to "institutional arrangements and inter-agency cooperation".[4] This is generally in line with category A notifications sent by countries to the WTO in the context of the TFA.[5]

---

[3] See the UN-OHRLLS website at http://unohrlls.org/.

[4] Transparency refers to measures that promote openness and accountability of government actions and include metrics such as publication of existing import–export regulations on the internet, stakeholder consultations on new draft regulations before finalization, and independent appeal mechanisms on customs rulings for traders. Formalities refer to simplification of trade procedures and comprise risk management in shipment inspections, pre-arrival processing, post-clearance audit, and expedited shipments. Transit facilitation includes limits on the physical inspection of transit goods, transit facilitation agreements with neighboring countries, and cooperation between agencies of countries involved in transit. Institutional cooperation refers to the cooperation of a national trade facilitation committee or similar body, cooperation between agencies within a country, and alignment of procedures and formalities with neighboring countries at border crossing points (ADB and ESCAP 2019).

[5] Developing economies can request more time in implementing the TFA. Category A means that developing members will implement the measure by 22 February 2017 and least-developed countries by 22 February 2018. Category B refers to the need for additional time to implement a measure, while category C refers to the need for both time and capacity building support to implement a measure (WTO TFA Database).

Meanwhile, the regional average level of implementation of "paperless trade" or digital trade facilitation measures is close to 55%. This includes measures such as single window and e-payment of customs duties. However, while the legal framework to enable paperless trade has improved in many economies, the average implementation rate of "cross-border paperless trade" is at 32%. Many developing countries have yet to begin implementing measures in this group.

Sustainable trade facilitation can be measured through trade facilitation for SMEs, for agriculture, and for women's engagement in trade. Figure 5.3 shows that agricultural trade facilitation measures have an implementation rate of nearly 50%. However, few countries have developed trade facilitation measures for the specific needs of SMEs (37%) and women (23%).

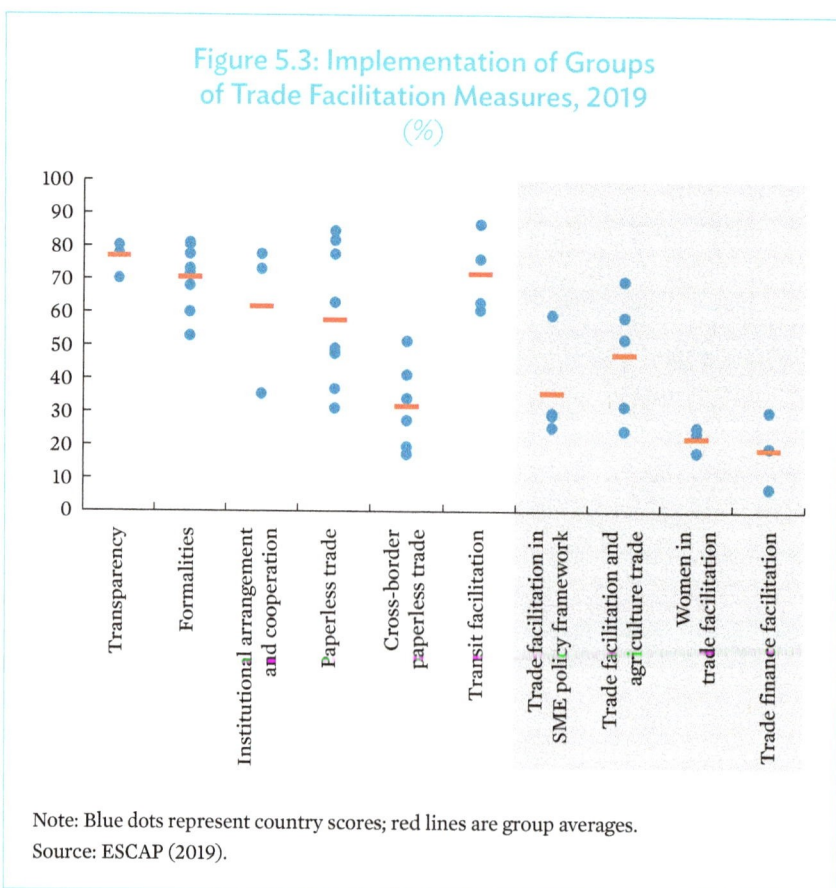

Figure 5.3: Implementation of Groups of Trade Facilitation Measures, 2019 (%)

Note: Blue dots represent country scores; red lines are group averages.
Source: ESCAP (2019).

Connectivity to Facilitate Trade

International trade is becoming a complex interaction between people and firms, with supply chains crisscrossing countries and regions. Good performance in trade requires connectivity, not only roads, rails, and seas, but also in financial markets and information processing. Inadequate transport and logistics infrastructure can hamper a country's competitiveness. Several studies have highlighted the importance of infrastructure to growth, its role in facilitating trade and lowering transaction costs (Ismail and Mahyideen 2015; Limao and Venables 2001), and its impact to the poor. Better infrastructure also promotes market integration (Vickerman 2002) and facilitates gains from increasing returns to scale and agglomeration.

Infrastructure is a major facilitator of trade in Asian economies. Connecting Asia's developing countries through physical infrastructure, particularly in the smaller and landlocked economies, can reduce the development gap among Asian economies. The potential gains are substantial: a virtuous circle whereby greater regional cooperation in trade and logistics bolsters Asia's economic growth and integration, which fosters greater investment in regional infrastructure. Increased connectivity can promote human development by increasing access to better jobs, education, and health services. Asia, to maintain its competitiveness and address its increasingly sophisticated production networks, needs efficient, fast, and reliable infrastructure connections that facilitate free movement of goods and people within countries and across borders.

Although Asia's infrastructure overall has improved considerably in recent decades, it has not kept pace with the region's rapid economic development and population growth. Road networks in Asia grew 5% annually from 2001 to 2010, much faster than the Organisation for Economic Co-operation and Development (OECD) countries (ADB 2017a). Yet, the region remains below the world average on quantity and quality of infrastructure (ADB 2017a). To sustain economic growth momentum and eradicate poverty, ADB (2017a) estimated that developing Asia would need to invest $22.6 trillion in infrastructure from 2016 to 2030, or $1.5 trillion annually, equivalent to 5.1% of projected GDP. When one adds the costs of climate change mitigation (particularly for more efficient and cleaner power generation and electricity transmission) and adaptation (especially "climate proofing," mainly transport and water and more climate-resilient infrastructure), cost rises to $26.2 trillion, or $1.7 trillion per year.

An inter-subregional comparison using the World Bank's Logistics Performance Index (Figure 5.4) shows that, overall, East and Southeast Asian economies perform better than economies in South and Central Asia and the Pacific. But they still significantly lag behind high-income countries. In the international trading arena, among all subregions, the Pacific had the lowest logistical performance on trade- and transport-related infrastructure, which includes ports, railroads, roads, and information technology.

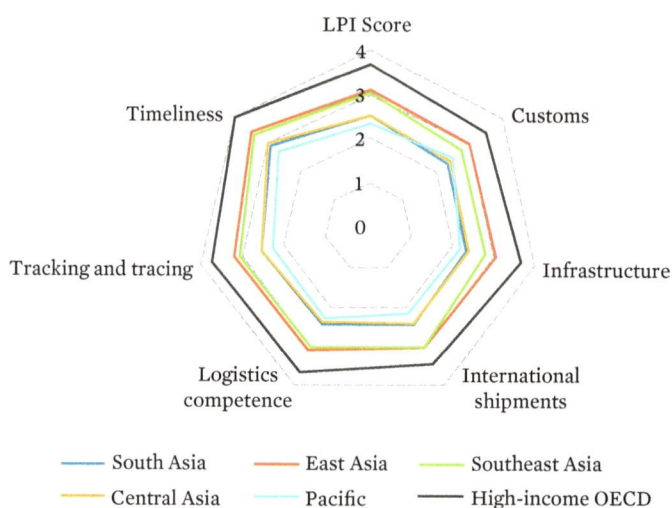

Figure 5.4: Logistics Performance Index by Subregion

OECD = Organisation for Economic Co-operation and Development.
Note: Pacific includes Fiji, Papua New Guinea, and Solomon Islands.
Source: World Bank Logistics Performance Index (LPI) 2018.

Cross-border connectivity has also been promoted through regional and subregional cooperation initiatives such as ASEAN, the Central Asia Regional Economic Cooperation (CAREC), the South Asia Subregional Economic Cooperation (SASEC), and the Greater Mekong Subregion. The Asian Highway network, for example, is a regional transport cooperation initiative to support the development of Euro–Asia transport links and improve connectivity for landlocked countries. It is comprised of 141,000 kilometers of roads from Tokyo, Japan in the east to Kapikule, Turkey in the west and from Denpasar, Indonesia in the south to Torpynovka, Russian Federation in the north.

In Central Asia, the six CAREC corridors link the region's key economic hubs and connect to other Eurasian countries. Three main economic corridors link the Greater Mekong Subregion: (i) North–South Economic Corridor from Kunming, People's Republic of China (PRC) to Bangkok, Thailand through northwest Lao People's Democratic Republic (PDR); (ii) the East–West Economic Corridor from Da Nang Port in Viet Nam, through the Lao PDR and Thailand, then to Myanmar; and (iii) the Southern Economic Corridor linking Cambodia with six provinces in Thailand, four regions in Viet Nam, and six provinces in the Lao PDR. Plans are under way to expand the network and coverage of these corridors.

SASEC members have developed economic corridors and efforts are being taken to promote synergies between these routes to improve cross-border links. The SASEC Operational Plan 2016–2025 introduced economic corridor development as a new strategic area of cooperation and identified strategic objectives and operational priorities for transport, trade facilitation, and energy.

Regional efforts to build cross-border infrastructure, however, is difficult given the nature of regional public goods when no proper market mechanism exists for their provision. Although developing economies generally recognize the benefits of regional public goods such as cross-border infrastructure, stakeholders may resist collective action in practice because they lack clear understanding of the shared benefits and are hindered by difficulties in balancing national and regional interests.

Challenges for Inclusive Trade

Developing economies face a key challenge in improving trade facilitation measures to reduce trade costs and realize their trade potential for inclusive trade and economic growth. While Asia and the Pacific economies have substantially reduced tariffs, nontariff and technical barriers to trade remain significant. Trade facilitation has emerged as a key instrument for reducing trade costs, including hard and soft infrastructure to reduce border transit costs and processing times. Trade facilitation eases cross-border movement of goods by cutting costs and simplifying trade procedures (OECD 2005).

It rests on four pillars: (i) transparency, (ii) simplification, (iii) harmonization, and (iv) standardization.

Trade facilitation initiatives reduce prices through simpler, transparent border procedures; it also lowers direct costs by raising efficiency among interacting businesses and administering agencies. This enables more firms to participate in regional and global value chains. For instance, SMEs are more vulnerable to financial and efficiency costs than large firms. They have fewer human resources, information, and capital. Many SMEs are also owned by women, especially in rural and agricultural settings. Lowering trade costs can enhance their participation in international trade. Developing countries stand to achieve the largest relative gains from trade facilitation. This is especially true for non-OECD countries with high trade-to-GDP ratios, which are therefore highly sensitive to changes in import and export costs.

Micro, Small, and Medium-sized Enterprises

Micro, small, and medium-sized enterprises (MSMEs) have long been recognized as engines of growth in developing and developed countries: they can create jobs, strengthen competition, introduce innovative technologies, and boost productivity (Kritikos 2014). Indeed, MSMEs account for a significant share of firms and employment in most economies.

Figures from the World Bank Enterprise Surveys show that from 2009 to 2018, SME employment in developing Asia accounted for 46.8% of total employment stock. Employment within SMEs also expanded more than large firms, 8.4%–9.4% compared with 5.3%, and accounted for more than 60% of the expansion. In aggregate, SMEs accounted for more than 60% of total net job creation (Table 5.2). While MSMEs employ most workers in most Asian economies, their contribution to GDP lags, with contributions ranging from 16.2% of GDP in Afghanistan to around 40% in Singapore and Thailand.

However, MSMEs do not participate in global value chains as much as large firms. Data show that one in five SMEs in developing Asia export, while more than one-third of large firms do. Similarly, material inputs or supplies of foreign origin in production are used by over 60% of large firms, but less than half of SMEs. These patterns show that small firms take less part in global value chains, either directly and indirectly, than large firms in developing Asia (Figure 5.5) and more needs to be done to support their integration.

Table 5.2: Employment by Firm Size, Developing Asia

Firm Size	Employment Share (%)	Employment Expansion			Employment Contraction			Net Job Creation	
		Firms that Expanded (%)	Expansion (%)	Share in Expansion (%)	Firms that Contracted (%)	Contraction (%)	Share in Contraction (%)	Net Change (%)	Share (%)
All	100	47.2	8.5		16.0	2.9		5.5	
Small (1–19)	16.3	45.6	9.4	26.7	14.7	2.6	21.9	6.8	30.6
Medium (20–99)	30.5	51.7	8.4	36.0	18.4	2.9	35.2	6.4	37.5
Large (100+)	53.2	57.6	5.3	39.2	19.4	2.1	41.6	3.1	25.6

Note: Figures for employment expansion, employment contraction, and net job creation refer to median values, and hence may not equal 100.

Source: ADB calculations using data from World Bank. Enterprise Surveys. http://www.enterprisesurveys.org (accessed March 2019).

Figure 5.5: Participation of Firms in Global Value Chains, Developing Asia

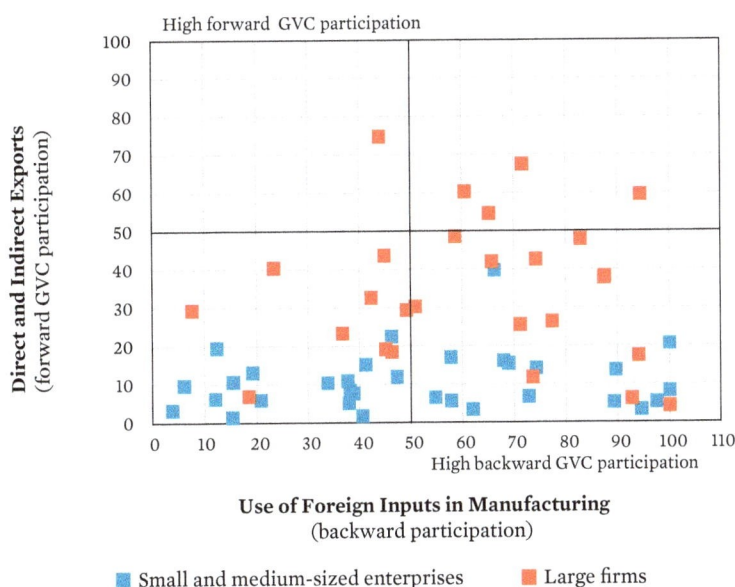

GVC = global value chain.

Note: Each square represents a country point estimate of firms participating in GVCs.

Source: World Bank. Enterprise Surveys. http://www.enterprisesurveys.org (accessed March 2019).

MSMEs face greater challenges in engaging in international markets, particularly in their exposure to trade costs, and are less equipped than large firms to manage risks. For instance, it takes longer for SMEs in developing Asia to clear exports through customs. Similarly, female-owned MSMEs tend to suffer disproportionately more than their male counterparts from trade-related fixed costs such as nontariff measures, primarily due to supply-side capacity constraints.

Overall, the resource disadvantage of smaller firms acts as a key constraint to their integration in global value chains. Other general challenges include difficulty in achieving economies of scale in acquiring inputs; lack of information on potential markets and opportunities that may require them to supply large volumes at consistent quality, homogenous standards, and at regular intervals; and difficulty in accessing services such as training, market intelligence, and logistics (ADB 2015, 33).

Further, besides country-specific barriers for entry, Table 5.3 lays out the major challenges to SME participation in global value chains.

Table 5.3: Major Challenges to SME Participation in Global Value Chains

Challenges	Capabilities and Limitations

Competition	• Small operations, resulting in relatively high cost of production
	• Lack of consumer preferences and inability to access lead firms:
	  – Lack of market intelligence (e.g., business opportunities, prospective customers, competition status, channels and distribution, local regulations and practices, and taxation)
	  – Inability to network
	  – Inability to meet large demands
	  – Uncompetitive price, quality, and/or delivery
	• Inadequate institutional support and assistance
	• Lack of necessary staffing and financial resources

Internationalization	• Inability to internationalize operation due to limited capacity to analyze, penetrate, and segment foreign markets • Technical limitations to act as suppliers to foreign buyers/investors • Cost and know-how to meet the growing number of products and sustainability standards
Trade liberalization	• Lack of knowledge about free trade agreements: – Lack of knowledge and skills to react to the agreements • Less awareness of opportunities and challenges derived from various trade agreements
Managerial skills	• Lack of knowledge about new strategies and techniques – Inability to orient new design and production • Inability to allow time and staffing to acquire new skills • Lack of knowledge to use e-commerce • Inability to hire appropriately qualified and talented people • Inability to combat anticompetitive practices

Source: ADB (2015. 34).

Trade and Economic Empowerment of Women

Trade can help empower women through better economic opportunities, technological upgrading, socioeconomic empowerment, and labor reforms (ADB 2017b; ADBI 2017; Cagatay and Erturk 2004; Fontana 2004; von Hagen 2014; Jobes 2010).

Greater trade openness is associated with higher incidence of paid employment. Evidence also suggests that women's participation in exporting firms as owners and employees is higher than in firms that do not export (Figure 5.6). Similarly, foreign-owned firms tend to employ more women than local firms, while globally engaged firms in Asia also tend to have better employment growth. Overall, countries with liberal trade regimes have lower unemployment than others (Figure 5.7).[6]

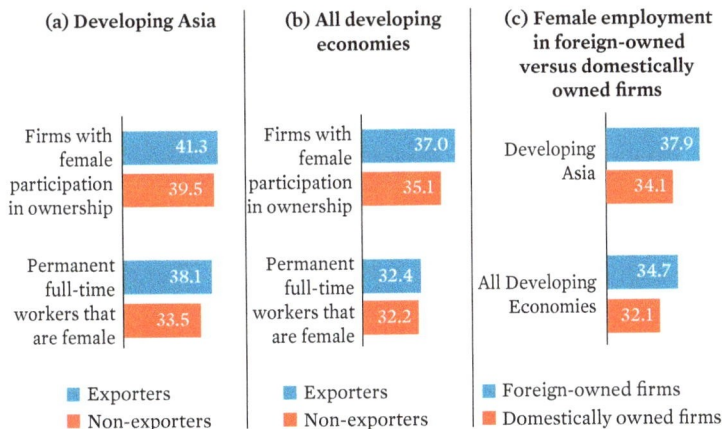

Figure 5.6: Female Firm Ownership and Employment in Globally Engaged and Domestic Firms, Developing Economies (% of firms)

Notes: World and regional averages are computed by taking a simple average of country point estimates. For each economy, only the latest available year of survey data are used in this computation. Developing Asia does not include Brunei Darussalam; Cook Islands; Hong Kong, China; Kiribati; Marshall Islands; Nauru; Palau; Republic of Korea; Singapore; Turkmenistan; and Tuvalu, as data are unavailable.

Source: ADB calculations using data from World Bank. Enterprise Surveys. http://www.enterprisesurveys.org (accessed March 2019).

[6] See for example Moore and Ranjan (2005); Dutt, Mitra, and Ranjan (2009); and Felbermayr, Prat, and Schmerer (2011).

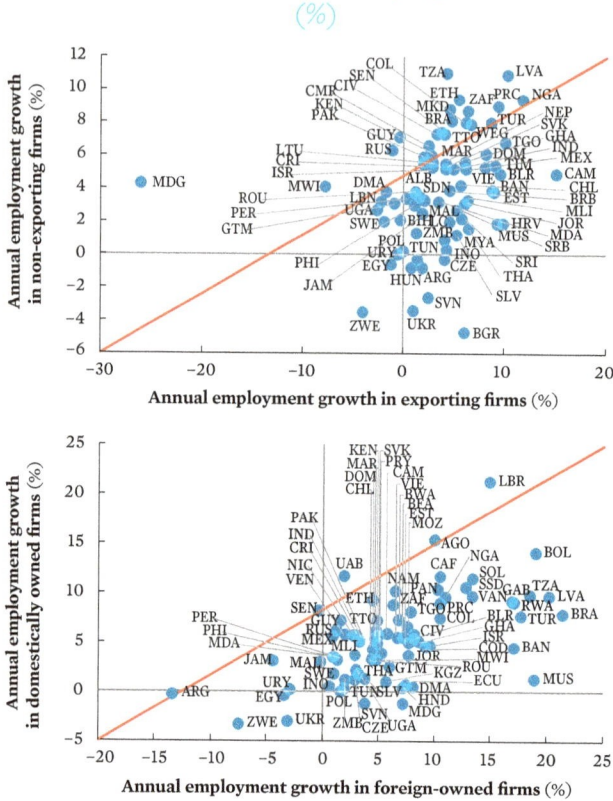

Figure 5.7: Employment Growth in Globally Engaged and Domestic Firms, Developing Economies (%)

AGO = Angola, ARG = Argentina, BAN = Bangladesh, BFA = Burkina Faso, BLR = Belarus, BOL = Bolivia, BRA = Brazil, BWA = Botswana, CAF = Central African Republic, CAM = Cambodia, CHL = Chile, PRC = People's Republic of China, CIV = Côte d'Ivoire, COD = Democratic Republic of Congo, COL = Colombia, CRI = Costa Rica, CZE = Czech Republic, DMA = Dominica, DOM = Dominican Republic, ECU = Ecuador, EGY = Egypt, EST = Estonia, ETH = Ethiopia, GAB = Gabon, GHA = Ghana, GTM = Guatemala, GUY = Guyana, HND = Honduras, IND = India, INO = Indonesia, ISR = Israel, JAM = Jamaica, JOR = Jordan, KEN = Kenya, KGZ = Kyrgyz Republic, LBR = Liberia, LVA = Latvia, MAL = Malaysia, MAR = Morocco, MDA = Moldova, MDG = Madagascar, MEX = Mexico, MLI = Mali, MOZ = Mozambique, MUS = Mauritius, MWI = Malawi, NAM = Namibia, NGA = Nigeria, NIC = Nicaragua, PAK = Pakistan, PAN = Panama, PER = Peru, PHI = Philippines, POL = Poland, PRY = Paraguay, ROU = Romania, RUS = Russian Federation, RWA = Rwanda, SEN = Senegal, SLV = El Salvador, SOL = Solomon Islands, SSD = South Sudan, SVK = Slovakia, SVN = Slovenia, SWE = Sweden, TGO = Togo, THA= Thailand, TTO = Trinidad and Tobago, TUN = Tunisia, TUR = Turkey, TZA = Tanzania, UZB = Uzbekistan, UGA = Uganda, UKR = Ukraine, URY = Uruguay, VAN = Vanuatu, VEN = Venezuela, VIE = Viet Nam, ZAF = South Africa, ZMB = Zambia, ZME = Zimbabwe.

Source: World Bank. Enterprise Surveys. http://www.enterprisesurveys.org (accessed March 2019).

Trade and participation in global value chains can foster technology and skills transfer. Job creation in export markets, especially skill-intensive jobs, can create incentives for training and educational opportunities (Heath and Mobarak 2015). For instance, in villages in India where services outsourcing has expanded employment for young women, girls are more likely to be in school than they would be in villages where no such trade links exist (WTO 2017b). International standards and practices can also foster inclusiveness of skills development opportunities. Similarly, trade liberalization in education services can help increase its supply and investment, and so improve quality and access to opportunities, especially for women.

A study on the impact of economic incentives on women in rural PRC shows that increasing returns for tea production not only increased their incomes, but also the survival of girls in tea-producing regions (Qian 2008). In Bangladesh, the rise of the export-oriented garment industry, whose workforce is 80% women, increased education for girls age 5 to 9 and reduced the number of teenage girls getting married (Heath and Mobarak 2015). These examples show that trade policy has a positive impact on women's lives that goes beyond economic benefits. Trade policy affects not only other targets of the UN Sustainable Development Goals, such as health and education, but the essence of gender inequality: the way that women are perceived in society and the opportunities that come their way.

Constraints for Women in Trade and Global Value Chains

While women face common challenges such as limited access to productive resources, they also face specific gender-based constraints that limit their ability to benefit from trade opportunities. Female producers and traders with lower basic education levels and skills training must overcome more constraints in accessing international markets than male counterparts. This is especially difficult for women in the rural economy, where limited education and literacy hinder their ability to comply with complicated border procedures, making them vulnerable to extortion by border officials. Areas with weak governance put them at greater risk when trading across borders.

Women's relative disadvantage in access to productive resources such as land and finance is a key factor hindering their participation in international markets. Access to finance significantly determines women's participation in international markets, in that they need capital to take part in trade-related activities. Lack of collateral and restrictions on land ownership also often limit women's access to finance.

Another gender-based constraint is the relative exclusion of women from traditional, male-dominated distribution networks. The success of any exporting or importing activity normally requires interaction with distribution networks. However, women often have limited access to the market networks and role models essential for equipping them in the culture of business and trade. One study shows that firms owned by men are more likely to find customers through traditional contact networks, whereas female-owned firms must search through other means (World Bank and WTO 2015). Digital technologies and platforms, particularly mobile phones and the internet, are increasingly playing a significant role in overcoming these constraints, underscoring the importance of digital connectivity for women, especially in rural areas.

Services Trade Barriers Fall Slowly

For services, barriers to trade are also falling. Data for Asian countries from the OECD's Services Trade Restrictiveness Index, indicates a gradual and welcome reduction in barriers over the 5 years to 2020 in most services, especially those relating to digital networks and to the transport and distribution supply chain (Figure 5.8). Barriers still vary widely, however, particularly in rail freight transport and courier services, and in professional services such as accounting and legal services.

Despite the decline, barriers to trade and investment in services are still wider and higher than barriers in merchandise trade. Integrated and coherent policies, with greater trade liberalization and regulatory reform, are critical for services trade. Not only do they promote productivity and competitiveness, they also help form productive linkages between services sectors and the general economy. Instances of regulatory reform in telecommunications, energy, transport, and financial services have boosted services trade in many of the region's economies (ADB 2017b).

The Role of Digitalization in Trade

The rapid advancement of digital technologies has transformed the growth and tradability of services. As these technologies rise, along with greater tradability of traditional services, it has helped new services emerge.

Figure 5.8: Changes in Trade Restrictiveness by Services Sector, 2014–2018

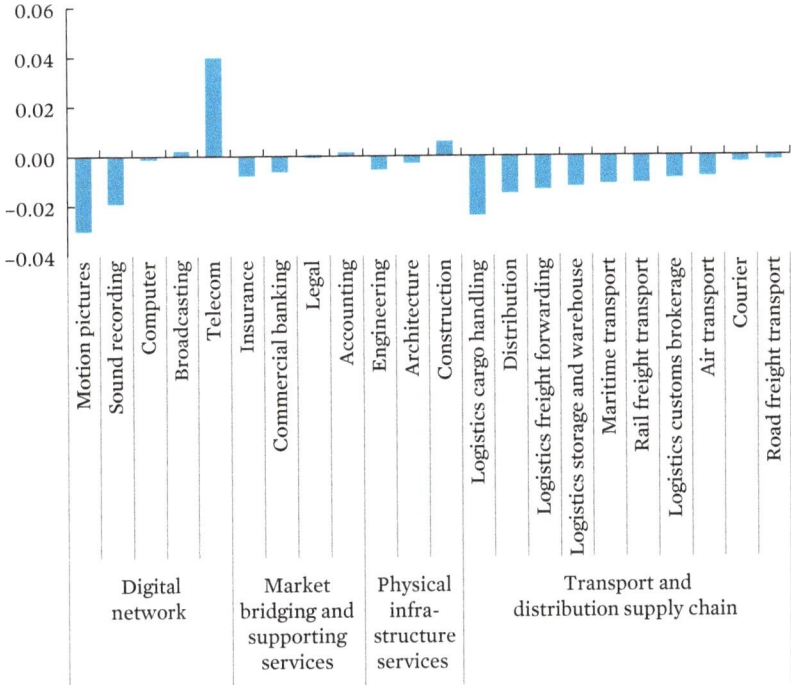

Notes: The Services Trade Restrictiveness Index (STRI) is derived by quantifying the qualitative information in the regulatory database as binary scores. The resulting sector indexes take values between 0 (complete openness to trade and investment) and 1 (total market closure to foreign services providers). Asia and Pacific countries with available data include Australia, the People's Republic of China, India, Indonesia, Japan, Malaysia, New Zealand, and the Republic of Korea.

Source: Organisation for Economic Co-operation and Development. Services Trade Restrictiveness Index dataset. https://stats.oecd.org/Index.aspx?DataSetCode=STRI (accessed May 2019).

Information and communication technology (ICT) services have formed the backbone of digital trade by supplying network infrastructure and underpinning the digitalization of other services. At the same time, innovative technologies have fostered the proliferation of new digitally enabled services that build on data-driven solutions such as big data analytics or cloud computing (OECD 2017b).

Asia's total trade in ICT and digitally deliverable services (or ICT-enabled services) increased from $429.8 billion in 2005 to $1.3 trillion in 2017. This accounted for over two-fifths of the region's trade in services from 2005 to 2017. Since 2005, Asia has consistently accounted for around a fifth of global trade in such services. Over the last 10 years, trade in ICT services in the region has grown by 12.4% a year, higher than the average global growth rate of 8%; trade in digitally deliverable services also grew robustly, at 9.2%, slightly below the 9.6% global average.

Notwithstanding the strong growth of e-commerce in Asia and the region's stellar performance in digitalization, digital trade restrictiveness remains a huge barrier to capitalizing the digital economy and leveraging trade for more inclusive, sustainable development. Figure 5.9 shows digital trade restrictiveness for selected economies in Asia, based on data from the European Centre for International Political Economy's Digital Trade Restrictiveness Index. The index covers 64 countries and includes many trade policy restrictions in the digital economy, varying from tariffs on digital products, restrictions on digital services and investments, restrictions on the movement of data, and restrictions on e-commerce. The index shows that digital trade restrictiveness varies widely within the region, with some of its economies among those with the most restrictive policy regimes and others among those with the greatest digital trade openness.

The PRC, India, Indonesia, and Viet Nam—countries with the largest and/or fastest-growing e-commerce markets—ironically are also among countries with the most restrictive policy regimes on digital trade. Notably, the PRC has the most restrictive policy regime for digital trade, both regionally and globally. The country applies a wide range of restrictive measures in many policy areas covered in the index, including public procurement, foreign investment, intellectual property rights, competition policy, intermediary liability, content access and standards, and quantitative trade and e-commerce restrictions (ECIPE 2018).

Similarly, India has restrictive policies in public procurement and standard setting; high tariffs on digital goods; and burdensome barriers in policy fields such as taxation and subsidies, foreign investment, and intellectual property rights. India also uses trade defense measures on digital products, yet its data policies remain relatively open, which has helped the country become a large exporter of ICT services in recent years.

Figure 5.9: Digital Trade Restrictiveness Index in Selected Asian Economies

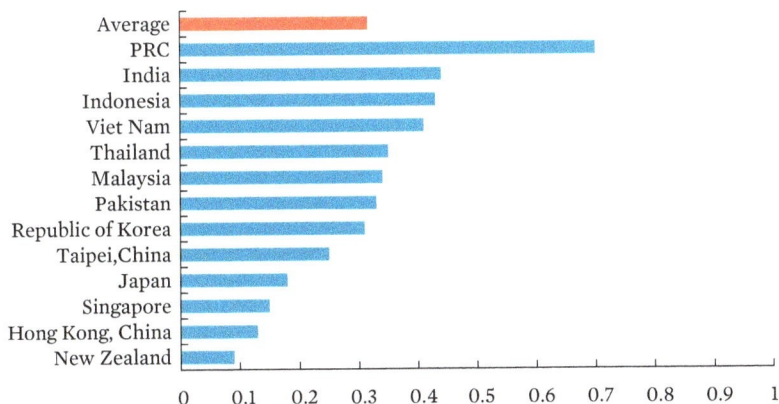

PRC = People's Republic of China.

Note: The index ranges from 0 (i.e., completely open) to 1 (i.e., virtually restricted), with increasing values representing higher levels of digital trade costs for businesses.

Source: European Centre for International Political Economy. https://ecipe.org/ (accessed May 2019).

Meanwhile, Indonesia applies highly restrictive measures in areas such as public procurement, intellectual property rights, intermediary liability, content access, quantitative trade restrictions, and standards, and is particularly restrictive in e-commerce. Viet Nam applies restrictive policy measures on foreign investment, competition policy, and movement of data, and has stringent business licensing and registration requirements (ECIPE 2018). Overall, these restrictions may in part reflect the predominance of domestic e-commerce and slow growth of cross-border e-commerce in these countries even as overall growth in e-commerce is high.

Trade barriers that may hold back innovation and obstacles to the movement of ICT and ICT-enabled services across borders must also be tackled to fully realize the benefits of digitalization. Reflecting on the policy environment of these countries—which are also among major traders of ICT and digitally deliverable services—the region's landscape for digital trade in services is diverse and intricate, including in regulations across countries (Figure 5.10).

Figure 5.10: Digital Services Trade Restrictiveness Index in Selected Asian Economies

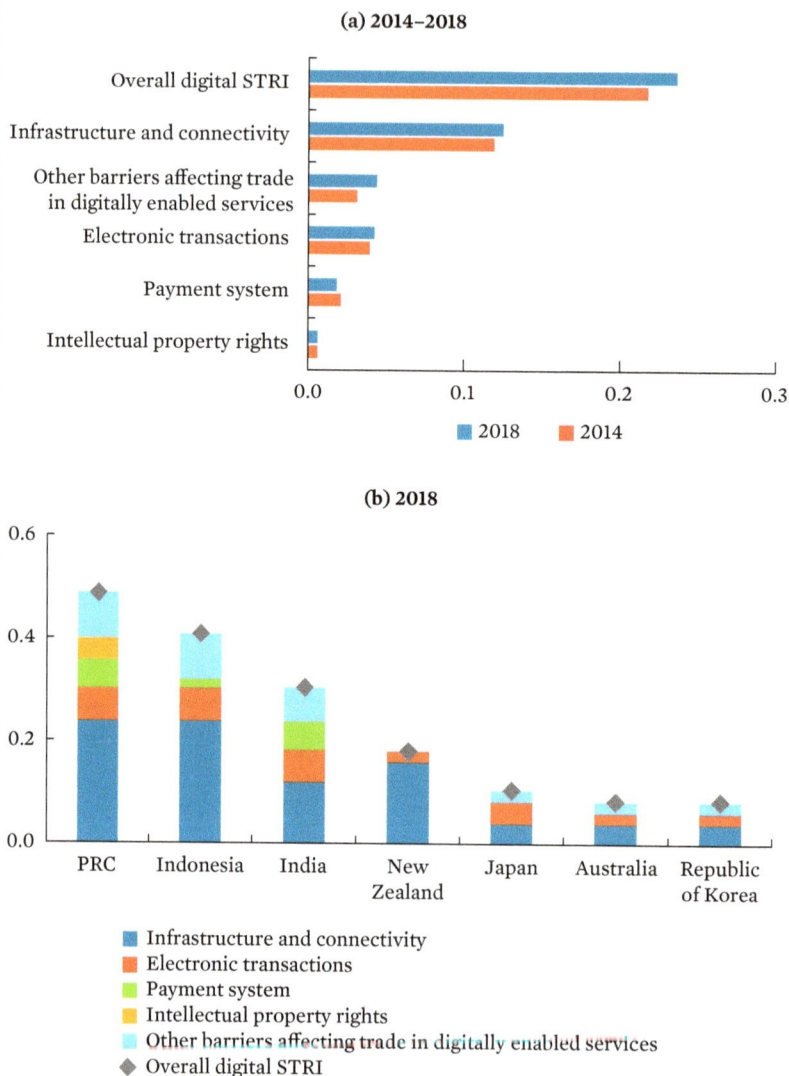

(a) 2014–2018

(b) 2018

PRC = People's Republic of China.

Note: Services Trade Restrictiveness Index (STRI) takes a value from 0 to 1. Complete openness to trade and investment gives a score of 0 and being completely closed to foreign services providers yields a score of 1.

Source: OECD. Digital Services Trade Restrictiveness Index Database. https://stats.oecd.org/Index.aspx?DataSetCode=STRI_DIGITAL (accessed May 2019).

The challenges from this are most pronounced in access to infrastructure and connectivity, differences in electronic transactions such as standards on electronic contracts, and other barriers that hamper trade in digitally enabled services such as commercial or local presence requirements and a lack of effective redress mechanisms against anticompetitive practices online.

The role of digitalization as an accelerator of sustainable and more inclusive development is widely and increasingly recognized. ICT primarily contribute in helping economies to build resilient infrastructure, promote inclusive and sustainable industrialization, and foster innovation and diversification. Moreover, ICT, e-commerce, and other digital platforms can be leveraged to promote entrepreneurship, including the empowerment of women as entrepreneurs and traders.

Beyond its economic benefits, digitalization has important impacts on broader socioeconomic development. Among others, it can foster greater social inclusion by widening access to key public services such as health, education, and financial services and improving their quality, coverage, and delivery. Digitalization itself offers new opportunities for better quality education and skills development and allows consumers to benefit from a greater diversity of products and services and lower prices.

Digital trade offers a range of opportunities for MSMEs to better access international markets and play more active roles in global value chains, giving them leverage to grow sustainably and contribute to inclusive development.

First, digital technologies, and ultimately digital trade, can benefit and empower MSMEs through several channels. Foremost is through the reduction of barriers and costs to trade. Recent studies have shown that internet access can reduce trade barriers and costs for all firms, especially for SMEs in services (Cusolito, Safadi, and Tagioni 2016). Digital technologies can also ease constraints that disproportionally make it difficult for small firms to enter international markets.

Second, digital technologies and networks can supplement traditional finance for MSMEs. This comes through online and mobile banking (in which e-commerce platforms prove to be useful channels for provision), and new financing tools such as crowdfunding (Ganne and Lundquist 2019). Blockchain also offers new opportunities for MSMEs to access trade finance by helping small firms build a credit history and allowing peer-to-peer transactions as an alternative to more expensive services using intermediaries, such as banks (Ganne 2018).

Third, digital technologies can facilitate MSME access to information, thus helping them obtain better market information and deal with legal and regulatory compliance requirements. For instance, government services and regulations (such as business and export requirements, tax compliance codes, and the like) can now be accessed online and necessary applications submitted using e-government services.

Fourth, e-commerce platforms can facilitate MSME participation in global value chains. Lendle and Olarreaga (2014) shows that more than 80% of eBay sellers are exporters, whereas only 10% of small firms using traditional non-platform methods are exporters. Studies have also shown that SMEs using e-commerce tend to sustain their export markets for longer than those that do not (ITC 2016).

Finally, digital technologies and networks can open new business opportunities for MSMEs—especially in rural areas and for female-owned firms. They can also promote new business structures that can serve as platforms for the international participation of MSMEs. ICT tools and services have led to the emergence of small and young firms that operate globally from inception, or the so-called micro-multinationals (Cusolito, Safadi, and Tagioni 2016). In particular, the tools are Skype for communications, Google and Dropbox for file sharing, LinkedIn for finding talent, PayPal for transactions, and eBay and Amazon for sales, have helped small and new entrants in global markets.

Policy Considerations

The global trade slowdown, adoption of trade protectionist policies in parts of the world, and widening social and income inequalities present a major challenge for developing countries, especially those with narrow industrial and private sector bases for generating jobs and diversifying exports. To support diversification, economies with a few concentrated sectors must tackle issues related to limited industrial or manufacturing capacity, poor international competitiveness, and transport and network infrastructure challenges, among others. Interventions are needed to support building economic infrastructure, enhancing trade facilitation initiatives, and policy reforms to integrate digital technology and access to finance for MSMEs and women to enable the benefits of open trade to be shared more equitably.

Economic Infrastructure

Support is needed for narrowing transport and ICT infrastructure gaps and overcoming connectivity challenges faced by developing Asian economies, especially those with geographic constraints and underdeveloped digital trade. This requires establishing a business environment conducive to digital trade, and strengthening the capacity of domestic institutions for digital and paperless trade while improving domestic e-commerce strategies and facilitating digital trade.

The role of digitalization as an accelerator of more inclusive development is increasingly recognized. ICT, e-commerce, and other digital platforms can be leveraged to reduce information and market friction, reduce economic costs for MSMEs, create new economic opportunities, and promote entrepreneurship. The center of gravity of global e-commerce markets continues to shift toward Asia and the Pacific, with the region accounting for 59% of global online retail sales, dominated by the PRC. Cross-border online shopping keeps on growing, while digital technologies used in trade facilitation are supporting greater trade integration around the globe.

Support for economic infrastructure can help reduce women's poverty (including time poverty), enable women to enjoy basic human rights, and more broadly help reduce inequalities. Improving transportation facilities can increase women's mobility and access to markets, decent work, and services (ADB 2013). Improving women's access to reliable and affordable modern energy supplies can reduce their unpaid work, allow more time for paid work, and improve health and well-being (OECD-DAC Network on Gender Equality 2016). Similarly, enhancing women's access to communications infrastructure and services (e.g., mobile phones, internet use, digital platforms, digital financial services) can help them harness the benefits of the digital economy, including through increased employment opportunities or income-generating activities, and improved access to information and government services.

Trade Facilitation

Tariff reductions and trade facilitation initiatives can help MSMEs better engage with international markets. Complex customs procedures have been particularly detrimental to SMEs (WTO 2016). Minimum thresholds on production or sales have also posed specific barriers for SMEs involved in e-commerce, which may have frequent low-volume shipments of low-value items on which customs duties must still be paid (Suominen 2017). Policies that reduce import tariffs and facilitate border procedures can help MSMEs participate in global value chains (Cusolito, Safadi, and Tagioni 2016).

Enhancing digital trade facilitation measures is essential to accelerate growth and promote the inclusiveness of digital trade. Encouraging inclusiveness, the potential reduction in trade costs can disproportionately benefit MSMEs, especially those in least developed and geographically challenged economies, female-owned firms, and those in rural areas. Establishing a supportive regulatory and legal environment is also integral to facilitating digital trade. ICT-enabled trade is not exempt from traditional tariff and nontariff barriers to goods and services trade. For digital trade to occur, lowering entry barriers and eliminating market access restrictions to goods and services are crucial. Further, a regulatory framework is needed—particularly in telecommunications—that fosters competition among services providers and encompasses legislation on e-commerce transactions, consumer protection, data protection/privacy, and cybercrime.

According to the 2019 UN Global Survey on Digital and Sustainable Trade Facilitation, most countries in Asia and the Pacific are implementing trade facilitation measures to improve transparency, streamline trade formalities, and enhance interagency cooperation. Customs services in virtually all countries have developed computerized systems to speed up clearance while improving control. Nearly 70% of the region's economies are also working on national electronic single windows.[7]

However, much remains to be done. At least one-third of the countries working on national electronic single windows are only at the planning and/or pilot stage. Implementation of cross-border (bilateral, subregional, or regional) paperless trade systems also remains mostly at the pilot stage—a notable exception being ASEAN members, who began exchanging live preferential certificates of origins through the ASEAN Single Window in November 2018.[8] The assessment presented, based on the latest data available, confirms that digital trade facilitation measures will bring substantial benefits to the

---

[7] See ESCAP (2019).

[8] For more information see http://asw.asean.org/index.php/news/item/launch-of-the-asean-single-window-live-operation.

countries in Asia and the Pacific. Implementation of paperless and cross-border paperless trade measures may reduce international trade costs in the region by up to 16% on average, higher than the 9% that is expected from implementation of the WTO TFA (ADB and ESCAP 2019).

Policies Geared toward Inclusiveness

Access to Finance for MSMEs and Women

Gaining access to global markets is an important way to foster growth and realize the enormous potential of MSMEs to support inclusive and sustainable development. Participation in global production networks does not just expose these firms to a larger customer base, it can also provide a range of other opportunities, including but not limited to: (i) increased technical capacity; (ii) increased demand for existing products and services, greater utilization of operational capacity, and improvement of production efficiency; and (iii) greater access to and cooperation with other enterprises—both upstream and downstream—which can help build credibility and so make it easier to get finance and attract investors and human resources (Yuhua and Bayhaqi 2013).

Global experience and firm-level data show that MSMEs are largely constrained by access to finance. The latest figures show 96.7 million, or 43% of formal MSMEs in developing Asia, have unmet financing needs. The gap in the region is estimated at $2.6 trillion and is largest in East Asia. Similarly, compared with men, female-owned and -led businesses tend to face more hurdles getting credit (ADB 2018, ADB 2015).

An ADB survey notes that about 74% of rejections of trade finance proposals are from MSMEs. Female-owned firms were rejected 2.5 times more than male-owned firms (Di Caprio, Kim, and Beck 2017). Furthermore, these enterprises are less likely to take loans from formal financial institutions such as banks and they tend to borrow on less favorable terms and for shorter durations. To fill the financing gap, most resort to internal sources, such as personal savings, borrowing from friends and relatives, and internal profit (ADB and ESCAP 2019; Harvie, Oum, and Dionisius 2013). The lack of financial access can be primarily attributed to these firms' weak credit histories and limited assets or resources as collateral for borrowing.

Targeted interventions and innovative financing models are therefore important to meet the needs of MSMEs at different stages of their business cycles and to encourage their participation in global value chains. Because women's access to finance is hampered by customary laws (especially on land ownership), more viable options include financing tools that use a firm's valued assets as collateral for loans—such as movables and accounts receivable—rather than real estate (ADB 2015). Gender-sensitive microfinance[9] and trade finance[10] are essential support for smaller and female-owned firms to develop and internationalize.

Trade Digitalization

Digital connectivity is emerging as an important driver of inclusive economic growth, and economies in Asia and the Pacific are rapidly becoming leaders in the global market for ICT. The first building block for leveraging digital trade to promote inclusive development is strengthening the efficiency, reliability, affordability, and accessibility of digital infrastructure and services. In Asia, mobile cellular subscription rates in 2017 had expanded to 100 subscriptions per 100 people, from 7 in 2000. Subscription rates have risen steadily across subregions, although they vary widely. Complementary measures, such as national broadband and e-commerce strategies, are also necessary.

The experience of many Asian economies demonstrates that well-targeted telecommunications reforms can make ICT services more available, affordable, and inclusive. These have specifically included expanding ownership of mobile phones, improving transparency in regulations and legal frameworks, and increasing competition among service providers to

[9] As a case in point, a microfinance expansion project in Papua New Guinea is helping rural communities access financial services. It aims to strengthen industry regulation and the capacity of lenders to widen their range of financial services and products in rural areas, focusing on lending to micro and small enterprises, especially to women. The project also supports financial literacy: over 200,000 clients and potential clients having received such training (47% of them women). Similarly, in Cambodia, an ADB project established and strengthened credit businesses of 122 savings groups and 15 agricultural cooperatives that have provided finance to 3,200 beneficiaries. The project also helped establish/strengthen about 400 agribusinesses and significantly boosted access to loans for women. In Tajikistan, a microfinance project provided credit to 16,000 women (44% of total borrowers) enabling them to engage in entrepreneurial activities, increase their incomes, and broaden their income sources.

[10] For example, ADB's Trade Finance Program—which includes the features of strong gender and SMEs—has been helping women and SMEs participate in global and regional value chains, often by supporting their access to finance along supply chain transactions or providing guarantees.

improve market access and entry. Consumer protection and confidence, the establishment of regulatory bodies, and efforts to improve mobile broadband networks are among other needed reforms (ADB 2017a).

Nonetheless, government capacity weighs on the reform agenda, while regional initiatives to harmonize regulations can also be hampered by disparate legal frameworks and the digital divide between countries. The increasingly cross-border nature of e-commerce and rapid growth of digital trade in services calls for intensified regional efforts to modernize and harmonize regulations.[11] With the increasing role of digitally deliverable services in boosting trade growth and promoting inclusive development, enhancing digital trade in services is ever more vital. Ultimately, securing policy coherence and the convergence of actions between and among Asia's economies in improving digital regulations and connectivity infrastructure are key to creating an enabling environment for digital trade in services.

Digital technologies also hold great potential in facilitating access to finance. Technologies like artificial intelligence and machine learning can enable a digital trade finance platform to significantly benefit SMEs. This can reduce transaction and information costs relating to business history and collateral. Analytics using these technologies, for example, can transform many nonfinancial transaction records into useful information in a digital lending platform to help determine whether to approve SME loans. Banks also benefit from automated processes, which could yield savings of $2.5 billion to $6 billion and increase revenues by 20% (ADB and ESCAP 2019).

Despite these benefits, digitalization faces high implementation costs. Based on the International Chamber of Commerce survey, about 40% of banks do not view digitalization as part of their agenda, while it remains at the developing stage among 50% of respondent banks (ICC 2018). The cost of digitizing securely exchanged and validated information is high as it requires an overhaul of well-integrated and long-standing processes. This is even more difficult for banks that are based in developing economies. Moreover, the fragmented way that digitalization has emerged creates

---

[11] The e-ASEAN Initiative of the ASEAN provides a good example. An agreement in 2000 made ASEAN the first developing region to prepare a harmonized e-commerce legal framework across jurisdictions (UNCTAD 2013). Other landmarks included the ASEAN ICT Masterplan 2015 for harmonized e-commerce laws in each member country to create ICT conducive to businesses and to secure transactions throughout the group. UNCTAD (2013) notes that progress toward harmonization has been strongest in electronic transactions laws, with nine member countries having legislation in place and Cambodia now putting a draft law into effect, and progress on laws covering cybercrime, domain names, and dispute resolution.

problems of interoperability and compatibility among various systems. International digital standards and laws have yet to be adopted to enable various systems to communicate with each other and ensure security and proper accountability.

Supporting digitalization in finance provision requires assistance by multilateral development banks and governments to build ICT infrastructure and regulatory reforms. Wider technology adoption can also be enhanced through coordination among banks, firms, and regulators. This enables regulators to create policies that enable innovation, mutual benefits, and seamless transactions while establishing standards of compliance and security. Coordination should also focus on the interoperability of various systems of government agencies, banks, and borrowing firms to enable electronic exchange of information and services. Interoperability should also be implemented internationally in support of cross-border trade.

Global Initiatives to Support Inclusive Trade

The availability of international agreements helps coordinate reforms and implement standardized regulations globally. The Aid for Trade (AfT) Initiative is an important global instrument under the WTO because it helps developing economies engage in international trade. Started in 2005, the AfT aims to help developing economies build trade-related infrastructure and supply-side capacity by increasing the available resources for developing countries to integrate with the global economy. AfT can also help tackle the general and specific constraints that women and smaller firms must overcome to fully benefit from international trade.

AfT can contribute to MSME development and empowerment through several channels. The WTO's monitoring and evaluation exercise reveals key areas of support: improving access to foreign markets and global value chains, providing access to finance, upgrading business skills, improving access to information, and supporting the growth and development of women. This highlights that empowering women can have a multiplier effect on empowering MSMEs. AfT can also promote gender equality and empower women by expanding their access to trade and economic opportunities—by increasing gender mainstreaming in aid for economic infrastructure and helping to improve gender targets in trade policies and regulations. AfT can help to strengthen country ownership of integrated gender equality programs and ensure they are aligned with national and regional priorities, while improving institutional capacity to implement them.

Integrating and scaling up that focus in other official development assistance priority areas, besides AfT, is also essential. While gender equality cuts across all areas of sustainable development and is not limited to trade-related activities, a strategic focus on gender in development interventions can significantly boost volumes of gender-targeted aid and, hence, help empower women.

References

Asian Development Bank (ADB). 2013. *Gender Tool Kit: Transport—Maximizing the Benefits of Improved Mobility for All*. Manila.

——. 2015. *Women in the Workforce: An Unmet Potential in Asia and the Pacific*. Manila.

——. 2017a. *Meeting Asia's Infrastructure Needs*. Manila.

——. 2017b. *Aid for Trade in Asia and the Pacific: Promoting Connectivity for Inclusive Development*. Manila.

——. 2018. *Women and Business in the Pacific*. Manila.

Asian Development Bank and United Nations Economic and Social Commission for Asia and the Pacific (ADB and ESCAP). 2019. *Asia–Pacific Trade Facilitation Report 2019: Bridging Trade Finance Gaps through Technology*. Manila: Asian Development Bank.

——. 2019. *Asia–Pacific Trade Facilitation Report 2019: Bridging Trade Finance Gaps through Technology*. Manila: Asian Development Bank.

Asian Development Bank Institute (ADBI). 2017. *Win-Win: How International Trade Can Help Meet the Sustainable Goals*. Tokyo: ADBI.

Cagatay, N. and K. Erturk. 2004. Gender and Globalization: A Macroeconomic Perspective. *International Labour Organization Working Paper Series*. No. 19. Geneva.

Cusolito, A. P., R. Safadi, and D. Tagioni. 2016. *Inclusive Global Value Chains—Policy Options for Small and Medium Enterprises and Low-Income Countries*. OECD/World Bank.

Di Caprio, A., K. Kim, and S. Beck. 2017. 2017 Trade Finance Gaps, Growth, and Jobs Survey. *ADB Briefs*. No. 83. Manila: ADB. http://dx.doi.org/10.22617/BRF178995-2.

Dutt, P., D. Mitra, and P. Ranjan. 2009. International Trade and Unemployment: Theory and Cross-National Evidence. *Journal of International Economics*. 78 (1). pp. 32–44.

ESCAP–World Bank Trade Cost Database. www.unescap.org/resources/escap-world-bank-trade-cost-database.

European Centre for International Political Economy (ECIPE). 2018. *Digital Trade Restrictiveness Index*. Brussels. https://ecipe.org/dte/dte-report/.

Felbermayr, G., J. Prat, and H. J. Schmerer. 2011. Trade and Unemployment: What Do the Data Say? *European Economic Review*. 55 (60). pp. 741–58.

Fontana, M. 2004. Modeling the Effects of Trade on Women and at Home: Comparative Perspectives. *Economie Internationale*. 99 (3). pp. 49–80.

Ganne, E. 2018. *Can Blockchain Revolutionize International Trade?* Geneva: WTO.

Ganne, E. and K. Lundquist. 2019. The Digital Economy, GVCs and SMEs. In *Global Value Chain Development Report 2019: Technological Innovation, Supply Chain Trade, and Workers in a Globalized World*. World Trade Organization. Geneva: WTO. pp. 121–39.

Harvie, C., S. Oum, and N. Dionisius. 2013. Small and Medium Enterprises' Access to Finance: Evidence from Selected Asian Economies. *ERIA Discussion Paper Series*. No. 2013–23. October. Jakarta: Economic Research Institute for ASEAN and East Asia.

Heath, R. and A. M. Mobarak. 2015. Manufacturing Growth and the Lives of Bangladeshi Women. *Journal of Development Economics*. 115 (C). pp. 1–15.

Ismail, N. W. and J. M. Mahyideen. 2015. The Impact of Infrastructure on Trade and Economic Growth in Selected Economies in Asia. *ADBI Working Paper Series*. No. 553. https://www.adb.org/sites/default/files/publication/177093/adbi-wp553.pdf.

International Trade Center (ITC). 2016. *Bringing SMEs onto the e-Commerce Highway*. Geneva: ITC.

Jobes, K. 2010. *Expanding Trade: Empowering Women. Are We Missing a Trick? Why Gender Matters for Trade*. Washington, DC: World Bank.

Kritikos, A. 2014. *Entrepreneurs and Their Impacts on Jobs and Economic Growth*. IZA World of Labor. https://wol.iza.org/uploads/articles/8/pdfs/entrepreneurs-and-their-impact-on-jobs-andeconomic-growth.pdf.

Lendle, A. and M. Olarreaga. 2014. Can Online Markets Make Trade More Inclusive? *Inter-American Development Bank Discussion Papers Series*. No. 349. Washington, DC.

Limao, N. and A. J. Venables. 2001. Infrastructure, Geographical Disadvantage, Transport Costs, and Trade. *The World Bank Economic Review*. 15 (3). pp. 451-479. http://documents.worldbank.org/curated/en/662351468331778084/Infrastructure-geographical-disadvantage-transport-costs-and-trade.

Moore, M. and P. Ranjan. 2005. Globalization and Skill-Biased Technological Change: Implications for Unemployment and Wage Inequality. *Economic Journal*. 115 (503). pp. 391–422.

Organisation for Economic Co-operation and Development (OECD). Digital Services Trade Restrictiveness Index Database. https://stats.oecd.org/Index.aspx?DataSetCode=STRI_DIGITAL.

——. Services Trade Restrictiveness Index dataset. https://stats.oecd.org/Index.aspx?DataSetCode=STRI.

——. 2005. The Economic Impact of Trade Facilitation. *OECD Trade Policy Working Paper Series*. No. 21. http://www.oecd.org/officialdocuments/publicdisplaydocumentpdf/?cote=TD/TC/WP(2005)12/FINAL&docLanguage=En.

——. 2017. *OECD Digital Economy Outlook 2017*. Paris: OECD Publishing. http://dx.doi.org/10.1787/9789264276284-en.

OECD–DAC Network on Gender Equality. 2016. *Tracking the Money for Women's Economic Empowerment: Still a Drop in the Ocean*. https://www.oecd.org/dac/gender-development/Tracking-the-money-for-womens-economic-empowerment.pdf.

Suominen, K. 2017. *The Silver Bullet for Fueling Small Business Exports in the Ecommerce Era: A plurilateral on De Minimis*. Manuscript. https://

katisuominen.files.wordpress.com/2017/04/de-minimis-plurilateral-suominen-april-2017.pdf.

United Nations Conference on Trade and Development (UNCTAD). 2013. *Review of e-commerce Legislation Harmonization in the Association of Southeast Asian Nations.* Geneva. https://unctad.org/en/pages/PublicationWebflyer.aspx?publicationid=623.

United Nations Economic and Social Commission for Asia and the Pacific (ESCAP). 2019. Digital and Sustainable Trade Facilitation Implementation in Asia and the Pacific: 2019 Update. *ESCAP Trade Insights.* No. 28. Bangkok.

United Nations Office of the High Representative for the Least Developed Countries, Landlocked Developing Countries and Small Island Developing States (UN-OHRLLS) website. http://unohrlls.org/.

Vickerman, R. 2002. Restructuring of Transportation Networks. In G. Atalik and M. M. Fischer, eds. *Regional Development Reconsidered.* Berlin: Springer. World Bank. 2001.

von Hagen, M. 2014. *Trade and Gender—Exploring a Reciprocal Relationship.* Kathmandu, Nepal: Deutsche Gesellschaft fur Internationale Zusammenarbeit (GIZ). https://www.OECD.org/dac/gender-development/GIZ_Trade%20and%20Gender_Exploring%20a%20reciprocal%20relationship.pdf.

World Bank and World Trade Organization. 2015. *The Role of Trade in Ending Poverty.* Geneva: World Trade Organization.

World Bank. Enterprise Surveys. http://www.enterprisesurveys.org.

World Trade Organization (WTO). *2016. World Trade Report 2016: Levelling the Playing Field for SMEs.* Geneva: WTO.

———. 2017. *World Trade Report 2017.* Geneva: WTO.

Yuhua, Z. and A. Bayhaqi. 2013. SMEs' Participation in Global Production Chains. *APEC Policy Support Unit Issues Paper Series.* No. 3. February. APEC Secretariat, Singapore.

Factory Asia: The Determinants of Multinational Activity in the Context of Global Value Chains

6

Natalia Ramondo[1]

Complex global value chains (GVC), in which intermediate goods and services are traded across internationally fragmented production processes, are an important feature of the global economy. Multinational corporations, as the main organizers and coordinators of GVCs, are at the center, with the cross-border trade of inputs and final goods arranged through their networks, contractual partners, and suppliers. GVC–trade related to multinationals makes up about 80% of global trade. Countries in East and Southeast Asia are more present in GVCs than other regions of the world, with the People's Republic of China (PRC) the biggest host for multinationals and Japan their biggest source country.

This chapter brings new evidence on the determinants of the activity of affiliates of multinational firms in Asia, in the context of the GVC. The analysis relies on a unique firm-level data set from Dun & Bradstreet with comprehensive coverage of countries in the region. The key feature of the data that makes the analysis possible is information provided on firms' engagement in international trade, which overcomes the main challenge in the literature so far. Having these data, the traditional country and industry determinants of different types of foreign direct investment (FDI)—comparative advantage, integration, and institutional factors—can be tested very precisely for a large set of countries. Production fragmentation considerations (input–output links, as in Alfaro and Charlton 2009) can also be considered, along with measures of engagement in the GVC such as a country's exports' upstreamness, and measured of value-added trade.

[1] I thank Davin Chor for his very helpful discussion as well as participants at the 2016 Asian Development Bank Conference on Economic Development: The Role of Foreign Direct Investment in Economic Development. This paper was prepared for the theme chapter of ADB's *Asian Economic Integration Report 2016* under the direction and supervision of Fahad Khan.

The importance of understanding the functioning of the GVC, and hence, the role of the multinational as its main actor, is undeniable. First, the attachment and type of engagement to the GVC seems to matter for development. The United Nations Conference on Trade and Development (UNCTAD) (2013) reports that countries with a higher growth in GVC participation had a median growth rate of gross domestic product (GDP) per capita of 3.3% from 1990 to 2010, compared with less than 1% for the median country that did not have increased participation. Moreover, countries that not only increased their engagement in the GVC, but also did so with high value-added activities, grew fastest.[2] Second, the GVC is an important cross-country transmission channel for shocks. As recent papers have demonstrated, increasing interdependence of economies through supplier linkages has created more synchronized business cycles. A natural disaster shock, such as the Tohoku earthquake that hit Japan in 2011, hit production in affiliates of Japanese multinationals in the United States (US), as well as of other firms in the US economy related by networks to the Japanese affiliates, and went hand-in-hand with the decrease in imports from Japan (Boehm, Flaaen, and Pandalai-Nayar 2015). Finally, GVCs create different incentives for lobbying for trade policy. Two producers at different stages of the production process (e.g., input production and assembly) are indeed in conflict about which goods should be protected from imports; even two firms in the same industry may end up with opposite interests in trade policy only because they made different location choices for different stages of production.[3] Hence, the increasing—and type of—engagement of a country in the GVC may reshape the political process through which trade policy is made (Blanchard, Bown, and Johnson 2016).

Firm-level drivers and location and industry determinants of multinationals linked to trade activities are key for policy makers in understanding the factors influencing the participation of countries and multinationals in the GVC.

Traditionally, the activity of multinational affiliates has been divided into two types: market-seeking activities (horizontal FDI) and low-cost-seeking activities (vertical FDI). Not only are these two activities non-exclusive, but

---

[2] Global value chains (GVC) participation is measured by UNCTAD as the foreign content of exports of a country plus the content of exports consumed in foreign countries, while the domestic value-added share of exports is the measure used for type of attachment to the GVC. In the following sections, we calculate similar statistics with our data.

[3] This is the case of Nike and New Balance, athletic footwear producers: while Nike produces and assembles all the footwear abroad, New Balance assembles—and sometimes, fully manufactures—some of its shoes in the United States.

the way multinationals use affiliated and unaffiliated parties is increasingly complex. It is not anymore about the decision of where to produce and/or integrate an input in the production of a final good at the headquarter; it is about how to integrate and where to locate a multidimensional GVC with final goods directed to markets worldwide. As transportation, administrative, and communication costs decrease, it is more and more feasible for the multinational to separate different stages of production across space, and from final consumers. As a result, vertical FDI should be understood more broadly as production fragmentation—not necessarily between two parties of the same corporation (like Intel), but between unrelated parties (like Apple–Foxconn) and hence, involving all types of trade flows.

Our data, by recording if a plant is engaged in international trade activities or not, distinguish between plants dedicated to serving local and international markets. Foreign affiliates engaged in international trade are referred to in this chapter as GVC–FDI. Moreover, by having the industry of operations of the plants and of their parent firms, information can be extracted from input–output tables and the presence of production fragmentation within the corporation can be established—this is called an input–output link. Finally, worth mentioning is that the data include the same detailed information for domestic plants, and these data are used in the analysis in this chapter.

First, we find that the engagement of a country in GVC–trade is positively related to GVC–FDI. This finding is robust to different measures of GVC–trade and to various specifications. Second, it is more likely to find trade-oriented foreign affiliates among large plants in poorer countries with exports in more downstream sectors, weaker rule of law, and a low cost to export. Moreover, in the spirit of Heckscher–Ohlin models of trade, these affiliates are in labor-intensive industries in relatively labor abundant countries. Third, the number of affiliates engaged in international trade is positively related to more of those affiliates having strong input–output links with their parent; the effect is stronger for the PRC. Finally, stronger input–output links among domestic firms in an industry seems to attract foreign firms, regardless of their activity.

Literature Review

Traditionally, there are two explanations for the location choices of the multinational, which give rise to the traditional motives for FDI, horizontal FDI, and vertical FDI. Markusen (1984) focuses on the public nonrival nature of knowledge (an ownership advantage) within the firm. Hence, the multinational relied on exploiting economies of scale by replicating the same production activity across production locations; the blueprint, once developed, can be combined with immobile factors in multiple locations by a single firm. This type of multinational activity, because it involves replicating the same activity in multiple countries, it is referred to as "horizontal FDI."

The proximity-concentration tradeoff theory arises from adding trade to the traditional horizontal framework (Horstmann and Markusen 1992; Brainard 1997). It explains the choice of overseas production over exports as motivated by proximity to consumers (either final consumers or other good producers downstream), or specialized suppliers, at the expense of scale: the choice is between lower variable costs from avoiding trade versus higher fixed costs from operating a new plant. The prediction of this theory is that horizontal FDI will prevail over trade the higher transport costs and trade barriers, and the larger the host market.[4]

Horizontal FDI theories assume similarity across countries in factor price differences. In contrast, theories that predict vertical expansion abroad (Helpman 1984, 1985) rely on differences in factor proportions across countries and on the assumption that headquarters and production activities have different factor intensities, in the spirit of the Heckscher–Ohlin models. The tests for horizontal versus vertical FDI motives are very limited because detailed data on the activities of multinationals' affiliates is lacking. For instance, Carr, Markusen, and Maskus (2001) analyze the sensitivity of total US affiliate sales in the host market to a set of country variables that the theory predicts should have a bigger effect on one type of FDI than the other. Their results show that affiliate sales are larger in countries more similar to the US in size, but decrease as the cost of investing in the host country falls, and with the cost of importing back goods from the host country (increasing with the cost of exporting to the host country). They interpret these results as evidence of the prevalence of horizontal FDI, but this is far from a conclusive test.

---

[4] Recent developments have incorporated other considerations to the traditional motives of FDI. In particular, Helpman, Melitz, and Yeaple (2004) have developed a model of firms that are heterogeneous in productivity and faced to the proximity-concentration tradeoff. The most productive firms in an economy will decide to open affiliates abroad, in line with the data, and industries with higher firm heterogeneity will show relatively more firms deciding to become multinationals over exporters.

In the vertical FDI side, the game-changing work by Antras (2003) introduced contract-theory considerations into the sourcing decisions of firms and incorporated features of the institutional environment. More precisely, firms in industries with more relation-specific investments, as defined by Nunn (2007), are more likely to keep the different stages of production within the boundaries of the firm. The interaction between industries with different contract intensity and countries with different institutional strengths (e.g., degree of contract enforcement) produces predictions about the location of "vertical" affiliates.[5]   The empirical literature that followed Antras's work has been fully devoted to analyze the determinants of intra-firm trade against arm-length trade. The analysis of the determinants of intra-firm trade were carried as a direct test of the theory by Antras (2003). Among others, one can find papers by Hanson, Mataloni, and Slaughter (2001, 2005); Yeaple (2006); and Nunn and Trefler (2008, 2014) on the activity of US multinationals. While the first two papers use data from the Bureau of Economic Analysis on the activity of US affiliates and parents in terms of their sales and purchases, the third paper uses custom data from the US Bureau of Census on related and unrelated party trade.

Latest developments in the literature have used more sophisticated data to address the determinants of vertical FDI versus horizontal FDI. This has tried to overcome the limitations of the data regarding a detailed account of the activities of multinationals' affiliates, and introduced information on the input and output links across industries, using input–output tables.

Notably, Alfaro and Charlton (2009) introduce vertical linkages by integrating input–output relationships into the analysis of affiliate location. They show there is a tendency for parents to open "vertically linked" affiliates; that is, in an input–output sense, affiliates are very similar to their parents. They conclude that vertical FDI is more prevalent than previously thought. They cannot, however, provide direct evidence on trade links between parents and affiliates. Ramondo, Rappoport, and Ruhl (2015) show that "vertically linked" affiliates are not necessarily sending inputs to the parent; input–output links may be a poor proxy for intra-firm trade linkages. Their findings, however, point to the complexity of the GVC; the multinational intertwines in-house and third-party suppliers along all the stages of the GVC.

---

[5] Another theoretical development for vertical FDI is Helpman, Grossman, and Szeidl (2006), who introduce firm heterogeneity into a framework with three countries in which firms choose to do vertical FDI in the South and horizontal FDI in the North.

The value of the results in Alfaro and Charlton (2009), confirmed by
Ramondo, Rodriguez-Clare, and Tintelnot (2015), is indeed to show a
lot of production fragmentation occurs between multinational parents
and affiliates.

A more recent paper by Alfaro et al. (2015) tries to tackle the complexity of
the GVC and how the multinational chooses to outsource or integrate its
different stages. Using data on affiliates' and parents' industries, together with
the input–output matrix, they try to circumvent the lack of data on affiliates'
trade flows to make inferences about the determinants of such decisions.
By looking at *all* industry codes of the multinational, and comparing them
with ones needed to produce a final product, as dictated by the input–output
matrix, they infer the inputs that the multinational may have chosen to
outsource to third parties. They link these decisions of outsourcing versus
in-house production to contractual environments of countries, specificity of
investment of sectors, and elasticities of demands of the final good, in the
spirit of Antras (2003) and Antras and Chor (2013).

At the same time, an incipient literature devoted to statistics on value-
added trade—as opposed to gross trade—has been developed to reflect the
increasing complexity of the GVC. The concern was that gross exports did
not accurately reflect which location was truly "producing" value. Given
the increasing fragmentation of production, trade in inputs increased
exponentially—and with it, the back-and-forth and double counting of flows.
An early attempt was Hummels, Ishii, and Yi (2001), who measured the
degree of vertical specialization by calculating the import content of exports
of a country. More recent developments started bringing into the picture
world input–output tables. Johnson and Noguera (2012); Johnson (2014);
Koopman, Wang, and Wei (2014); and Wang, Wei, and Zhu (2014) construct
different measures of value-added trade, which are explained in detail
below. Antras et al. (2012), and Antras and Chor (2013) develop measures of
the upstreamness of exports, both for a country and for an industry.

Finally, a new literature has developed quantitative models of multinational
activity that contemplate complex strategies for these firms. By applying
statistical techniques introduced by Eaton and Kortum (2002), Ramondo
and Rodriguez-Clare (2013); Arkolakis, Ramondo, Rodriguez-Clare, and
Yeaple (2014); Tintelnot (2015); and Alviarez (2015) build models in which
firms not only replicate production abroad to serve the host market, but also
ship goods back home and to third-party countries, and receive goods from

the parent company. These quantitative general equilibrium models are suitable to perform welfare calculations of the activities of multinationals.

Empirical Analysis

Three types of data are used for the analysis. First, data on the activities of plants that distinguish between plants that only direct their sales to the host market of operations and plants that serve the international market, both for foreign and domestic plants located in Asia. Second, a measure of the degree of production fragmentation within a corporation: information on the industry of operation of parents and affiliates plants is combined with data from the input–output matrix for the US. Finally, data from the literature on value-added trade are used on the engagement of a country in GVC–trade.

Data

Data on the activity of multinationals. We use firm-level data from *WorldBase*, sold by Dun & Bradstreet.[6] These data provide a rich resource for very detailed measures of multinational activity. This data set has been used in several academic papers (Alfaro and Charlton 2009; Fajgelbaum, Grossman, and Helpman 2015; and Alfaro et al. 2015, more recently), and policy reports and books, such as "Synchronized factories—Latin America and the Caribbean in the Era of Global Value Chains" by the IADB (edited by Juan Blyde).[7]

The unit of observation in WorldBase is the establishment, not the firm. As explained in Alfaro and Charlton (2009), "establishments, like firms, have their own addresses, business names, and managers, but might be partly or wholly owned by other firms." We use a cross-section of establishments for 2015. For each establishment, the following information is available:

- industry code: four-digit SIC code of the primary industry in which the establishment operates;[8]
- country of operation of the establishment;

---

[6] The data were acquired from Advanced Data Technology, Dennis Jacques (d.f.jacques@att.net).

[7] See Alfaro and Charlton (2009) for an analysis of the coverage of WorldBase.

[8] Industry SIC codes are converted to NAICS 2002 codes.

- sales and/or employment; and
- international trade dummies: three variables indicating if the establishment only exports, only imports, or both exports and imports.

We restrict the sample to establishments reporting to a "global ultimate headquarter" (GUH); for some observations, the GUH and subsidiary are the same entity (i.e., these are most of the non-multinational establishments). Foreign establishments are those that report to a GUH located in a different country.[9] Where an establishment identified as GUH is operating in the "holding companies" sector, we replace the primary industry code for the secondary industry code of operations where that is available. Finally, we are able to link establishments belonging to the same GUH within and across countries. Branches are not included. We also restrict the sample to establishments in the mining, manufacturing, and business services sectors, belonging to GUH in any sector.[10] The country coverage for destination countries is restricted to selected Asian economies, while the list of origin countries includes mainly the Organisation for Economic Co-operation and Development economies and emerging investors.[11]

We are left with 230,130 observations on establishments. Table 6.1 presents a summary of the fraction of plants that are foreign and/or exporters and/ or importers, across sectors. These shares are in line with observations in

[9] Regional headquarters are not included. For instance, if a plant in the PRC reports to a regional headquarters in Hong Kong, China, which in turn belongs to a global ultimate headquarter in the US, the plant in the PRC is recorded as belonging to a GUH in the US.

[10] Since we convert the four-digit SIC industry classification to four-digit NAICS, we end up with an extra sector called "other sectors" that gathers some NAICS agricultural industry code and some code in services other than business services. These end up being very few observations.

[11] Our coverage in terms of countries is the following. We focus on establishments operating in the following Asian economies: Afghanistan; Armenia; Australia; Azerbaijan; Bangladesh; Brunei Darussalam; Cambodia; the PRC; Georgia; Hong Kong, China; India; Indonesia; Japan; Kazakhstan; the Republic of Korea; the Kyrgyz Republic; Malaysia; Nepal, New Zealand; Pakistan; the Philippines; Singapore; Sri Lanka; Taipei,China; Thailand; Uzbekistan; and Viet Nam. On the origin side, we focus on GUHs from the following economies: Australia; Austria; Belgium; Brazil; Canada; the PRC; Switzerland; Denmark; Spain; Finland; France; United Kingdom; Germany; Hong Kong, China; India; Indonesia; Ireland; Israel; Italy; Japan; the Republic of Korea; Luxembourg; Mexico; Malaysia; the Netherlands; Norway; New Zealand; Portugal; the Russian Federation; Singapore; Sweden; Thailand; Turkey; Taipei,China; the US; and South Africa. For economies that are both in the destination and origin list, we have observations for domestic establishments. Given the list of origin and destination economies, the data permit an analysis of outward FDI for some economies in Asia, particularly, the PRC and India.

the literature: the fraction of exporters is almost 20% overall, but increases to more than 60% among foreign plants and decreases to 15% for domestic plants. As expected, the highest percentages are found in manufacturing—the bulk of the data—for which overall exporters represent a 24% of total plants. The number of foreign plants is also in line with the common wisdom in the literature: they represent 10% of the total number of plants in our sample.

Table 6.1: Summary Statistics, WorldBase

Fraction of Exporters/ Importers	All Sectors	Mining	Manufacturing	Business Services	Other
Fraction of exporters, all	0.19	0.12	0.24	0.07	0.14
among foreign plants	0.63	0.38	0.74	0.28	0.24
among domestic plants	0.15	0.10	0.19	0.05	0.12
Fraction of importers, all	0.18	0.11	0.24	0.04	0.09
among foreign plants	0.65	0.36	0.79	0.21	0.13
among domestic plants	0.14	0.09	0.18	0.04	0.08
Fraction of exporters and importers, all	0.15	0.09	0.20	0.03	0.05
among foreign plants	0.57	0.30	0.70	0.14	0.09
among domestic plants	0.11	0.07	0.15	0.02	0.04
Fraction of foreign plants	0.09	0.07	0.10	0.07	0.20
Total number of plants	**230,130**	**5,958**	**161,418**	**61,280**	**1,474**

Note "Services" refers to business services only. "Other sectors" includes some categories of the agricultural and services sectors.
Source: Author's calculations using data from Dun & Bradstreet. D&B WorldBase.

These descriptive statistics pool all data together. Thus, in Table 6.2, we present descriptive statistics by economy. Notice that the large economies in the region (panel A) have both domestic and foreign plants. This sub-sample of economies carries the analysis to include domestic establishments and, as explained below, quality checks on the data can be made. Countries in panel B, only have data on foreign plants (i.e., plants with GUHs in a different country). Some of those countries, which are the poorest in Asia, have very few data points; nonetheless, these are kept in the analysis.

Table 6.2: Summary Statistics by Economy, WorldBase

| Economy | As Share of All Plants | | As Share of Domestic Plants | | As Share of Foreign Plants | | |
	Foreign	Exporters	Importers	Exporters and Importers	Exporters	Importers	Exporters and Importers
Panel A							
Australia	0.129	0.123	0.106	0.068	0.225	0.216	0.151
PRC	0.228	0.376	0.375	0.317	0.815	0.878	0.789
Hong Kong, China	0.410	0.480	0.340	0.278	0.480	0.292	0.237
Indonesia	0.498	0.367	0.320	0.230	0.521	0.524	0.415
India	0.022	0.155	0.144	0.111	0.469	0.392	0.350
Japan	0.008	0.033	0.033	0.026	0.202	0.310	0.183
Korea, Rep. of	0.136	0.448	0.326	0.283	0.438	0.447	0.356
Malaysia	0.634	0.598	0.598	0.478	0.711	0.694	0.648
New Zealand	0.111	0.200	0.200	0.100	0.000	0.200	0.000
Singapore	0.407	0.358	0.356	0.301	0.518	0.446	0.403
Thailand	0.306	0.433	0.378	0.304	0.722	0.784	0.661
Taipei,China	0.223	0.825	0.836	0.767	0.766	0.835	0.740
Panel B							
Afghanistan					0.000	0.000	0.000
Armenia					0.000	0.000	0.000
Azerbaijan					0.000	0.000	0.000
Bangladesh					0.100	0.400	0.100
Brunei Darussalam					0.167	0.500	0.167
Georgia					0.417	0.500	0.333
Kazakhstan					1.000	0.000	0.000
Kyrgyz Republic					0.000	0.000	0.000
Cambodia					0.407	0.481	0.370
Sri Lanka					0.357	0.357	0.286
Nepal					0.000	0.000	0.000
Pakistan					0.000	0.231	0.000
Philippines					0.661	0.729	0.579
Uzbekistan					0.286	0.000	0.000
Viet Nam					0.757	0.835	0.699

PRC = People's Republic of China.

Note: Panel A lists economies for which we have observations on domestic and foreign plants, while panel B lists economies for which we only have observations on foreign plants. Some economies in panel B have very few observations: Afghanistan 1; Armenia 4; Azerbaijan 8; Kazakhstan 1; the Kyrgyz Republic 3; and Nepal 4.

Source: Author's calculations using data from Dun & Bradstreet. D&B WorldBase.

It is reassuring that for the PRC, the fraction of foreign plants that export is around 82%, very similar to that reported by Defever and Riano (2015). Japan has the lowest penetration of foreign firms, as expected, and Viet Nam has among the highest shares of export-oriented foreign plants.

We use both the data on domestic and foreign establishments to further document well-established facts about exporters in the literature. This is meant to test the quality of the variable indicating the level of engagement in international trade of a given plant. We document that (i) exporters are larger than domestic firms, (ii) foreign establishments are larger than domestic establishments, and (iii) foreign affiliates that export are larger than affiliates that do not export (Figure 6.1). It is reassuring about the quality of the data that these standard facts in the literature hold here. Fact (i) has been documented extensively, starting by the early work of Bernard and Jensen (1997), for many countries for which firm-level data are available; it is also the reason for being for the Melitz model of trade. Fact (ii) has been documented with firm-level data by Helpman, Melitz, and Yeaple (2004), and for several other countries. Finally, fact (iii) is less documented since it is difficult to find data for the activities of multinationals at the firm level, even for one country. Researchers using the data for US multinationals from the Bureau of Economic Analysis have been able to document this fact (for instance, see Ramondo, Rappoport, and Ruhl [2015]).

Data on input–output links. An important variable in the analysis is our measure of production fragmentation within a corporation. We use the input–output table for the US for 2002, from the Bureau of Economic Analysis, and take the direct requirement coefficient between industry i and j. These coefficients indicate the amount of inputs produced by i that goes into the production of one dollar of output of industry j. We measure the input–output (IO) link between the (primary) industry of the affiliate and the (primary) industry of the parent by considering the direct requirement coefficient between their two industries: when the industry of the affiliate is upstream, we denote it by dr_{ap}, and when it is downstream from the industry of the parent, dr_{pa}. We say that there is strong a IO link between parent and affiliate when the direct requirement coefficient is bigger than zero—we make the appropriate distinction for upstream and downstream links. We restrict our attention to input–output links in the manufacturing sector.

Data on value-added trade. Now, we turn to the description of data on value-added trade. GVCs are associated with sequential production in which countries import intermediate goods, add value, and export final or intermediate goods to another country.

Figure 6.1: Exporters and Foreign Affiliates in WorldBase

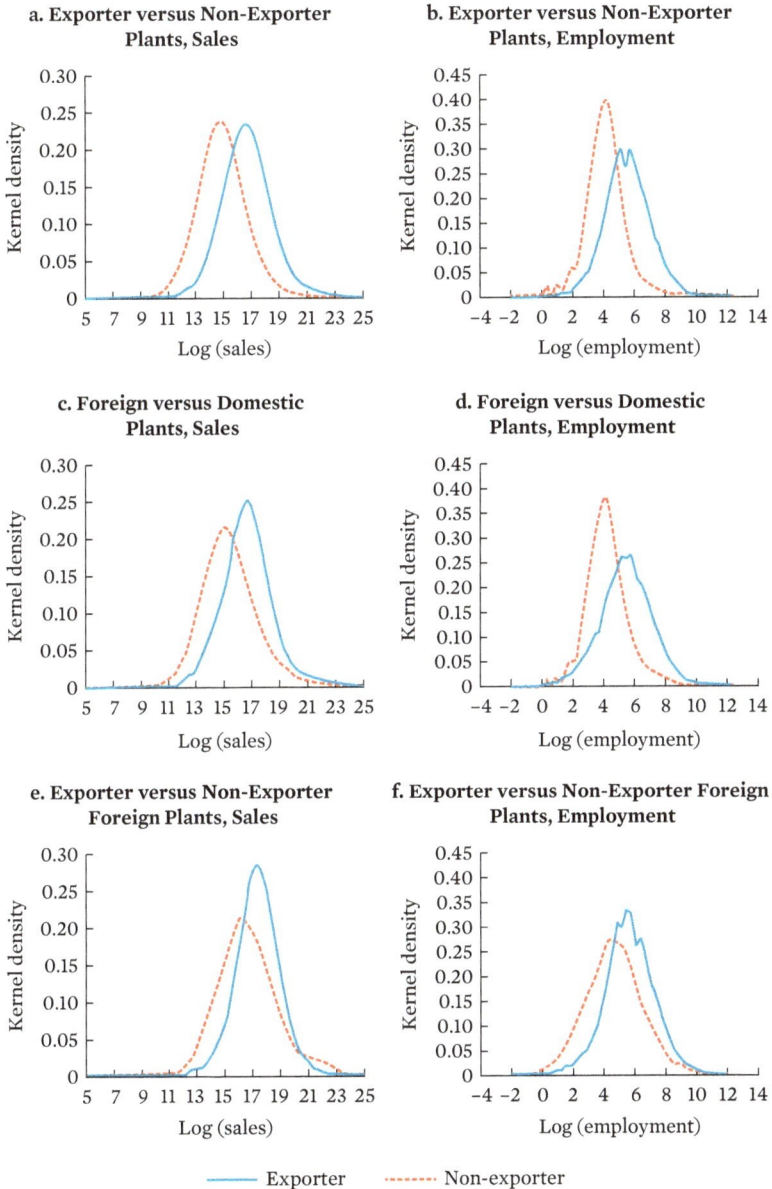

**a. Exporter versus Non-Exporter
Plants, Sales**

**b. Exporter versus Non-Exporter
Plants, Employment**

**c. Foreign versus Domestic
Plants, Sales**

**d. Foreign versus Domestic
Plants, Employment**

**e. Exporter versus Non-Exporter
Foreign Plants, Sales**

**f. Exporter versus Non-Exporter Foreign
Plants, Employment**

——— Exporter   -------- Non-exporter

Source: Author's calculations using data from Dun & Bradstreet. D&B WorldBase.

The more fragmented the production chain is, the more trade in intermediate goods should be observed, as well as a little bit of value added in different locations. Studies on the GVC have been done for very specific goods such as iPad and iPhone (Dedrick, Kraemer, and Linden 2010). Being only one good, the authors were able to calculate how much each participating country adds to the total final value of these goods. Such calculations reveal that the PRC, for instance, which has a high export flow in terms of gross value, only contributes to less than 4% of value added to the total value of an iPad. This happens because the iPad is produced through a long sequential production chain that involves many locations: the PRC receives many of the parts to assemble the iPad from other countries. Capturing this phenomenon more generally is not easy and requires very detailed data.

The crudest measure of GVC participation is trade in intermediate goods, as a share of total trade. The presumption that more trade in intermediate goods reflects more fragmentation of production, and hence, a higher participation in GVCs.

In their recent paper, Wang, Wei, and Zhu (2014) propose as a measure of value-added trade at the bilateral country-sector level the ratio of domestic value added that is exported and stays abroad.[12] The higher the share of valued added that is exported, and not re-exported, the lower the degree of vertical specialization. However, Wang, Wei, and Zhu (2014) explain that value-added export (VAX) may not capture important features of the international fragmentation of production. Two countries, in a given industry, may have the same VAX ratio but for very different reasons. For example, total electronics exports from the PRC and the US may have an identical VAX ratio, say 0.5, but occupy very different positions in the GVC. In the PRC case, this is because half of gross exports reflect foreign value added (e.g., value added from Japan, the Republic of Korea, and the US). In contrast, for US exports, half of the gross exports are US value added in intermediate goods used by other countries to produce goods that are re-exported to the US. In this example, only half of the US value added that is initially exported is ultimately absorbed abroad; the US VAX ratio is 0.5 even if it does not use any foreign value added in the production of its electronics exports.

Wang, Wei, and Zhu (2014) decompose the gross value of exports in several terms: domestic value added (DVA) that is ultimately absorbed abroad—an inverse measure of vertical specialization; foreign value added used in the

---

[12] This measure is always between 0 and 1.

production for exports (FVA); returned domestic value, or the portion of domestic value added that is initially exported and returned home embedded in imports (RDV); and pure double counted terms due to the back-and-forth intermediate goods trade (PDC). We use their measures of DVA and RDV, as a share of gross exports, which are available for 35 industries, including services industries, and 46 countries. We use their measures in our analysis in two ways: first, as dependent variables to briefly analyze the country and industry determinants of what we call GVC–trade; and second, as explanatory variables in the empirical analysis of the determinants of the activities of multinationals. The data are from the ADB Multi Regional Input–Output Tables, which produced a substantial extension in terms of time and country coverage of the World Input–Output Database.

Other Controls

Country-level variables used as controls in the analysis can be (broadly) divided in three groups: comparative advantages, institutions, and integration factors. The first group of controls includes variables such as the difference in real GDP per capita between source and host country, the difference in capital-labor ratios between source and host country, the share of skilled labor in total employment. The second group of controls includes indices of institutional quality (e.g., rule of law, level of corruption) and financial development, as used by Rajan and Zingales (1998) and Manova (2013). Integration factors include proxies for trade costs, such as distance and other common "gravity" variables, regional trade agreements, the cost to export and import, logistic infrastructure, and average applied tariffs. Most of these variables are from the World Development Indicators, World Governance Indicators, and the World Bank's Doing Business report for 2013. The degree of upstreamness of exports of a country, is also considered. This variable is constructed by Antras et al. (2012) and combine a measure of the upstreamness in production of each industry with the sectoral composition of exports. Basically, the measure of an industry position in the production process is aggregated to the country level using the share of exports in each industry. This variable ranges from 1.3 for Bangladesh to 3.36 for Kazakhstan, with a mean of 2, which corresponds to India.

Industry variables are also included in some parts of the analysis and interacted with the country variables. Research and development intensity of the industry, and other variables such as skill and capital intensities—which indicate the "factor intensity" of the industry—are included. These variables are from the US.

Table A6.1 has the complete list of the variables used in the analysis, and their sources.

Descriptive Analysis

Global Value Chain Trade in Asia

We start by showing some of the broad patterns observed in the data for measures of global value chain (GVC)–trade. A couple of examples illustrate how the measures of value-added trade work. First, Figure 6.2 shows the evolution of the VAX ratio, from Johnson (2014), an average across all the countries for which the data are available over 1995–2009—Asian countries, and selected individual countries. The figure also shows the evolution of the share of trade in intermediate goods; the pattern is very similar to the one observed for the VAX ratio.

The evolution of the VAX ratio hints that vertical specialization, or fragmentation of production, across borders has dramatically increased in the last 20 years. The same pattern is observed for Asian countries, even though their average share is 10 percentage points higher than the world average. This trend, however, masks a high degree of heterogeneity across countries. Figure 6.2b shows the VAX ratio for selected countries and compares two Asian countries, the PRC and India, with two Latin American countries, Mexico and Brazil. Mexico presents the lowest VAX ratio of the group—while Brazil has the highest—throughout the period, although both are fairly stable. In contrast, the PRC and India present drastic decreases in their VAX ratios indicating their increasing participation in the GVC.

Table 6.3 summarizes the shares of domestic and foreign value added of exports (DVA and FVA, respectively), and return domestic value (RDV). It is worth noting that the PRC and India substantially increased their shares of RDV, indicating outsourcing activities, such as assembly, to other countries may be occurring, providing those countries with inputs belonging to sectors more upstream in the production process.[13]

---

[13] The degree of export upstreamness of a country's exports is positively related to the DVA share; that is, if a country tends to produce in earlier stages of the GVC, the more the domestic value it adds to its exports.

Figure 6.2: Value-Added Export Ratios and Trade in Intermediate Goods

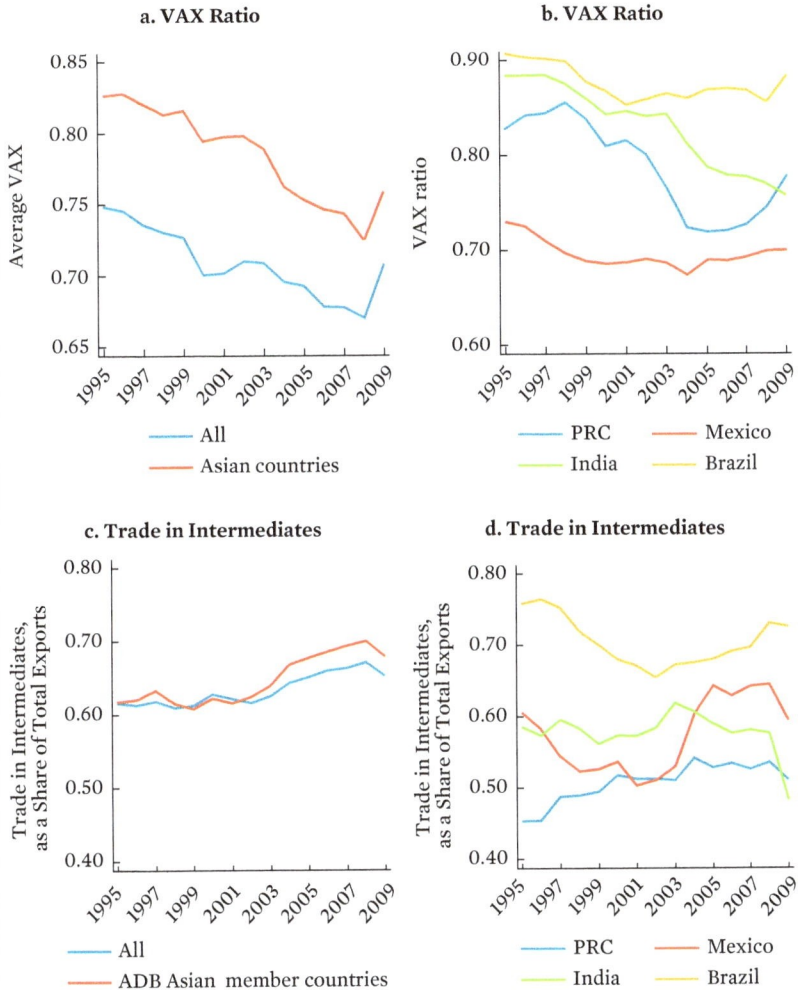

a. VAX Ratio

b. VAX Ratio

c. Trade in Intermediates

d. Trade in Intermediates

ADB = Asian Development Bank, PRC = People's Republic of China, VAX = value-added export.

Notes: The VAX ratio is the value added of exports as a share of gross exports, while trade in intermediate goods is a share of total trade, from Johnson (2014). The left panels show an average across countries, all and in Asia.

Source: Johnson, R. 2014. Five Facts about Value-Added Exports and Implications for Macroeconomics and Trade Research. *Journal of Economic Perspective.* 28 (2). pp. 119–42.

Table 6.3: Summary Statistics, Global Value Chain Trade

Value	All	ADB Members	Asian Members	Non Members	PRC	India
DVA						
2000	0.771	0.801	0.804	0.754	0.860	0.860
2014	0.782	0.814	0.810	0.768	0.851	0.876
FVA						
2000	0.166	0.140	0.142	0.181	0.102	0.103
2014	0.164	0.088	0.143	0.177	0.109	0.095
RDV						
2000	0.0043	0.0076	0.0031	0.0015	0.0050	0.0013
2014	0.0037	0.0128	0.0030	0.0018	0.0073	0.0027

DVA = domestic value added, FVA = foreign value added, PRC = People's Republic of China, RDV = return domestic value.

Note: DVA, FVA, and RDV of exports, are as shares of gross exports, an average across sectors and country-pairs.

Source: Author's calculations using data from Dun & Bradstreet. D&B WorldBase.

Global Value Chain–Foreign Direct Investment in Asia

We start by documenting broad patterns from the *WorldBase* data set regarding FDI and GVC–FDI.

Top country-pairs and industries for GVC–FDI. First, Tables 6.4 and 6.5 show the most popular economy-pairs and most popular industries of affiliates dedicated to GVC–FDI (i.e., with both import and export activities). Indeed, Japan is the most popular source of GVC–FDI, while the PRC is the most popular destination. In terms of industries, affiliates engaged in GVC–FDI are mainly in the motor vehicle components sector, electronics, machinery, and chemicals. Interestingly, a business service sector—telemarketing bureaus—shows up as the top eighth.

Outward FDI and outward GVC–FDI, selected sources. The diagrams in Figure 6.3 show the main destination of affiliates in Asia for Japanese, American, Chinese, and Indian multinationals. As expected, for Japan and the US, the main destination in Asia is the PRC, as a large and relatively cheap market. Of course, the share is higher for Japan due to its geographical proximity to the PRC. Less developed Asian countries such as Viet Nam and Indonesia are also popular destinations in Asia for Japanese multinationals, while the second most popular destination in Asia for US multinationals is Australia, an English-speaking country.

Table 6.4: GVC–FDI: Most Common Economy Pairs

Affiliate Economies	GUH Economy	Number of Affiliates that Import and Export
15. Singapore	Japan	164
14. Philippines	Japan	171
13. Malaysia	Japan	175
12. PRC	France	177
11. Taipei,China	Japan	212
10. Indonesia	Japan	214
9. Thailand	Japan	258
8. Viet Nam	Japan	306
7. PRC	Singapore	337
6. PRC	Republic of Korea	358
5. PRC	Taipei,China	401
4. PRC	Germany	625
3. PRC	United States	646
2. PRC	Hong Kong, China	1,314
1. PRC	Japan	2,260

FDI = foreign direct investment, GUH = global ultimate headquarters, GVC = global value chain, PRC = People's Republic of China.
Source: Author's calculations using data from Dun & Bradstreet. D&B WorldBase.

Table 6.5: GVC–FDI: Most Common Industries

Affiliate Industry	Number of Affiliates that Import and Export
15. Computer systems design services	391
14. Other engine equipment	395
13. All other miscellaneous general purpose machinery	433
12. All other petroleum and coal products	434
11. Plastics material and resin	465
10. Ethyl alcohol	477
9. Farm machinery and equipment	490
8. Telemarketing bureaus	532
7. Custom computer programming services	542
6. Semiconductor and related device	694
5. Paint and coating	710
4. Pharmaceutical preparation	859
3. Plastics pipe and pipe fitting	980
2. Other electronic component	1,358
1. Motor vehicle brake system	1,925

FDI = foreign direct investment, GVC = global value chain.
Source: Author's calculations using data from Dun & Bradstreet. D&B WorldBase.

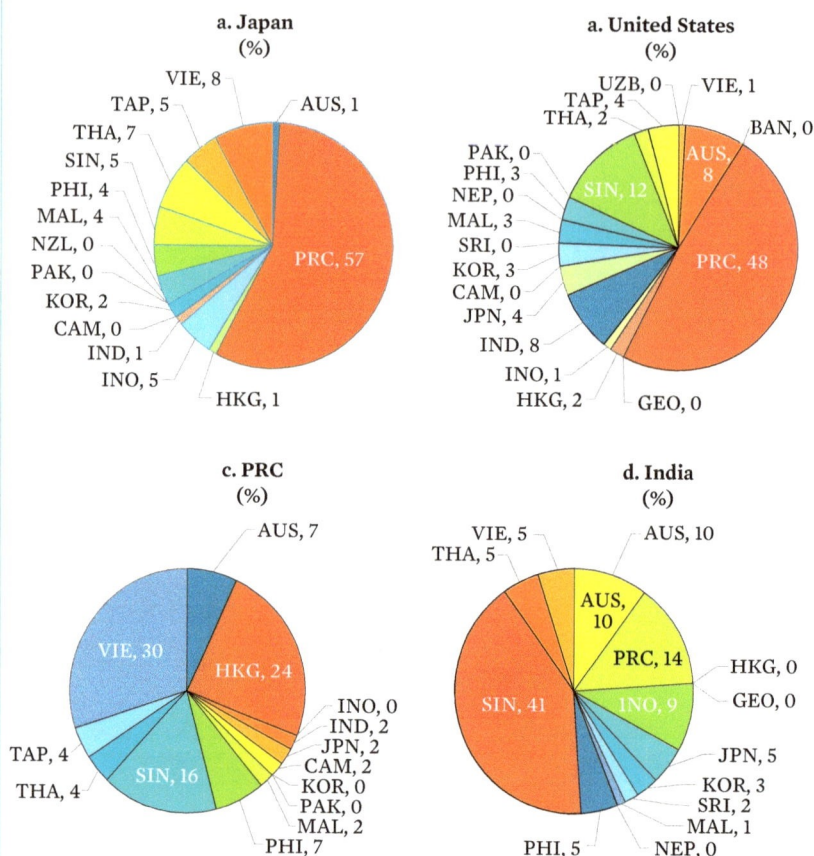

Figure 6.3: Outward GVC–FDI—Selected Source Economies

a. Japan (%)

a. United States (%)

c. PRC (%)

d. India (%)

AUS = Australia; BAN = Bangladesh; CAM = Cambodia; FDI = foreign direct investment; GEO = Georgia; GVC = global value chain; HKG = Hong Kong, China; IND = India; INO = Indonesia; JPN = Japan; KOR = Republic of Korea; MAL = Malaysia; NEP = Nepal; NZL = New Zealand; PAK = Pakistan; PHI = Philippines; PRC = People's Republic of China; SIN = Singapore; SRI = Sri Lanka; TAP = Taipei,China; THA = Thailand; UZB = Uzbekistan; VIE = Viet Nam.

Notes: Number of affiliates, in each economy, as a share of the total number of affiliates belonging to global ultimate headquarters from each of the selected economies.

Source: Author's calculations using data from Dun & Bradstreet. D&B WorldBase.

The PRC concentrates almost 30% of its foreign affiliates in Australia—the richest country in the area. That Hong Kong, China is the second most popular destination for PRC multinationals in our data set is not surprising: UNCTAD points out to a high flow of round-about FDI between the PRC and Hong Kong, China. The poorer countries in Asia account for more than 15% of outward FDI from the PRC. Indian multinationals in our data set choose Singapore, an economy specialized in the services sector, as their most popular destination. Perhaps, this distinct pattern is linked to the findings in Table 6.6, which shows that outward FDI for India is concentrated in business services: More than 50% of Indian affiliates abroad are in that sector, according to our data. The table also shows that Japanese multinationals in Asia are heavily concentrated in manufacturing, while PRC affiliates abroad are more diversified, and have a strong presence in mining.

Table 6.6: Outward Foreign Direct Investment: Selected Origin Economies, by Sector

Economies	Share of Foreign Plants in			
	Mining	Manufacturing	Business Services	Other
PRC	0.163	0.465	0.298	0.074
India	0.036	0.378	0.562	0.024
Thailand	0.029	0.619	0.105	0.248
Malaysia	0.041	0.589	0.342	0.027
Indonesia	0.100	0.500	0.400	0.000
Japan	0.012	0.885	0.096	0.007
Republic of Korea	0.010	0.913	0.069	0.008
Hong Kong, China	0.007	0.919	0.070	0.003
Taipei,China	0.003	0.935	0.054	0.008
Singapore	0.018	0.783	0.174	0.025
Australia	0.058	0.527	0.397	0.018
United States	0.016	0.590	0.388	0.006
Brazil	0.094	0.406	N/A	0.500
South Africa	0.167	0.444	0.333	0.056

PRC = People's Republic of China.
Note: Each row shows the fraction of affiliates from country n abroad in each sector. Each row should sum up to one.
Source: Author's calculations using data from Dun & Bradstreet. D&B WorldBase.

Inward FDI, selected host economies. Table 6.7 shows patterns across sectors of inward FDI for selected receiving economies. Interestingly, while inward FDI in the PRC and Viet Nam is concentrated in manufacturing, foreign affiliates in Hong Kong, China; Singapore; and especially India, are concentrated in business services. The pattern for GVC–FDI (i.e., affiliates engaged in both export and import activities) is similar to the overall distribution of FDI across sectors for each country (which is not shown).

Table 6.7: Inward Foreign Direct Investment: Selected Host Economies, by Sector

Economies	Share of Foreign Plants in			
	Mining	Manufacturing	Business Services	Other
PRC	0.006	0.924	0.069	0.001
India	0.012	0.587	0.399	0.002
Viet Nam	0.010	0.921	0.069	0.000
Malaysia	0.027	0.821	0.139	0.013
Singapore	0.022	0.460	0.494	0.025
Taipei,China	0.030	0.835	0.134	0.000
Hong Kong, China	0.007	0.172	0.817	0.004
Indonesia	0.044	0.831	0.091	0.034
Thailand	0.024	0.916	0.060	0.000
Republic of Korea	0.020	0.815	0.158	0.007
Japan	0.012	0.551	0.437	0.000
Australia	0.076	0.474	0.377	0.073

PRC = People's Republic of China.
Note: Each row shows the fraction of affiliates from country n abroad in each sector. Each row should sum up to one.
Source: Author's calculations using data from Dun & Bradstreet. D&B WorldBase.

GVC–FDI and source countries. Table 6.8 highlights an important issue regarding the origin of global ultimate headquarters (GUHs) and the activity of affiliates. We analyze whether there is any difference in engagement in GVC–FDI between affiliates with Asian and non-Asian GUH. We also look at differences between affiliates belonging to GUHs in developing Asian countries and the rest of the world.[14] Even though in a minority, foreign affiliates belonging to a GUH of Asian origin are much more engaged in international trade than affiliates abroad belonging to non-Asian GUHs. The effect is coming from affiliates belonging to multinationals from developed

[14] The group of developing Asian countries includes India, Indonesia, Malaysia, the PRC, and Thailand.

Asian countries (e.g., Japan and the Republic of Korea): Foreign affiliates of GUHs from developing Asia are less engaged in international trade than ones belonging to the rest of the world. The last two columns of the table shows statistics for affiliates of GUHs belonging to the PRC and India. The fraction of PRC affiliates abroad engaged in GVC–FDI is substantially smaller than those for India.

Table 6.8: Summary Statistics, by GUH Origin

Plants	Asia	Outside Asia	Developing Asia[a]	Rest of the World	PRC	India
All plants	203,132	26,998	86,094	144,036	31,297	52,008
Foreign plants (share of total)	0.05	0.37	0.01	0.14	0.007	0.005
Fraction that exports	0.73	0.52	0.43	0.63	0.35	0.48
Fraction that imports	0.76	0.53	0.37	0.66	0.27	0.37
Fraction that imports and exports	0.67	0.45	0.29	0.58	0.21	0.32

GUH = global ultimate headquarters, PRC = People's Republic of China.
[a] Includes India, Indonesia, Malaysia, the PRC, and Thailand.
Source: Author's calculations using data from Dun & Bradstreet. D&B WorldBase.

GVC–FDI and country and industry characteristics. The next figures and tables explore the relation between characteristics of the host country and engagement in the GVC. In particular, and novel in the literature, we document the relationship between GVC–trade and GVC–FDI.

We start by exploring the relationship between some important host country characteristics and GVC–FDI, overall and across sectors. Table 6.9 shows the average share of affiliates of foreign multinationals that are trade-oriented (i.e., have exports and imports), for two country groups with a value of a given characteristic below/above the median across countries. Overall, GVC–FDI is concentrated in countries with exports in more downstream sectors, weak rule of law, lower cost to export/import, lower capital–labor ratio, and lower income. This pattern repeats if we look by sector—and is less pronounced in the business service sector. The last three variables in the table are bilateral variables: countries have much more GVC–FDI if the foreign value added in their exports to the source country of affiliates, on average, is high, and their capital–labor ratio and real GDP per capita, with respect to the source country of the affiliates, is low.

Table 6.9: GVC–FDI and Country Characteristics

Sectors	All		Mining		Manufacturing		Business Services	
Country Variable wrt to Median	Low	High	Low	High	Low	High	Low	High
Export upstreamness	0.71	0.39	0.67	0.30	0.75	0.42	0.47	0.33
Rule of law	0.69	0.24	0.57	0.19	0.70	0.24	0.58	0.25
Cost to export (and import)	0.64	0.27	0.54	0.20	0.68	0.31	0.46	0.24
Capital–labor ratio (K/L)	0.61	0.32	0.37	0.34	0.66	0.32	0.43	0.31
Real GDP p.c. (rgdpl)	0.66	0.30	0.55	0.23	0.68	0.33	0.51	0.28
FVA share	0.16	0.64	0.15	0.54	0.16	0.68	0.16	0.48
KLd/KLo	0.64	0.29	0.44	0.23	0.67	0.30	0.46	0.29
rgdpld/rgdplo	0.63	0.32	0.48	0.22	0.67	0.35	0.44	0.30

FDI = foreign direct investment, GDP = gross domestic product, GVC = global value chain.
Note: Low/high refers to group of countries with the country characteristic in the rows below/above the median. The numbers shown in the columns refer to the average fraction of foreign affiliates that export and import in each group of countries, for all and each sector separately. The variable KLd/KLo (rgdpld/rgdplo) refers to the ratio of the capital–labor ratio (real GDP per capita) between the destination and origin country. The foreign value added (FVA) share is the bilateral foreign value added in exports from the host to the source country, as a share of gross bilateral exports.
Source: Author's calculations.

Table 6.10 presents an exhaustive list of country characteristics (averages) for two groups of plants: those engaged in international trade and those devoted to serving the market of operations for domestic and foreign plants. Country characteristics can be grouped into variables related to integration, comparative advantage, institutional environment (both governance and business environment), and GVC–trade.

Some differences are stark. First, plants engaged in international trade are located in countries with substantially lower cost to export—and import—and more so for foreign plants. While tariffs (at least in aggregate) and bilateral regional trade agreements do not seem to play major roles in attracting GVC–FDI, the presence of a bilateral investment treaty—particularly regarding the investor-state-of-dispute—and a double taxation treaty does.

Second, regarding comparative advantage motives, plants engaged in international trade are located in poorer countries, in line with the findings of the literature on horizontal versus vertical FDI, and in (unskilled) labor abundant countries. Moreover, these host countries have substantially lower development and capital than the countries from which the plants come from.

Table 6.10: GVC and Country Characteristics: Foreign and Domestic Firms

Country-level Variable	Average, All Plants		Average, Foreign Plants	
	Imports and Exports	Only Domestic Sales	Imports and Exports	Only Domestic Sale
Integration Variables				
Trade restrictiveness index	0.05	0.05	0.05	0.05
Burden of customs procedures	4.42	4.52	4.43	4.77
Cost to export ($ per container)	685	892	577	752
Cost to import ($ per container)	751	1,029	622	804
Number of documents to export	6.53	4.77	6.74	5.24
Number of documents to import	5.94	6.34	5.35	5.83
Logistics performance index	3.48	3.72	3.48	3.57
Quality of port infrastructure	4.56	4.79	4.55	4.93
Applied tariff rate	3.34	1.92	3.53	2.48
RTAs			0.34	0.36
BITs			0.55	0.38
BITs, investor-state-of-dispute			1.9	1.7
DTTs			0.91	0.78
Comparative Advantage Variables				
Real GDP per capita (rgdpl)	14,118	22,020	13,006	24,227
K-L ratio	89,872	176,996	76,379	156,101
Average year schooling	7.64	9.00	7.61	8.73
log rgdpl, host rel. to source	−0.44	−0.03	−1.32	−0.75
log K-L ratio, host relative to source	−0.50	−0.04	−1.51	−0.78
Institutional variables rule of law	0.10	0.83	−0.09	0.68
Regulatory quality	0.12	0.61	0.05	0.76
Government effectiveness	0.36	0.95	0.27	0.87
Control of corruption	0.06	0.84	−0.05	0.69
Political stability	−0.28	0.25	−0.29	0.23
Voice and accountability	−0.51	0.60	−0.95	0.12
Days required to enforce a contract	345	356	390	353

continued on next page

Table 6.10 continued

Country-level Variable	Average, All Plants		Average, Foreign Plants	
	Imports and Exports	Only Domestic Sales	Imports and Exports	Only Domestic Sale
Number of procedures to register a business start-up	5.26	3.6	6.6	4.45
Cost of business start-up procedures (% of GNI)	7.1	3.1	8.6	4.7
Days to get electricity	50.4	61.8	57.9	58.9
Days required to register property	18.6	8.8	27.1	16.4
Days required to start business	11.9	5.1	17.1	8.2
Time spent dealing with government regulations	0.90	0.90	0.90	0.90
Hours required to prepare and pay taxes	222	134	304	168
Private credit (% of GDP)	0.81	1.09	0.46	0.91
GVC–Trade Variables				
DVA share	0.72	0.79	0.72	0.79
FVA share	0.21	0.16	0.21	0.16
Export upstreamness (overall)	1.99	2.05	1.97	2.20

BIT = bilateral investment treaty, DTT = double taxation treaty, DVA = domestic value added, FVA = foreign value added, GDP = gross domestic product, GNI = gross national income, GVC = global value chain, K-L = capital–labor, RTA = regional trade agreement.

Note: "Time spent dealing with government regulations" is measured in percentage of senior management time. Integration variables (expect for RTAs, BITs, and DTTs) and institutional variables are from the World Bank (World Governance Indicators and World Development Indicators), for 2013. DVA and FVA shares refer to the domestic and foreign value added, respectively, as a share of gross exports, at the bilateral level.

Source: Author's calculations.

Figure 6.4 shows in more detail the relationship between the difference in real GDP per capita between host and source country and the fraction of foreign affiliates engaged in bilateral international trade. On average, a source country with an income of double that of the host country has a 17% larger fraction of GVC–FDI (i.e., affiliates that both export and import, as a share of the total number of affiliates from the same source). Additionally, Figure 6.4b shows that a traditional motive, such as distance between host and source markets, have a negative effect on GVC–FDI: Country-pairs twice as far have a 12% lower fraction of affiliates engaged in GVC–FDI.

Figure 6.4: Comparative Advantage, Geography, and GVC–FDI

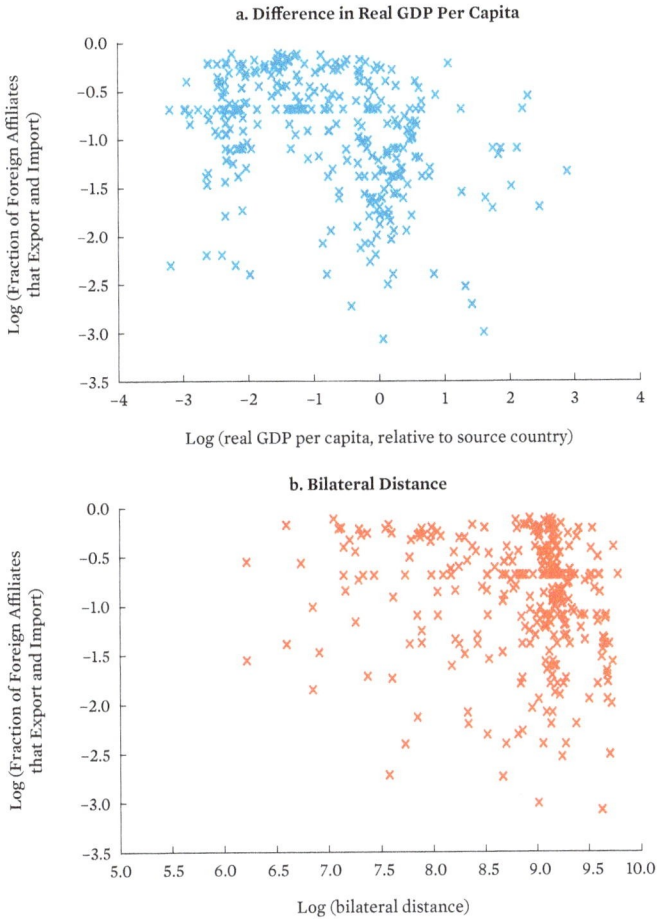

FDI = foreign direct investment, GDP = gross domestic product, GVC = global value chain.

Notes: The y-axis variable i is the number of affiliates in "country" c belonging to parents in n that export, as a share of total affiliates in country c belonging to parents in n. The x-axis variable is the log (real GDP per capita) and log (bilateral distance) for panels a and b, respectively, of the host relative to the source economy. In all cases origin and destination countries are different ($c \neq n$). The OLS coefficient for a fitted line is -0.17 (standard error: 0.03) for the top chart and -0.12 (standard error: 0.05) for the bottom panel chart.

Sources: Author's calculations using data from ADB Multiregional Input–Output Tables; and methodology by Wang, Wei, and Zhu (2014); Institute for Research on the International Economy. http://www.cepii.fr/ CEPII/en/cepii/cepii.asp (accessed July 2016); Penn World Tables 8.1. http://cid.econ.ucdavis.edu/pwt.html (accessed July 2016); and World Bank, World Development Indicators. http://data.worldbank.org/ data-catalog/world-development-indicators (accessed July 2016).

Third, institutional variables capturing governance aspects of the host country all present lower averages in countries where affiliates engaged in international trade are located. This is also the case for the variables related to "doing business" in the country. This is intuitive because firms care more about the "rule of law" when their activities are directly linked to the domestic market; if their main activity is to export, the institutional environment may matter less—particularly because these affiliates may be "shielded" from the regulatory and business environment of the country of production through special legislation and special economic zones (SEZs). Table 6.11 shows the SEZs and GVC–FDI in developing Asian countries: even if the number of observations is low, more SEZs are associated with more GVC–FDI.

Table 6.11: Special Economic Zones and GVC–FDI

Countries	Number of SEZs	SEZ per square kilometer	GVC–FDI (%)
Bangladesh	8	0.00006	10
Cambodia	14	0.00008	41
India	199	0.00007	47
Kazakhstan	10	0.000004	100
PRC	1,475	0.00016	82
Philippines	312	0.001041	66
Sri Lanka	12	0.00019	36

FDI = foreign direct investment, GVC = global value chain, PRC = People's Republic of China, SEZ = special economic zone.
Note: The number of SEZ is for 2014. GVC–FDI refers to the fraction of foreign affiliates in the country that exports, as a percentage of foreign affiliates in the country.
Source: ADB. 2016. *Asian Economic Integration Report*. Manila.

Finally, trade-oriented affiliates are located in countries with exports concentrated in more downstream sectors and with less domestic—and more foreign—value added. Figure 6.5 explores in more detail the relationship between GVC–trade and GVC–FDI. GVC–trade is measured in four ways: bilateral DVA share, bilateral FVA share, difference in export upstreamness between the host and source country, and differences in DVA shares between host and source countries. Figures 6.5a and 6.5b show the two sides of the same token: the DVA and FVA content of exports in the host country is correlated with the fraction of trade-oriented foreign plants, at the bilateral level. That is, when a country is part of a GVC that is twice as fragmented, as manifested in a lower DVA (and higher FVA), it attracts three times as many affiliates engaged in GVC–FDI; if we consider FVA shares instead, the magnitude of the effect is 55%.

Figure 6.5: Trade and GVC–FDI, Bilateral Level

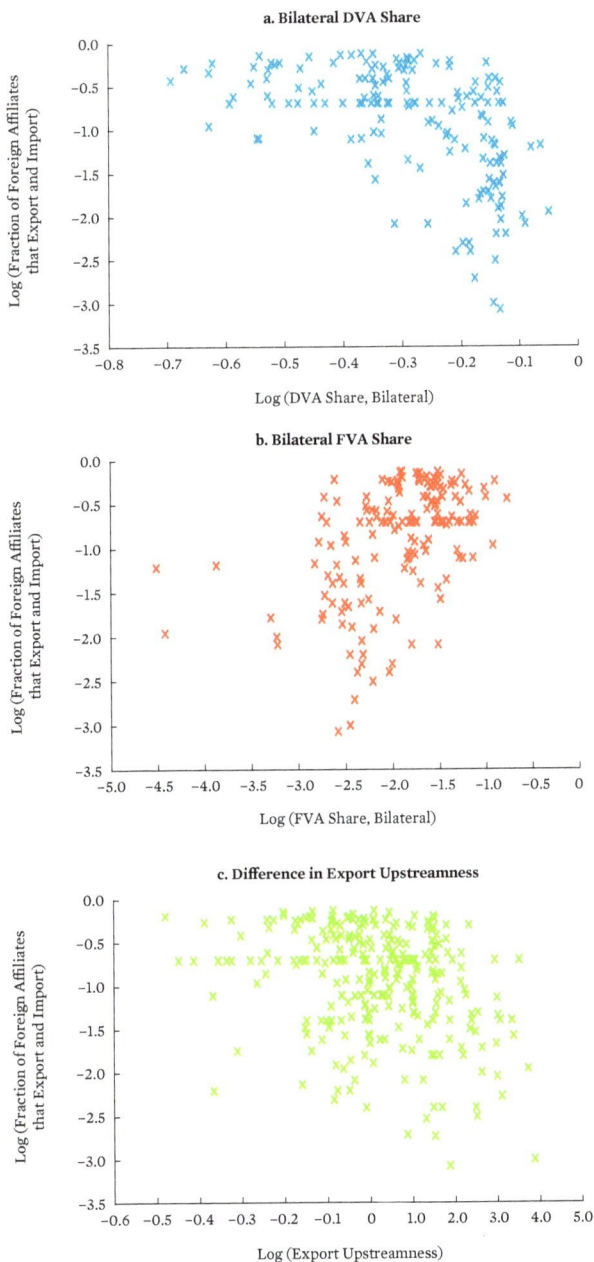

a. Bilateral DVA Share

Y-axis: Log (Fraction of Foreign Affiliates that Export and Import)

X-axis: Log (DVA Share, Bilateral)

b. Bilateral FVA Share

Y-axis: Log (Fraction of Foreign Affiliates that Export and Import)

X-axis: Log (FVA Share, Bilateral)

c. Difference in Export Upstreamness

Y-axis: Log (Fraction of Foreign Affiliates that Export and Import)

X-axis: Log (Export Upstreamness)

continued on next page

Figure 6.5 continued

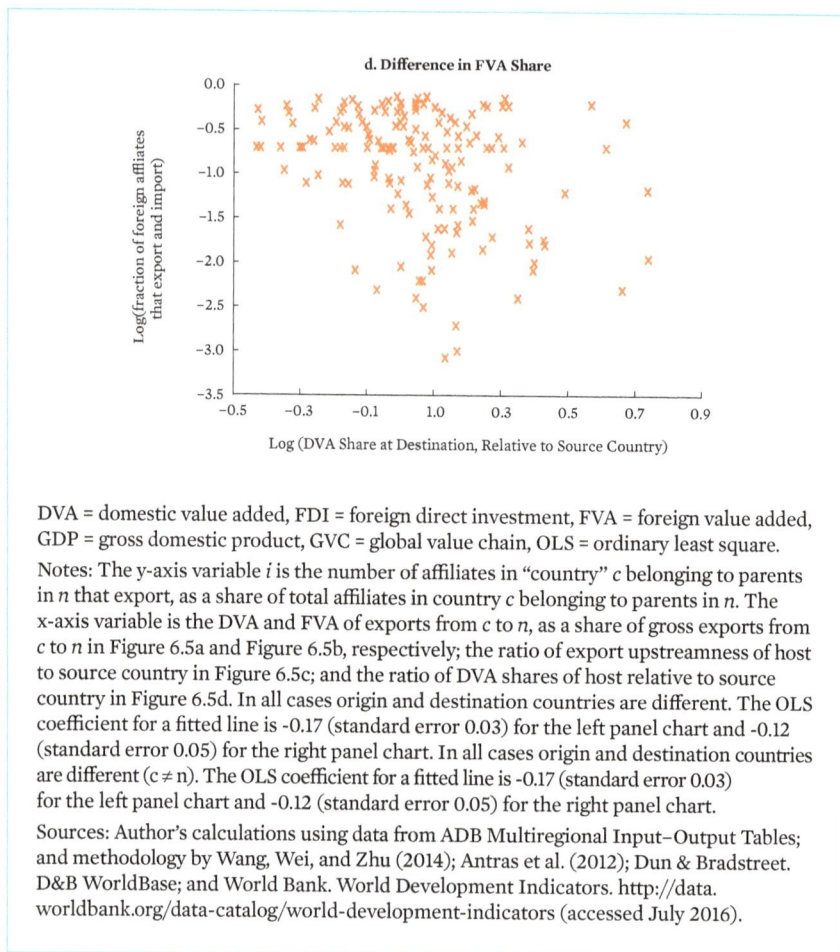

d. Difference in FVA Share

DVA = domestic value added, FDI = foreign direct investment, FVA = foreign value added, GDP = gross domestic product, GVC = global value chain, OLS = ordinary least square.

Notes: The y-axis variable i is the number of affiliates in "country" c belonging to parents in n that export, as a share of total affiliates in country c belonging to parents in n. The x-axis variable is the DVA and FVA of exports from c to n, as a share of gross exports from c to n in Figure 6.5a and Figure 6.5b, respectively; the ratio of export upstreamness of host to source country in Figure 6.5c; and the ratio of DVA shares of host relative to source country in Figure 6.5d. In all cases origin and destination countries are different. The OLS coefficient for a fitted line is -0.17 (standard error 0.03) for the left panel chart and -0.12 (standard error 0.05) for the right panel chart. In all cases origin and destination countries are different ($c \neq n$). The OLS coefficient for a fitted line is -0.17 (standard error 0.03) for the left panel chart and -0.12 (standard error 0.05) for the right panel chart.

Sources: Author's calculations using data from ADB Multiregional Input–Output Tables; and methodology by Wang, Wei, and Zhu (2014); Antras et al. (2012); Dun & Bradstreet. D&B WorldBase; and World Bank. World Development Indicators. http://data.worldbank.org/data-catalog/world-development-indicators (accessed July 2016).

Moreover, Figure 6.5b shows that the higher the level of export upstreamness of the host relative to the source country of the affiliates, the more intense is the GVC–FDI activity of those affiliates in the host country. Conversely, countries with a small share of GVC–FDI tend to have exports in more upstream sectors than the source countries of foreign affiliates; multinationals do not locate their exporter affiliates in those countries. The effects are large: increasing the difference in exports upstreamness from the median (1) to the 99th percentile (1.24), implies an increase in the fraction of trade-oriented foreign affiliates of 30% (e.g., from the 60% share of GVC–FDI from Germany in Viet Nam, to the one from the PRC in Viet Nam of 77%).

Finally, if one looks at the differences in DVA shares between exports of the host relative to the source country of the affiliates, the results are similar: the lower the share of local value added embedded in exports of the host country of the affiliates—relative to the source country—the higher the fraction of affiliates engaged in GVC–FDI. All this is extremely suggestive evidence that trade-oriented affiliates of multinationals are part of the GVC. These relations are now explored more formally.

GVC and growth. The last descriptive results explore the following question: Is there a relationship between engagement in the GVC, both through FDI and trade, and a country's growth? Some evidence is provided in Table 6.12. Low/high FDI refers to countries with sales of foreign plants, as a share of total sales, below/above the median share across countries; low/high GVC–FDI refers to countries with a fraction of foreign plants that export below/above the median share across countries; and low/high GVC–trade refers to countries with a DVA share above/below the median share across countries. For countries in each group, the median annual (average) growth rate of real GDP per capita, from 2000 to 2010, is computed. Even though observations are not many, the results are suggestive: countries with high engagement in GVC–FDI, GVC–trade, and/or high presence of large foreign plants grew more. Attracting large foreign plants that engage in GVC–FDI seems to be really important for higher growth: the median country with high GVC–FDI grew substantially faster than the median country with a low level of attraction of foreign plants engaged in export activities.

Table 6.12: Engagement in the GVC and Growth

GVC Engagement	Low	High	Observations
GVC–Trade	2.1%	3.3%	8
GVC–FDI	2.8%	3.6%	27
FDI Intensity	2.5%	3.4%	12

DVA = domestic value added, FDI = foreign direct investment, GVC = global value chain.

Note: Annual average growth rate of real GDP per capita, for 2000-2010, median among countries in each group. Low/high FDI intensity refers to countries with sales of foreign plants, as a share of total sales, below/above the median share across countries. Low/high GVC–FDI refers to countries with a fraction of foreign plants that export below/above the median share across countries. Low/high GVC–trade refers to countries with DVA shares above/below the median across countries.

Sources: Author's calculations using data from ADB Multiregional Input–Output Tables; and methodology by Wang, Wei, and Zhu (2014); and Dun & Bradstreet. D&B WorldBase.

Econometric Analysis

Determinants of GVC–FDI

Country and industry determinants. We now turn to the regression analysis of the determinants of GVC–FDI. In the first set of regressions, we use as our dependent variable a dummy variable that indicates whether the establishment exports and imports (1) or not (0). As shown in the descriptive section, most establishments have both sides of international trade flows; only a few only export or only import. This regression is the baseline regression of this chapter: it precisely captures at the affiliate level domestic versus trade-oriented activities, and it informs, as it could not be done before, the literature on horizontal versus vertical FDI.

Controls in this regression include variables at the affiliate level, country level, country-pair level, and interactions between country and industry variables; in absorbed by industry effects. Alternately, industry-level variables, and their interaction with country variables, are considered and country-level factors are subsumed in fixed effects.

Among country-level variables, we include integration, institutional, and comparative advantage variables, and some related to GVC–trade, including the upstreamness of exports and the share of domestic value in exports. The specification is estimated for all plants in the data and for plants with GUHs in a different country (i.e., foreign affiliates of multinationals). Results are shown in Tables 6.13 and 6.14.

Plants engaged in international trade are consistently larger than plants devoted to serving their market of operations: a 10% larger plant in sales is 30% more likely to be engaged in international trade activities. The estimates suggest that we should find these plants more often in smaller economies, but the effect is somewhat smaller for foreign plants. Because it is common to assume that there are fixed costs of opening and operating a plant, that multinationals have plants in smaller markets suggests their fixed costs might be somehow smaller, and it may well be—as suggested by the seminal work of Markusen (1984)—that economies of scale operate at the multinational level, not the plant level. Another possibility is that the size of the market in which they decide to open affiliates is not very important because multinationals use those locations to serve the global market, not only Asia; in other words, they have a much larger market than other (non-multinational) exporters in the region.

Table 6.13: Determinants of GVC–FDI: Country Variables
(ordinary least squares)

Country-level Variable	Dependent Variable: D (exports >0 and imports >0)									
	(1)	(2)	(3)	(4)	(5)	(6)	(7)	(8)	(9)	(10)
Log (affiliate sales)	0.030**	0.023**	0.030**	0.046**	0.029**	0.038**	0.036**	0.037**	0.044**	0.038**
	(0.001)	(0.001)	(0.001)	(0.002)	(0.001)	(0.002)	(0.002)	(0.002)	(0.003)	(0.002)
Log (real GDP)	-0.055**	-0.129**	-0.009*	-0.104**	0.013**	-0.030**	-0.092**	0.013**	-0.059**	0.032**
	(0.003)	(0.005)	(0.004)	(0.006)	(0.004)	(0.005)	(0.007)	(0.005)	(0.008)	(0.004)
Log (real GDP per capital)	0.780**	-0.001	0.570**	1.082**	0.121**	0.714**	0.095	0.671**	0.940**	0.150*
	(0.028)	(0.048)	(0.029)	(0.026)	(0.043)	(0.046)	(0.076)	(0.052)	(0.069)	(0.061)
Log (capital–labor ratio)	-0.517**	-0.089	-0.667**	-1.225**	-0.363**	-0.495**	-0.173+	-0.777**	-1.056**	-0.525**
	(0.029)	(0.058)	(0.032)	(0.030)	(0.032)	(0.053)	(0.092)	(0.062)	(0.084)	(0.056)
Log (years of schooling)	-0.006+	-0.038**	-0.005	0.063**	0.062**	-0.010+	-0.029**	0.021**	0.053**	0.118**
	(0.004)	(0.005)	(0.004)	(0.006)	(0.009)	(0.005)	(0.008)	(0.007)	(0.009)	(0.013)
Rule of law	-0.425**					-0.296**				
	(0.014)					(0.016)				
Private credit		0.227**					0.227**			
		(0.025)					(0.030)			
Trade restrictiveness index (host economy)			-3.397**					-3.446**		
			(0.261)					(0.269)		
Export upstreamness				-0.704**					-0.548**	
				(0.031)					(0.043)	
× Capital intensity of industry				-0.002					0.009+	
				(0.003)					(0.005)	
Exporter DVA share					-1.852**					-1.034**
					(0.071)					(0.085)

continued on next page

Table 6.13 continued

Country-level Variable					Dependent Variable: D (exports >0 and imports >0)					
	(1)	(2)	(3)	(4)	(5)	(6)	(7)	(8)	(9)	(10)
D(Asian GUH)	1.058**	-0.005	-0.062**	-0.945**	-0.881**	0.118	-0.009	0.032	-0.190*	0.124
	(0.171)	(0.021)	(0.015)	(0.068)	(0.073)	(0.232)	(0.029)	(0.020)	(0.074)	(0.087)
× Rule of law	0.229**					0.012				
	(0.019)					(0.024)				
× Log (real GDP per capita)	-0.131**					-0.012				
	(0.019)					(0.025)				
× Private credit		-0.028					0.003			
		(0.020)					(0.028)			
× Trade restrictiveness index			0.136					-0.097		
			(0.268)					(0.393)		
× Export upstreamness				0.403**					0.108**	
				(0.033)					(0.038)	
× Export DVA share					0.998**					-0.151
					(0.093)					(0.118)
Observations	60,138	41,814	57,852	34,683	56,000	17,126	8,581	15,458	12,256	14,344
R-squared	0.395	0.321	0.378	0.370	0.402	0.351	0.283	0.355	0.200	0.375
Sample	all	all	all	all	all	foreign	foreign	foreign	foreign	foreign

DVA = domestic value added, GDP = gross domestic product, GUH = global ultimate headquarters.

Notes: The dependent variable is a dummy variable equal to one if the plant reports export and import activity. Country-level variables are for the country the plant is located. The variable "private credit" refers to private credit as share of GDP. The variable "TRI" refers to the trade restrictiveness index from the World Bank. The variable "exp. upstreamness" refers to the level of export upstreamness of the host country. DVA is calculated as a share of gross exports of the destination country, at the country level, an average across years, for all sectors. The dummy D(Asian GUH) equals one if the plant belongs to a GUH in Asia. kl indicates the (log) capital intensity, with respect to labor, of the industry of the affiliate. In columns 1–5, domestic plants which are also GUHs are excluded. All specifications with affiliate industry fixed effects. Standard errors, clustered at the parent level, in parentheses. Levels of significance are denoted by ** p<0.01, * p<0.05, + p<0.1.

Source: Author's calculations.

Table 6.14: Determinants of GVC–FDI: Industry Variables
(ordinary least squares)

Country-level Variable	Dependent Variable: D(exports>0 & imports >0)					
	(1)	(2)	(3)	(4)	(5)	(6)
Log (affiliate sales)	0.046**	0.047**	0.049**	0.049**	0.050**	0.050 **
	(0.002)	(0.002)	(0.002)	(0.003)	(0.003)	(0.003)
Log (capital intensity of industry)	−0.197**	−0.054**	−0.038**	−0.177*	−0.056*	−0.047 *
	(0.072)	(0.014)	(0.015)	(0.083)	(0.022)	(0.022)
× Export upstreamness	0.068*			0.060+		
	(0.028)			(0.035)		
Log (SL)	0.019	0.031*	0.016	−0.009	−0.008	−0.020
	(0.013)	(0.016)	(0.016)	(0.024)	(0.025)	(0.026)
R&D	0.593**	0.247	0.486*	0.351	0.335	0.483
	(0.179)	(0.192)	(0.198)	(0.330)	(0.351)	(0.344)
D(DRAP > 0 & DRPA > 0)	0.005			0.026+		
	(0.009)			(0.015)		
Average DRAP		0.736*			0.343	
		(0.311)			(0.340)	
Average DRPA			1.335*			0.807
			(0.545)			(0.645)
D (Asian GUH)	−0.198+	−0.249**	−0.190*	−0.484**	−0.472**	−0.444 **
	(0.104)	(0.071)	(0.079)	(0.120)	(0.117)	(0.125)
× Log (capital intensity of industry)	0.047*	0.016	0.009	0.055*	0.053*	0.047*
	(0.021)	(0.015)	(0.016)	(0.023)	(0.022)	(0.023)
× Average DRAP		0.303			−0.224	
		(0.331)			(0.368)	
× Average DRPA			−0.654			−0.047
			(0.599)			(0.755)
Observations	17,607	17,607	17,607	6,393	6,393	6,393
R-squared	0.424	0.354	0.351	0.220	0.219	0.220
Sample	all	all	all	foreign	foreign	foreign

DRAP = direct requirement coefficient from affiliate industry to parent industry; DRPA = direct requirement coefficient from parent industry to affiliate industry; GUH = global ultimate headquarters; R&D = research and development; SL = skill intensity of industry, nonproduction employment over total employment.

Notes: The dependent variable is a dummy variable equal to one if the establishment reports export and import activity. The variable "kl" refers to the (log) capital intensity of the industry, relative to labor, while *sl* refers to the (log) skill intensity of the industry, relative to (unskilled) labor. The dummy D(*drap* > 0 & *drpa* > 0) is equal to one when both direct requirement coefficients (i.e., when the affiliate is upstream and downstream of the parent) are higher than zero. Avg *drap* (*drpa*) refers to the average direct requirement coefficient of the industry of the affiliate, with respect to downstream (upstream) industries. The dummy D(Asian GUH) is one if the plant has an Asian GUH. Only plants that are not GUH and in the manufacturing sector. All specifications with source and destination fixed effects. Standard errors, clustered at the parent level, in parentheses. Levels of significance are denoted by ** p<0.01, * p<0.05, + p<0.1.

Source: Author's calculations.

Richer markets—contrary to what was seen in raw statistics—also attract more trade-oriented plants, once we control for the capital–labor ratio, the size of the market, and other industry characteristics. Consistent with the descriptive evidence, a higher capital–labor ratio at destination is associated with less trade-engaged plants. This suggests that, in Asia, GVC–FDI seeks labor-abundant countries. The quality of institutions, captured by the rule of law index, is an important factor in creating plants oriented to serving the domestic market; the association is weaker for foreign plants. The availability of private credit in a country also seems to matter in attracting trade-oriented plants. As expected, the degree of trade restrictiveness deters the creation of trade-oriented plants.

Turning to the factors related to GVC–trade, the estimates suggest that countries with exports in more upstream sectors are less likely to have trade-oriented plants. For instance, when the level of export upstreamness goes from the 50th percentile to the 95th percentile (this is like giving Japan the levels of export upstreamness of Australia), the probability of observing a foreign plant that exports decreases by more than 35% (from a mean of 45% to 30%). The effect is slightly mitigated in capital-intensive industries for the case of foreign plants. Similarly, the DVA share of a country's exports is associated negatively with the presence of GVC–FDI: an increase in the DVA bilateral share from the median (0.74) to the 95th percentile (0.88)—this is like giving the DVA share in exports from India to the PRC, the share from India to Japan—is associated with a decrease in GVC–FDI of 16% (e.g., from the mean for Chinese affiliates abroad to the mean for Indian affiliates abroad).

The last rows of the table are devoted to explore more systematically the differences in the impact of country variables depending on the origin of the affiliates' GUHs. The coefficient on the dummy indicating Asian and non-Asian affiliates is either negative or insignificant among foreign affiliates, once we control for host-market characteristics, in contrast with the raw statistics that states showed that Asian multinationals were more likely to be engaged in GVC–FDI. This result, most likely, points to a selection effect: Asian GUHs choose to locate their affiliates in markets that are friendlier to trade activities; once those characteristics are controlled, there is nothing special about belonging to an Asian corporation in terms of engagement in GVC–FDI.

The only variable that presents a significant difference between Asian and non-Asian GUH origins, when only foreign plants are considered, is the export upstreamness of a receiving country: The negative effect on GVC–FDI is significantly dampened for affiliates of Asian GUHs. That is, a country with exports in more upstream sectors is less likely to attract GVC–FDI, but if the affiliate belongs to an Asia GUH, that likelihood increases. Similarly, the estimates suggest that if the foreign affiliate belongs to an Asian GUH, given everything else, is less likely to be engaged in GVC–FDI, but if the host country is specialized in more upstream sectors, that likelihood increases.

Industry factors affecting GVC–FDI are shown in Table 6.14. GVC–FDI is attracted by less capital-intensive industries; the skill intensity of an industry and the level of R&D intensity do not seem to matter for GVC–FDI, but both factors seem to matter more for the trade engagement of domestic plants. Input–output links between the industry of the affiliate and the industry of the parent are positively, but weakly, related to GVC–FDI. When we consider the average direct requirement coefficient of the industry of the affiliate when that industry is upstream (avg dr_{ap}) or downstream (avg dr_{pa}), alternately, we find a positive association between being a more important input for other industries—or being a more important output for other industries—and the likelihood that a plant engages in international trade. Moving from the median industry (with avg dr_{ap} = 0.016) to the 90th percentile industry (with avg dr_{ap} = 0.076) increases the probability of observing a plant that exports and imports by more than 6%.

Finally, distinguishing between Asian and non-Asian GUH origins does not affect the results for input–output links, but it matters for the effect of capital intensity: plants of Asian GUHs are more likely to export and import if they are in more capital-intensive industries, relative to plants belonging to GUHs from other origins. Again, the coefficient on the dummy indicating Asian origin of the GUH is significantly negative: once we control for the industry characteristics of the affiliate, being Asian decreases the likelihood of the affiliate of being engaged in GVC–FDI. As above, the explanation can be based on selection: these Asian multinationals choose to open affiliates in industries that more easily engage in GVC–FDI; once we control for those industry features, affiliates of Asian GUHs are more likely to be horizontal (this may be due to a better knowledge of the local Asian markets).

Gravity. We turn now to investigate a standard relationship in the trade and multinational literature: the gravity equation. This equation states that the flow of firms (or goods) between two countries should be inversely proportional to bilateral resistance factors, such as geographical distance. Following the state-of-the-art in estimating gravity equations, we subsumed destination and origin country factors in two sets of country-fixed effects.

The regressions shown in Table 6.15 are meant to establish "gravity" facts for Asian countries, using direct measures of *bilateral* affiliates activity, such as sales, and of bilateral GVC–FDI. A similar analysis using variables directly related to the activity of affiliates of multinationals, not balance of payment FDI flows (or FDI stocks), is presented in Ramondo (2014) and Ramondo, Rodriguez-Clare, and Tintelnot (2015). The main difference with their work is that, thanks to the access to WorldBase, the sample of country-pairs involving countries in Asia has significant detail.

Specifications in all columns of Table 6.15 are aggregated at the bilateral level; that is, the dependent variable is, for instance in columns 1–3, sales of affiliates in country n belonging to GUHs in country i. Moreover, we augment the standard gravity specification by a variable related to GVC–trade: the *bilateral* domestic value-added embedded in gross exports from the host to the origin country of the foreign affiliates (columns 3 and 6 in Table 6.15).

The effects of distance are negative and the coefficient is closer to one, as found in the literature. However, the effect of distance drops and lose significance in the case of GVC–FDI (columns 4–6), most likely because distance refers to proximity between the country of the affiliate and the one of its GUH, but exports/imports can be to/from any other country. Sharing a language has a positive effect on the bilateral activity of affiliates of multinationals, as does belonging to the same regional trade agreement and having signed a double taxation treaty. Having an regional trade agreement or a double taxation treaty between countries does not affect the fraction of affiliates that are trade-oriented, and the presence of a bilateral investment treaty between two countries discourages trade-related affiliates' activities in favor of horizontal FDI.[15]

Differences in income between the origin and destination countries significantly encourage multinational activity when the destination is the poorer country and, as shown above, also encourage trade-related activities of affiliates. Similarly, GVC–FDI at the bilateral level increases with the labor abundance of the receiving country, relative to the source country.

---

[15] This does not contradict the findings in Table 6.10 that show that trade-oriented affiliates are located in countries that, on average, signed more bilateral investment treaties; the result in Table 6.15, apart from including several other controls and being at the country-pair level, is about the intensive margin of GVC–FDI—i.e., bilateral investment treaties affect the fraction of trade-engaged affiliates.

Table 6.15: Determinants of Bilateral FDI and GVC–FDI: Gravity (ordinary least squares)

Country-level Variable	Affiliate Sales			Fraction of Affiliates with Exports and Imports		
	(1)	(2)	(3)	(4)	(5)	(6)
Log (distance)	–1.360**	–1.360**	–1.093*	0.069	0.069	0.131
	(0.284)	(0.284)	(0.461)	(0.085)	(0.085)	(0.173)
D(shared language)	0.801**	0.801**	1.209*	0.071	0.071	0.039
	(0.296)	(0.296)	(0.548)	(0.099)	(0.099)	(0.162)
D(shared colonial past)	0.349	0.349	–0.211	–0.047	–0.047	–0.096
	(0.400)	(0.400)	(0.510)	(0.113)	(0.113)	(0.147)
D(RTA)	1.724**	1.724**	1.347**	0.013	0.013	–0.005
	(0.276)	(0.276)	(0.452)	(0.108)	(0.108)	(0.168)
D(DTT)	0.621*	0.621*	0.389	0.115	0.115	0.009
	(0.282)	(0.282)	(0.403)	(0.092)	(0.092)	(0.123)
D(BIT)	–0.296	–0.296	0.527	–0.228**	–0.228**	–0.301*
	(0.246)	(0.246)	(0.350)	(0.078)	(0.078)	(0.119)
$\text{Log}\,(rgdpl_d / rgdpl_o)$	–7.398**			–0.675**		
	(1.633)			(0.068)		
KL_d / KL_o		–7.237**			–0.667**	
		(1.597)			(0.067)	
Log (DVA share)			3.347			–0.415
			(2.428)			(0.679)
Observations	409	409	205	331	331	1821
R-squared	0.735	0.735	0.753	0.592	0.592	0.634

BIT = dummy equals one if bilateral investment treaty in force btw two countries, DTT = dummy equals one if bilateral double taxation treaty in force btw two countries, DVA = domestic value added, KL = capital–labor ratio, RTA = dummy equals one if two countries are part of the same regional trade agreement in force, rgdpl = real GDP per capita.

Notes: The dependent variable is a measure of the activity of affiliate of multinational firms, affiliate sales, as well as the number of foreign affiliates that export and import, as a share of the total number of foreign affiliates, from source country i in destination country n. The variable Log (DVA share) in exports from the host country of the affiliate to the origin country, an average across years, for all sectors. All specifications with source and destination fixed effects. Robust standard errors in parentheses. Levels of significance are denoted by ** $p<0.01$, * $p<0.05$, + $p<0.1$.

Source: Author's calculations.

Finally, DVA shares are in general positively associated to the activity of foreign plants in a host country: when DVA shares are larger it means that the host country adds more value domestically in its exports to a given source country of the affiliates; this indicates less fragmentation of production and a richer network of domestic firms, which may be an attraction factor for foreign plants.

Determinants of GVC–Trade

We now carry a similar analysis to the one for GVC–FDI but for GVC–trade. We use as our measure of GVC–trade the share of DVA in gross exports, at the bilateral-sector level, for 2000, 2005, 2011, and 2014. We consider specifications with all the countries in the sample, as in Wang, Wei, and Zhu (2014), and as a sub-sample of only Asian countries. We further show results by sector (manufacturing and mining).

Table 6.16 considers country factors that may affect the DVA share of exports. Richer exporter countries have in general higher DVA shares, but for Asian countries the relationship is reversed: richer countries are associated with lower DVA shares. This is interesting as it speaks to the fact that countries more engaged in Factory Asia are better off in the region. The market size of the exporter impacts positively, as expected, the share of DVA of exports.

The capital intensity of the exporter affects the share of DVA positively in manufacturing, but negatively in mining: countries with higher capital–labor ratios add more value to exports domestically if the good is a manufacturing good. This is the same as saying that relatively labor-abundant countries have lower DVA shares and hence are more engaged in the GVC. The exporter's level of human capital, measured as the average years of schooling of the population in a country, reinforces its engagement in the GVC—except for manufacturing in Asia, where relatively unskilled labor is the appealing feature for the GVC linked to Factory Asia. The degree of upstreamness of exports is positively and strongly correlated with adding more value domestically; that is, countries that on average are specialized in more upstream sectors are less engaged in the GVC. A better rule of law in a country seems to stimulate participation in the GVC, but, consistent with the findings in Table 6.13, the opposite is true for the manufacturing sector in Asia. Finally, the presence of more private credit—which cannot be evaluated among Asian countries because of collinearity—also seems to stimulate engagement in the GVC in manufacturing as the share of DVA in exports is lower.

Table 6.16: Determinants of GVC–Trade: Country Characteristics (ordinary least squares)

Country-level Variable	Dependent Variable: DVA as a Share of Gross Exports					
	(1)	(2)	(3)	(4)	(5)	(6)
Log (real GDP per capita)	0.023**	0.019*	0.135**	-0.069**	-0.101**	0.138+
	(0.008)	(0.009)	(0.011)	(0.018)	(0.024)	(0.072)
Log (real GDP)	0.031**	0.038**	0.013**	0.063**	0.089**	0.011**
	(0.001)	(0.001)	(0.002)	(0.001)	(0.002)	(0.004)
Log (capital–labor ratio)	0.014*	0.027**	-0.099**	0.019+	0.033*	-0.146**
	(0.006)	(0.007)	(0.009)	(0.010)	(0.014)	(0.046)
Years of schooling	-0.013**	-0.015**	-0.021**	0.001	0.007**	-0.017+
	(0.001)	(0.001)	(0.001)	(0.002)	(0.003)	(0.009)
Rule of law	-0.021**	-0.019**	-0.048**	0.043**	0.045**	-0.019+
	(0.004)	(0.005)	(0.005)	(0.004)	(0.005)	(0.010)
Export upstreamness	0.052**	0.081**	0.099**	0.164**	0.242**	0.216**
	(0.005)	(0.007)	(0.008)	(0.005)	(0.008)	(0.008)
Private credit	-0.011*	-0.014*	0.020**			
	(0.005)	(0.007)	(0.006)			
Observations	183,068	79,597	5,362	42,195	20,539	1,249
R-squared	0.670	0.577	0.420	0.690	0.675	0.647
Sample industries	all	mfg	mining	all	mfg	mining
Sample countries	all	all	all	Asia	Asia	Asia

DVA = domestic value added, GDP = gross domestic product, GVC = global value chain.

Notes: Observations are at the bilateral country-sector level, for different years. Controls refer to the exporter country. All specifications with importer and industry-year fixed effects. Robust standard errors, clustered by importerexporter, in parentheses. Levels of significance are denoted by ** $p<0.01$, * $p<0.05$, + $p<0.1$.

Source: Author's calculations.

The effects of country size, capital–labor ratio, real GDP per capita, rule of law, and the level of upstreamness of exports in Table 6.16 are in line with that observed in Table 6.13: exports in more upstream sectors were associated with less trade-oriented affiliates; countries with less labor had less exporters and relatively larger and poorer markets.[16]

---

[16] As our sample on GVC–FDI is for Asia and most observations are in manufacturing, results in Table 6.13 are comparable to the results in Table 6.16, column 5.

Turning to the bilateral factors affecting the domestic value-added share of gross exports, in Table 6.17, distance plays a positive role. The further away countries are, the higher the domestic content of exports. Additionally, if the exporter has higher income per capita than the importer, the domestic value added share of exports is lower than if the opposite is true. Finally, if the exporter is relatively more capital abundant than the importer, the DVA share is higher than if the exporter were more labor abundant than the importer. Results are consistent with the findings in Table 6.15, in which more GVC–FDI activities were associated with a large difference in factor endowments favoring labor, as is the case for GVC–trade.

Table 6.17: Determinants of GVC–Trade: Gravity (ordinary least squares)

	Dependent Variable: DVA as Share of Gross Exports					
	(1)	(2)	(3)	(4)	(5)	(6)
Log (distance)	0.005**	0.004**	0.009**	0.002	0.002	0.005
	(0.001)	(0.001)	(0.002)	(0.003)	(0.002)	(0.004)
D(shared language)	−0.007**	−0.005*	−0.008*	−0.007+	−0.003	−0.006
	(0.002)	(0.002)	(0.004)	(0.004)	(0.004)	(0.006)
D(shared colonial past)	0.005*	0.003	0.004	0.004	−0.001	0.000
	(0.002)	(0.002)	(0.004)	(0.004)	(0.002)	(0.004)
D(RTA)	0.003**	0.000	0.001	0.002	0.002+	0.004
	(0.001)	(0.001)	(0.002)	(0.003)	(0.001)	(0.003)
Log $(rgdpl_e/rgdpl_i)$	−0.022	−0.032*	−0.097**	0.040	−0.034*	−0.188*
	(0.018)	(0.014)	(0.028)	(0.042)	(0.014)	(0.081)
Log (KL_e/KL_i)	0.022	0.030*	0.093**	−0.036	0.030*	0.178*
	(0.018)	(0.013)	(0.027)	(0.040)	(0.013)	(0.078)
Observations	168,266	73,951	4,988	37,095	18,060	1,112
R-squared	0.281	0.469	0.832	0.271	0.514	0.684
Sample industries	all	mfg	mining	all	mfg	mining
Sample countries	all	all	all	Asia	Asia	Asia

DVA = domestic value added, GVC = global value chain, KL = capital–labor ratio, rgdpl = real GDP per capita, RTA = regional trade agreement.
Notes: Observations are at the bilateral country-sector level, for different years. All specifications with exporter and importer fixed effects. Standard errors, clustered by importer–exporter, in parentheses. Levels of significance are denoted by ** p<0.01, * p<0.05, + p<0.1.
Source: Author's calculations.

GVC–FDI and Production Fragmentation

Next, we explore the relation between engagement in GVC–FDI and the degree of production fragmentation within the corporation, measured by the input–output links between the industries of operations of the parent and the affiliate. The analysis is similar to one in Alfaro and Charlton (2009) and Ramondo, Rodriguez-Clare, and Tintelnot (2015). The novel feature of the analysis is that our data allow us to go a step further and associate the production fragmentation observed between the parent and its affiliate directly with the trade activities of the affiliate. We restrict the analysis to manufacturing plants belonging to parents that also operate in manufacturing. We include plants both with GUHs in the same and different country, but we exclude (domestic) plants that are their own GUH.

This part of the analysis can be seen as a deeper exploration into an important characteristic of industries—and industry-pairs: the strength of their links with other industries. We will interpret the presence of stronger input–output links between two industries as more scope for production fragmentation and hence more potential to be part of the GVC.

We start by showing in Table 6.18 the economy–industry pairs observed in our data with the strongest input–output links between parents and affiliates. Not surprisingly, such pairs involve affiliates in the semiconductor sector in the PRC that belong to Japanese parents that produce in the (downstream) electrical equipment sector.[17] Mostly, the strongest pairs are in the electronic and car sectors and involve affiliates in the PRC of parents located in Japan and other developed countries. This table pairs well with Tables 6.3 and 6.4 that show that affiliates with trade activities are concentrated in the motor vehicle brake system sector and the sector producing electronic components, located in the PRC and belonging to parents from Japan.

Next, we establish the Alfaro-Charlton fact for affiliates located in Asia. That is, we establish that more multinational activity is observed in industry pairs with strong input–output links. We aggregate the firm-level data in the following way to construct the dependent variable: affiliates operating in country ca and industry ka belonging to parents in country cp and industry kp.

---

[17] The industry classification of four-digit NAICS is coarse; many affiliate–parent pairs belong to the same four-digit industry which, in itself, indicates strong input–output links since most industries use the inputs they produce within the same industry. Those industries pairs are not included in Table 6.18.

Table 6.18: Production Fragmentation: Most Common Economy–Industry Pairs

Economy (Affiliate)	Economy (Parent)	Industry of Affiliate	Industry of Parent
15. PRC	Japan	Other electrical equipment and component	Semiconductors and other electronic component
14. PRC	Japan	Motor vehicle parts	Plastic products
13. PRC	Japan	Motor vehicle parts	Semiconductors and other electronic component
12. PRC	Japan	Semiconductors and other electronic component	Other electrical equipment and component
11. PRC	Taipei,China	Communications equipment	Semiconductors and other electronic component
10. PRC	Taipei,China	Computer and peripheral equipment	Semiconductors and other electronic component
9. PRC	Republic of Korea	Semiconductors and other electronic component	Communications equipment
8. PRC	Japan	Semiconductors and other electronic component	Motor vehicle parts
7. PRC	Japan	Semiconductors and other electronic component	Communications equipment
6. PRC	Japan	Metal working machinery	Plastic products
5. PRC	Japan	Other fabricated metal products	Motor vehicle parts
4. PRC	Germany	Electrical equipment	Navigational, measuring, electromedical, and control instruments
3. PRC	Taipei,China	Semiconductors and other electronic component	Computer and peripheral equipment
2. PRC	US	Basic chemical	Other general purpose machinery
1. PRC	Japan	Semiconductors and other electronic component	Electrical equipment

PRC = People's Republic of China, US = United States.

Notes: Industry pairs in manufacturing only, at four-digit NAICS. Pairs sorted by the direct requirement coefficient between the industry of the affiliate (upstream) and the parent (downstream), drap.

Source: Author's calculations.

We use three measures of affiliates' activity in the 4-tupla $ca \times ka \times cp \times kp$: number of affiliates, sales of affiliates, and affiliates' employment.

Figure 6.6a, taken from Ramondo, Rodriguez-Clare, and Tintelnot (2015), summarizes the characteristics of the direct requirements coefficients, from the 2002 US input–output table. The x-axis is the industry code of the using (downstream) industry, and the y-axis is the industry code of the producing (upstream) industry. The bubble's size is proportional to that of the direct requirements coefficient of the industry pair. It is clear from the figure that most industries require inputs from similar industries: the entries in the direct requirements table tend to be largest on or near the diagonal. Figures 6.6b and 6.6c plots the distribution of industry pairs for the parent–affiliate pairs in the data, for all plants, and for plants with foreign GUHs. The bubble's size is proportional to the number of parent–affiliate observations in that industry pair. Combining these figures suggests that parents own affiliates in similar industries, and these industries are important producers of intermediate inputs for each other.

Figure 6.6: Production Fragmentation—Direct Requirements Coefficients and Parent–Affiliate Activity

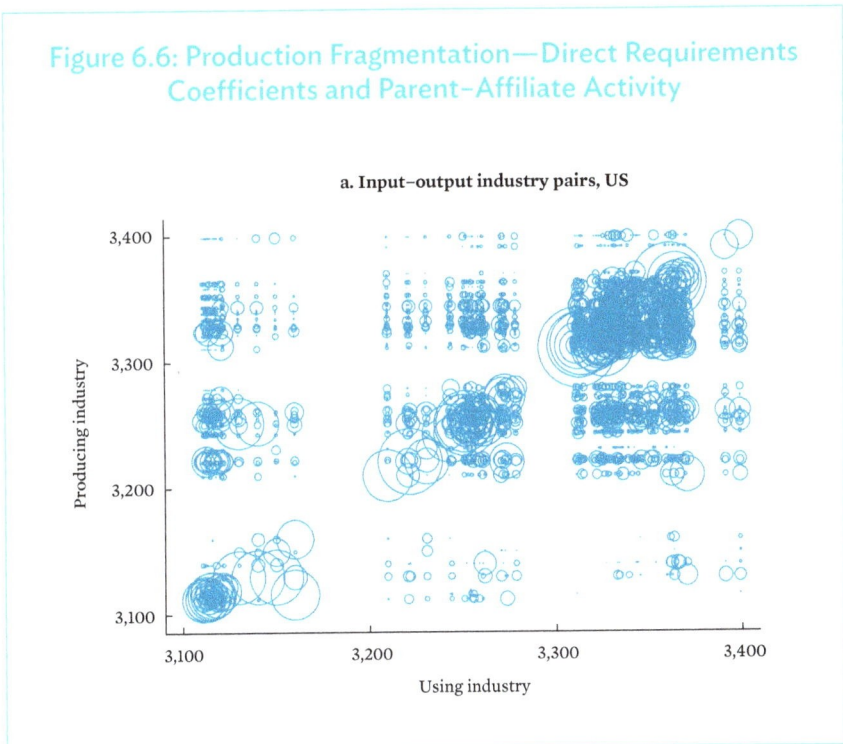

a. Input–output industry pairs, US

continued on next page

Figure 6.6 continued

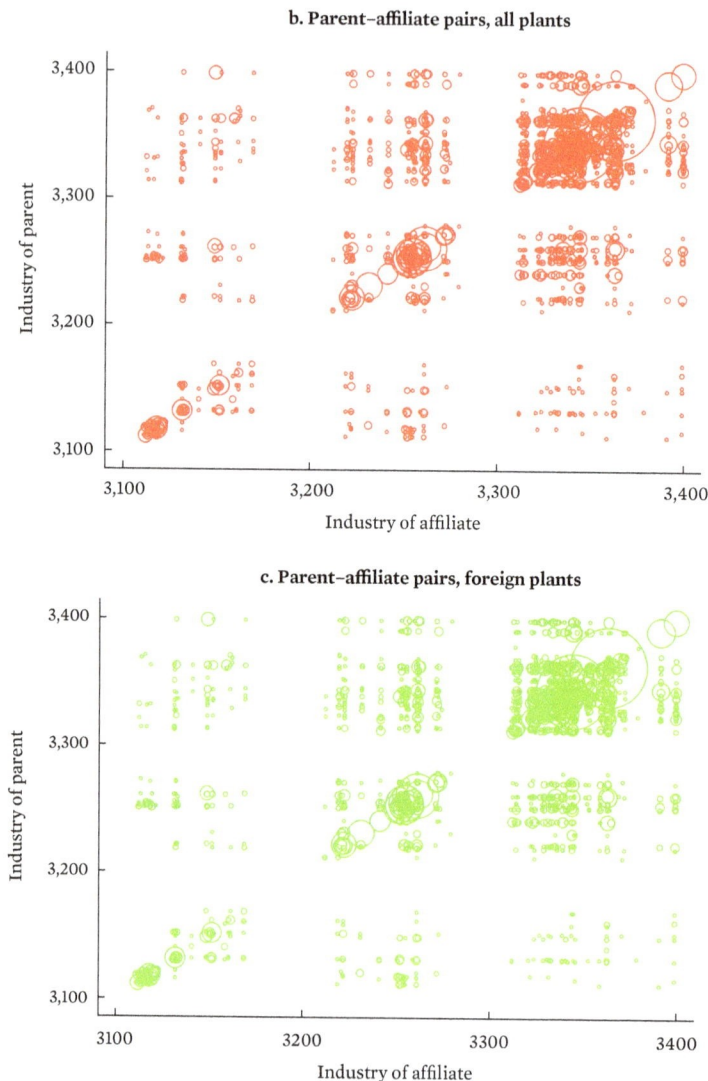

b. Parent–affiliate pairs, all plants

c. Parent–affiliate pairs, foreign plants

Notes: Figure 6.6a: Direct requirements coefficients for industry pairs in 2002, from the US input–output matrix; bubbles are proportional to the size of the direct requirements coefficient. Figure 6.6b: Frequency of the industries of parent–affiliate pairs, all plants; bubbles are proportional to the number of parent–affiliate pairs in a given industry pair. Figure 6.6c: Frequency of the industries of parent–affiliate pairs, plants with parents in a different country; bubbles are proportional to the number of parent–affiliate pairs in a given industry pair. The direct requirements coefficient is the value of goods needed from the producing (upstream) industry to produce $1 of output in the using (downstream) industry. Manufacturing industries only.

Source: Author's calculations.

More than 95% of manufacturing affiliates operate in industries with a strong input–output link with the industry of the parent; only 5% of plants present zero direct requirement coefficients with the parent (against almost 50% in the input–output matrix). The distribution is skewed: while the mean of *drap* is 0.20, the median is 0.06—similarly for *dpa*; less than a third of observations are above the mean. Summing up, this is the visualization of the Alfaro-Charlton's fact: parents own establishments, both domestic and abroad, in industries that are closely related in terms of input–output links.

Table 6.19 presents the formal results. Similar to the results in Alfaro and Charlton (2009) and Ramondo, Rodriguez-Clare, and Tintelnot (2015), multinational activity—and more generally the activity of multi-establishment firms—is associated with production chains between parents and affiliates. An increase in *drap* from 0.06 (the median) to 0.3 (the 75th percentile) is associated with an increase in sales of affiliates in a given 4-tupla of 18%; the effect is halved when only plants with foreign parents are considered.

Table 6.19: Production Fragmentation and the Boundaries of the Firm
(ordinary least squares)

Country-Level Variable	Log (Number of Affiliates) (1)	Log (Sales of Affiliates) (2)	Log (Employees of Affiliates) (3)	Log (Number of Affiliates) (4)	Log (Sales of Affiliates) (5)	Log (Employees of Affiliates) (6)
drap	0.624**	0.813**	0.804**	0.304**	0.399+	0.389+
	(0.113)	(0.211)	(0.173)	(0.095)	(0.228)	(0.200)
drpa	0.427**	0.975**	0.759**	0.181*	0.541**	0.365*
	(0.101)	(0.202)	(0.161)	(0.077)	(0.200)	(0.165)
Observations	7,837	6,999	6,999	4,127	3,682	3,682
R-squared	0.219	0.157	0.254	0.110	0.077	0.158
Sample	all plants	all plants	all plants	foreign plants	foreign plants	foreign plants

drap = direct requirement coefficient from affiliate industry to parent industry, drpa = direct requirement coefficient from parent industry to affiliate industry.

Notes: The dependent variable is a measure of the activity of affiliates operating in industry k and country n belonging to firms in industry l country i. Only affiliate–parent pairs in the manufacturing sector are included. Columns 1–3 includes all plants, while columns 4–6 only plants with parents in a different country. Only plants that are not parent companies are included. All regressions with origin country-fixed effects, destination country-fixed effects, and parent industry-fixed effects. Standard errors, clustered at the parent–affiliate industry level, in parentheses. Levels of significance are denoted by ** $p<0.01$, * $p<0.05$, + $p<0.1$.

Source: Author's calculations.

Next, we explore in more detail the characteristics of plants that present strong input–output links with their parents. Table 6.20 shows the result formally: a plant with a *drap* = 1 (above the 95th percentile) has 25% more sales than a plant with no input–output link with its parent. The effects for foreign plants are of similar magnitude. Hence, production fragmentation seems to be associated to larger plants, probably because of economies of scale playing a role.[18]

Table 6.20: Production Fragmentation and Affiliate Size (ordinary least squares)

Country-Level Variable	Dependent Variable: Log (Affiliate Sales)			
	(1)	(2)	(3)	(4)
drap	0.250**		0.221*	
	(0.054)		(0.087)	
drpa		0.217**		0.286**
		(0.059)		(0.098)
Observations	19,225	19,225	6,787	19,225
R-sq	0.039	0.039	0.055	0.056
Sample	all	all	foreign	foreign

drap = direct requirement coefficient from affiliate industry to parent industry; drpa = direct requirement coefficient from parent industry to affiliate industry.

Notes: The dependent variable is at the firm level. The variable *drap* (*drpa*) denotes the direct requirement coefficient between the industry of the affiliate and parent when the affiliate is in the upstream (downstream) industry. Columns 1–2 include all plants, while columns 3–4 include only plants with parents in a different country. Only affiliate–parent pairs in the manufacturing sector and only plants that are not parent companies are included. All specifications with origin and destination fired effects. Standard errors, clustered at the parent level, in parentheses. Levels of significance are denoted by ** p<0.01, * p<0.05, + p<0.1.

Source: Author's calculations.

Second: Are these production chains between parent and affiliate plants associated with GVC–FDI at the level of the 4-tupla, *ca* × *ka* × *cp* × *kp*? Table 6.21 presents the results.

---

[18] Note the fundamental difference between results in Tables 6.19 and 6.20: the latter one links the size of the *individual* affiliate to the strength of the input–output links of its industry of operation (and that of its parent), while the former links the amount of FDI activity—both at the extensive and intensive margin—in a given 4-tupla with those same input–output links between industry pairs.

Table 6.21: Production Fragmentation and GVC–FDI
(ordinary least squares)

Country-Level Variable	Dependent Variable: Number of Affiliates with							
	Exports and Imports		Exports	Imports	Exports and Imports		Exports	Imports
	(1)	(2)	(3)	(4)	(5)	(6)	(7)	(8)
Number of affiliates with:								
drap > 0 and *drpa* > 0	0.274**	0.055 **			0.797**	0.547**		
	(0.054)	(0.015)			(0.031)	(0.057)		
× D(PRC)		0.420 **				0.292**		
		(0.047)				(0.036)		
drap > 0			0.313**				0.806**	
			(0.055)				(0.031)	
drpa > 0				0.347**				0.868**
				(0.066)				(0.034)
Observations	18,165	18,165	18,165	18,165	8,741	8,741	8,741	8,741
R-squared	0.370	0.553	0.402	0.417	0.625	0.634	0.624	0.636
Sample	all	all	all	all	foreign	foreign	foreign	foreign

drap = direct requirement coefficient from affiliate industry to parent industry; drpa = direct requirement coefficient from parent industry to affiliate industry, FDI = foreign direct investment, GVC = global value chain, PRC = People's Republic of China.

Notes: The dependent variable is the number of plants operating in industry *ka* and country *ca* belonging to parents in industry *kp* and country *cp* with different types of international trade exposure. Similar for the control dummies. The dummy D(PRC) is one when the plant is located in the PRC. Columns 5–8 include all plants, while columns 9–12 include only plants with parents in a different country. Only affiliate–parent pairs in the manufacturing sector and only plants that are not parent companies are included. All specifications with origin and destination fixed effects. Standard errors, clustered at the parent–affiliate industry level, in parentheses. Levels of significance are denoted by ** $p<0.01$, * $p<0.05$, + $p<0.1$.

Source: Author's calculations.

There is a strong positive association between the number of plants with both non-zero upstream and downstream links with the parent and affiliate plants that both export and import. Interestingly, results are stronger if the plant is located in the PRC: if we added 10 more plants with strong input–output links with their parents, the probability in the PRC that the plant exports and imports would increase by almost 5% overall, and 3% if the plant were foreign. Additionally, the number of plants upstream of the parent in the production chain is significantly and positively associated with the exporter status of the plant—and also the case when the importer status of the plant and production-chain relations in which the affiliate is downstream of the parent are considered. The coefficients when only foreign plants are considered are much higher and always strongly significant. This result simply suggests that more GVC–FDI is found in industries with richer networks of input–output links, and hence, with more scope for segmenting production, and hence, being part of the GVC.

Let us interpret the coefficients in more detail. For instance, take column 1: the median bin has one plant engaged in international trade, while the 90th percentile bin has two plants and the 95th percentile has four plants (one of the bins with the most plants is the one involving Chinese plants of Japanese parents in the auto parts industry, with 150 plants). Moving from the median bin to the 95th percentile bin implies an increase of 3.6 plants with strong input–output links with their parent—which is equivalent to moving from the median bin to more than the 90th percentile bin in terms of the distribution of the number of plants with strong input–output links with their parents (the bin with the largest number of plants with strong input–output links with their parent involves, precisely, the auto parts industry and Chinese plants of Japanese multinationals, with 169 plants). Magnitudes are similar for the remaining columns. These results are indeed suggestive of the engagement of a plant in international trade activities being related to production fragmentation.

In the last set of results, we explore the relation between the presence of production fragmentation in a host economy and the attraction of multinational activity, and in particular, of trade-related multinational activities. This set of results can be interpreted as part of the set of characteristics of an industry–country pair that may be potential attraction factors for GVC–FDI.

Table 6.22 tests the results formally, including an interaction between the capital intensity of the industry and the relative capital abundance of the country, and a dummy for the PRC, and affiliate-country and affiliate-industry fixed effects.[19] Besides the fact that variables are counts in Table 6.21 and shares in Table 6.22, the crucial difference between the tables is that while Table 6.21 uses the sample of all plants and foreign plants, respectively, to construct both the control and dependent variables, at the 4-tupla level.

---

[19] The interaction between capital intensity of the industry and capital abundance of the country is meant to capture Heckscher-Ohlin type effects: countries that are relatively capital abundant should concentrate activities that are capital intensive.

Table 6.22 uses as dependent variable *only* the number of *foreign* plants and as control, *only* the number of *domestic* plants, in an industry–country pair.

Table 6.22: Multinational Activity, GVC–FDI, and Domestic Input–Output Links
(ordinary least squares)

Country-Level Variable	Dependent Variable (in logs)			
	Number of Foreign Affiliates as Share of All Plants		Number of Foreign Affiliates with Export and Imports as Share of Foreign Plants	
	(1)	(2)	(3)	(4)
(Log) Share of domestic affiliates	0.279**	0.294**	0.065	0.071
with *drap* > 0 and *drpa* > 0	(0.066)	(0.066)	(0.057)	(0.057)
× D(PRC)	–0.342+	–0.352+	–0.217+	–0.200+
	(0.191)	(0.194)	(0.115)	(0.120)
kl × log (KL)		0.035**		–0.000
		(0.011)		(0.000)
Observations	451	435	407	407
R-squared	0.866	0.869	0.588	0.589

drap = direct requirement coefficient from affiliate industry to parent industry; drpa = direct requirement coefficient from parent industry to affiliate industry, FDI = foreign direct investment, GVC = global value chain, KL = capital–labor ratio, PRC = People's Republic of China.

Notes: The dependent variable in columns 1–2 is the (log) number of foreign affiliates as a share of total plants operating in industry *k* and country *n*, while in columns 3–4 the dependent variable refers to the number of foreign affiliates that export and import as a share of total foreign plants operating in industry *k* and country *n* (GVC–FDI). The independent variable is the (log) number of domestic affiliates as a share of total domestic plants operating in industry *k* and country *n* that a have positive direct requirement coefficients with their parent, both upstream and downstream. The dummy D(PRC) is one when country *n* is the People's Republic of China. The variable *kl* × log *KL* is the interaction between the capital intensity of industry *k* and the capital–labor ratio for country *n*. Only domestic affiliates in the manufacturing sector and that are not parents are included. All regressions with destination country and affiliate-industry fixed effects. Standard errors, clustered at the industry-country level, in parentheses. Levels of significance are denoted by ** p<0.01, * p<0.05, + p<0.1.

Source: Author's calculations.

Results for the activity of multinational affiliates that survive and are strong: a 10% increase in the fraction of domestic affiliates with strong input–output links with their (domestic) parents increases the share of foreign affiliates in the industry by almost 30%. The effect is reversed for the PRC: stronger production fragmentation among domestic PRC firms proportionally decrease the number of foreign plants in the industry. For GVC–FDI, the relation observed in the figure is not significant once we add other controls; but for the PRC the relationship turns negative (i.e., proportionally more domestic plants with input–output links with their PRC parent are associated with proportionally less foreign plants engaged in international trade). This result can be because the PRC market heavily regulates foreign entry when is aimed at the local market.

All in all, these results suggest that industries (and countries) in which there is more scope for production fragmentation have larger and more international-trade oriented plants. Additionally, the results suggest that the strength of the GVC among domestic firms in the host industry may attract FDI, regardless whether it is horizontal or GVC–FDI.

Concluding Remarks

This chapter has explored a novel relation between what we call global value chain–foreign direct investment (GVC–FDI) and GVC–trade. Using detailed data for affiliates in Asia, the presence of affiliates of foreign multinationals engaged in trade activities was found to be positively associated with a country's engagement in GVC–trade, measured either by the upstreamness of exports or the share of domestic value added in gross exports. Exploration of the country and industry determinants of trade-oriented host market-oriented affiliates' activities revealed that traditional comparative advantage considerations are at play: affiliates in poorer, labor-abundant countries, and specialized in labor-intensive activities, are more likely to be trade-oriented. Moreover, these affiliates are more likely to be located in markets with weaker rule of law and low cost of exports (and imports). Bilateral investment treaties do not seem to be crucial for these affiliates—as special economic zones seem to be—but these treaties are important for attracting foreign plants in general.

We have added to the traditional motives of foreign affiliates, looking to variables related to production fragmentation within the corporation. We find that affiliates that have input–output links with their parents are larger— and this is not particularly different for affiliates engaged in international trade activities. These input–output links are more likely to be observed in industries and countries with more affiliates engaged in GVC–FDI, suggesting that indeed the international trade activity of foreign affiliates is linked to the GVC in Asia. Finally, a new motive for attracting FDI has been uncovered: the presence of more domestic plants with strong input–output links with their parents in a country and industry is positive associated with more foreign affiliates. This entails that a tight network of input–output relationship among firms in the host country is important for attracting foreign multinationals.

References

Alfaro, L., P. Antras, D. Chor, and P. Conconi. 2015. Internalizing Global Value Chains: A Firm-Level Analysis. Unpublished.

Alfaro, L. and A. Charlton. 2009. Intra-industry Foreign Direct Investment. *American Economic Review*. 104 (2). pp. 459–494.

Alviarez, V. 2015. Multinational Production and Comparative Advantage. Manuscript, UBC.

Antras, P. and D. Chor. 2013. Organizing the Global Value Chain. *Econometrica*. 81 (6). pp. 2127–2204.

Antras, P., D. Chor, T. Fally, and R. Hillberry. 2012. Measuring Upstreamness of Production and Trade. *American Economic Review Papers and Proceedings*. 102 (3). pp. 412–16.

Antras, P. 2003. Firms, Contracts, and Trade Structure. *Quarterly Journal of Economics*. 118 (4). pp. 1375–18.

Antras, P. and E. Helpman. 2004. Global Sourcing. *Journal of Political Economy*. 112 (3). pp. 552–80.

Arkolakis, C., N. Ramondo, A. Rodriguez-Clare, and S. Yeaple. 2014. Innovation and Production in the Global Economy. Penn State University. Unpublished.

Bernard, A. and J. B. Jensen. 1997. Exporters, Skills Upgrading, and the Wage Gap. *Journal of International Economics*. 42 (1–2). pp. 3–31.

Blanchard, E., C. Bown, and R. Johnson. 2016. Global Supply Chains and Trade Policy. *NBER Working Paper Series*. No. 21883.

Boehm, C., A. Flaaen, and N. Pandalai-Nayar. 2015. The Role of Global Supply Chains in the Transmission of Shocks: Firm-level Evidence from the 2011 Tohoku Earthquake. *VOX CEPR Policy Portal*.

Brainard, S. L. 1997. An Empirical Assessment of the Proximity-Concentration Tradeoff Between Multinational Sales and Trade. *American Economic Review*. 87 (4). pp. 520–44.

Carr, D. L., J. R. Markusen, and K. E. Maskus. 2001. Estimating the Knowledge-Capital Model of the Multinational Enterprise. *American Economic Review.* 91 (3). pp. 693–708.

Dedrick, K., K. L. Kraemer, and G. Linden. 2010. Who Profits from Innovation in Global Value Chains?: A Study of the Ipod and Notebook PCs. *Industrial and Corporate Change.* 19 (1). pp. 81–116.

Defever, F. and A. Riano. 2015. Protectionism through Exporting: Subsidies with Export Share Requirements in China. *Centre for Economic Performance Discussion Papers.* No. 1182. London School of Economics.

Eaton, J. and S. Kortum. 2012. Technology, Geography, and Trade. *Econometrica.* 70 (5). pp. 1741–79.

Fajgelbaum, P., G. Grossman, and E. Helpman. 2015. A Linder Hypothesis for Foreign Direct Investment. *Review of Economic Studies.* 82 (1). pp. 83–121.

Grossman, G., E. Helpman, and A. Szeidl. 2006. Optimal Integration Strategies for the Multinational Firm. *Journal of International Economics.* 70 (1). pp. 216–38.

Hanson, G., R. Mataloni, and M. Slaughter. 2001. Expansion Strategies of US Multinational Firms. In D. Rodrik and S. Collins, eds. *Brookings Trade Forum.* pp. 245–82. Brookings Institution, Washington, DC.

———. 2005. Vertical Production Networks in Multinational Firms. *Review of Economics and Statistics.* 87 (4). pp. 664–78.

Helpman, E. 1984. A Simple Theory of Trade with Multinational Corporations. *Journal of Political Economy.* 92 (3). pp. 451–71.

———. 1985. Multinational Corporations and Trade Structure. *Review of Economic Studies.* 52 (3). pp. 443-57.

Helpman, E., M. Melitz, and S. R. Yeaple. 2004. Export versus FDI with Heterogenous Firms. *American Economic Review.* 94 (1). pp. 300–16.

Horstmann, I. and J. Markusen. 1992. Endogenous Market Structures in International Trade (natura facit saltum). *Journal of International Economics*. 32 (1–2). pp. 109–29.

Hummels, D., J. Ishii, and K. Yi. 2001. The Nature of Growth of Vertical Specialization in World Trade. *Journal of International Economics*. 54 (1). pp. 75–96.

Inter-American Development Bank. 2015. "Synchronized Factories—Latin America and the Caribbean in the Era of Global Value Chains." Edited by Juan S. Blyde. Washington, DC.

Johnson, R. and G. Noguera. 2012. Accounting for Intermediates: Production Sharing and Trade in Value Added. *Journal of International Economics* 86 (2). pp. 224–36.

Johnson, R. 2014. Five Facts about Value-Added Exports and Implications for Macroeconomics and Trade Research. *Journal of Economic Perspective*. 28 (2). pp. 119–42.

Koopman, R., Z. Wang, and S. Wei. 2014. Tracing Value-Added and Double Counting in Gross Exports. *American Economic Review*. 104 (2). pp. 459–94.

Manova, K. 2013. Credit Constraints, Heterogeneous Firms, and International Trade. *Review of Economic Studies*. 80 (2). pp. 711–44.

Markusen, J. 1984. Multinationals, Multi-Plant Economies, and the Gains from Trade. *Journal of International Economics*. 16 (3–4). pp. 205–26.

Nunn, N. 2007. Relationship-Specificity, Incomplete Contracts, and the Pattern of Trade. *Quarterly Journal of Economics*. 122 (2). pp. 569–600.

Nunn, N. and D. Trefler. 2008. The Boundaries of the Multinational Firm: An Empirical Analysis. In E. Helpman, D. Marin, and T. Verdier, eds. *The Organization of Firms in a Global Economy*. Harvard University Press. pp. 55–83.

——. 2014. Domestic Institutions as a Source of Comparative Advantage. In G. Gopinah, E. Helpman, and K. Rogoff, eds. *Handbook of International Economics Vol. 4*. Chapter 5. pp. 263–315.

Rajan, R. and L. Zingales. 1998. Financial Dependence and Growth. *American Economic Review*. 88 (3). p. 559–86.

Ramondo, N., V. Rappoport, and K. Ruhl. 2016. Intrafirm Trade and Vertical Fragmentation in US Multinational Corporations. *Journal of International Economics*. 98 (1). pp. 51–59.

Ramondo, N. 2014. A Quantitative Approach to Multinational Production. *Journal of International Economics*. 93 (1). pp. 108–22.

Ramondo, N. and A. Rodriguez-Clare. 2013. Trade, Multinational Production, and the Gains from Openness. *Journal of Political Economy*. 121 (2). pp. 273–322.

Ramondo, N., A. Rodriguez-Clare, and F. Tintelnot. 2015. Multinational Production: Data and Stylized Facts. *American Economic Review Papers and Proceedings*. 105 (5). pp. 530–36.

Tintelnot, F. 2015. Global Production with Export Platforms. University of Chicago. Unpublished.

United Nations Conference on Trade and Development (UNCTAD). 2013. *World Investment Report 2013—Global Value Chains: Investment and Trade for Development*. Geneva.

Wang, Z, S. Wei, and K. Zhu. 2014. Quantifying International Production Sharing at the Bilateral and Sector Level. *NBER Working Papers*. No. 19677. National Bureau of Economic Research, Cambridge, MA.

Yeaple, S. 2006. Offshoring, Foreign Direct Investment, and the Structure of US Trade. *Journal of European Economic Association*. 4 (2–3). pp. 602–11.

APPENDIX A6

Table A6.1: Description of Variables

Variable Name	Source	Description
aff sales	D&B	affiliate sales
applied tariff rate	WDI, WB	weighted mean, all sectors, 2013
average time to clear exports through customs	WDI, WB	2013
BITs	ADB	dummy equal one if bilateral investment treaty in force between two countries, 2013
burden of customs procedure	WDI, WB	2013
control of corruption	WGI, WB	index: −2.5 (lowest) to 2.5, 2013
cost of business start-up processing	WDI, WB	% of GNI, 2013
cost to export	WDI, WB	in $ per container, 2013
cost to import	WDI, WB	in $ per container, 2013
D(shared colonial past)	CEPII	dummy equal one if two countries share colonial past
D(shared language)	CEPII	dummy equal one if two countries share a language
days required to enforce a contract	WDI, WB	2013
days required to get electricity	WDI, WB	2013
days required to register property	WDI, WB	2013
days required to start-up a business	WDI, WB	2013
doc to export	WDI, WB	number of documents, 2013
doc to import	WDI, WB	number of documents, 2013
drap	BEA	direct req coeff from affiliate industry to parent industry, input–output matrix, US 2002
drpa	BEA	direct req coeff from parent industry to affiliate industry, input–output matrix, US 2002

continued on next page

Table A6.1 continued

Variable Name	Source	Description
DTTs	ADB	dummy equal one if bilateral DTT in force between two countries, 2013
DVA share	ADB MRIO	domestic value added in exports, as share of gross exports, bilateral level, average 2005-10-14
exp. upstr	Antras et al	host country's export upstreamness
FVA share	ADB MRIO	foreign value added in exports, as share of gross exports, bilateral level, average 2005-10-14
government effectiveness	WGI, WB	index: –2.5 (lowest) to 2.5, 2013
hours spent to prepare and pay taxes	WDI, WB	2013
KL	PWT (8.0)	capital–labor ratio for host country, 2005
kl	NBER	capital intensity of industry, capital stock over total employment, US, average 2000–2005
Logistics performance index	WDI, WB	logistics performance index quality, 2013
number of procedure to register a business	WDI, WB	number of documents, 2013
political stability	WGI, WB	index: –2.5 (lowest) to 2.5, 2013
priv. credit	Beck et al	private credit, as % of GDP, in host country
quality of ports infrastructure	WDI, WB	quality of ports infrastructure,2013
R&D	NBER	R&D intensity of industry, measured by expenditures, US, average 2000–2005
RDV share	ADB MRIO	return value added in exports, as share of gross exports, bilateral level, average 2005-10-14
regulatory quality	WGI, WB	index: –2.5 (lowest) to 2.5, 2013
rgdp	PWT (8.1)	real GDP, expenditure based, average 2005–2011
rgdpl	PWT (8.1)	real GDP per capita, average 2005–2011
RTA	ADB	dummy equal one if two countries are part of the same regional trade agreement in force, 2013

continued on next page

Table A6.1 continued

Variable Name	Source	Description
rule of law	WGI, WB	index: −2.5 (lowest) to 2.5, 2013
sl	NBER	skill intensity of industry, non-production employment over total employment, US, average 2000–2005
time spent dealing with government regulation	WDI, WB	% of senior manager time, 2013
TRI	WB	host country trade restrictiveness index, 2009
voice and accountability	WGI, WB	index: −2.5 (lowest) to 2.5, 2013
yr. sch.	Barro–Lee	average years of schooling in host country, average 1996–2005

ADB = Asian Development Bank, BEA = Bureau of Economic Analysis, CEPII = Centre d'Études Prospectives et d'Informations Internationales (the French Research Center in International Economics), D&B = Dun and Bradstreet, GDP = gross domestic product, GNI = gross national income, MRIO = Multi-Regional Input–Output Tables, NBER = National Bureau of Economic Research, PWT = Penn World Tables, WB = World Bank, WDI = World Development Indicators, WGI = World Governance Index.

Source: Author's compilation.

Policy Factors Influencing FDI Inflows: A Comprehensive Analysis

7

Hyun-Hoon Lee

Introduction

Many studies have found that foreign direct investment (FDI) can play a positive role in spurring economic growth and income of host countries. For example, Javorcik (2004), Cheung and Lin (2004), and Haskel et al. (2007) find positive spillover effects of FDI on innovation activity and productivity of domestic firms. Huttunen (2007) also find that foreign firms pay higher wages than domestic firms. Since FDI is expected to have positive welfare impacts on the host countries, investment policy measures in many countries have been geared toward investment liberalization, promotion, and facilitation (United Nations Conference on Trade and Development [UNCTAD] 2015).

FDI can take the form of investment in new assets (greenfield investment) or acquisition of existing assets (mergers and acquisitions [M&A]). Because of their distinctive characteristics, the two FDI modes may have different welfare effects in host countries. Wang and Wong (2009) find that greenfield FDI promotes economic growth while M&As promote growth only when the host country has an adequate level of human capital. Harms and Méon (2011) also find that while greenfield investment substantially enhances growth, M&As have no effect, at best. But Ashraf, Herzer, and Nunnenkamp (2015) find that greenfield FDI has no statistically significant effect on total factor productivity, while M&As have a positive effect in the sample of both developed and developing host countries of FDI.

The question is then to understand how different institutional and policy factors have different effects on FDI so that policy makers can properly design a policy framework to attract FDI, particularly orienting multinational enterprises to invest in the country in a certain way (Byun, Lee, and Park 2012). Many studies have linked institutional/governance variables with "aggregate" FDI. For example, Schneider and Frey (1985) and Edwards (1992) claim that political instability deters FDI flows. Daude and Stein (2007) find that the unpredictability of laws, regulations and policies, excessive regulatory burden, government instability, and lack of commitment are important institutional aspects that play a major role in deterring FDI.

Similarly, Busse and Hefeker (2007) find that government stability, internal and external conflicts, corruption, ethnic tension, law and order, democratic accountability, and quality of bureaucracy are important determinants of FDI inflows. Hayakawa, Kimura, and Lee (2013), using overall FDI inflows to 89 developing countries from 1985 to 2007, find that internal conflict, corruption, military involvement in politics, and bureaucratic quality are strongly associated with FDI inflows to developing countries.

However, most studies have focused on institutional/governance factors on FDI and only few studies have examined how different policies of host countries influence FDI inflows to these countries. For example, using the World Bank's Ease of Doing Business (EoDB) ranking, Jayasuriya (2011) shows that there is a positive relationship between EoDB ranking and FDI inflows, but when the sample is restricted to developing countries, the relationship becomes insignificant. In contrast, Corcoran and Gillanders (2015) show that the overall Doing Business is highly significant in attracting FDI.

EoDB is not a direct measure of a country's FDI policies as it measures a country's business regulatory environments that may influence both domestic investment and FDI inflows. Utilizing PricewaterhouseCoopers country reports on FDI policies, Wei (2000) constructs two measures of government policies toward FDI in 49 countries: FDI restrictions index and FDI incentives index. Specifically, FDI restrictions index was created based on the presence of restrictions in four sub-areas such as (i) controls on foreign exchange transactions, (ii) exclusion of foreign firms from certain strategic sectors, (iii) exclusion of foreign firms from other sectors, and (iv) restrictions on the share of foreign ownership. Similarly, an FDI incentives index was created based on the presence or absence of FDI promoting policies in four areas: (i) special incentives for foreigners to invest in certain industries or certain geographic areas; (ii) tax concessions specific to foreign firms; (iii) cash grants, subsidized loans, reduced rent for land use, or other nontax concessions, when these are specific to foreign firms; and (iv) special promotion for exports (including the existence of export processing zones, special economic zones, and the like). Wei (2000) shows empirically that FDI inflows are negatively related to FDI restrictions index and positively related to FDI incentives.

Two points are noteworthy. First, most studies on the effects of governance and policies on FDI focus on aggregate FDI despite that its two entry modes may have different welfare effects in the host countries.[1] Second, most studies focus mostly on institutional variables such as political stability and corruption and less on business environments or FDI policy variables of host countries which might have a more direct impact on FDI decisions of multinationals.

Against this background, this chapter empirically evaluates how different institutional and policy factors influence FDI flows in the modes of greenfield versus M&A to developing countries. In particular, this report assesses (i) host-country specific factors such as institutional/governance indicators and business environments, and (ii) bilateral pair-specific factors such as regional trade agreements (RTAs) and bilateral investment treaties (BITs).

Most studies have focused on FDI flows from all foreign countries or particularly from high-income countries. However, multinationals from emerging countries have increased their foreign investments in recent years. With a relatively poor governance quality and business environment of their home countries, emerging market multinationals may be regarded less favorably than firms of host countries. Depending upon the income of potential host countries, multinationals may also behave differently. That is, foreign investors may respond more sensitively to the local governance and business environment of developing countries than to those of high-income countries. Some studies have also found that determinants of FDI flows are not the same in different sectors. For example, multinationals investing in the primary sector may consider less importantly local governance and business environment (Walsh and Yu 2010).

---

[1] Many studies examine country-specific determinants of greenfield and mergers and acquisitions (M&A) investments but few focus on policy factors. For example, Neto, Brandao, and Cerqueira (2010), Byun, Lee, and Park (2012), and Davies, Desbordes, and Ray (2015). There are also few studies that focus on one particular mode of FDI. For example, using bilateral M&A data from 1990 to 2001, Gassebner and Méon (2010) present evidence that political risk decreases M&A inflows but they do not compare how M&A is different from greenfield FDI.

The study in this chapter empirically assesses how the two modes of FDI flows from high-income to developing countries respond differently to various institutional and policy factors of host countries in different sectors. As a comparison, this study will also assess the effects of local institutional and policy factors on FDI flows between high-income countries as well as from emerging countries to developing or high-income countries.

For this purpose, bilateral greenfield and M&A investments are utilized from 26 high-income countries (24 Organisation for Economic Co-operation and Development [OECD] countries and Hong Kong, China and Singapore)[2] to 97 developing countries[3] and 45 high-income countries for 2003–2015, and applies Poisson Pseudo-Maximum Likelihood (PPML) estimation to the gravity model. As a comparison, FDI flows from 10 major emerging investors[4] to 97 developing countries and 45 high-income countries are compared for the same period.

First, this chapter describes the data on greenfield investment and M&A investments and the key institutional and policy variables used in the regression analysis.

Descriptive Statistics

Bilateral Greenfield and M&A Investments

We use data on bilateral greenfield and M&A investments. The former was acquired from fDi Markets (Financial Times Ltd.) and the latter from Zephyr. The counts and dollar values of greenfield and M&A investments are available from these two sources. However, for M&A investment, the values are often not reported for confidentiality reasons. A complete set of counts and dollar values is reported in the case of greenfield investment, but when the investing company does not release the dollar value, the data

---

[2]   Among the 35 OECD member countries, 11 countries are excluded because the size of their FDI is small (e.g., Chile) or because their income level is not high (e.g., Mexico and Turkey).

[3]   Developing countries in this chapter include "low income," "lower middle income," and "upper middle income" countries, while high-income countries include "high-income" countries classified by the World Bank (2015).

[4]   The People's Republic of China (PRC), India, the Russian Federation, Malaysia, South Africa, Turkey, Brazil, Thailand, Mexico, and Poland. These 10 emerging countries are also included as developing country hosts. Note that Mexico and Turkey are OECD member countries but their per capita income level is below $10,000 in 2015 and hence are included here as emerging source countries rather than high-income source countries.

provider (fDi Intelligence) estimates the value by an algorithm.[5] Thus, the dollar values of greenfield investment may not be as accurate as its counts.

Therefore, we use data on the counts of bilateral greenfield and M&A investments conducted by 26 high-income countries and 10 major emerging countries. Tables 7.1a and 7.1b report the list of all source countries included in the present study. Table 7.1a lists the ranking of source countries according to total greenfield FDI during 2004–2015, while Table 7.1b according to total cross-border M&A. The 36 countries conducted 137,624 counts of greenfield investment projects and 129,205 counts of M&A deals during 2004–2015. With 34,777 counts, the United States (US) was the number one greenfield investor followed by the United Kingdom (UK), Germany, Japan, and France. These five investors account for 58.7% of the total count. These countries are also major acquirers during the period. The PRC and India ranked 10th and 11th in greenfield investment but their investment each amounts to less than one-tenth of that of the US. The total count of greenfield investment made by the 10 emerging countries is only about one-tenth of that of the 36 source countries. In the case of cross-border M&A, the share of the 10 emerging countries is even smaller.

Figure 7.1 shows the trend of greenfield investment and M&A investments conducted by the 36 countries during 2004–2015. There were fewer cases of cross-border M&A than greenfield investment in the early years of 2000s, but M&A overtook greenfield investment in more recent years. Figures 7.2a and 7.2b show the trend of the two different modes of FDI, from high-income countries versus emerging countries. Both greenfield and M&A investments from emerging countries have increased gradually throughout the entire period but have remained considerably smaller than those from high-income countries.

The 36 countries made greenfield investments in 213 economies during 2004–2015, Table 7.2a lists the 40 major hosting economies of greenfield investment. They received 85% of total greenfield investments from the 36 countries (117,566 of 137,624). With 13,308 counts, the US is the largest recipient of greenfield investment accounting for almost 10% of the total counts. Among the developing countries, the PRC, India, the Russian Federation, Brazil, Mexico, Viet Nam, Romania, Thailand, and Malaysia are major recipients of greenfield investment.

---

[5]   The algorithm looks at projects in the same country/sector/activity with actual jobs and capital expenditure data and then removes the smallest 5% of projects and largest 5% of projects to create a data set for estimates. If there are less than five projects in the data set, then the algorithm takes the regional data. Where fewer than five projects are in the data set, the algorithm takes the global data set (an internal description provided by fDi Intelligence).

Table 7.1a: Ranking of Source Economies According to Total Greenfield FDI, 2004–2015

Ranking	Income Level	Source Economy	Greenfield FDI	Cross-Border M&A
1	High-income	United States	34,777	37,383
2	High-income	United Kingdom	13,832	16,590
3	High-income	Germany	13,347	7,128
4	High-income	Japan	10,924	4,229
5	High-income	France	7,946	6,321
6	High-income	Switzerland	4,674	6,375
7	High-income	Spain	4,339	2,222
8	High-income	Netherlands	4,197	5,010
9	High-income	Canada	4,163	5,231
10	Emerging	People's Republic of China	3,657	1,860
11	Emerging	India	3,434	1,413
12	High-income	Italy	2,988	1,569
13	High-income	Sweden	2,782	3,257
14	High-income	Republic of Korea	2,515	832
15	High-income	Austria	2,253	1,355
16	High-income	Australia	2,095	3,269
17	High-income	Denmark	1,678	1,521
18	High-income	Finland	1,661	1,511
19	High-income	Ireland	1,636	1,316
20	High-income	Belgium	1,611	2,277
21	Emerging	Russian Federation	1,609	1,543
22	High-income	Singapore	1,579	4,265
23	High-income	Hong Kong, China	1,411	3,707
24	High-income	Norway	1,202	2,004
25	High-income	Luxembourg	1,135	2,142
26	Emerging	Malaysia	898	991
27	Emerging	South Africa	763	679
28	Emerging	Brazil	719	363
29	Emerging	Turkey	705	207
30	High-income	Portugal	619	343
31	Emerging	Thailand	508	240
32	High-income	New Zealand	428	426
33	Emerging	Mexico	411	342
34	High-income	Czech Republic	410	315
35	Emerging	Poland	384	519
36	High-income	Greece	334	450
	High-income total		**124,536**	**121,048**
	Emerging total		**13,088**	**8,157**
	All countries total		**137,624**	**129,205**

FDI = foreign direct investment, M&A = merger and acquisition.

Source: Compiled by author from fDi Market (Financial Times Ltd.) for greenfield investment and from the Zephyr Database for M&A investment.

Table 7.1b: Ranking of Source Economies According to Total Cross-Border M&A, 2004–2015

Ranking	Income Level	Source Economy	Cross-Border M&A	Greenfield FDI
1	High-income	United States	37,383	34,777
2	High-income	United Kingdom	16,590	13,832
3	High-income	Germany	7,128	13,347
4	High-income	Switzerland	6,375	4,674
5	High-income	France	6,321	7,946
6	High-income	Canada	5,231	4,163
7	High-income	Netherlands	5,010	4,197
8	High-income	Singapore	4,265	1,579
9	High-income	Japan	4,229	10,924
10	High-income	Hong Kong, China	3,707	1,411
11	High-income	Australia	3,269	2,095
12	High-income	Sweden	3,257	2,782
13	High-income	Belgium	2,277	1,611
14	High-income	Spain	2,222	4,339
15	High-income	Luxembourg	2,142	1,135
16	High-income	Norway	2,004	1,202
17	Emerging	People's Republic of China	1,860	3,657
18	High-income	Italy	1,569	2,988
19	Emerging	Russian Federation	1,543	1,609
20	High-income	Denmark	1,521	1,678
21	High-income	Finland	1,511	1,661
22	Emerging	India	1,413	3,434
23	High-income	Austria	1,355	2,253
24	High-income	Ireland	1,316	1,636
25	Emerging	Malaysia	991	898
26	High-income	Republic of Korea	832	2,515
27	Emerging	South Africa	679	763
28	Emerging	Poland	519	384
29	High-income	Greece	450	334
30	High-income	New Zealand	426	428
31	Emerging	Brazil	363	719
32	High-income	Portugal	343	619
33	Emerging	Mexico	342	411
34	High-income	Czech Republic	315	410
35	Emerging	Thailand	240	508
36	Emerging	Turkey	207	705
	High-income total		121,048	124,536
	Emerging total		8,157	13,088
	All countries total		129,205	137,624

FDI = foreign direct investment, M&A = merger and acquisition.

Source: Compiled by author from fDi Market (Financial Times Ltd.) for greenfield investment and from the Zephyr Database for M&A investment.

Figure 7.1: Trend of Greenfield and M&A Investments, 2004–2015 (Counts)

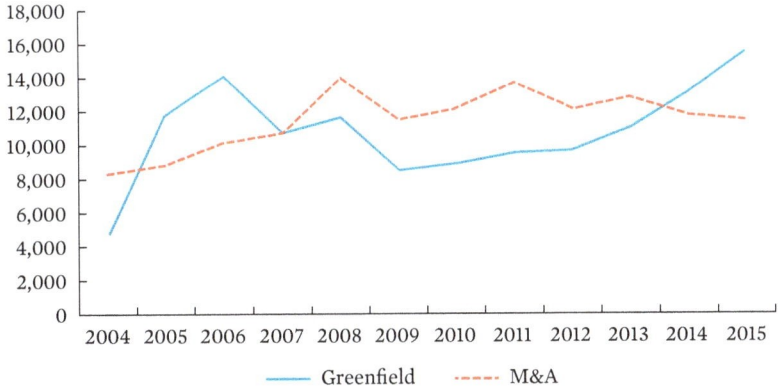

M&A = merger and acquisition.
Source: Authors' calculation using data from fDi Market (Financial Times Ltd.) for greenfield investment and from the Zephyr Database for M&A investment.

Figure 7.2a: Trend of Greenfield FDI from High-Income versus Emerging Countries, 2004–2015 (Counts)

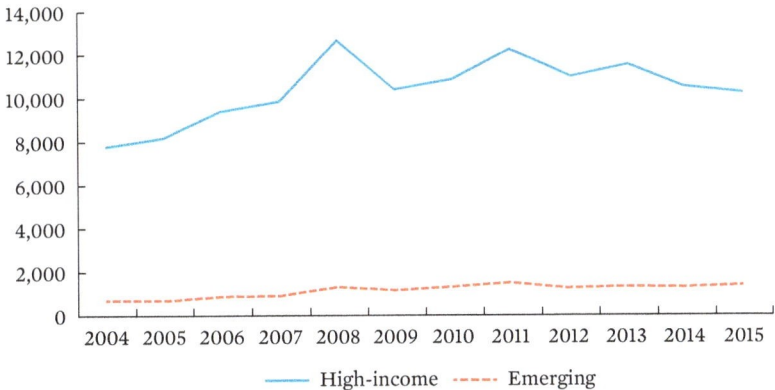

FDI = foreign direct investment.
Source: Authors' calculation using data from fDi Market (Financial Times Ltd.).

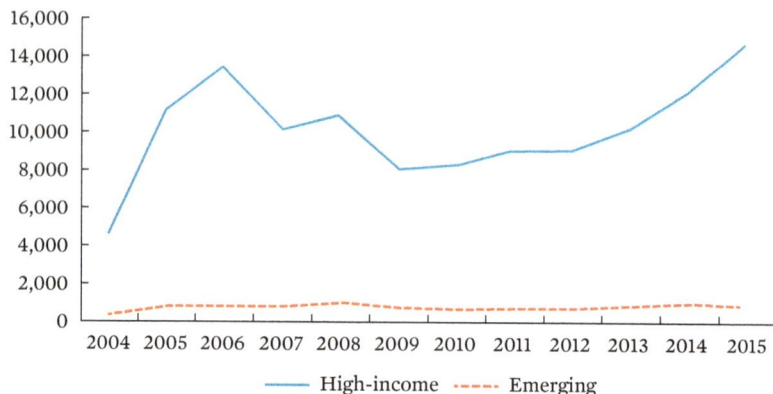

Figure 7.2b: Trend of Cross-Border M&A from High-Income versus Emerging Countries, 2004–2015 (Counts)

M&A = merger and acquisition.
Source: Authors' calculation using data from Zephyr Database.

Table 7.2b lists the 40 major hosts of M&A investment which account for 89% of 129,205 deals made in 213 economies during 2004–2015. The US received the most cross-border M&A investments, followed by the UK and the PRC. Only 12 developing countries are among the 40 major hosts of M&A investments. Compared to greenfield investment, cross-border M&A is less common in developing countries than in high-income countries.

Regression analyses examine the determinants of greenfield and M&A investments from 26 high-income countries and 10 emerging countries to 97 developing countries and 45 high-income countries, respectively, for which the data for explanatory variables are available.[6] Table 7.3a presents the top 40 country pairs for greenfield investment during 2004–2014. The US–PRC pair shows the largest amount of greenfield investment flows, followed by US–UK, US–India, UK–US, and the Japan–PRC pair, which are all large countries in terms of population and gross domestic product (GDP). Thus, we can see that gravity works well in bilateral greenfield investments. Table 7.3b presents the corresponding pairs for M&A investments.

---

[6] 97 developing hosts include the 10 emerging countries which are considered as source countries, while 45 high-income hosts include the 26 high-income countries which are also considered as source countries.

Table 7.2a: 40 Major Hosts of Greenfield FDI, 2004–2015

Ranking	Income level	Host economy	Greenfield FDI	Cross-Border M&A
1	High-income	United States	13,308	16,748
2	Developing	People's Republic of China	12,951	7,013
3	High-income	United Kingdom	9,066	15,255
4	Developing	India	8,004	4,918
5	High-income	Germany	6,917	6,624
6	High-income	France	4,724	5,189
7	Developing	Russian Federation	3,456	2, 115
8	High-income	Singapore	3,452	1,369
9	Developing	Brazil	3,355	2,006
10	High-income	Spain	3,254	2,871
11	Developing	Mexico	3,222	825
12	High-income	United Arab Emirates	3,215	415
13	High-income	Poland	2,891	1,059
14	High-income	Australia	2,864	5,236
15	High-income	Canada	2,681	6,433
16	Developing	Viet Nam	2,231	521
17	Developing	Romania	2,089	644
18	High-income	Hong Kong, China	1,982	1,127
19	Developing	Thailand	1,899	448
20	High-income	Japan	1,731	2,543
21	High-income	Netherlands	1,724	4,040
22	High-income	Ireland	1,666	1,293
23	Developing	Malaysia	1,654	890
24	High-income	Belgium	1,562	1,871
25	High-income	Hungary	1,480	480
26	High-income	Italy	1,457	3,759
27	High-income	Czech Republic	1,395	753
28	Developing	Indonesia	1,393	923
29	Developing	Turkey	1,260	628
30	Developing	South Africa	1,211	967
31	Developing	Philippines	1,186	298
32	High-income	Republic of Korea	1,173	1,800
33	High-income	Switzerland	1,168	1,864
34	Developing	Bulgaria	953	1,312
35	Developing	Argentina	925	485
36	High-income	Sweden	831	2,648
37	High-income	Taipei,China	826	375
38	High-income	Slovak Republic	806	221
39	High-income	Austria	802	816
40	Developing	Colombia	792	339

FDI = foreign direct investment, M&A = merger and acquisition.

Source: Authors' calculation using data from fDi Market (Financial Times Ltd.) for greenfield investment and from the Zephyr Database for M&A investment.

Table 7.2b: 40 Major Hosts of Cross-Border M&A, 2004–2015

Ranking	Income level	Host economy	Cross-Border M&A	Greenfield FDI
1	High-income	United States	16,748	13,308
2	High-income	United Kingdom	15,255	9,066
3	Developing	People's Republic of China	7,013	12,951
4	High-income	Germany	6,624	6,917
5	High-income	Canada	6,433	2,681
6	High-income	Australia	5,238	2,864
7	High-income	France	5,189	4,724
8	Developing	India	4,918	8,004
9	High-income	Netherlands	4,040	1,724
10	High-income	Italy	3,759	1,467
11	High-income	Spain	2,871	3,254
12	High-income	Sweden	2,648	831
13	High-income	Japan	2,543	1,731
14	Developing	Russian Federation	2,115	3,456
15	Developing	Brazil	2,006	3,355
16	High-income	Belgium	1,871	1,562
17	High-income	Switzerland	1,864	1,168
18	High-income	Republic of Korea	1,800	1,173
19	High-income	Israel	1,711	331
20	High-income	Norway	1,567	298
21	High-income	Finland	1,414	675
22	High-income	Singapore	1,369	3,452
23	High-income	Denmark	1,336	712
24	Developing	Bulgaria	1,312	953
25	High-income	Ireland	1,293	1,666
26	High-income	Hong Kong, China	1,127	1,982
27	High-income	Poland	1,059	2,891
28	Developing	South Africa	967	1,211
29	High-income	New Zealand	926	388
30	Developing	Indonesia	923	1,393
31	Developing	Malaysia	890	1,654
32	Developing	Mexico	825	3,222
33	High-income	Austria	816	802
34	High-income	Portugal	808	494
35	Developing	Ukraine	763	771
36	High-income	Czech Republic	753	1,395
37	Developing	Romania	644	2,089
38	Developing	Turkey	628	1,260
39	High-income	Luxembourg	610	186
40	High-income	Cyprus	526	80

FDI = foreign direct investment, M&A = merger and acquisition.

Source: Authors' calculation using data from fDi Market (Financial Times Ltd.) for greenfield investment and from the Zephyr Database for M&A investment.

The top five country pairs are all high-income countries except the US–PRC pair that ranked fifth. In fact, for M&A investment, there are only six country pairs which include developing countries as host countries, whereas in greenfield investment, there are 13 pairs which include developing countries as host countries. Therefore, compared to greenfield investment, cross-border M&A is less common between high-income and developing countries. This finding is consistent with Nocke and Yeaple (2008) who claim that most FDI takes the form of cross-border M&A when production cost differences between home and host countries are small, while greenfield investment plays a more important role for FDI from high-cost to low-cost countries.

This chapter aims to assess how FDI flows into primary sector and services sector are different from those into other sector (mostly manufacturing sector). Tables 7.4a and 7.4b list all industries and their respective sectoral classification according to the size of greenfield FDI and cross-border M&A. Primary sector includes coal, oil, and natural gas, metals, and minerals, while services sector includes business services, communications, financial services, health care, leisure and entertainment, personal services, public and social service, software and information technology (IT) services, and warehousing and storage.[7] Data provided by Zephyr are matched with industries classified by fDi Markets. In both modes of FDI, primary sector accounts for about 10% or less of total counts. Primary sector is the largest in greenfield FDI while in M&A, primary sector and services sector are similar in size.

Figures 7.3a and 7.3b illustrate the sectoral trend of the two different modes of FDI, from the 26 high-income countries and 10 emerging countries included in our study as source countries. Greenfield investment to other sector has remained larger than that to services sector during 2004–2015, while cross-border M&A to services sector surpassed that to other sector since 2012. Both greenfield and M&A investments to primary sector have remained substantially small throughout the whole period.

---

[7]   Some industries classified by fDi Markets are not clear enough to be reclassified into the three sectors of primary, manufacturing, and services. For example, "automotive OEM" industry, which includes mostly manufactured products such as automobiles, also includes "motor vehicle and parts deals," which appears to be part of services sector. However, the share of such ambiguous sub-industries is very small, so in this chapter only obvious industries are reclassified into primary sector and services sector and the remaining industries are classified as "other sector," which can be regarded as "manufacturing sector."

Table 7.3a: 40 Major Economy Pairs for Greenfield FDI, 2003–2015

Ranking	Source Economy	Host Economy	Greenfield FDI	Cross-Border M&A
1	US	PRC	3,870	2,692
2	US	UK	3,791	7,155
3	US	IND	3,017	2,581
4	UK	US	2,404	3,752
5	JPN	PRC	1,924	592
6	US	DEU	1,712	1,835
7	DEU	US	1,706	1,341
8	JPN	US	1,487	1,266
9	US	CAN	1,408	4,416
10	CAN	US	1,333	2,863
11	US	FRA	1,325	1,592
12	DEU	PRC	1,282	151
13	US	MEX	1,191	387
14	US	SGP	1,114	327
15	US	AUS	1,020	2,119
16	US	BRA	971	871
17	FRA	US	920	989
18	UK	PRC	914	288
19	UK	IND	892	455
20	US	IRL	889	434
21	US	ARE	861	115
22	JPN	THA	814	111
23	US	JPN	770	1,296
24	JPN	IND	763	215
25	DEU	IND	762	182
26	CHE	DEU	732	719
27	DEU	UK	730	1,038
28	DEU	FRA	714	330
29	US	NLD	694	1,163
30	US	ESP	687	638
31	US	HKG	650	245
32	UK	DEU	643	1,206
33	US	RUS	612	397
34	FRA	PRC	611	184
35	FRA	UK	611	1,003
36	UK	ARE	607	72
37	UK	AUS	586	815
38	JPN	VNM	586	124
39	UK	SGP	555	101
40	US	POL	548	145

ARE = United Arab Emirates; AUS = Australia; BRA = Brazil; CAN = Canada; CHE = Switzerland; DEU = Germany; ESP = Spain; FDI = foreign direct investment; FRA = France; HKG = Hong Kong, China; IND = India; IRL = Israel; JPN = Japan; M&A = merger and acquisition; MEX = Mexico; NLD = Netherlands; POL = Poland; PRC = People's Republic of China; RUS = Russian Federation; SGP = Singapore; THA = Thailand; UK = United Kingdom; US = United States; VNM = Viet Nam.

Source: Authors' calculation using data from fDi Market (Financial Times Ltd.) for greenfield investment and from the Zephyr Database for M&A investment.

Table 7.3b: 40 Major Economy Pairs for Cross-Border M&A, 2003–2015

Ranking	Source Economy	Host Economy	Cross-Border M&A	Greenfield FDI
1	US	UK	7,155	3,791
2	US	CAN	4,416	1,408
3	UK	US	3,752	2,404
4	CAN	US	2,863	1,333
5	US	PRC	2,692	3,870
6	US	IND	2,581	3,017
7	US	AUS	2,119	1,020
8	US	DEU	1,835	1,712
9	US	FRA	1,592	1,325
10	CHE	US	1,498	465
11	HKG	PRC	1,448	487
12	DEU	US	1,341	1,706
13	US	JPN	1,296	770
14	JPN	US	1,266	1,487
15	UK	DEU	1,206	643
16	US	NLD	1163	694
17	US	ISR	1142	204
18	UK	FRA	1109	536
19	CHE	UK	1099	204
20	DEU	UK	1038	730
21	FRA	UK	1003	611
22	AUS	UK	992	239
23	FRA	US	989	920
24	US	ITA	892	362
25	US	BRA	871	971
26	UK	AUS	815	586
27	SGP	PRC	736	340
28	US	KOR	729	449
29	CHE	DEU	719	732
30	UK	NLD	678	200
31	UK	ITA	665	182
32	US	ESP	638	687
33	UK	CAN	631	250
34	JPN	PRC	592	1,924
35	UK	ESP	560	363
36	US	SWE	546	206
37	NLD	US	530	407
38	AUS	NZL	522	85
39	UK	IRL	496	335
40	FRA	DEU	492	460

AUS = Australia; BRA = Brazil; CAN = Canada; CHE = Switzerland; DEU = Germany; ESP = Spain; FDI = foreign direct investment; FRA = France; HKG = Hong Kong, China; IND = India, IRL = Israel; ITA = Italy; JPN = Japan; KOR = Republic of Korea; M&A = merger and acquisition; NLD = Netherlands; NZL = New Zealand; PRC = People's Republic of China; SGP = Singapore; SWE = Sweden; UK = United Kingdom; US = United States.

Source: Authors' calculation using data from fDi Market (Financial Times Ltd.) for greenfield investment and from the Zephyr Database for M&A investment.

Table 7.4a: Industrial Classification According to the Size of Greenfield FDI

Sector	Industry	Greenfield FDI	Cross-Border M&A
Services	Software and IT services	18,559	13,828
Services	Business services	15,077	18,901
Services	Financial services	11,790	11,163
Others	Industrial machinery, equipment, and tools	8,954	5,902
Services	Communications	7,185	14,489
Others	Transportation	6,331	3,692
Others	Automotive components	5,669	1,700
Others	Chemicals	5,390	3,135
Primary	Metals	5,116	6,077
Others	Food and tobacco	4,525	4,388
Others	Electronic components	4,438	1,519
Others	Real estate	4,291	4,821
Primary	Coal, oil, and natural gas	3,157	6,370
Others	Hotels and tourism	3,025	1,639
Others	Plastics	3,003	1,096
Others	Automotive OEM	2,846	491
Others	Alternative renewable energy	2,663	1,499
Others	Consumer products	2,618	7,470
Others	Pharmaceuticals	2,494	2,580
Others	Textiles	1,821	2,257
Others	Medical devices	1,713	1,900
Others	Business machines and equipment	1,500	765
Others	Consumer electronics	1,556	835
Others	Semiconductors	1,467	2,919
Others	Aerospace	1,460	329
Others	Building and construction materials	1,232	697
Services	Paper, printing, and packaging	1,223	1,051
Others	Rubber	1,154	294
Others	Beverages	1,051	1,646
Services	Warehousing and storage	1,003	356
Others	Non-automotive transport OEM	929	461
Others	Biotechnology	807	2,297
Others	Engine and turbines	717	316
Others	Ceramics and glass	711	539
Others	Health care	612	1,157
Others	Wood products	510	428
Primary	Minerals	372	699

continued on next page

Table 7.4a continued

Sector	Industry	Greenfield FDI	Cross-Border M&A
Services	Leisure and entertainment	347	932
Others	Space and defense	248	19
Services	Personal services	0	265
Others	Unclassified	0	235
Services	Public and social services	0	48
Services total		**55,184**	**59,033**
Primary total		**8,645**	**13,146**
Others total		**73,795**	**57,026**
All industries total		**137,624**	**129,205**

FDI = foreign direct investment, IT = information technology, M&A = merger and acquisition, OEM = original equipment manufacturer.
Source: Authors' calculation using data from fDi Market (Financial Times Ltd.) for greenfield investment and from the Zephyr Database for M&A investment.

Table 7.4b: Industrial Classification According to the Size of Cross-Border M&A

Sector	Industry	Cross-Border M&A	Greenfield FDI
Services	Business services	16,901	15,077
Services	Communications	14,489	7,185
Services	Software and IT services	13,828	18,559
Services	Financial services	11,163	11,790
Others	Consumer products	7,470	2,618
Primary	Coal, oil, and natural gas	6,370	3,157
Primary	Metals	6,077	5,116
Others	Industrial machinery, equipment, and tools	5,902	8,954
Others	Real estate	4,821	4,291
Others	Food and tobacco	4,388	4,525
Others	Transportation	3,692	6,331
Others	Chemicals	3,135	5,390
Others	Semiconductors	2,919	1,467
Others	Pharmaceuticals	2,580	2,494
Others	Biotechnology	2,297	807
Others	Textiles	2,257	1,821
Others	Medical devices	1,900	1,713
Others	Automotive components	1,700	5,669
Others	Beverages	1,646	1,051

continued on next page

Table 7.4b continued

Sector	Industry	Cross-Border M&A	Greenfield FDI
Others	Hotels and tourism	1,639	3,025
Others	Electronic components	1,519	4,438
Others	Alternative/Renewable energy	1,499	2,663
Others	Health care	1,157	612
Others	Plastics	1,096	3,003
Services	Paper, printing, and packaging	1,051	1,223
Services	Leisure and entertainment	932	347
Others	Consumer electronics	835	1,556
Others	Business machines and equipment	765	1,560
Primary	Minerals	699	372
Others	Building and construction materials	697	1,232
Others	Ceramics and glass	539	711
Others	Automotive OEM	491	2,846
Others	Non-automotive transport OEM	461	929
Others	Wood products	428	510
Services	Warehousing and storage	356	1,003
Others	Aerospace	329	1,460
Others	Engines and turbines	316	717
Others	Rubber	294	1,154
Services	Personal services	265	0
Others	Unclassified	235	0
Services	Public and social service	48	0
Others	Space and defense	19	248
Services total		**59,033**	**55,184**
Primary total		**13,146**	**8,645**
Others total		**57,026**	**73,795**
All industries total		**129,205**	**137,624**

FDI = foreign direct investment, IT = information technology, M&A = merger and acquisition, OEM = original equipment manufacturer.

Source: Authors' calculation using data from fDi Market (Financial Times Ltd.) for greenfield investment and from the Zephyr Database for M&A investment.

Figure 7.3a: Trend of Greenfield FDI by Sector, 2004–2015 (Counts)

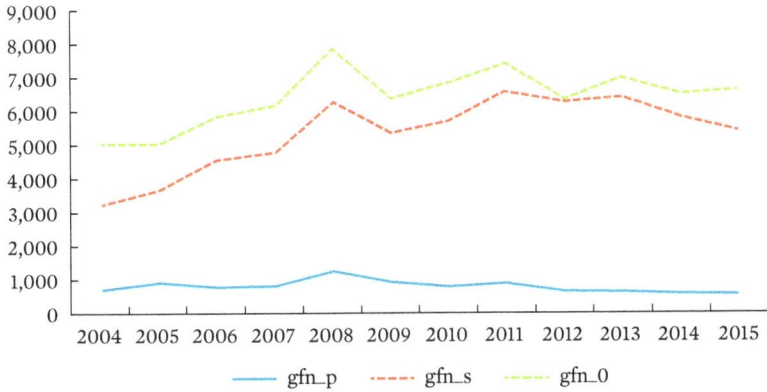

FDI = foreign direct investment, gfn_o = greenfield investment to other sector, gfn_p = greenfield investment to primary sector, gfn_s = greenfield investment to services sector.
Source: Authors' calculation using data from fDi Market (Financial Times Ltd.).

Figure 7.3b: Trend of Cross-Border M&A by Sector, 2004–2015 (Counts)

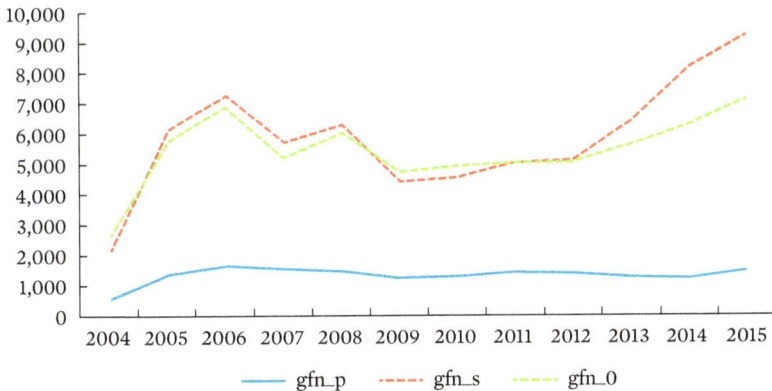

M&A = merger and acquisition, man_o = cross-border M&A to other sector, man_p = cross-border M&A to primary sector, man_s = cross-border M&A to services sector.
Source: Authors' calculation using data from fDi Market (Financial Times Ltd.).

Institutional and Policy Variables

In the regression analyses, we use different institutional and policy variables alternatively in the gravity equations for bilateral greenfield investment and M&A investment. Specifically, we use one set of institutional variables and two sets of policy variables which are all host-country specific. In addition, we investigate the impact of pair-specific policy variables for RTA and BIT.

World Bank's Worldwide Governance Indicators

For assessment of host country's institutional quality on investment inflows, we utilize World Bank's Worldwide Governance Indicators (WGI), which are annually available from 1996 for 215 countries and territories. WGIs are comprised of six indicators: (i) voice and accountability, (ii) political stability and absence of violence/terrorism, (iii) government effectiveness, (iv) regulatory quality, (v) rule of law, and (vi) control of corruption. See Table A7.2 for detailed explanations about WGIs. These aggregate indicators are constructed based on different data sources produced by a variety of different organizations. Each indicator ranges from –2.5 to 2.5, with higher score for higher quality of governance/institution.[8] For easier comparison with other policy measures, we transform the WGIs to range from 0 to 100, by adding 2.5 and then multiplying them by 20.

Some studies have utilized WGIs to investigate institutional determinants of FDI and found that a wide range of institutions including corruption do matter for inward FDI (among others, Globerman and Shapiro 2004; Bénassy-Quéré, Coupet, and Mayer 2007; Buchanan, Le, and Rishi 2012). The six indicators are highly correlated with each other. Therefore, similarly to Globerman and Shapiro (2002; 2004), we create an aggregate measure as a simple average of the six indicators and use it as an overall governance infrastructure measure in the regression analysis. We also include each of them alternatively in the regression so as to assess which component of governance infrastructure matters more in influencing FDI inflows. In order to mitigate potential endogeneity of WGIs, we match the averages of FDI data for 2004–2006, 2007–2009, 2010–2012, and 2013–2015 with the WGI data for the preceding year of each subperiod (i.e., 2003, 2006, 2009, and 2012).

---

[8] For the methodology of the WGI, the reader is referred to Kaufmann, Kraay, and Mastruzzi (2011). See also Thomas (2009) for a critical review.

Table A7.1 lists all economies with their respective average value of WGIs during the years of 2003, 2006, 2009, and 2012. The average value of WGIs for all high-income economies was 70.2, while that for developing economies was 41.2. Thus, the governance quality of high-income economies is generally higher than that of developing economies.

Among the 97 developing economies, Chile ranked first with a score of 73.2 followed by Mauritius, Botswana, Lithuania, and Uruguay. Democratic Republic of Congo, Myanmar, Iraq, Sudan, and Chad ranked in the bottom with scores from 17.5 to 23.6. Among the high-income economies, Finland ranked first with 88.0, followed by Denmark, Sweden, New Zealand, and Switzerland, while Equatorial Guinea, Saudi Arabia, Bahrain, Trinidad and Tobago, and Kuwait scored from 25.5 to 53.5, ranking at the bottom among the high-income economies.

World Bank's Ease of Doing Business

A country's business regulatory environment may influence not only domestic investment but also FDI it attracts. The World Bank's Ease of Doing Business (EoDB) reports have been ranking countries annually since 2003. The Doing Business 2016 reports include 10 components: (i) starting a business, (ii) dealing with construction permits, (iii) getting electricity, (iv) registering property, (v) getting credit, (vi) protecting minority investors, (vii) paying taxes, (viii) trading across borders, (ix) enforcing contracts, and (x) resolving insolvency. See Table A7.3 for detailed explanations about EoDBs. Each indicator ranges from 0 to 100, with higher score representing better environment for doing business.[9]

Using the official rankings from 2006 to 2009, Jayasuriya (2011) shows a positive relationship between EoDB ranking and FDI inflows. However, when the sample is restricted to developing countries, the results suggest that an improved ranking has, on average, an insignificant influence on FDI inflows. Using the Doing Business rank for 2004–2009, Corcoran and Gillanders (2015) show that the overall Doing Business is significant in attracting FDI. They further show that the relationship is driven by the "ease of trading across borders" component and that the relationship is significant for middle-income countries, but not for the world's poorest region, Sub-Saharan Africa, or for the OECD countries.

---

[9] For the methodology of the EoDB, the reader is referred to http://www.doingbusiness.org/methodology.

Among the 10 components, the "registering property" component has been added since the 2005 Report whereas the components of "registering property," "protecting minority investors," "paying taxes," "trading across borders," and "dealing with construction permits" have been added since the 2006 Report. The "getting electricity" component has been added only since 2011 reports.

Therefore, in the regression analysis, we drop the "getting electricity" component and use the nine indicators for 2006, 2009 and 2012, contained in 2007, 2010, and 2013 reports, respectively, and match them with the averages of FDI data for 2007–2009, 2010–2012, and 2013–2015.[10] Similarly to the case of WGIs, we first use an overall measure of EoDB as an average of the nine indicators of EoDB and also each of the nine EoDB indicators as an explanatory variable, alternatively.

EoDB ranges between 1 and 100, with higher value for more favorable business environments. As seen in Table A7.1, with an average score of 71.9, ease of doing business indicator for high-income economies was much higher than that for overall developing economies whose average score was 53.5. Among the 97 developing economies, Malaysia, Lithuania, Latvia, Georgia, and Mauritius ranked highest, in a range of 73.8 ~ 70.8, comparable to those of Belgium, Switzerland, Israel, and Portugal. In contrast, Chad, Libya, Democratic Republic of Congo, Venezuela, and Guinea ranked at the bottom, with a range of 28.6 to 36.2. Among the high-income economies, Singapore; New Zealand; Hong Kong, China; the US; and Ireland had the best environment for doing business, while Equatorial Guinea, Croatia, Brunei Darussalam, Trinidad and Tobago, and Greece had the worst environment for doing business (see Table A7.1).

Regional Trade Agreement

There have been many theoretical and empirical studies that investigate the effects of regional trade agreements (RTAs) on FDI. Most theoretical studies have shown that RTA increases investments not only from intra-block firms but also from outside firms (e.g., Motta and Norman, 1996; Ekholm, Forslid, and Markusen 2007; and Ito 2013).

---

[10] The data for all sets of indicators in each year's Doing Business Report are for the previous year. (i.e., the data in 2004 Report is for year 2003, and so forth.).

Using US data for 1985–1999, Chen (2009) finds that RTAs increase outside multinationals' incentive to invest in the participating countries, especially in those that are integrated with larger markets and have lower production costs. Similarly, Kreinin and Plummer (2008) find that RTAs have had a positive and significant effect on FDI in the cases of European Union, North American Free Trade Agreement, Southern Common Market, and Association of Southeast Asian Nations. Using bilateral outward FDI stock from 20 OECD countries to 60 host countries for 1982–1999, Yeyati, Stein, and Daude (2003) find that only the countries in the RTA that offer a more attractive overall environment for FDI are likely to attract more FDI. Using bilateral flow data between 25 OECD and 45 high-income and 95 developing countries for 2003–2012, Chala and Lee (2015) find that common membership in RTAs promotes bilateral greenfield investment only in OECD-developing country pairs.

Some researchers investigate how RTA effects differ for different country groupings. Using bilateral outward FDI between 24 home and 28 host European countries, Baltagi, Egger, and Pfaffermayr (2008) find that RTA for a given home country exerts positive effects on FDI in Eastern European host countries where vertical FDI prevails and negative effects on Western European host countries where horizontal FDI prevails. Based on the knowledge capital model, Jang (2011) finds that bilateral free trade agreement (FTA) decreases bilateral FDI in the OECD–OECD country pairs but increases bilateral outward FDI in the OECD–non–OECD country pairs where skill difference is large and vertical FDI prevails. Chala and Lee (2015) also find that RTAs may discourage greenfield investment between OECD and high-income countries, while they promote greenfield investment between OECD and developing countries.

While most studies ignore the actual content of RTAs, Berger et al. (2013) analyze the impact of modalities on FDI. Using bilateral FDI flows between 28 home and 83 host countries for 1978–2004, they find that RTAs increase FDI only if the RTAs offer liberal admission rules and that RTAs without strong investment provisions may even discourage FDI.

None of the abovementioned studies examine how differently an RTA affects greenfield investment versus M&A investment. In a theoretical analysis, Kim (2009) examines the impacts of RTA on the FDI entry mode of multinational firm focusing on greenfield investment versus cross-border M&A. Based on an oligopoly market structure, he shows that the formation of an FTA between home and host countries eliminates the tariff-jumping advantage of greenfield investment, so discouraging greenfield investment.

According to the date of entry into force, we compile an RTA dummy variable referring to the WTO's RTA database.11 As with other variables, we match the RTA dummies for 2003, 2006, 2009, and 2012 with the averages of FDI data for 2004–2006, 2007–2009, 2010–2012, and 2013–2015.

Bilateral Investment Treaty

Bilateral investment treaty (BIT) is an international agreement establishing legally binding terms and conditions for FDI. Many BITs set forth actionable standards of conduct that applied to governments in their treatment of investors from other states, including: (i) fair and equitable treatment (most-favored-nation treatment), (ii) protection from expropriation, and (iii) free transfer of means and full protection and security.[12]

Accordingly, BITs are expected to promote FDI inflows between signatories. In developing countries, in particular, BITs may compensate for less developed local institutions and can be expected to promote FDI inflows. Many studies, however, have produced ambiguous results on the effectiveness of BITs in promoting FDI inflows. For example, Busse, Koniger, and Nunnenkamp (2010) find that BITs promote FDI flows to developing countries and may even substitute for weak domestic institutions, but Tobin and Rose-Ackerman (2005) conclude that BITs do not encourage FDI except at low levels of political risk. In particular, Tobin and Rose-Ackerman reject the view that BITs are a substitute for a favorable local business environment, whereas Neumayer and Spess (2005) report some limited evidence to this effect.

None of the previous studies has investigated how BITs influence greenfield investment and M&As differentially. Because there is no theoretical model that predicts differential effects of BITs on greenfield versus M&A investments, we do not make any a priori hypothesis and take this as an empirical question.

Our bilateral investment treaty data are taken from the website of the United Nations Conference on Trade and Development (UNCTAD). Our BIT variable is a dummy variable taking the value of one for a ratified BIT

---

[11] World Trade Organization. Regional trade agreements. https://www.wto.org/english/tratop_e/region_e/region_e.htm.

[12] Legal Information Institute, Cornell University Law School (https://www.law.cornell.edu/wex/bilateral_investment_treaty).

between the source and the host country.[13] In order to mitigate potential reverse causality, we match the BIT dummies for 2003, 2006, 2009, and 2012 with the averages of FDI data for 2003–2005, 2006–2008, 2009–2011, and 2012–2014.

Empirical Specification

The Gravity Model

The main purpose of this chapter is to assess how different kinds of institutional and policy factors affect the two different types of FDI inflows (greenfield versus M&A) from high-income countries and emerging countries, respectively, to high-income and developing countries, respectively. For this purpose, a bilateral panel data set of greenfield and M&A investments is constructed from 26 high-income economies (24 OECD countries as well as Singapore and Hong Kong, China) to 97 developing economies and 45 high-income economies for the whole period 2003–2015.[14] We then apply the gravity model to estimate the impact of policy factors on FDI flows.

The simple gravity equation pioneered by Tinbergen (1962) and Pöyhönen (1963) posits that the volume of trade between two countries is positively related to their masses (GDPs) and inversely related to the distance between them. The gravity equation is the workhorse model for the empirical literature in international trade because it fits very well to the data, not only for trade in goods but also for various kinds of cross-border transactions such as services, capital, and labor.

As Baldwin (2006) noted, the gravity model possesses "more theoretical foundation than any other trade model." Most notably, Anderson and van Wincoop (2003) generated general theoretical foundations for the gravity equation based on differentiated products and homothetic preferences. Based on different assumptions, Eaton and Kortum (2002), Helpman et al. (2008), Melitz and Ottaviano (2008), and Chaney (2008, 2013) also proposed theoretical gravity models for trade in goods. Aviat and Coeurdacier (2005),

---

[13] BITs are not the same as some BITs impose more discipline on host countries. It is beyond the scope of the present paper to differentiate the BITs. The main focus here is to fully utilize the "structural" gravity model and assess how BITs may have a differential effect on greenfield investment versus M&As.

[14] See Table A7.1 for the list of economies.

Martin and Rey (2004, 2006), and Coeurdacier and Martin (2009) derived a gravity equation for trade in assets with financial transaction costs.

Some authors have also extended the gravity model to explain cross-border FDI flows. For example, by introducing a third country to the standard knowledge capital model of multinationals with skilled and unskilled labor, Bergstrand and Egger (2007) suggest a theoretical rationale for estimating gravity equations for FDI flows and foreign affiliate sales. Head and Ries (2008) also develop a gravity model for cross-border M&A based on the idea of an international market for corporate control. From three different models of multinational firms, Kleinert and Toubal (2010) derive a gravity equation that can be applied to the analysis of sales of foreign affiliates of multinational firms.

Most theoretical formulations of the gravity equation specify Y_{ijt}, flows of transactions from origin i to destination j, as the product of country and bilateral-specific terms:

$$Y_{ijt} = \alpha_t \frac{M_{it} M_{jt}}{D_{ijt}} \qquad (1)$$

M_{it} and M_{jt} measure the attributes of origin i and destination j at a specific point in time t and α_t is a common time-specific factor. D_{ijt} reflects transaction costs between i and j at time t. In our application, Y_{ijt} is bilateral FDI flows (greenfield or M&A) from origin i to destination j at time t. We consider two different types of bilateral FDI flows: new greenfield FDI projects and new cross-border M&A deals.

In our application, we specify the host country-specific terms, M_{jt} as

$M_{jt} = \eta \ POLICY_{jt} + \gamma_1 \ln POP_{jt} + \gamma_2 \ln PCGDP_{jt} + \gamma_3 \ln POP_{jt} + \gamma_4 \ GROWTH_{jt} + \gamma_4 \ INFLATION_{jt}$

where POP_{jt} and $PCGDP_{jt}$ are, respectively, the population and per capita GDP (PCGDP) of host countries and $GROWTH_{jt}$ and $INFLATION_{jt}$ are, respectively, GDP growth rate and inflation rate of host countries.[15]

---

[15] As will be discussed in the following, the home country-specific terms, M_{jt} will be absorbed by home-year fixed effects which account for multilateral resistance.

It should be noted that institutional and policy variables are likely to be highly correlated with the level of economic development and hence without including a variable that captures the level of economic development, any positive relation with a policy variable and FDI flows may reflect a positive relation with the level of economic development and FDI flows. Therefore, noting that GDP is a product of GDP per capita and population, we include the logs of GDP per capita and population separately. Population, GDP per capita, GDP growth rate, and inflation rates approximated by consumer price index are all drawn from the World Bank's World Development Indicators.

Higher GDP per capita and greater population represent the attractiveness of a host market in the case of market-seeking FDI. Therefore, in this case, these two variables are expected to have a positive association with FDI. However, when multinationals aim to exploit low wages in the host countries of their investment, the GDP per capita may have a negative association with FDI.

GDP growth rate and inflation rates are included in order to capture the short-term fluctuations of macroeconomic conditions of host countries. Globerman and Sapiro (2004) find that economic growth is an important determinant of aggregate FDI, but not of the cross-border M&A flows. Higher inflation rates may suggest greater macroeconomic instability of the host country and the currency value of the host country may become weaker against other currencies, resulting in a lower value of local firms in terms of foreign currencies. This may increase or decrease multinationals' incentives to invest in this country, depending on their motives (and modes) of FDI.

We also specify the bilateral term as

$$D_{ijt} = \beta_1 \ln RTA_{ijt} + \beta_2 \ln BIT_{ijt} + \theta PAIR_{ij} + u_{drt}$$

where RTA_{ijt} and BIT_{ijt} indicate whether both countries are members of a bilateral/regional trade agreement or a bilateral investment treaty, respectively, and $PAIR_{ij}$ indicates bilateral fixed effects between countries i and j.

PAIR includes log of geographic distance between source and host countries, a common language dummy and also a dummy for contiguity. Kogut and Singh (1988) argue that cultural factors have a more important influence on cross-border M&A than greenfield investment because unlike greenfield investment, cross-border M&A often requires the utilization of existing personnel, management and organizational culture.

Three Econometric Issues

There are three main issues for a consistent estimation of the coefficients for the institutional and policy variables in the gravity framework. First, many pairs of countries do not exert FDI flows and hence enter with zeros. Taking logs of the dependent variable would drop zero observation and result in biased estimates given that zero flows may indicate that fixed costs exceed expected variable profits (Razin, Rubinstein, and Sadka 2004; and Davis and Kristjánsdóttir 2010). Based on the property that the expected value of the logarithm of a random variable is different from the logarithm of its expected value (i.e., $E[\ln(y)] \neq \ln E[y]$), Santos Silva and Tenreyro (2006) argue that estimating a log-linearized gravity equation by ordinary least squares (OLS) results in bias. They also argue that OLS would be inconsistent in the presence of heteroskedasticity, which is highly likely in practice.

Santos Silva and Tenreyro (2006) have suggested that a gravity equation be estimated in its multiplicative form:

$$Y_i = \exp(x_i \beta) + \varepsilon_i \qquad (2)$$

where Y_i is a dependent variable with a non-negative value such that $E[\varepsilon_i | x] = 0$. This formulation can be estimated using the Poisson Pseudo-Maximum Likelihood (PPML) estimator. As PPML has received increasing recognition in estimating the gravity model, we also utilize PPML in our study.[16]

Our second concern relates to the endogeneity of policy variables. That is, FDI inflows may cause the policy makers of host countries to make their FDI environment more favorable to foreign investment. We design three tactics to account for this concern. First, as an effort to reduce random volatility of FDI flows and to obtain fewer cases of zero values, we reduce the time dimension to four periods by taking the mean of the dependent variable for years 2004–2006, 2007–2009, 2010–2012, and 2013–2015. And then we match the dependent variable with the policy variables and other

---

[16] For various discussions on PPML, see http://privatewww.essex.ac.uk/~jmcss/LGW.html.

explanatory variables for the preceding year of each subperiod (i.e., 2003, 2006, 2009, and 2012), thus allowing for both contemporaneous and lagged effects (1–2 years) of policy factors on FDI inflows to accrue.

Our third concern is that "structural" gravity models consistent with theory require that estimation of a gravity equation account for not only bilateral distance and transaction costs but also "multilateral resistance" (Anderson and van Wincoop 2003). This issue has been addressed in the empirical literature by including source-year and host-year fixed effects in the panel data estimations. However, including a full set of time-varying source and host country fixed effects is not feasible for our purposes because with host-year fixed effects, host country-specific policy variables would not be measured. Therefore, we only include source-year fixed effects for source countries' outward multilateral resistance. Arguably, FDI decisions are made by multinationals of source countries and hence host countries' inward multilateral resistance (i.e., host-year fixed effects) does not matter much.

As for the estimation of time-varying pair-specific policy variables (i.e., RTA and BIT dummy variables), we include a full set of time-varying source and host country fixed effects as well as bilateral pair fixed effects. This specification is consistent with Anderson and van Wincoop (2003)'s "structural" gravity models in that it incorporates a full set of multilateral resistance effects. This specification is also consistent with Baier and Bergstrand (2007) who estimate the gravity equation with time-varying multilateral terms and bilateral fixed effects to account for an endogeneity problem when they assess the effects of RTAs on bilateral trade.

Empirical Results

Effects of Governance on FDI

Table 7.5 reports the estimated results for overall World Governance Index (WGI) as an average of six WGIs. Reported in columns (1)–(4) are the results when the dependent variable is the number of greenfield investment projects, while in columns (5)–(8) are the results for cross-border M&As. Within each group of FDI, the first two columns report the results when the source countries are high-income countries and the next two columns report the results when the source countries are emerging economies.

As explained in the previous section, each equation includes source country-period fixed effects as well as period fixed effects. Our focus variable, overall WGI, has a positive and highly significant coefficient in all equations, irrespective of the mode of FDI and income group of source or host countries. However, it appears that multinationals from high-income countries, as compared to those from emerging countries, are more responsive to the local governance quality. In particular, its coefficient is larger when source countries are high-income countries and hosts are developing countries. In the case of greenfield investment flows from high-income to developing countries, if a host country's overall WGI is 1 point higher than that for another country, holding all other variables the same, the number of greenfield investment in this country is on average 4.9% (= 100*(EXP(0.048)-1)) greater than another country.[17] Therefore, if the Philippines' overall governance were not the level of 40.6 but were the level of Malaysia (56.8), greenfield flows from the 26 high-income countries to the Philippines would have been 80% (= 16.2*100*(EXP(0.048)-1)) greater during the whole period of 2004–2015. At the same time with the WGI level of Malaysia, M&A investment flows from the 26 high-income countries to the Philippines would have been 119% (= 16.2*100*(EXP(0.071)-1)) greater during the same period.

We also include an RTA dummy and a BIT dummy as bilateral policy variables, but do not put much emphasis on the estimated results because they are not obtained after fully accounting for bilateral fixed effects as well as source- and host-county-period fixed effects. A full structural gravity model is estimated subsequently for these two bilateral policy variables.

Among the control variables, population and GDP per capita of host countries enter with highly significant positive coefficients, suggesting that countries with a large market size and high income receive more greenfield investments.[18] Growth rate also enters with a statistically significant positive coefficient in the equations for greenfield investment, suggesting that countries with a greater market potential also receives more greenfield investments. An exception is when sources are emerging countries and hosts are developing countries. On the other hand, high inflation deters greenfield investment only when it flows from high-income to developing countries.

---

[17] Even if the dependent variable is not in logarithm, the estimated coefficients obtained by the PPML still can be interpreted as percentage changes of the dependent variable.

[18] Note that time-varying variables of source countries are displaced because source country-period fixed effects are included.

Table 7.5: Effects of World Bank's World Governance Index on FDI

	Greenfield Investment				Cross-Border M&A			
Source	High-Income		Emerging		High-Income		Emerging	
Host	High-Income	Developing	High-Income	Developing	High-Income	Developing	High-Income	Developing
	(1)	(2)	(3)	(4)	(5)	(6)	(7)	(8)
Overall World Governance Index - host (expected sign = plus)	0.032*** (0.006)	0.048*** (0.004)	0.028** (0.012)	0.020*** (0.006)	0.044*** (0.008)	0.071*** (0.007)	0.040*** (0.011)	0.042*** (0.009)
RTA between source and host (= 1 if yes)	0.425*** (0.156)	0.140 (0.110)	−0.238 (0.276)	0.641*** (0.144)	0.753*** (0.182)	−0.265** (0.121)	0.033 (0.207)	0.530*** (0.163)
BIT between source and host (= 1 if yes)	0.350** (0.153)	−0.025 (0.089)	−0.042 (0.255)	0.901*** (0.155)	−0.393** (0.160)	−0.240** (0.117)	−0.078 (0.203)	1.361*** (0.197)
lnPopulation - host	0.750*** (0.050)	0.903*** (0.020)	0.747*** (0.061)	0.475*** (0.033)	0.768*** (0.055)	1.009*** (0.035)	0.644*** (0.077)	0.477*** (0.052)
lnPCGDP - host	0.067 (0.154)	0.505*** (0.053)	0.437** (0.200)	0.316*** (0.066)	0.190 (0.182)	0.524*** (0.085)	0.495*** (0.174)	0.203* (0.104)
Growth rate - host	0.071*** (0.017)	0.033*** (0.009)	0.079*** (0.027)	0.013 (0.017)	−0.028 (0.032)	−0.015 (0.019)	−0.002 (0.039)	−0.072** (0.033)

continued on next page

Table 7.5 continued

Source	Greenfield Investment				Cross-Border M&A			
	High-Income		Emerging		High-Income		Emerging	
Host	High-Income	Developing	High-Income	Developing	High-Income	Developing	High-Income	Developing
	(1)	(2)	(3)	(4)	(5)	(6)	(7)	(8)
Inflation rate - host	0.132***	-0.024***	0.150***	0.006	0.113***	-0.008	0.129***	0.002
	(0.026)	(0.009)	(0.035)	(0.008)	(0.033)	(0.011)	(0.041)	(0.015)
lnDistance between source and host	0.098	-0.690***	-0.602**	0.504***	0.009	-1.266***	-0.616***	-0.656***
	(0.111)	(0.073)	(0.254)	(0.100)	(0.133)	(0.089)	(0.137)	(0.105)
Common language (= 1 if yes)	0.802***	0.636***	0.725***	0.914***	1.001***	0.932***	1.517***	1.212***
	(0.195)	(0.117)	(0.240)	(0.182)	(0.274)	(0.166)	(0.187)	(0.222)
Contiguity (= 1 if yes)	0.414	-0.248	0.439	0.697***	0.129	-1.084***	0.424	1.134***
	(0.254)	(0.211)	(0.356)	(0.160)	(0.302)	(0.301)	(0.275)	(0.251)
Constant	-12.493***	-12.558***	-13.561***	-7.467***	-13.578***	-10.371***	-13.541***	-6.892***
	(0.000)	(0.000)	(0.000)	(0.000)	(0.000)	(0.000)	(0.000)	(0.000)
Observation	4,272	8,976	1,780	3,740	4,272	8,976	1,780	3,740
R-squared	(0.632)	(0.811)	(0.579)	(0.526)	(0.606)	(0.797)	(0.664)	(0.400)

BIT = bilateral investment treaty, FDI = foreign direct investment, M&A = merger and acquisition, RTA = regional trade agreement.

Notes: Estimates are obtained with Poisson Pseudo-Maximum Likelihood (PPML) estimator. Source country-period fixed effects and period fixed effects are included but not shown for brevity. Standard errors in parenthesis are based on clustering by country-pair. ***, **, and * indicate the significance levels of 1%, 5%, and 10%, respectively.

Source: Author's calculations.

In contrast, high-income countries with high inflation appear to receive a greater amount of both greenfield and M&A investments. Bilateral distance yields significant negative coefficients in all equations, except in the equations when both sources and hosts are high-income countries in both modes of FDI. In all equations, common language yields significant positive coefficients. The contiguity variable does not appear to matter in greenfield investment.

As explained in the previous section, WGI has six components. We replaced the overall WGI with each of the six WGIs and re-ran the eight regressions, yielding 48 estimated coefficients for the six WGIs. Table 7.6 reports the results. For the sake of comparison, column (1) of the table also reports the estimated coefficients for the overall WGI, which are identical to the results reported in Table 7.5. When the host countries are developing countries, investors from high-income countries, as compared to those from emerging countries, appear to be more responsive to all sub-indicators of host country's governance quality in both types of FDI, in both the size of estimated coefficients and their statistical significance level. This is particularly evident when hosts are developing countries and when FDI is in the mode of cross-border M&A. When source countries are high-income countries and hosts are developing countries, "regulatory quality" and "government effectiveness" of host developing countries appear to be particularly important for both greenfield and cross-border M&A investments.

Table 7.7 reports the estimated coefficients for the overall WGI when the dependent variable is the number of greenfield and cross-border M&A investments in different sectors. When hosts are developing countries, multinationals from both high-income countries and emerging markets appear to be least responsive to local governance quality when they invest in the primary sector irrespective of the entry mode. When hosts are high-income countries, the result seems somewhat at odds: both greenfield and M&A investment flows to services sector are least responsive to local governance quality.

Effects of Business Environments on FDI

We now turn to the effects of host country's business environments on FDI inflows. Table 7.8 reports the estimated results when the average value of the World Bank's Ease of Doing Business (EoDB) is added to the equation reported in Table 7.5.

Table 7.6: Effects of Sub-Indicators of Governance on FDI

FDI	Source	Host	WGI Average (1)	Voice and Accountability (2)	Political Stability (3)	Government Effectiveness (4)	Regulatory Quality (5)	Rule of Law (6)	Control Corruption (7)
Greenfield investment	High-income	High-income	0.032*** (0.006)	0.002 (0.005)	0.020*** (0.005)	0.031*** (0.005)	0.042*** (0.007)	0.032*** (0.007)	0.026*** (0.004)
		Developing	0.048*** (0.004)	0.017*** (0.003)	0.025*** (0.004)	0.039*** (0.004)	0.046*** (0.004)	0.030*** (0.003)	0.027*** (0.004)
	Emerging	High-income	0.028** (0.012)	−0.007 (0.007)	0.014* (0.008)	0.029*** (0.007)	0.039*** (0.013)	0.032*** (0.015)	0.032*** (0.007)
		Developing	0.020*** (0.006)	0.011*** (0.004)	0.015*** (0.005)	0.005 (0.006)	0.020*** (0.005)	0.004 (0.005)	0.008* (0.005)
Cross-border M&A	High-income	High-income	0.044*** (0.008)	0.036*** (0.005)	−0.002 (0.004)	0.034*** (0.006)	0.054*** (0.008)	0.040*** (0.005)	0.030*** (0.005)
		Developing	0.071*** (0.007)	0.033*** (0.006)	0.036*** (0.004)	0.049*** (0.007)	0.065*** (0.007)	0.043*** (0.006)	0.040*** (0.007)

continued on next page

Table 7.6 continued

FDI	Source	Host	WGI Average (1)	Voice and Accountability (2)	Political Stability (3)	Government Effectiveness (4)	Regulatory Quality (5)	Rule of Law (6)	Control Corruption (7)
	Emerging	High-income	0.040***	0.020***	−0.007	0.036***	0.056***	0.042***	0.026***
			(0.011)	(0.006)	(0.008)	(0.007)	(0.011)	(0.011)	(0.007)
		Developing	0.042***	0.029***	0.019***	0.021***	0.045***	0.017**	0.017**
			(0.009)	(0.005)	(0.006)	(0.008)	(0.009)	(0.007)	(0.008)

FDI = foreign direct investment, M&A = merger and acquisition, WGI = World Governance Index.

Notes: Estimates are obtained with Poisson Pseudo-Maximum Likelihood (PPML) estimator from the specifications of Table 7.5, replacing overall WGI with each of the components of WGI. As in Table 7.5, all equations include host country-specific and pair-specific control variables as well as source country-period fixed effects and period fixed effects but not shown for brevity. Standard errors in parenthesis are based on clustering by country-pair. ***, **, and * indicate the significance levels of 1%, 5%, and 10%, respectively.

Source: Author's calculations.

Table 7.7: Effects of WGI on FDI in Different Sectors

Source	Host	Greenfield Investment				Cross-Border M&A			
		All	Primary Sector	Service Sector	Other	All	Primary Sector	Service Sector	Other
		(1)	(2)	(3)	(4)	(5)	(6)	(7)	(8)
High-income	High-income	0.032***	0.038***	0.023***	0.039***	0.044***	0.089***	0.039***	0.038***
		(0.006)	(0.007)	(0.007)	(0.005)	(0.008)	(0.013)	(0.010)	(0.007)
	Developing	0.428***	0.032***	0.051***	0.048***	0.071***	0.034***	0.077***	0.075***
		(0.004)	(0.005)	(0.005)	(0.004)	(0.007)	(0.008)	(0.009)	(0.007)
Emerging	High-income	0.028**	0.022*	0.014	0.045***	0.040**	0.167***	0.023**	0.032***
		(0.012)	(0.013)	(0.011)	(0.017)	(0.011)	(0.049)	(0.010)	(0.010)
	Developing	0.020***	0.011	0.022***	0.020***	0.042***	0.022*	0.045***	0.047***
		(0.006)	(0.008)	(0.007)	(0.007)	(0.009)	(0.012)	(0.013)	(0.009)

M&A = merger and acquisition, WGI = world governance index.

Notes: Estimates are obtained with Poisson Pseudo-Maximum Likelihood (PPML) estimator from the specifications of Table 7.5, replacing overall WGI in the equations for different sectors. As in Table 7.5, all equations include host country-specific and pair-specific control variables as well as source country-period fixed effects and period fixed effects but not shown for brevity. Standard errors in parenthesis are based on clustering by country-pair. ***, **, and * indicate the significance levels of 1%, 5%, and 10%, respectively.

Source: Author's calculations.

As in Table 7.5, reported in columns (1)–(4) are the results when the dependent variable is the number of greenfield investment projects, while in columns (5)–(8) are the results for cross-border M&As. Within each group of FDI, the first two columns report the results when the source countries are high-income countries and the following two columns report the results when the source countries are emerging countries. Each equation includes source country-period fixed effects and period fixed effects.

With inclusion of overall EoDB, estimated coefficients of overall WGI remain similar and continue to be highly significant in most equations. However, overall EoDB carries a statistically significant positive coefficient only when sources are high-income countries and hosts are developing countries in the equation for greenfield investment. Thus, multinationals from high-income countries tend to be more responsive to business environment of developing hosts than of high-income hosts. In contrast, multinationals from emerging economies appear to be less concerned with local business environments.

Specifically, if the Philippines' overall EoDB were not the level of 50.5 but were close to the level of Malaysia (73.8), greenfield flows from the 26 high-income economies to the Philippines would have been 52% (= 23.3*100*(EXP(0.022)-1)) larger during the whole period of 2004–2015 (see Table A7.1). Also, if the Philippines' overall governance were not the level of 40.6 but were close to that of Malaysia (56.8), greenfield flows from high-income economies to the Philippines would have been 71% (= 16.2*100*(EXP(0.043)-1)) larger during the whole period of 2003–2015. Therefore, if the overall governance and doing business environment levels of the Philippines were the same as those of Malaysia, the number of greenfield investment made by the 26 high-income economies in the Philippines would have been more than doubled (i.e., 123% larger).

Table 7.9 reports the results when we replace the overall EoDB with each of the nine EoDBs. We first focus on the results estimated for greenfield investment flows to developing countries. When sources are high-income countries, greenfield investment is positively associated with the host country's "starting business," "registering property," "getting credit," "trading across borders," and "enforcing contracts." In contrast, greenfield investment from emerging economies appear to be concerned mostly with "dealing with business construction" in developing hosts. Indeed, emerging economies' greenfield investment in high-income countries is also positively associated with "dealing with business construction."

Table 7.8: Effects of World Bank's Ease of Doing Business Index on FDI

Source	Greenfield Investment				Cross-Border M&A			
	High-Income		Emerging		High-Income		Emerging	
Host	High-Income	Developing	High-Income	Developing	High-Income	Developing	High-Income	Developing
	(1)	(2)	(3)	(4)	(5)	(6)	(7)	(8)
Overall Ease of Doing Business Index - host (expected sign = plus)	0.005	0.022	−0.002	−0.001	0.004	0.009	−0.007	−0.014
	(0.011)	(0.007)	(0.014)	(0.010)	(0.012)	(0.007)	(0.012)	(0.016)
Overall World Governance Index - host (expected sign = plus)	0.026***	0.043***	0.031*	0.021***	0.042***	0.072***	0.044***	0.051***
	(0.010)	(0.005)	(0.018)	(0.007)	(0.013)	(0.008)	(0.013)	(0.011)
RTA between source and host (=1 if yes)	0.383***	0.081	−0.193	0.676***	0.706***	−0.299***	0.052	0.543***
	(0.157)	(0.110)	(0.275)	(0.143)	(0.166)	(0.125)	(0.209)	(0.179)
BIT between source and host (=1 if yes)	0.319**	−0.118	0.012	0.797***	−0.545***	−0.378***	−0.114	1.343***
	(0.160)	(0.103)	(0.245)	(0.163)	(0.168)	(0.131)	(0.202)	(0.202)
lnPopulation - host	0.758***	0.982***	0.804***	0.467***	0.755***	1.038***	0.669***	0.489***
	(0.048)	(0.021)	(0.078)	(0.033)	(0.046)	(0.040)	(0.082)	(0.049)
lnPCGDP - host	0.248	0.413***	0.646***	0.313***	0.143	0.433***	0.565***	0.193
	(0.178)	(0.061)	(0.195)	(0.085)	(0.201)	(0.086)	(0.190)	(0.124)
Growth rate - host	0.087***	0.021*	0.125***	0.005	−0.052*	−0.036*	0.000	−0.125***
	(0.020)	(0.011)	(0.026)	(0.020)	(0.028)	(0.022)	(0.054)	(0.033)

continued on next page

Table 7.8 continued

	Greenfield Investment				Cross-Border M&A			
	High-Income		Emerging		High-Income		Emerging	
Source								
Host	High-Income	Developing	High-Income	Developing	High-Income	Developing	High-Income	Developing
	(1)	(2)	(3)	(4)	(5)	(6)	(7)	(8)
Inflation rate - host	0.167***	0.024**	0.224***	0.002	0.160***	-0.017	0.148***	-0.008
	(0.027)	(0.009)	(0.033)	(0.010)	(0.035)	(0.013)	(0.050)	(0.016)
lnDistance between source and host	0.094	-0.651***	0.566***	-0.471***	0.057	-1.296***	-0.640***	-0.650***
	(0.118)	(0.078)	(0.247)	(0.102)	(0.127)	(0.094)	(0.139)	(0.111)
Common language (=1 if yes)	0.754***	0.609***	0.565***	0.927***	0.785***	0.951***	1.652***	1.342***
	(0.200)	(0.115)	(0.255)	(0.183)	(0.200)	(0.167)	(0.225)	(0.221)
Contiguity (=1 if yes)	0.474*	-0.250	0.500	0.655***	0.433**	-1.272***	0.399	0.992***
	(0.244)	(0.180)	(0.350)	(0.158)	(0.214)	(0.339)	(0.262)	(0.246)
Constant	-14.535***	-13.506***	-17.457***	-7.450***	-13.457***	-10.251***	-14.282***	-6.385***
	(1.762)	(0.661)	(2.412)	(1.256)	(2.165)	(1.069)	(2.994)	(1.777)
Observation	3,096	6,792	1,290	2,830	3,096	6,792	1,290	2,830
R-squared	0.641	0.841	0.610	0.543	0.717	0.815	0.652	0.420

BIT = bilateral investment treaty, FDI = foreign direct investment, M&A = merger and acquisition, RTA = regional trade agreement.
Notes: Estimates are obtained with Poisson Pseudo-Maximum Likelihood (PPML) estimator. Source country-period fixed effects and period fixed effects are included but not shown for brevity. Standard errors in parenthesis are based on clustering by country-pair. ***, **, and * indicate the significance levels of 1%, 5%, and 10%, respectively.
Source: Author's calculations.

Looking on the results for cross-border M&A, we find that there are fewer sub-indicators of EoDB which are statistically significant. When sources are high-income countries, none is significantly positive when hosts are also high-income countries, while "starting business," "registering property," "getting credit," and "protecting minority investors" are significantly positive when hosts are developing countries.

Next, we investigate if local governance quality and business environment are complementary or substitutes. For this purpose, we add an interaction term of the overall WGI with each of EoDBs in the equations for greenfield investment when sources are high-income countries and hosts are developing countries. The results are summarized in Table 7.10. We find that the direct effect of overall EoDB is positive and significant. However, the coefficient of the interaction term (EoDB*WGI_ave) is significant with a negative sign. Thus, the marginal effect of overall EoDB on greenfield investment (= 0.096 – 0.002*WGI_ave) becomes smaller as overall WGI becomes greater. For example, at 34.7 of WGI_ave (bottom quartile), the marginal effect of EoDB is 0.40 and statistically significant, while at 47.4 of WGI_ave (top quartile), the marginal effect of EoDB is –0.0048 and statistically insignificant. This suggests that for the country with high WGI, EoDB does not have a discernable association with greenfield investment. For the country with very low WGI, however, EoDB has a statistically significant positive association with greenfield investment. Thus, a favorable local business environment may substitute for poor local governance in encouraging greenfield investment to the developing countries characterized with very poor local governance.

This finding is illustrated in Figure 7.4, which plots overall EoDB against the logarithm of the predicted value of the number of greenfield investment. Figure 7.4a plots the fitted values when WGI_ave < 34.7 (bottom quartile), while Figure 7.4b plots the fitted values when WGI_ave > 34.7. The predicted value of the number of greenfield investment is increasing in the value of EoDB_ave for countries characterized by a very low quality of governance. In contrast, for countries with a high quality of governance, EoDB does not appear to have such a positive association with greenfield investment. Hence, the between-country relationship of overall EoDB with greenfield investment is positive and such a positive relationship is particularly strong in countries where their governance quality is low.

Table 7.9: Effects of Sub-Indicators of EoDB on FDI

FDI	Source	Host	EoDB Average (1)	Starting Business (2)	Dealing with Business Construction (3)	Registering Property (4)	Getting Credit (5)	Protecting Minority Investor (6)	Paying Taxes (7)	Trading Across Borders (8)	Enforcing Contracts (9)	Resolving Insolvency (10)
Greenfield investment	High-income	High-income	0.005	-0.009*	0.007	-0.003	0.006	-0.003	0.019	0.028***	0.007	-0.007**
			(0.011)	(0.005)	(0.005)	(0.004)	(0.004)	(0.004)	(0.005)	(0.009)	(0.006)	(0.003)
		Developing	0.022***	0.007	0.005	0.012***	0.008***	0.001	-0.002	0.011***	0.009**	0.000
			(0.007)	(0.003)	(0.004)	(0.004)	(0.002)	(0.005)	(0.003)	(0.003)	(0.004)	(0.002)
	Emerging	High-income	-0.002	-0.017	0.030**	0.003	0.005	-0.018	0.038***	0.017	0.007	-0.007**
			(0.014)	(0.012)	(0.0120)	(0.005)	(0.005)	(0.009)	(0.008)	(0.018)	(0.006)	(0.003)
		Developing	-0.001	-0.001	0.008**	0.000	-0.000	-0.001	-0.003	-0.003	0.007	0.007**
			(0.010)	(0.005)	(0.004)	(0.004)	(0.004)	(0.005)	(0.004)	(0.003)	(0.006)	(0.003)

continued on next page

Table 7.9 continued

FDI	Source	Host	EoDB Average (1)	Starting Business (2)	Dealing with Business Construction (3)	Registering Property (4)	Getting Credit (5)	Protecting Minority Investor (6)	Paying Taxes (7)	Trading Across Borders (8)	Enforcing Contracts (9)	Resolving Insolvency (10)
Cross-border M&A	High-income	High-income	0.004 (0.012)	0.011 (0.007)	0.000 (0.005)	-0.002 (0.004)	0.008 (0.005)	0.000 (0.004)	0.007 (0.006)	0.011 (0.011)	-0.010* (0.005)	0.000 (0.003)
		Developing	0.009 (0.007)	0.006* (0.003)	-0.014*** (0.004)	0.009** (0.004)	0.015*** (0.003)	0.010** (0.005)	0.003 (0.003)	-0.005 (0.004)	0.004 (0.005)	-0.002 (0.003)
	Emerging	High-income	-0.007 (0.012)	0.019** (0.009)	-0.011* (0.006)	-0.005 (0.005)	0.008 (0.005)	-0.001 (0.005)	0.007 (0.008)	-0.019 (0.019)	-0.010* (0.005)	0.000 (0.003)
		Developing	-0.014 (0.016)	0.008 (0.005)	-0.006 (0.006)	-0.005 (0.007)	0.010** (0.004)	0.006 (0.006)	-0.014** (0.006)	-0.008 (0.005)	-0.010 (0.005)	0.000 (0.003)

EoDB = ease of doing business, FDI = foreign direct investment, M&A = merger and acquisition.

Notes: Estimates are obtained with Poisson Pseudo-Maximum Likelihood (PPML) estimator from the specifications of Table 7.8, replacing Overall EoDB with each of the components of EoDB. As in Table 7.8, all equations include host country-specific and pair-specific control variables as well as source country-period fixed effects and period fixed effects but not shown for brevity. Standard errors in parenthesis are based on clustering by country-pair. ***, **, and * indicate the significance levels of 1%, 5%, and 10%, respectively.

Source: Author's calculations.

Table 7.10: Interaction Effects of EoDB and WGI on Greenfield FDI Flows from High-Income to Developing Countries

FDI	Governance Indicator	EoDB Average (1)	Starting Business (2)	Dealing with Business Construction (3)	Registering Property (4)	Getting Credit (5)	Protecting Minority Investor (6)	Paying Taxes (7)	Trading Across Borders (8)	Enforcing Contracts (9)	Resolving Insolvency (10)
Greenfield investment	EoDB	0.096***	0.012	0.026**	0.065***	0.012	0.008	0.048***	0.017*	0.069***	0.008
		(0.022)	(0.012)	(0.013)	(0.011)	(0.008)	(0.015)	(0.008)	(0.009)	(0.013)	(0.009)
	EoDB*WGI average	-0.002***	-0.000	-0.000*	-0.001***	-0.000	-0.000	-0.000***	-0.000	-0.001***	-0.000
		(0.000)	(0.000)	(0.000)	(0.000)	(0.000)	(0.000)	(0.000)	(0.000)	(0.000)	(0.000)
	WGI average	0.140***	0.059***	0.076***	0.130***	0.041***	0.053***	0.118***	0.050***	0.134***	0.053***
		(0.025)	(0.019)	(0.018)	(0.015)	(0.011)	(0.014)	(0.011)	(0.013)	(0.017)	(0.007)

EoDB = ease of doing business, FDI = foreign direct investment, WGI = World Governance Index.

Notes: Estimates are obtained with Poisson Pseudo-Maximum Likelihood (PPML) estimator from the specifications of Table 7.8, replacing Overall EoDB with each of the components of EoDB as well as their interaction terms with WGI average. As in Table 7.8, all equations include host country-specific and pair-specific control variables as well as source country-period fixed effects and period fixed effects but not shown for brevity. Standard errors in parenthesis are based on clustering by country-pair. ***, **, and * indicate the significance levels of 1%, 5%, and 10%, respectively.

Source: Author's calculations.

Figure 7.4: Predicted Number of Greenfield Investment due to Overall EoDB: When Sources Are High-Income and Hosts Are Developing Countries

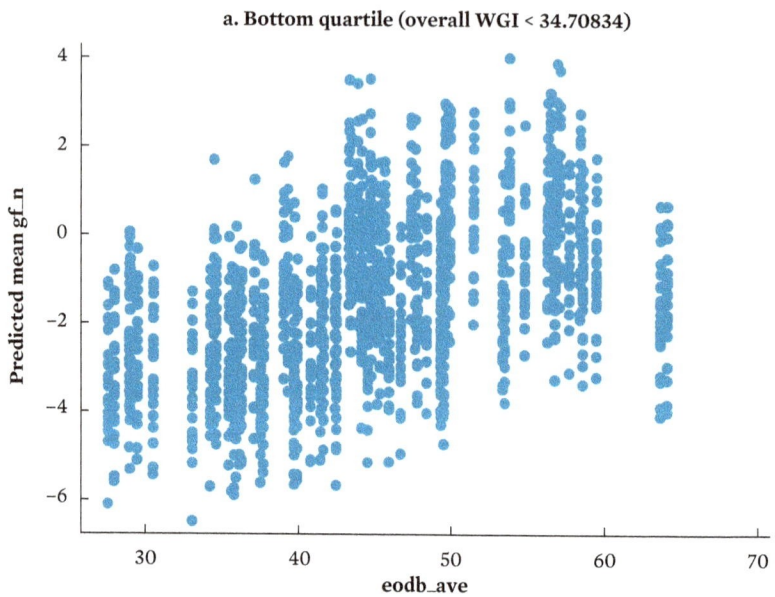

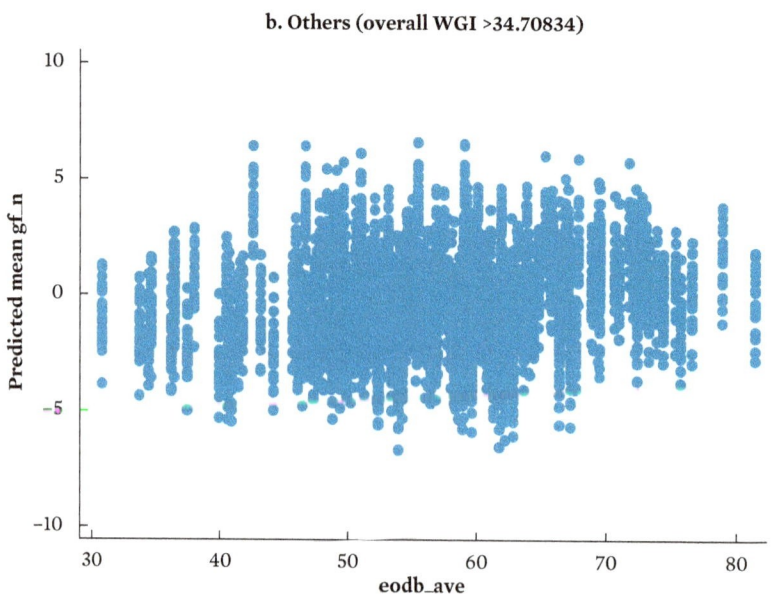

EoDB = ease of doing business, gf_n = logarithm of the predicted value of the number of greenfield investment, WGI = World Governance Index.
Source: Author's calculations.

Turning to sectoral results in Table 7.11, we focus on the case when sources are high-income countries and hosts are developing countries. We find that EoDB is positive and significant in primary sector and other sector, while it is positive but not significant in services sector.

Table 7.11: Effects of EoDB on FDI in Different Sectors

		Greenfield Investment				Cross-Border M&A			
		All	Primary Sector	Service Sector	Other	All	Primary Sector	Service Sector	Other
Source	Host	(1)	(2)	(3)	(4)	(5)	(6)	(7)	(8)
High-income	High-income	0.005	0.006	0.010	-0.000	0.004	-0.058***	0.018	0.002
		(0.011)	(0.008)	(0.012)	(0.010)	(0.012)	(0.016)	(0.014)	(0.011)
	Developing	0.022***	0.025**	0.008	0.031***	0.009	0.003	0.011	0.007
		(0.007)	(0.011)	(0.006)	(0.009)	(0.007)	(0.009)	(0.008)	(0.007)
Emerging	High-income	-0.002	0.023	0.014	-0.023	-0.007	-0.053**	0.024	-0.024*
		(0.014)	(0.016)	(0.013)	(0.017)	(0.012)	(0.021)	(0.015)	(0.014)
	Developing	-0.001	0.003	-0.001	-0.002	-0.014	-0.006	-0.019	-0.013
		(0.010)	(0.010)	(0.011)	(0.013)	(0.016)	(0.023)	(0.019)	(0.017)

EoDB = ease of doing business, M&A = merger and acquisition.
Notes: Estimates are obtained with Poisson Pseudo-Maximum Likelihood (PPML) estimator from the specifications of Table 7.8, including Overall EoDB in the equations for different sectors. As in Table 7.8, all equations include host country-specific and pair-specific control variables as well as source country-period fixed effects and period fixed effects but not shown for brevity. Standard errors in parenthesis are based on clustering by country-pair. ***, **, and * indicate the significance levels of 1%, 5%, and 10%, respectively.
Source: Author's calculations.

Effects of RTAs and BITs on FDI

For the estimation of RTA and BIT dummy variables, we include a full set of time-varying home and host country fixed effects as well as bilateral pair fixed effects, following Baier and Bergstrand (2007) who estimate the gravity equation with time-varying multilateral terms as well as bilateral fixed effects to account for an endogeneity problem when they assess the effects of RTAs on bilateral trade. This specification is consistent with "structural" gravity models by Anderson and van Wincoop (2003).

Table 7.12 summarizes the results for both greenfield and M&A investments. When the estimates are made for the whole group including both high-income and developing host countries, RTA has a positive and significant coefficient in the equation for the number of greenfield investments from high-income countries (column 1). Precisely, when any two countries' RTA becomes effective, the number of greenfield investment between the country pair increases by 10.4% in 3 years (= 100*(EXP(0.099)-1)). In order to assess if the RTA effect is different for developing countries, we re-ran the regressions with the interaction terms of RTA and BIT with the dummies for developing host countries and high-income host countries. As shown in column (2), RTA seems to increase greenfield investment only when the counterparts are developing host countries. This result is consistent with Chala and Lee (2015) and Lee and Ries (2016). For M&A investment, we do not find such differential effects.

Table 7.12: Effects of RTA and BIT on FDI

Source	Greenfield Investment				Cross-Border M&A			
	High-Income		Emerging		High-Income		Emerging	
	(1)	(2)	(3)	(4)	(5)	(6)	(7)	(8)
RTA between source and host (= 1 if yes)	0.099**		-0.279***		-0.066		0.154	
	(0.044)		(0.094)		(0.079)		(0.191)	
BIT between source and host (= 1 if yes)	0.050		0.214**		-0.136		0.068	
	(0.050)		(0.089)		(0.145)		(0.221)	
RTA * high-income host		-0.015		0.155		-0.159		-0.250
		(0.066)		(0.120)		(0.116)		(0.224)
RTA * Developing host		0.157**		-0.412***		0.055		0.510**
		(0.062)		(0.105)		(0.092)		(0.218)
BIT * high-income host		0.033		0.157		-0.190		0.265
		(0.087)		(0.168)		(0.355)		(0.248)
BIT * Developing host		0.050		0.227**		-0.118		-0.182
		(0.056)		(0.103)		(0.158)		(0.342)
Observation	9,302	9,302	3,202	3,202	6,966	6,966	2,015	2,015
R-squared	0.990	0.990	0.966	0.967	0.982	0.982	0.951	0.952

BIT = bilateral investment treaty, FDI = foreign direct investment, M&A = merger and acquisition, RTA = regional trade agreement.

Notes: Estimates are obtained with Poisson Pseudo-Maximum Likelihood (PPML) estimator. Spec 2 includes source country-period fixed effects and host country-period fixed effects as well as period fixed effects. Standard errors in parenthesis are based on clustering by country-pair. ***, **, and * indicate the significance levels of 1%, 5%, and 10%, respectively.

Source: Author's calculations.

When source countries are emerging countries, RTA dummy carries a negative and significant coefficient in the equation for greenfield investment, while BIT dummy carries a positive and significant coefficient in the same equation (Column 3). Such effects are due to the case when sources and hosts are both developing countries (Column 4). When the dependent variable is the number of M&A deals, we only find a significant positive coefficient for RTA when sources and hosts are both developing countries (Column 8).

Sectoral results for greenfield investment are reported in Table 7.13. When sources are high-income countries, RTA has a positive effect on greenfield investment flows to developing hosts in all three sectors. When sources are emerging countries, RTA has a highly significant positive effect on greenfield investment flows to services sector when hosts are high-income countries. Sectoral results for cross-border M&A investment are reported in Table 7.14. It appears that RTA has a marginally significant positive effect on M&A investment flows to other sector when hosts are developing countries.

Table 7.13: Effects of RTA and BIT on Greenfield FDI in Different Sectors

	Greenfield Investment							
	High-Income				Emerging			
	All	Primary Sector	Service Sector	Other	All	Primary Sector	Service Sector	Other
Source	(1)	(2)	(3)	(4)	(5)	(6)	(7)	(8)
RTA * high-income host	-0.015	0.267	0.103	-0.115	0.155	0.042	0.463***	-0.059
	(0.066)	(0.213)	(0.091)	(0.092)	(0.120)	(0.397)	(0.159)	(0.191)
RTA * Developing host	0.157**	0.223*	0.171*	0.176***	-0.412***	-0.293	-0.474**	-0.460***
	(0.062)	(0.135)	(0.088)	(0.067)	(0.105)	(0.282)	(0.202)	(0.133)
BIT * high-income host	0.033	0.904*	-0.174	0.069	0.157	0.064	0.161	0.140
	(0.087)	(0.481)	(0.142)	(0.111)	(0.168)	(0.693)	(0.233)	(0.207)
BIT * Developing host	0.050	-0.068	0.071	0.059	0.227**	0.575*	0.111	0.158
	(0.056)	(0.143)	(0.067)	(0.065)	(0.103)	(0.312)	(0.187)	(0.156)
Observation	9,302	4,375	7,088	7,569	3,202	1,246	2,140	2,324
R-squared	0.990	0.900	0.991	0.986	0.967	0.821	0.952	0.964

BIT = bilateral investment treaty, FDI = foreign direct investment, RTA = regional trade agreement.
Notes: Estimates are obtained with Poisson Pseudo-Maximum Likelihood (PPML) estimator. Spec 2 includes source country-period fixed effects and host country-period fixed effects as well as period fixed effects. Standard errors in parenthesis are based on clustering by country-pair. ***, **, and * indicate the significance levels of 1%, 5%, and 10%, respectively.
Source: Author's calculations.

Table 7.14: Effects of RTA and BIT on Cross-Border M&A in Different Sectors

	Cross-Border M&A							
	High-Income				Emerging			
Source	All	Primary Industry	Service Industry	Other	All	Primary Industry	Service Industry	Other
	(1)	(2)	(3)	(4)	(5)	(6)	(7)	(8)
RTA * high-income host	-0.159	-0.438**	-0.005	-0.003	-0.250	-0.704	-0.154	-0.692***
	(0.116)	(0.182)	(0.132)	(0.117)	(0.224)	(1.002)	(0.273)	(0.252)
RTA * Developing host	0.055	0.240	0.034	0.179*	0.510**	0.174	0.391	0.394
	(0.092)	(0.243)	(0.131)	(0.100)	(0.218)	(1.060)	(0.368)	(0.321)
BIT * high-income host	-0.190	-0.334	0.047	-0.564	0.265	0.404	0.078	0.285
	(0.355)	(0.565)	(0.327)	(0.424)	(0.248)	(0.863)	(0.475)	(0.303)
BIT * Developing host	-0.118	-0.276	0.000	-0.189	-0.182	0.859	-0.143	-1.031*
	(0.158)	(0.287)	(0.196)	(0.157)	(0.342)	(0.963)	(0.581)	(0.526)
Observation	6,966	3,386	5,228	5,292	2,015	641	1,287	1,480
R-squared	0.982	0.964	0.989	0.969	0.952	0.866	0.948	0.918

BIT = bilateral investment treaty, M&A = merger and acquisition, RTA = regional trade agreement.

Notes: Estimates are obtained with Poisson Pseudo-Maximum Likelihood (PPML) estimator. Spec 2 includes source country-period fixed effects and host country-period fixed effects as well as period fixed effects. Standard errors in parenthesis are based on clustering by country-pair. ***, **, and * indicate the significance levels of 1%, 5%, and 10%, respectively.

Source: Author's calculations.

Summary and Concluding Remarks

Many studies have found that foreign direct investment (FDI) can play a positive role in spurring economic growth and income of host countries. Given that FDI can take the form of greenfield investment or mergers and acquisitions (M&A), this chapter empirically evaluates how institutional and policy factors of host countries influence greenfield and M&A investments to developing countries.

This study empirically assesses how the two modes of FDI flows from high-income to developing countries respond differently to various institutional and policy factors of host countries in different sectors. As a comparison, this study also assesses the effects of local institutional and policy factors on FDI flows from high-income to high-income countries as well as from emerging countries to developing or high-income countries.

For this purpose, this chapter utilized bilateral greenfield and M&A investments from 26 high-income economies (24 OECD countries as well as Singapore and Hong Kong, China) to 97 developing countries and 45 high-income countries for the whole 2003–2015 period and applies Poisson Pseudo-Maximum Likelihood (PPML) estimation to the gravity model. As a comparison, FDI flows from 10 major emerging investors to 97 developing countries and 45 high-income countries were separately examined for the same period.

We offer a number of new findings:

(i) The quality of local governance exerts a highly significant positive effect on FDI, irrespective of its mode (greenfield versus M&A) and the income level of source or host countries. In particular, multinationals from high-income countries are more responsive to the local governance quality of developing countries than those from developing countries.

(ii) When hosts are developing countries, multinationals from both high-income countries and emerging markets are less responsive to local governance quality when they invest in the primary sector than in services or other sectors, irrespective of the mode of entry.

(iii) Multinationals from high-income countries tend to be more responsive to local business environment of developing hosts than of high-income hosts. In contrast, multinationals from emerging economies appear to be less concerned with local business environments.

(iv) A favorable business environment of host countries encourages a greater amount of greenfield investment flows from high-income countries to developing countries.

(v) If the overall governance and business environment levels of the Philippines were the same as those of Malaysia during 2004–2015, the number of greenfield investment from high-income countries to the Philippines would have been more than doubled in the period.

(vi) For the countries with a high quality of governance, local business environment does not have a discernable association with greenfield investment. For countries with very low governance quality, however, local business environment has a statistically

significant positive association with greenfield investment.
Therefore, a favorable local business environment may substitute
for poor local governance in encouraging greenfield investment
to the developing countries characterized with very poor
local governance.

(vii) Regional trade agreement increases greenfield investment from
high-income countries to developing countries.

References

Ashraf, A., D. Herzer, and P. Nunnenkamp. 2015. The Effects of Greenfield FDI and Cross-border M&As on Total Factor Productivity. *The World Economy*. Article first published online: 26 August 2015. DOI: 10.1111/twec.12321.

Aviat, A. and N. Coeurdacier. 2005. The Geography of Trade in Goods and Asset Holdings. *Journal of International Economics*. 71 (1). pp. 22–51.

Baier, S. L. and J. H. Bergstrand. 2007. Do Free Trade Agreements Actually Increase Members' International Trade? *Journal of International Economics*. 71 (1). pp. 72–95.

Baldwin, R. 2006. The Euro's Trade Effects. *European Central Bank Working Paper Series*. No. 594. Frankfurt.

Baltagi, B. H., P. Egger, and M. Pfaffermayr. 2008. Estimating Regional Trade Agreement Effects on FDI in an Interdependent World. *Journal of Econometrics*. 145 (1). pp. 194–208.

Bénassy-Quéré, A., M. Coupet, and T. Mayer. 2007. Institutional Determinants of Foreign Direct Investment. *The World Economy*. 30 (5). pp. 764–82.

Berger, A., M. Busse, P. Nunnenkamp, and M. Roy. 2013. Do Trade and Investment Agreements Lead to More FDI? Accounting for Key Provisions inside the Black Box. *International Economics and Economic Policy*. 10 (2). pp. 247–75.

Bergstrand, J. H. and P. Egger. 2007. A Knowledge-and-Physical-Capital Model of International Trade Flows, Foreign Direct Investment, and Multinational Enterprises. *Journal of International Economics*. 73 (2). pp. 278–308.

Buchanan, B. G., Q. V. Le, and M. Rishi. 2012. Foreign Direct Investment and Institutional Quality: Some Empirical Evidence. *International Review of Financial Analysis*. 21 (C). pp. 81–89.

Busse, M. and C. Hefeker. 2007. Political Risk, Institutions and Foreign Direct Investment. *European Journal of Political Economy*. 23 (2). pp. 397–415.

Busse, M., J. Königer, and P. Nunnenkamp. 2010. FDI Promotion through Bilateral Investment Treaties: More than a Bit? *Review of World Economics*. 146 (1). pp. 147–77.

Byun, H. S., H. H. Lee, and C. Park. 2012. Assessing Factors Affecting M&As versus Greenfield FDI in Emerging Countries. *ADB Economics Working Papers Series*. No. 293. Manila: Asian Development Bank.

Chala, B. W. and H. H. Lee. 2015. Do Regional Trade Agreements Increase Bilateral Greenfield Investment? *Journal of Economic Integration*. 30 (4). pp. 680–707.

Chaney, T. 2008. Distorted Gravity: The Intensive and Extensive Margins of International Trade. *American Economic Review*. 98 (4). pp. 1707–721.

Chen, M. X. 2009. Regional Economic Integration and Geographic Concentration of Multinational Firms. *European Economic Review*. 53 (3). pp. 355–75.

Cheung, K. and P. Lin. 2004. Spillover Effects of FDI on Innovation in China: Evidence from the Provincial Data. *China Economic Review*. 15 (1). pp. 25–44.

Corcoran, A. and R. Gillanders. 2015. Foreign Direct Investment and the East of Doing Business. *Review of World Economics*. 151 (1). pp. 103–26.

Coeurdacier, N. and P. Martin. 2009. The Geography of Asset Trade and the Euro: Insiders and Outsiders. *Journal of the Japanese and International Economics*. 23 (2). pp. 90–113.

Daude, C. and E. Stein. 2007. The Quality of Institutions and Foreign Direct Investment. *Economics and Politics*. 19 (3). pp. 317–44.

Davies, R. B., R. Desbordes, and A. Ray. 2015. Greenfield versus Merger and Acquisition FDI: Same Wine, Different Bottles. *University College Dublin School of Economics Working Papers Series*. No. 2015-02.

Davis, R. B. and H. Kristjánsdóttir. 2010. Fixed Costs, Foreign Direct Investment, and Gravity with Zeros. *Review of International Economics*. 18 (1). pp. 47–62.

Eaton, J. and S. Kortum. 2002. Technology, Geography, and Trade. *Econometrica*. 70 (5). pp. 1741–779.

Edwards, S. 1992. Capital Flows, Foreign Direct Investment, and Debt-Equity Swaps in Developing Countries. *National Bureau of Economic Research Working Papers Series*. No. 3497. Cambridge, MA: National Bureau of Economic Research.

Ekholm, K., R. Forslid, and J. R. Markusen. 2007. Export-Platform Foreign Direct Investment. *Journal of the European Economic Association*. 5 (4). pp. 776–95.

Gassebner, M. and P. G. Méon. 2010. Where Do Creditor Rights Matter? Creditor Rights, Political Constraints and Cross-border M&A Activity. *CEB Working Papers Series*. No. 10-019.

Globerman, S. and D. Shapiro. 2002. Global Foreign Direct Investment Flows: The Role of Governance Infrastructure. *World Development*. 30 (11). pp. 1899–919.

Harms, P. and P. G. Méon. 2011. An FDI is an FDI is an FDI? The Growth Effects of Greenfield Investment and Mergers and Acquisitions in Developing Countries. *Gerzensee Study Center Working Papers Series*. No. 11.10.

Haskel, J. E., S. C. Pereira, and M. J. Slaughter. 2007. Does Inward Foreign Direct Investment Boost the Productivity of Domestic Firms? *Review of Economics and Statistics*. 89 (3). pp. 482–96.

Hayakawa, K., F. Kimura, and H. H. Lee. 2013. How Does Country Risk Matter for Foreign Direct Investment? *Developing Economies*. 51 (1). pp. 60–78.

Huttunen, K. 2007. The Effect of Foreign Acquisition on Employment and Wages: Evidence from Finnish Establishments. *Review of Economics and Statistics*. 89 (3). pp. 497–509.

Ito, T. 2013. Export Platform Foreign Direct Investment: Theory and Evidence. *The World Economy*. 36 (5). pp. 563–81.

Jang, Y. J. 2011. The Impact of Bilateral Free Trade Agreements on Bilateral Foreign Direct Investment among Developed Countries. *The World Economy*. 34 (9). pp. 1628–651.

Jayasuriya, D. 2011. Improvements in the World Banks' Ease of Doing Business Rankings: Do They Translate into Greater Foreign Direct Investment Inflows? *World Bank Policy Research Working Papers Series*. No. 5787.

Javorcik, B. S. 2004. Does Foreign Direct Investment Increase the Productivity of Domestic Firms? In Search of Spillovers through Backward Linkages. *American Economic Review*. 94 (3). pp. 605–27.

Kaufmann, D., A. Kraay, and M. Mastruzzi. 2011. The Worldwide Governance Indicators: Methodology and Analytical Issues 1. *Hague Journal on the Rule of Law*. 3 (2). pp. 220–246.

Kim, Y. H. 2009. Cross-border M&A vs. Greenfield FDI: Economic Integration and Its Welfare Impact. *Journal of Policy Modeling*. 31 (1). pp. 87–101.

Kleinert, J. and F. Toubal. 2010. Gravity for FDI. *Review of International Economics*. 18 (1). pp. 1–13.

Kogut, B. and H. Singh. 1988. The Effect of National Culture on the Choice of Entry Mode. *Journal of International Business Studies*. 19 (3). pp. 411–32.

Kreinin, M. E. and M. G. Plummer. 2008. Effects of Regional Integration on FDI: An Empirical Approach. *Journal of Asian Economics*. 19 (5). pp. 447–54.

Krugman, P. 2000. Fire-sale FDI. In S. Edwards, ed. *Capital Flows and the Emerging Economies: Theory, Evidence, and Controversies*. University of Chicago Press. pp. 43–58.

Lee, H. H. and J. Ries. 2016. Aid for Trade and Greenfield Investment. *World Development*. 84 (C). pp. 206–18.

Martin, P. and H. Rey. 2004. Financial Super-markets: Size Matters for Asset Trade. *Journal of International Economics*. 64 (2). pp. 335–61.

————.2006. Globalization and Emerging Markets: With or Without Crash? *American Economic Review.* 96 (5). pp. 1631–651.

Motta, M. and G. Norman. 1996. Does Economic Integration Cause Foreign Direct Investment? *International Economic Review.* 37 (4). pp. 757–83.

Neto P., A. Brandão, and A. Cerqueira. 2010. The Macroeconomic Determinants of Cross Border Mergers and Acquisitions and Greenfield Investments. *The IUP Journal of Business Strategy.* 7 (1). pp. 21–57.

Neumayer, E. and L. Spess. 2005. Do Bilateral Investment Treaties Increase Foreign Direct Investment to Developing Countries? *World Development.* 33 (10). pp. 1567–585.

Nocke, V. and S. Yeaple. 2008. An Assignment Theory of Foreign Direct Investment. *Review of Economic Studies.* 75 (2). pp. 529–57.

Pöyhönen, P. 1963. A Tentative Model for the Volume of Trade Between Countries. *Weltwirtschaftliches Archiv.* 90 (1). pp. 93–100.

Razin, A., Y. Rubinstein, and E. Sadka. 2004. Fixed Costs and FDI: The Conflicting Effects of Productivity Shocks. *National Bureau of Economic Research Working Papers Series.* No. 10864.

Rose-Ackerman, S. and J. Tobin. 2005. Foreign Direct Investment and the Business Environment in Developing Countries: The Impact of Bilateral Investment Treaties. *Yale Law & Economics Research Papers Series.* No. 293.

Santos Silva, J. and S. Tenreyro. 2006. The Log of Gravity. *Review of Economics and Statistics.* 88 (4). pp. 641–58.

Schneider, F. and B. F. Frey. 1985. Economic and Political Determinants of Foreign Direct Investment. *World Development.* 13 (2). pp. 161–75.

Thomas, M. A. 2009. What Do the Worldwide Governance Indicators Measure. *The European Journal of Development Research.* 22 (1). pp. 31–54.

Tinbergen, J. 1962. *Shaping the World Economy: Suggestions for an International Economic Policy.* The Twentieth Century Fund.

United Nations Conference on Trade and Development (UNCTAD). 2015. *World Investment Report 2015: Reforming International Investment Governance*. Geneva.

Wang, M. and M. C. S. Wong. 2009. What Drives Economic Growth? The Case of Cross-Border M&A and Greenfield FDI Activities. *Kyklos*. 62 (2). pp. 316–30.

Walsh, J. P. and J. Yu. 2010. Determinants of Foreign Direct Investment: A Sectoral and Institutional Approach. *IMF Working Papers Series*. No. WP/10/187.

Wei, S. J. 2000. Local Corruption and Global Capital Flows. *Brookings Papers on Economic Activity*. 31 (2). pp. 303–54.

Yeyati, E. L., E. Stein, and C. Daude. 2003. Regional Integration and the Location of FDI. *Inter-American Development Bank Working Papers Series*. No. 492.

APPENDIX

Table A7.1: List of Economies with their WGI and EoDB Indices

High-Income Economies			High-Income Economies		
ISO-Code	Overall WGI	Overall EoDB	ISO-Code	Overall WGI	Overall EoDB
ARE	59.8	67.9	NOR	83.8	82.5
AUS	81.8	80.9	NZL	85.2	89.8
AUT	81.6	75.9	OMN	55.0	64.8
BEL	76.5	73.4	POL	63.2	65.0
BHR	52.4	66.0	PRT	71.0	71.3
BRN	61.1	58.9	QAT	62.0	68.2
CAN	82.5	82.7	SAU	43.0	63.8
CHE	84.4	73.2	SGP	79.4	91.9
CYP	70.8	68.8	SVK	64.6	68.9
CZE	67.5	62.8	SVN	69.3	62.1
DEU	79.0	77.9	SWE	85.3	80.1
DNK	86.7	83.4	TTO	53.1	59.3
ESP	68.6	70.0	USA	75.3	84.9
EST	70.2	75.0	**Average**	**70.2**	**71.9**
FIN	88.0	80.8			
FRA	74.0	68.0			
GBR	78.3	84.1	Developing Economies		
GNQ	25.5	43.1	ISO-Code	Overall WGI	Overall EoDB
GRC	60.7	59.7	ALB	43.3	57.1
HKG	78.4	87.6	ARM	45.2	62.6
HRV	57.2	57.0	BFA	43.3	39.2
HUN	66.3	65.3	BGD	31.4	49.4
IRL	79.6	84.6	BGR	54.0	67.0
ISL	82.8	80.2	BIH	42.9	51.8
ISR	61.2	71.5	BLZ	49.7	58.9
ITA	61.8	65.1	BOL	38.8	47.9
JPN	74.0	77.5	BRA	50.5	49.0
KOR	63.9	78.8	BWA	64.5	63.4
KWT	53.5	60.1	CHL	73.2	68.3
LUX	83.7	64.9	CHN	39.1	54.4
MLT	74.1	61.2	CMR	32.4	41.2
NLD	83.4	75.7			

continued on next page

Table A7.1 continued

Developing Economies			Developing Economies		
ISO-Code	Overall WGI	Overall EoDB	ISO-Code	Overall WGI	Overall EoDB
COG	28.1	36.0	LSO	46.7	49.6
COL	40.5	63.4	LTU	64.4	73.8
CPV	58.9	53.6	LVA	63.3	73.1
CRI	61.6	54.0	MAR	43.5	58.6
DOM	42.8	59.2	MDA	41.1	59.0
DZA	33.3	48.5	MDG	41.8	46.2
ECU	34.3	56.1	MEX	48.1	68.3
EGY	38.2	49.3	MLI	41.8	41.6
ETH	30.8	45.0	MMR	17.8	41.5
FJI	41.9	67.1	MNG	47.7	59.4
GAB	39.7	47.9	MOZ	43.7	50.3
GEO	44.8	72.2	MRT	37.9	40.9
GHA	50.7	60.7	MUS	65.5	70.8
GIN	25.8	36.2	MWI	42.9	49.8
GTM	37.7	56.2	MYS	56.8	73.8
GUY	42.3	57.9	NAM	56.2	61.6
HND	37.9	56.6	NER	37.5	37.2
HTI	25.5	38.4	NGA	26.9	43.9
IDN	37.9	54.0	NIC	39.2	53.2
IND	44.3	46.7	NPL	32.5	58.5
IRN	29.5	54.8	PAK	29.5	55.9
IRQ	18.8	44.8	PAN	51.4	62.9
JAM	49.2	60.8	PER	43.4	67.0
JOR	49.5	52.3	PHL	40.6	50.5
KAZ	38.3	56.0	PNG	35.7	53.7
KEN	35.9	55.7	PRY	34.7	57.2
KGZ	32.3	57.8	ROU	51.3	64.9
KHM	33.5	47.6	RUS	35.6	58.0
LAO	28.7	45.9	RWA	39.3	51.4
LBN	37.6	58.0	SDN	19.4	47.4
LBR	29.0	42.9	SEN	45.1	41.8
LBY	28.9	28.9	SLB	37.1	56.0
LKA	43.4	56.1	SLE	33.5	44.0

continued on next page

Table A7.1 continued

Developing Economies			Developing Economies		
ISO-Code	Overall WGI	Overall EoDB	ISO-Code	Overall WGI	Overall EoDB
SLV	46.8	58.1	UGA	38.0	49.6
SUR	48.4	40.5	UKR	39.0	43.1
SWZ	37.7	55.8	URY	64.3	57.0
SYC	52.6	62.1	VEN	27.1	35.7
TCD	23.6	28.6	VNM	39.3	57.2
TGO	30.9	37.8	ZAF	56.2	69.5
THA	46.4	70.2	ZAR	17.5	31.0
TUN	48.1	63.5	ZMB	42.7	57.0
TUR	48.4	63.1	**Average**	**41.2**	**53.5**
TZA	41.9	52.7			

EoDB = ease of doing business, WGI = World Governance Index.
Source: Compiled by author.

Table A7.2: World Bank's Worldwide Governance Indicators

Voice and Accountability

Capturing perceptions of the extent to which a country's citizens are able to participate in selecting their government, as well as freedom of expression, freedom of association, and a free media.

Political Stability and Absence of Violence/Terrorism

Capturing perceptions of the likelihood that the government will be destabilized or overthrown by unconstitutional or violent means, including politically motivated violence and terrorism.

Government Effectiveness

Capturing perceptions of the quality of public services, the quality of the civil service and the degree of its independence from political pressures, the quality of policy formulation and implementation, and the credibility of the government's commitment to such policies.

Regulatory Quality

Capturing perceptions of the ability of the government to formulate and implement sound policies and regulations that permit and promote private sector development.

Rule of Law

Capturing perceptions of the extent to which agents have confidence in and abide by the rules of society, and in particular the quality of contract enforcement, property rights, the police, and the courts, as well as the likelihood of crime and violence.

Control of Corruption

Capturing perceptions of the extent to which public power is exercised for private gain, including both petty and grand forms of corruption, as well as "capture" of the state by elites and private interests.

Source: Kaufmann, D., A. Kraay, and M. Mastruzzi (2010), "The Worldwide Governance Indicators: Methodology and Analytical Issues," Brookings Institution.

Table A7.3: World Bank's Ease of Doing Business Indicators

Starting a Business
Procedures to legally start and operate a company (number), time required to complete each procedure (calendar days), cost required to complete each procedure (% of income per capita), and paid-in minimum capita (% of income per capita).

Dealing with Construction Permits
Procedures to legally build a warehouse (number), time required to complete each procedure (calendar days), and cost required to complete each procedure (% of warehouse value).

Registering Property
Procedures to legally transfer title on immovable property (number), time required to complete each procedure (calendar days), and cost required to complete each procedure (% of property value).

Getting Credit
Strength of legal rights index (0–12), depth of credit information index (0–8), credit bureau coverage (% of adults), and credit registry coverage (% of adults).

Protecting Minority Investors
Extent of disclosure index (0–10), extent of directory liability index (0–10), ease of shareholder suits index (0–10), extent of conflict of interest regulation index (0–10), extent of shareholder rights index (0–10), extent of ownership and control index (0–10), extent of corporate transparency index (0–10), and extent of shareholder governance index (0–10).

Paying Taxes
Tax payments for a manufacturing company in a year (number per year adjusted for electronic and joint filing and payment), time required to comply with three major taxes (hours per year), and total tax rate (% of profit before all taxes).

Trading Across Borders
Documentary compliance, border compliance, and domestic transport

Enforcing Contracts
Time required to enforce a contract through the courts (calendar days), cost required to enforce a contract through the courts (% of claim), court structure and proceedings index (0–5), case management index (0–6), court automation index (0–4), alternative dispute resolution index (0–3), and quality of judicial processes index (0–18).

Resolving Insolvency
Time required to recover debt (years), cost required to recover debt (% of debtor's estate), outcome, and recovery rate for secured creditors (cents on the dollar).

Source: http://www.doingbusiness.org/methodology.

PART 3
FINANCIAL COOPERATION

"The lesson of history is that you do not get a sustained economic recovery as long as the financial system is in crisis."

Ben Bernanke, former chair of the Federal Reserve

Financial Cycles and Crises in Asia

8

Stijn Claessens

Introduction[1]

In decades prior to the global financial crisis, much of the policy, academic, and general views on financial cycles and macro-financial linkages was along the lines of "can safely ignore." As Stanley Fischer, then first deputy managing director of the International Monetary Fund (IMF), put it: "I wasn't used to thinking of the banking and financial sector as having such a critical role...Floating exchange rates, tightening budgets, liberalizing markets and worrying about wages were all according to the book... Tesobonos were not."[2] Olivier Blanchard, chief economist of the IMF in 2009, expressed a similar view in a paper in April that year: "In the interest of full disclosure: This is a first pass by an economist who, until recently, thought of financial intermediation as an issue of relatively little importance for economic fluctuations...".

The global financial crisis led to a major revision of general thinking and policy making on the links between macro and finance. And it has spurred, besides a more general debate, a truly new line of research. Before the crisis, there was a long shadow of two separate strands in academic literature, which carried to a significant degree over into the policy world. On the finance side, increasing trust was placed on the so-called "efficient financial markets" paradigm. And limited attention was given to how the various

---

[1] This is the written version of a keynote speech presented at the International Conference on "Financial Cycles, Systemic Risk, Interconnectedness, and Policy Options for Resilience," held on 8–9 September 2016 in Sydney, Australia, and organized by the ADB, RBA, UNSW. Many of the figures on Asia are provided by Benjamin Piven and Alex Tetra at the Federal Reserve Bank of New York. I would like to thank Sonja Fritz for her excellent assistance. The opinions expressed are those of the author and do not necessarily reflect the views of the Bank for International Settlements.

[2] As quoted in the Euromoney publication of September 1997.

forms of finance could be channels of transmission and sources of shocks themselves. And on the macroeconomic side, there were large intellectual investments in real business cycles and new-Keynesian models and related dynamic (stochastic) general equilibrium modeling exercises at policy making institutions, such as central banks. These typically did not include much in terms of financial channels, apart perhaps from the financial accelerator mechanism, and the macroeconomic view was most: "finance is a veil" and can safely be ignored. Neither of the two literature streams interacted much and certainly did not focus much on their intersection: macro-financial linkages.

The crisis has changed this in many ways. It has highlighted many questions, some old, some new, on both the demand side—defined as related to those agents in search of external financing for investment or consumption purposes—and the supply side—defined as related to those financial institutions and markets providing the various forms of external financing. The buildup to the crisis and its aftermath have shown that financial markets can be less than fully efficient and be subject to herding, behavioral, and other biases. Finance was thus shown not to be a veil, in that the supply side of finance was found to matter in originating and propagating shocks. Important and together, the global financial crisis and acknowledgments of prominent academics (e.g., Blanchard et al. 2016) and others of the failures in collective thinking have made for the recognition of the importance of macro-finance linkages. Spurred by the crisis, more empirical evidence has also been collected on macro-financial linkages and financial cycles, with much of this focused on the demand-side channels and some on supply side.

Still, there is no unified theoretical framework to consider macro-financial linkages and there are many empirical questions remaining. With that in mind, this paper sets out to do the following. It first reviews the analytical reasons for financial cycles and macro-financial linkages: why and how do financial cycles arise? It also reviews how one can go about measuring financial cycles. The paper in the next section then reviews financial cycles in general and, for emerging Asia specifically, reviews financial conditions in these countries. It reviews domestic as well as the cross-border dimensions of financial cycles. Finally, it draws on the lessons of financial crises, reviewing the causes and consequences of crises as well as what are good crisis management and prevention policies. The last section concludes.

Financial Cycles: Why? How to Measure?

Quite a few theories suggest that finance can affect the business cycle, but fewer theories can explain independently why financial cycles might arise. The theories that do suggest that finance affects the business cycle can be grouped under two headings. The first group is those about finance affecting demand, where demand is defined as the needs of agents in search of external financing for investment or consumption purposes. Here, the financial accelerator mechanisms are the key ones. And the second group is those coming about through the supply of finance, defined as financial institutions and markets providing the various forms of external financing. Here, in addition to some of the same financial accelerator mechanisms, movements and developments within the financial system are key.

There are also various empirical approaches to measuring financial cycles (and business cycles), which can be classified into two groups: (i) those relying on deviations of financial variables from their trends, and (ii) those relying on deviations from their levels. Both types of methods have their advantages and disadvantages and all require nuances in their use. I discuss research on these issues, ending with the challenging issue of the development of new theories of how financial cycles can arise independently and identifying their empirical relevance.

Theories of How Finance Affects the Business Cycle

On the demand side, the main theories suggesting that financial conditions affect real outcomes can be categorized under the financial accelerator mechanism. This mechanism describes how endogenous developments in financial markets, in response to real or financial shocks, can lead to aggregate amplification and propagation of shocks in the real economy. The mechanism's microeconomic main foundation is based on a large body of corporate finance theory. This states that due to "frictions"—largely stemming from information asymmetries and enforcement difficulties—the financial positions of agents (notably their levels of debt relative to wealth or net worth, i.e., leverage) affect their access to finance. This in turn means that shocks to agents' net worth affect their ability to invest or consume, which then means that shocks to commodity or asset prices, say, or to interest rates would have greater real economic outcomes.

There are many variations of these financial accelerator mechanisms, and some have been built into dynamic (stochastic) general equilibrium models, so-called D(S)GE models. The most well-known are the external finance premium—as developed by Bernanke and Gertler (1989), and put in a general equilibrium model by Bernanke, Gertler, and Gilchrist (1999)—and the collateral channel, as developed into a general equilibrium model by Kiyotaki and Moore (1997). In these analyses, as declines in net worth constrain the ability of corporations and households to obtain new loans, investment and consumption is adversely affected in the first round. As agents' access to financial services and output is affected by shocks, general equilibrium effects arise in these models. By allowing for the endogenous determination of asset prices, a small negative shock leading to an asset price decline gets amplified as it reduces the value of net worth and collateral for all borrowers, and thereby reduces aggregate availability of loans. This further depresses demand for the asset and its price and then reduces access to external financing in a second round as shocks persist and amplify, and spill over to other corporations or sectors.

This literature in many ways builds on earlier, more qualitative discussions spurred by the Great Depression. This period saw among many adverse economic outcomes price deflation, making the servicing of nominal debt more burdensome, and thereby adversely affecting aggregate demand. The seminal work here is Irving Fisher (1933), who provides a descriptive account of the linkages between the high leverage of borrowers and the severity of the downturn during the Depression. His "debt-deflation" mechanism narrates how a decrease in net worth induced by declines in asset prices can lead borrowers to reduce their spending and investment, which in turn causes activity to contract more and results in a cycle of falling output and deflation. More recently, a number of models have formalized and expanded on this mechanism.

The macroeconomic implications of financial market imperfections have also been studied in the context of open economy models, spurred by Krugman (1999). Similar to the case of a corporation or household in a closed economy, a country's ability to borrow is affected by its net worth because of financial market imperfections—probably more so than in the domestic context—since contracts are harder to enforce and information asymmetries are greater across borders. As a result, shocks can be even more amplified. The financial accelerator has been shown to be a quantitatively important mechanism in explaining the real effects of financial stress in open economy models. Gertler, Gilchrist, and Natalucci (2007), studying an open economy version of Bernanke, Gertler, and Gilchrist (1999) to analyze the behavior of the Korean economy during the 1997–1998 financial crisis, report that the financial accelerator mechanism explains half of the reduction in the Republic of Korea's output and that credit market frictions amplify the adverse effects of the crisis on investment.

The demand accelerator mechanism can also run through various, additional channels and a number of models now exist showing their general equilibrium impact. For example, various frictions can affect corporations' cash flow, working capital, access to trade finance, or default probabilities that also give rise to the so-called financial accelerator mechanism. There are also general equilibrium models with frictions related to heterogeneity, project and technological choices, productivity, and governance. Models have also shown how financial frictions can operate via labor markets and affect aggregate demand; for example, this can occur when firms' financing constraints affect hiring. Also, there can be effects on the supply of labor, such as when declines in house prices in combination with high mortgage debt make people less able to move jobs. And there can be frictions related to information and uncertainty as well as more generally to volatility, making for less precision in signals, which can tighten credit standards, and thereby adversely affect access to finance. Finally, limits to monetary policy, as in the presence of the zero lower bound, can exacerbate these various accelerator effects and dynamics.

While the ways the financial accelerator affects business cycles will vary by the specific mechanism, the overall way will most often be similar. In the case of an adverse shock, as net worth and asset prices decline and collateral becomes less valuable, borrowers (corporations, households, sovereigns) will have less access to finance, which worsens their real investment and consumption, and then, via adverse feedbacks, leads in aggregate to worse economic outcomes. In the worst cases, this can lead to "busts": asset prices drop sharply and credit declines drastically, creating external financing crunches with very adverse real consequences. In the case of favorable shocks, in contrast where net worth and asset prices increase, collateral becomes more valuable, and final borrowers have more access to finance—this leads to a strengthening of the real economy, with various positive feedback loops. Here one can even have "booms": asset prices and credit increase sharply and capital inflows may rise, leading to greatly amplified positive real consequences.

On the supply side, the financial system can be a source of shocks, amplification, and propagation itself, even when on the demand side there are no shocks affecting borrowers. Several channels can be distinguished. One is the traditional bank lending channel. Some borrowers (households, small and medium-sized enterprises) are more bank financing-dependent (because of information asymmetries, transaction costs, and others). As banks are affected by shocks, they will increase or decrease financing to these classes of borrowers. This has been one of the traditional channels of transmission of monetary policies, which has received new attention in light of unconventional monetary policy, such as quantitative easing, conducted by many central banks in advanced countries since the global financial crisis.

Another, but relatively less well-analyzed channel has been the bank capital channel. When banks have a capital shortfall or some impairment of their balance sheets, they will reduce their provision of credit. As external financing declines, and investment and consumption drop, aggregate adverse effects can come about (Van den Heuvel 2008). This channel relates also to regulatory policies, as when capital adequacy requirements are raised sharply and in turn induce a credit crunch. More generally, there can be supply effects through leverage and liquidity channels. These operate like the capital channel, not just for banks, but also for other nonbank financial intermediaries. In addition, supply effects can come about through indirect channels, as well as asset price changes beneficially or adversely affecting (common) exposures. All these channels show how the financial sector can create and amplify shocks. The basic operation, however, is the financial accelerator again: shocks to assets or equity affect financial institutions and markets, which then in turn amplify and propagate, leading to changes in external financing conditions for corporations, households, and sovereigns. There can be capital shocks, asset price shocks, or liquidity shocks. The mechanisms can also relate to fire sales, or to leverage cycles. The net effect is that, as they interact with the "standard" financial accelerator, there can be even more pronounced general equilibrium virtuous and vicious cycles, where the financial system can (also) become a (further) force for procyclicality.

Besides these consequences that have more of a time-series dimension, there can also be consequences arising from cross-sectional interconnections and exposures, including those related to "too-big-to-fail" banks or otherwise systemically important financial institutions and critical market infrastructure, and other forms of direct and indirect intra-financial system connections, including international. The overall impact of these (complex) interactions among financial intermediaries and markets, including through capital markets because of commonly traded securities, is a newer area of research, and these intra-system dynamics are not (yet) well understood. But clearly much scope for externalities and market failures exists within financial systems, leading not only to systemic risks, but also to potentially adverse real sector consequences. Recent research has indeed emphasized the importance of amplification through channels operating on the supply side of finance, including both financial institutions and markets (e.g., Brunnermeier and Pedersen 2009; Adrian and Shin 2011; and Geanakoplos 2010).

How to Measure Financial Cycles and Business Cycles?

There are two main, complementary approaches in the literature. One is the "classic cycle" approach, which looks for a turning point in the level of financial and real variables to identify significant turning points (so-called peaks and troughs). The other is the "growth-cycle" approach, which de-trends financial and real variables and then defines the cycle relative to this trend. I discuss both briefly.

The identification of cycles using the classic approach came from Burns and Mitchell (1946) and underlies the National Bureau of Economic Research (NBER) type of dating recessions (and expansions). While the relevant NBER-committee dates cycles using many variables and a more judgmental approach, researchers have developed algorithms to similarly determine peaks and troughs, the best known is the one based on and Bry and Boschan (1971) for gross domestic product (GDP), which became known as the BB algorithm. It has been popularized for business cycles by Harding and Pagan (2002a) in the form of a so-called BBQ algorithm to identify the turning points in quarterly series.

This approach allows for simple measures, which can then be used as input for further analyses. For example, it gives the average duration and typical pattern of a cycle, which are very relevant for policy. Its simplicity can also make it easy to explain the duration, amplitude, and slope of various macro-financial variables and (monetary and fiscal) policy. It can also be used to analyze boosts and busts (and financial crises) as extremes of such financial cycles. And it can be used to analyze the degree of business and financial cycles' synchronization within and across countries. For example, there is a concordance index (Harding and Pagan 2002b), which is the fraction of time any two series are in the same phase in their respective cycles. It can show the amplification across financial cycles within and across countries.

The other method of identifying cycles is trend-based. Using various methods, the idea is to measure credit "excessive" to a trend. Often this is done with the Hodrick-Prescott (HP) filter with a specific frequency range (typically a one-sided HP filter used with λ=400,000). This is used for example by the Basel Committee on Banking Supervision for determining the so-called credit-to-GDP gap, which in turn is used as input in triggering and setting the level of the countercyclical capital buffer. The credit gap performs relatively well as an early warning indicator of future crises.

More advanced time-series techniques are being used as well, such as latent dynamic factor, frequency domain, and multivariate factor analyses. Other related advanced techniques include state-space, spectrum representation, and Kalman filters. These techniques can include many more variables, i.e., various financial condition variables, to detect commonalities and obtain a unique financial cycle, without making many assumptions about the nature of the cycle. One advantage of some of these techniques is that one can robustly add variables (i.e., output gap estimates) to improve forecasting. Some can also be used to augment end points with forecasts before de-trending, which helps with the so-called end-of-period problem in filtering techniques (the latest, current observation will importantly drive the trend).

These two sets of methodologies each have their advantages and disadvantages and are really complementary. For one, it can be both the level and growth of credit that give rise to concerns: for example, the level of credit may matter as it proxies for the degree of leverage in an economy, whereas growth may matter as it indicates that the new debt is contributing less to growth (e.g., due to the lower productivity of financing for existing assets, such as housing, rather than new investment). Methodologies also have specific advantages and disadvantages. The level-based methodology is very simple but is not country-specific. This, on one hand, makes for easy cross-country comparisons, but, on the other, ignores issues such as that, for higher GDP-growth countries, where the level of GDP is less likely to decline, slowdowns can already be of a material consequence. And a developing country engaged in financial deepening can have high growth in credit, without necessarily raising financial or economic stability concerns.

For all, some choices must still be made. For example, the level and trend-based methodologies both have to indicate what the selection criteria are so that small deviations in the variables do not lead to too many cycles. The trend-based ones are more demanding in the choice of techniques, raising questions such as: should one use uni- or multivariate frequency filters; is the HP the best, and if so, with what filter, or is another technique better? If using multivariate approaches, what data should be included? Should one use market prices that are forward looking? How should one deal with end-of-period and new data? Can one distinguish short- vs. long-term trends? What is the best frequency of updating the trends? Again, these choices can greatly affect the exact financial cycles obtained. Furthermore, many approaches use (some) real quantities and asset prices, so the question arises as to what price index should be used to deflate. While measured financial cycles (and business cycles) thus vary by method used, there are nevertheless quite a few regularities, which we discuss next.

Financial Cycles in General and in Asia

In this section, I review the key characteristics of business and financial cycles in general, the patterns and overlaps in cycles, and the effects of financial cycles on the real economy, also considering various nuances. I then review the state of finance in Asia, especially in emerging markets, asking where countries are in their financial cycles, and what is the role of international factors in driving their financial cycles.

Business and Financial Cycles

To clarify, I use the classic definition of a business cycle and define a financial cycle accordingly. Figures 8.1 and 8.2 give these definitions graphically. Figure 8.1 defines the concepts of economic recession, expansion, and recovery as well as peaks and troughs; Figure 8.2 shows the equivalent financial cycle ones of contraction/downturn and upturn/boom.

In terms of the main stylized factors, business and financial cycles clearly display differing characteristics. Full business cycles are typically 6 to 8 years long, counting from peak to peak; a recession is typically 1 year and expansions are 5 years. Financial cycles can be much longer, 10–20 years, with booms even longer. It is also clear that financial cycles tend to be more volatile than business cycles, as measured for example by standard deviations. The contraction phases are especially deeper for financial cycles than those for business cycles (Figure 8.3). Downturns in house prices can be very long, and upturns in credit are typically long as well.

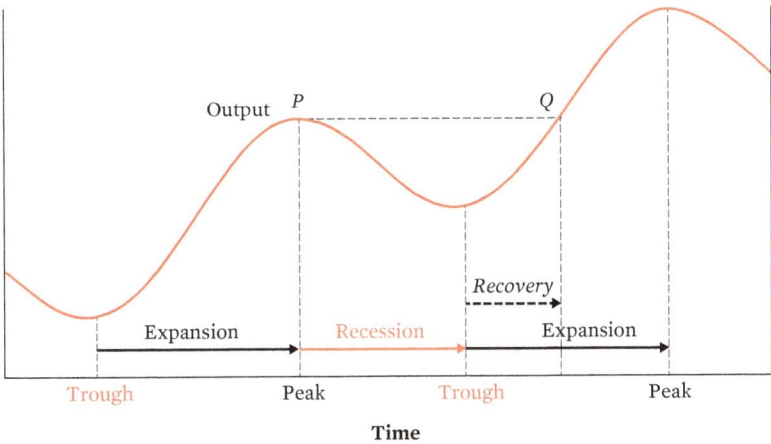

Figure 8.1: Definition of a Business Cycle

Source: Claessens, S., M. A. Kose, and M. E. Terrones. 2012. How Do Business and Financial Cycles Interact? *Journal of International Economics.* 87 (1). pp. 178–90.

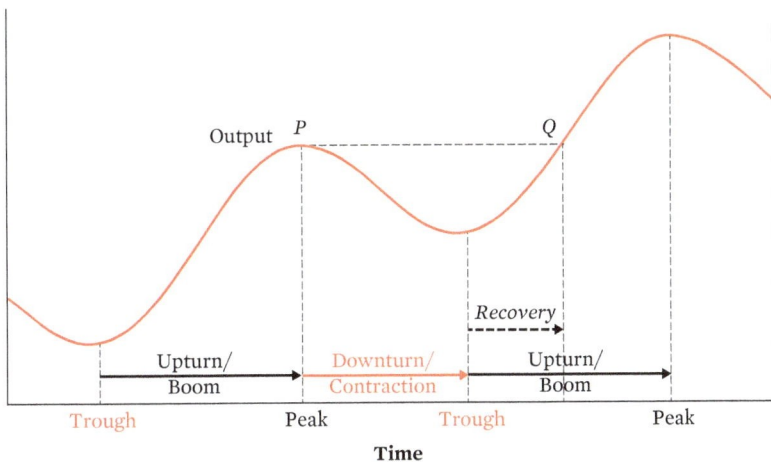

Figure 8.2: Definition of a Financial Cycle

Source: Claessens, S., M. A. Kose, and M. E. Terrones. 2012. How Do Business and Financial Cycles Interact? *Journal of International Economics.* 87 (1). pp. 178–90.

Importantly, financial cycles then reinforce each other, in that, credit, housing, or equity prices are more likely to be all in an upturn (or downturn). At the same time, it appears that the financial cycle is best captured by house

Figure 8.3: Average Amplitude of Financial Booms and Busts

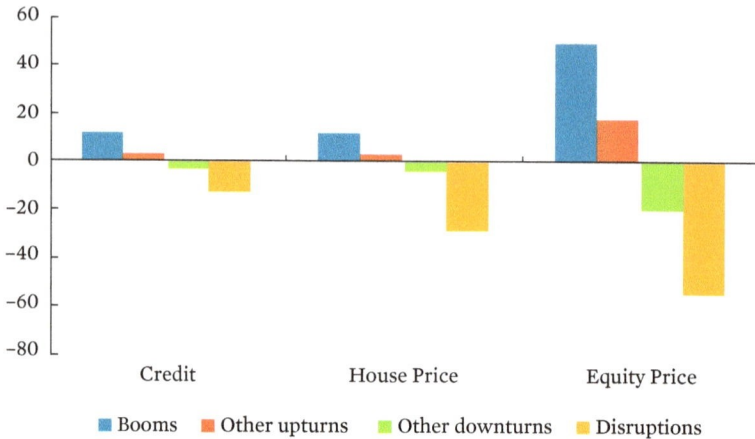

Notes: Figures reflect the average amplitude of upturns and downturns, measured in percentages. The amplitude for upturns (downturns) is calculated based on the 1-year change in each respective financial variable after its trough (peak). Booms are the top 25% of upturns calculated by amplitude. Disruptions (crunches, busts, and collapses) are the worst 25% of downturns calculated by amplitude. The data set includes 21 Organisation for Economic Co-operation and Development (OECD) countries and covers quarterly data from 1960 to 2007 and draws from International Monetary Fund's International Financial Statistics and the OECD (updated to account for data revisions).

Source: Claessens, S., M. A. Kose, and M. E. Terrones. 2012. How Do Business and Financial Cycles Interact? *Journal of International Economics.* 87 (1). pp. 178–90.

prices and credit, not by equity prices. Financial cycles also do tend to coincide globally. This likely reflects global factors as well as cross-border spillovers driving financial cycles globally. Of course, some of these patterns also apply to business cycles, where there are factors driving common recessions/recoveries. Most importantly, there is a high coincidence of financial cycle peaks with subsequent systemic financial crises.

Besides documenting the fact that financial booms and busts can be large, the main important empirical stylized fact documented by a number of authors is that the financial cycle impacts the business cycle, with at times strong interactions. Claessens, Kose, and Terrones (2009, 2011, and 2012), for example, analyze financial cycles and business cycles in 21 advanced countries and 23 emerging market countries from 1960 to 2007, using turning point analysis. Drehmann, Borio, and Tsatsaronis (2012) do so for seven advanced countries using a pre-specified frequency-based filter method in which the financial cycle is assumed to operate.

These and many other studies (see Taylor 2015 for a review) show that recessions with financial contractions are more severe, i.e., longer and deeper. Figure 8.4 shows how financial disruptions tend to amplify and lengthen recessions. At the same time, not all recessions coincide with financial cycle troughs; for example, the United States (US) had a recession in the early 2000s while the financial cycle was still expanding. However, it is clear that high credit expansion before a financial crisis stalls recovery after the crisis. And Figure 8.5 shows that credit and output contractions coincide most around the world, suggesting that credit developments are the most important to watch from a real sector perspective.

Business and financial cycles accentuate each other, and not just in recessions with financial disruptions. It is also clear that economic expansions with financial expansions are stronger and longer. Figure 8.6 shows how financial booms tend to enhance and lengthen expansions.

Figure 8.4: Impact of Financial Disruptions on Recessions

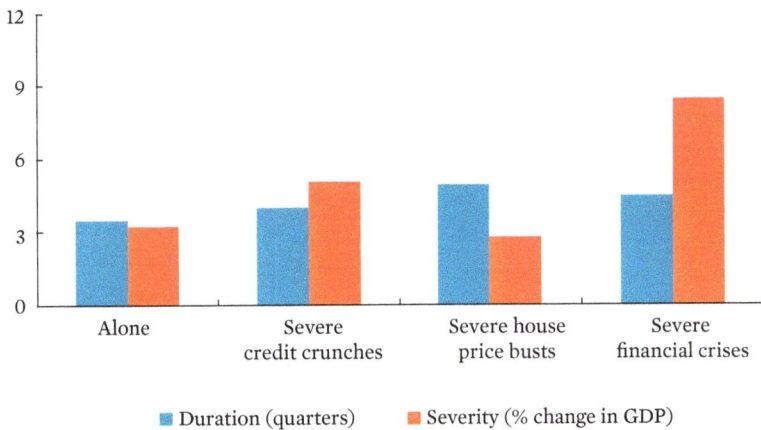

GDP = gross domestic product.

Notes: Severe credit crunches and equity or house price busts are in the top half of all crunch and bust episodes. Duration is the number of quarters from peak to trough in output. The data set includes 21 Organisation for Economic Co-operation and Development (OECD) countries and covers quarterly data from 1960 to 2007. It draws from International Monetary Fund's International Financial Statistics and OECD (updated to account for data revisions).

Source: Claessens, S., M. A. Kose, and M. E. Terrones. 2012. How Do Business and Financial Cycles Interact? *Journal of International Economics.* 87 (1). pp. 178–90.

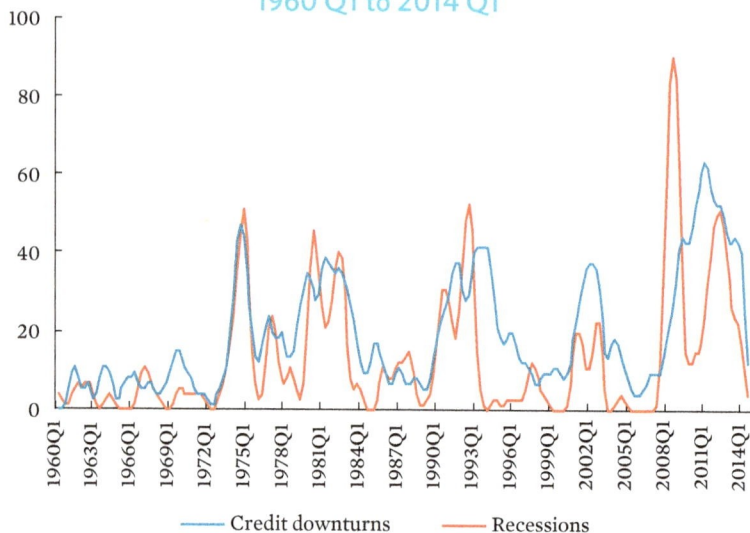

Figure 8.5: Recessions and Credit Downturns, 1960 Q1 to 2014 Q1

Q = quarter.
Source: Claessens, S., M. A. Kose, and M. E. Terrones. 2012. How Do Business and Financial Cycles Interact? *Journal of International Economics*. 87 (1). pp. 178–90.

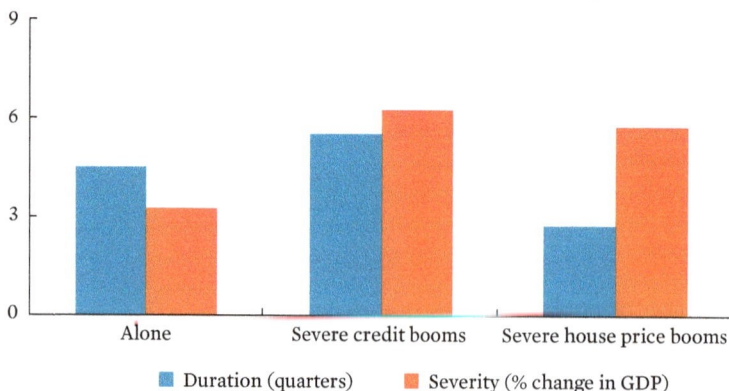

Figure 8.6: Impact of Financial Booms on Expansions

GDP = gross domestic product.
Notes: The data set includes 21 Organisation for Economic Co-operation and Development (OECD) countries and covers quarterly data from 1960 to 2007. It draws from International Financial Statistics and OECD (updated to account for data revisions).
Source: Claessens, S., M. A. Kose, and M. E. Terrones. 2012. How Do Business and Financial Cycles Interact? *Journal of International Economics*. 87 (1). pp. 178–90.

But while these stylized facts are now fairly well established, there is as of (yet) limited understanding of what causes financial booms and triggers busts. Booms can have multiple triggers, some domestic, like productivity increases and financial liberalization, and some external, like shocks to commodity prices and global interest rates triggering changes in capital flows. Many have tried to explain the cyclical movements in asset and credit markets and found some proximate causes, such as financial liberalization, productivity gains, and a variety of distortions, such as weak supervision and regulation, underpriced deposit insurance, and poorly designed safety nets. However, many puzzles remain about what drives bubbles and booms in the first place.

This relates in part to the limited knowledge on the role of frictions during "normal" cycles. It also relates to the seemingly large nonlinearities arising in times of financial turmoil, where what appear to be small perturbations can lead to large financial and economic consequences. As such, the best prevention strategies remain unclear in many respects. More generally, nuances and judgment in the use of the "financial cycle" measured remain necessary, especially for policy. For one, it is also risky to rely on pure data (mining). Correlations can arise due to other factors. For example, fundamentals (shocks) and policy actions (fiscal, monetary) may create relations between business and financial cycles that are not necessarily worrisome. Internationally, via risk sharing and otherwise, one can get co-movements in financial variables, even without a real connection between two economies. Also, there are many second-best situations, say where in case financial markets develop more, this does not necessarily need to lead to higher welfare. And there is much heterogeneity in terms of countries' cyclical positions, structural features, and variations in financial systems, making tailoring of the measurements of financial cycles necessary.

Importantly, in part as the theoretical framework for what is driving financial cycles is limited, there is also no formal benchmark of what a good or bad financial cycle is, i.e., it is unclear how one defines "excessive." This also means that it is unclear what should be done about short-term movements. Should one ignore those movements, but how about if they continue, important as financial cycles are very low frequency? All this is more challenging as one cannot expect a single, standard financial cycle measure. Compare for example the two measures in Figure 8.7; one based solely on credit growth and house prices, and the other solely on equity prices and bond yields, all as of 2014 (Sandri 2014). Both measures of the "financial gaps" are compared to the standard output gap measure for each country, which is of course the same in both Figures 8.7a and 8.7b. Figure 8.7a shows that if one uses the financial cycle gap measure based on credit growth and house prices, then the set of countries for which the financial

Figure 8.7: Economic and Financial Gaps by Basis

a. Credit growth and house prices

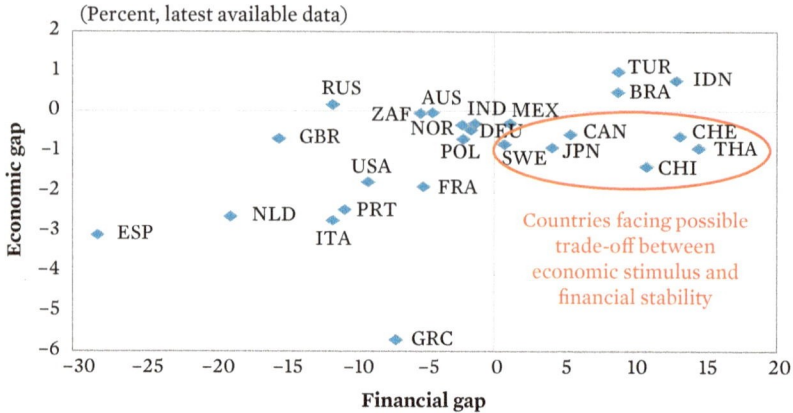

(Percent, latest available data)

Countries facing possible trade-off between economic stimulus and financial stability

Note: The "economic gap" is the average between the output gap and the deviation of the 2015 inflation forecast from target. The "financial gap" is the average between the credit-to-GDP gap and the property price gap.

b. Equity prices and bond yields

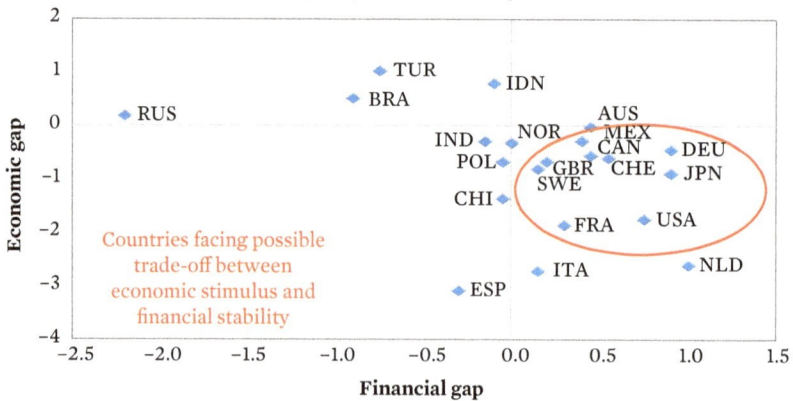

Countries facing possible trade-off between economic stimulus and financial stability

AUS = Australia, BRA = Brazil, CAN = Canada, CHI = People's Republic of China, CHE = Chile, DEU = Germany, ESP = Spain, FRA = France, GBR = Great Britain, IND = India, IDN = Indonesia, ITA = Italy, JPN = Japan, MEX = Mexico, NLD = Netherlands, NOR = Norway, POL = Poland, PRT = Portugal, RUS = Russian Federation, SWE = Sweden, THA = Thailand, TUR = Turkey, USA = United States of America, ZAF = South Africa.

Note: The "economic gap" is the average between the output gap and the deviation of the 2015 inflation forecast from target. The "financial gap" is the average between the gap measures of equity required returns and sovereign term premiums (refer to International Monetary Fund's Global Financial Stability Report, October 2014).

Source: Sandri, D. 2014. Business and Financial Cycles. Mimeo. IMF.

and economic gap measures indicate a different "impulse"—thus measures affecting both economic and financial stability could potentially conflict—is relatively small. The story in Figure 8.7b based on the financial cycle gap derived from equity prices and bond yields is quite different: here many more countries are at risk of potential conflicts between economic and financial stability measures. Which of the two financial cycle measures is "correct" we do not know. All of this is to exemplify that one needs to be able to tell the story of the "why and what" the financial cycle stands for.

Financial Cycles and Financial Conditions in Asia

I next review the state of financial cycles in Asia, and focus on the emerging markets in the region. I also review financial sectoral conditions in emerging Asia, including corporate sector and household credit, and banking system conditions, in terms of capitalization, nonperforming loans, and profitability and valuation.

Financial cycles in emerging Asia are generally still in the expansion phase. Credit has continued to increase across most of emerging Asia lately (Figure 8.8). And as credit continues to increase and deviate significantly

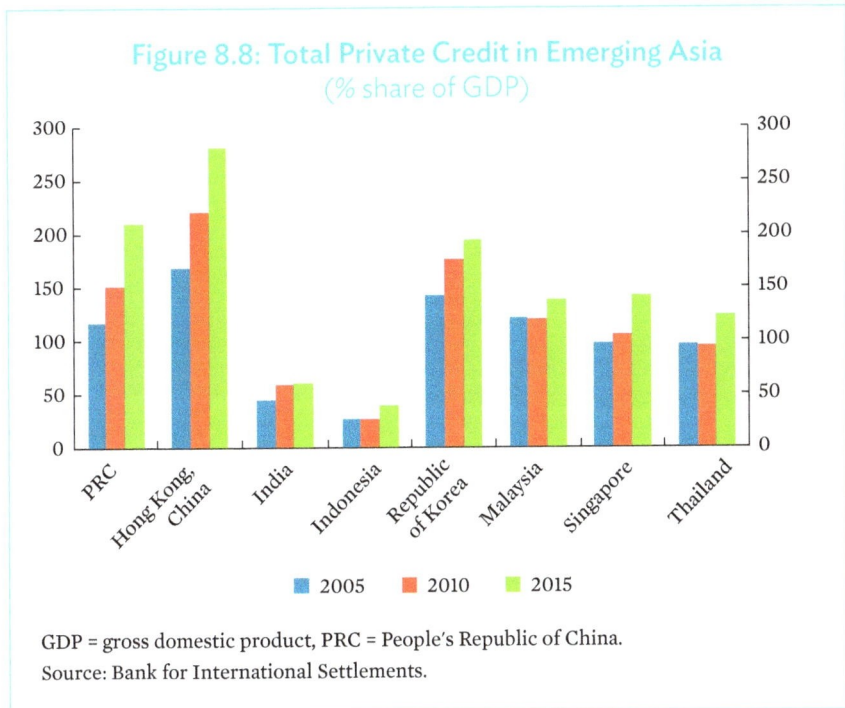

Figure 8.8: Total Private Credit in Emerging Asia
(% share of GDP)

GDP = gross domestic product, PRC = People's Republic of China.
Source: Bank for International Settlements.

from its long-run trends, credit gaps are highly positive and widening in several countries (Figure 8.9). As they do, there may be in some countries concerns of unsustainable credit booms. Also, while credit in emerging Asia is largely still limited to the corporate sector, this is becoming less so as economies become more developed (Figure 8.10). With corporate leverage rising in many countries (Figure 8.11), the high leverage combined with the slower economic growth, including of exports, are lowering debt service capacity (Figure 8.12), raising some questions about debt at risk. High leverage and slower growth have already squeezed corporate earnings, and debt service capacity has deteriorated markedly since 2012 (particularly in the People's Republic of China [PRC], India, Indonesia, and the Republic of Korea). As such, if growth further moderates amid muted exports and more sluggish industrial production, the operating environment for corporations in emerging Asia would become increasingly challenging.

Figure 8.9: Deviation of Credit-to-GDP from Long-Run Trend (%)

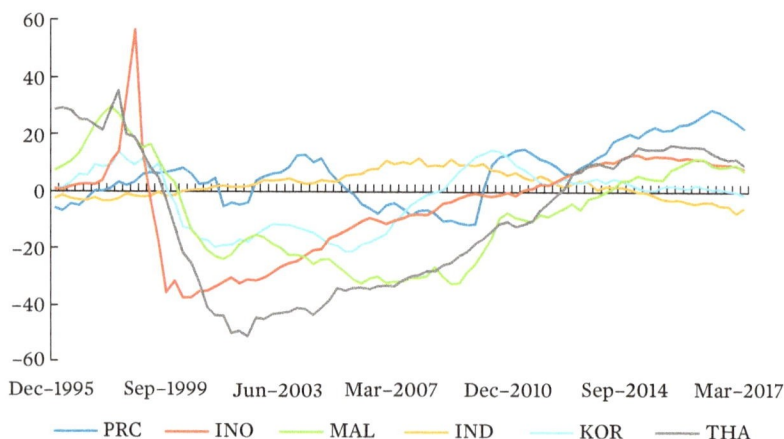

GDP = gross domestic product, IND = India, INO = Indonesia, KOR = Republic of Korea, MAL = Malaysia, PRC = People's Republic of China, THA = Thailand.

Notes: The credit-to-GDP ratio, published in the Bank for International Settlements database of total credit to the private nonfinancial sector, captures total borrowing from all domestic and foreign sources. In terms of financial instruments, credit covers the core debt, which is here equal to loans and debt securities. A credit-to-GDP gap is defined as the difference between the credit-to-GDP ratio and its long-term trend, in percentage points. The long-term trend is calculated using a one-sided Hodrick-Prescott filter with a smoothing parameter of 400,000.

Source: Bank for International Settlements, https://www.bis.org/ (accessed September 2017).

Figure 8.10: Household versus Corporate Credit in Emerging Asia (% share of total)

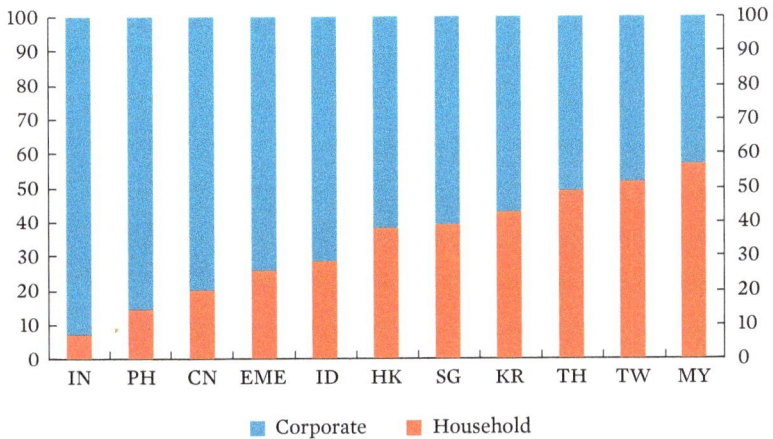

CN = People's Republic of China; EME = Emerging Asia; HK = Hong Kong, China; ID = Indonesia; IN = India; KR = Republic of Korea; MY = Malaysia; PH = Philippines; SG = Singapore; TH = Thailand; TW = Taipei,China.

Sources: IMF, World Bank; national sources.

Figure 8.11: Corporate Leverage in Emerging Asia (ratio, debt to EBITDA)

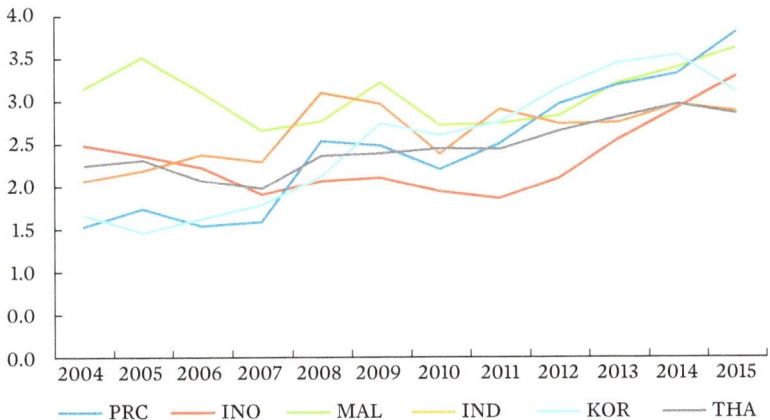

EBITDA = earnings before interest, tax, depreciation, and amortization; IND = India; INO = Indonesia; KOR = Republic of Korea; MAL = Malaysia; PRC = People's Republic of China; THA = Thailand.

Source: S&P Capital IQ.

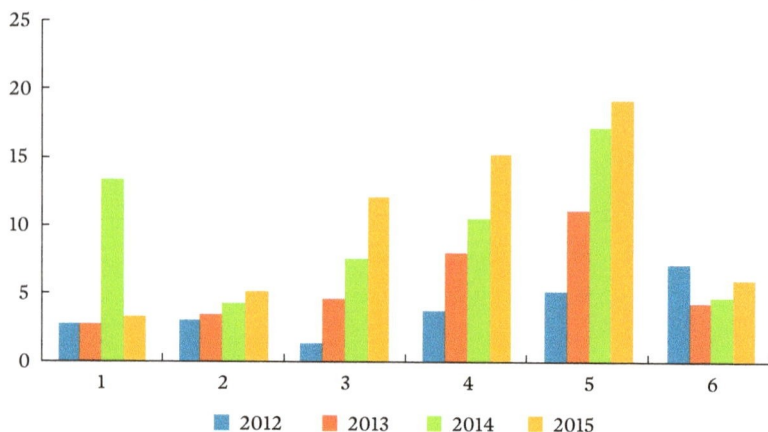

Figure 8.12: Debt at Risk in Emerging Asia
(Listed company debt with an ICR [EBITDA/Interest]<1)

EBITDA = earnings before interest, tax, depreciation, and amortization; ICR = interest coverage ratio.
Note: Data are as of December 2015.
Source: S&P Capital IQ; International financial institution estimates.

While bank credit risk is primarily concentrated in the corporate sector, in some economies household debt is high and household leverage elevated (and rising) (Figure 8.13). In most economies in the region, rising household leverage has been accompanied by significant property price appreciation. More recently, property price growth has decelerated, in part as a result of macroprudential tightening, rising housing supply, and weakening GDP and credit growth (Figure 8.14). With house price appreciation slowing in many economies, the decelerating property price appreciation poses additional downside risks for banks in some economies.

The combination of high corporate leverage, significant asset price volatility, and slowing growth have begun to pressure bank asset quality in some economies (i.e., the PRC; Indonesia; Thailand; and, to a lesser extent, Hong Kong, China and Singapore), albeit most often from a low base. Nevertheless, nonperforming loans are growing in many economies across the region and default risks are rising, creating vulnerabilities (Figure 8.15). Given the size of recent credit buildups in emerging Asia, nonperforming loans could rise significantly over the next few years, with the PRC, Malaysia, and Indonesia particularly appearing vulnerable (Figure 8.16).

Figure 8.13: Household Debt as Share of GDP (%)

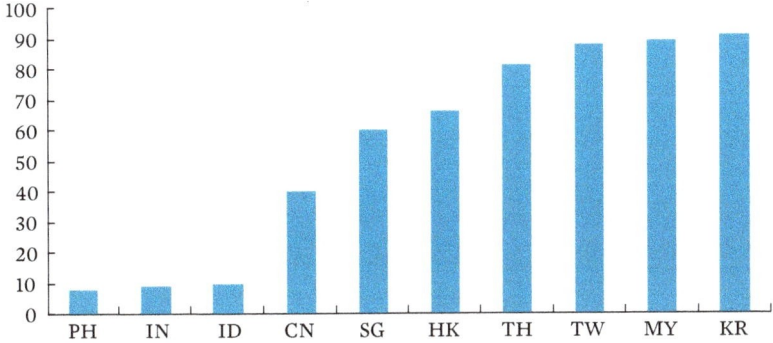

CN = People's Republic of China; GDP = gross domestic product; HK = Hong Kong, China; ID = Indonesia; IN = India; KR = Republic of Korea; MY = Malaysia; PH = Philippines; SG = Singapore; TH = Thailand; TW = Taipei,China.
Sources: CEIC; Federal Reserve Bank of New York calculations.

Figure 8.14: Average Annual Growth of House Prices in Emerging Asia (year on year, % average annual growth)

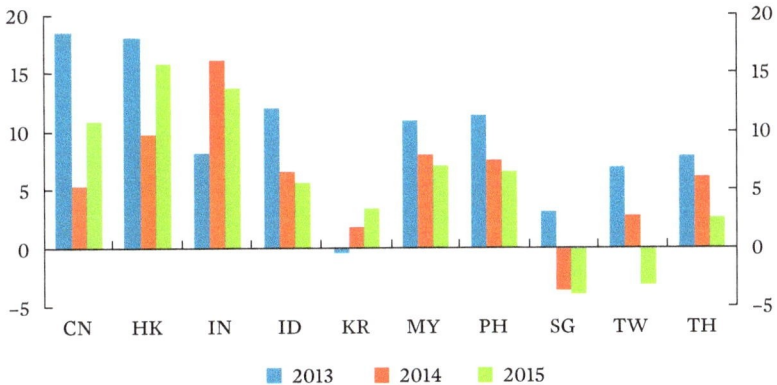

CN = People's Republic of China; HK = Hong Kong, China; ID = Indonesia; IN = India; KR = Republic of Korea; MY = Malaysia; PH = Philippines; SG = Singapore; TH = Thailand; TW = Taipei,China.
Sources: Bank for International Settlements; Cesa-Bianchi (2013); national sources.

Figure 8.15: Growth of Nonperforming Loans in Emerging Asia
(%, year-on-year)

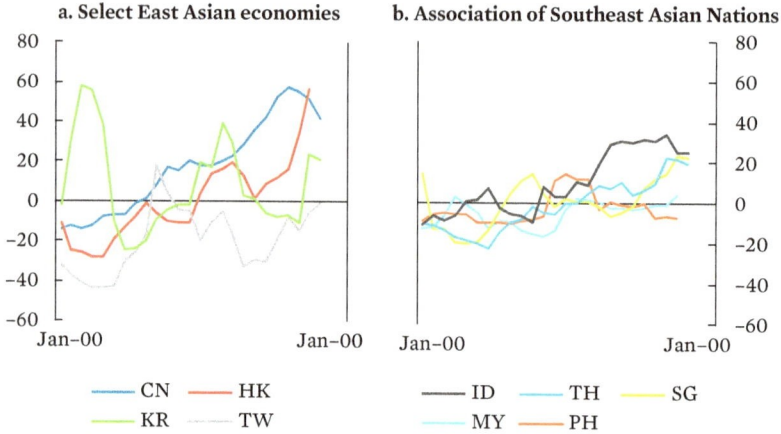

a. Select East Asian economies

b. Association of Southeast Asian Nations

Legend: CN — HK — KR — TW

ID — TH — SG — MY — PH

CN = People's Republic of China; HK = Hong Kong, China; ID = Indonesia; IN = India; KR = Republic of Korea; MY = Malaysia; PH = Philippines; SG = Singapore; TH = Thailand; TW = Taipei,China.

Sources: National sources; bank financials.

Figure 8.16: EPLs and LLRs in Emerging Asia
(% of total loans)

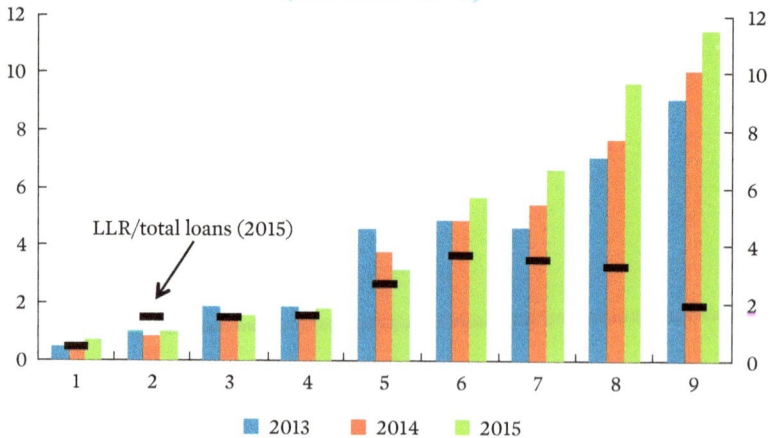

LLR/total loans (2015)

Legend: ■ 2013   ■ 2014   ■ 2015

EPL = estimated problem loan, LLR = loan loss reserve.

Note: Federal Reserve Bank of New York estimated problem loans include loans classified as special mention, restructured loans, and repossessed assets. LLRs are as of the end of 2015.

Sources: Company financials; Federal Reserve Bank of New York estimates.

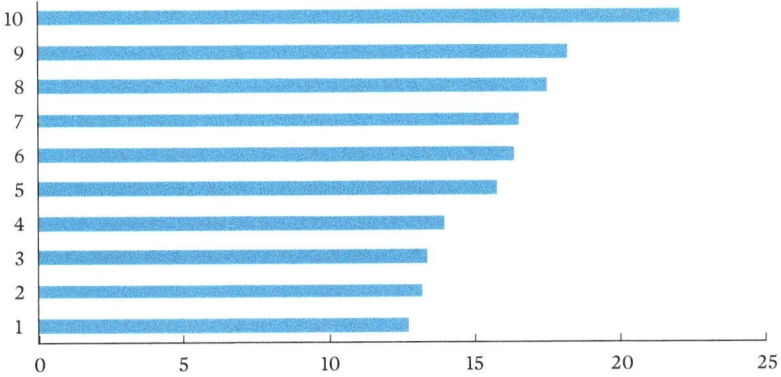

Figure 8.17: Capital Adequacy Ratio in Emerging Asia
(%, total capital as share of risk-weighted assets)

Sources: CEIC; Federal Reserve Bank of New York calculations; company reports.

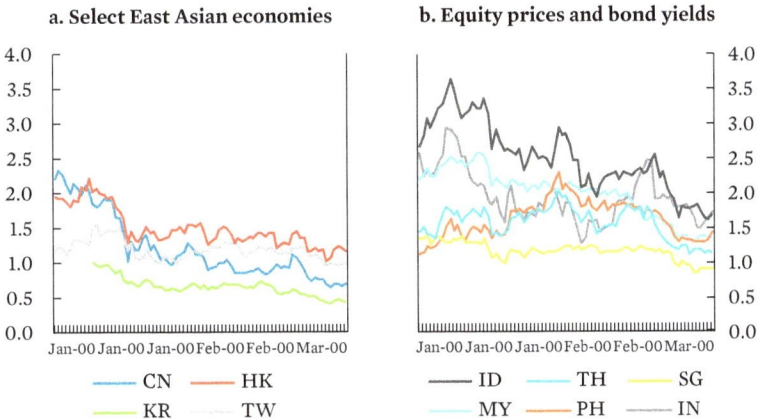

Figure 8.18: Bank Valuations in Emerging Asia
(price-to-book ratio)

a. Select East Asian economies

b. Equity prices and bond yields

CN = People's Republic of China; HK = Hong Kong, China; ID = Indonesia; IN = India;
KR = Republic of Korea; MY = Malaysia; PH = Philippines; SG = Singapore; TH = Thailand;
TW = Taipei,China.
Note: Computed using unweighted average of listed banks.
Source: Bloomberg.

Overall bank capitalization is very strong in emerging Asia, however. And, in general, banks in the region remain sufficiently capitalized to withstand a moderate rise in loan-loss provisioning consistent with a deceleration in trend economic growth and rising nonperforming loans—although such a scenario would likely weigh on profitability (Figure 8.17). Under a more severe scenario, however, bank capital support to address (expected) losses could be required in selected countries, raising potential contingent fiscal liabilities. Market valuations also suggest some concern about banks' profitability (Figure 8.18).

International Dimensions of Financial Cycles

There has been much discussion about a global financial cycle, which has been found in the form of commonality in credit (Figure 8.19), asset prices and financial conditions more generally around the world (Rey 2013). This global financial cycle appears to be in part driven by financial and economic conditions in the major financial centers, the US, the eurozone, Japan, and the United Kingdom (G4). Although the specific factors and their importance vary across studies, a consensus has emerged on the role of US monetary policy, the supply of global liquidity (especially in US dollars), the state of G4 banking systems, and global risk aversion in helping explain the high synchronicity of capital flows (see further Milesi-Ferretti et al. 2011; Shin 2012; Rey 2013; Cerutti, Claessens, and Ratnovski 2016; among others). It also affects emerging Asia. But there are differences in sensitivity to global factors by type of capital flow and across countries in general (Cerutti, Claessens, and Puy 2015).

For one, sensitivities to common dynamics vary greatly across type of flow. Only bank-related and portfolio bond and equity inflows co-move substantially across emerging markets, while foreign direct investment and flows to nonbanks do not. Second, sensitivities vary by country, and emerging Asia is no exception here. Figure 8.20 shows the differences in sensitivities. Some emerging markets display very low sensitivity to the common dynamics in all types of flows, others, such as Brazil, South Africa, and Turkey are highly sensitive to all types. Another group, including countries such as India, Mexico, Pakistan, the Philippines, and Uruguay, displays a high sensitivity to only one (or two) types. We also find that once we control for the presence of the emerging markets common factor, regional common factors among emerging markets are less important.

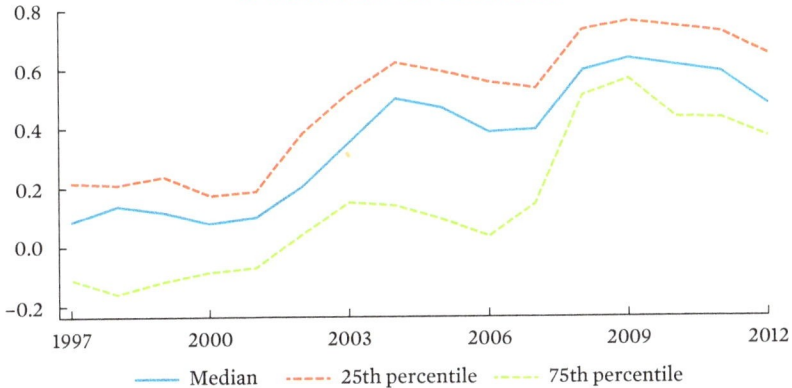

Figure 8.19: Correlation of Credit Growth between G4 and non-G4 Countries

G4 = United States, eurozone, Japan, and United Kingdom.
Source: Cerutti, E., S. Claessens, and L. Ratnovski. 2016. *Global Liquidity and Drivers of Cross-Border Bank Flows.* Paper prepared for the 63rd Economic Policy Panel meeting. The Netherlands. 22–23 April.

Cerutti, Claessens, and Puy (2015) analyze how macroeconomic and institutional fundamentals and financial market characteristics relate to the observed cross-country heterogeneity in sensitivities to common factors. They do not find that, in general, "good" fundamentals, in the form of a high quality of institutions or low public debt, tend to insulate countries from changes in global conditions. Rather, financial market characteristics more robustly explain the cross-sectional dispersion in sensitivities (Figure 8.21). In particular, for emerging markets that rely heavily on international mutual funds in their portfolio flows (both equity and bond), inflows are more sensitive to changes in global conditions. Similarly, bank inflows to emerging markets relying on global banks are significantly more sensitive to global liquidity factors. And inclusion in a global index and greater liquidity of the local equity market make these inflows more sensitive.

The fact that macro fundamentals have little power explaining sensitivities, while liquidity and the lender or investor base proxy do, has important implications. It means that watching one's lender or investor base is crucial. The fact that the sensitivity of flows is more about market characteristics and lender and investor conditions than about (institutional) fundamentals, is consistent with recent literature on procyclical international investors, such as micro-based evidence on mutual funds by Raddatz and Schmukler (2012)

Figure 8.20: Global Factor Sensitivities in Emerging Asia

Economies	Equity	Bond	Bank
Turkey	0.56	0.42	0.42
South Africa	0.46	0.58	0.5
Israel	0.17	0.36	−0.03
Argentina	0.37	0.14	0.32
Brazil	0.58	0.52	0.46
Chile	−0.06	0.15	0.19
Colombia	0.16	0.02	0.23
Mexico	0.3	0.38	0.27
Peru	0.27	0.33	0.45
Uruguay	−0.09	0.44	0.02
Venezuela, Rep. Bol.	−0.06	0.29	−0.18
India	0.67	0.16	0.23
China, People's Rep. of	0.41	−0.08	0.57
Indonesia	0.51	0.69	0.43
Korea, Republic of	0.49	0.27	0.43
Malaysia	0.38	0.29	0.45
Pakistan	0.9	0.4	0.12
Philippines	0.64	0.36	0.19
Thailand	0.58	0.36	0.4
Belarus	0.02	0.22	0.2
Kazakhstan	0.62	0.43	−0.09
Bulgaria	0.45	0.04	0.18
Russian Federation	0.29	0.36	0.39
Ukraine	0.22	0.31	0.2
Czech Republic	0.14	0.41	0.43
Slovak Republic	−0.05	0.44	0.2
Estonia	0.13	−0.22	−0.05
Latvia	0.12	0.25	0.1
Hungary	−0.07	0.43	−0.14
Lithuania	−0.09	0.35	−0.12
Croatia	0.21	0.12	−0.4
Slovenia	0.64	0.22	0.13
Poland	0.21	0.49	−0.12
Romania	0.6	0.34	−0.02

Notes: Three types of flows are sensitive: equity, bonds, and banks. Country sensitivity varies by flow. Some are high in all three, some in one or two.

Source: Cerutti, E., S. Claessens, and D. Puy. 2015. Push Factors and Capital Flows to Emerging Markets: Why Knowing Your Lender Matters More Than Fundamentals. *IMF Working Paper Series*. 15/127. Washington, DC: International Monetary Fund.

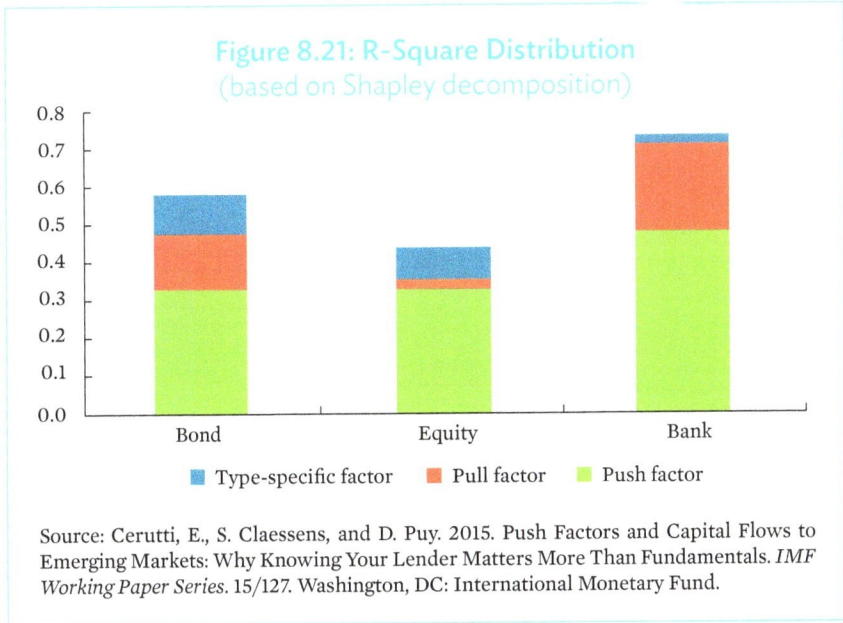

Figure 8.21: R-Square Distribution
(based on Shapley decomposition)

Legend: Type-specific factor · Pull factor · Push factor

Source: Cerutti, E., S. Claessens, and D. Puy. 2015. Push Factors and Capital Flows to Emerging Markets: Why Knowing Your Lender Matters More Than Fundamentals. *IMF Working Paper Series*. 15/127. Washington, DC: International Monetary Fund.

and the work on banking flows by Bruno and Shin (2015). It qualifies the view that good fundamentals reduce the exposure of emerging markets to global conditions. And it has major implications in that emerging markets need to monitor and know their lenders and investors, as their mandates, incentives, and constraints matter greatly. It should be noted, though, that higher sensitivity does not necessarily mean macro risks, since it can be that the level of flows is relatively small, even though the variance and sensitivity are high. Put differently, high sensitivities are problematic if flows are macro-relevant. And other factors might amplify (or dampen) effects of a high sensitivity; for example, countries may be able to offset volatility in capital inflows through local investors changing their investment abroad, i.e., engaging in offsetting capital outflows.

Financial Crises

Having discussed financial cycles and financial conditions in emerging Asia, I now turn to financial crises. Financial crises are in some sense manifestations of intense financial cycles, so there are clear patterns and lessons. But there are also specific reasons to worry about financial crises. There are two main specific motivations. One, crises can have large and long-lasting effects on the real economy, the global financial crisis being one case in point, but it has been seen many times before, as shown by Reinhart and Rogoff (2009a). Figure 8.22 shows these effects where banking crises are found to be especially costly. Second, financial crises have happened over centuries and have affected many countries, as Reinhart and Rogoff (2009b) show authoritatively in their book *This Time Is Different*. Figure 8.23 shows this pattern. As crises have affected countries for centuries, history has been a great laboratory for researchers to study crises, and there are thus many lessons for policy makers specific to financial crises. Together, this means that we both should and can learn from past crises. Yet, unfortunately, we should also expect crises to recur. While there are many aspects regarding financial crises to review, I highlight four key questions many analysts have tried to answer.[3]

Figure 8.22: Output Evolution after Banking and Currency Crises
(% of pre-crisis trend)

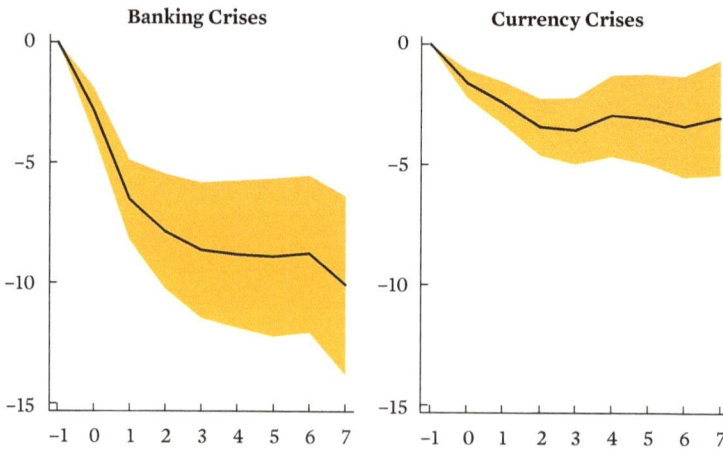

Note: Figure reports mean difference from year t = –1; 90% confidence interval for estimated mean; first year of crisis at t = 0; years on x-axis.
Source: International Monetary Fund (2009).

---

[3] See further Claessens et al. 2014 for a collection of 19 chapters and 6 parts in *Financial Crises, Causes, Consequences and Policy Responses*, on which this draws.

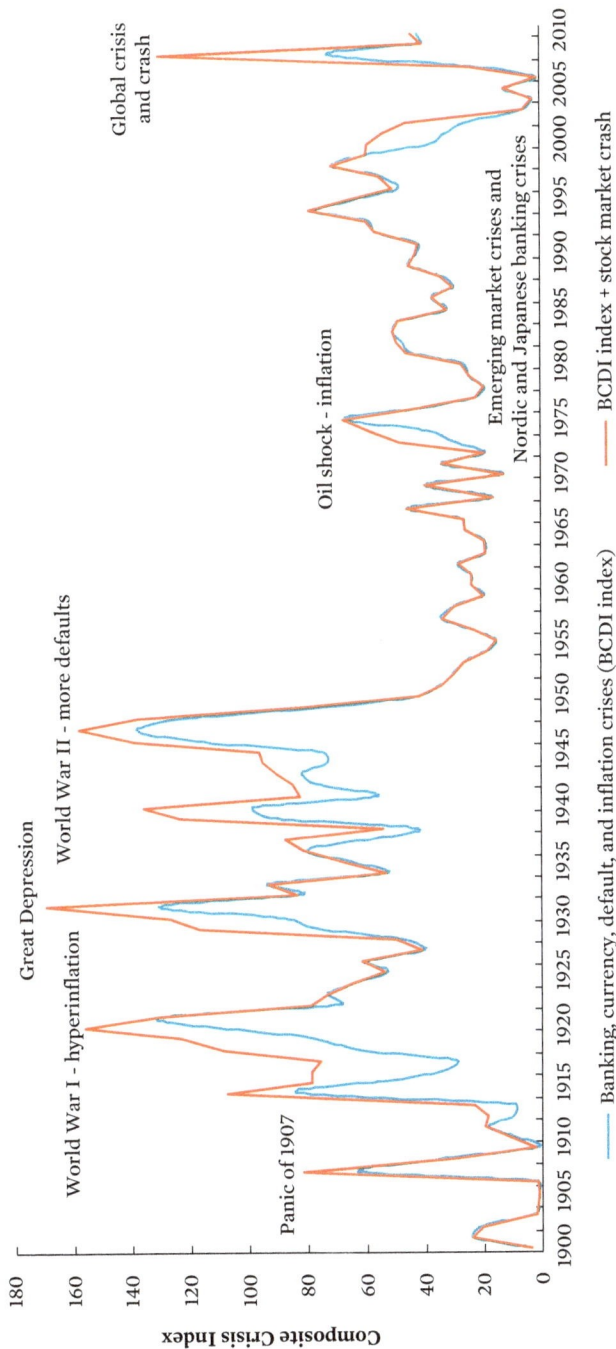

Figure 8.23: Varieties of Crises—World Aggregate, 1900–2010

Note: The composite crisis index measures banking, currency, sovereign default, inflation crises, and stock market crashes (weighted by their share of world income).

Source: Reinhart, C. and K. Rogoff. 2009a. The Aftermath of Financial Crises. *American Economic Review.* 99 (2), pp. 466–472.

What Are the Patterns in Financial Crises and What Causes Them?

Financial crises come in many forms: debt, banking, currency, inflation, and sovereign crises are the most prominent. As noted, many crises of various types have occurred over the centuries. Crises also come in (regional) waves: Latin America, Asia, and then lately the US and Europe (Figure 8.24). Crises were more common in emerging markets in the past, but the global financial crisis, of course, has predominantly affected advanced countries. While causes vary, the various types of financial crisis can be related. Banking, currency, and sovereign crises can overlap since one can lead to the other (Figure 8.25). For example, a bank crisis can spill over into a sovereign crisis, since there are multiple links between a sovereign and its banks. Many banking crises also come along with debt and currency crises. Still, identifying crises is both a science and an art and, as a consequence, samples vary and so do related consequences.

While crises are diverse, there are common causes to crises and research provides insights into the recognizable early signals or alarm bells possibly indicating one on the horizon. Importantly, crises are often preceded by booms in asset prices, including house prices, and credit, as in the latest house price boom and bust (Figure 8.26). As noted, detecting these booms is hard as they can be long, longer than business cycles, and there are various theories about the types of crises.

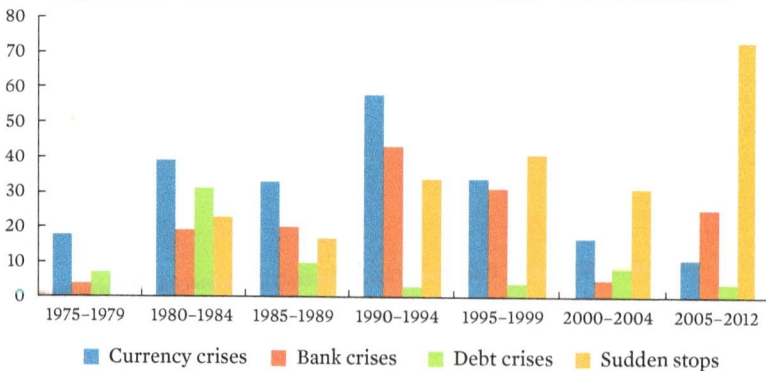

Figure 8.24: Number of Financial Crises—All Countries

Sources: Laeven, L. and F. Valencia. 2008. Systemic Banking Crises: A New Database. *IMF Working Paper Series*. 08/224. Washington, DC: International Monetary Fund; and 2012. Systemic Banking Crises Database: An Update. *IMF Working Paper Series*. 12/163. Washington, DC: International Monetary Fund (for data on banking, currency, and debt crises); and Forbes, K. and F. Warnock. 2012. Capital Flow Waves: Surges, Stops, Flight, and Retrenchment. *Journal of International Economics*. 88 (2). pp. 235-51 (for sudden stops).

Figure 8.25: Crises Overlap, by Type

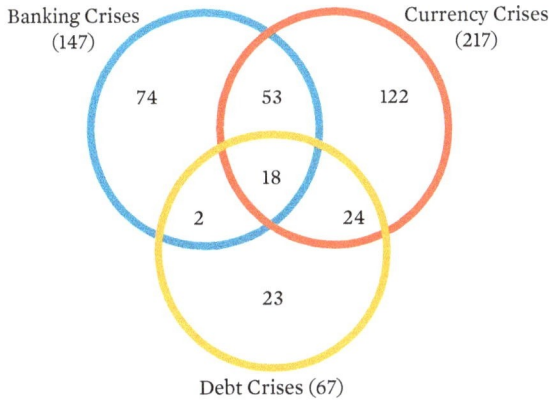

Banking Crises
(147)

Currency Crises
(217)

74   53   122

18

2   24

23

Debt Crises (67)

Source: Author.

Figure 8.26: Housing Boom–Bust—Selected Countries

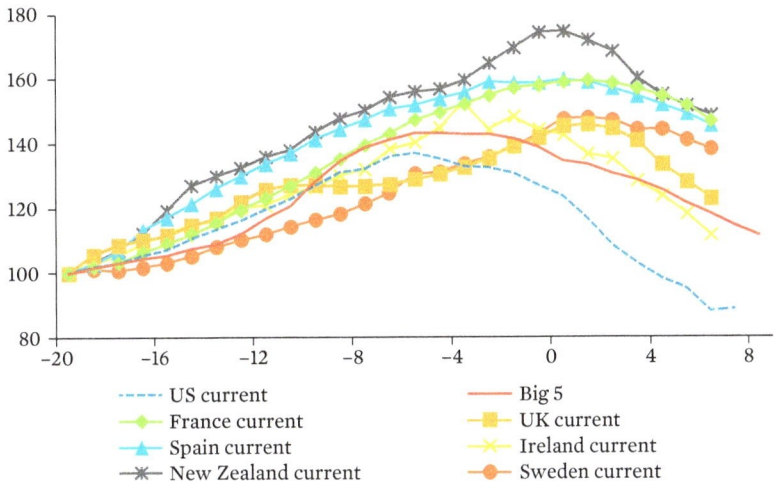

- - - - US current
—◆— France current
—▲— Spain current
—✳— New Zealand current

——— Big 5
—■— UK current
—✕— Ireland current
—●— Sweden current

UK = United Kingdom, US = United States.

Sources: Bank for International Settlements, Organisation for Economic Co-operation and Development, and Haver Analytics.

While, as also noted in the review of financial cycles, many puzzles remain, in a nutshell, crises can stem from vulnerabilities in private or public sectors' balance sheets and be triggered by shocks that have domestic or external origins.

What Are the Effects of Crises?

There are really two parts to this: short-term and medium-term effects. Let me elaborate on each of these. The short-term macroeconomic and financial implications of crises are severe, and with many commonalities across various types. Irrespective of its origins, a crisis is often an amalgam of events, including substantial drops in credit volume and asset prices, severe disruptions in financial intermediation with large-scale balance sheet problems, and often a need for substantial government and international support. Financial variables, such as asset prices and credit, usually see drops across types of crises, albeit with variations in terms of duration and severity. These financial busts can be long, with the recent house busts matching past crises patterns. And although driven by a variety of factors, in their economic consequences, crises are often followed by poor growth, as after the latest global financial crisis. After the initial financial turmoil, crises are typically followed by recessions (Figure 8.27), which last long and have large output losses (Figures 8.28 and 8.29), while other macroeconomic variables register significant declines as well.

Besides their negative short-run effects, crises often have adverse medium- to long-run effects on the real economy, in emerging markets and advanced countries alike (Figures 8.30–8.33). Output tends to be depressed substantially and persistently following crises, with no rebound, on average, to the pre-crisis trend in the medium term. Sudden stops in capital flows seem to be the worst, especially for emerging markets. However, growth eventually returns to its pre-crisis rate for most economies. The depressed output path tends to result from long-lasting reductions of roughly equal proportions in the employment rate, the capital-to-labor ratio, and total factor productivity. In the short term, the output loss is mainly accounted for by total factor productivity losses, but, unlike employment and the capital-to-labor ratio, the level of total factor productivity recovers somewhat to its pre-crisis trend in the medium term. But crises can also lead to much reform and growth, which pays over the longer-run (Figures 8.34–8.35).

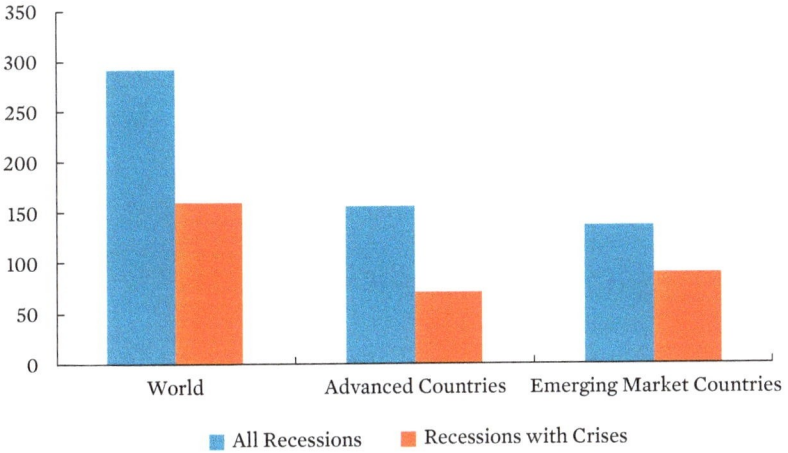

Figure 8.27: Number of Recessions with and without Crises

Source: Claessens, S., M. A. Kose, and M. E. Terrones. 2012. How Do Business and Financial Cycles Interact? *Journal of International Economics.* 87 (1). pp. 178–90.

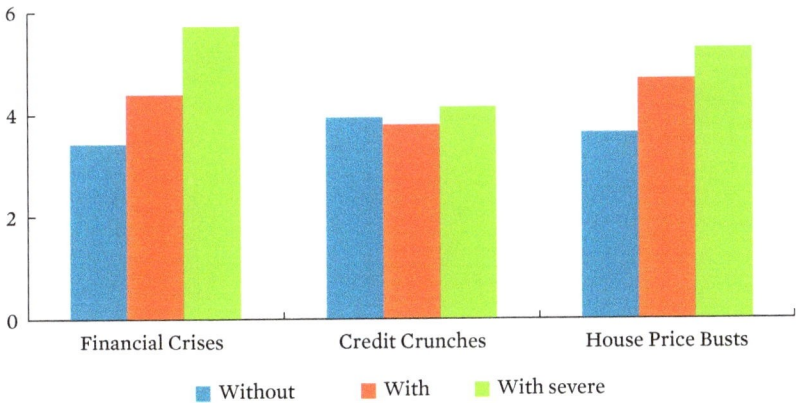

Figure 8.28: Number of Quarters a Recession Lasts with or without Crises

Source: Claessens, S., M. A. Kose, and M. E. Terrones. 2012. How Do Business and Financial Cycles Interact? *Journal of International Economics.* 87 (1). pp. 178–90.

Figure 8.29: GDP Loss over Recovery Period from Recession

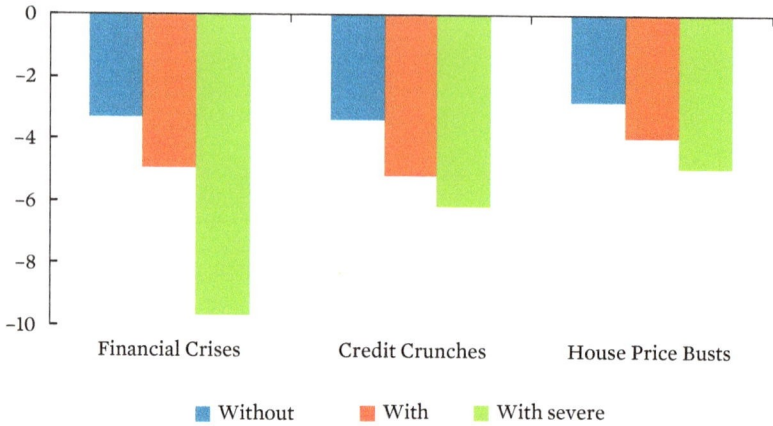

GDP = gross domestic product.
Source: Claessens, S., M. A. Kose, and M. E. Terrones. 2012. How Do Business and Financial Cycles Interact? *Journal of International Economics*. 87 (1). pp. 178–90.

Figure 8.30: Actual GDP versus Pre-Crisis Trend— Republic of Korea

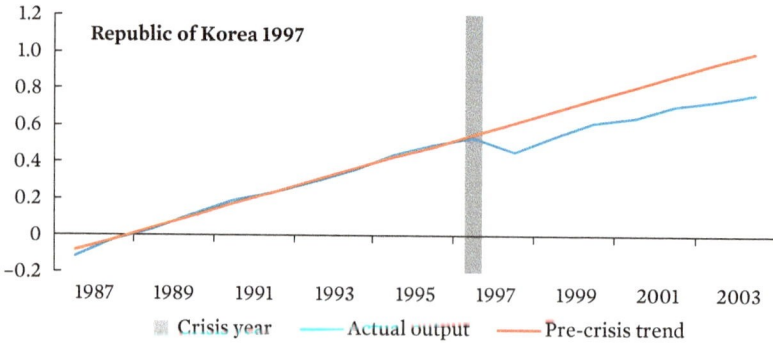

GDP = gross domestic product.
Source: International Monetary Fund (2009).

Figure 8.31: Actual GDP versus Pre-Crisis Trend—Sweden

Sweden 1991

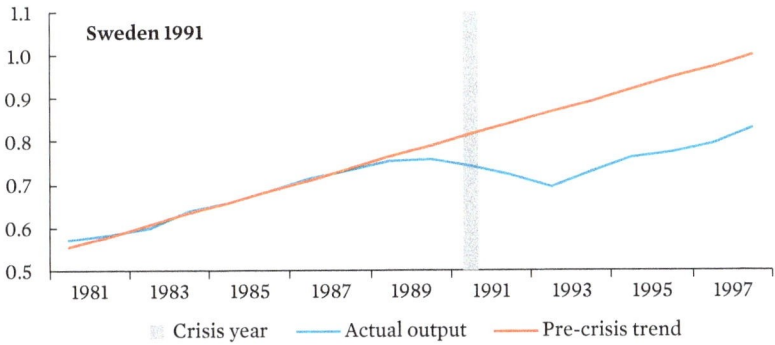

Crisis year — Actual output — Pre-crisis trend

GDP = gross domestic product.
Source: International Monetary Fund (2009).

Figure 8.32: Actual GDP versus Pre-Crisis Trend—Japan

Japan 1997

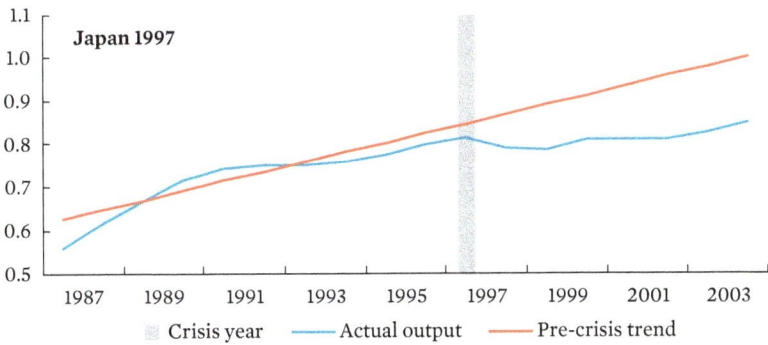

Crisis year — Actual output — Pre-crisis trend

GDP = gross domestic product.
Source: International Monetary Fund (2009).

Figure 8.33: Actual GDP versus Pre-Crisis Trend—Thailand

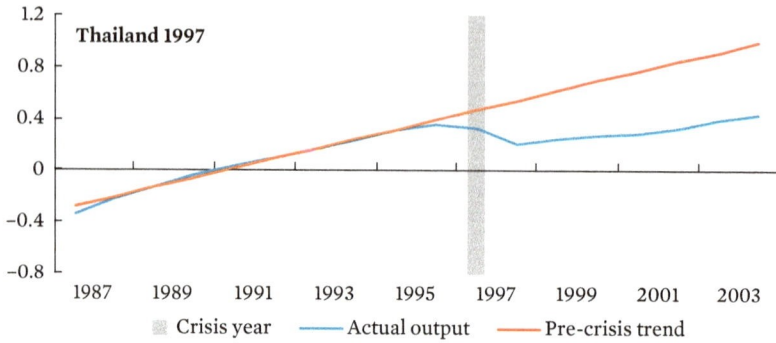

GDP = gross domestic product.
Source: International Monetary Fund (2009).

Figure 8.34: Actual GDP versus Pre-Crisis Trend—Chile

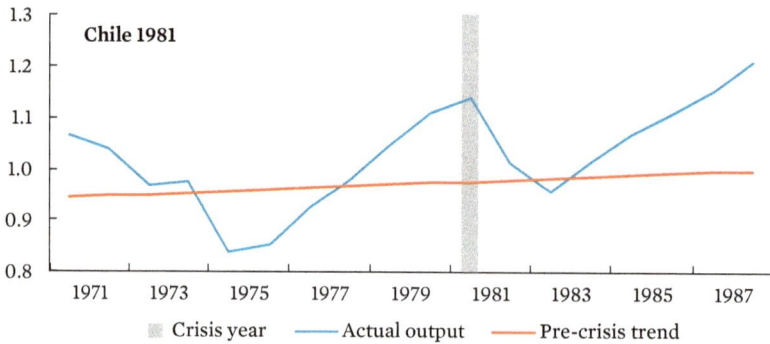

GDP = gross domestic product.
Source: International Monetary Fund (2009).

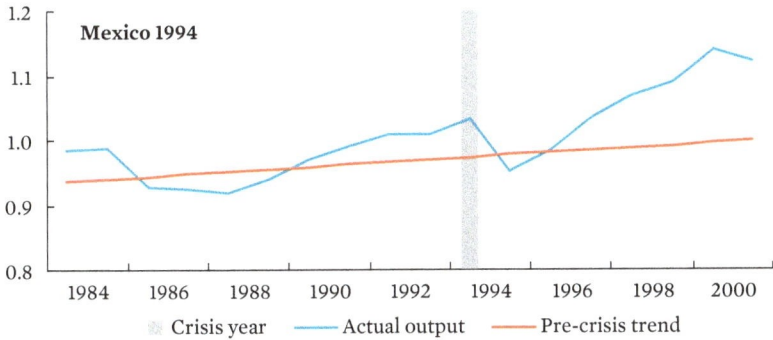

Figure 8.35: Actual GDP versus Pre-Crisis Trend—Mexico

GDP = gross domestic product.
Source: International Monetary Fund (2009).

What Policies Can Help to Remedy the Consequences of Crises?

Policies used to remedy the consequences of a crisis can be grouped into two sets. The first involves containment policies, deployed during the early stages of a crisis. This phase is often characterized by deteriorating sentiment on the viability of the financial system and the economic prospects of the country in the short term. It may involve runs on banks, on entire markets, and even on the domestic currency. Typically, at this stage it is difficult to tell whether the crisis reflects just liquidity shortages or solvency problems. To buy time to determine the true nature of the crisis, governments resort to policies such as emergency liquidity provision to banks, other financial intermediaries, and even entire markets. They often announce guarantees on bank liabilities and in extreme cases governments use deposit freezes and capital controls, and many even default on their debts. These policies come with benefits, but can also have large costs, importantly, as they limit restructuring options.

The second set of policies encompasses the resolution phase. This typically covers mainly banks, corporations, households, and sometimes sovereign restructuring. By this stage, governments have had time to design a plan to address the various solvency problems and enact necessary changes in legislation or secured funding for restructuring. This phase includes policies such as recapitalization of banks with public funds, closure of insolvent institutions, restructuring of viable ones, setting new institutional arrangements, such as asset management companies, as well as restructuring of private debt, including of households and corporations. Not all these policies are used in every crisis, but they are the most common.

The effect of these interventions on economic costs and the fiscal accounts depends, to a large extent, on the mix. Guarantees on bank liabilities can contain liquidity pressures on banks, for example, without involving a disbursement of public funds upfront, but come with potentially substantial fiscal contingencies. In contrast, direct capital injections impact the public purse directly, but some resources can be recovered in the future when public shareholdings are returned to private hands. The timing of the policy mix can also affect the full fiscal costs of a crisis. If fiscal and monetary policies are used aggressively to avoid a sharp contraction in economic activity, as was in the recent financial crisis, this may discourage more active and deeper restructuring of banks, households, and corporations. This in turn has the risk of prolonging the crisis and depressing growth for a prolonged period, and can then increase indirect fiscal and economic costs.

What Should Policy Makers Be Doing to Prevent Crises?

As noted, important lessons have been learned about financial vulnerabilities, notably the role of excessive credit growth—perhaps the single most important predictor of a crisis, the role of excessive maturity mismatches, and excessive exposure to exchange rate risk. Also, we know more about the consequences of crises on the real economy and the effectiveness of policies used to resolve them. While not an ideal prescriptive, these lessons help in designing policies to prevent booms and reducing the incidence of crises in the future. Since many measures are well-known and being implemented, I will not provide the full list here (see Blanchard et al. 2016 for a general review and Claessens and Kodres 2017 for an evaluation of financial reforms), but it covers the following three broad areas:

Macroeconomic: Including to revisit the "Great Moderation" paradigm of fiscal and monetary policies and considering the scope for macroprudential regulations.

Financial: Including to enhance micro-prudential regulation and supervision, notably to reduce "too-big-to-fail" financial integration and improve resolution; address the shadow banking system; upgrade and adapt the legal and institutional environment; and review the financial system's infrastructure, including clearing of derivatives, use of central clearing counterparts, and so on.

Revamping international financial architecture: Including to enhance the provision of global liquidity and the safety net, improve cross-border banking resolution, with burden sharing, and make information provision better in general.

While progress has been made, we cannot claim that crises can be avoided at all costs. Despite new regulations, better supervision, and other advances, it will remain difficult to prevent and predict crises. Just as the policy tool kit evolves, the nature and types of crises evolve and change as causes shift over time. While improvements are made in some respects, financial markets respond and vulnerabilities shift over time elsewhere. Complexity in financial markets and institutions makes the identification of new vulnerabilities challenging. Also, financial crises are to a large extent a natural consequence of financial development, which is generally good. Therefore, while prevention efforts are important, it is unlikely that they will ever be effective enough to eradicate crises completely. The world is simply too complex for that.

There are deeper issues too that policy makers cannot easily tackle. Systems, that is people, are always learning. Collective misreading means that optimism often prevails, warnings are ignored, and patterns recur. Importantly, while patterns recur, the view will often prevail that there will not be bad consequences this time. As Britain's Queen Elizabeth asked in 2009: "'Why did no one see it coming?" This is part of the "This time is different" symptom, as the title of Reinhart and Rogoff's book highlights. And crises can reflect deeper problems. Political economy, inequality, and globalization have been mentioned. A key message therefore is, since financial crises will recur, as they are hard to prevent and predict, crisis management matters too, especially as this analysis shows, approaches vary in their efficiency.

Overall Open Questions

While there are many important lessons regarding financial cycles and crises, many questions remain. There are some regularities in financial cycles, but these are mostly known *ex post*, as in the recent house price booms and busts in advanced countries. Although the procyclicality of leverage among financial institutions, as highlighted by its increase during the run up to the 2007–2009 crisis followed by the sharp deleveraging in its aftermath, has been extensively documented, its exact causes have yet to be identified. Similarly, there are many questions on financial crises. For one, they recur, often in waves, suggesting markets and policy makers do not learn from the past or that causes keep shifting. A major challenge to explain in the immediate lead up to a crisis is the sharp, nonlinear behavior of financial markets in response to "small" shocks. Why crises involve disruptions to such a degree that aggregate liquidity shortages occur, and transmission of monetary policy is disrupted, remains a puzzle. Although credit crunches are, in part, attributable to capital shortages at financial institutions, such shortages do not seem to fully explain why lenders become overly risk averse following a crisis. And why financial spillovers across entities (institutions, markets, countries, and so on) are much more potent than most fundamentals suggest (in other words, why there is so much contagion) is an open question.

This lack of knowledge of the forces shaping the dynamics before and during periods of financial stress also greatly complicates the design of proper policy responses. Financial crises remain not only hard to prevent and predict, but how best to manage them is an open question. Clearly, approaches vary in efficiency, but "what works best when" is not fully clear. Some research shows that countercyclical policies might mitigate the costs and reduce the duration of recessions. Others find limited effects associated with expansionary policies. And some argue that such policies can worsen recession outcomes. Although valuable lessons have been learned about crisis resolution, countries are still far from adopting the "best" practices to respond to financial turmoil. It is clear now that open bank assistance without proper restructuring and recapitalization is not an efficient way of dealing with an ailing banking system. Excessive liquidity support and guarantees of bank liabilities cannot substitute for proper restructuring and recapitalization either, because most banking crises involve solvency problems, not just liquidity shortfalls. Still, in spite of this understanding, some countries did not adopt these policy responses, including in the crises since 2007, suggesting that there are deeper factors that research has not been able to uncover or address. Moreover, since crises are likely to reappear, countries will need (more) financial and debt restructuring, including sovereign restructuring. Yet many issues related to restructuring of both household debt and sovereign debt require more sophisticated theoretical and empirical approaches. The research and policy agendas are thus large.

References

Adrian, T. and H. S. Shin. 2011. Financial Intermediaries and Monetary Economics. In Benjamin Friedman and Michael Woodford eds. *Handbook of Monetary Economics*. Amsterdam: Elsevier.

Bernanke, B. and M. Gertler. 1989. Agency Costs, Net Worth, and Business Fluctuations. *American Economic Review*. 79 (1). pp. 14–31.

Bernanke, B., M. Gertler, and S. Gilchrist. 1999. The Financial Accelerator in a Quantitative Business Cycle Framework. In J. B. Taylor and M. Woodford, eds. *Handbook of Macroeconomics*. 1 (C). pp. 1341–93. Amsterdam: Elsevier.

Blanchard, O. J. 2009. State of Macro. *Annual Review of Economics*. 1 (1). pp. 209–28.

Blanchard, O. J., R. Rajan, K. Rogoff, and L. H. Summers, eds. 2016. *Progress and Confusion: The State of Macroeconomic Policy*. Cambridge, MA: MIT Press.

Brunnermeier, M. and L. Pedersen. 2009. Market Liquidity and Funding Liquidity. *Review of Financial Studies*. 22 (6). pp. 2201–238.

Bruno, V. and H. S. Shin. 2015. Capital Flows and the Risk-taking Channel of Monetary Policy. *Journal of Monetary Economics*. 71 (April). pp. 119–32.

Burns, A. F. and W. C. Mitchell. 1946. *Measuring Business Cycles*. New York: NBER.

Cerutti, E., S. Claessens, and L. Ratnovski. 2016. *Global Liquidity and Drivers of Cross-Border Bank Flows*. Paper prepared for the 63rd Economic Policy Panel meeting. The Netherlands. 22–23 April.

Cerutti, E., S. Claessens, and D. Puy. 2015. Push Factors and Capital Flows to Emerging Markets: Why Knowing Your Lender Matters More Than Fundamentals. *IMF Working Paper Series*. 15/127. Washington, DC: International Monetary Fund.

Cesa-Bianchi, A. 2013. Housing Cycles and Macroeconomic Fluctuations: A Global Perspective. *Journal of International Money and Finance*. 37 (C). pp. 215–38.

Claessens, S., M. A. Kose, and M. E. Terrones. 2009. What Happens During Recessions, Crunches, and Busts? *Economic Policy*. 24 (60). pp. 653–700.

——. 2011. Financial Cycles: What? How? When? In R. H. Clarida and F. Giavazzi, eds. *NBER International Seminar on Macroeconomics 2010*. 7. pp. 303–44.

——. 2012. How Do Business and Financial Cycles Interact? *Journal of International Economics*. 87 (1). pp. 178–90.

Claessens, S., M. Kose, L. Laeven, and F. Valencia, eds. 2014. *Financial Crises: Causes, Consequences, and Policy Responses*. Washington, DC: International Monetary Fund.

Claessens, S. and L. E. Kodres. 2017. The Regulatory Responses to the Global Financial Crisis: Some Uncomfortable Questions. In E. Balleisen, L. Bennear, K. Krawiec, and J. Wiener, eds. *Policy Shock: Regulatory Responses to Oil Spills, Nuclear Accidents, and Financial Meltdowns*. Cambridge: Cambridge University Press.

Drehmann, M., C. Borio, and K. Tsatsaronis. 2012. Characterising the Financial Cycle: Don't Lose Sight of the Medium Term! *BIS Working Papers*. No. 380. Basel.

Fisher, I. 1933. The Debt-Deflation Theory of Great Depressions. *Econometrica*. 1 (4). pp. 337–57.

Forbes, K. and F. Warnock. 2012. Capital Flow Waves: Surges, Stops, Flight, and Retrenchment. *Journal of International Economics*. 88 (2). pp. 235–51.

Geanakoplos, J. 2010. The Leverage Cycle. In D. Acemoglu, K. Rogoff, and M. Woodford, eds. *NBER Macroeconomic Annual 2009*. 24. pp. 1–65.

Gertler, M., S. Gilchrist, and F. M. Natalucci. 2007. External Constraints on Monetary Policy and the Financial Accelerator. *Journal of Money, Credit and Banking*. 39 (2-3). pp. 295–330.

Harding, D. and A. Pagan. 2002a. Dissecting the Cycle: A Methodological Investigation. *Journal of Monetary Economics*. 49 (2). pp. 365–81.

———. 2002b. A Comparison of Two Business Cycle Dating Methods. *Journal of Economic Dynamics and Control*. 27 (9). pp. 1681–690.

International Monetary Fund (IMF). 2009. What's the Damage? Medium-Term Output Dynamics after Financial Crises. In IMF. *World Economic Outlook October 2009: Sustaining the Recovery*. Washington, DC: International Monetary Fund.

Kiyotaki, N. and J. Moore. 1997. Credit Cycles. *Journal of Political Economics*. 105 (2). pp. 211–248.

———. 1999. Balance Sheets, the Transfer Problem, and Financial Crises. *International Tax and Public Finance*. 6 (4). pp. 459–72.

Laeven, L. and F. Valencia. 2008. Systemic Banking Crises: A New Database. *IMF Working Paper Series*. 08/224. Washington, DC: International Monetary Fund.

———. 2012. Systemic Banking Crises Database: An Update. *IMF Working Paper Series*. 12/163. Washington, DC: International Monetary Fund.

Milesi-Ferretti, G. M., C. Tille, G. I. P. Ottaviano, and M. O. Ravn. 2011. The Great Retrenchment: International Capital Flows during the Global Financial Crisis. *Economic Policy*. 26 (66). pp. 285–342.

Raddatz C. and S.L. Schmukler. 2012. On the International Transmission of Shocks: Micro–Evidence From Mutual Fund Portfolios. *Working Papers Central Bank of Chile*. 668. Central Bank of Chile.

Reinhart, C. and K. Rogoff. 2009a. The Aftermath of Financial Crises. *American Economic Review*. 99 (2). pp. 466–472.

———. 2009b. *This Time Is Different: Eight Centuries of Financial Folly*. Princeton Press.

———. 2014. Financial and Sovereign Debt Crises: Some Lessons Learned and Those Forgotten. In S. Claessens, M. Kose, Luc Laeven, and F. Valencia, eds. *Financial Crises: Causes, Consequences, and Policy Responses.* Washington, DC: International Monetary Fund. pp. 141–155.

Rey, H. 2013. Dilemma not Trilemma: The Global Financial Cycle and Monetary Policy Independence. In *Proceedings of the 2013 Federal Reserve Bank of Kansas City Economic Symposium at Jackson Hole.* pp. 285–333.

Sandri, D. 2014. *Business and Financial Cycles.* Mimeo. IMF.

Shin, H. S. 2012. Global Banking Glut and Loan Risk Premium. Mundell-Fleming Lecture. *IMF Economic Review.* 60 (2). pp. 155–92.

Taylor, A. 2015. Credit, Financial Stability, and the Macroeconomy. *Annual Review of Economics.* 7 (1). pp. 309–39.

Van den Heuvel, S. J. 2008. The Welfare Cost of Bank Capital Requirements. *Journal of Monetary Economics.* 55 (2). pp. 298–320.

Three Decades of International Financial Crises: What Have We Learned and What Still Needs to Be Done?

9

Ross P. Buckley, Emilios Avgouleas, and Douglas W. Arner

Introduction[1]

This chapter was initially written to commemorate the 20th anniversary of the Asian financial crisis, which started in 1997, because those who do not learn from crises risk repeating history. For example, most experts agree that the global financial crisis of 2008 would have affected East Asia far more severely had the region not learned many of the lessons of its earlier troubles. Indeed, more than a decade after 2008, the region has internalized and acted on even more of the lessons of 1997.

Few experts predicted the Asian crisis—or the 2008 global financial crisis for that matter or the 2020 coronavirus disease (COVID-19) crisis—and certainly we do not pretend to be sufficiently equipped to predict the next one. Yet history teaches there will be another, and probably sooner rather than later. In the decade since the global financial crisis there has been an ongoing eurozone crisis, now subsumed into the COVID-19 crisis.

Fragility that periodically erupts into a full-blown financial crisis appears to be an integral feature of market-based financial systems in spite of the emergence of sophisticated risk management tools and regulatory systems. If anything, the increased frequency of modern crises underscores how difficult it is to diversify away systemic risk and that perceptions of perfectly stable financial systems are normally flawed, even if the source of the next crisis remains well concealed to the expert eye.

[1] The authors are grateful for very helpful comments and suggestions by Junkyu Lee and Peter Rosenkranz, and also thank the participants of the ADB-ADBI Conference under the theme "20 Years after the Asian Financial Crisis: Lessons, Challenges, and the Way Forward" in Tokyo on 13–14 April 2017 for valuable remarks and discussion. The authors also greatly acknowledge the invaluable research assistance of Evan Gibson, Jessica Chapman, and Sarah Webster.

We thus write to compare and contrast these three crises of the past 3 decades (the Asian financial crisis, the global financial crisis, and the eurozone crisis), and examine their respective causes and policy responses, both to distill the lessons to be learned and to identify what more can be done to strengthen our financial systems. Admission of the inevitability of the next financial crisis in no way suggests that analysis of earlier crises is futile. Although impossible to forecast a financial crisis with a high degree of accuracy and certainty, still, earlier crises always leave lessons useful in preparation for the next one. We should take every opportunity to learn and work to build stronger, more effective financial systems, with the COVID-19 crisis highlighting just how significant this can be.

The Asian Financial Crisis

In 1997–1998, Asia experienced its worst financial crisis of the 20th century. A period of exceptional economic growth and substantial capital inflow in the mid-1990s was punctuated by a crisis which engulfed economies including Indonesia, the Republic of Korea, and Thailand. The problems began in Thailand in June 1997. Foreign money flooded into the country and fueled speculative markets in real estate and stocks and heavy domestic consumption that contributed to a massive current account deficit (Feldstein 1999).[2] Thailand tried to defend the value of its currency but was forced to allow it to float in July and its value plummeted (Arensman 1997). In the following weeks, the contagion spread to Malaysia and the Philippines, to Indonesia and the Republic of Korea over the next months, and eventually around the world to Brazil and the Russian Federation, and to the United States (US) through the near collapse of Long-Term Capital Management, then the world's largest hedge fund (Blustein 1997).

This section reviews the crisis and considers (i) its causes, (ii) the effectiveness of policy responses to nonperforming loans (NPLs), and (iii) its lessons.

Overview of the Asian Financial Crisis

The Asian financial crisis was not a conventional debt crisis. It differed from the 1982 developing country debt crisis and the Mexican peso crisis of 1994–1995, in that the troublesome indebtedness was that of the private

---

[2]   See Martin Feldstein, "A Self-Help Guide for Emerging Markets", *Foreign Affairs*, March/April 1999. See also P. Passell, "Economic Scene; For a New Generation of Asian Tigers, A Harsh Currency Lesson", *The New York Times*, 24 July 1997, D-2, col. 1.

sector, not the public or quasi-public, and that it occurred within "a benign international environment with low interest rates and solid growth in output and exports" (World Bank 1998). Furthermore, debt levels in East Asia, especially relative to the export earnings that allow the servicing of foreign currency denominated loans, were not ruinously high by any means. Initially this was a banking crisis that evolved into a currency crisis, which developed into a more generalized economic crisis, at least for Indonesia, the Republic of Korea, and Thailand, the three most severely affected countries.

Causes of the Asian Financial Crisis

The four principal causes of the crisis were (i) the type and extent of indebtedness, (ii) financial sector weaknesses, (iii) fixed local exchange rates, and (iv) a region-wide loss of confidence, which eventually spread to emerging market economies worldwide. Each will be considered briefly.

Type and Extent of Indebtedness

Short-term debt contributed significantly to East Asia's economic problems, particularly foreign-held debt denominated in a local currency. Short-term indebtedness increased significantly in 1995 and 1996 across the region, with the increase concentrated in Indonesia and Thailand (World Bank 1997). The ratio of short-term to total debt in the countries of the region in mid-1997 ranged from 67% in the Republic of Korea and 46% in Thailand, to 19% in the Philippines (World Bank 1997).

The primary problem with foreign investment in the short-term debt of emerging markets is the fluidity of the investment (Soulard 1994). Adverse economic news is likely to halt the rolling over of outstanding debt upon maturity, resulting in net capital outflows. This risk is analogous to capital flight. The secondary problem is that these outflows may foment a collapse in investor confidence.

When foreign-held short-term debt is denominated in a local currency, volatility is heightened because a substantial devaluation will decimate a local currency portfolio if denominated in a major global currency (as is most often the case). Accordingly, the first signs of a pending devaluation will prompt a severe sell-off. The reliance on local currency short-term bonds intensified the crisis once it commenced (World Bank 1998).

The extent of indebtedness in East Asia was the product in part of excess liquidity in the developed world. Similarly, each of the lending booms in Latin America were predicated upon excess liquidity in the northern hemisphere (Dawson 1990, 237 244; Marichal 1989, 95; Stallings 1987, 294–295). The story was precisely the same in Asia. Western capital poured into East Asian countries in record quantities in the 2 years to June 1997. East Asian stocks and bonds were being acquired by US and European investors scornful of the low interest rates on offer in their home countries and fearful that the US stock market had reached unsustainable heights (Blustein 1997). Liquidity was at a peak in the US and flowed into emerging market economies (Pettis 1998a, 1998b).

Financial Sector Weaknesses

Failure to intermediate capital flows effectively. One of the few traits shared among the five principal nations at the center of the Asian financial crisis was an underdeveloped and inadequately regulated domestic financial sector (Arner 2007). The local financial system proved unable to serve as an effective intermediary and allocate funds to productive uses. Capital inflows often ended up in property and stock market investments, driving up the price of those assets in speculative bubbles (Sugisaki 1998). Such speculative investments often cannot generate the foreign currency reserves needed to repay foreign currency debt. Indeed, a useful indicator of whether capital flows to an emerging market economy are excessive may be the destination of the funds. When the majority of incoming foreign capital is funding a boom in the local stock and/or real estate markets, it is time for local regulators to adopt measures to make their nation a less attractive destination for short-term foreign capital, what would be termed "macroprudential measures" in the aftermath of the global financial crisis, including measures to reduce leverage as well as capital flows.

Faced with a steep yield curve, local banks succumbed to the dangerous temptation to borrow short and lend long and largely did so without hedging their foreign exchange exposures, relying on the perceived permanence of fixed exchange rate systems. But regulatory standards were inadequate across the region (World Bank 1998) and doubts about the resilience of individual financial systems were exacerbated by a marked and habitual lack of transparency. Insufficient disclosure and a lack of adequate prudential regulation were compounded by the moral hazard engendered by the crony capitalism prevalent in the region. Local banks were often controlled by people with strong connections to the ruling political party which influenced

Three Decades of International Financial Crises:
What Have We Learned and What Still Needs to Be Done?

347

their lending decisions ("crony lending"). In addition, the choice of highly risky, lucrative funding strategies by the banks in the region was strongly influenced by the prospect of a local bailout, given also their management's strong political connections.

This meant that indiscriminate international borrowing and domestic lending had been common throughout the region, and when the bubble burst, domestic banks were in crisis in many countries, particularly Indonesia, the Republic of Korea, and Thailand (Dornbusch 1997, 26; Garran 1997). The productive capacity of the region and ensuing credit boom had far outstripped the sophistication and regulation of its financial sectors.

Premature liberalization of domestic financial markets. In Thailand's case, foreign money had flooded into the economy: (i) directly as institutional investors invested in stocks and bonds, particularly short-term local market bonds, and (ii) indirectly as Thai banks borrowed heavily from their foreign counterparts through the Bangkok International Banking Facility established in 1993 (Chow 1997). With the benefit of hindsight, the Bangkok International Banking Facility was established too early, before effective micro- or macro-prudential controls and supervision were in place and functioning well. As the International Monetary Fund (IMF) identified: "a robust financial system underpinned by effective regulation and supervision of financial institutions" (IMF 1998) is the overriding precondition to an economy liberalizing its financial system and capital controls. Indonesia, the Republic of Korea, and Thailand opened their financial systems to international capital flows without reinforcing the stability of the domestic financial sector in a sequenced manner (IMF 1998, 6).

The dangers of premature liberalization of local financial markets are apparent when considering the minimal effect the crisis had had on Taipei,China (Welle-Strand, Chen, and Ball 2011), which was also one of the Asian tiger economies at the time. Taipei,China's financial sector was closed to foreign banks and its financial markets largely closed to foreign speculators.[3] Its heavily controlled financial markets and huge foreign exchange reserves served it exceedingly well. Taipei,China's experience underlines that appropriate regulation and supervision must precede financial market liberalization. It also highlighted another important lesson:

---

[3] Taipei,China's total external debt only increased from $17 billion in 1989 to $34 billion in 1997, while the Republic of Korea increased from $42 billion to $143 billion. Taipei,China's inward investment to international reserve ratio was 15% in 1997, whereas the Republic of Korea's was 372%. See Hsiao and Hsiao (2001).

the importance of self-insurance against volatility through accumulation of large foreign exchange reserves. Malaysia's experience with imposition of capital controls—while highly controversial at the time—is now seen as an effective choice in an evolutionary process of financial market liberalization and integration into global financial markets,

Fixed Exchange Rates

Fixed exchange rates appeal to developing countries because they stabilize costs of credit (Viscio 1998; Bustelo, Garcia, and Olivié 1999) and inflation, providing discipline against government fiscal and monetary policies (Feldstein 1999; Eichengreen and Hausmann 1999). They are helpful in breaking the wage-price-currency spirals (that have led to ruinous inflation cycles in nations such as Argentina), promoting exports (through slightly undervalued exchange rates), and achieving a stable external environment in times of export-led growth (Viscio 1998).

However, fixed exchange rates pose their own political and economic problems, particularly in the context of emerging markets in the process of integrating into the global financial system, as highlighted through the idea of the "impossible trinity." When an economy with a fixed exchange rate is performing less strongly than that of the economy it uses to peg its currency, either the peg will require adjustment or the fixed currency will become overvalued inhibiting competitiveness. Choosing to devalue the currency is difficult for politicians, as it risks inflation and may be viewed domestically as a failure in economic leadership. Accordingly, it is easy, with a fixed rate regime, for a currency to become overvalued, as occurred in Mexico in 1993–1994, in Indonesia and Thailand in 1996–1997, in the Russian Federation in 1997–1998, and in Argentina in 2000–2001 (Blinder 1999).

The other problem with fixed exchange rates is that they have the potential to both encourage excessive borrowing in foreign currency as well as heighten risks of speculative attacks. The combination of the two can trigger destabilizing debt issues, as highlighted in the 1997 Asian crisis. Borrowers choose to take the lower interest rates that are usually on offer abroad and trust the fixed exchange rate to deal with the currency risk. As the Asian financial crisis demonstrated conclusively, this behavior is highly risky and masks the real cost of borrowing in a foreign currency: the currency risk does not disappear merely because one's domestic currency is pegged to a foreign currency.

A pure floating exchange rate is not strictly necessary; a managed flexible rate, provided it is managed in a sensible and market responsive manner, is usually sufficient. However, in the contemporary world of massive capital flows, a fixed rate is an invitation to trouble. The overwhelming policy lesson of the Asian financial crisis is that flexible exchange rates provide a real measure of protection against currency crises and accompanying economic problems (Meyer 1999).

Region-Wide Loss of Confidence Triggers Contagion

The severity of the Asian crisis exceeded the combined effect of its various causes (World Bank 1998) and can only be explained by a region-wide loss of confidence that led to contagion to emerging markets, both across and beyond the region. This was the common factor that turned the distinct economic troubles of five countries into a regional crisis (World Bank 1998). The tendency to view emerging markets as one asset class or entity was well manifested in the "tequila effect" of 1995 in which Mexico's peso crisis resulted in a sell-off across the entire emerging markets sector—in nations as diverse as Argentina, Hungary, the Philippines, and Thailand (Buckley 1999). Accordingly, from the perspective of each investor, loss of confidence in the entire region, and thus contagious exodus from lending and investment in Southeast Asian economies, was rational. It led to an outflow of capital—both domestic capital flight and a halt in external re-financing, which triggered currency depreciation, and to massive, unhedged, foreign exchange exposures and severely damaged balance sheets of local corporations (World Bank 1998).

Accumulation of Nonperforming Loans and Policy Responses

The Asian financial crisis teaches some specific lessons about the economic and structural imbalances which propagate a fertile environment for the multiplication of nonperforming loans (NPLs) and how NPLs should be managed. Essentially, weaknesses in loan underwriting and bank governance before the crisis caused a surge in NPLs which, combined with inadequate capital ratios, triggered insolvencies necessitating banking sector restructurings (Buckley and Arner 2011). Asia was affected by a twin crisis that combined excesses in borrowing and lending with fixed exchange rates, which could not be maintained in the face of large and volatile capital flows. It was thus a combination of a private sector banking solvency crisis and a currency crisis. At its initial stages, however, it was not a sovereign debt crisis, an improper diagnosis by the IMF and others which has been subsequently accepted and reflected in resolution approaches.

The two countries most deeply affected by the crisis—Indonesia (Takayasu and Yokoe 2000) and Thailand (Laplamwanit 1999; Julian 2000)—had NPL ratios averaging over 13% leading into the crisis. In the People's Republic of China's (PRC), the NPL ratio was particularly high, at over 20%, but its economy was detached from regional vulnerabilities because of its closed financial system and capital account (Wang 1999). In addition, the cause of the high NPL accumulation was largely historical, relating to the process of transition. The high NPL ratios (with the exception of the PRC) was indicative of the inadequate prudential regulation the banking sector was subject to and poor credit standards banks in the region applied to their lending. Evidence of poor credit standards was present prior to the crisis on the basis of several indicators, especially in Indonesia and Thailand, and an early warning system focusing on NPLs would have easily caught them even before the eruption of a full-blown crisis.

A common theme across all countries was the concentration of collateral in one asset class, the property sector, through direct and indirect lending (Richardson 2017).[4] Loans collateralized by property are particularly vulnerable to falling values during the downward phase of the credit cycle. This can cause a sudden and sharp spike in banking sector NPLs, destabilizing balance sheets, and therefore capital adequacy ratios, that in extreme cases can lead to bank insolvency.

Similarly, the capital adequacy ratios of the countries most affected by the crisis (while consistent with the Basel capital standards at the time) were insufficient at 8% to 10% to absorb the high level of NPLs (Kawai 2003).

Following these prudential weaknesses when the crisis reached a stage at which banks required balance sheet and business model restructuring to address solvency, a common problem facing all relevant countries was the underdevelopment or non-existence of NPL and bank resolution regimes. The Republic of Korea[5] and Malaysia (Furuoka et al. 2012) fared better than Indonesia and Thailand through proactively implementing comprehensive

---

[4]   Also see Senhadji and Collyns (2002).

[5]   The Korea Asset Management Corporation created an NPL resolution fund to facilitate purchases of NPLs. See Kihwan (2006). https://www.imf.org/external/np/seminars/eng/2006/cpem/pdf/kihwan.pdf.

Three Decades of International Financial Crises:
What Have We Learned and What Still Needs to Be Done?

351

and structured resolution plans, laws, and regulations focusing on recapitalizing banks and managing NPLs through asset management companies. In contrast, Thailand was slow to respond to the unfolding crisis (Laplamwanit 1999; Jungjaturapit 2008) and Indonesia was particularly slow in implementing reforms (Sherlock 1988).[6]

Analysis of Policy Responses

The Asian financial crisis demonstrated that restructuring the banking sector by focusing on closures rather than managing NPLs is not constructive in many cases, particularly in the context of a systemic crisis. At the point that confidence evaporated at both the international and domestic levels, intensifying the crisis due to the procyclical effect it caused, the most affected jurisdictions were simultaneously experiencing a high level of bank closures. Arguably, bank restructurings can tackle pressing problems of financial institution solvency. Yet, such consolidation at the wrong moment can also lead to a dearth of liquidity. Paradoxically, mass bank closures, which intensified instead of stemming panic, were a condition of the IMF's support program, notwithstanding that these were non-viable financial institutions (IMF 2000; Fischer 1988). Indonesia[7] and Thailand[8] had the highest levels of closures and deepest and longest disruptions of financial stability, as well as excessive use of public funds to bail out their banking sectors. NPL ratios and bank closures peaked simultaneously in those jurisdictions.[9] However, a concentration of bank closures in Thailand did not correlate with a drop in NPL ratios in the short term.[10]

To manage the large volumes of NPLs, asset management companies were created in Indonesia, Malaysia, and Thailand.[11] The use of these proved instrumental in cleansing bank balance sheets of NPLs, strengthening capital

---

[6] For the Indonesian government's lack of commitment and actual strategy to implement reforms, see Ranta (2017).

[7] As a part of the IMF support program, the Indonesian government closed 16 banks in 1997 alone.

[8] As a part of the IMF support program, the Thai government closed 56 bankrupt finance companies in 1997, see Kawai (2003); also see Wong et al. 2010.

[9] At the end of 1997, Thailand's NPL/total loans ratio was 22.6% and Indonesia's was 7.2%. See Kawai (2003). Also see Gochoco-Bautista, Oh, and Rhee (2000).

[10] While the bank closures took place in 1997, NPL levels continued to rise sharply. Thailand's NPL ratio reached 50.1% in January 1999. Takayasu and Yokoe (2000).

[11] The Financial Restructuring Authority in Thailand, the Indonesian Bank Restructuring Agency, and Danaharta in Malaysia. See Noerlina and Dewi (2003).

ratios in the longer term, stabilizing banking sectors, and aiding the recovery of the region's economies. Each jurisdiction required enacting or amending legislation to establish asset management companies, except for Republic of Korea, where the existing state-owned asset management company, Korea Asset Management Corporation, was reorganized (Kihwan 2006).

Lessons of the Asian Financial Crisis

There are at least six enduring lessons from the Asian financial crisis:

(i)   Contagion: Loss of confidence can spread easily, acting as a channel for the cross-border propagation of financial stability risks, exacerbating the vulnerabilities of domestic financial systems.

(ii)   Fixed exchange rates are a high-risk strategy and some form of floating rate is generally much to be preferred.

(iii) The denomination of most of an economy's foreign debt in foreign currency is risky, particularly in the absence of markets for hedging.

(iv)   Much of the debt needs of emerging markets should be funded with long-term local currency denominated instruments.

(v)   The infrastructure and regulation of local capital markets need to be developed extensively.

(vi)   Capital tends to flow recklessly to emerging markets in times of surplus liquidity in the developed world.

Each lesson will be considered in turn.

Cross-Border Contagion

Whether due to artificial groupings by investment houses (e.g., "emerging markets"), or due to genuine economic and financial links (Terada-Hagiwara and Pasadilla 2004), or due to the simple fact that much of modern finance presents strong links of interconnectedness (Seth, Sarkar, and Mohanty 2001), cross-border contagion is a real risk factor for domestic financial systems. The best protective measure, apart from restrictions on short-term capital flows, is to build a well-regulated financial system with adequately capitalized financial institutions, combined with adequate levels of foreign currency reserves. The latter would act as a form of self-insurance against volatility. Augmenting cooperation structures for cross-border crisis management should be seen as a priority for Asian countries and of equal importance to regional arrangements to mutualize self-insurance through

Three Decades of International Financial Crises:
What Have We Learned and What Still Needs to Be Done?

353

pooling and/or access to foreign exchange reserves to manage possible liquidity crises (Liu, Lejot, and Arner 2013), of which the region has become a leading example through the Chiang Mai Initiative (Eichengreen 2003), its multilateralization (CMIM),[12] and the associated ASEAN+3 Macroeconomic Research Office (AMRO).[13]

The Benefits of Floating Exchange Rates

The attractiveness of fixed exchange rate regimes is understandable. However, their disadvantages outweigh their advantages. Currencies attached to fixed exchange rates may become overvalued either due to expansive fiscal policies that may prove inconsistent with a fixed exchange rate regime or due to loss of competitiveness that gives rise to balance of payments imbalances. But currencies attached to a fixed exchange rate are often politically difficult to devalue when they become overvalued, as they naturally tend to do over time. Overvalued currencies lead to a worsening of current account deficits, capital flight, and currency crises.[14] Floating exchange rates provide—while still subject to volatility—generally better results. Given the volumes of global currency flows (over $5 trillion per day according to the Bank for International Settlements) (BIS 2016), floating exchange rates nonetheless benefit from strong financial systems and availability of foreign exchange reserves and liquidity arrangements, allowing the better weathering of periodic international volatility and crises.

The (High) Risks of Foreign Currency Borrowing

Borrowing in foreign currency imposes a tremendous currency risk on the borrower's economy. At the time of the Asian financial crisis, large-scale hedging was extremely expensive and rarely done,[15] whatever the need to do so. Denominating loans and bonds in foreign currency increases

---

[12] In March 2014, the Chiang Mai Initiative developed into the CMIM Agreement, a multilateral currency swap agreement among Association of Southeast Asian Nations (ASEAN) plus 3 (ASEAN+3) countries (ASEAN+3 Macroeconomic Research Office 2007).

[13] In May 2011, AMRO was founded as the regional surveillance unit of ASEAN+3, directly responsible for regional economic surveillance and overseeing the CMIM. See Rana, Chia, and Jinjarak (2012).

[14] For a discussion of the difficulty in devaluing fixed exchange rates due to competing government objectives, see Obstfeld and Rogoff (1995). For an analysis of government credibility and devaluation through the Latin America example, see Welch and McLeod (1993).

[15] For an analysis of an unprecedented increase in short-term foreign liabilities at the onset of the Asian financial crisis, see Chang and Velasco (1998). Also see Schwartz (2002).

indebtedness as it encourages lenders to discount the currency risk. The
Asian financial crisis demonstrated that if the currency risk is with the
borrower because of the denomination of the debt, in times of trouble it is
transferred to the lender by the incapacity of the borrower to service the
debt. The need is therefore clear to develop local currency denominated
financing channels, including both equity and debt, as well as markets for
hedging foreign currency exposures.

The Need for Long-Term Local Currency Capital

The next lesson touches on the pressing need for emerging market
economies to raise long-term capital in their own currencies. Prior to 1997,
foreign currency borrowing from banks as well as short-term bond issuance
was a major source of local currency capital, as local lenders borrowed in
international markets to on-lend in domestic currencies along with major
local borrowers likewise directly accessing primarily US dollar markets.[16]
However, the short tenor of these instruments brings tremendous instability.
Long-term local currency capital markets allow emerging market debtors
to raise capital with the currency risk shifted on the investors. Returns to
investors will be greater when times are good, as debtors will have to pay
more to borrow in their currency, and less when times are bad, through the
operation of the exchange rate. This repayment profile is well adapted to
avert crises.

Many regional economies have learned this lesson, with the PRC, Indonesia,
and the Republic of Korea, in particular, devoting considerable effort to the
development of local currency sovereign bond markets. These efforts have
received very important support at the regional level through the ASEAN+3
Asian Bond Markets Initiative.[17]

The Need to Develop Local Capital Markets

Bond and equity markets transfer risks directly to investors, not through
banks. This is desirable because concentrating risk in an industry as unstable
as banking is perilous. In addition, in emerging market economies, banks
are often subject to pressure to make finance available to certain debtors

---

[16] For a breakdown of debt structure in the ASEAN+3 countries in facing the Asian financial
crisis, see Liu (2007). Also see Stevens (2007).

[17] Launched by ASEAN+3 in 2003, the Asian Bond Markets Initiative created a regional bond
guarantee system and established a regional settlement and clearance infrastructure. See
Goswami and Sharma (2011).

for non-commercial reasons (Harwood, Pomerleano, and Litan 1999). This form of crony capitalism has generally been seen as a major contributing factor to the scale of the Asian financial crisis (Lee 1999; Singh and Ann Zammit. 2006; Rajan and Zingales 1998). Once again, this has been a major area of focus in the region, both in individual economies and regionally, in ASEAN (Reserve Bank of Australia 2003; BIS 2011; Park 2016). In the latter, in addition to the ASEAN+3 Bond Market Initiative and its debt market focus, the ASEAN Capital Markets Forum (Goswami and Sharma 2011)[18] and its Implementation Plan has provided important support,[19] as have related initiatives in the context of the Asia-Pacific Economic Cooperation targeting funds and listing. In each case, these build on international work, in particular, through International Organisation of Securities Commissions and are influenced by European Union (EU) experiences, both positive (particularly before the global financial crisis) and negative (particularly since the global financial crisis) (Poli 2014; Liu, Lejot, and Arner 2013; Kaeochotchuangkul, Benjapongsapun, and Ammarapala n.d.).

International Capital Flows and Trade Imbalances

Emerging market financial crises are often preceded by a period of high liquidity in developed markets, which in turn chase yields in other markets, often resulting in overlending translating into excessive debt levels that eventually resolves through currency, banking, or sovereign debt problems[20] The primary task of local and international bank regulators—to maintain the safety and soundness of their domestic financial systems—requires vigilance and control over the amount international banks and institutional investors are lending to and investing in emerging market economies. Given the manner in which global trade has developed since 1998 (particularly since the PRC's accession to the World Trade Organization in 2001), trade imbalances generating financial flows from the developing world are now a concern for developed economies too and a major element underlying the global financial crisis (Caballero and Krishnamurthy 2009).

---

[18] The Asian Bond Market Forum was launched in 2010 as a common platform to support harmonization of regulation concerning cross-border bond transactions and the standardization of market practices. See Goswami and Sharma (2011).

[19] Launched in 2015, the "Implementation Plan to Promote the Development of an Integrated Capital Market to Achieve the Objectives of the AEC Blueprint 2015" focused on adopting international standards, progressive liberalization, and sequencing regional initiatives. See Phuvanatnaranubala (2009).

[20] See Reinhart and Rogoff (2011), Kindleberger (1978), and Minsky (1992).

The Global Financial Crisis

The Asian financial crisis highlighted how global financial imbalances foster instability. As lessons were not learned, financial imbalances also fueled the global financial crisis. Both crises were, in part, associated with improperly designed regulatory systems supporting overinvestment in real estate (Arner 2009) and it was such overinvestment that provided the initial trigger in both cases. The global financial crisis began as a domestic mortgage crisis in the US, which rapidly spread throughout the world after the failure of Lehman Brothers and AIG. Financial institutions lost confidence in dealing with one another and funding markets froze. This prompted regulators around the world to not only focus on recapitalizing financial institutions—including those not normally subject to bailouts—but also becoming the liquidity provider of last resort for markets.

This section reviews the crisis and considers (i) the causes, (ii) the policy responses, and (iii) lessons of the global financial crisis.

Causes of the Global Financial Crisis

The five principal causes of the global financial crisis were: (i) excessive leverage fueled by lax monetary policies, (ii) poorly functioning credit markets that underpriced risk, (iii) a disconnect between regulatory structures and the financial system, (iv) misaligned incentives, and (v) interconnectedness that facilitated the global transmission of systemic risk.[21] Each of these was underpinned by excessive reliance on quantitative risk management mechanisms (Arner 2009). Each is considered briefly.

Excessive Leverage

From 2000 to 2007, borrowers; lenders; arrangers of transactions; and credit support providers such as insurance companies, investors, and credit rating agencies all combined in an environment of low interest rates, very easily available capital and regulatory distraction to push lending and borrowing to new levels of excess, notably in the US, the United Kingdom (UK), and key eurozone countries such as Italy and Spain (Avgouleas 2015).

---

[21] See Avgouleas (2012a), Chapter 2, in which flawed financial innovations coupled with flawed science are further added as a cause of the global financial crisis.

Three Decades of International Financial Crises:
What Have We Learned and What Still Needs to Be Done?

357

Leverage had, first, been identified as a destabilizing factor for financial systems by Hyman Minsky, who showed its deleterious consequences for defaults and debt overhang.[22] This was an argument further refined by US economists, who have shown the importance of the leverage cycle on the price of collateral and, in turn, the volatility of the latter in causing financial instability (Geanakoplos 2010). As if high leverage levels were not enough, global credit markets in the wake of the global financial crisis presented a number of other structural weaknesses that would play a key role in bringing about a crisis of unusually large magnitude.

United States Subprime Mortgage Market

Excessive borrowing and lending were particularly concentrated in real estate markets. In the US, consumer borrowers of lesser credit quality (including the now infamous subprime lending, of which the most extreme example was "NINJA" borrowers—no income, and no job or assets) became popular targets of bank credit products, mostly subprime mortgages (Arner 2009). Securitization and the perception that credit risk could be perfectly hedged on a portfolio basis—especially with the support of credit default swaps—allowed banks to accelerate consumer lending to all members of society regardless of risk (Arner 2009), a false security augmented by false assumptions about the actual risk sharing impact of securitization (Rajan 2005; Keys et al. 2010).

Underpinning these lending practices were guarantees, purchases, and securitization of so-called "conforming loans" by the US-government-sponsored enterprises: Fannie Mae and Freddie Mac (Arner 2009). These institutions posed systemic risk because of their central role in US mortgage markets and being the largest issuers of US government agency debt securities (Arner 2009). When subprime mortgagors began defaulting in large numbers, Fannie Mae and Freddie Mac were unable to honor their guarantees and faced bankruptcy. The re-nationalization of these institutions averted their default and a systemic crisis, yet eroded confidence in markets and prompted the eventual failures of Lehman Brothers and AIG (Arner 2009).

---

[22] For a restatement and a summary of the "financial instability hypothesis," see Minsky (1992).

Other Asset Classes

Excessive lending and leverage was not limited to real estate. Investors pursued yield with little consideration of risk. Arrangers and advisors, such as credit ratings agencies, were more than willing participants in their quest to earn fees (Arner 2009), and investors followed their advice either due to heuristics or rational herding (Avgouleas 2009). Debt securities manufactured by the securitization process were repackaged and resold to financial institutions and institutional investors (including insurance companies and pension funds) in the US and around the world (Arner 2009). When the market for these securities collapsed, the systemic repercussions reached all corners of the globe.

Malfunctioning Credit Markets

One of the key causes of the global financial crisis was a run on short-term funding markets, which banks had used exceedingly by 2008 or the so-called run on the repo (Gorton and Metrick 2009). A liquidity crunch meant that large volumes of short-term funding could not be renewed or rolled over,[23] which sent shockwaves around the system, with the prospect of default looming for both key Wall Street and High Street banks. Another manifestation of malfunctioning credit markets was the market for asset-backed securities where risk was substantially underpriced and underwriting standards very loose. Securitization was the foundation of universal banks' "originate-and-distribute" model, whereby assets (e.g., mortgages) could be repackaged and sold to investors, with the proceeds funding the origination of further assets to repeat the distribution cycle (Arner 2009; Schwarcz 2009a).

Misaligned incentives led to excessive risk taking and socially damaging outcomes (Avgouleas 2012a; Schwarcz 2009b). Furthermore, securitization instruments, markets, and methodologies were very complex and lacked transparency, obscuring the underlying risks (Schwarcz 2008). Poor loan origination practices and unregulated nonbanks and shadow banks were at the heart of the subprime mortgage crisis (Segoviano et al. 2013).

---

[23] On the importance of this parameter, see Brunnermeier (2009) and Brunnermeier and Pedersen (2009).

Derivatives

Securitization played a substantial role in amplifying systemic risk by facilitating excessive leverage and risk concentration across the financial system (Segoviano et al. 2013). Derivatives were critical in supporting the securitization structure because these instruments were designed as a hedge or insurance to reduce the risk of the underlying asset (e.g., subprime mortgages). Growth in securitization before the global financial crisis coincided with the ballooning of derivatives markets (Masciantonio and Andrea Tiseno 2012). The Basel II framework provided real opportunities to game regulatory requirements. Thus, it incentivized the increased use of credit derivatives to mitigate risks, which resulted in heightened counterparty risk among financial institutions (e.g., banks) and major dealers (e.g., Lehman Brothers, Bear Stearns, Merrill Lynch, UBS, RBS, Citigroup, and AIG) (Arner 2009).

Prior to the global financial crisis, over-the-counter derivatives markets were generally regulated by the private sector through a model premised on the paradigmatic example of private ordering promoted by the International Swaps and Derivatives Association, with limited public supervision, which was mainly undertaken through monitoring major bank participants (Arner 2011). Derivatives markets lacked transparency. This defect was made evident when regulators failed to identify Bear Stearns' or AIG's massive unhedged bets against a collapse in the subprime mortgage market (Mishkin 2010). When AIG—the largest issuer of credit default swaps—was unable to honor its commitments, securitization structures unwound rapidly, reconcentrating credit risk into the financial system at a time when it was extremely vulnerable, exposing the lethal web of global credit market interconnectedness (Avgouleas 2012b).

Credit Rating Agencies

Credit ratings agencies played a critical role in supporting the securitization structures by rating the securities (which were sold to investors largely on the basis of rating-based judgments with levels of due diligence expected in debt markets differing dramatically from acceptable levels in the equity markets) based on a tranche of mortgages' cash flows and risk profile. However, credit ratings agencies had conflicts of interest, including that the client paying the fee for the security's rating was the issuer. It was later revealed that some securitized products were awarded higher ratings than fundamentals suggested and that "ratings shopping" may have resulted in upwardly biased ratings.[24] This masked the risk of the underlying subprime mortgages. Before the global financial crisis, credit ratings agencies were unregulated, being subject only to the International Organization of Securities Commissions (IOSCO) Code of Conduct which advocated mitigating potential conflicts of interest in general terms only (Arner 2009). Thus, these conflicts of interest were not subject to any meaningful regulatory deterrent.

Disconnect between Regulatory Structures and the Financial System

Regulatory gaps and arbitrage played a central role in the global financial crisis (Arner 2011). Financial regulatory structures did not reflect the structure of the financial system. This was most evident in macroprudential supervisory failure, blurred financial demarcations of regulatory boundaries, and the procyclical nature of certain regulations (Weber et al. 2014).

Macroprudential Supervisory Failure

Before the global financial crisis, regulators essentially sought to ensure the safety and soundness of a financial system by ensuring the safety and soundness of each significant financial institution in the system. This is known as microprudential regulation. It is an approach that neglected potential interactions between those institutions, especially of the type highlighted by the global financial crisis, or so-called endogenous risk (Brunnermeier et al. 2009), and interaction between the financial system and the macroeconomic cycle and between credit supply and asset bubbles. Monitoring these aspects of the financial system and guarding against risks arising in this context came to be known as macroprudential regulation (Hanson, Kashyap, and Stein 2011; Freixas, Laeven, and Peydró 2015). The adoption of a macroprudential approach is conceived to offer the authorities, in principle, a means of better protecting the economy against the consequences of financial instability. If asset bubbles and other forms of macroeconomic volatility can be identified at an early enough stage, then it may be possible for corrective measures to be taken (Cranston et al. 2018).[25]

Before the global financial crisis, regulatory structures neglected macroprudential or systemic risk across the financial system including that generated by regulated banks, shadow banks, financial instruments

---

[24] See Figure 6 in Masciantonio and Tiseno (2012).

[25] See Chapter 2 in Cranston et al. (2018).

(e.g., derivatives), and systemically important financial institutions. In the period before the global financial crisis, the regulatory focus was on microprudential regulation—the safety and soundness of individual institutions—and monetary stability, not the risks across the financial system (i.e., the cross-sectoral dimension) or how risks aggregate over time (i.e., the time dimension) (Arner 2011). This was exemplified by regulators' decision to allow Lehman Brothers to fail in the belief that the investment bank did not pose a systemic risk. A flawed belief since it was Lehman Brothers' failure, and that of AIG, that triggered the systemic phase of the crisis.

Blurred Financial Demarcations

In the US, commercial banks and investment banks had been legislatively separated since the Great Depression of the 1930s. Deregulation in the late 1990s fueled the rise of universal banking (e.g., Citigroup), combining the previously segregated business models and the growth of international financial behemoths.[26] When the global financial crisis unfolded, universal banks had large exposures to a range of toxic assets, notably through securitization. Coupled with dysfunctional interbank markets, a liquidity crunch, and insufficient capital buffers, consequential deleveraging severely strained balance sheets, which led to many institutions, such as Citigroup, UBS, RBS, requiring government recapitalizations (Masciantonio and Tiseno 2012), reinforcing the too-big-to-fail impact (Avgouleas 2010). Securitization created linkages with nonbank financial institutions: investment banks (e.g., Lehman Brothers, Merrill Lynch, Bear Stearns) and insurance companies (e.g., AIG). Similar to the banking system, the regulatory structure was not designed for these risks. When securitization structures unwound, this resulted in the widespread failure of bank and nonbank financial institutions.

Procyclical Regulation

Weaknesses in capital and liquidity, combined with excess leverage, were central causes of the global financial crisis (Arner 2011). Basel II had a number of procyclical design faults: greater recognition of quantitative risk modeling; reliance on credit ratings; and regulatory recognition of credit risk mitigation techniques, especially credit derivatives. The adoption of quantitative risk modeling for risk management (i.e., capital held against market risk) proved inadequate when subjected to circumstances of extreme

---

[26] See Chapter 14 in Avgouleas (2016c).

market stress ("black swan" events). Reliance on credit ratings in determining required levels of bank capital enhanced the procyclicality of capital regulation, because when credit ratings were downgraded aggressively, this led to higher capital requirements (Arner 2009). Insufficient Basel II capital buffers amplified these structural weaknesses.

Accounting standards during the global financial crisis were market-based (i.e., market-to-market). These standards had a procyclical effect, as financial institutions had to continually revalue assets downward as more institutions deleveraged, creating ever greater and more solvency-threatening losses (Arner 2011). These in turn required greater capital buffers, with Basel II once again amplifying the downward spiral in market confidence.

Global Transmission of Systemic Risk

Too Big to Fail

As mentioned previously, the decision to allow Lehman Brothers to fail was based on the presumption it would not pose a systemic risk and would support market discipline. In the event, this belief proved disastrously misplaced. Unwinding the firm's positions in equity, debt, and derivatives markets around the world dramatically increased uncertainty (i.e., if Lehman Brothers could fail, any institution could fail), which shattered already weak confidence among financial market participants. Around the same time, Bank of America agreed to acquire Merrill Lynch, the third-largest US investment bank (Arner 2009).

Derivatives were instrumental in the near collapse of AIG, which triggered the systemic phase of the crisis (Arner 2011). These derivative exposures created connections between the shadow and regulated banking systems, which facilitated the transmission of systemic risk (Gibson 2014). If AIG had been allowed to default on its derivatives, the resultant systemic risk would probably have caused the insolvency of many of the world's largest financial institutions (Arner 2009). Nonetheless, these events, in collaboration with the uncertainty, loss of confidence, adverse selection, and losses resulting from the demise of Lehman Brothers, did cause precipitous market price falls and a nearly complete freeze in markets' ability to refinance exposures. These developments threatened, in the absence of government intervention, a complete breakdown of the global financial system (Arner 2009).

A Domestic Regulatory Approach in a Global Financial System

The nature of the crisis required not merely domestic responses, but also international coordination. In particular, information gaps in relation to cross-border institutions and their supervision were exposed; the soft-law bodies setting the standards for the global financial systems lacked any supervisory capacity and other cross-border crisis management systems were non-existent (Avgouleas 2012b).[27] The systemic phase of crisis was triggered by the failure of large complex global financial conglomerates (e.g., Lehman Brothers, AIG), which was intensified by international and domestic legal and regulatory structures that lacked appropriate arrangements to manage their failure (Arner 2009).

Financial Funding Market Failures

Reliance on short-term interbank, money market, and capital market funding caused severe financial system liquidity strains when these markets became dysfunctional. This was evident before the collapse of Lehman Brothers. Northern Rock in the UK and Bear Stearns in the US had been unable to fund their business models, eventually requiring resolution through government intervention. Following the collapse of Lehman Brothers, financial funding market illiquidity became central to the systemic phase of the crisis (Arner 2009). The traditional regulatory approach of focusing on bank insolvency obscured initial responses as financial market illiquidity affected all financial institutions. Financial institutions became increasingly wary of dealing with one another, especially in short-term interbank borrowing and lending. At the same time, markets began to scrutinize institutions viewed as heavily exposed, such as monoline insurers and insurance companies dealing extensively in credit default swaps, investment banks, mortgage lenders, quasi-public mortgage market institutions (e.g., Fannie Mae and Freddie Mac), and banking groups (Arner 2009).

An Analysis of Policy Responses

Globally systemically important banks became fragile from an over exposure to subprime mortgages and related financial instruments (e.g., derivatives), or plain reckless lending, mostly to the real estate sector, complicating bank rescues. Despite central bank actions to bolster short-term liquidity markets

---

[27] See Chapter 4 in Avgouleas (2012b).

to avoid a collapse of the financial system, initial regulatory approaches were calibrated far too narrowly and were not very effective (Arner 2009), since they pursued two *prima facie* conflicting objectives: to stabilize the system, on the one hand and, on the other, to punish reckless (or worse) bankers. Delays in calibrating the appropriate liquidity mechanisms were partially responsible for the credit crisis becoming a systemic crisis (Arner 2009). The approach of the authorities to rescue systemically important financial institutions was very different to the approach adopted by the IMF in the Asian crisis (Arner, Avgouleas, and Gibson 2017), where governments were required to take drastic steps to close financial institutions and address nonperforming assets.

Approaches differed from jurisdiction to jurisdiction, but the underlying premise was to strengthen balance sheets and stabilize financial systems, which eventually enabled banks to resume lending. The use of asset management companies and/or guarantees was preferred. No bailout approach proved superior, as the choice depended on market factors, the financial position of the government involved, and the ability to retain or reinforce confidence in the failing financial institution. For example, hesitation in the UK was analogous to that in Indonesia and Thailand, and in each case this hesitation eroded confidence and diminished the success of the delayed bailout of RBS (Arner, Avgouleas, and Gibson 2017).

From 2008 onward, the Group of 20 (G-20) assumed the leading role in coordinating post-global-financial-crisis responses and financial regulatory reforms, substituting for the Group of Seven, which had taken on this role after the Asian financial crisis. Similar to the emerging-markets-focused approach adopted after the Asian financial crisis, these post-global-financial-crisis reforms have resulted mainly from domestic implementation of internationally agreed approaches, albeit with a focus on developed economies and global financial markets (Arner 2011; Buckley and Arner 2011). International cooperation and coordination, setting financial standards, and monitoring implementation was assigned to the Financial Stability Board (FSB), a renamed and strengthened evolution of the Financial Stability Forum that had been established in the wake of the Asian financial crisis (Arner 2011).

Following a number of summits, the G-20 and FSB established the core elements of the new regulatory framework:

(i)   building high-quality capital and liquidity standards and mitigating procyclicality;

(ii)   addressing systemically important financial institutions through, among other things, structural reform and new resolution regimes;

(iii) improving over-the-counter derivative markets through centralization of trading and clearing and a new regulatory framework dealing with risk management;

(iv)   strengthening accounting standards, especially relative to calculation of capital and risk and forward-looking provisions for new lending by means of adoption of IFRS 9;[28]

(v)   strengthening adherence to international supervisory and regulatory standards through regular peer reviews;

(vi)   reforming management compensation practices to redress perverse incentives and support financial stability;

(vii) developing macroprudential frameworks and tools; and

(viii) expanding and refining the regulatory perimeter.

Frameworks for specific global financial crisis issues were outsourced in the immediate aftermath of the crisis to international organizations, including the Basel Committee on Banking Supervision, IOSCO, and the International Association of Insurance Supervisors. For example, the Basel Committee on Banking Supervision released Basel III in 2010 and IOSCO released a much revised set of *Objectives and Principles of Securities Regulation* in 2012. Implementation of these reforms is ongoing and their effectiveness cannot yet be fully gauged. However, more recently we see an increasing divergence in national regulatory practices and a reluctance to abide especially with the Basel capital adequacy framework, which some jurisdictions, including at least to some extent the US, are beginning to question.

Lessons from the Global Financial Crisis

Setting aside highly significant systemic and microprudential concerns relating to bankers' incentives and financial sector culture, which are outside the scope of this paper, five main lessons can be drawn from the global financial crisis:

(i)   Securitization cannot mitigate market risks in the absence of regulation correcting incentives.

---

[28] International Financial Reporting Standards (IFRS) are accounting standards issued by the IFRS Foundation and the International Accounting Standards Board. IFRS 9 addresses the accounting for financial instruments and covers classification and measurement of financial instruments, impairment of financial assets, and hedge accounting.

(ii)   Comprehensive regulation of the financial system is needed to augment its resilience though that may come at the expense of clarity as financial stability regulation has become overly complex.

(iii)   Regulations should guard against moral hazard, especially too-big-to-fail institutions and should not be procyclical, a charge that was launched against Basel II capital standards (and credit ratings).

(iv)   Systemic risks need to be detected and mitigated but, as this may be exceedingly difficult, a prophylactic approach that leads to ex-ante building of adequate capital and liquidity buffers is probably the best regulatory strategy.

(v)   A flexible, speedy, and comprehensive framework is needed to resolve financial institutions, with special attention given to systemically important financial institutions.

Each lesson is considered in detail.

Securitization Regulation Should Mitigate Market Risks

Prior to the global financial crisis, securitization was often abused and its inherent risks obscured. The lesson from this experience is that securitization should lead to simple and transparent structures that promote disclosure; and credit ratings agencies should be regulated to avoid or at least mitigate conflicts of interest when assigning ratings to securitization-related financial instruments (Arner 2009). Securitization has an important potential role in the financial system—especially in access to finance and support for economic growth—but regulation to ensure transparency and align incentives is necessary.

Comprehensive Regulation of the Financial System Is Needed

The second lesson from the global financial crisis is that regulatory gaps, overlaps, and divisions in a number of jurisdictions, especially the US, presented opportunities for regulatory avoidance and arbitrage. Regulatory structures were flawed in scope and coverage (Arner 2011). All financial institutions, including all service providers (e.g., credit ratings agencies), and financial instruments (e.g., derivatives) should be regulated to discourage regulatory arbitrage. This may involve developing new and enhancing existing financial market infrastructures. Regulatory structures must be designed to address unregulated areas that pose substantial risks, such as shadow banking and off-balance sheet treatments. The scope of financial regulation must be broadened to dispel traditional preconceptions of particular institutions undertaking specific financial activities. Regulation and supervision must be suitably flexible to recognize and address any financial activity emanating from any institution. This is a particular challenge going forward given the impact of technology on finance (i.e., FinTech) in avoiding regulatory arbitrage, ensuring a level playing field, and protecting against risks arising from new directions and participants (Zetzsche et al. 2017).

Designing Regulations which are not Procyclical in Crisis Conditions

Certain Basel II regulations and "mark-to-market" accounting standards proved to be procyclical under crisis conditions. Procyclicality was further enhanced when assets and credit ratings were devalued and downgraded. To strengthen balance sheets in crisis conditions, the robustness of capital, liquidity, and leverage requirements should be tested *ex ante,* and risk management must be improved to insulate institutions against asset devaluations in the event of economic downturns or when an asset bubble bursts. Adopting forward-looking accounting standards on top of these prudential requirements will further mitigate procyclicality (Novoa, Scarlata, and Sole 2009). Countercyclical requirements and capital requirements calibrated for systemically important financial institutions should be built over a period to buttress balance sheets with an additional buffer against credit rating downgrades or outright asset value write-offs. Basel III has addressed some of these issues in the banking system. Reporting and related stress testing of systems provides important opportunities for increased use of technology in both compliance and regulatory monitoring through regulatory technology (RegTech) approaches (Arner, Barberis, and Buckley 2017).

Effective Detection and Mitigation of Systemic Risk

Regulation of market infrastructure. Preventing and addressing systemic risk is a fundamental aspect of financial regulatory design, which was exposed as a critical design flaw of the regulatory structure before the global financial crisis. The lessons are that supervisors must have the capacity to identify and regulate systemically important financial institutions to mitigate transmission of systemic risk, and be equipped with the tools and mechanisms to ensure that funding markets remain liquid in all market conditions. Furthermore, financial instruments which have the propensity to become systemic risk conduits, such as derivatives, require regulation that facilitates transparency and disclosure, and financial market infrastructure that can interrupt the transmission of systemic risk (e.g., central counterparty clearinghouses). Market infrastructure is a particular focus of many new FinTech developments, posing new challenges for regulators but also offering new opportunities to design better systems, including through the use of RegTech (Arner, Barberis, and Buckley 2016).

Macroprudential supervision. Effective macroprudential supervision is critical. Under this framework, regulators have responsibility to look at the resilience of the financial system as a whole and the way it interacts with the wider economy, including the possible formation of asset bubbles. Supervisors need to be equipped with the tools and mechanisms to assess and manage risks across the financial system and which aggregate over time.[29] In this context, a number of new measures, such as leverage ratios, countercyclical capital requirements, and lending controls, (like loan-to-value and loan-to-income ratios) have both a micro- (institutional stability) and macroprudential (systemic stability) effect (Avgouleas, 2012).[30] Related reporting requirements for financial institutions and the resulting new data sets available to regulators offer very important opportunities for new RegTech analytical approaches, including big data and artificial intelligence.

A Framework to Resolve Systemically Important Financial Institutions

Domestic arrangements and powers. The absence of an effective systemically important financial institution resolution mechanism was key to the systemic phase of the global financial crisis (e.g., Lehman Brothers and AIG). The G-20 recognized that one of the greatest failures of international and domestic regulation was the lack of appropriate arrangements to deal with the failure of large complex financial conglomerates (Arner 2011). This involves assessing the risks posed from interactions and interconnections. The primary lesson of the global financial crisis is to have arrangements in place to either prevent or manage a failure. To prevent or manage a failure requires a supervisor (including a designated resolution supervisor) being equipped with a range of resolution powers including to replace management; terminate, continue, or assign contracts; purchase or sell assets; write down debt and restructure bank operations; ensure continuity of essential services; override shareholder rights; establish a bridge institution or asset management vehicle; carry out a bail-in within a resolution; suspend payments to unsecured creditors and customers; and impose an effective and

---

[29] For a detailed discussion, see Taylor, Arner, and Gibson (2019).

[30] See Chapter 2 in Cranston et al. 2018.

orderly liquidation (FSB 2011). This is broadly the approach now adopted by the FSB. While the FSB approach focuses primarily on globally systemically important financial institutions, both the global financial crisis and the Asian financial crisis highlight the necessity of individual jurisdictions putting in place appropriate contingency plans and resolution systems particularly for domestic systemically important financial institutions (Weber et al. 2014). In addition, region-based discussions are also necessary in addressing cross-border concerns particularly for regionally systemically important financial institutions—a major issue in the eurozone crisis discussed in the following section and also an important area of focus of ASEAN in the context of the ASEAN Banking Integration Framework.

Reinforcing international cooperation. Reinforcing international cooperation is particularly pertinent in financial crisis management involving the resolution of systemically important financial institutions which operate across borders. Resolution arrangements should focus on the underlying objective of preventing serious financial instability which would have an adverse effect on a country's real economy (Arner 2011). Problematically, financial crisis management is biased toward domestic concerns. Therefore, the best approach is to formulate a pre-determined contingency plan which accounts for cross-border risks and is constantly being revised to keep up-to-date with ongoing market developments, often referred to as "living wills" (Avgouleas, Goodhart, and Schoenmaker 2013). But it should be under constant supervisory monitoring and supported by regular meetings between domestic supervisors (home and abroad), the sharing of information, and ensuring that supervisors have the powers and tools to restructure and resolve all financial instructions (Arner 2011). This approach has been endorsed by the G-20, the IMF, the FSB, and most other transnational regulatory networks. Similar approaches have also been developed in the EU, particularly as a result of the eurozone crisis and need to be a major focus as Asia increasingly seeks to liberalize cross-border financial institution operations in the context of the ASEAN Banking Integration Framework as well as bilateral (e.g., ASEAN–Hong Kong, China) and wider efforts (e.g., ASEAN+3, Asia-Pacific Economic Cooperation).

The Eurozone Crisis

The 2008 global financial crisis spread to most developed economies, including those of the EU. Unfortunately, despite decades of effort to build a single financial market, almost all EU jurisdictions lacked proper crisis resolution mechanisms, especially in cross-border dimensions of a crisis. This led to a threat of widespread bank failures in certain EU member states and near collapse of their financial systems. The banking crisis eventually morphed into a sovereign debt crisis due to the "doom loop" in countries such as Cyprus, Ireland, and Spain, where the banks had overextended themselves with reckless lending. At the same time, the markets declined to roll over Greek debt, necessitating placing the country under an IMF and EU rescue program. While the latter failed to achieve its macroeconomic objectives, it was, nevertheless, adequate to eventually stem the fear of a string of sovereign bankruptcies within the eurozone. Today, in the wake of the eurozone financial crisis, the 2016 Brexit vote, and the COVID-19 crisis, the EU is at a crossroads. It has to decide whether the road to recovery runs through closer integration of financial policies to follow recent centralization of bank supervision and resolution in the European Banking Union, or whether to take a path of fragmentation with a gradual return to controlled forms of protectionism in the pursuit of narrow national interest, although the latter is bound to endanger the single market (Avgouleas and Arner 2017). Therefore, the policy dilemmas facing the EU and contemporary institution building within the eurozone provide a key window into the future of both global and regional financial integration. This section will examine (i) how the crisis should be conceptualized, (ii) its primary causes, and (iii) the lessons it teaches about the need for centralized supervision in financially integrated markets.

Conceptualizing the Crisis

The eurozone crisis should be seen as a sequence of four interlocking crises resulting from imbalanced integration. First, the use of the single currency exacerbated intra-EU competitiveness gaps, leading to a competitiveness crisis which also led to widening fiscal deficits resulting in debt accumulations (particularly in Greece, Italy, Portugal, and Spain) that were financed by the surpluses of the northern countries. As recycled surpluses were invested in the bonds of deficit countries (Greece, Italy) and the banking systems of the eurozone periphery (Ireland, Spain) where they financed massive real estate bubbles, they led to accumulation of unsustainable levels of public and private debt (Avgouleas 2012a).

The eurozone crisis signaled a fundamental shift in the political dynamics underpinning the EU. While remedies for the crisis—austerity, more integration, mutualization of eurozone members' debt, and other measures—

Three Decades of International Financial Crises:
What Have We Learned and What Still Needs to Be Done?

371

remain the topic of heated discussion, one remedy was uncontroversial. All agree that the eurozone crisis would have been less severe if eurozone members could have found a way to break the link between bank debt and sovereign indebtedness. The fact that many EU banks had invested in EU member state bonds and were also hurt by the continuous recession ravaging the periphery of the eurozone only made things worse. Since its establishment, the European Economic and Monetary Union (EMU) lacked these crucial supporting institutions that could have helped it to restore financial stability during times of acute uncertainty and market volatility (Bergsten and Kirkegaard 2012). More specifically, the EMU lacked suitable institutions that could absorb liquidity shocks, due to a collapse of confidence in the prospects of a member state's economy, and cross-border supervisory and resolution structures that could effectively deal with the cross-border spillover effects of a bank collapse.

Causes of the Eurozone Crisis

Inadequacy of Regulatory Architecture

The EU constitutes the most advanced global laboratory for regional economic, legal, and political integration (Wouters and Ramopoulos 2012). The establishment of a single currency area (the eurozone) and the pan-European presence of a number of large banks with large cross-border operations lent urgency to questions about long-term protection of EU-wide financial stability in the absence of appropriate institutional arrangements. The so-called financial stability trilemma holds (Schoenmaker 2011; Thygesen 2003) that the three objectives of financial stability, single (financial) market integration, and national regulation cannot be pursued successfully simultaneously; one of these objectives has to give way to safeguard the other two.[31] In spite of assertions to the contrary (Padoa-Schioppa 2000), the eurozone crisis has proven a common currency area is not viable without building, at the same time, transnational supervisory structures in the fields of fiscal monitoring and responsibility and bank supervision and resolution. This lesson has been well understood in Asia, with discussions of any potential for a single regional currency having ceased since the onset of the eurozone crisis.

---

[31] Lastra and Louis (2013) describe the same trade off as an "inconsistent quartet" of policy objectives.

Therefore, while the establishment of pan-European banks has been a potent integrative factor for the EU, it was inevitable that the concurrent presence of pan-European banks and decentralized and incoherent regulatory structures would not be able to prevent financial instability across the single market, especially across the single currency area, in the event of serious market turbulence. In Asia, while discussions of any form of Asian monetary union have largely ceased, discussions regarding financial market integration—particularly in ASEAN—continue, highlighting the very direct significance of EU experiences in this respect, both positive as well as negative.

While the nature of the regulatory architecture itself may or may not be an important cause of a financial crisis, institutional design is certainly very important for the prevention and resolution of a major financial crisis. Prevention is dealt with through a framework of systemic risk control and robust prudential regulations. Crisis management and resolution, on the other hand, require established supervisory and resolution structures, which in an integrated market, must have a cross-border remit to override the principle of home country control (Garicano and Lastra 2010). A careful look at the developmental phase of European institution building reveals this has been a process of experimentation rather than design. This experience provides important lessons for Asia—particularly ASEAN—in building regional markets.

In spite of the vast amount of effort expended in developing both the EU single financial market and EMU, important design features necessary to support financial stability had not been put in place or were not sufficiently robust, particularly in relation to resolution of cross-border financial institutions, deposit guarantee arrangements, regulation and supervision, and fiscal arrangements and affairs. Clearly, because of the political economy of Asia, institutional centralization of the sort now pursued in the EU is not feasible. Nonetheless, as a result of the eurozone crisis, the key issues that have to be considered during the design phase of an integrated regional financial market are now much clearer.

Home-Country Control and Minimum Harmonization

The premise of home-country control and the principle of minimum harmonization were bound to undermine at some point the stability of the EU banking system. Minimum harmonization left the EU with an incomplete regulatory framework, since, in many cases, it merely augmented rather than replaced pre-existing national laws (Avgouleas 2000).

The eurozone crisis brought home with devastating force the potential risks of financial market integration, reflecting the main findings of the financial stability trilemma. Moreover, financial integration leads financial institutions operating in the single market to develop very tight links of interconnectedness, allowing shocks appearing in one part of the market to be transmitted widely and quickly across all other parts. Examples of such rapid transmission of shocks included the failure of Icelandic banks, the botched rescue of Fortis bank, the threat of collapse of the financial systems of Ireland and Spain, and the possibility of a sovereign default (e.g., Greece), or of a chain of sovereign defaults. Each of those crises brought serious tremors to European markets and exposed their fragility and the dearth of policy options available to eurozone decision makers.

In the EU, the diversity of member state economies and issues arising out of inherent contradictions between national policy priorities meant a relatively low degree of responsiveness to the crisis at the initial stages, and lots of confusion. This became evident as soon as some EMU states, which experienced a more severe crisis than other members, had to adopt policies based on their own national needs and interests—which may not necessarily have been in conformity with single-market policies. For example, lack of common deposit insurance in a well-integrated banking market at a time of cross-border crisis led to several conflicting policy choices and responses in an effort by the states to protect their own citizens, with the Icelandic banking crisis and the fracture of Fortis as leading examples (Avgouleas, Arner, and Asharaff 2014).

From the standpoint of Asia, with its even greater disparity in economic size, development, political arrangements, and social and cultural contexts, such risks must be considered at the outset of any regional financial process, not only to minimize the chances of crisis and maximize economic benefits, but also to manage potentially severe political consequences.

Regulatory Responses to the Eurozone Crisis

It was not until the 2008 global financial crisis, and not in earnest until the outbreak of the eurozone crisis in 2010, that the vexed issue of preservation of financial stability in an integrated market came to the forefront of EU policy makers' attention. Both crises have emphasized the need to revisit existing models of financial market integration with a view to enriching them with institutions and structures that underpin financial stability and economic growth.

When the global financial crisis broke out with force, European financial stability was hampered by a number of pre-existing problems which had simply been ignored for far too long. These included colossal pre-crisis public and private debt loads, a flawed macroeconomic framework, and absence of institutions capable of effectively handling a cross-border banking crisis. The eurozone's framework assumed that any macroeconomic or banking system stability shocks could be dealt with at the national level without requiring transfers from the strongest to the weaker members of the eurozone, due to the no bailout clause in the EMU Treaty. Consequently, the outbreak of the sovereign debt crisis in the eurozone in 2010 meant that the EU had to enter into the most transformative phase of its history.

The EU has had to devise mechanisms, in the midst of crisis, first, to prevent an immediate meltdown of its banking sector and the chain of sovereign bankruptcies that would have ensued, and, second, to reform its flawed institutions to prevent the eurozone architecture from collapsing. Eurozone members, in other words, had to build both a crisis-fighting capacity and bailout funding mechanisms. This led to the establishment of the European Financial Stability Facility, now superseded by the European Stability Mechanism. At the same time, serious steps have been taken to build a European Banking Union based on structures safeguarding centralization of bank supervision and uniform deposit insurance arrangements, and centralization of crisis resolution.

Since 2011, the EU as a whole has embarked on a number of initiatives to build an integrated surveillance framework in the implementation of fiscal policies under the Stability and Growth Pact to strengthen economic governance and to ensure budgetary discipline, and the implementation of structural reforms. In addition, the European Parliament and the European Council adopted a "six-pack" set of legislative acts aimed at strengthening the eurozone's economic governance by reduction of deficits through tighter control of national finances.[32] The reforms represented the most comprehensive reinforcement of economic governance in the EU and the eurozone since the launch of the EMU almost 20 years before. This legislative package aims at concrete and decisive steps toward ensuring fiscal discipline to stabilize the EU economy and to avert new crises.

---

[32] The legislative six-pack set of European economic governance architecture reforms comprised five regulations and one directive, proposed by the European Commission to come into force on 13 December 2011.

Three Decades of International Financial Crises:
What Have We Learned and What Still Needs to Be Done?

375

Important measures have been adopted, chief of which is the implementation of a European Banking Union among the eurozone members. European Central Bank (ECB) activism through its quantitative easing program and the ultimately unused "Outright Monetary Transactions" eventually stabilized sovereign debt markets. Further, the implementation of mandatory bail-ins through the EU bank recovery and resolution directive aims to contain the impact of the banking crisis on sovereigns by making bailouts nearly impossible.[33]

Breaking the vicious circle of bank debt becoming sovereign debt is a matter of utmost importance for the survival of the eurozone. EU members need to complete the adjustment of internal and external imbalances, to repair financial sectors, and to achieve sustainable public finances (EU 2012). Piling up debt in their effort to bail out Europe's ailing banks only makes things worse. In addition, it raises the cost of borrowing for eurozone members to unsustainable levels, necessitating continuous bailouts by the wealthier members of the eurozone in an effort to keep the EMU from breaking up. However, such sovereign bailouts are both very expensive and highly unpopular with the citizens of lender countries (EU 2012). A comprehensive EU mandate on structural reform of the EU banking sector may take some time as the EU faces so many existential problems on numerous fronts. The COVID-19 crisis is making resolutions more difficult.

From the Asian standpoint, perhaps the central feature for consideration is how to avoid entanglement of domestic fiscal and financial arrangements in future crises, whether regional or in individual economies. Such planning at the same time needs to consider how resources can be pooled to reduce the risk and severity of volatility and crisis as well as support economic integration and balanced development.

From the many EU regulatory reforms, three initiatives stand out. First, the most important gaps in the eurozone institutional edifice were remedied through the establishment of the first (and most significant) pillar of the European Banking Union, the Single Supervisory Mechanism, run by the ECB. Centralization of supervision for eurozone banks through the Single Supervisory Mechanism means that the ECB is now the prudential supervisor of the eurozone banking sector. Under the Single Supervisory Mechanism Regulation of October 2013, the ECB is vested with the necessary investigatory

---

[33] Directive 2014/59/EU establishing a framework for the recovery and resolution of credit institutions and investment firms OJ 201 4 L 173/190.

and supervisory powers. Second, EU plans for the harmonization of member state resolution laws and introduction of integrated resolution structures are being implemented. The Single Resolution Mechanism established by Regulation (EU) No. 806/2014 is aimed at safeguarding the continuity of essential banking operations, protecting depositors, client assets, and public funds, and minimizing risks to financial stability. This mechanism should be more efficient than a network of national resolution authorities, particularly in cross-border failures, given the need for speed and credibility in addressing issues amid crisis. Third, the development of common EU rulebooks for the single market by the European Supervisory Authorities is a laudatory development that is proceeding rapidly.

While from the standpoint of Asia—even within ASEAN—the level of centralization being pursued in the EU as a result of the eurozone crisis is not politically feasible, the process nonetheless highlights the three key areas which need to be considered in further Asian financial integration efforts: (i) harmonization of domestic regulatory systems, (ii) supervision of cross-border financial institutions, and (iii) arrangements to address cross-border financial institution failures. Each of these should be seen as essential preconditions to integration, in the same way that the Asian financial crisis strongly demonstrated the necessity of strengthening domestic financial systems prior to liberalization.

Lessons of the Eurozone Crisis

The EU crisis response in the development and functioning of single market operations has emphasized the need to improve international and regional coordination on fiscal, monetary, and financial policies affecting other states.

Financial stability risks are magnified within integrated cross-border markets. The cascading effects of the eurozone crisis are a vivid reminder of the contagion risk in a highly integrated system (ADB 2012). Thus, it should not be controversial, even though it does challenge orthodox thinking, to argue that financial integration—in contrast to the general consensus regarding trade integration—is not always beneficial. Despite the increased importance of enhanced regionalism and integration, policy formulation must take a balanced view. The European crisis provides deep insight into the risks of integration and identifies mistakes that should not be repeated in the adoption of integration plans elsewhere, chiefly in ASEAN.

The European experience has demonstrated that centralization of bank supervision and resolution within a single currency zone is an essential condition for a functional monetary union (although it is no panacea). It has clearly exposed the weaknesses of regulatory structures along national lines when these have to deal with integrated cross-border financial markets. The soundness and credibility of domestic policies are not substitutes for regional commitments, even though, when reform of domestic policies is "blocked," regional commitments can help to "tie hands" and exert external pressure. Further, rather than imposing strict benchmarks and milestones to meet the idiosyncrasies of individual economies, the integration framework should facilitate and encourage the growth of regional economies while allowing the market to work freely.

The EU faces a number of hard choices, including the intractable tradeoff between national sovereignty and collective financial stability. Establishment of the European Banking Union within the boundaries of the eurozone—which includes a single supervisor, a single resolution authority and, in the future, a pan-European deposit guarantee scheme—has clearly tilted the balance toward further centralization and pooling of sovereignty. With the decision of the United Kingdom to leave the EU, discussions are now moving forward in the context of regional securities and insurance supervisory arrangements as well. This highlights the level of sovereignty concessions necessary to support an effective single market. This is even more so when the single market is underpinned by common currency arrangements. In that case, a fiscal union to smooth out trade imbalances and to contain shocks in the financial sector seems essential (Bénassy-Quéré, Ragot, and Wolff 2016).

This level of sovereignty sacrifice though is beyond the capacity of most national polities, including the UK, as has been clearly demonstrated by Brexit, a point that has certainly not gone unnoticed in Asia.

Brief Anatomy of Responses to the Crises and Critical Comparisons

The three crises analyzed here are quite distinctive. Nevertheless, they share common causes, including high leverage in the financial system, undercapitalized banks, weak lending standards, asset bubbles of varied nature and force, captured or weak regulators, a self-reinforcing negative loop between banks and their sovereigns, and lax monetary environments. And there are common lessons, principally the need ahead of time for frameworks and systems to address the main forms of financial crisis, including currency, banking or financial, current account or competitiveness, and sovereign debt crises. But before examining lessons, it is reasonable to provide a critical overview of crisis responses mostly comprising *ex post* remedial steps and legislative and regulatory reforms.

Commonalities and Differences in Crisis Prevention and Crisis Management

The biggest similarities in a way are between the two regional crises (Asian financial crisis and eurozone crisis) rather than between them and the global financial crisis, as the prospect of financial sector and sovereign bankruptcy loomed large in both cases. But there have been marked differences in approach in these two crises.

Strengthening Supervision and Resolution, Tackling Nonperforming Loans to Restore Confidence

Whereas in the Asian financial crisis a deep intervention in the financial sector and a resolve to tackle NPLs through asset management companies came early, in the eurozone measures to strengthen the supervision of the financial sector (e.g., the Single Supervisory Mechanism) came later in the crisis and the same delayed response is also seen in crisis management measures like the European Stability Mechanism and the Single Resolution Mechanism. On the other hand, the eurozone periphery is still grappling with a serious NPL problem. Thus, whereas in the Asian financial crisis confidence in the banking sector was restored relatively early, in the eurozone this has been a drawn-out process.

Deposit and Currency Runs

Arguably, while the run on deposits in the eurozone periphery was not dissimilar to the panic experienced by East Asian countries during the Asian financial crisis, the eurozone did not experience a run on the common currency and thus did not have to take measures to stem short-term capital flows, and nor did it have to raise interest rates to stem investor flight.

Levels of Legal Autonomy in Designing Bank Rescue Policies

While states affected by the Asian financial crisis had retained legal and legislative autonomy and flexibility, in spite of IMF oversight, eurozone countries have to comply with EU legal restrictions on state aid and public bailouts—to some extent replaced by compulsory bail-ins—and a largely predetermined bank resolution script based in EU legislation (the bank recovery and resolution directive).[34] Yet the EU approach to its banking crisis has been far from uniform. For every bail-in centered bank resolution (e.g., Cyprus, Denmark), the EU can also show a series of public rescues, e.g., Germany, Greece, and Italy, in the Asian mode, but unlike the Asian blueprint, very few bank closures.

Central Bank Intervention: Extraordinary Monetary Policies and the Lender of Last Resort

While eurozone member states, like Asian countries, lack a common treasury, the former share a central bank. It was the ECB's threat to buy as much as needed of its member's debt, the so-called Outright Monetary Transactions program (ECB 2012), that eventually calmed bond markets and brought down sovereign debt premiums. This proclaimed policy, alongside a truly massive asset purchase and quantitative easing (QE) program (Jones 2015) implemented by the ECB seems to have worked miracles in stabilizing previously volatile markets for sovereign lending in the EU. In addition, during both the global financial crisis and the eurozone crisis, central banks cast aside any concerns about moral hazard and became especially liberal lenders of last resort; chiefly, again, the US Federal Reserve, but the ECB as well (Avgouleas 2016b).

It is widely accepted that the ECB's QE has smoothed out liquidity shortages within the eurozone financial system. Extraordinary monetary policy measures, often in substitution of fiscal policy measures, have been a feature of both the global financial crisis and the eurozone responses, where QE was used very extensively by central banks (especially the US Federal Reserve and the Bank of England) to alleviate the credit crunch. On the other hand, there is no evidence of use of QE and loose monetary policy in general in the Asian financial crisis. On the contrary, faced with a currency crisis, East Asian countries raised interest rates, thereby tightening rather than loosening money supply. This is, of course, an important distinction, since the robust growth rates that East Asian countries have posted since 2008 (and for the two prior decades) might constitute a strong lesson against the dominant (Kindleberger 1978, Friedman and Schwartz 1963) liquidity supply

---

[34] Directive 2014/59/EU establishing a framework for the recovery and resolution of credit institutions and investment firms OJ 201 4 L 173/190.

paradigm relative to economic crisis prevention and resolution. This policy contrast could mean that robust macroeconomic fundamentals and rapid implementation of reforms may be as important for alleviation of liquidity shortages in the economy as central bank intervention is in the medium term. In addition, macroeconomic adjustments and rapid implementation of financial sector reforms come with none of the financial stability risks that a loose monetary policy brings. Surprisingly, this policy contrast has remained largely unexplored in economics to this day and no empirical data appears to be available as to which liquidity or confidence restoration paradigm is the most effective (Avgouleas 2016a).

Structural and Resolution Frameworks to Limit Too-Big-To-Fail Institutions

In several jurisdictions—especially the US and the UK—the universal banking business models operated by major banks, which combined commercial banking and deposit taking with investment and trading activity in securities and derivatives markets, came under attack. Not only was it considered as one of the reasons that made banks too-big-to-fail (TBTF), but it was also thought to be a channel for systemic risk propagation from one market segment to another, raising the levels of market fragility both at the institutional and the systemic level (Avgouleas 2010). As a result, both the US and the UK have passed structural reform legislation (the so-called Volcker Rule in the US Dodd Frank Act and ring-fencing through the UK Banking Act 2013). Both sets of legislation aim to downsize and otherwise restrict the operations of TBTF institutions, although the model of activity or business entity separation that each jurisdiction has followed is quite different, with the UK's ring-fencing model being the more draconian.

As mentioned, when the global financial crisis erupted in 2008 a series of public bailouts took place, whereby the state took a direct stake in banks, or nationalized them outright (Arner, Avgouleas, and Gibson 2017). But, in contrast with the Asian financial crisis, asset management companies seem to have been out of favor. International (e.g., FSB) and national regulators moved fast to pass resolution standards (e.g., FSB Key Attributes) that minimized the room for public rescues, eliminated the so-called TBTF subsidy that large financial institutions were found to enjoy in their funding base making them more profitable than smaller competitors (Weber et al. 2014).

Derivatives Markets Reform

Furthermore, while financial sector leverage was a feature of all three crises, the trigger for the global financial crisis was the combined effect of bad lending (subprime mortgages) and complex (innovative) financial products. So, the markets for complex derivatives and securitized debt had to be dealt with through an additional wave of regulation. Whereas the Asian financial crisis and the eurozone crises were merely the product of outright bad bank lending and its impact on sovereign indebtedness, therefore, derivatives market infrastructure reforms have not been seen as critical.

Augmented Governance, Compensation, and Prudential Standards

Finally, all three crises have been followed with a tightening of supervisory structures and augmented supervisory standards, including higher levels of capital and liquidity reserves, as well as the introduction of a macroprudential or systemic approach to regulation. In addition, banks' governance and risk management techniques have been overhauled as a reaction to all three crises. As compensation structures in the banking sector were found to be flawed generating perverse incentives, strong measures have been adopted to deal with this cardinal problem, leading to a realignment of bank management's incentives with financial stability goals.

Looking Forward

Taken together the differences between the specific triggers and origins of the three crises may be greater than their similarities, which suggests that our next crisis (and history teaches there will always be another), will be different in its causes and consequences than any of these three. And in terms of remedial policies, in spite of several similarities, the differing approaches when it came to tackling NPLs and the use of the monetary tool, place differences in crisis response policies into sharp relief. In fact, the most critical divide centers on whether rapid macroeconomic adjustment (as in the Asian financial crisis, and to some extent the eurozone crisis) or use of extraordinary monetary measures is the best way to restore confidence and stabilize liquidity conditions. In the context of the COVID-19 crisis, the focus is initially the latter in order to avoid a health and economic crisis becoming a financial crisis.

Nevertheless, three important lessons or recommendations for Asia stand out.

First, in an increasingly globalized world, formal international cooperation in financial stability and cross-border bank supervision and resolution might in the long run come to be seen as a necessary ingredient of national prosperity whenever national financial markets are closely integrated.[35] At the same time, in today's environment, tensions regarding sovereignty at various levels make this unlikely outside of the EU (following the exit of the UK).

While Asia—even in the context of ASEAN—is unlikely to be willing to accept the level of sovereignty sacrifice necessary for the creation of a true single regional financial market based on a regional currency (parallel to the EU Single Market), economic and financial cooperation and coordination in the region remain essential. Beyond the G-20 context, this is most likely in the context of ASEAN, ASEAN+3, Executives' Meeting of East Asia-Pacific Central Banks (EMEAP), and perhaps the Shanghai Cooperation Organisation. As integration continues, it is essential for parallel discussion to take place not only on liberalization, but also crisis preparation, with a stronger role for the ASEAN+3 Macroeconomic Research Office (AMRO) and/or through further development of the various regional forums of the international standard setting bodies, such as the FSB Asia Regional Consultative Group.

Second, it is always prudent to prepare for the next financial crisis. The only working assumption about which any regulator can be confident is that there will be one—and its precise nature and timing will be exceptionally difficult to predict, as can be seen from the COVID-19 crisis. Building a robust crisis management, early intervention and resolution framework should be seen as the paramount responsibility of regulators and public policy planners in the region. In addition to the effective implementation of the FSB and Basel frameworks, Asian countries should also design their own mechanisms for national and cross-border liquidity relief to cope with the next crisis. Liquidity has fleeting properties, whether as foreign money inflows or financial system funding, and can easily disappear when the economy is exposed to short-term shocks or emerging structural weaknesses, or the financial system suffers a run due to a confidence crisis. In the same context, even for stable economies, financial regulators should remain watchful of interconnectedness risks and the possibility of contagion from the shadow banking sector that may quickly undermine the stability of the regulated

---

[35] For an example of such a model for the governance of global financial markets (albeit one that requires an enormous amount of trust on behalf of international regulatory community), see Chapter 9 in Avgouleas (2012b).

Three Decades of International Financial Crises:
What Have We Learned and What Still Needs to Be Done?

383

sector. This is particularly true as a result of sustainability crises, such as COVID-19.

While Asia focused on improving regulation in the aftermath of the Asian financial crisis, with very good results during the global financial crisis, which left the region largely unscathed, it has made relatively less progress in resolution mechanisms. As such, at the domestic level, continued emphasis on improving regulation and building financial infrastructure and implementing financial safety nets, including resolution frameworks, needs to continue. This is especially the case in the region's developing members, which should be guided by the experiences—positive and negative—of its emerging and developed members. At the same time, as the PRC's financial system continues to integrate internationally and regionally, this raises new risks both for the PRC as well as for the region. Regionally, as integration efforts continue, there is a consequent necessity to build a framework to deal with potential crises of the major forms identified: currency, banking or financial, current account or competitiveness, and sovereign debt.

In crisis prevention, approaches vary in each context. For currency crises, a flexible exchange rate, backed by reasonably large foreign exchange reserves, is probably the best starting point, supplemented by bilateral and regional arrangements under AMRO and the CMIM, as well as precautionary international lines from the IMF and possibly others, such as the New Development Bank and major currency central banks. For banking and financial crises, the starting point is regulation, with a focus on participation in international standard setting processes, development of regional implementations and, most importantly, focusing on domestic arrangements. For current account or competitiveness crises, at the regional level, AMRO offers a macroeconomic monitoring arrangement to supplement the international monitoring of the IMF. But at the end of the day this—as once again shown in the EU—is a domestic focus in the first instance. The same applies to sovereign debt crises, but, as already noted, development of domestic and regional financial systems to support local currency financing and risk management can play a very important role.

Third, if in spite of the above protective measures an economic disturbance or a financial sector shock develops into a full-blown financial crisis, then the speed of the policy response and the decisiveness of public institutions matters greatly for the restoration of confidence. Tested remedies, such as asset management companies, which provide a radical solution to overstretched bank balance sheets, ought not to be discarded on grounds of moral hazard and bailout subsidies. On the contrary, affected countries should instead try to build a transparent framework which distributes losses equitably and prudently targeting rapid restoration of confidence in the health of the financial system, avoiding the type of creditor runs experienced in all three crises discussed in this chapter.

Much of the great expansion of regulation in the aftermath of the global financial crisis has been well adopted to prevent another one. But loopholes remain, especially in the regulatory perimeter, with most shadow banking activity remaining unregulated and in terms of cross-border supervision. If anything, these issues are greater across most of Asia than in the G-20, raising risks but also presenting opportunities for increased cooperation, coordination, and monitoring in the region. In particular, as finance technology (FinTech) continues to transform Asian financial systems at an increasing rate, issues relating to appropriate treatment of new technologies and new participants beyond traditional financial institutions such as information technology, communications, e-commerce, and social media firms becomes even more important in Asia than in the developed markets of Europe or North America. The needs for financial inclusion and financial development are higher, the opportunities for leapfrogging are greater, and the risks that arise are potentially far more significant, domestically and regionally. Improving the technology and abilities of regulators across the region through regulatory technology (RegTech) must be a major focus. (Arner, Buckley, and Zetzsche 2018). After all, financial innovation and liberalization are often central to financial crises. And FinTech is likely to be no exception to this traditional cycle, with COVID-19 dramatically increasing digitization.

In summary, we have a globalized financial system that was designed by John Maynard Keynes and Harry Dexter White in the early to mid-1940s, to be a series of lightly interconnected national systems. Ever since the system began to globalize in the 1980s, we have been working to accommodate new regulatory settings to the new, profoundly different reality of a globalized financial system. But while we have made much progress, we also have a long way to go. In Asia, geopolitics and economics—particularly the rise of India, ASEAN, and even more critically of the PRC—highlight that the nature of global market integration has changed, with significant implications for crisis prevention and management. As we learned in the Asian financial crisis, Asia must take steps to secure its own success and to protect itself from financial crises, from whatever source they derive. COVID-19 is likely to drive this forward.

Three Decades of International Financial Crises:
What Have We Learned and What Still Needs to Be Done?

385

So what could realistically be considered as possible areas of concrete action in the coming years in Asia? Given how loose is Asian integration in institutional infrastructure and what a tortuous affair EU institutional integration has been, deeper integration may not be expected in the absence of substantial political will, which normally only arises in the aftermath of a major disaster, such as the three crises considered in this paper or a seismic event such as Brexit or COVID-19. In fact, it was the Asian financial crisis which largely triggered much of the East Asian financial development and integration activity which has taken place over the past 20 years, in particular the evolution of EMEAP, CMIM, AMRO, ASEAN+3 Bond Market Initiative, ASEAN Capital Market Development Plan, and ASEAN Banking Integration Framework. Likewise, the Asian financial crisis caused a strong focus on financial stability and step-by-step integration across the region in domestic, regional, and international initiatives, including the regional preference for foreign exchange reserve accumulation. Those efforts served the region very well in the global financial crisis, with many of the post-Asian-financial-crisis predilections adopted globally after the global financial crisis.

Going forward, the most likely source of a major transformative event in our view are the region's large economies: the PRC and India, with ASEAN potentially a third. While the PRC has already emerged as one of the world's largest and most important economies, India is likely to also do so over the coming decades. The evolution of these two major economies and powers will pose huge challenges to the region, particularly for smaller economies, which are likely to be impacted by potential economic, financial, or political spillovers and likely contagion. Most of the region's currencies are already more directly impacted by the yuan than the dollar, given increasing trade relations with the PRC. This means that in some ways a regional currency is emerging, in the same way the pound sterling, US dollar, and the Deutsche mark did over the previous 150 years. The internationalization of the renminbi for the region is already a significant reality. Likewise, as the PRC's financial system and capital account is gradually liberalized and Chinese financial institutions expand across the region (in the same way that UK, US, and European financial institutions followed their national enterprises across the world), the PRC, in particular, will assume an ever-increasing financial role in the region. It has already stepped into many of the spaces previously occupied by US and European financial institutions in the region, in the wake of the global financial crisis. This trend may well be enhanced with the planned establishment of the PRC's central bank digital currency.

The outsize dominance of Southeast Asian financial systems by foreign institutions (in future perhaps predominantly Chinese) will require careful consideration and step-by-step processes to manage integration with the PRC, and eventually India too, and manage the consequential reactions in ASEAN. Arguably, the PRC's rise serves the same sort of incentive to regional integration which the rise of the US in the post-war period played in the evolution of the EU.

The first step in any crisis management approach is, of course, prevention, but this should also be combined with management and resolution. Cooperation in cross-border and cross-sectoral systemic risk monitoring should be revisited, and supervisory colleges should be strengthened by establishing a coherent structure for micro-prudential supervision cooperation. This should be followed with a crisis management structure and knowledgeable regulators with a role in standard setting.

CMIM is primarily a mechanism to share surplus foreign exchange reserves in order to manage international currency volatility. It is a liquidity arrangement and thus useful in managing liquidity-based banking or financial, currency, and sovereign debt crises. As such, it has a clear role and function and one which justifies further development. In particular, both expansion of resources combined with greater institutionalization should be pursued, with an expansion of AMRO and the development of a treaty-based framework for its operation.

AMRO of course extends beyond merely serving as a platform for the CMIM and plays an important preventative role. This role likewise should be expanded and augmented in the context of a treaty-based framework in order to provide more extensive and more effective macroeconomic monitoring across the region. This sort of macroeconomic monitoring provides an important preventative function in the context, particularly, of sovereign debt crises but also in the context of competitiveness or balance of payments crises and currency crises.

AMRO would thus become a regional liquidity and macroeconomic surveillance mechanism based on a treaty based framework. It could thus be opened to participation beyond ASEAN+3, potentially extending across the region. In this new role it could complement the Asian Development Bank (ADB) and the Asian Infrastructure Investment Bank as well the Bretton Woods institutions and the New Development Bank.

In addition to liquidity and macroeconomic surveillance, the global financial crisis, in particular, has highlighted the importance of financial

Three Decades of International Financial Crises:
What Have We Learned and What Still Needs to Be Done?

387

stability arrangements, particularly from the macroprudential standpoint, domestically, regionally, and internationally. Since the global financial crisis, new or reformed financial stability and macroprudential arrangements have been put in place, including the FSB internationally and the European Systemic Risk Board in the EU.

Apart from the widening of the Chiang Mai Initiative, the region should consider having a regional systemic risk council supported by country central banks in the mode of the European Systemic Risk Board. The latter is backed by the ECB and it operates on the basis of an EU statute, although it is a soft-law body (i.e., it has no standing under EU law). The responsibilities of an "Asian Systemic Risk Council" (or at least an "ASEAN Systemic Risk Council") would fit very well in an Asian framework for systemic risk detection, including serving warning and signaling functions, but will require Asian central banks to participate and share data. Initially this would be an arrangement which would not entail any loss of sovereignty but instead only the sharing of confidential information and the issuance of confidential warnings to members. It could be included within the institutional expansion of AMRO. However, EMEAP may well in time prove to be a more appropriate institutional environment, given its history, related activities, and deep personal relationships between central banks from the more developed financial jurisdictions of the region.

Such an Asian Systemic Risk Council would be particularly timely given the challenge of the rise of FinTech across the region, both from the standpoint of cybersecurity and potential digital identity and electronic know-your-customer utilities to the rapid expansion particularly of Chinese e-commerce and social media firms such as Alibaba and Tencent into finance across the region—the so-called "TechFins" (Zetzsche et al. 2018). The region is already a leader in this area and is likely to face many demands to develop harmonized frameworks to allow FinTech and TechFin firms to expand across the region, particularly in the aftermath of COVID-19. At the same time, these firms not only bring opportunities, they bring risks. This has been most clearly demonstrated by the rise of cybersecurity concerns across the region, most pointedly in the Bangladesh central bank robbery of 2016 and related international concerns, with the result of restricting access of regional financial institutions to international networks through historical correspondent banking relationships.

In addition, given shadow banking's importance and cross-border links (including through FinTechs and TechFins), a future Asian Systemic Risk

Council would have a valuable role as a systemic risk data consolidator and impartial monitor.

Further, a future Asian Systemic Risk Council could serve as a secretariat for regional colleges of supervisors. For banks active in the region, on a cross-border basis, colleges of supervisors ought to be strengthened and the Asian Systemic Risk Council could coordinate the work of colleges. When a crisis hits, such a body could prove invaluable, especially when it comes to coordinated bank rescues or resolutions on a subsidiary-by-subsidiary basis. Naturally, it will not involve any form of burden sharing, but it could have evolved as a trusted venue for information sharing and could be utilized as trusted venue for rescue or resolution cooperation.

The Asian Systemic Risk Council could also become the principal forum for consultation and the coordinated feeding back of policy responses to Basel and the FSB of regional considerations.

In domestic implementation of international and regional financial regulatory standards, ADB itself would be the lead—as it largely already is today—in supporting domestic and regional reform processes. Further, ADB, in cooperation with the IMF and the World Bank, must become a major agent of change in bank corporate governance cultures across the region, augmenting bank management accountability.

In resolution, too-big-to-fail avoidance of bail-ins on a systemic basis does not mean that creditors (with the exception of depositors) should always escape lightly. Asian jurisdictions ought to introduce or upgrade bank resolution regimes and not overly rely on bailouts (at least in principle).

Finally, a culture of transparency, openness, and cooperation ought to be pursued in all future integration initiatives in the Asian market. Since the risks are increasingly regional (and global), purely country-based responses may prove largely obsolete when a cross-border crisis hits. Recognizing that financial stability in the region can easily fall victim to "tragedy-of-the commons" behaviors is an important first step. Like trade and environmental protection, regional financial stability closely binds the prosperity of Asian nations—as evidenced most clearly in the Asia financial crisis. Therefore, it offers a very fertile ground to augment interaction between national regulatory authorities, central banks, and governments in Asia, giving rise to a wider economic cooperation impetus for the benefit of all nations in the region.

References

Arensman, R. 1997. Economy Stall in Thailand Has a Familiar Look. *The Denver Post*. 2 November.

Arner, D. W. 2007. *Financial Stability, Economic Growth and the Role of Law*. Cambridge: Cambridge University Press.

——. 2009. The Global Credit Crisis of 2008: Causes and Consequences. *The International Lawyer*. 43 (1). pp. 91–136.

——. 2011. Adaptation and Resilience in Global Financial Regulation. *North Carolina Law Review*. 89 (5). pp. 1579–628.

Arner, D. W., E. Avgouleas, and E. Gibson. 2017. Overstating Moral Hazard: Lessons from Two Decades of Banking Crises. *University of Hong Kong Faculty of Law Research Paper Series*. No. 2017/003.

Arner, D. W., J. N. Barberis, and R. P. Buckley. 2016. The Evolution of FinTech: A New Post-Crisis Paradigm? *Georgetown Journal of International Law*. 47 (4). pp. 1271–319. https://www.ssrn.com/abstract=2676553

——. 2017. FinTech, RegTech and the Reconceptualisation of Financial Regulation. *Northwestern Journal of International Law and Business*. 37 (3): 371-414. https://www.ssrn.com/abstract=2847806

Arner, D. W., R. P. Buckley, and D. Zetzsche. 2018. *FinTech for Financial Inclusion: A Framework for Digital Financial Transformation*. An Alliance for Financial Inclusion Special Report. Kuala Lumpur.

ASEAN+3 Macroeconomic Research Office (AMRO). 2007. ASEAN+3 Region: 20 Years after the Asian Financial Crisis. In AMRO. *ASEAN+3 Regional Economic Outlook 2017*. Singapore: ASEAN+3 Macroeconomic Research Office.

Asian Development Bank (ADB). 2012. *Asian Economic Integration Monitor*. Manila: ADB.

Avgouleas, E. 2000. The Harmonisation of Rules of Conduct in EU Financial Markets: Economic Analysis, Subsidiarity and Investor Protection. *European Law Journal*. 6 (1). pp. 72–92.

——. 2009. The Global Financial Crisis, Behavioural Finance and Financial Regulation: In Search of a New Orthodoxy." *Journal of Corporate Law Studies*. 9 (1). pp. 23–59.

——. 2010. *The Reform of 'Too-Big-To-Fail' Bank: A New Regulatory Model for the Institutional Separation of 'Casino' from 'Utility' Banking.* Paper presented at the 7th EUROFRAME Conference on Economic Policy Issues in the European Union. 11–12 June. University of Amsterdam.

——. 2012a. *Eurozone Crisis and Sovereign Debt Restructuring: Intellectual Fallacies and New Lines of Research.* Paper presented at the Society of International Economic Law: 3rd Biennial Global Conference. Centre for International Law and Faculty of Law, National University of Singapore. July.

——. 2012b. *Governance of Global Financial Markets: The Law, the Economics, the Politics.* Cambridge: Cambridge University Press.

——. 2015. Bank Leverage Ratios and Financial Stability: A Micro- and Macroprudential Perspective. *Levy Economics Institute Working Paper Series*. No. WP 849.

——. 2016a. Central Banks, Financial Stability and Legal Liability—The Central Banking Contract. Keynote address to the Annual Conference of the Society of Legal Scholars, Banking and Financial Law Section, Oxford University. 6 September.

——. 2016b. Fundamentals of Bank Supervision and the Lender of Last Resort in the Post-2008 Era: A Critical Appraisal and Forward Looking Recommendations. *University of Edinburgh School of Law Legal Studies Research Paper Series*. No. 2016/24.

——. 2016c. Large Systemic Banks and Fractional Reserve Banking. Chapter 14 in R. Buckley, E. Avgouleas, and D. Arner, eds. *Reconceptualising Global Finance and its Regulation.* Cambridge: Cambridge University Press.

Avgouleas, E. and D. Arner. 2017. Eurozone Debt Crisis and the European Banking Union: 'Hard Choices', 'Intolerable Dilemmas' and the Question of Sovereignty. *The International Lawyer*. 50 (1). pp. 29–67.

Avgouleas, E., C. Goodhart, and D. Schoenmaker. 2013. Bank Resolution Plans as a Catalyst for Global Financial Reform. *Journal of Financial Stability* 9 (2). pp. 210–18.

Avgouleas, E., D. Arner, and U. Asharaff. 2014. Regional Financial Arrangements Lessons from the Eurozone Crisis for East Asia. In I. J. Azis and H. S. Shin, eds. *Global Shock, Asian Vulnerability and Financial Reform*. Cheltenham: Edward Elgar.

Bank for International Settlements (BIS). 2011. Weathering Financial Crises: Bond Markets in Asia and the Pacific. Paper presented at the BOJ-BIS High Level Seminar on "The Development on Regional Capital Markets." 21–22 November.

———. 2016. Triennial Central Bank Survey of Foreign Exchange and OTC Derivative Markets in 2016. 11 December. http://www.bis.org/publ/rpfx16.htm.

Bénassy-Quéré, A., X. Ragot, and G. Wolff. 2016. Which Fiscal Union for the Euro Area? *Bruegel Policy Contribution*. Issue 2016/05. 12 February.

Bergsten, C. F. and J. F. Kirkegaard. 2012. The Coming Resolution of the European Crisis. *Peterson Institute for International Economics Policy Brief Series*. No. 12-1.

Blinder, A. S. 1999. Eight Steps to a New Financial Order. *Foreign Affairs*. 78 (5). pp. 50–63.

Blustein, P. 1997. Investors Reconsider Big Emerging-Markets Bets. *The Washington Post*. 20 July.

Brunnermeier, M. K. 2009. Deciphering the Liquidity and Credit Crunch 2007–2008. *Journal of Economic Perspectives*. 23 (1). pp. 77–100.

Brunnermeier, M. K., A. Crockett, C. Goodhart, A. D. Persaud, and H. S. Shin. 2009. *The Fundamental Principles of Financial Regulation: Geneva Reports on the World Economy 11*. Geneva: International Center for Monetary and Banking Studies.

Brunnermeier, M. K. and L. H. Pedersen. 2009. Market Liquidity and Funding Liquidity. *Review of Financial Studies*. 22 (6). pp. 2201–238.

Buckley, R. P. 1999. *Emerging Markets Debt: An Analysis of the Secondary Market*. London: Kluwer.

Buckley, R. P. and D. Arner. 2011. *From Crisis to Crisis: The Global Financial System and Regulatory Failure*. London: Kluwer.

Bustelo, P., C. Garcia, and I. Olivié. 1999. Global and Domestic Factors of Financial Crises in Emerging Economies: Lessons from the East Asian Episodes (1997–1999). *ICEI Working Paper Series*. No. 16. Madrid: Instituto Complutense De Estudios Internacionales.

Caballero, R. J. and A. Krishnamurthy. 2009. Global Imbalances and Financial Fragility. *NBER Working Paper Series*. No. 14688.

Chang, R. and A. Velasco. 1998. The 1997–98 Financial Crisis: Why in Asia? Why Not in Latin America? Unpublished paper. http://citeseerx.ist.psu.edu/viewdoc/download?doi=10.1.1.468.5775&rep=rep1&type=pdf.

Chow, H. 1997. Crawling from the Wreckage. *Emerging Markets Investor*. 4 (15).

Cranston, R., E. Avgouleas, K. van Zwieten, C. Hare, and T. van Sante. 2018. *Principles of Banking Law*. Oxford: Oxford University Press. Chapter 2.

Dawson, F. G. 1990. *The First Latin American Debt Crisis: The City of London and the 1822–1825 Loan Bubble*. New Haven: Yale University press.

Dornbusch, R. 1997. A Bail-Out Won't Do the Trick in Korea. *Business Week*. 8 December.

European Central Bank (ECB). 2012. Technical Features of Outright Monetary Transactions. Press release. 6 September.

Eichengreen, B. 2003. What to Do with the Chiang Mai Initiative. *Asian Economic Papers*. 2 (1). pp. 1–49.

Eichengreen, B. and R. Hausmann. 1999. Exchange Rates and Financial Fragility. *NBER Working Paper Series*. No 7418. November.

European Union (EU). 2012. *European Economic Forecast: Autumn 2012*. Commission Directorate-General for Economic and Financial Affairs.

Feldstein, M. 1999. *A Self-Help Guide for Emerging Markets*. Foreign Affairs. March/April.

Financial Stability Board (FSB). 2011. *Key Attributes of Effective Resolution Regimes for Financial Institutions*. FSB paper.

Fischer, S. 1988. The Asian Crisis: A View from the IMF. Speech delivered at the Midwinter Conference of the Banker's Association of Foreign Trade. Washington, DC 22 Jan.

Freixas, X., L. Laeven, and J. L. Peydró. 2015. *Systemic Risk, Crises, and Macroprudential Regulation*. Boston: MIT Press.

Friedman, M. and A. J. Schwartz. 1963. *A Monetary History of the United States, 1867–1960*. Princeton: Princeton University Press.

Furuoka, F., B. Lim, C. Jikunan, and M. C. Lo. 2012. Economic Crisis and Response: Case Study of Malaysia's Response to Asian Financial Crisis. *Journal of Contemporary Eastern Asia*. 11 (1). pp. 43–56.

Garicano, L. and R. M. Lastra. 2010. Towards a New Architecture for Financial Stability: Seven Principles. *Journal of International Economic Law*. 13 (3). pp. 597–621.

Garran, R. 1997. "Korea Crisis." The Australian, November 19.

Geanakoplos, J. 2010. Solving the Present Crisis and Managing the Leverage Cycle. *Federal Reserve Bank of New York Economic Policy Review*. August. pp. 101–31.

Gibson, E. C. 2014. Managing Financial Stability and Liquidity Risks in Hong Kong's Banking System: What is the Optimum Supervisory Model? PhD dissertation. University of Hong Kong.

Gochoco-Bautista, M. S, S. Oh, and S. G. Rhee. 2000. In the Eye of the Asian Financial Maelstrom: Banking Sector Reforms in the Asia-Pacific Region. In Asian Development Bank. *Rising to the Challenge in Asia: A Study of Financial Markets*. Manila.

Gorton, G. B. and A. Metrick. 2009. Securitized Banking and the Run on Repo. *NBER Working Paper Series*. No. 15223.

Goswami, M. and S. Sharma. 2011. The Development of Local Debt Markets in Asia. *IMF Working Paper Series*. No. 11/132.

Hanson, S. G., A. K. Kashyap, and J. C. Stein. 2011. A Macroprudential Approach to Financial Regulation. *The Journal of Economic Perspectives*. 25 (1). pp. 3–28.

Harwood, A., M. Pomerleano, and R. E. Litan. 1999. The Crisis in Emerging Financial Markets: A World Bank-Brookings Conference Report. *Brookings*. 1 May. http://www.brookings.edu/research/the-crisis-in-emerging-financial-markets-a-world-bank-group-brookings-conference-report/.

Hsiao, F. S. T. and M. W. Hsiao. 2001. Capital Flows and Exchange Rates. Journal of Asian Economics. 12 (3). pp. 353–81.

International Monetary Fund (IMF). 1998. *World Economic Outlook*. Washington, DC: IMF.

——. 2000. *Recovery from the Asian Crisis and the Role of the IMF*. June. https://www.imf.org/external/np/exr/ib/2000/062300.htm.

Jones, C. 2015. European Central Bank Unleashes Quantitative Easing. *FT.com*. 22 January.

Julian, C. C. 2000. The Impact of the Asian Economic Crisis in Thailand. *Managerial Finance*. 26 (4): 39–48.

Jungjaturapit, K. 2008. Has Thailand Learned from the Asian Crisis of 1997? Major Themes in Economics. 10 (5). pp. 35–64.

Kaeochotchuangkul, I., T. Benjapongsapun, and V. Ammarapala. n.d. *Lessons Learned from the European Union (EU) Debt Crisis to the ASEAN Economic Community (AEC)*. Thammasat University.

Kawai, M. 2003. Bank and Corporate Restructuring in Crisis-Affected East Asia: from Systemic Collapse to Reconstruction. In G. de Brouwer, ed. *Financial Markets and Policies in East Asia*. London: Routledge.

Three Decades of International Financial Crises:
What Have We Learned and What Still Needs to Be Done?

395

Keys, B., T. Mukherjee, A. Seru, and V. Vig. 2010. Did Securitization Lead to Lax Screening? Evidence from Subprime Mortgage Loans. *Quarterly Journal of Monetary Economics*. 125 (1). pp. 307–62.

Kihwan, K. 2006. *The 1997–98 Korean Financial Crisis: Causes, Policy Response, and Lessons*. Speech delivered at the High Level Seminar on Crisis Prevention in Emerging Markets. IMF and the Government of Singapore, Singapore. 10–11 July. https://www.imf.org/external/np/seminars/eng/2006/cpem/pdf/kihwan.pdf.

Kindleberger, C. 1978. *Manias, Panics and Crashes: A History of Financial Crises*. New York: Macmillan.

Laplamwanit, N. 1999. *A Good Look at the Thai Financial Crisis in 1997–98*. Paper. http://www.columbia.edu/cu/thai/html/financial97_98.html.

Lastra, R. M. and J. V. Louis. 2013. European Economic and Monetary Union: History, Trends and Prospects. *Yearbook of European Law*: 32 (1). pp. 57–206.

Lee, E. 1999. The Debate on the Causes of the Asian Crisis: Crony Capitalism Versus International System Failure. *Internationale Politik und Gesellschaft*. 2 (1999): 162–167.

Liu, Q., P. Lejot, and D. Arner. 2013. *Finance in Asia: Institutions, Regulation and Policy*. Abington: Routledge.

Liu, W. 2007. Short-Term Foreign Funds, a Comparative Study between China and Victim Countries of 1997 Asian Financial Crisis. *Global Journal of Finance and Banking Issues*. 1 (1). pp. 41–55.

Marichal, C. 1989. *A Century of Debt Crisis in Latin America: From Independence to the Great Depression, 1820-1930*. Princeton, NJ: Princeton University Press.

Masciantonio, S. and A. Tiseno. 2012. *The Rise and Fall of Universal Banking: Ups and Downs of a Sample of Large and Complex Financial Institutions Since the Late '90s*. 74th International Atlantic Economic Conference. 14 October.

Meyer, L. H. 1999. Lessons from the Asian Crisis: A Central Banker's Perspective. *Levy Economics Institute Working Paper Series*. No. 276. August.

Minsky, H. P. 1992. The Financial Instability Hypothesis. *Jerome Levy Economics Institute of Bard College Working Paper Series*. No. 74.

Mishkin, F. S. 2010. Over the Cliff: From the Subprime to the Global Financial Crisis. *NBER Working Paper Series*. No. 16609.

Noerlina and S. C. Dewi. 2003. Asian Financial Crisis: Overview of Asian Crisis and Recovery Progress. *The Winners*. 4 (1). pp. 13–17.

Novoa, A., J. Scarlata, and J. Sole. 2009. Procyclicality and Fair Value Accounting. *IMF Working Paper Series*. No. WP/09/39.

Obstfeld, M. and K. Rogoff. 1995. The Mirage of Fixed Exchange Rates. *Journal of Economic Perspectives*. 9 (4). pp. 79–81.

Padoa-Schioppa, T. 2000. *The Road to Monetary Union in Europe: The Emperor, the Kings and the Genies*. Oxford: Oxford University Press.

Park, C. Y. 2016. Developing Local Currency Bond Markets in Asia. *ADB Economics Working Paper Series*. No. 495. Manila.

Passell, P. 1997. Economic Scene; For a New Generation of Asian Tigers, A Harsh Currency Lesson. *The New York Times*. 24 July.

Pettis, M. 1998a. Can Financial Crises be Prevented? Unfinished paper. June.

———. 1998b. "The New Dance of the Millions: The Asian Crisis." *Challenge, Taylor and Francis Journals*. 41 (4). pp. 90–100.

Phuvanatnaranubala, T. 2009. Implementation Plan for ASEAN Capital Markets Integration. Speech delivered at the 2nd OECD Southeast Asian Regional Forum. Bangkok. 27 April.

Poli, E. 2014. Is the European Model Relevant for ASEAN? *Istituto Affari Internazionali Working Paper Series*. No. 14/13.

Three Decades of International Financial Crises:
What Have We Learned and What Still Needs to Be Done?

397

Rajan, R. 2005. Has Financial Development Made the World Riskier? *Proceedings*. Federal Reserve Bank of Kansas City. August. pp. 313–369.

Rajan, R. G. and L. Zingales. 1998. Which Capitalism? Lessons from the East Asian Crisis. *Journal of Applied Corporate Finance*. 11 (3). pp. 40–48.

Rana, P. B., W. Chia, and Y. Jinjarak. 2012. Monetary Integration in ASEAN+3: A Perception Survey of Opinion Leaders. *Journal of Asian Economics*. 23 (1). pp. 1–12.

Ranta, P. 2017. Malaysia's and Indonesia's Recovery from the Asian Financial Crisis—Comparison and Causes behind the Recovery. Bachelor of Business Thesis. Metropolia University of Applied Sciences. Helsinki.

Reinhart, C. M. and K. S. Rogoff. 2011. From Financial Crash to Debt Crisis. *American Economic Review*. 101 (5). pp. 1676–1706.

Reserve Bank of Australia. 2003. Bond Market Development in East Asia. *Reserve Bank of Australia Bulletin*. http://www.rba.gov.au/publications/bulletin/2003/dec/1.html.

Richardson, D. 2017. *Asian Financial Crisis*. The Parliament of Australia. http://www.aph.gov.au/About_Parliament/Parliamentary_Departments/Parliamentary_Library/Publications_Archive/CIB/CIB9798/98cib23.

Schoenmaker, D. 2011. The Financial Trilemma. *Discussion Paper*. Duisenberg School of Finance Amsterdam & Finance Department, Vrije Universiteit Amsterdam, Tinbergen Institute.

Schwarcz, S. 2008. Disclosure's Failure in the Subprime Mortgage Crisis. *Utah Law Review*. pp. 1109–122.

——. 2009a. Understanding the 'Subprime' Financial Crisis. *South Carolina Law Review*. 60 (3). pp. 549–72.

——. 2009b. Conflicts and Financial Collapse: The Problem of Secondary-Management Agency Costs. *Yale Journal on Regulation*. 26 (2). pp. 457–70.

Schwartz, H. 2002. The Long(term) and Short(term) of the Asian Financial Crises. In R. Starrs, ed. *Nations Under Siege: Globalization and Nationalism in Asia*. London: Macmillan.

Segoviano, M., B. Jones, P. Lindner, and J. Blankenheim. 2013. Securitization: Lessons Learned and the Road Ahead. *IMF Working Paper Series*. No. WP/13/255.

Senhadji, A. S. and C. Collyns. 2002. Lending Booms, Real Estate Bubbles and the Asian Crisis. *IMF Working Paper Series*. No. 02/20.

Seth, R., A. Sarkar, and S. K. Mohanty. 2001. Loan Flows, Contagion Effects, and East Asian Crisis. *Journal of Emerging Markets*. 6 (3). pp. 42–54.

Sherlock, S. 1988. Crisis in Indonesia: Economy, Society and Politics. *Current Issues Brief*. Parliament of Australia.

Singh, A. and A. Zammit. 2006. Corporate Governance, Crony Capitalism and Economics: Should the US Business Model Replace the Asian Way of 'Doing Business?" *Corporate Governance: An International Review*. 14 (4). pp. 220–233.

Soulard, A. 1994. The Role of Multilateral Financial Institutions in Bringing Developing Companies to U.S. Markets. *Fordham International Law Journal*. 17 (5). pp. 145–151.

Stallings, B. 1987. *Banker to the Third World: U.S. Portfolio Investment in Latin America, 1900–1986*. Oakland, CA: University of California Press.

Stevens, G. 2007. The Asian Crisis: A Retrospective. Speech delivered at the Anika Foundation Luncheon Supported by the Australian Business Economists and Macquarie Bank. Sydney. 18 July.

Sugisaki, S. 1998. Economic Crises in Asia. Address at the 1998 Harvard Asia Business Conference. Harvard Business School. 30 January.

Takayasu, K. and Y. Yokoe. 2000. Non-Performing Loan Issue Crucial to Asia's Economic Resurgence. *RIM* 44. https://www.jri.co.jp/english/periodical/rim/1999/RIMe199903npl/.

Taylor, M. W., D. W. Arner, and E. C. Gibson. 2019. Central Banks' New Macroprudential Consensus. In D. G. Mayes, P. L. Siklos, and J. Sturn, eds. *The Oxford Handbook of the Economics of Central Banking*. Oxford: Oxford University Press.

Three Decades of International Financial Crises:
What Have We Learned and What Still Needs to Be Done?

399

Terada-Hagiwara, A. and G. O. Pasadilla. 2004. Experience of Asian Asset Management Companies: Do They Increase Moral Hazard? – Evidence from Thailand. *ERD Working Paper Series*. No. 55. Manila.

Thygesen, N. 2003. Comments on the Political Economy of Financial Harmonisation in Europe. In J. Kremer, D. Schoenmaker and P. Wierts, eds. *Financial Supervision in Europe*. Cheltenham: Edward Elgar.

Viscio, I. 1998. The Recent Experience with Capital Flows to Emerging Market Economies. *OECD Economic Outlook*. 65 (1). pp. 177–95.

Wang, H. 1999. The Asian Financial Crisis and Financial Reforms in China. *Pacific Review*. 12 (4). pp. 537–56.

Weber, R., D. Arner, E. Gibson, and S. Baumann. 2014. Addressing Systemic Risk: Financial Regulatory Design. *Texas International Law Journal*. 49 (149). pp. 149–200.

Welch, J. H. and D. McLeod. 1993. The Costs and Benefits of Fixed Dollar Exchange Rates in Latin America. *Economic and Financial Policy Review*. 1. pp. 31–44.

Welle-Strand, A., P. Chen, and G. Ball. 2011. East Asia. 28 (4). pp. 329–50.

Wong, R. Y. C., E. C. Chang, A. K. F. Siu, Y. F. Luk, P. S. Tso, and W. C. Kwan. 2010. *Asian Financial Crisis: Causes and Development*. Hong Kong Institute of Economics and Business Strategy, The University of Hong Kong.

World Bank. 1997. *Global Development Finance (Vol. 1)*. Washington, DC: World Bank.

———. 1998. *Global Development Finance (Vol. 1)*. Washington, DC: World Bank.

Wouters, J. and T. Ramopoulos. 2012. The G20 and Global Economic Governance: Lessons from Multilevel European Governance? *Journal of International Economic Law*. 15 (3). pp. 751–75.

Zetzsche, D. A., R. P. Buckley, J. N. Barberis, and D. W. Arner. 2017. Regulating a Revolution: From FinTech and Regulatory Sandboxes to RegTech and

Smart Regulation. *Fordham Journal of Corporate & Financial Law.* 23 (1). pp. 31–103.

——. 2018. From FinTech to TechFin: The Regulatory Challenges of Data-Driven Finance. *New York University Journal of Law & Business.* 14 (2). pp. 393–446.

Financial Integration in Asia and the Pacific: Challenges and Prospects

10

Cyn-Young Park, Peter Rosenkranz, and Mara Claire Tayag[1]

Regional cooperation and integration (RCI) is an important strategy for attaining national development goals. It can be critical in accelerating economic growth, reducing poverty and economic disparities, raising productivity and employment, and strengthening institutions. It narrows gaps between the developing member countries of the Asian Development Bank (ADB) by deepening trade integration and building intraregional supply chains and stronger financial links, enabling slow-moving economies to speed their own expansion. ADB, in approving the RCI Operational Plan for 2016–2020, recognized RCI as an important platform for developing member countries to work together to unlock their vast economic potential.

In 2017, ADB's Asian Economic Integration Report unveiled a new composite index—the Asia-Pacific Regional Cooperation and Integration Index (ARCII)—to track progress of RCI in Asia and the Pacific.[2] Understanding where the region stands on RCI is an important step toward unlocking economic potential and maximizing its benefits. Policy makers also need mechanisms to monitor and evaluate progress against set goals. The ARCII aims to assess the extent to which each economy is integrated into the region, to identify the strengths and weaknesses of multiple regional integration drivers, and to track progress in a comprehensive and systematic manner. Reflecting the multifaceted nature of RCI, the ARCII combines 26 indicators categorized into six RCI dimensions: (i) trade and investment, (ii) money and finance, (iii) regional value chains, (iv) infrastructure and connectivity, (v) movement of people, and (vi) institutional and social integration. In turn,

[1] The authors thank Monica Melchor, Ana Kristel Lapid, Clemence Faith Cruz, and Pilar Dayag for their excellent research assistance.

[2] In this chapter, Asia and the Pacific (hereinafter referred to as Asia) includes ADB's 45 developing members plus Australia, Japan, and New Zealand. For a more detailed discussion of the ARCII methodology and concepts, see Chapter 7: Asia-Pacific Regional Cooperation and Integration Index of ADB. 2017. *Asian Economic Integration Report 2017*. Manila.

the ARCII allows comparative analysis of the regional integration process by different countries and subregions in these six RCI dimensions.

Figures 10.1 and 10.2 show RCI progress varies by subregion and by dimension. While the region has maintained stable overall ARCII over the past decade, Central Asia, East Asia, and South Asia have made progress. By dimension, trade and investment and movement of people appear to be the most forceful and stable foundation for regional integration in Asia. Over time, the infrastructure and connectivity dimension has strengthened as a major contributor. However, together with institutional and social integration, the money and finance dimension has shown very low integration.

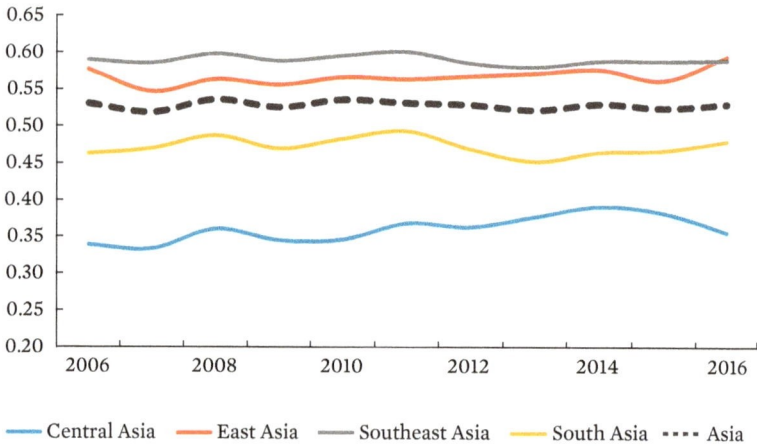

Figure 10.1: Asia-Pacific Regional Cooperation and Integration Index, 2006–2016

Source: Park, C. and R. Claveria. 2018. Constructing the Asia-Pacific Regional Integration Index: A Panel Approach. *ADB Economics Working Paper Series*. No. 544. Manila: Asian Development Bank.

Financial integration, in theory, offers many benefits, among which are better consumption smoothing through international risk sharing, more efficient allocation of capital for investment, and improvements in macroeconomic and financial discipline. Potential gains of financial integration such as allocation efficiency and risk diversification can be larger where financial integration is global. With free flow of capital and low transaction costs, global markets

Figure 10.2: Asia-Pacific Regional Cooperation and Integration Index by Dimension

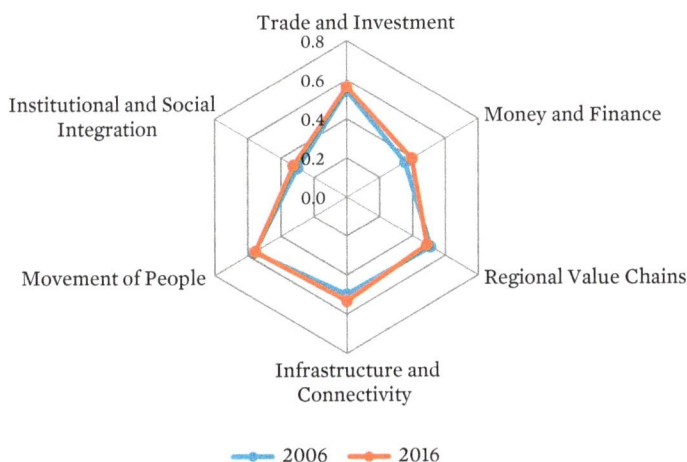

Note: The index combines 26 indicators categorized into six regional cooperation and integration dimensions: (i) trade and investment, (ii) money and finance, (iii) regional value chains, (iv) infrastructure and connectivity, (v) movement of people, and (vi) institutional and social integration.

Source: Park, C. and R. Claveria. 2018. Constructing the Asia-Pacific Regional Integration Index: A Panel Approach. *ADB Economics Working Paper Series*. No. 544. Manila: Asian Development Bank.

can become deeper, more liquid, and more diversified. However, financial integration is less than complete. This is largely due to market frictions that include high transaction costs and information asymmetry, while past crisis episodes serve to highlight the risk of cross-border financial contagion in practice.

Earlier studies also noted some important hurdles to financial integration in Asia. First, Forbes and Rigobon (2002) noted Asia lacks an anchor country or financial centers that can mediate financial transactions within the region. Although Singapore and Hong Kong, China are important financial centers in East Asia and Southeast Asia, they have served the clients of major international capital markets rather than local capital markets, and so have done more to help the region's financial markets become globally integrated than to integrate with one another. Second, Eichengreen and Park (2005) provided evidence that a lower level of capital market liberalization and the underdevelopment of financial markets and institutions, particularly in potential lending countries, explained most of the difference between intra-Europe and intra-East Asia integration in cross-border bank lending. Third, to enhance regional market integration, Asia may need further financial and monetary cooperation for exchange rate and financial stability. Chelley-Steeley and Steeley (1999) presented evidence that the abolition of exchange controls helped equity markets become more closely integrated in Europe. Danthine, Giavazzi, and von Thadden (2000) and Fratzscher (2001) also provided evidence that the introduction of the euro has deepened financial integration in the eurozone.

The case for the regional integration of financial markets centers on how it allows the region's economies to benefit from allocation efficiency and risk diversification. Although the benefits may increase where integration is global, limited regional integration compared to global integration may also help contain the risk of unfettered financial flows. Investors may be more familiar with regional financial assets—with similar economic structure and investment culture—and find it easier to assess related risks. At the same time, the availability of regional financial products and services—for example through local currency bond markets—could help improve financial resilience to external shocks by channeling savings to fund the region's investment needs. Finally, deeper trade integration among geographically close economies can improve information sharing and add peer pressure to promote financial development and stability.

This chapter offers an overview of the progress of financial integration in Asia since the 1997–1998 Asian financial crisis, including during the 2008–2009 global financial crisis, and discusses challenges and prospects of the region's financial integration. The trends and patterns of financial integration in Asia are assessed using measures based on quantity and price, and the degree of financial integration is analyzed to estimate the potential contagion effects from regional and global shocks in regional equity and bond markets. Policy implications for ADB financial sector operations are also analyzed.

Trends and Patterns of Financial Integration in Asia

Both price and quantity measures can be used to assess the degree of financial integration in Asia since the 1990s. Typically, increased international financial flows, cross-border asset holdings, and convergence in asset prices suggest deeper financial integration. We estimate the degrees of financial integration of Asian economies at regional and global levels.

Trends of Financial Openness and Financial Flows

A wave of financial deregulation and capital account liberalization since the 1990s has led capital flows to emerging market economies to surge, driven by private capital from a variety of sources. Asia has been no exception. The region attracted around 15% of total global financial inflows leading up to the 1997–1998 crisis. After falling sharply to –15.9% in 1998 (reflecting the crisis effect), the share recovered quickly, averaging 9.0% from 2003 to 2007. Although the share fell again during the global financial crisis, it recovered sharply and surpassed levels achieved before the crisis, reaching a peak of 33.7% of total global financial inflows in 2013. Since then inflows to Asia have declined, settling at about 12% of the global total in 2017.

Figures 10.3a and 10.3b show the trends of *de jure* and *de facto* financial openness in Asia. Figure 10.3a presents the average Chinn-Ito index (KAOPEN) across Asia, which is an index measuring an economy's degree of capital account openness.[3] Figure 10.3b presents the sum of foreign assets and liabilities as a percentage of GDP. Although some Asian economies still maintain various types of controls on cross-border capital flows, financial openness overall has increased with growing liberalization of capital accounts in many regional economies.

Asia has been able to attract an increasing share of global foreign direct investment (FDI) inflows, from the annual average of 18.5% of the global FDI inflows for 1990–1994 to 26.6% for 2015–2017 (Figure 10.4a). Portfolio investment flows to the region rose from 6.3% to 16.1% between the two periods (Figure 10.4b). Other investment inflows by nonresidents are much more volatile, recording large net outflows during times of financial turmoil during 1995–1999 and 2010–2014, underlining the region's financial vulnerability associated with increasing cross-border banking flows (Figure 10.4c).

---

[3] The index was introduced in Chinn and Ito (2006). KAOPEN is based on the binary dummy variables that codify the tabulation of restrictions on cross-border financial transactions reported in the IMF's Annual Report on Exchange Arrangements and Exchange Restrictions. This index takes on higher values the more open the country is to cross-border capital transactions. By construction, the series has a mean of zero.

Figure 10.3: Measures of Financial Openness—Asia

(a) Average Chinn-Ito Index: Capital Account Openness

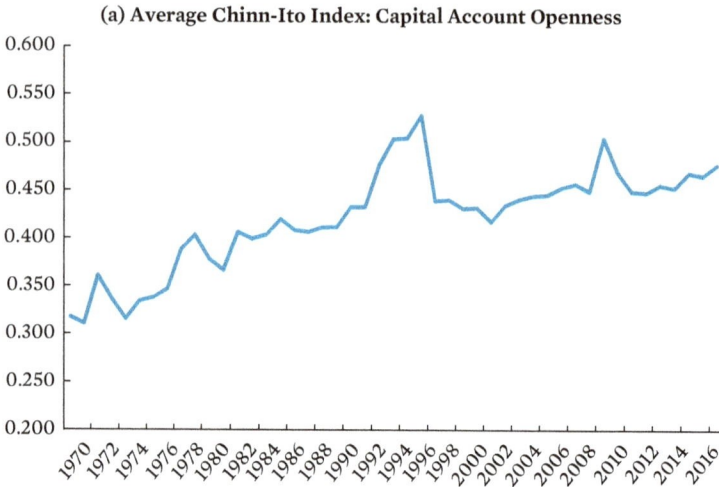

Source: Chinn, M.D. and H. Ito. 2006. What Matters for Financial Development? Capital Controls, Institutions, and Interactions. *Journal of Development Economics* 81(1): pp. 163–192.

(b) Total Foreign Assets and Liabilities—Asia (% of GDP)

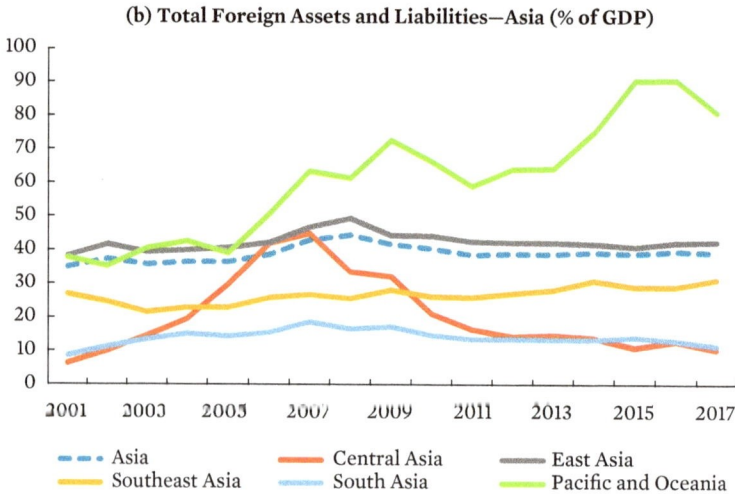

GDP = gross domestic product.

Sources: International Monetary Fund. International Financial Statistics. data.imf.org/IFS (accessed November 2018); and national sources.

Figure 10.4: Nonresident Financial Flows to Asia, By Type
(% of total global inflows, annual average)

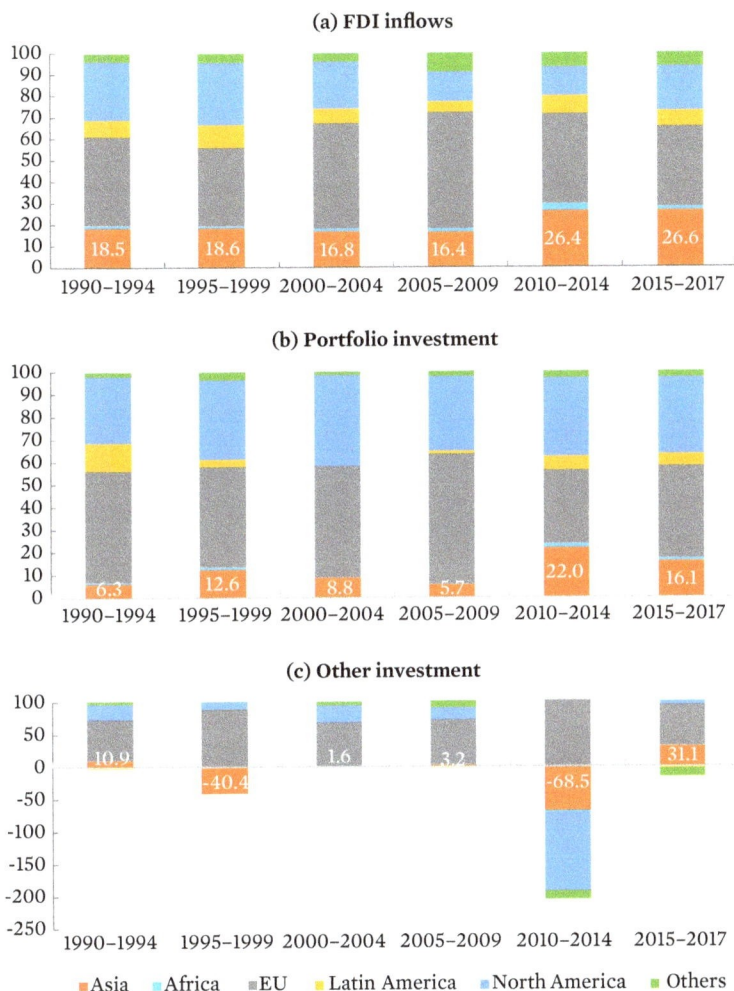

(a) FDI inflows

	1990–1994	1995–1999	2000–2004	2005–2009	2010–2014	2015–2017
Asia	18.5	18.6	16.8	16.4	26.4	26.6

(b) Portfolio investment

	1990–1994	1995–1999	2000–2004	2005–2009	2010–2014	2015–2017
Asia	6.3	12.6	8.8	5.7	22.0	16.1

(c) Other investment

	1990–1994	1995–1999	2000–2004	2005–2009	2010–2014	2015–2017
Asia	10.9	-40.4	1.6	3.2	-68.5	31.1

■ Asia ■ Africa ■ EU ■ Latin America ■ North America ■ Others

EU = European Union, FDI = foreign direct investment.

Notes: Based on Balance of Payments and International Investment Position Manual Sixth Edition (BPM6). Portfolio investment refers to the sum of equity and debt security investment. Other investment is a residual category that includes currency and deposits; loans (including use of IMF credit and loans from the IMF); nonlife insurance technical reserves, life insurance and annuities entitlements, pension entitlements, and provisions for calls under standardized guarantees; trade credit and advances; other accounts receivable; and special drawing rights allocations.

Source: International Monetary Fund. Balance of Payments Statistics. https://www.imf.org/external/datamapper/datasets/BOP (accessed November 2018).

Patterns of Cross-Border Financial Asset Holdings

Asia's growing financial integration, both regionally and globally, is underpinned by continued strengthening and expansion of cross-border financial linkages. Cross-border asset holdings[4] in Asia increased from 2009 to 2018 (Figure 10.5) by $7.6 trillion, from $9.8 trillion in 2009 to $17.4 trillion in 2018.

The share of intraregional assets held within Asia also rose slightly, from 19.4% in 2009 to 24.0% in 2018. Intraregional shares for all asset classes, except portfolio equity, increased. As a share of total cross-border assets, portfolio equity holdings increased significantly, from 17.1% in 2009 to 24.0% in 2018.

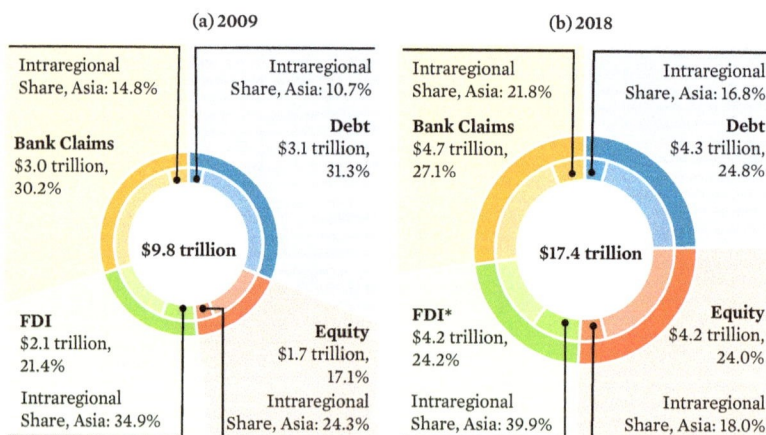

Figure 10.5: Cross-Border Assets—Asia

* = Data as of December 2017, FDI = foreign direct investment.

Notes: FDI assets refer to outward FDI holdings. Asia includes ADB regional members for which data are available.

Sources: ADB calculations using data from Bank for International Settlements. Locational Banking Statistics. https://www.bis.org/statistics/bankstats.htm (accessed September 2019); International Monetary Fund (IMF). Coordinated Direct Investment Survey. http://data.imf.org/CDIS (accessed May 2019); and IMF. Coordinated Portfolio Investment Survey. http://data.imf.org/CPIS (accessed September 2019).

---

[4] Asia's cross-border asset holdings refer to the stock of outbound portfolio debt, portfolio equity, FDI, and cross-border bank claims. Asia's cross-border liabilities refer to the stock of inward portfolio debt, portfolio equity, FDI, and cross-border bank liabilities.

In contrast, portfolio debt investment fell from 31.3% of cross-border assets in 2009 to 24.8% in 2018, indicating that cross-border equity holdings rose faster than portfolio debt holdings. Meanwhile, Asia's cross-border bank claims accounted for 27.1% of cross-border assets, the largest share, in 2018, while cross-border debt assets were 31.3% in 2009, the biggest share that year.

Total cross-border liabilities also grew, rising by $8.5 trillion, from $9.5 trillion in 2009 to $18.0 trillion in 2018 and continue to be linked more strongly to the rest of the world (Figure 10.6). The share of liabilities from outside the region stayed at about 70% through the 9 years. FDI accounted for more than 40% of total cross-border liabilities for both years. The intraregional share of Asia's cross-border liabilities for bank lending increased by 5.3 percentage points, and by 1.5 percentage points for debt, while that for portfolio equity and FDI decreased from 2009 to 2018.

Figure 10.6: Cross-Border Liabilities—Asia

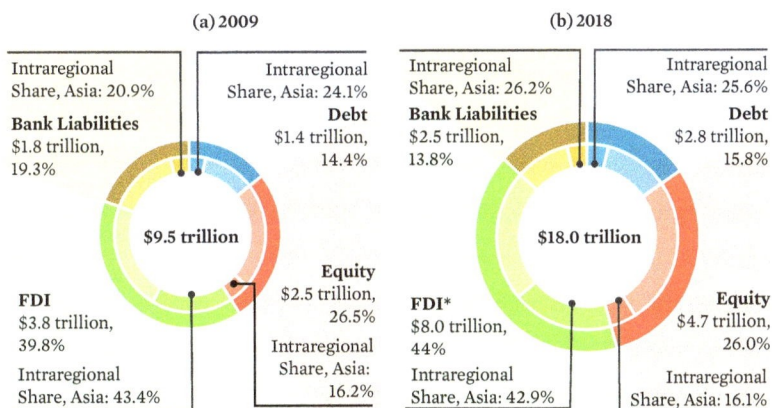

(a) 2009

Intraregional Share, Asia: 20.9%
Bank Liabilities $1.8 trillion, 19.3%

Intraregional Share, Asia: 24.1%
Debt $1.4 trillion, 14.4%

$9.5 trillion

FDI $3.8 trillion, 39.8%
Intraregional Share, Asia: 43.4%

Equity $2.5 trillion, 26.5%
Intraregional Share, Asia: 16.2%

(b) 2018

Intraregional Share, Asia: 26.2%
Bank Liabilities $2.5 trillion, 13.8%

Intraregional Share, Asia: 25.6%
Debt $2.8 trillion, 15.8%

$18.0 trillion

FDI* $8.0 trillion, 44%
Intraregional Share, Asia: 42.9%

Equity $4.7 trillion, 26.0%
Intraregional Share, Asia: 16.1%

* = Data as of December 2017, FDI = foreign direct investment.

Notes: FDI liabilities refer to inward FDI holdings. Asia includes ADB regional members for which data are available.

Sources: ADB calculations using data from Bank for International Settlements. Locational Banking Statistics. https://www.bis.org/statistics/bankstats.htm (accessed September 2019); International Monetary Fund (IMF). Coordinated Direct Investment Survey. http://data.imf.org/CDIS (accessed May 2019); and IMF. Coordinated Portfolio Investment Survey. http://data.imf.org/CPIS (accessed September 2019).

Outward Portfolio Investment

Asia's foreign portfolio investment exposure continues to expand. This trend is predominantly driven by increased portfolio equity investment outside the region, according to the Coordinated Portfolio Investment Survey of the International Monetary Fund (IMF).[5] This has resulted in the intraregional share in outward equity investment declining since 2007. The intraregional share of outward debt investment increased until 2014, before falling for the next 2 years and edging up in 2017.

Figure 10.7: Outward Portfolio Investment—Asia

a: Outward Portfolio Equity Investment   **b: Outward Portfolio Debt Investment**

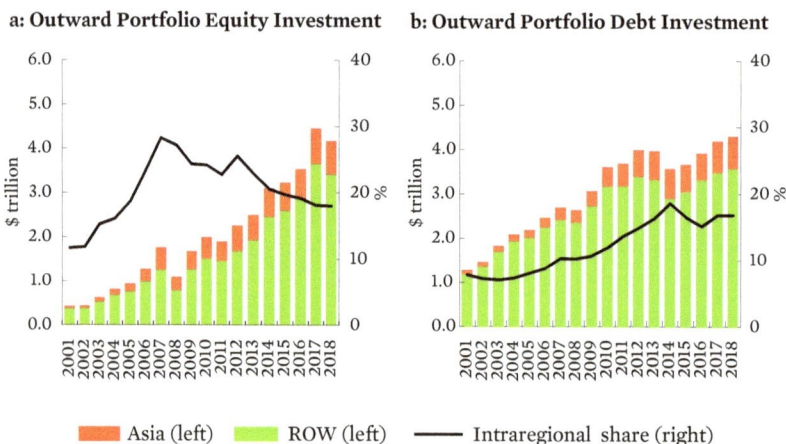

Asia (left)   ROW (left)   —— Intraregional share (right)

ROW = rest of the world.

Note: Asia includes Asian Development Bank (ADB) regional members for which data are available.

Source: ADB. 2019. *Asian Economic Integration Report 2019/2020*. Manila.

---

[5] For the portfolio investment data used in this study, Asia's reporting economies include Australia; Bangladesh (data beginning 2014); Hong Kong, China; India (data beginning 2003); Indonesia; Japan; Kazakhstan; Malaysia; Mongolia (data beginning 2010); New Zealand; Pakistan (data beginning 2002); Palau (data beginning 2014); the Philippines; the Republic of Korea; Singapore; Thailand; and Vanuatu (data from 2001–2005). The People's Republic of China is excluded due to lack of comparable data for 2001–2014.

Asia's outward portfolio equity investment averaged 16.5% annual growth from 2001 to 2018, way ahead of the 7.7% annual growth in portfolio debt investment over those years. Regional investor appetite for equities since 2010 has seen global equity markets recover from their sharp decline a decade ago. Indeed, outward portfolio equity investment reached $4.2 trillion in 2018, jumping almost tenfold from $430 billion in 2001 (Figure 10.7a). Portfolio equity investment from Asia to the rest of the world led the rise, reaching $3.4 trillion in 2018 from $380 billion in 2001. The intraregional share fell to 18.0% in 2018, down from a 28.3% peak in 2007.

Asia's outward portfolio debt investment outstanding rose to $4.3 trillion in 2018 from $1.3 trillion in 2001. The intraregional share rose to 16.8% in 2018 from 7.8% in 2001 (Figure 10.7b).

Outside the region, the preferred portfolio investment destinations are the Cayman Islands, European Union (EU), and the United States (US). Within the region, Australia, Japan, and the People's Republic of China (PRC) remain popular.

Inward Portfolio Investment

Outstanding portfolio equity investment into Asia reached $4.7 trillion in 2018, outstripping inward debt investment of $2.8 trillion (Figure 10.8). Inward portfolio equity investment grew an average 15.5% a year from 2001–2018. Investors from the US and the EU, in particular, increased their exposure, indicating their appetite for realizing strong returns in emerging economies' equity markets. That said, the intraregional share also increased from 7.6% in 2001 to 16.1% in 2018.

Meanwhile, portfolio debt investment into Asia reached $2.8 trillion in 2018, and again the US and the EU were the primary portfolio investors. The intraregional share of Asian debt holdings dipped to 25.6% in 2018, from 29.2% peak of 2013.

Inter- and Intra-Subregional Portfolio Investment

East Asia is the most prominent source and destination for intraregional portfolio investment, while Oceania (Australia and New Zealand) remain popular with regional securities investors.

Figure 10.8: Inward Portfolio Investment—Asia

a: Inward Portfolio Equity Investment **b: Inward Portfolio Debt Investment**

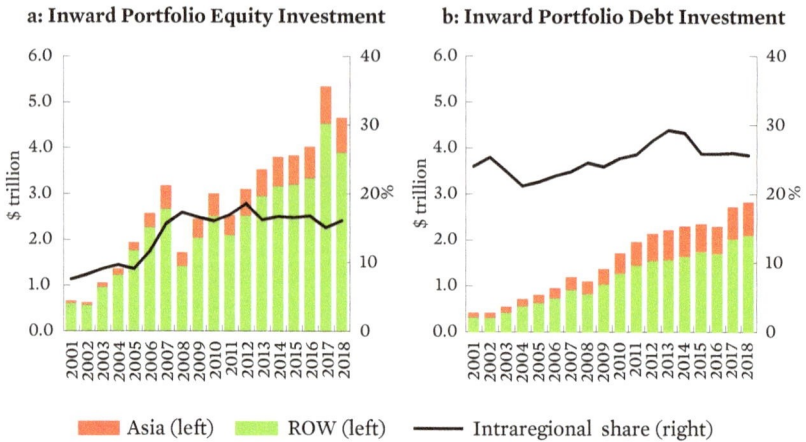

Asia (left)   ROW (left)   ―― Intraregional share (right)

ROW = rest of the world.

Note: Asia includes Asian Development Bank (ADB) regional members for which data are available.

Source: ADB. 2019. *Asian Economic Integration Report 2019/2020*. Manila.

East Asia represents the destination for 70.3% ($528.2 billion) of total intraregional portfolio equity investment outstanding in 2018 (Figure 10.9), with the PRC the target for 40% of that. Southeast Asia represents the next largest subregion (12.0%), with Singapore taking $39.1 billion in 2018, followed by Indonesia ($17.5 billion), Thailand ($11.4 billion), and Malaysia ($9.6 billion).

East Asia also continues to be favored by intraregional investors of portfolio debt (Figure 10.10), driven by significant investment in the PRC. In 2018, debt investment to East Asia amounted to 48.1% of intraregional investment outstanding, although down 4.0 percentage points from 2013. Oceania also remained a popular destination for intraregional debt investment, at $212.4 billion in 2018, driven by interest in Australia, with its intraregional share increasing from 25% in 2013 to 27.1% in 2018.

A marked rise was also seen in debt investment from Oceania, which almost tripled from $16.8 billion in 2013 to $44.5 billion in 2018. Most of that came from Australia ($35.6 billion).

Figure 10.9: Inter- and Intra-Subregional Portfolio Equity Investment—Asia

a: 2013
Total = $572.6 billion

b: 2018
Total = $751.0 billion

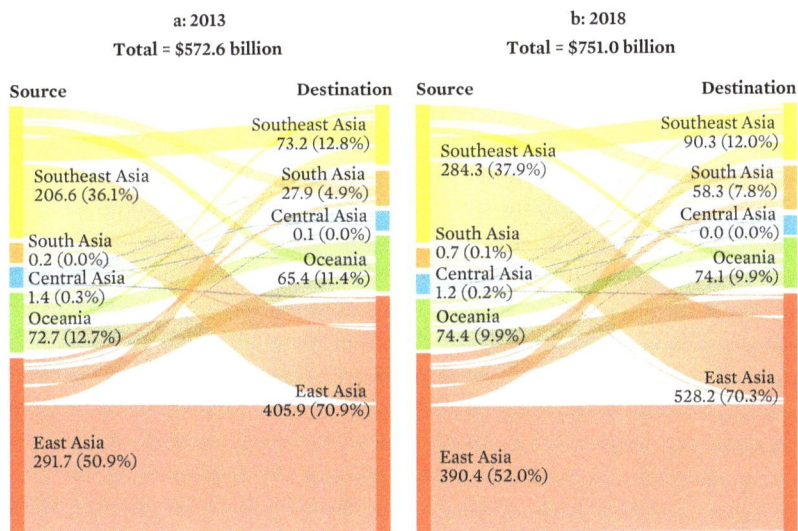

Notes: Figures in parentheses indicate the percent share of the total. Source economies for subregions are as follows: Central Asia includes Kazakhstan. East Asia includes Hong Kong, China; Japan; Mongolia; and the Republic of Korea. Oceania includes Australia and New Zealand. South Asia includes Bangladesh, India, and Pakistan. Southeast Asia includes Indonesia, Malaysia, the Philippines, Singapore, and Thailand. Asia includes Central Asia, East Asia, Oceania, South Asia, and Southeast Asia.

Source: Asian Development Bank. 2019. *Asian Economic Integration Report 2019/2020*. Manila.

Cross-Border Bank Holdings[6]

Asia's cross-border bank claims rose to $4.7 trillion in 2018 from $1.3 trillion in 2001 (Figure 10.11a), with most remaining on economies outside the region. However, the intraregional share rose moderately from 17.8% in 2001 to 20.8% in 2018. In contrast, the region's cross-border bank liabilities decreased slightly from a $2.4 trillion peak in 2012 to $2.5 trillion in 2018 (Figure 10.11b). Most of the region's bank liabilities continue to come from outside the region, but the intraregional share increased from 18.8% in 2011 to 26.2% in 2018. This trend suggests that regional banks have increasingly met the demand for cross-border financing in the region.

[6] Asia's reporting economies include Australia; Japan; the Republic of Korea (data beginning 2005); the Philippines (data beginning 2016); and Taipei,China. Hong Kong, China is excluded due to lack of comparable data for 2001–2013.

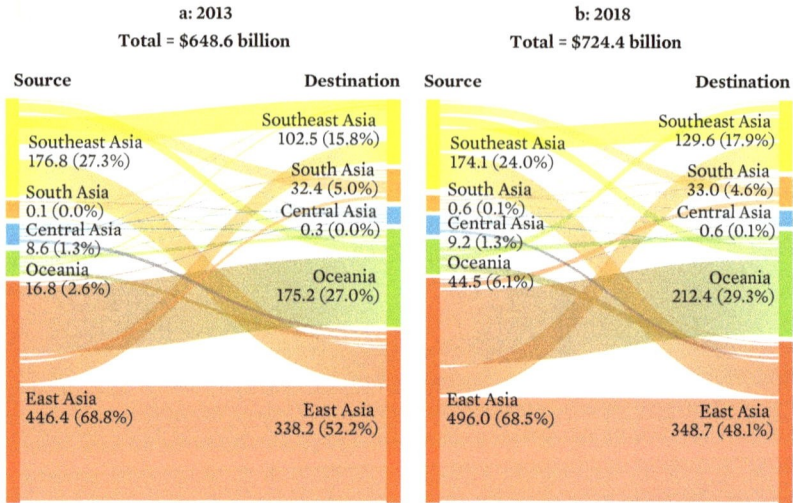

Figure 10.10: Inter- and Intra-Subregional Portfolio Debt Investment—Asia

Notes: Figures in parentheses indicate the percent share of the total. Source economies for subregions are as follows: Central Asia includes Kazakhstan. East Asia includes Hong Kong, China; Japan; Mongolia; and the Republic of Korea. Oceania includes Australia and New Zealand. South Asia includes Bangladesh, India, and Pakistan. Southeast Asia includes Indonesia, Malaysia, the Philippines, Singapore, and Thailand. Asia includes Central Asia, East Asia, Oceania, South Asia, and Southeast Asia.

Source: Asian Development Bank. 2019. *Asian Economic Integration Report 2019/2020*. Manila.

Cross-Border Co-Movement of Equity and Bond Markets

If financial markets are fully integrated, assets with similar risk characteristics should be priced similarly (after adjusting for risks). In other words, greater financial integration should be accompanied by a closer co-movement of prices.

Table 10.1 reports simple averages of stock return correlations of different subregions with regional and global stock markets, over two different periods, before and after the global financial crisis. The results suggest that Asian financial markets are generally becoming more integrated both regionally and globally over time, as correlations of most Asian financial markets with others in and beyond the region are stronger than they were before the global financial crisis. The correlations of Asian markets with global markets have also generally increased more than intraregional correlations.

Figure 10.11: Cross-Border Bank Holdings—Asia

a: Cross-Border Bank Claims

b: Cross-Border Bank Liabilities

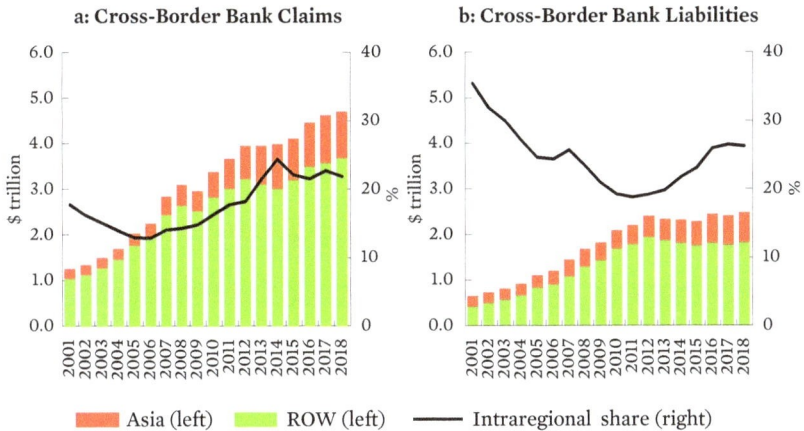

Asia (left)   ROW (left)   —— Intraregional share (right)

ROW = rest of the world.

Notes: Asia's reporting economies include Australia; Japan; the Republic of Korea (data beginning 2005); the Philippines (data beginning 2016); and Taipei,China. Hong Kong, China is excluded because comparable data for 2001–2013 is lacking. Asian partner economies include Asian Development Bank (ADB) regional members for which data are available.

Source: ADB. 2019. *Asian Economic Integration Report 2019/2020*. Manila.

Figures 10.12a and 10.12b show σ-convergence of total bond market returns within and beyond Asia. Asian bond returns have gradually converged over the sample period, with noticeable divergence during the 2008–2009 global financial crisis and the 2013 taper tantrum (Figure 10.12a). Moreover, σ-convergence shows strong convergence of Asia's bond returns with US bond returns over time (Figure 10.12b), even below Asia's intraregional dispersion. The Asia–EU dispersion was higher compared to that of Asia–US. After rising considerably during the global financial crisis, exceeding Asia's intraregional dispersion, the Asia–EU σ-convergence declined steadily except for the significant increase experienced in 2014–15, a time during which the Greece crisis regained momentum causing Greece sovereign bond yields to rise.

The trend of convergence across regional economies' local currency bond markets represents the integration of Asian local currency bond markets with the global market, reflecting the effect of the growing participation of international investors in Asian local currency markets. As the region's local currency bonds have become a part of international investors'

Table 10.1: Average Simple Correlation of Stock Price Index Weekly Returns—Asia with Asia and Asia with the World

Region	Asia			World		
	Pre-GFC Jan 1999 – Sep 2007	Post-GFC Jul 2009 – Nov 2018	**	Pre-GFC Jan 1999 – Sep 2007	Post-GFC Jul 2009 – Nov 2018	**
Central Asia	0.16	0.22	▲	0.04	0.23	▲
East Asia	0.40	0.49	▲	0.42	0.58	▲
Southeast Asia	0.37	0.44	▲	0.35	0.50	▲
South Asia	0.19	0.21	▲	0.18	0.22	▲
Oceania	0.11	0.03	▼	0.17	0.07	▼
Asia	0.30	0.34	▲	0.29	0.39	▲

** = direction of change in simple correlation between the pre- and post-global financial crisis, ▼ = decrease, ▲ = increase, — = no change, GFC = global financial crisis.

Notes:

(i)   Asia includes Central Asia, East Asia, Oceania, South Asia, and Southeast Asia. Central Asia includes Georgia, Kazakhstan, and the Kyrgyz Republic. East Asia includes the People's Republic of China; Hong Kong, China; Japan; the Republic of Korea; Mongolia; and Taipei,China. Oceania includes Australia and New Zealand. Southeast Asia includes Indonesia, the Lao People's Democratic Republic, Malaysia, the Philippines, Singapore, Thailand, and Viet Nam. South Asia includes Bangladesh, India, Nepal, Pakistan, and Sri Lanka.

(ii) Values refer to the average of pair-wise correlations. Weekly returns (in local currency converted to US dollar) are computed as the natural logarithm difference between weekly average of daily stock price index for the current week, and the weekly average of the daily stock price index from the previous week. World returns calculated from MSCI All-Country World Index.

Sources: Asian Development Bank calculations using data from Bloomberg; CEIC, Haver, Stooq. https://stooq.com/q/?s=ˆsti (accessed November 2018); and International Monetary Fund. World Economic Outlook Database. https://www.imf.org/external/pubs/ft/weo/2018/01/weodata/index.aspx (accessed November 2018).

investment portfolio, their dollar returns are increasingly priced against the international benchmark for low risks (i.e., the US returns) and therefore show greater convergence. The higher returns required for Asian local currency bonds over US or EU bonds during times of financial turbulence create divergence of the international bond markets. However, this trend of international convergence may not be an indication of regional integration across local currency bond markets in Asia. Growing bilateral convergence between each local currency bond market and the US would also generate stronger convergence among local currency bond markets across Asia.

Figure 10.12: σ-Convergence of Total Bond Return Indexes—Asia

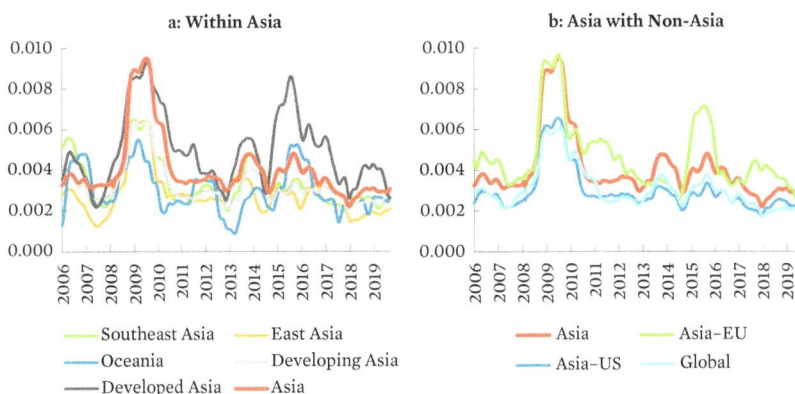

a: Within Asia

b: Asia with Non-Asia

Southeast Asia — East Asia
Oceania — Developing Asia
Developed Asia — Asia

Asia — Asia–EU
Asia–US — Global

EU = European Union, US = United States.

Notes:

(i) Values refer to the unweighted mean of individual economy's σ-convergence, included in the subregion. Each economy's σ-convergence is the simple mean of all its pair-wise standard deviation. Data are filtered using Hodrick-Prescott method.

(ii) East Asia includes Hong Kong, China; Japan; the People's Republic of China; the Republic of Korea; and Taipei,China. Oceania includes Australia and New Zealand. Southeast Asia includes Indonesia, Malaysia, the Philippines, Singapore, and Thailand. Developed Asia includes Japan and Oceania. Developing Asia includes East Asia excluding Japan, India, Kazakhstan, and Southeast Asia. Asia includes developed and developing Asia.

(iii) JP Morgan Asia Diversified bond return index was used for developing Asia, and Bloomberg Barclays bond return indexes for developed Asia, euro area, US, and the world. All bond return indexes are comprised of local currency government-issued bonds converted to US dollars.

Sources: Asian Development Bank (ADB). 2019. *Asian Economic Integration Report 2019/2020*. Manila; and methodology by Espinoza, Raphael, Oral Williams, and Ananthakrishnan Prasad. 2010. Regional Financial Integration in the GCC. *International Monetary Fund Working Paper*. No.10/90. Washington, DC: International Monetary Fund; and Park, C. 2013. Asian Capital Market Integration: Theory and Evidence. *ADB Economics Working Paper Series*. No. 351. Manila: ADB.

Financial Integration and Risk of Contagion

While freer capital mobility is welfare enhancing in theory, a deepening of financial integration may also facilitate the cross-border transmission of a financial shock. Past crises have been the testimony for the risk of such contagion. More worrisome is that financial instability may have an impact on the real side of the economy, resulting in a substantial reduction in economic growth.

Financial integration in emerging Asia either regionally or globally may increase the potential for the financial transmission of external shocks. But direct evidence on this point is patchy. If regional equity or bond markets are fully integrated with global markets and there is no country-specific disturbance, stock or bond returns should only react to news common to all markets. We examine the extent of financial integration of the individual equity and bond markets in emerging Asia with other markets within and beyond the region by analyzing the reaction of these markets to regional and global shocks.

Figure 10.13: Share of Variance in Equity Returns Explained by Global and Regional Shocks—Asian Markets (%)

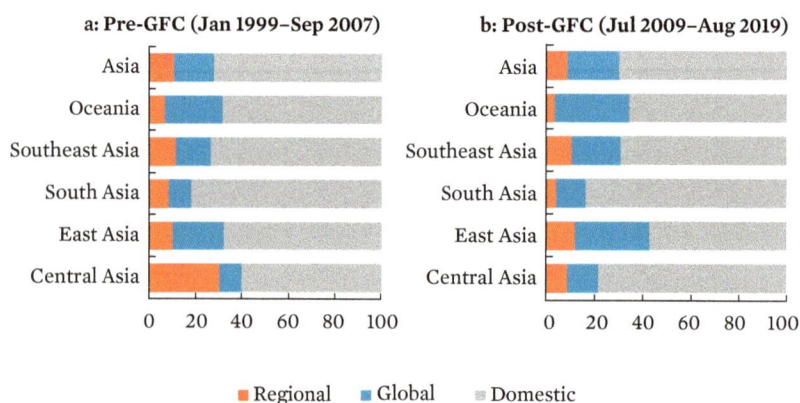

GFC = global financial crisis, PRC = People's Republic of China.

Notes: Asia includes Central Asia, East Asia, Oceania, South Asia, and Southeast Asia. Central Asia includes Georgia, Kazakhstan, and the Kyrgyz Republic. East Asia includes Hong Kong, China; Japan; Mongolia; the People's Republic of China; the Republic of Korea; and Taipei,China. Oceania includes Australia and New Zealand. South Asia includes Bangladesh, India, Nepal, Pakistan, and Sri Lanka. Southeast Asia includes Indonesia, the Lao People's Democratic Republic, Malaysia, the Philippines, Singapore, Thailand, and Viet Nam. Weekly returns are computed as the natural logarithm difference between weekly average of daily stock price index for the current week, and the weekly average of the daily stock price index from the previous week.

Sources: Asian Development Bank calculations using data from Bloomberg; CEIC; Stooq. Stooq Online. http://stooq.com/q/d/_s=^sti (accessed September 2019); World Bank. World Development Indicators. https://data.worldbank.org/indicator/ny.gdp.mktp.cd (accessed September 2019); and methodology by Park, C. and J. Lee. 2011. Financial Integration in Emerging Asia: Challenges and Prospects. *Asian Economic Policy Review.* 6 (2). pp. 176–198.

Empirical results show that tighter global financial integration translates into increased spillovers from a global shock on returns and volatilities of regional equities (Figures 10.13 and 10.14). The growing share of variance explained by external (both global and regional) shocks suggests the growing degree of integration of the local portfolio asset markets with global and regional markets. This increasing sensitivity to external shocks—seen especially in the region's equity markets—is underscored by the elevated exposure to international investors especially from outside the region (as discussed in page 408). In contrast to Asian equity markets, global and regional shocks have limited impact on Asian local currency bond markets. Nevertheless, the relative importance of the combined global and regional shocks was on average greater after the global financial crisis than before.

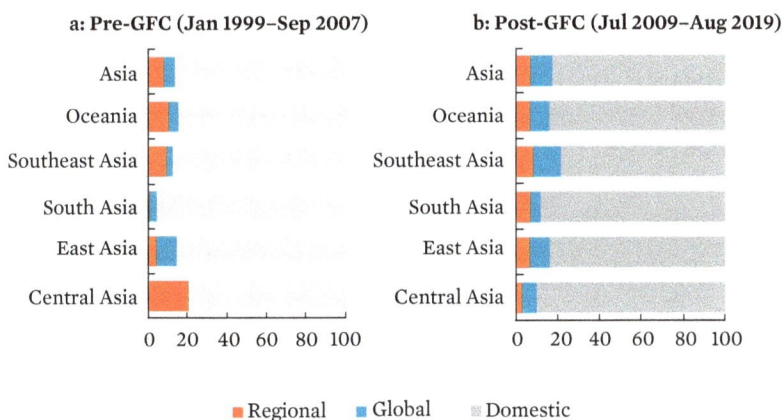

Figure 10.14: Share of Variance in Bond Returns Explained by Global and Regional Shocks—Asian Markets (%)

GFC = global financial crisis.
Notes: Asia includes Central Asia, East Asia, South Asia, Southeast Asia, and Oceania. Central Asia includes Kazakhstan. East Asia includes Hong Kong, China; Japan; the People's Republic of China; and the Republic of Korea. South Asia includes India. Southeast Asia includes Indonesia, Malaysia, the Philippines, Singapore, and Thailand. Oceania includes Australia and New Zealand. JP Morgan Asia Diversified bond return index was used for all economies, except for Australia and Japan where Bloomberg Barclays bond return indexes were used. All bond return indexes are comprised of local currency government-issued bonds.
Sources: Asian Development Bank calculations using data from Bloomberg; CEIC; International Monetary Fund. World Economic Outlook Database. https://www.imf.org/external/pubs/ft/weo/2018/01/weodata/index.aspx (accessed September 2019); and methodology by Park, C. and J. Lee. 2011. Financial Integration in Emerging Asia: Challenges and Prospects. *Asian Economic Policy Review*. 6 (2). pp. 176–198.

Implications for ADB Financial Sector Operations

Unfinished Reforms for Better Financial Efficiency, Inclusivity, and Stability

After the 1997–1998 Asian financial crisis, many Asian economies, particularly in East Asia and Southeast Asia, took extraordinary steps to improve their domestic financial systems and promote regional financial integration. They saw the crisis as an opportunity to deepen financial cooperation and integration—both as a safeguard against spillovers from global market instability and to provide a platform for regional financial market development. Some regional initiatives are noteworthy, such as the ASEAN+3 Economic Review and Policy Dialogue, the Chiang Mai Initiative, the Asian Bond Markets Initiative, and the Asian Bond Fund Initiative.

However, much can still be done to improve financial integration. A number of studies find that the region's financial markets remain largely fragmented and provide evidence that its financial markets are more integrated with global markets than with each other (Kim, Lee, and Shin 2008; Hinojales and Park 2011; and Park and Lee 2011). This study supports those findings. The region's financial markets also lack depth and breadth due to fragmentation and limited availability of regional financial products. Further financial integration would require liberalization of capital accounts, promotion of common standards for financial transactions, and the establishment of financial infrastructure to support cross-border transactions.

Despite progress over the past few decades, the region's finance sectors and markets continue to face major developmental challenges. First, the region's finance sectors and markets lag behind the development of the real sector of the economy. Although wide variation exists across countries and subregions, on average, there is room for further expansion of finance sectors and markets in most developing economies in the region (Figure 10.15). The situation is much worse for lower-income economies, where the size of financial assets is much smaller with very little development of nonbank financial institutions (Figure 10.16) and where financial inclusion is the lowest (Figure 10.17a). The banking systems in many developing countries—particularly in Central Asia, South Asia, Southeast Asia, and the Pacific—have a limited number of branches and automated teller machines (Figure 10.17b), and so are failing to provide adequate access for the public (Mylenko 2010).

Figure 10.15: Financial Market Development—Developing Asia (% of GDP)

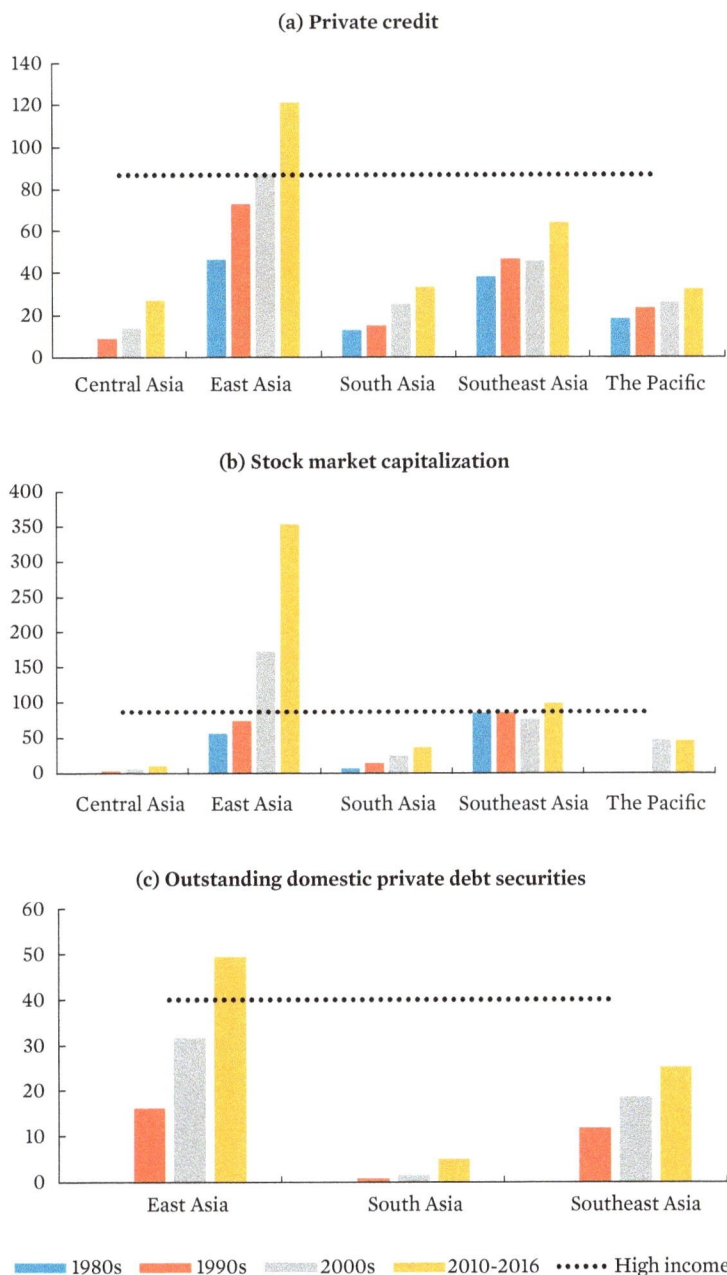

(a) Private credit

(b) Stock market capitalization

(c) Outstanding domestic private debt securities

Legend: 1980s   1990s   2000s   2010-2016   •••••• High income

continued on next page

Figure 10.15: continued

> Black horizontal dotted line indicates 2010–2016 average for high-income economies of the world (based on World Bank's Global Financial Development Database definition).
>
> GDP = gross domestic product.
>
> Notes:
>
> (i)   *Private credit by deposit money banks:* The financial resources provided to the private sector by domestic money banks as a share of GDP. Domestic money banks comprise commercial banks and other financial institutions that accept transferable deposits, such as demand deposits. Central Asia includes Armenia, Azerbaijan, Georgia, Kazakhstan, the Kyrgyz Republic, and Tajikistan. East Asia includes Hong Kong, China; the Republic of Korea; Mongolia; and the People's Republic of China (PRC). South Asia includes Afghanistan, Bangladesh, Bhutan, India, Maldives, Nepal, Pakistan, and Sri Lanka. Southeast Asia includes Brunei Darussalam, Cambodia, Indonesia, the Lao People's Democratic Republic, Malaysia, Myanmar, the Philippines, Singapore, Thailand, Timor-Leste, and Viet Nam. The Pacific includes the Federated States of Micronesia, Fiji, Papua New Guinea, Samoa, Solomon Islands, Tonga, and Vanuatu.
>
> (ii) *Stock market capitalization:* Total value of all listed shares in a stock market as a percentage of GDP. Central Asia includes Armenia, Azerbaijan, Georgia, Kazakhstan, and the Kyrgyz Republic. East Asia includes Hong Kong, China; the Republic of Korea; Mongolia; and the PRC. South Asia includes Bangladesh, India, Nepal, Pakistan, and Sri Lanka. Southeast Asia includes Indonesia, Malaysia, the Philippines, Singapore, Thailand, and Viet Nam. The Pacific includes Fiji and Papua New Guinea.
>
> (iii) *Outstanding domestic private debt securities:* Total amount of domestic private debt securities (amount outstanding) issued in domestic markets as a share of GDP. It covers data on long-term bonds and notes, commercial paper and other short-term notes. East Asia includes Hong Kong, China; the Republic of Korea; and the PRC. South Asia includes India. Southeast Asia includes Indonesia, Malaysia, the Philippines, Singapore, and Thailand.
>
> Source: World Bank. Global Financial Development Database. https://www.worldbank.org/en/publication/gfdr/data/global-financial-development-database (accessed May 2019).

Second, the region's financial systems remain dominated by banking systems especially among low- and middle-income economies, which can undermine structural resilience and systemic stability (Figure 10.18). The 1997–1998 Asian financial crisis highlighted the risk of heavy reliance on bank lending, which limited financial diversity and threatened financial stability. The absence of well-developed domestic capital markets constrains the availability of alternative sources for stable long-term corporate financing and so increases risks to the overburdened banking system that stem from maturity and currency mismatches.

Third, basic financial infrastructure, including legal and institutional frameworks and governance systems, remains underdeveloped in most low-income developing countries. Rapidly growing middle-income

Figure 10.16: Financial Sector Assets of Selected Asian Economies, 2016 (% of GDP)

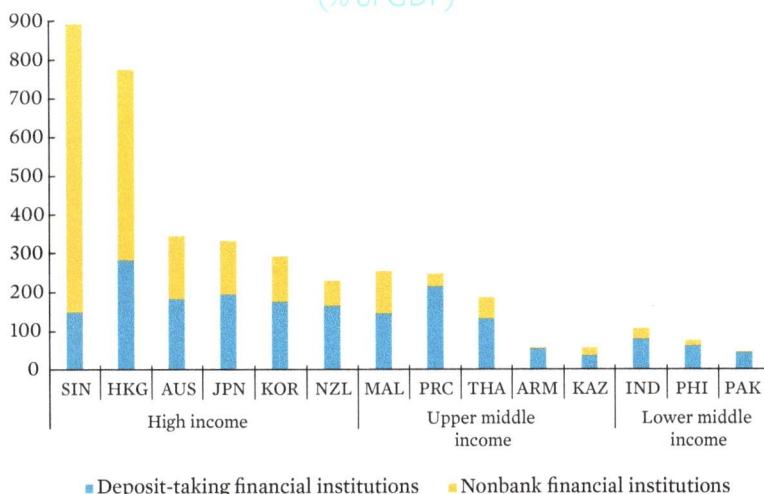

ARM = Armenia; AUS = Australia; GDP = gross domestic product; HKG = Hong Kong, China; IND = India; JPN = Japan; KAZ = Kazakhstan; KOR = Republic of Korea; MAL = Malaysia; NZL = New Zealand; PAK = Pakistan; PHI = Philippines; PRC = People's Republic of China; SIN = Singapore; THA = Thailand.

Notes:

(i)   *Deposit-taking financial institutions' assets to GDP (%)*: Total assets held by deposit-taking financial institutions as a share of GDP. Assets include claims on domestic real nonfinance sector which includes central, state and local governments, nonfinancial public enterprises' and private sector. Deposit-taking financial institutions comprise commercial banks and other financial institutions that accept transferable deposits, such as demand deposits.

(ii) *Nonbank financial institutions' assets to GDP (%)*: Total assets held by mutual funds, pension funds, and insurance companies. Data for mutual funds: 2014 for Armenia, Kazakhstan, and Thailand. Data for pension funds: 2015 for Pakistan. Data for insurance company assets: 2015 for Australia, New Zealand, and Thailand; 2014 for India and Pakistan.

Sources: International Monetary Fund. International Financial Statistics (downloaded using CEIC, accessed May 2019); and World Bank. Global Financial Development Database. https://www.worldbank.org/en/publication/gfdr/data/global-financial-development-database (accessed May 2019).

economies—for example, India, Indonesia, the Philippines, and Thailand— have strengthened financial infrastructure such as electronic payment systems, credit information bureaus, and collateral registries in the past decade, which has helped make banking operations more efficient and

Figure 10.17: Financial Inclusion Indicators—Asia

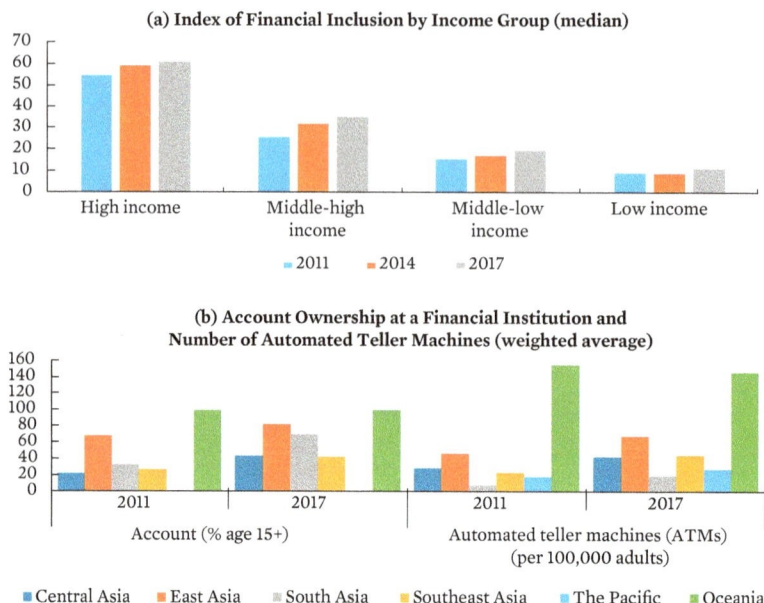

(a) Index of Financial Inclusion by Income Group (median)

■ 2011 ■ 2014 ■ 2017

(b) Account Ownership at a Financial Institution and Number of Automated Teller Machines (weighted average)

■ Central Asia ■ East Asia ■ South Asia ■ Southeast Asia ■ The Pacific ■ Oceania

Notes:
(i) Asia (or Asia and the Pacific) refers to Asian Development Bank (ADB) regional members (developing and advanced) with available data.

(ii) The Index of Financial Inclusion, which follows the methodology of Park and Mercado (2018), is a composite index covering the following indicators: (a) Access: account (% age 15+), credit card (% age 15+), debit card (% age 15+), and mobile money (% age 15+); (b) Availability: branches per 100,000 population and ATMs per 100,000 population; and (c) Usage: borrower (% age 15+), saver (% age 15+), and credit (% age 15+). High-income group consists of Australia; Hong Kong, China; Japan; the Republic of Korea; New Zealand; and Singapore. Middle-high income group consists of Azerbaijan, the People's Republic of China, Kazakhstan, Malaysia, and Thailand. Middle-low income group consists of Armenia, Bangladesh, Bhutan, Cambodia, Georgia, India, Indonesia, the Kyrgyz Republic, the Lao People's Democratic Republic, Mongolia, Myanmar, Pakistan, the Philippines, Sri Lanka, Tajikistan, Uzbekistan, and Viet Nam. Low-income group consists of Afghanistan and Nepal. Data are unavailable or patchy for Pacific developing member countries (Pacific DMCs) of ADB.

(iii) Data for account ownership are unavailable for Brunei Darussalam, Bhutan, Maldives, and all Pacific DMCs. Data for number of ATMs are unavailable for Cook Islands; Hong Kong, China; Kiribati; the Marshall Islands; Nauru; Palau; Papua New Guinea; Taipei,China; Tajikistan; Turkmenistan; Tuvalu; Uzbekistan; and Vanuatu.

Sources: World Bank. Global Findex database. https://globalfindex.worldbank.org/ (accessed May 2019); and Park, C. and R.V. Mercado, Jr. 2018. Financial Inclusion: New Measurement and Cross-Country Impact Assessment. *ADB Economics Working Paper Series*. No. 539. Manila: ADB.

Figure 10.18: Corporate Financing—Developing Asia
(% of total)

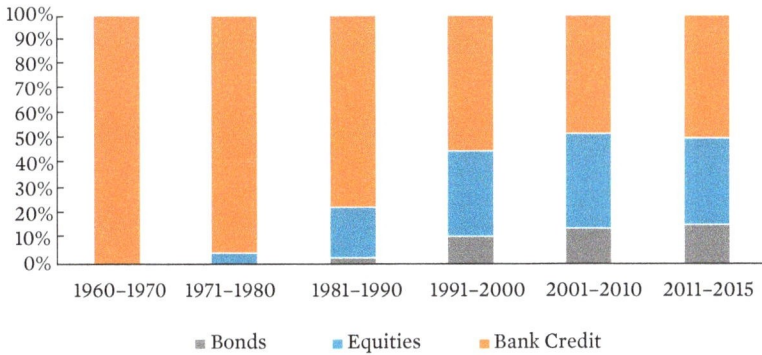

Notes: Developing Asia includes Central Asia, East Asia, South Asia, Southeast Asia, and the Pacific. Central Asia includes Armenia, Georgia, Kazakhstan, the Kyrgyz Republic, and Tajikistan. East Asia includes Hong Kong, China; Mongolia; the People's Republic of China; and the Republic of Korea. South Asia includes Afghanistan, Bangladesh, Bhutan, India, Maldives, Nepal, Pakistan, and Sri Lanka. Southeast Asia includes Brunei Darussalam, Cambodia, Indonesia, the Lao People's Democratic Republic, Malaysia, Myanmar, the Philippines, Singapore, Timor-Leste, Thailand, and Viet Nam. The Pacific includes Fiji, Papua New Guinea, Samoa, Solomon Islands, Tonga, and Vanuatu.

Source: World Bank. Global Financial Development Database. https://www.worldbank.org/en/publication/gfdr/data/global-financial-development-database (accessed November 2018).

boosted public confidence in the banking and financial systems. However, the situation in many developing economies in the region leaves a lot to be desired and hinders efficient functioning of finance sectors and markets.

Finally, the region's finance sectors and markets remain largely fragmented, hampering the deepening and broadening of regional financial markets and services and therefore effectively preventing savings from being mobilized to meet the region's vast investment needs. Asia is a net saver and exports significant capital to advanced economies (Table 10.2). This already presents an irony—that capital flows from low-income to high-income economies. What is more ironic, however, is that some regional economies in need of external funding for investment are importing these necessary funds from outside the region. This reflects the inability of the region's financial systems to channel surplus funds within the region effectively, leaving it vulnerable to swings in external credit and financial conditions.

Table 10.2: Savings and Investment—Asia, 2017

Economies	Levels ($ billion)			% of GDP		
	Savings	GDCF	Net Savings	Savings	GDCF	Net Savings
Asia	10,004	9,172	832	37.7	34.6	3.1
Japan	1,353	1,166	187	27.8	23.9	3.8
Emerging Asia	8,091	7,436	655	41.8	38.4	3.4
PRC	5,752	5,336	417	47.0	43.6	3.4
India	799	797	3	30.7	30.6	0.1
NIEs*	799	641	158	36.4	29.2	7.2
Hong Kong, China	91	76	15	26.6	22.3	4.3
Korea, Republic of	553	476	77	36.1	31.1	5.0
Singapore	156	90	66	48.1	27.6	20.4
ASEAN-5	740	662	78	31.9	28.5	3.3
Indonesia	314	340	-26	30.9	33.4	-2.6
Malaysia	90	80	9	28.5	25.6	3.0
Philippines	137	79	58	43.8	25.1	18.6
Thailand	145	104	41	31.8	22.8	9.0
Viet Nam	55	59	-5	24.4	26.6	-2.2

*Excluding Taipei,China. Japan figures are for 2016.

ASEAN = Association of Southeast Asian Nations, GDP = gross domestic product, GDCF = gross domestic capital formation, NIEs = newly industrialized economies, PRC = People's Republic of China.

Notes:
(i) Asia (or Asia and the Pacific) refers to ADB's regional members (developing and advanced) with available data. Emerging Asia includes the PRC, India, NIEs, and ASEAN-5.
(ii) Gross savings (current $) is calculated as gross national income less total consumption, plus net transfers.
(iii) Gross domestic capital formation (current $) consists of outlays on additions to the fixed assets of the economy plus net changes in the level of inventories. Fixed assets include land improvements (fences, ditches, drains, and so on); plant, machinery, and equipment purchases; and the construction of roads, railways, and the like, including schools, offices, hospitals, private residential dwellings, and commercial and industrial buildings. Inventories are stocks of goods held by firms to meet temporary or unexpected fluctuations in production or sales, and "work in progress." According to the 1993 System of National Accounts, net acquisitions of valuables are also considered capital formation.
(iv) Net savings: Gross savings minus gross domestic capital formation.

Source: World Bank. World Development Indicators. https://databank.worldbank.org/data/source/world-development-indicators (accessed February 2019).

The experience of the global financial crisis underscores both new and unfinished items on the reform agenda as the environment where financial institutions do business and markets function continues to transform through innovation and globalization. Broadening finance sectors and deepening markets are important for creating more efficient and resilient domestic financial systems in the long term. The scope of banking businesses and financial services is limited in many of the region's developing economies. Authorities therefore need to promote greater public access to banking and encourage banks and other financial institutions to diversify savings instruments and to provide credits to traditionally underserved sectors such as households and small and medium-sized enterprises (SMEs). They also need to allow diverse products to develop for better risk management.

Across the region, finance sector development and integration should aim at three important reform priorities. The reforms need to be implemented through an interplay of policies at national and regional level. Indeed, sound domestic financial development provides the foundation for advancing regional financial market development and thus integration.

First, efficient and well-functioning finance sectors and markets are needed to support economic growth and development. In this context, it is important to foster financial depth and diversity to help meet the diverse needs of savers and investors and boost financial efficiency. Second, appropriate regulation and adequate supervisory capacity should be in place to ensure financial stability. Both micro- and macro-prudential measures need to be considered to safeguard financial stability amid rapidly developing financial innovations and globalizing financial markets. In that regard, is it essential that Asian economies continue toward adopting Basel III reform measures, which are aimed at strengthening regulation, supervision, and risk management of the banking sector (Figure 10.19). Specific measures are related to capital, liquidity, and disclosure requirements. Third is the drive to enhance financial access to contribute to inclusive growth.

Reform Priorities by Subregion

Southeast Asia

Challenges to the finance sector in Southeast Asian economies include a weak investment climate, underdeveloped capital markets, and a lack of financial inclusion. ADB support has consequently been shaped to tackle

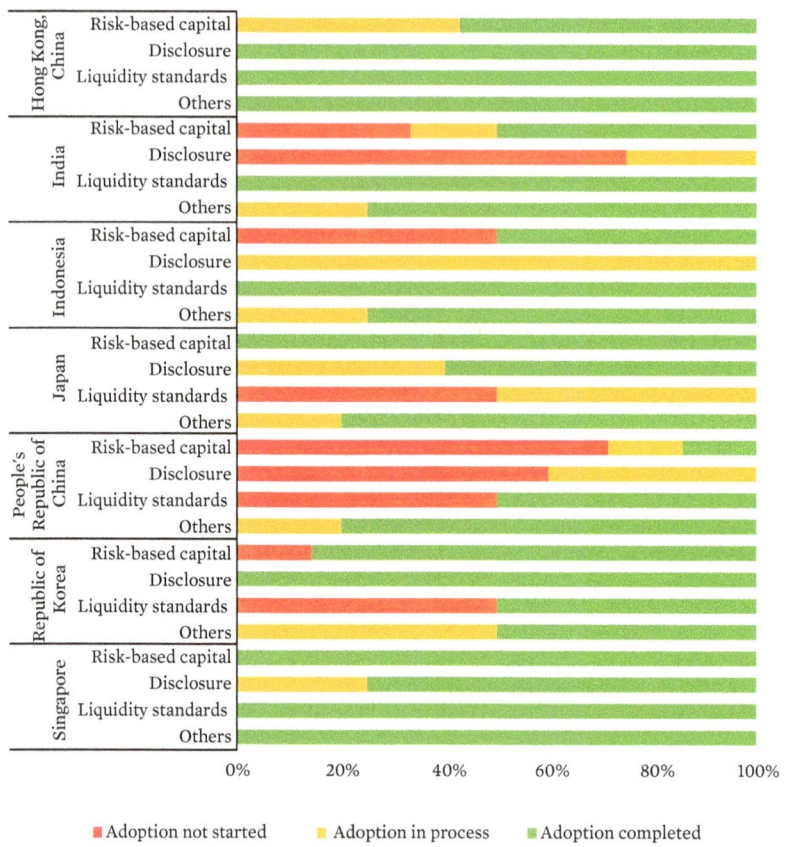

Figure 10.19: Summary of Adoption Status of Basel III Standards—Asia, by Major Basel III Standards

Notes: Asia refers to covered countries for which data are available. Status classifications are applicable to Basel standards whose deadlines have lapsed. The category "Others" includes standards on leverage ratio, systemically important bank requirements, interest rate risk in the banking book, and large exposures. Adoption not started covers standards whose draft regulations are not yet published. Adoption in process covers standards where draft or final regulations are published. Finally, standards are said to be completely adopted when final rules are both published and implemented.

Source: Bank for International Settlements. 2019. *Seventeenth Progress Report on Adoption of the Basel Regulatory Framework.* https://www.bis.org/bcbs/publ/d478.pdf.

these weaknesses, to address low financial inclusion in certain economies, furthering the development of capital markets, and more broadly improving the capacity of financial institutions.

Financial inclusion is low across economies in Southeast Asia and is consequently a priority for ADB in this subregion. In Indonesia and the Philippines, only about a third of individuals have an account at a formal institution. Financial inclusion is also limited in Thailand and Viet Nam. In response, reforms to increase inclusiveness and access to finance have been pursued in Cambodia, Indonesia, the Philippines, Thailand, and Viet Nam.

- ADB support in Indonesia, the Philippines, Thailand, and Viet Nam is targeted at improving access to financial services in formal institutions—such as increasing the number of adults with bank accounts. Measures to expand access to economic opportunities are moreover directed at underserved populations, including small farmers and fisherfolk in the Philippines, the poorest 40% of the population in Indonesia and Viet Nam, and rural and ethnic minorities in Viet Nam.
- In Cambodia, ADB is helping to increase the number of new microfinance loan accounts and expand the number of end borrowers reached.
- In Thailand, financial inclusion outcomes include the increased use of appropriate financial services by all, a decline in the percentage of the population without a bank account, and an increase in pension. Further development of microfinance institutions moreover aims to enhance financial inclusion.

ADB also provides support for finance sector policy reforms aiming to increase the efficiency of the finance sector across economies in Southeast Asia.

- In Cambodia, ADB areas of intervention include finance sector policies, reforms to central bank capacity development and payment systems, and insurance development.
- In Indonesia, capital market reforms are among priority areas of the ADB–Indonesia country partnership strategy for 2016–2019, in line with broader efforts to develop the finance sector. Such reforms are rooted in Indonesia's underdeveloped finance sector—which is regarded as inefficient with costly domestic lending and relatively small and foreign-dominated bond and equity markets.
- In the Philippines, capacity development of financial institutions to support capital market development has been targeted.
- In Thailand, finance sector strategies and policies to create more diversified and well-governed financial markets relate to

microfinance institutional development, nonformal microfinance institutions, mortgage markets and services, and pensions.

- In Timor-Leste, targets to enhance finance sector development and improve the availability and efficiency of financial services include increasing the ratio of bank credit to the private sector to non-oil GDP to 70% by 2025.

South Asia

Challenges in South Asia feature funding constraints to the private sector, underdeveloped capital markets, and constrained financial inclusion. ADB support in these areas comprises efforts to enhance macrofinancial stability, further the reform of underdeveloped capital markets and financial institutions, and mitigate critical constraints to financial inclusion. Some efforts include:

- Increased private sector lending and funding to SMEs to further private sector development is a priority across the subregion. Objectives relating to increasing private sector development are articulated in the country partnership strategies of Afghanistan, Bangladesh, Bhutan, India, Nepal, Pakistan, and Sri Lanka. Such targets center on mobilizing resources to support private sector-led growth, including increased private sector lending and growth in the share of loans to SMEs.
- Further development of capital markets and financial institutions was identified as a core area of ADB support in Bhutan and Pakistan for enhancing finance sector efficiency. In Bhutan, ADB areas of intervention include money markets, microfinance institutional development, long-term debt such as export credits, pensions, and finance sector policies. Interventions are motivated by the lack of prudential regulations in the country's banking and financial systems, underdeveloped capital markets, and insufficient deepening of its equity and debt markets, and the further need to improve its pension and insurance sectors. Pakistan likewise faces weaknesses in a finance sector that is heavily bank-dominated and serves large public sector requirements for borrowing.
- Macrofinancial stability was laid out as a goal in Bhutan. Macrofinancial risks have worsened through an India rupee liquidity shortage following the economy's rapid structural transformation, a buildup in public spending, inadequate liquidity management, and the effects of a heavily bank-based and underdeveloped

finance sector, which together have intensified financial instability. Consequently, targets laid out in the ADB–Bhutan country partnership strategy for 2014–2018 include the raising of gross international reserves, containing growth in domestic credit, and maintaining the bank nonperforming loan ratio at less than 10%.

- In India, country partnership strategy priorities include improvements in institutions and the investment climate and a deepening of regional connectivity to improve the potential for direct and foreign investment and boost connectivity between domestic and international markets.
- Financial inclusion was laid out as a goal in Bangladesh, India, Pakistan, and Sri Lanka. Such targets include the expansion of financial access to underserved segments, including women and agriculture-based and SME borrowers. Financial inclusion is a critical constraint in Pakistan in particular, as 10% of adults and only 3% of women have an account at a formal financial institution—less than a third of the South Asia average.

Central Asia

Economies in Central Asia must tackle financing constraints to SMEs, as well as barriers to financial inclusion, weaknesses in their finance sector development, and weak investment climates. These are shaping ADB support in the subregion.

- Georgia faces weaknesses in its finance sector development, particularly nonbank financial institutions subject to unfavorable legal and regulatory frameworks. Moreover, further capital market development is needed in government securities and corporate bond markets. Consequently, objectives laid out in the ADB–Georgia country partnership strategy report include increasing nonbank finance sector financial intermediation and increasing the use of efficient and reliable services by micro, small, and medium-sized enterprises (MSMEs). Specific targets include increasing bank credit to GDP, raising domestic savings as a percentage of GDP, and enhancing access to financing through local equity markets.
- Improving financial inclusion is a goal in Kazakhstan and Georgia. In Kazakhstan, easing access for MSMEs is a priority area and the target is to increase to 25% the share of MSMEs using bank credit to finance operations by 2021. Access to finance for microenterprises and SMEs is limited. In Georgia, ADB support is geared toward improving

private sector access to finance, including for MSMEs in agribusiness, retail, manufacturing, and tourism. In addition, the country's limited affordable bank financing hinders financial inclusion.

- Improving the investment climate is a goal in Kazakhstan, the Kyrgyz Republic, Tajikistan, and Turkmenistan. Embedded in this objective are targets to improve global rankings in the ease of doing business, to increase internationally recognized quality certifications of firms, and to increase linkages between regional and global trade networks. Putting in place funding and technical support to further private sector development is a further goal in Uzbekistan, with ADB involvement centering on building an enabling environment for private sector growth.

East Asia

Challenges in East Asian economies include a lack of efficiency in finance sector infrastructure and oversight frameworks, and obstacles to financial stability that stem from a high buildup of nonperforming loans in certain economies. Therefore, ADB efforts in this subregion include measures to strengthen finance sector resilience and to expand access to SMEs and underserved populations.

- Enhancing financial inclusion is a priority area in Mongolia. It has set a target to increase access to SME finance—in particular, increasing SME loan accounts in the banking sector by 15% by 2020. Strengthening finance sector resilience has been also highlighted in the ADB country partnership strategy report with Mongolia. Financial stability in Mongolia has been strained by heavy dollarization, weak financial supervision, and inadequate provisioning. Moreover, this has been compounded by a worsening external environment characterized by plummeting FDI, falling commodity prices, and a moderation of growth in the PRC—all of which have contributed to undermining macroeconomic stability and the deterioration of public finances.
- In the PRC, the focus is on increasing the availability of finance to the rural sector and SMEs and expanding social protection coverage—in particular, achieving full basic pension insurance coverage by 2020. Increased financial inclusion is critical, with low-income groups and SMEs having limited access to financial services and with an underdeveloped micro and rural financial system worsening financial system disparities. Improving finance sector

efficiency is another key area in the ADB–PRC country partnership strategy report. ADB involvement centers on strengthening finance sector infrastructure and oversight frameworks.

The Pacific

Challenges in Pacific island economies include lack of finance sector efficiency—owing to underperforming state-owned enterprises, insufficient financial inclusion, and underdeveloped capital markets. ADB involvement in the finance sectors of Pacific economies has been extensive, covering efforts to improve the business environment and improve the financial efficiency of state-owned enterprises, enhance financial stability and resilience, and counteract a lack of financial inclusion.

A key outcome of ADB involvement in the Pacific relates to enabling the business environment. Outcome indicators include increasing the financial efficiency of state-run firms—average return on assets and average return on equity, in Papua New Guinea and Samoa in particular—and increasing the ease of starting and doing business.

- In Kiribati, targets to improve the efficiency and effectiveness of state-run firms include reducing fiscal allocations to and contingent liabilities from state-run firms and completing their restructurings.
- In Papua New Guinea, areas for ADB intervention include support for reform of state-owned enterprises and corporatization and the reform of regulatory and legislative barriers to financial access.

Measures to increase the efficiency of the finance sector are embedded in ADB partnership with Pacific countries, as are those to provide financial and technical support for private sector expansion. ADB seeks to further such efforts through its flagship regional technical assistance programs—the Pacific Private Sector Development Initiative, the Pacific Business Investment Facility, and the Pacific Economic Management program. Constraints involve a critical shortage of commercial finance impeding businesses of all sizes, including SMEs. The Pacific Business Investment Facility and ADB Trade Finance Program seek to address these funding constraints.

- In Solomon Islands, ADB interventions include private sector development, microfinance, and public finance and expenditure management.

Financial sector programs have been established in the subregion to enhance financial stability and resilience. These include the ADB Financial Sector Program aiming to facilitate reforms in the financial and banking sector, including building fiscal sustainability and strengthening public financial management with the view to enhance financial stability in the Marshall Islands; a Private Sector Development TA and loan extended in the early 2000s in the Federated States of Micronesia; and programs on Strengthening Banking and Corporation Laws, Small Business Development and Microfinance, and Fiscal and Financial Reform in Nauru.

Financial inclusion is a concern in Solomon Islands and Vanuatu. Measures to counteract the lack of financial inclusion consist of targets to increase the proportion of the adult population with a bank account.

Conclusions and Policy Implications

Overall, both quantity and price measures of financial integration suggest an increasing degree of openness and integration of finance sectors and markets within Asia and between Asia and the world. First, capital flows in and out of Asia have consistently increased, with Asia's holdings of cross-border assets and liabilities rising within and beyond the region. Alongside growing integration, asset prices have also converged. Second, while Asian investors have increasingly held more foreign equities and debts over the past decade, the intraregional share of outward portfolio investment has fallen short of that of foreign direct investment or trade. Third, Asian equity markets appear to be more internationally integrated than Asian bond markets. The visible increases in the cross-country correlations of Asian equity markets with other Asian markets as well as with markets in the US and Europe are also indicative of a strengthening of regional and global integration. Local currency bond markets, in contrast, remain generally segmented from overseas markets.

Further financial integration would require liberalization of capital accounts, the promotion of common standards for financial transactions, and establishment of financial infrastructure that can support cross-border transactions.

An understanding of the degree and dynamics of financial integration in Asia is important for shaping the region's policies, not only for economic growth and development but also for financial stability. As markets become increasingly integrated regionally and globally, any convulsion in global financial markets and significant developments in major industrial economies will likely influence the region's equity and bond markets. The results also suggest that market co-movements increase during times of stress.

In the wake of the global financial crisis, a consensus has emerged to support more balanced and sustainable growth worldwide, with further development of domestic and regional financial markets and institutions among the key elements. Experience and research demonstrate that a well-designed institutional framework for finance is crucial for achieving the twin objectives of supporting economic growth and financial stability. Effective regulation and supervision, for example through the adoption of Basel III standards, is the basic foundation for finance sector development and sophistication, while a reliable institutional framework is essential to lay down rules for financial transactions and to support finance sector development. Without an appropriate legal and institutional framework, effective finance will not develop. Past episodes of financial crises underscore the importance of ensuring financial stability while being prepared for times of financial distress and crisis. In such times, an effective resolution framework supports prompt responses to troubled institutions, helps contain the spread of the financial troubles, and cushions the impact of crises.

Asian equity markets, particularly those with tight financial linkages to the global market, have demonstrated vulnerabilities to abrupt swings in global investor sentiment and the reversal of foreign portfolio investment flows. To maintain investor confidence, sound macroeconomic management is a must. Despite visible improvement in depth and breadth across Asian equity markets, further policy efforts are needed to strengthen market resilience. This requires steps to foster deeper and more liquid domestic capital markets, including: broadening the investor base; encouraging the development of more diverse local financial products; improving legal, regulatory, and institutional frameworks; upgrading governance and transparency; and establishing sound market infrastructure and institutions.

Past crisis experiences have proven that cooperation is essential in responding to systemic failure. Cooperation is similarly requisite to ensure regional and global financial stability. Several areas for regional cooperation in finance are vital. The first is liquidity provisioning, where the expanded ASEAN+3's $120 billion Chiang Mai Initiative Multilateralization (CMIM) is a good example. Over the past decades since the Asian financial crisis, it has grown from a series of bilateral swap arrangements to a more formal institution-like structure—with set contributions, voting rights, and drawdown limits. Second, and related, is macroeconomic and financial surveillance. The enhancement of the ASEAN+3 Macroeconomic Research Office in support of the CMIM is a visible step in this direction. Third, growing cross-border banking activities highlight the need for regulatory cooperation at the regional level. In that vein, supervisory colleges for regionally active foreign banks can be an effective regional cooperation tool to strengthen cross-border supervision in Asia.

And finally, developing vibrant local currency bond markets is crucial to more efficiently channel the region's vast resources. Their development can mitigate the global shortage of sound and liquid financial assets, lessen the probability that a currency depreciation will morph into a full-blown financial crisis, and help unwind global imbalances by reducing the current massive inflows into other debt markets, for example, US securities. In addition, in economies with low foreign reserves, developed local currency bond markets can reduce reliance on foreign currency debt, and shrink currency mismatches.

References

Asian Development Bank (ADB). 2008. *Emerging Asian Regionalism: A Partnership for Shared Prosperity*. Manila.

——. 2017. *Asian Economic Integration Report 2017*. Manila.

——. 2018. *Asian Economic Integration Report 2018*. Manila.

——. 2019. *Asian Economic Integration Report 2019/2020*. Manila.

Bank for International Settlements. 2019. *Seventeenth Progress Report on Adoption of the Basel Regulatory Framework*. https://www.bis.org/bcbs/publ/d478.pdf.

——. Locational Banking Statistics. https://www.bis.org/statistics/bankstats.htm (accessed September 2019).

Chelley-Steeley, P. L. and J. M. Steeley. 1999. Changes in the Comovement of European Equity Markets. *Economic Inquiry*. 37 (3). pp. 473–88.

Chinn, M. D. and H. Ito. 2006. What Matters for Financial Development? Capital Controls, Institutions, and Interactions. *Journal of Development Economics*. 81 (1). pp. 163–92.

Danthine, J., F. Giavazzi, and E. von Thadden. 2000. European Financial Markets after EMU: A First Assessment. *CEPR Discussion Paper. 2413*. London: Center for Economic Policy Research.

Eichengreen, B. and Y. C. Park. 2005. Financial Liberalization and Capital Market Integration in East Asia. In Y. C. Park, ed. *A New Financial Market Structure for East Asia*. Cheltenham: Edward Elgar.

Espinoza, R., O. Williams, and A. Prasad. 2010. Regional Financial Integration in the GCC. *IMF Working Paper*. No.10/90. Washington, DC: International Monetary Fund.

Forbes, K. and R. Rigobon. 2002. No Contagion, Only Interdependence: Measuring Stock Market Comovements. *The Journal of Finance, American Finance Association*. 57 (3). pp. 2223–2261.

Fratzscher, M. 2001. Financial Market Integration in Europe: On the Effects of EMU on Stock Markets. *European Central Bank Working Paper*. No. 48. Frankfurt: European Central Bank.

Hinojales, M. and C. Park. 2011. Stock Market Integration: Emerging East Asia's Experience. In M. Devereux, P. Lane, C. Park, and S. Wei, eds. *The Dynamics of Asian Financial Integration: Facts and Analytics*. Manila: Asian Development Bank.

International Monetary Fund (IMF). Balance of Payments Statistics. https://www.imf.org/external/datamapper/datasets/BOP (accessed November 2018).

——. Coordinated Direct Investment Survey. http://data.imf.org/CDIS (accessed May 2019).

——. Coordinated Portfolio Investment Survey. http://data.imf.org/CPIS (accessed September 2019).

——. World Economic Outlook Database. https://www.imf.org/external/pubs/ft/weo/2018/01/weodata/index.aspx (accessed November 2018).

Kim, S., J. Lee, and K. Shin. 2008. Regional and Global Financial Integration in East Asia. In B. Eichengreen, Y. C. Park, and C. Wyplosz, eds. *China, Asia and the New World Economy*. Oxford: Oxford University Press.

Mylenko, N. 2010. *Financial Access 2010: The State of Financial Inclusion Through the Crisis* (English). Washington, DC: World Bank.

Park, C. and J. Lee. 2011. Financial Integration in Emerging Asia: Challenges and Prospects. *Asian Economic Policy Review*. 6 (2). pp. 176–98.

Park, C. 2013. Asian Capital Market Integration: Theory and Evidence. *ADB Economics Working Paper Series*. No. 351. Manila: Asian Development Bank.

Park, C. and R. Claveria. 2018. Constructing the Asia-Pacific Regional Integration Index: A Panel Approach. *ADB Economics Working Paper Series*. No. 544. Manila: Asian Development Bank.

Park, C. and R. V. Mercado, Jr. 2018. Financial Inclusion: New Measurement and Cross-Country Impact Assessment. *ADB Economics Working Paper Series*. No. 539. Manila: Asian Development Bank.

Stooq. https://stooq.com/q/?s=ˆsti (accessed November 2018).

World Bank. Global Findex database. https://globalfindex.worldbank.org/ (accessed May 2019).

——. Global Financial Development Database. https://www.worldbank.org/en/publication/gfdr/data/global-financial-development-database (accessed November 2018 and May 2019).

——. World Development Indicators. https://databank.worldbank.org/data/source/world-development-indicators (accessed February 2019).

PART 4
BUILDING RESILIENCE

"And we have called consistently for the two essential ingredients for conquering this virus: national unity and global solidarity."

Dr. Tedros Adhanom Ghebreyesus, Director-General, World Health Organization

Global Shortage of Personal Protective Equipment amid COVID-19: Supply Chains, Bottlenecks, and Policy Implications

11

Cyn-Young Park, Kijin Kim, Susann Roth, Steven Beck, Jong Woo Kang, and Mara Claire Tayag (Asian Development Bank); and Michael Griffin (World Health Organization)[1]

The coronavirus disease (COVID-19) pandemic took a significant toll on people's lives, communities, economies, and jobs. Starting as a health crisis, it quickly evolved to pose serious threats to the global economy, trade, and finance, with the estimated economic impacts at the time of this chapter was written ranging from $5.8 trillion to $8.8 trillion globally (Park et al. 2020).

The scale of the pandemic that emerged from the initial outbreak led to a dramatic increase in demand for masks, goggles, gowns, gloves, and other personal protective equipment (PPE). Surging demand, partly joined with panic buying, hoarding, and misuse of PPE in the pandemic, is disrupting global supplies and putting lives at risk. The spike quickly overwhelmed global production capacity, depleted stockpiles, prompted significant price increases, and led to production backlogs of 4–6 months in fulfilling orders.

The World Health Organization (WHO) in March 2020 estimated that 89 million medical masks were required for the COVID-19 response each month, along with 76 million examination gloves and 1.6 million medical goggles (WHO 2020). The most significant challenge was to ensure that critical PPE products were sourced and allocated to frontline health workers and other responders in affected countries, especially those most vulnerable to the spread of the coronavirus. WHO, in the first 2 months of the pandemic, shipped nearly half a million sets of PPE to 47 countries, but supplies depleted rapidly. To meet rising global demand as the crisis spread, WHO in March 2020 estimated that PPE manufacturing needed to be increased by 40% and urged governments to act quickly.

---

[1] Excellent research support was provided by Joshua Anthony Gapay, Benjamin Endriga, Marife Lou Bacate, Zemma Ardaniel, Ana Kristel Lapid, Concepcion Latoja, and Clemence Fatima Cruz.

Crucial Need to Understand How Supply Chains Operate

Supply chain disruptions for PPE are particularly risky for medical personnel as COVID-19 rapidly spreads. If not adequately protected, health care workers who are the frontline defense against coronavirus can infect patients or colleagues. The need to be quarantined after exposure quickly depletes the health workforce.

Medical supply chains are essential elements of a well-functioning health system. To respond to infectious disease effectively, health supply systems should be designed to swiftly and reliably source and deliver essential health commodities, including vaccines and medicines and PPE for health care workers, which are needed during outbreaks, epidemics, and pandemics.

The coronavirus pandemic exposed the vulnerabilities of supply chains across many industries. Over the past few years, health care systems in many advanced economies have encouraged or forced the offshoring of PPE production to low-cost providers in Asia and the Pacific, including the People's Republic of China (PRC). In the United States (US), 95% of surgical masks and 70% of respirators are produced overseas (McKenna 2020). Amid the COVID-19 outbreak in the PRC, factory shutdowns and bans on travel and PPE exports put significant strain on global PPE supply chains, while the evolving pandemic nature of COVID-19 led to political and technical constraints in supplying the market. To improve inventory management efficiency, the just-in-time system was also implemented worldwide for materials critical for PPE products, resulting in an overall reduction in national stocks. Although many recent business practices such as the geographic expansion of suppliers, single-sourcing, and just-in-time replenishment are considered positive for economic and cost efficiency, these practices contrast with the idea of pandemic planning and stockpiling. Absent strategic stockpiles and secure supply chain management, PPE stocks are insufficient to meet the surge in demand for PPE during disease outbreaks (ICT 2008).

PPE Market Overview

PPE and pharmaceutical manufacturing in Asia and the Pacific is significant. Prominent producers operate in the PRC, while India meets about 20% of global demand for medicines and vaccines; the Republic of Korea remains among the most significant pharmaceutical manufacturing markets, and

Singapore is a regional hub for international pharmaceutical companies (Mordor Intelligence 2020).

PPE refers to clothing and equipment designed to protect the wearer from injury or spread of infection. Key PPE items—including N95 masks, surgical masks, gowns, and goggles—are essential for health care workers. Most of the raw materials and inputs used to produce PPE are outsourced to low-cost suppliers. Production of these items often requires imports of raw materials such as cotton fiber, polyester, and polyamide produced by manufacturers around the world.

The global market for PPE in the health sector was estimated to be worth $2.5 billion in 2018. Gloves have the highest share of sales revenue at 25%, followed by suits or coveralls at 22%. Face masks and hats came in third with a share of 14% (Figure 11.1). By region, in 2018 the US had the largest market share (33%), followed by Asia and the Pacific (28%), and Europe (22%).

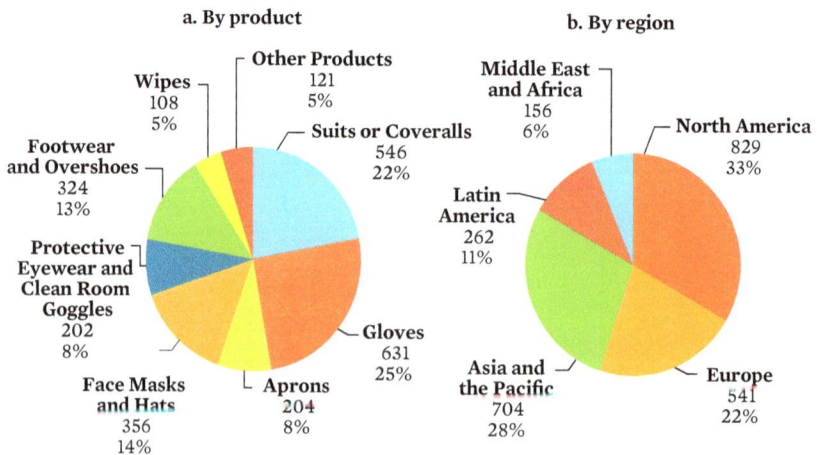

Figure 11.1: Market Share by PPE Product and Region (revenue $ million, %)

a. By product

- Wipes 108 5%
- Other Products 121 5%
- Footwear and Overshoes 324 13%
- Suits or Coveralls 546 22%
- Protective Eyewear and Clean Room Goggles 202 8%
- Face Masks and Hats 356 14%
- Aprons 204 8%
- Gloves 631 25%

b. By region

- Middle East and Africa 156 6%
- North America 829 33%
- Latin America 262 11%
- Asia and the Pacific 704 28%
- Europe 541 22%

PPE = personal protective equipment.
Source: Mordor Intelligence. 2020. *Protective Clothing Market for Life Sciences Industry (2019–2024)*. https://www.mordorintelligence.com.

The greatest concentration of mask production is in the PRC, reportedly accounting for about half the global production capacity. Some sources indicate it could be even as much as 80%–90%. For gloves that comply with WHO standards, the distribution of manufacturing capacity is more diverse. Although the PRC produces significant amounts of gloves, the greatest production capacities are in Indonesia, Malaysia, and Thailand. Small production capacities are scattered across various countries such as the Philippines and Turkey. Any increase in production capacity is estimated to be 20%–40%, with a ramp-up period of about 3–4 months. In many smaller countries, however, quality assurance standards do not meet WHO technical specifications.

Snapshot of PPE Supply Chains Based on Trade Flows

Given the complexity of PPE products and its supply chains, this chapter provides only a snapshot of select supply chains of PPE products in critical shortage, making the most of publicly available information. Figure 11.2 presents global trade networks for six kinds of PPE based on the six-digit Harmonized System (HS) codes: (i) HS 630790 including surgical masks, (ii) HS 392690 including respirators, (iii) HS 621010 including surgical gowns, (iv) HS 392620 including protective suits, (v) HS 900490 including protective goggles, and (vi) HS 401511 including surgical gloves.[2] The size of the circles represents total trade of the item, and the thickness of the lines denotes the importance of bilateral trade flows between economies.

The trade network maps show high geographic and regional concentration in the PPE supply chain. Three regional clusters emerge: Asia, Europe, and the United States. While the PRC, Germany, and the US are the main producers, the PRC appears to play a central role in producing and exporting many PPE products to Asia and the rest of the world. In particular, the PRC is the world's largest exporter in commodity groups that include masks, gowns, protective suits, and goggles. Malaysia, Thailand, and the PRC are the top three exporters of surgical gloves in the world. Within Europe, major PPE suppliers are Belgium, France, Germany, Italy, the Netherlands,

---

[2] It should be noted that there are some caveats in this approach. The six-digit commodity codes used here are still highly aggregated and may include other items. The specific items are identifiable at the 8-10 digit codes, but their classification vary significantly among the tariff schedules of different economies; hence the same items may appear in multiple commodity groups.

Figure 11.2: Global Trade Networks of Select PPE Products, 2018

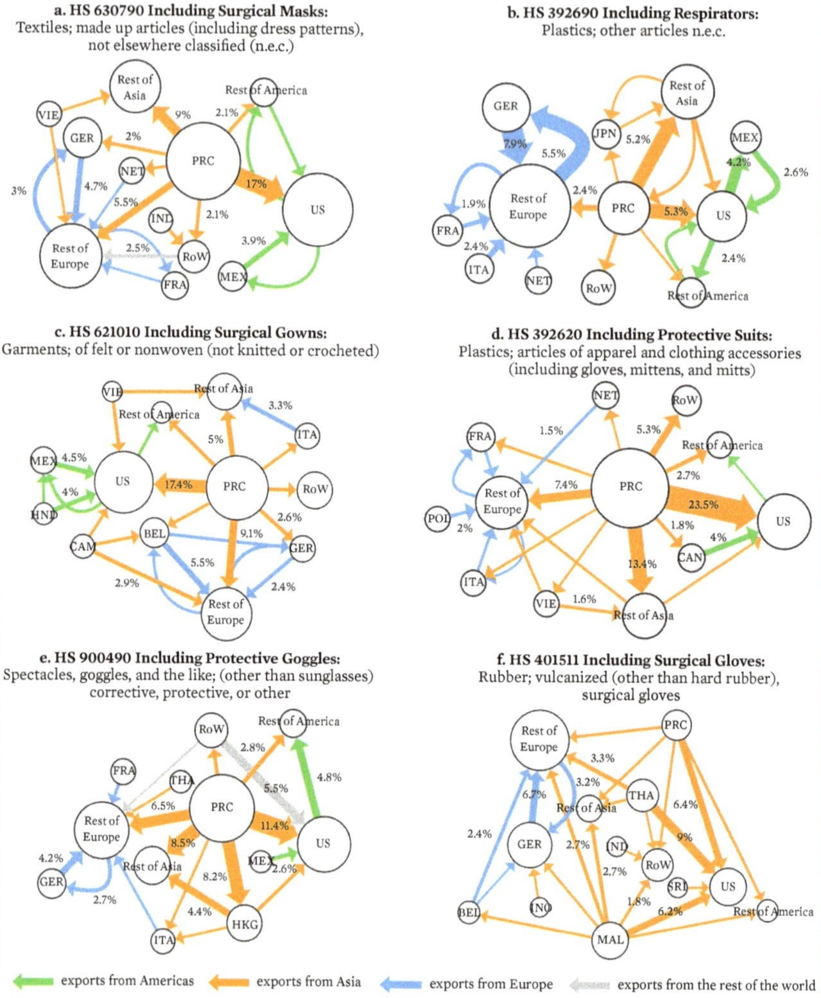
a. HS 630790 Including Surgical Masks:
Textiles; made up articles (including dress patterns), not elsewhere classified (n.e.c.)
Rest of Asia
Rest of America
VIE
GER
PRC
NET
US
IND
Rest of Europe
RoW
FRA
MEX
9%
2.1%
2%
3%
4.7%
5.5%
17%
2.1%
3.9%
2.5%
b. HS 392690 Including Respirators:
Plastics; other articles n.e.c.
GER
Rest of Asia
JPN
MEX
Rest of Europe
PRC
US
FRA
ITA
NET
RoW
Rest of America
7.9%
5.5%
5.2%
4.2%
2.6%
2.4%
1.9%
5.3%
2.4%
2.4%
c. HS 621010 Including Surgical Gowns:
Garments; of felt or nonwoven (not knitted or crocheted)
VIE
Rest of Asia
Rest of America
ITA
MEX
US
PRC
RoW
HND
CAM
BEL
GER
Rest of Europe
3.3%
5%
4.5%
4%
17.4%
2.6%
9.1%
5.5%
2.9%
2.4%
d. HS 392620 Including Protective Suits:
Plastics; articles of apparel and clothing accessories (including gloves, mittens, and mitts)
NET
RoW
FRA
Rest of America
Rest of Europe
PRC
POL
US
CAN
ITA
VIE
Rest of Asia
1.5%
5.3%
2.7%
7.4%
23.5%
2%
1.8%
4%
13.4%
1.6%
e. HS 900490 Including Protective Goggles:
Spectacles, goggles, and the like; (other than sunglasses) corrective, protective, or other
RoW
Rest of America
FRA
THA
PRC
Rest of Europe
US
GER
Rest of Asia
MEX
ITA
HKG
2.8%
4.8%
5.5%
6.5%
11.4%
8.5%
4.2%
2.6%
8.2%
2.7%
4.4%
f. HS 401511 Including Surgical Gloves:
Rubber; vulcanized (other than hard rubber), surgical gloves
Rest of Europe
PRC
3.3%
3.2%
THA
6.7%
Rest of Asia
6.4%
2.4%
GER
IND
9%
RoW
2.7%
2.7%
SRI
US
BEL
INO
1.8%
6.2%
Rest of America
MAL
exports from Americas
exports from Asia
exports from Europe
exports from the rest of the world

BEL = Belgium; CAM = Cambodia; CAN = Canada; FRA = France; GER = Germany; HKG = Hong Kong, China; HND = Honduras; HS = Harmonized System; IND = India; INO = Indonesia; ITA = Italy; JPN = Japan; MAL = Malaysia; MEX = Mexico; NET = Netherlands; POL = Poland; PPE = personal protective equipment; PRC = People's Republic of China; RoW = rest of the world; SRI = Sri Lanka; THA = Thailand; US = United States; VIE = Viet Nam; n.e.c. = not elsewhere classified.

Notes: The size of the nodes represents the economy's total trade (exports plus imports) of the concerned commodity group. The thickness of the lines represents the value of the flow of goods between economies. Some lines show the share of exports to the total global exports of the commodity group. For clarity, only exports with high values are represented by the lines.

Source: ADB calculations using data from United Nations Commodity Trade Database. https://comtrade.un.org (accessed 22 March 2020).

and Poland. Other European countries import from these countries and from the PRC. Although the US is the largest buyer of PPE produced in the PRC (and of gloves from Malaysia), it is still the major producer and at the core of the regional supply value chain for many PPE products in North and South America.

Abrupt, large supply disruptions from the PRC, as the major supplier in the trade network, will have spillovers throughout the world. Trade restrictions and export bans also exacerbate the stresses in PPE production and supplies. Given the PRC's strong centrality in the regional PPE supply chain, supply disruptions from the PRC will likely have substantial impact on regional supplies. On the other hand, Europe has its own regional PPE capacity and sources somewhat diversified among suppliers. This may help the region withstand the supply shock originating from Asia. However, production capacity in Europe is unlikely to meet a demand surge associated with the rapid spread of COVID-19. The US also depends heavily on overseas production and is expected to face a critical shortage of PPE.

Sources of Significant Supply Chain Bottlenecks

The PPE supply chain has not been properly functioning to meet a surge in demand due to the constraints in production and logistics. Prices of PPE products rose dramatically in the first few months of the COVID-19 outbreak: a sixfold increase for surgical masks, threefold for respirators, and a doubling in the price of gowns (WHO 2020). There was a backlog of 4–6 months for supply orders globally, and raw materials ran short. Export bans for PPE and key materials were implemented in many countries.

Below are major sources of the identified backlogs in the production and distribution of PPE, with a focus on face masks (also shown in Figure 11.3).

- **Raw materials.** A surge in demand for N95 masks led to a shortage of the key component, nonwoven polypropylene. In the PRC, the shortage of melt-blown fabric was a serious bottleneck in downstream processes for making high-level N95 masks.
- **Machines.** A bottleneck of melt-blown production lines appeared, and the time taken in building production lines was also a constraint. For example, it takes about half a year at least to assemble a single machine production line to make melt-blown fabric.

- **Geographic concentration of manufacturers.** The high dependence on the PRC as a production hub meant that worker quarantines led to manufacturer shutdowns. The PRC accounted for half the global supply of masks, with a daily production of about 20 million units before the outbreak.
- **Export bans.** The global shortage of face masks was worsened by export bans of masks and key materials in economies including Bangladesh; Canada; Czech Republic; Egypt; France; Germany; India; Indonesia; Iran; Japan; Jordan; Kazakhstan; Kenya; Malaysia; Pakistan; Poland; the PRC; the Russian Federation; the Republic of Korea; Taipei,China; Thailand; and Ukraine. As of 18 March 2020, export bans were in place in 22 economies.
- **Other bottlenecks.** Transport and shipping constraints caused by roadblocks and quarantine measures, and lower availability of transportation and freight containers, hoarding, profiteering, and limited workforce capacity due to illness, also contributed to the shortage.

Figure 11.3: An Illustration of PPE Supply Chain Bottlenecks

This figure illustrates the case of face masks produced by Medicom, Inc., a PPE manufacturer based in Canada with offices in the United States; the Netherlands (European arm); and Hong Kong, China (Asian arm).

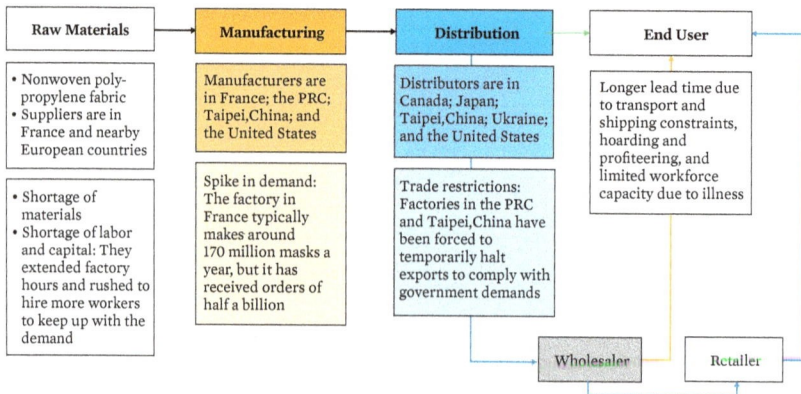

Raw Materials	Manufacturing	Distribution	End User
• Nonwoven polypropylene fabric • Suppliers are in France and nearby European countries	Manufacturers are in France; the PRC; Taipei,China; and the United States	Distributors are in Canada; Japan; Taipei,China; Ukraine; and the United States	Longer lead time due to transport and shipping constraints, hoarding and profiteering, and limited workforce capacity due to illness
• Shortage of materials • Shortage of labor and capital: They extended factory hours and rushed to hire more workers to keep up with the demand	Spike in demand: The factory in France typically makes around 170 million masks a year, but it has received orders of half a billion	Trade restrictions: Factories in the PRC and Taipei,China have been forced to temporarily halt exports to comply with government demands	

Wholesaler   Retailer

PPE = personal protective equipment, PRC = People's Republic of China.
Sources: Asian Development Bank based on L. Alderman 2020. As Coronavirus Spreads, Face Mask Makers Go Into Overdrive. *The New York Times.* 29 February; E. Feng and A. Cheng. 2020. COVID-19 Has Caused a Shortage of Face Masks. But They're Surprisingly Hard to Make. *National Public Radio.* 16 March; A. Hufford and M. Evans. 2020. Critical Component of Protective Masks in Short Supply. *The Wall Street Journal.* 7 March; B. Henneberry. n.d. How Surgical Masks Are Made. Thomas. https://www.thomasnet.com/articles/other/how-surgicalmasks-are-made/.

Responses to PPE Supply Chain Bottlenecks

Country Responses

Countries gave urgent support for firms to expand production capacity. The Government of the PRC introduced measures to boost production of face masks by aiding the purchase of raw materials and the hiring of workers as well as offering tax breaks for manufacturers. By March 2020, the PRC was producing 200 million face masks a day—more than 10 times what was being made at the start of February. Local authorities granted new licenses to allow more factories to produce masks, including high-grade ones used by health care professionals, while the local government in Jiangxi Province invested about $507,000 to help companies buy medical materials. In Japan, the government provided support for companies to increase capital investment in mask production, while securing supply of over 600 million masks per month (Ministry of Trade, Economy, and Industry of Japan 2020).

Extraordinary measures were also taken to ramp up production capacity by reorienting the manufacturers of nonmedical device for PPE production. In the PRC, automobile companies were asked to produce masks and other types of PPE. For instance, SAIC-GM-Wuling, a General Motors venture, built 14 production lines for masks with a daily capacity of 1.7 million masks. Truckmaker Shaanxi Automobile Group Co. started producing goggles with 3,000 units of daily capacity. The smartphone maker Xiaomi produced thermometers and other equipment (Bloomberg 2020). In the United Kingdom, more than 60 manufacturers including Airbus, Jaguar Land Rover, and Rolls-Royce were sent blueprints for manufacturing up to 20,000 ventilators for COVID-19 patients (Davies 2020). Major US automakers such as Ford and General Motors also worked with medical device manufacturers to make more ventilators and respirators (Bushey, Edgecliffe-Johnson, and Stacey 2020).

ADB Support in the COVID-19 Fight

Support from the Asian Development Bank (ADB) for its developing member countries (DMCs) to respond to the pandemic and the related economic crisis focused on finance, knowledge, and partnerships. ADB took a three-pronged approach: (i) support countries' immediate needs to respond to the pandemic and its secondary effects; (ii) strengthen sector-wide pandemic preparedness, stabilize economies, and strengthen health systems; and (iii) address systemic constraints limiting effective responses, working with the private sector and international organizations like the United Nations (UN).

On 13 April 2020, ADB announced a $20 billion package to address the needs of its DMCs as they responded to the COVID-19 pandemic. The package tripled the $6.5 billion assistance announced on 18 March 2020. ADB support aimed to provide emergency responses such as the procurement of medical equipment and supplies, and to address the mid- to long-term economic impact of COVID-19 transmitted through various channels (See Table 11.1 for the list of projects approved as of 20 April 2020).

Among these measures, the Supply Chain Finance Program dedicated $200 million to support companies that make and distribute medicines and other items needed to combat COVID-19 (ADB 2020). The program aimed to contribute to stabilizing the supply chain for products to protect against COVID-19, including N95 masks, COVID-19 test kits, gloves, PPE for health care providers, ventilators, hygiene items, and the like (collectively called COVID-19 Critical Goods). ADB assistance targeted channeling funds to manufacturers, their suppliers, and distributors of critical goods through post-shipment post-acceptance finance, pre-shipment loans, and distributor financing (Figure 11.4).

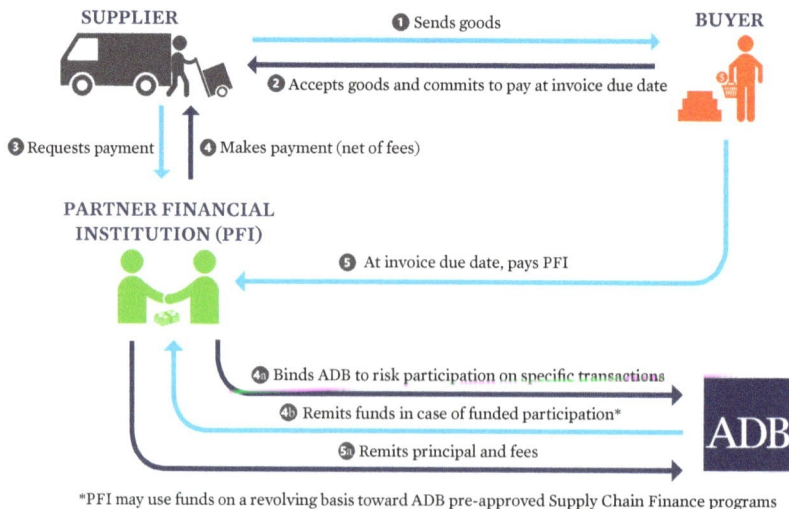

Figure 11.4: How the Supply Chain Finance Program Works

*PFI may use funds on a revolving basis toward ADB pre-approved Supply Chain Finance programs

Source: Asian Development Bank. Supply Chain Finance Program. https://www.adb. org/site/trade-finance-program/scfp.

Table 11.1: Asian Development Bank's Responses to COVID-19, as of 20 April 2020

Target DMCs	Project title	Amount ($ million)	Approval date
Afghanistan	Emergency Assistance Grant for COVID-19 Pandemic Response	40	15-Apr-20
Bangladesh	Re-allocation from Skills for Employment Investment Program	1.33	31-Mar-20
Federated States of Micronesia	COVID-19 Emergency Response	0.47	31-Mar-20
Indonesia	COVID-19 Emergency Response	3	20-Mar-20
Maldives	COVID-19 Emergency Response	0.5	25-Mar-20
	COVID-19 Emergency Response	1	25-Mar-20
	Support for Improving the Preparedness and Response to Novel Coronavirus Outbreak	0.23	02-Mar-20
Mongolia	Re-allocation from Fifth Health Sector Development Project	1.4	13-Feb-20
	Re-allocation from Regional Improvement of Border Services Project	0.08	12-Mar-20
Nauru	COVID-19 Emergency Response	0.32	31-Mar-20
	Repurposed funds from National Disaster Risk Management Fund	50	07-Apr-20
Pakistan	COVID-19 Emergency Response	2	30-Mar-20
	Re-allocation from Preparing Health Sector Assessment	0.01	23-Mar-20
	COVID-19 Emergency Response	3	13-Mar-20
Philippines	Implementing a Rapid Emergency Supplies Provision (RESP) Assistance to Design a Sustainable Solution for COVID-19 Impact Areas in the National Capital Region, Through a Public Private Collaboration	5	27-Mar-20
	COVID-19 Emergency Response (Nonsovereign)	18.6	20-Feb-20
People's Rep. of China	COVID-19 Emergency Energy Supply (Nonsovereign)	20	30-Mar-20
Marshall Islands	COVID-19 Emergency Response	0.37	31-Mar-20
Samoa	Pacific Disaster Resilience Program	2.9	15-Apr-20
Sri Lanka	Re-allocation from Health Systems Enhancement Project	0.6	25-Mar-20
Tajikistan	Re-allocation from Maternal and Child Health Integrated Care	0.1	13-Mar-20

continued on next page

Table 11.1: continued

Target DMCs	Project title	Amount ($ million)	Approval date
Tonga	Pacific Disaster Resilience Program (Phase 2)	6	15-Apr-20
	COVID-19 Emergency Response	0.47	06-Apr-20
Tuvalu	COVID-19 Emergency Response	0.37	31-Mar-20
Uzbekistan	Re-allocation from Primary Health Care Improvement Project	18	08-Apr-20
DMCs	Regional Support to Address the Outbreak of Coronavirus Disease 2019 and Potential Outbreaks of Other Communicable Diseases	2	25-Feb-20
		2	25-Mar-20
		44	08-Apr-20
	Strengthening Regional Health Cooperation in the Greater Mekong Subregion (Supplementary)	2	07-Feb-20
	Supply Chain Finance (Nonsovereign)	200	12-Mar-20
	Trade Finance Program—Additional Financing (Nonsovereign)	800	13-Apr-20
	Microfinance Risk Participation and Guarantee Program—Additional Financing (Nonsovereign)	260	13-Apr-20

DMC = developing member country.
Source: Asian Development Bank.

An $800 million increase in ADB's Trade Finance Program was also mobilized. The program is seen as an effective crisis response vehicle because it has strong relationships with many banks, both inside developing Asia and globally, the latter particularly helpful to mobilize cofinancing, involving private sector resources to leverage the impact of ADB's direct support. These ties with banks through the program enable fast and effective support through local banking systems.

Policy Implications

Lessons from Past Experiences

Recent epidemics and pandemics, including the 2009 H1N1 influenza pandemic and the 2014 Ebola virus epidemic, have provided important lessons in improving readiness of PPE supply. Transparent and comprehensive information about the availability of products on the market, production capacity, and supply responses was critical for PPE readiness during these outbreaks, epidemics, and even more so for pandemics. Ensuring guidance on appropriate use of PPE (through proper care, maintenance, and disposal) also proved helpful in avoiding wastage. The absence of a system-wide mechanism to track the amount of PPE circulating in markets and in use, and to centrally monitor orders to support future preparedness was a key challenge. Lessons learned from the past experiences suggest strategies that include (Patel et al. 2017):

- **Monitoring PPE use and distribution and centralizing visibility on orders placed.** It helps to safeguard effective delivery of patient care during an emergency response and allow distributors and manufacturers to better detect duplicate orders and forecast product demand at national, regional, and global levels. Surge capacity can be facilitated, while trade and logistics support can be prioritized even during pandemics.
- **Improving just-in-time supply system and sharing responsibility.** Stockpiles (international, national, and local) should be designed to address demands in an acute outbreak, epidemic, and pandemic, while production capacity can be raised to meet needs for PPE supply. For outbreaks in one country, it is much easier to source additional supplies from other countries, but during pandemics this is difficult since all countries are affected.
- **Improving domestic manufacturing surge capacity at the time of an event.** Government health systems must be tested before epidemics or pandemics happen.
- **Sharing information and communicating regularly.** An efficient, low-burden mechanism for governments and private sector partners to share situational and supply information needs to be developed.

Although lessons from the past are highly relevant, it is important to reinforce efforts to address the supply chain disruption of PPE under new circumstances. Worldwide supply chain networks have been a key feature of globalization from which multinational corporations seeking low-cost supplies have benefited mostly. Offshoring, lean manufacturing, and just-in-time inventory—proven measures to cut costs—may have stretched the global supply chain to breaking point in times of stress. These business practices now make firms extremely vulnerable to disruptions in parts of the supply chain or where trade restrictions are in place.

After the crisis is over, countries may want to consider maintaining adequate PPE stocks and enough surge capacity to be able to ramp up national production. It is important for countries to work together to improve resource allocation and production capacity within and across borders. Given interdependence along the supply chain network, export bans and trade restrictions on key materials and PPE should be avoided while the cross-border logistics of these types of freights are streamlined. As countries will likely face different infection curves at any given time, efficient resource allocation at a global scale will help support the national health security of individual countries while minimizing strains on limited domestic resources.

The Role of Multilateral Development Banks

The COVID-19 pandemic exposed the weakest or weaker links in the PPE supply chain. Given the acute global shortage of PPE, swift international support and cooperation for building a seamless pipeline to ensure continuity of supply was critical. Multilateral development banks including ADB are best off providing support on the following three fronts:

Help to Increase National PPE Production and Logistics Capacity, and Regional Cooperation

ADB provides funding and assistance to increase investment aimed at increasing production and capacity throughout the supply chain for PPE. ADB can provide funding to incentivize public–private partnerships to develop efficient and effective production and logistics strategies so that PPE supplies are directed to those in critical need, including health care workers. This includes developing local production capacity and mobilizing the diverse sources of supply for PPE needs during outbreaks in DMCs. Problems in the PPE supply chain were evident during the H1N1 pandemic, where PPE production was concentrated mostly in the PRC. Financing mechanisms are available but need to be expanded. Countries need guarantees to make advanced payments for supplies.

Regional cooperation mechanisms across subregions and economic cooperation clusters should be upscaled. The public goods aspect of secure PPE supply chain under pandemic conditions underpins the call for strengthening the role of regional institutions in regional or global mechanisms for epidemic and pandemic response. By strengthening collaboration with established mechanisms like the Pandemic Supply Chain Network coordinated by WHO, multilateral development banks can play a role in effective coordination with member countries at the regional level. It is essential to acquire national and local supply chain market information and share it with the members in the common regional network so that they can manage timely and more efficient responses at the onset of a disease outbreak and mitigate the spread beyond the initial outbreak.

Strengthening Supply Chain and Trade Finance Programs for MSMEs

Micro, small, and medium-sized enterprises (MSMEs) are particularly vulnerable to the economic and trade impact of COVID-19. Many of the PPE and supply manufacturers in the region are also MSMEs. Some were forced to close their businesses and lay off their employees, while many had difficulty with their cash flows. Surveys in Asia reported that many small businesses experienced supply chain disruptions, sales and trade reductions, and liquidity and working capital constraints. Trade finance programs also help facilitate trade of MSMEs in the supply chain (Myers 2020; AuManufacturing 2020; The Times of India 2020). ADB's Trade Finance Program and Supply Chain Finance Program have more roles to play in financing MSMEs in developing economies to support their domestic and international trade.

However, experts recognize that procurement of supply is a bigger challenge than financing. Globally, the WHO-led Pandemic Preparedness Network (PPN) is working on political solutions to lift export bans and on rationalization of the trade and supply of key materials so that countries get allocations based on epidemiological profiles (incidence of disease and the country risk profile) and for developing countries to get much-needed supplies. The PPN procures on behalf of partners like the World Bank and countries across the world, bringing attention to the failure of markets to deliver PPE supplies. The PPN is also helping countries with demand projections and mediating between buyers and sellers in a transparent manner and organizing logistics while flight bans are in place. For complicated supplies like ventilators, countries are looking into leasing and using refurbished units; it is important to ensure capacity is available to operate machines.

Target Aid to Support Vulnerable Groups

ADB can swiftly provide a range of grants and concessional financing for programs targeted at vulnerable groups such as women, children, and the elderly. There are growing concerns that COVID-19 would disproportionately affect women. Majority of health care professionals and workers are women. For example, women account for 60% of health care jobs in South and

Southeast Asia.[3] They make up about 80% of the nursing workforce where PPE supply is critical because patient interactions are intense. More broadly, women are often the primary caregivers for families. Should national health care systems be stretched by widespread infections, many patients will have to be cared for at home. Caring for the sick in the family will add to the social burden, while increasing the risk of infection for women.

The poorest and most vulnerable people are likely to be more exposed to infection risks, job and income losses, and suffer more from inadequate medical treatments. Aid can further support in providing masks and other PPE to community health centers and public clinics that are playing a critical frontline role for these groups.

[3] The figures are based on the national force survey data in seven countries: Bangladesh, India, Indonesia, the Philippines, Sri Lanka, Thailand, and Viet Nam.

References

Alderman, L. 2020. As Coronavirus Spreads, Face Mask Makers Go Into Overdrive. *The New York Times*. 29 February. https:// www.nytimes. com/2020/02/06/business/coronavirus-facemasks.html?action=click& module=RelatedLinks&pgtype=Article.

Asian Development Bank (ADB). 2020. ADB to Provide $200 Million to Support Strained Supply Chains in Fight Against COVID-19. News Release. 12 March. https://www.adb.org/news/adb-provide-200millionsupport-strained-supply-chains-fight-againstcovid-19.

AuManufacturing. 2020. Coronavirus, Bushfires, Drought Contribute to Biggest Drop in Manufacturing Conditions in Two Decades: Survey. 19 March. https://www.aumanufacturing. com.au/coronavirus-bushfires-droughtcontribute-to-biggest-drop-in-manufacturing-conditionsin-two-decadessurvey.

Bloomberg. 2020. Chinese Carmakers Are Now Making Face Masks, Prompted by Coronavirus. 10 February. https://www. bloomberg.com/news/articles/2020-02-10/carmakersmoonlight-as-mask-manufacturers-to-fight-coronavirus.

Bushey, C., A. Edgecliffe-Johnson, and K. Stacey. 2020. Trump Invokes Federal Law to Compel General Motors to Make Ventilators. *Financial Times*. 28 March. https://www.ft.com/ content/9328d358-1588-4498-97d9-0dd43255a076.

Davies, R. 2020. UK Government Sends Ventilator Blueprints to Major Manufacturers. *The Guardian*. 16 March. https://www. theguardian. com/business/2020/mar/16/vauxhall-ownerpsa-car-shuts-european-plants-amid-coronavirus-fears.

Feng, E., and A. Cheng. 2020. COVID-19 Has Caused a Shortage of Face Masks. But They're Surprisingly Hard to Make. *National Public Radio*. 16 March. https://www.npr.org/sections/goatsandsoda/2020/03/16/814929294/covid-19-has-caused-a-shortage-of-face-masks-but-theyre-surprisingly-hard-to-mak.

Henneberry, B. n.d. How Surgical Masks Are Made. *Thomas*. https://www. thomasnet.com/articles/other/how-surgicalmasks-are-made/.

Hufford, A., and M. Evans. 2020. Critical Component of Protective Masks in Short Supply. *The Wall Street Journal*. 7 March. https://www.wsj.com/articles/coronavirus-pressures-supplychain-for-protective-masks-11583552527.

Infection Control Today (ICT). 2008. US Pandemic Could Severely Strain Face Mask, Other PPE Supply Pipeline. 4 October. https://www.infectioncontroltoday.com/personal-protective-equipment/us-pandemic-couldseverely-strain-face-mask-other-ppe-supply-pipeline.

McKenna, M. 2020. Amid Coronavirus Fears, a Mask Shortage Could Spread Globally. *Wired*. 4 Feb. https://www.wired.com/story/amid-coronavirus-fears-a-mask-shortage-could-spread-globally/.

Ministry of Trade, Economy, and Industry (Japan). 2020. Seventeenth Meeting of the Novel Coronavirus Response Headquarters. 5 March. https://www.meti.go.jp/english/ covid-19/mask.html.

Mordor Intelligence. 2020. *Protective Clothing Market for Life Sciences Industry (2019–2024)*. https://www.mordorintelligence.com.

Myers, S. L. 2020. As Coronavirus Slams Small Business, a Noodle Shop Fights for Life. *The New York Times*. 27 February. https://www.nytimes.com/2020/02/27/business/chinacoronavirus-noodles-small-business.html.

Park, C., J. Villafuerte, A. Abiad, B. Narayan, E. Banzon, A. Aftab, and M. C. Tayag. 2020. Updated Assessment of the Potential Economic Impact of COVID-19. *ADB Briefs*. No. 133. Manila: ADB.

Patel, A., M. M. D'Alessandro, K. J. Ireland, W. G. Burel, E. B. Wencil, and S. A. Rasmussen. 2017. Personal Protective Equipment Supply Chain: Lessons Learned from Recent Public Health Emergency Responses. *Health Security* 15 (3). pp. 244–252.

The Times of India. 2020. 71% of Small Business See Demand Fall: Survey. 20 March. https://timesofindia.indiatimes.com/business/india-business/71-of-small-biz-see-demand-fallsurvey/articleshow/74720910.cms.

World Health Organization. 2020. Shortage of Personal Protective Equipment
Endangering Health Workers Worldwide. News Release. 3 March.
https://www.who.int/news-room/detail/03-03-2020-shortage-of-
personal-protectiveequipment-endangering-health-workers-worldwide.

Managing Health Threats through Regional and Intersectoral Cooperation

12

Megan Counahan, Sonalini Khetrapal, Jane Parry, Gerard Servais, and Susann Roth

As the coronavirus disease (COVID-19) pandemic has starkly illustrated, parts of the Asia and Pacific region are hot spots for emerging and re-emerging infectious diseases. Factors such as growing antimicrobial resistance and the health impacts of climate change and frequent natural disasters pose threats to regional health security. Regional cooperation is essential to protect health security. Investments in and beyond the health sector—and for health security as a regional public good—are also needed to address these regional risks.

Although regional cooperation and integration have helped bring many benefits to developing member countries (DMC) of the Asian Development Bank (ADB), with cross-boundary infrastructure, intraregional investment, and labor mobility all improving over the last 2 decades of economic growth, there are numerous pressing threats to human health. Emerging and re-emerging communicable diseases and increasing antimicrobial resistance are among them, while natural disasters and increasing adverse events from climate change add to the complexity of the cooperation challenges (United Nations Economic and Social Commission for Asia and the Pacific [ESCAP] 2017a).

The solutions for increased health security risk rely on both transboundary cooperation and cross-sectoral support on issues such as transport, urban planning, labor, environment, agriculture, and social policy (Box 12.1).

Reduced disease brings benefits to everyone, and these ultimately spread across countries. This is especially so in areas with constant movement of goods, services, and labor across borders—such as in the Greater Mekong Subregion (GMS). The challenge is ensuring that collective action necessary for health is taken both at national and regional levels (Smith 2003). Successfully addressing regional health security as a regional public good relies on political commitment translated into government actions supported through sustained financing.

<hr />

Box 12.1: What Is Health Security?

The World Health Organization (WHO) defines health security as: "the proactive and reactive activities required to minimize the vulnerability to acute public health events that endanger the collective health of populations living across geographical regions and international borders."[a]

Health security commonly incorporates a wide range of health risks, including emerging diseases, social determinants of health like poverty, and social and environmental factors (Figure 12.1.1).[b]

Figure 12.1.1: Understanding Health Security

EMERGING DISEASES HUMANITARIAN EMERGENCIES NATURAL DISASTERS
CONFLICT HEALTH RADIOACTIVE DANGERS POVERTY
ENVIRONMENTAL CHANGE SECURITY FOOD INSECURITY
VIOLENCE INFECTIOUS DISEASES CHEMICAL ACCIDENTS

WHO defines...

" the activities required, both proactive and reactive, to minimize vulnerability to acute public health events that endanger the collective health of populations living across geographical regions and international boundaries. "

[a] WHO. 2007. *World Health Report 2007.* Geneva: WHO. http://www.who.int/whr/2007/overview/en/.
[b] Y.W. Chen et al. 2009. The Nature of International Health Security. *Asia Pacific Journal of Clinical Nutrition* 18(4): 679–683.
Source: Asian Development Bank.

<hr />

Threats to Health Security in Asia and the Pacific

Hot Spots for Emerging and Re-emerging Communicable Disease

Over the past 30 years, about 60% of all known human infectious diseases and 75% of emerging infectious diseases affecting people have been zoonotic—diseases that originate from animals (WHO 2010). The most recent evidence at the time of publication suggested that while the intermediary host was less clear, the SARS-CoV-2 virus responsible for causing COVID-19 likely originated from a bat reservoir (Andersen et al. 2020). Zoonotic diseases not only threaten the health of millions of people each year, but can also have disastrous impacts on livestock and economies. In recent years, disease outbreaks, from severe acute respiratory syndrome (SARS), avian influenza, Middle East respiratory syndrome (MERS), Ebola virus disease, and Zika virus disease, have shown how emerging and re-emerging pathogens can cause severe social and economic disruption, and present threats across national borders.

The 2003 SARS outbreak, for example, infected an estimated 8,000 people and killed 800, and at the same time devastated the Asia and Pacific region's tourism and aviation sectors, taking a human and economic toll as far away from the epicenter as Canada (Lee and McKibbin 2004, Health Canada 2003). During an avian influenza outbreak in 2009, 12% of the annual poultry stock (some 50 million birds) died or were culled in Viet Nam, heavily impacting households and the national economy (Keusch et al. 2009). Similarly, the MERS outbreak cost the Republic of Korea in terms of lost tourism and trade revenue, and by depressing domestic consumer spending.

All of these are likely to be dwarfed by the impact of COVID-19, which emerged in the People's Republic of China (PRC) in late 2019. As of May 2020, the UN Department of Economic and Social Affairs Economic Analysis projected the world economy would shrink by 3.2% for the year as a whole, reducing gross domestic product (GDP) growth in developed countries by as much as 5.0% and in developing countries by 0.7% (UN Department of Economic and Social Affairs 2020). ADB analysis using the Global Trade Analysis Project model put the estimated global economic impact of COVID-19 as high as $5.8 trillion (6.4% of global GDP), assuming the pandemic was contained within 3 months, and $8.8 trillion (9.7% of global GDP) within 6 months (ADB 2020a). The analysis puts the potential economic impact in Asia and the Pacific at an estimated $1.7 trillion (6.2% of regional GDP) under a 3-month scenario and $2.5 trillion (9.3% of regional GDP) under a 6-month scenario, accounting for 30% of the global decline in output.

Countries in Southeast Asia and parts of the Pacific are predicted to be hot spots for emerging disease, as the result of conditions that include close proximity of human and domestic husbandry; climate; poverty; high population density; and insufficient disease surveillance, diagnostic capacity, and outbreak reporting (Box 12.2). This is particularly so for zoonoses, vector-borne diseases, and drug-resistant pathogens (Jones et al. 2008).

Demand for a protein-rich diet has fueled the market for meat (World Livestock 2013). Production has increased dramatically in developing countries, where per capita meat consumption has increased threefold since the early 1960s and egg consumption has increased fivefold (Horby, Pfeiffer, and Oshitani 2013). Asia accounts for 70% of this growth. Denser livestock production methods and less diversity increase the risk of disease spreading among animals and the risk of newly emerging zoonoses. With much of livestock production in East and Southeast Asia being small-scale, isolating farm animals from wildlife—the recommended practice of the Food and Agriculture Organization of the United Nations—is often impossible.

Box 12.2: What Are Emerging Diseases?

The World Health Organization (WHO) defines emerging diseases as "newly recognized, newly evolved or occurred previously but have shown an increase in incidence or expansion of geographical, vector or host range" and include those showing drug (including antimicrobial) resistance.[a] Emerging infectious diseases result from complex systems where biological, social, ecological, and technological processes interconnect to enable microbes to exploit new ecological opportunities.[b] Increasing antimicrobial resistance adds to the challenge—by making it harder to provide effective prevention and treatment of infections and to stay ahead of the evolving changes.

[a] WHO. *Emerging Zoonoses*. Geneva. http://www.who.int/zoonoses/emerging_zoonoses/en/.

[b] R. J. Coker et al. 2011. Emerging Infectious Diseases in Southeast Asia: Regional Challenges to Control. *The Lancet*. 377 (9765). pp. 599–609. https://www.thelancet.com/pdfs/journals/lancet/PIIS0140-6736(10)62004-1.pdf.

Source: Asian Development Bank.

For emerging and re-emerging infectious diseases (those former major public health threats and are becoming so again, such as malaria and tuberculosis), real-time surveillance at a subnational level, including the ability to collect and test (human and animal) samples rapidly and precisely, is needed to identify and track outbreaks. Coupled with national and regional reporting and systems for response, this will help control outbreaks. Since surveillance, testing, diagnosis, and control of zoonotic disease take place at the interface between animal and humans, systematic communication and substantial coordination between human, wildlife, and veterinary health services are vital (World Bank 2012).

Antimicrobial Resistance Is Rampant

Antimicrobial resistance is another major threat to global health security. Antimicrobial resistance is the ability of microorganisms (bacteria, viruses, and some parasites) to stop an antimicrobial agent (antibiotics, antivirals, and antimalarial medicines) from working against it, rendering standard treatments ineffective. While antimicrobial resistance occurs over time, and usually through genetic changes, the misuse and overuse of antimicrobial medicines accelerate this process.[1]

Falsified or substandard medicines also play a part. In many places, antimicrobial medicines, particularly antibiotics, are overused and misused in human and animals, and often given without consideration of the broader impact on the ecology. Significant quantities of antimicrobial medicines are used in animal husbandry and fishing for therapeutic and nontherapeutic purposes. Traces of these excessively used antibiotics then enter the food chain, exacerbating antibiotic resistance in humans.

South Asia and Southeast Asia are home to the highest number of major bacterial pathogens for which there is antimicrobial resistance, including multidrug-resistant tuberculosis (Bhatia and Narain 2010; Song 2005). The prevalence of antimicrobial resistance of major bacterial pathogens has been accelerating and is a serious threat to global public health. For example, in 2016, there were an estimated 600,000 new cases of multidrug- and rifampicin-resistant tuberculosis. Drug resistance has complicated HIV and malaria treatment, and antimicrobial resistances are on the rise as well.

The COVID-19 pandemic will likely exacerbate this crisis. Although this is a viral infection, as with other viral respiratory diseases, patients are often co-infected with bacterial pneumonia that sometimes is caused by drug-resistant bacteria. Of the almost 300,000 deaths caused by the 2009 H1N1 influenza pandemic, from 29% to as much as 55% were due to secondary

---

[1] World Health Organization (WHO). *Antimicrobial Resistance*. Geneva. http://www.who.int/antimicrobial-resistance/en/.

bacterial pneumonia (Roos 2012; Morris, Cleary, and Clarke 2017). COVID-19 may follow a similar pattern. Data from Wuhan, the city in the PRC where the virus that causes the disease emerged, showed that one in every seven patients hospitalized with the disease acquired a secondary bacterial infection (Zhou et al. 2020).

Climate Change and Natural Disasters Increase Threats to Health

Climate change impacts the ecosystem by increasing the incidence, scale, frequency, and complexity of disasters.[2] These disasters can lead to increased risks for outbreaks, as people (and their livestock) are displaced, medical treatment is interrupted, and health systems impacted. Natural disasters have made a significant impact on health security on a global scale. Asia and the Pacific, with 60% of the world's population, is highly vulnerable. Countries in the region struggle to reduce disaster risk (Table 12.1). Since 1970, and as shown in Figure 12.1, disasters in Asia and the Pacific, such as earthquakes, storms, and floods, have killed 2 million people—contributing 57% of the global death toll and a cost of $1.3 trillion (ESCAP 2017b).

Table 12.1: Disaster-Affected Populations by Yearly Average and Country

Rank	Country	Affected Population Per Million People, Per Year	
		2005–2015	2020–2030 estimate
1	Bangladesh	5,430	5,329
2	Philippines	6,079	5,043
3	Viet Nam	3,615	3,237
4	Lao People's Democratic Republic	3,034	2,702
5	Bhutan	2,929	2,679
6	Myanmar	2,452	2,058
7	Nepal	1,933	1,885
8	India	1,907	1,794
9	Cambodia	1,732	1,581
10	Republic of Korea	1,456	1,250

Source: United Nations Economic and Social Commission for Asia and the Pacific. 2017. *Asia-Pacific Disaster Report*. Bangkok.

[2] WHO. *Climate Change and Human Health.* http://www.who.int/globalchange/en.

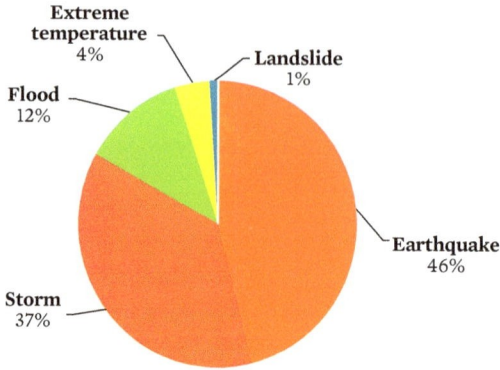

Figure 12.1: Fatalities from Asia and the Pacific Natural Disasters, 1970–2018

Note: Percentages are of the total around 2.03 million recorded fatalities.

Source: The Emergency Events Database, cited in UN Economic and Social Commission for Asia and the Pacific. 2019. The Disaster Riskscape Across Asia-Pacific: Pathways for Resilience, Inclusion and Empowerment. *Asia-Pacific Disaster Report 2019.* Bangkok. https://www.unescap.org/sites/default/files/publications/Asia-Pacific%20Disaster%20Report%202019_full%20version.pdf.

Drivers of Health Security Threats in Asia and the Pacific

Urban Areas Are Growing

From 2000 to 2024, the world's total population is projected to grow by 1.76 billion, with 86% expected to take place in urban areas of low- and middle-income countries (UN 2006). It is estimated that by 2050, Asia and the Pacific will be home to 3.2 billion urban dwellers (UN Human Settlements Programme and ESCAP 2015). In 2018, almost 600 million people, about one in three urban residents in Asia, were living in slums and informal settlements.[3] People living in slums are the most vulnerable to health risks (WHO 2016a). Poor housing conditions, congestion, and lack of access to safe water and sanitation—all typical characteristics of slums—increase the risk of communicable disease (Adiga et al. 2018). The COVID-19 pandemic illustrates the role of social inequality in vulnerability to disease (Riley, Raphael, and Snyder 2020).

[3] United Nations Department of Economic and Social Affairs. Sustainable Development Goals Overview 11: Sustainable Cities and Communities. Make Cities and Human Settlements Inclusive, Safe, Resilient and Sustainable. New York. https://unstats.un.org/sdgs/report/2019/goal-11/.

Overcrowding is a prominent risk factor of rapid communicable disease transmission, and crowded sleeping areas are associated with influenza in young children (Irfan et al. 2017; Doshi 2015). Tuberculosis is among the diseases especially affecting urban poor population groups. Only investment in improving their determinants of health (for example, their living conditions) will help to stop it. Poor air quality due to pollution is also associated with greater risk of respiratory disease, including from COVID-19 infection (Zhu et al. 2020). Overburdened urban health systems are unprepared for disease outbreaks. Improving urban health risk management, including active surveillance, and reinforcing local health systems can reduce the impact of infectious disease outbreaks, disasters, and public health emergencies (WHO/UN-HABITAT 2016).

As Trade Increases, So Does Population Mobility

Rapidly increasing labor migration threatens health security. The number of international migrants—people residing in a country other than their country of birth—is estimated to be almost 272 million globally in 2020, the highest-ever recorded (UN International Organization for Migration [IOM] 2020a). ADB reports that over a third of international migrants worldwide in 2017 (258 million) originated from Asia and the Pacific, making the region the largest source. International migrants from the region almost doubled from 48.3 million in 1990 to 86.9 million in 2017. The total number of migrants residing in Asia and the Pacific stood at 42.4 million in 2017, with about 71% from economies in the region (ADB 2019).

Migrants, particularly those in the informal sector, often have limited access to health services. They are unable to access national health systems and are commonly not included in outreach or health education, nor considered for national health planning and policy development. Even Thailand—a country that has made considerable effort to make health care accessible to migrants regardless of their legal status—faces challenges. The sheer number of migrant workers makes them difficult to reach. According to the IOM, the country hosts an estimated 4 million to 5 million migrants, both legal and undocumented (IOM 2020b). Failure to invest in migrant health can have devastating effects on national health security, as the example of the COVID-19 epidemic in Singapore illustrates. Having initially controlled the outbreak among its population very well, the government overlooked the city's migrant workers, who account for 1.4 million of the city state's 5.8 million population—less than 25% of the total. As of 22 May, migrant workers accounted for 85% of all its COVID-19 cases as the disease ripped through their cramped, unhygienic dormitories (Bismonte 2020).

As many governments in Asia and the Pacific continue working toward greater ease of travel across borders—improving road infrastructure, growing cross-border trade, and increasing private investment and construction activities—the possible health and disease impacts on mobile and migrant populations need to be addressed collaboratively at a regional level.

Health Systems Need Strengthening

As signatories to the International Health Regulations (WHO 2005), governments acknowledge that investing in health systems will yield direct health and economic benefits and help protect populations from emerging health threats. However, the challenge is daunting. In Asia and the Pacific, the average total health expenditure as a percentage of GDP is low, at 5.3% for East Asia and the Pacific (excluding high-income countries) and 4.4% for South Asia.[4] In absolute terms, domestic health spending has held relatively constant, irrespective of the rate of economic growth. Although ADB's DMC average health expenditure as a percentage of GDP is nearly 6%, significant variation exists, and a worryingly large number of countries continue to underinvest (Oliver Wyman n.d.).

At the same time DMCs' health budgets are being stretched by falling donor expenditure in health and the increasing need to tackle the growing prevalence of noncommunicable diseases, which are rapidly becoming national priorities. While noncommunicable diseases place additional strain on already underfunded health systems, they can also provide an opportunity to strengthen patient-centric care. However, it is difficult for DMCs to move the focus away from "quick-fix" solutions. The underlying strengthening of health systems, which is necessary to bring sustained change, is more challenging and needs to involve outside actors such as finance ministries. Weaknesses in health systems have been highlighted during the COVID-19 pandemic. Recovering from the impact of the COVID-19 pandemic and being ready for future pandemics will require investment in public health emergency preparedness. ESCAP estimates that the region will need $880 million a year through 2030 in emergency preparedness, risk management, and response (ESCAP 2020).

---

[4] World Bank. 2014. *Health Expenditure,* Total, as percentage of GDP. Washington, DC. https://data.worldbank.org/indicator/SH.XPD.CHEX.GD.ZS.

Strengthening health systems is an important building block for health security. It improves data collection on surveillance and monitoring of infectious diseases, regulation of the private sector and harnessing its potential, and regulation of the medicines supply chain. These can address not only the health risks to a country's own population, but also its regional and international obligations to protect health security (Figure 12.2).

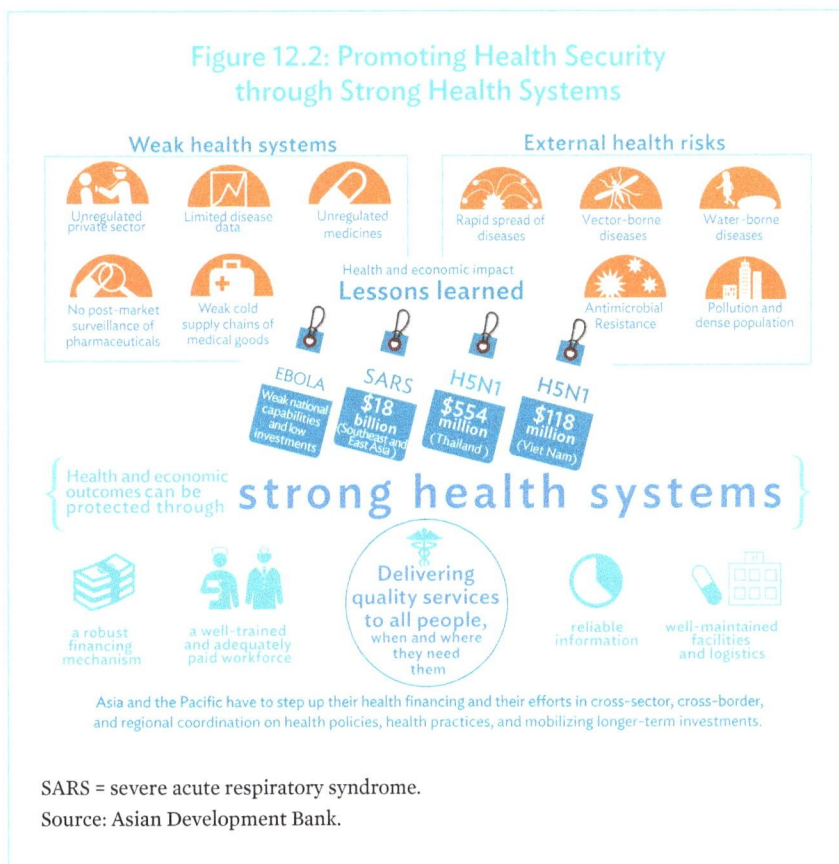

Figure 12.2: Promoting Health Security through Strong Health Systems

Weak health systems

- Unregulated private sector
- Limited disease data
- Unregulated medicines
- No post-market surveillance of pharmaceuticals
- Weak cold supply chains of medical goods

External health risks

- Rapid spread of diseases
- Vector-borne diseases
- Water-borne diseases
- Antimicrobial Resistance
- Pollution and dense population

Health and economic impact

Lessons learned

- EBOLA — Weak national capabilities and low investments
- SARS — $18 billion (Southeast and East Asia)
- H5N1 — $554 million (Thailand)
- H5N1 — $118 million (Viet Nam)

Health and economic outcomes can be protected through **strong health systems**

- a robust financing mechanism
- a well-trained and adequately paid workforce
- **Delivering quality services to all people, when and where they need them**
- reliable information
- well-maintained facilities and logistics

Asia and the Pacific have to step up their health financing and their efforts in cross-sector, cross-border, and regional coordination on health policies, health practices, and mobilizing longer-term investments.

SARS = severe acute respiratory syndrome.
Source: Asian Development Bank.

Health Security in the Age of COVID-19

On 30 January 2020, WHO declared a public health emergency of international concern due to the rapidly spreading novel coronavirus 2019-nCoV, subsequently named SARS-CoV-2, the cause of COVID-19. When a pandemic was declared on 12 March, there were more than 125,000 confirmed cases and 4,613 confirmed deaths worldwide (WHO 2020a).

By 15 May, according to WHO data, there were over 4.4 million confirmed COVID-19 cases globally, and over 86,800 deaths had been recorded (WHO 2020b). The disease was continuing its global sweep, and as the countries hit earliest, such as the PRC, Italy, and the Republic of Korea were cautiously lifting restrictions put in place to control the spread of the disease; many others, especially in developing countries, were bracing for the worse yet to come. Scientists had been warning for decades that the world was likely to experience a major infectious disease outbreak, likely zoonotic in origin. Indeed, this concern was at the heart of the Global Health Security Agenda (Box 12.3 on page 486). Yet public health spending and pandemic preparedness plans for individual nations show that often their predictions fell victim to limited resources, shifting public health priorities, and the uncertain time frame for new epidemics (Gronvall 2020).

COVID-19 has dispelled any doubt that a zoonosis could have a devastating impact on human health. It demonstrates the importance of reliable epidemiological data to understand new infectious diseases and their infectious potential, fatality rates, and at-risk populations. Increasing rates of noncommunicable diseases and their risk factors have made more people vulnerable to COVID-19. The pandemic has demonstrated the importance of linkages between diseases and highlighted the danger of not considering communicable and noncommunicable diseases in tandem.

As well as highlighting the fundamental need for cross-border and multilateral support and cooperation in health security, the pandemic raised other important health security issues. It exacerbated existing public challenges, including combating antimicrobial resistance (Box 12.3), and ensuring public health measures such as immunization and HIV services are in place to address infectious diseases. It highlighted the delicate and sometimes contentious balance between individual rights and health security. It also challenged the moral framework for decision-making. When the COVID-19 pandemic started, many governments took an unprecedented "whatever it takes" approach to protect the elderly and children and the most vulnerable population groups. The pandemic may also present opportunities for a new and better direction in global health and health security.

The Need for Improving Transnational Cooperation

COVID-19 has put investment needs for regional health security into sharp relief. It is difficult to imagine a more compelling illustration of health security as a regional and global public good. The pandemic has shown how communities, even when separated into sovereign states, are interconnected, mutually reliant, and only as strong as their weakest link. The shutdown of international borders and the unprecedented disruption to global supply chains as countries attempted to bring their respective outbreaks under control, and show how any semblance of normal trade, population movement, and regional cooperation can exist only when there is a certain level of health security. The pandemic proved the need for better regional and global coordination on health security to coordinate policy decisions and use scientific evidence to manage the spread of infections.

The COVID-19 pandemic has indeed prompted greater regional cooperation. The policy actions of three groupings illustrate how each facilitated coordinated regional responses.

Association of Southeast Asian Nations. The Special Association of Southeast Asian Nations (ASEAN) Plus Three Summit on Coronavirus Disease 2019 (COVID-19) was held on 14 April 2020. In a statement after the summit, ASEAN Plus Three (APT) reaffirmed members' "shared commitment to strengthen solidarity, enhance cooperation and mutual support among the APT countries to control and contain the spread of the pandemic, addressing the adverse impact of the pandemic on our societies and economies" (ASEAN 2020a). The resolutions that emerged from the meeting included:

- Strengthening the early warning system in the region for pandemics and other epidemic diseases as well as regular, timely, and transparent exchange of real-time information, sharing experiences and best practices, mutual technical support; and support a strong, collective response for control and treatment to harness synergies for curbing COVID-19.
- Improving national and regional capacities to prepare for and respond to pandemics, including the protection of health care workers and other frontline personnel, and to provide adequate medicines and medical supplies, especially diagnostic tools, personal protective equipment (PPE), and medical equipment.
- Consideration about setting up a regional stockpile of essential medical supplies to respond to emergency needs, and drawing on existing regional emergency reserve facilities, including warehouses managed by the ASEAN Coordinating Centre for Humanitarian Assistance on disaster management.
- Support for ongoing regional efforts by the APT health cooperation sector and by ASEAN to enhance capacities to prevent, detect,

and respond to public health threats, leveraging the International Health Regulations (2005) and existing mechanisms, including, among others, the ASEAN Emergency Operations Center Network for public health emergencies and the ASEAN BioDiaspora Virtual Centre.

- Strengthening scientific cooperation in epidemiological research, including through the APT Field Epidemiology Training Network, and coordination involving the private sector, toward the rapid development, manufacturing, and distribution of diagnostics antiviral medicines and vaccines, while following the objectives of efficiency, safety, equity accessibility, and affordability—and sharing and leveraging digital technologies and innovation to promote a science-based response to combating COVID-19.

The organization continued to work on COVID-19-related issues after the summit, reaffirming the 30 April commitment and publishing a Risk Assessment for International Dissemination of COVID-19 to the ASEAN Region in May 2020 (ASEAN 2020b).

South Asian Association for Regional Cooperation. On 15 March 2020, the South Asia Association for Regional Cooperation (SAARC) held its first high-level meeting since 2014. Although not an official summit, seven national leaders and Pakistan's health minister attended the videoconference, which was telecast live on YouTube and broadcast on television throughout the region (SAARC 2020). India's Prime Minister launched a COVID-19 emergency fund with an initial contribution of $10 million, and more than $8 million in voluntary contributions from most SAARC members was added.

Central Asia Regional Economic Cooperation. Central Asia Regional Economic Cooperation (CAREC) countries have been in constant communication, sharing information and experiences in containing COVID-19. The PRC and Kazakhstan extended support to neighbors by sending medical teams and equipment. Central Asian countries have deliberated joint actions to ensure the free movement of food supplies, agricultural products, and humanitarian and medical supplies during the crises.

The CAREC 2030 strategy includes health as an operational priority to help CAREC countries address pandemic risks, control communicable diseases, and reduce the burden of noncommunicable diseases through regional cooperation (ADB 2017). For this purpose, a forthcoming scoping study on CAREC health cooperation (supported by ADB) will identify forward-looking approaches to respond to health threats in the region. These include strengthening regional health security, improving health information systems and human resources, improving access to medicine and health services, enhancing health care for migrant workers, and strengthening interregional cooperation with non-CAREC countries. It will be essential to draw lessons from the ongoing COVID-19 pandemic and accelerate efforts to jointly tackle common health threats, given the CAREC region's vulnerability to repeated disease outbreaks. Technical assistance of about $4 million is being provided by ADB to help CAREC countries be better prepared for future public health threats like the COVID-19 pandemic.

Public Health Service Disruptions

The COVID-19 pandemic threatened to disrupt the provision of essential health services because it has created supply and demand barriers. The UN Children's Fund (UNICEF) warned that more than 1 million children under 5 years than usual could die over 6 months due to weakened health systems and the disruption of services during the COVID-19 pandemic (Robertson et al. 2020). Disruption of immunization services, even for brief periods, is a particular worry. Interrupted immunization will increase the numbers of susceptible individuals and raise the likelihood of outbreak-prone diseases that vaccines could have prevented, according to WHO (WHO 2020c).

One of WHO's guiding principles in its advice to member states is that immunization is a priority health service that should, as far as possible, be safeguarded during the COVID-19 pandemic. However, major constraints hamper continued provision in low- and middle-income countries (Fields 2020). These include disruptions to vaccine supplies because of reduced air transport from manufacturing sites, and to services at a time community-based outreach to remote populations is suspended. As health workers are diverted to the pandemic response, practical barriers to working safely include the shortages of PPE and the limited transport options to get to work. On the demand side, turnout for immunization is reduced when caregivers heed stay-at-home orders and avoid contact with the health system.

Similarly, service disruptions for tackling malaria and HIV have implications for global health security. WHO has reported suspension of insecticide-treated net and indoor residual spraying campaigns because of concerns around exposure to COVID-19 (WHO 2020d). Modeling by a group convened by WHO and the

Joint UN Programme on HIV/AIDS estimates that a 6-month interruption in antiretroviral therapy services and supplies for people living with HIV could lead to more than 500,000 extra deaths from AIDS-related illnesses in sub-Saharan Africa in 2020–2021, effectively setting the clock on AIDS-related deaths back to 2008, when the region recorded more than 950,000 AIDS-related deaths (Joint UN Programme on HIV 2020).

The implication for health security is countries need systems that ensure essential health services are provided and that enough resources are available to manage them separately from health emergencies such as major infectious disease outbreaks and epidemics.

The COVID-19 pandemic has revealed fundamental shortcomings in public health services and a reliance on hospital and curative services. As a result, hospitals have become infection hot spots for COVID-19, infecting a significant share of the health workforce.

The Ethical Minefield of Immunity Passports to Manage Health Security Threats

As the COVID-19 pandemic has progressed, countries have grappled with what the "new normal" might look like. A lack of definitive evidence about post-infection immunity to COVID-19 notwithstanding, the idea of a COVID-19 immunity passport or immunity-based license has been suggested. This would give people with immunity greater freedom of movement, either within a community or across a national border, than those naive to the disease. On one hand, immunity passports can be seen as an artificial restriction on who can and cannot participate in social, civic, and economic activities (Phelan 2020). They carry the risk of creating a perverse incentive for people to become infected, particularly those who cannot afford to be excluded from the workforce. This, in turn, risks compounding existing gender, race, ethnicity, and nationality inequities.

How to ensure that such passports, especially in digital form, are difficult to falsify or trade, while protecting the privacy and human rights of the holder, are also contentious and unresolved issues. On the other hand, immunity passports can, and some would say should, be compared to the alternative: enforcing strict public health restrictions for many months or permitting activities that increase the risk of further outbreaks. Both scenarios also exacerbate inequalities and impose serious social and economic burdens (Persad and Emanuel 2020).

Immunity passports have been used before, when considering mandatory yellow fever and other disease vaccinations when entering certain countries in the context of International Health Regulations (IHR) 2005. Immunity passports will become relevant if a COVID-19 vaccine is available and accessible. Similar ethical and privacy-related issues have emerged about contact tracking systems using apps on mobile phones.

COVID-19 Diagnostics, Therapeutics, and Vaccine Regulation and Supply Chain Issues

Soon after the SARS-CoV-2 virus was identified, scientists in multiple locations geared up to work on developing diagnostics and antibody tests, therapeutics, and a vaccine. The pace of development in all three areas has been breath taking and unprecedented. As these products enter the global supply chain, strong regulatory systems and well-managed supply chains are more important than ever. Global regulatory coordination is critical for ensuring that safe and effective products can be licensed and brought to market as quickly as possible, reaching those who need them, regardless of the stage of development of a country's health system.

This is particularly important given the need to ensure that access to COVID-19 diagnostics, treatment, and vaccines remains equitable. The urgent need to develop different diagnostic tools, or attempts to repurpose existing medicines or those already in development, puts pressure on regulatory bodies to respond faster than ever. It expedites market approvals on an emergency basis, highlighting the need for robust regulatory systems that ensure quality and safety are as important as access (Duke-NUS Medical School Centre of Regulatory Excellence 2020).

Existing partnerships between regulators and reliance practices under which regulators in resource-constrained settings share data and rely on each other's regulation of medical products, can be utilized to increase pandemic responsiveness. However, even this cannot solve all problems faced by regulatory agencies, particularly in low- and middle-income countries. Because COVID-19 is a truly global pandemic, unlike the localized Ebola or Zika outbreaks, for example, demand for related medical products is global, meaning no single manufacturer can meet demand. This raises regulatory issues because low-income country regulators may not be regulating the same version of a medical product that has already gained approval from a regulatory agency with which they have a reliance agreement.

Early Lessons from the COVID-19 Pandemic

Stress testing of preparedness. WHO IHR (2005) requires that countries ensure timely sharing of information about events that may cross borders and threaten international public health. Countries are requested to report annually to the World Health Assembly on their capacities. The Joint External Evaluation is part of WHO's process to help countries assess their ability to prevent, detect, and respond to public health threats such as infectious disease outbreaks. The evaluation tool includes 19 technical areas with 48 indicators.

Using indicators derived from IHR reporting requirements, a 2018 study of the Joint External Evaluation data found that many nations were still unprepared for the next outbreak with pandemic potential (Gupta et al. 2018). This highlights the urgent need for greater capacity building and collaboration between countries to strengthen global preparedness for outbreaks and other health emergencies.

The COVID-19 pandemic has galvanized an unprecedented mobilization of the scientific community and the use of digital tools for sharing information. New and evolving knowledge has never been shared as fast as it is now, through preprint servers, and open access to COVID-19 content in peer-reviewed journals. Since January 2020, more than 7,000 papers on the subject have been published.

A new development paradigm. Just as the scientific community has had to adapt rapidly to a new, more urgent research environment, so the development sector has had to pivot quickly toward new ways of working (UN Development Programme Eurasia 2020). An optimist may even call it a "COVID dividend," i.e., "the value we will reap from the reforms, changes in behavior and other innovations which were caused, prompted or dramatically accelerated by the COVID-19 pandemic that deliver sustained improvements in the social, economic, environmental, institutional, personal, and community dimensions of our lives." (Stewart-Weeks 2020). Some of these have been "simple" solutions such as remote meetings tools to overcome inability to travel or congregate. Other more complex solutions, such as the promotion of universal basic income, have arguably brought about paradigm shifts.

The pandemic has upended traditional ideas about expertise in the field of health security and chimes with growing calls to "decolonize" global health

(Green 2019). Some of the world's most highly developed countries have spectacularly failed to control COVID-19 inside their own borders, while other middle-income countries have done far better. The pool of expertise in public health, especially in health security, is truly global.

COVID has highlighted the need to work with the private sector to create more market transparency—for example, related to COVID-19 supplies. This became tragically apparent when health systems all over the world scrambled to source essential supplies of PPE for health care and other workers in key sectors. The market's failure to respond resulted in different health systems within the same country competing for the same supplies, and also resulted in substandard and unsafe protective products being sold and distributed, and in some cases, used.

Many issues have universally applied so far in the COVID-19 pandemic. WHO takes the role of the world's technical public health agency, and as the provider of normative guidance. It is a centralized source of data on national-level epidemics and response. Both regional bodies and national governments have taken the lead in managing the epidemic at country level. However, the job of practically tackling the COVID-19 epidemic falls to local governments and communities themselves. The epidemic has shown how these, the smallest units of governance, are arguably the most important to manage health security.

ADB Support for Regional Health Security

ADB has supported regional public goods for health security for more than 20 years and has long recognized the importance of investing in collective action to reduce regional health risks. The combination of persistent and increasing public health threats, and the requirement for countries to meet the obligations of the IHR (2005), present an opportunity for ADB to assist them in achieving these complementary goals.

ADB is well-placed to help strengthen health security as a regional public good (Figure 12.3). It can structure long-term financing and convene partners across public and private sectors and across borders to design and implement successful health projects for Asia and the Pacific's socioeconomic development. Under its new corporate Strategy 2030, ADB will continue to support regional public goods for health.

Figure 12.3: How ADB Makes a Difference to Regional Health Security

ADB = Asian Development Bank, DMC = developing member country.
Source: Asian Development Bank.

ADB's investment history shows it is moving toward systematic and targeted investments to strengthen health security. In 2003, ADB supported countries to respond to SARS, and in 2006 it provided about $40 million in grant financing for the avian influenza response, which helped countries take the lessons learned from SARS and cooperate on disease surveillance and response. ADB has also managed disease-specific trust funds to combat specific communicable disease threats such as HIV and malaria through a health system strengthening approach.[5]

---

[5] ADB Cooperation Fund for Fighting HIV/AIDS. https://aric.adb.org/initiative/adb-cooperation-fund-for-fighting-hiv-aids and ADB Regional Malaria and Other Communicable Disease Threats Trust Fund https://www.adb.org/site/funds/funds/rmtf.

The Cooperation Fund for Fighting HIV/AIDS in Asia and the Pacific

In 2005, the Cooperation Fund for Fighting HIV/AIDS in Asia and the Pacific (Trust Fund) was established with a $19.2 million grant from the Government of Sweden (ADB 2015a). The objective of the grant, to be utilized by the end of 2014, was to support DMCs to develop a comprehensive AIDS response, partnering with ADB in areas that played to ADB's strategic value and advantages, and to benefit the subregions, countries, and communities most vulnerable to HIV. The trust fund worked with governments in 17 countries and with numerous partner organizations on regional and cross-border projects. Community mobilization projects in particular had a strong health security element.

Greater Mekong Subregion. Several of the Trust Fund's projects aimed to capitalize on infrastructure projects to access otherwise hard-to-reach groups with HIV prevention programs. Project staff from the Ministries of Public Works and Transport of Cambodia, the Lao People's Democratic Republic (Lao PDR), and Viet Nam were trained to mainstream HIV risk mitigation into transport and road development projects. Training tools for construction workers and affected communities, and practice guidelines for integrating HIV prevention in the infrastructure sector, were developed and widely disseminated. They continue to be used by ADB transport staff and consultants in the Greater Mekong Subregion (GMS).

Other Trust Fund projects demonstrated ADB's ability to work with nongovernment organizations to promote health security. The Raks Thai Foundation implemented an ADB project to strengthen collaboration among community-based organizations in regional HIV prevention, care, and treatment programs, with a focus on the health of mobile populations. ADB was able to capitalize on the organization's well-established access to local and regional stakeholders and target communities in a project covering the six countries of the GMS.

In the PRC, an HIV prevention and action program was launched in Yunnan province and Guangxi Zhuang Autonomous Region. The project focused on construction sites and provided materials and training for field and peer educators, as well as HIV prevention materials tailored to construction workers. Because the road project extended to the border with Myanmar, undocumented immigrants from that country were incorporated into the target group.

Papua New Guinea. A Trust Fund project focused on Lae Port, which successfully engaged with a private sector entity, the Lae Chamber of

Commerce as implementing partner to implement HIV prevention practices in the workplace and promote awareness of HIV in high-risk settings through training of peer educators.

Regional Malaria and Other Communicable Disease Threats Trust Fund

When the Regional Malaria and Other Communicable Disease Threats Trust Fund (RMTF) was established in December 2013, its remit was to support DMCs in creating multicountry, cross-border, and multisector responses to urgent malaria and other communicable disease issues (ADB 2015b and 2018a). In 2015, the fund moved from supporting the control of malaria to eliminating the disease by strengthening health systems in a process that would reduce other communicable disease threats. Two factors led to this decision: first, growing resistance to artemisinin-based combination therapy—the last line of simple-to-use and effective malaria drugs—had been detected in four GMS countries: Cambodia, Myanmar, Thailand, and Viet Nam. Second, it became clear that with the right health system building blocks in place, eliminating malaria in Asia and the Pacific was technically feasible. The Global Fund's Regional Artemisinin-resistance Initiative (RAI) was launched in 2013. RAI helped Cambodia, the Lao PDR, Myanmar, Thailand, and Viet Nam to achieve a 91% reduction in malaria deaths from 2012 to 2017. RAI's second phase started in 2018. The $242 million grant over 3 years is the Global Fund's largest regional grant, and the first with the defined goal of disease elimination from a specific area. ADB is a member of the RAI regional Steering Committee.

The rationale was that achieving elimination in Asia and the Pacific would prevent resistance reaching the African continent. Over the next 5 years, the project funded projects under six broad domains. The fund had key successes in each area:

Leadership: Galvanized malaria elimination leadership at the highest level and provided decision support for accountability.

Financing: Introduced innovative mechanisms for malaria elimination financing and donor collaboration.

Medicines: Supported regulatory and disease control bodies to work more effectively, and strengthened post-market surveillance of anti-malarials, and collaboration between regional counterparts (ADB 2018b and 2016a).

Information systems: Stimulated the appetite for transformational digital interventions and improved capacity, resulting in increased surveillance and automated reporting of malaria and communicable diseases (ADB 2016b, 2016c, 2018c–2018h).[6]

Laboratory diagnostics and surveillance: Convened partners within countries and across borders to work toward the common goal of eliminating malaria (ADB 2018i).

Promotion and prevention: Strengthened the role of health impact assessment for malaria prevention in infrastructure projects and special economic zones in border areas (ADB 2016d, 2018j, 2018k).

Greater Mekong Subregion Health Security Project

The GMS Health Security Project is composed of four loans to Cambodia, the Lao PDR, Myanmar, and Viet Nam, and a grant to the Lao PDR.[7] The project builds on interventions focusing on communicable disease control in Cambodia, the Lao PDR, and Viet Nam, and now including Myanmar.

The funding will strengthen GMS public health security. The project has three outputs: (1) improvement of regional cooperation and communicable disease control in border areas, (2) strengthening of national disease surveillance and outbreak response systems, and (3) better laboratory services and hospital infection prevention and control (Figure 12.4).

ADB Projects Related to COVID-19

ADB is supporting its DMC response to COVID-19 outbreaks through finance, knowledge, and partnerships. It has earmarked $20 billion to the task and introduced measures to streamline operations to make the delivery of assistance quicker and more flexible (ADB 2020b). These projects also have health security dimensions (Table 12.2).

---

[6] ADB, SIL-Asia *Digital Health Investment: Costing Tool.* http://sil-asia.org/costing-tool/ and the ADB, SIL-*Asia Digital Health Terminology Guide.* http://sil-asia.org/digital-health-terminology-guide/.

[7] ADB. Regional: Greater Mekong Subregion Health Security Project. https://www.adb.org/projects/48118-002/main.

Figure 12.4: The Greater Mekong Subregion Health Security Project, 2017–2022

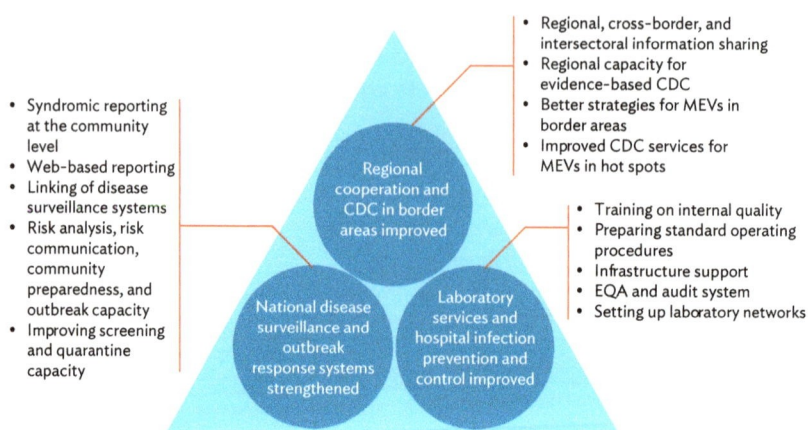

- Syndromic reporting at the community level
- Web-based reporting
- Linking of disease surveillance systems
- Risk analysis, risk communication, community preparedness, and outbreak capacity
- Improving screening and quarantine capacity

- Regional, cross-border, and intersectoral information sharing
- Regional capacity for evidence-based CDC
- Better strategies for MEVs in border areas
- Improved CDC services for MEVs in hot spots

- Training on internal quality
- Preparing standard operating procedures
- Infrastructure support
- EQA and audit system
- Setting up laboratory networks

Regional cooperation and CDC in border areas improved

National disease surveillance and outbreak response systems strengthened

Laboratory services and hospital infection prevention and control improved

CDC = communicable disease control, MEV = migrant and mobile people, ethnic minorities, and other vulnerable groups, EQA = external quality assessment.
Source: Asian Development Bank.

Table 12.2: COVID-19-Related ADB Projects

DMC (country)	Project name and number	Project type	Amount ($ million)
Control of communicable disease			
Afghanistan	Emergency Assistance for COVID-19 Pandemic Response Sovereign (Public) Project 54190-001[a]	Grant	40
Tonga	COVID-19 Emergency Response 54135-002[c]	Grant	0.47
Regional: Federated States of Micronesia, Nauru, Marshall Islands, Tuvalu	COVID-19 Emergency Response 54135-001[d]	Grant	0.32 0.37 0.47 0.37
Pakistan	COVID-19 Emergency Response 54199-001[e]	Grant	2
Maldives	COVID-19 Emergency Response 54155-001[f]	Grant	0.5

continued on next page

Table 12.2: *continued*

DMC (country)	Project name and number	Project type	Amount ($ million)
Mongolia	COVID-19 Emergency Response 54145-001[g]	Grant	1
Indonesia	COVID-19 Emergency Response 54150-001[h]	Grant	3
Philippines	COVID-19 Emergency Response 54133-001[i]	Grant	3
Mongolia	Support for Improving the Preparedness and Response to Novel Coronavirus Outbreak 54102-001[j]	Technical Assistance	0.225
Health system development			
Bangladesh	COVID-19 Response Emergency Assistance Project Sovereign (Public) Project 54173-001[b]	Loan	100
Regional	Regional Support to Address the Outbreak of Coronavirus Disease 2019 and Potential Outbreaks of Other Communicable Diseases 54079-001[k]	Technical Assistance	48
People's Republic of China	COVID-19 Emergency Response Project 54077-001[l]	Loan	CNY 130

[a] ADB. 2020. Afghanistan: Emergency Assistance for COVID-19 Pandemic Response. Manila. https://www.adb.org/projects/54190-001/main.

[b] ADB. 2020. Bangladesh: COVID-19 Response Emergency Assistance Project. Manila. https://www.adb.org/projects/54173-001/main.

[c] ADB. 2020. Tonga: COVID-19 Emergency Response. Manila. https://www.adb.org/projects/54135-002/main.

[d] ADB. 2020. Regional: Federated States of Micronesia, Nauru, Marshall Islands, Tuvalu: COVID-19 Emergency Response. Manila. https://www.adb.org/projects/54135-001/main#project-overview.

[e] ADB. 2020. Pakistan: COVID-19 Emergency Response. Manila. https://www.adb.org/projects/54199-001/main.

[f] ADB. 2020. Maldives: COVID-19 Emergency Response. Manila. https://www.adb.org/projects/54155-001/main.

[g] ADB. 2020. Mongolia: COVID-19 Emergency Response. Manila. https://www.adb.org/projects/54145-001/main.

[h] ADB. 2020. Indonesia: COVID-19 Emergency Response. Manila. https://www.adb.org/projects/54150-001/main.

[i] ADB. 2020. Philippines: COVID-19 Emergency Response. Manila. https://www.adb.org/projects/54133-001/main#project-overview.

[j] ADB. 2020. Mongolia: Support for Improving the Preparedness and Response to Novel Coronavirus Outbreak. Manila. https://www.adb.org/projects/54102-001/main.

[k] ADB. 2020. Regional: Regional Support to Address the Outbreak of Coronavirus Disease 2019 and Potential Outbreaks of Other Communicable Diseases. Manila. https://www.adb.org/projects/54079-001/main.

[l] ADB. 2020. China, People's Republic of: COVID-19 Emergency Response. Manila. https://www.adb.org/projects/54077-001/main.

Next Steps in Asia and the Pacific: Investing in Regional Health Security

Stronger Links with Global Agendas, Including Universal Health Coverage

Sustainable Development Goal 3, set by the UN, includes the targets to "achieve universal health coverage, including financial risk protection, access to quality essential health care services, and access to safe, effective, quality, and affordable essential medicines and vaccines for all." This necessitates linkages to health systems strengthening including health information and in turn strengthening health security (ADB 2015c).

Build Regional Governance and Reach for Convergence of Policies

Regional public goods can only be realized with regional effort and cooperation. The region will be able to cooperate better for health security if more countries establish regional surveillance, reporting and disease management policies, and governance processes that seamlessly transfer across national borders.

Increase Cross-Sector Approaches and Activities

Enhancing cross-border collaboration at the subnational level is key, as is integrated border development that brings several sectors together in a coordinated fashion. This requires a cohesive action plan for the multiple facets involved, including agriculture, food, and climate change. Financing institutions need to generate cross-sectoral partnerships for continued commitment at the country level.

Make Upstream Investments in Health Systems Strengthening

Preparing for the inevitability of health emergencies minimizes the impact on health, the health system, and the economy. Looking upstream and addressing weaknesses in the health system such as health financing, information, and reach are crucial to achieving this (ADB 2016e). Efforts to strengthen health security and health systems need to be integrated across the system to promote sustainability, efficiency, and effectiveness of a country's preparedness efforts, while avoiding the creation of a vertical health security silo.[8]

Areas of focus for this could include improved regulatory and governance structures, medicines, diagnostic tools and medical equipment quality and supply chain, active surveillance, diagnostics at the point of care, and service delivery to the last mile, infection prevention and control, resilient infrastructure as well as collaborating beyond the health sector to address the environmental and socioeconomic determinants of health.

Invest in Surge Capacity

Preparing for disease outbreaks should include building regional buffer stocks of key essential medicines and ensuring there is surge capacity within the health system's work force, from major hospitals down to community health workers. One way of doing this is to explore the establishment of regional workforce hubs, which promote cross-border registration of health workers to allow for surge capacity and training opportunities. The public and private sectors must work together to capitalize on their respective strengths. This requires that the public sector provides an enabling environment with a sound legal accountability and regulatory framework for the private and public sectors to collaborate. Often, the expectations between private and public sectors are not clearly set and communicated, and the performance measures and accountability toward each other are not well-defined.

Use Digital Tools for Surveillance

Information and communication technology, geospatial technologies, digital diagnostic equipment and laboratory information systems networks, mobile applications for disease surveillance and reporting, and electronic health records with unique health identifiers that can securely identify patients without exposing private data, wherever and whenever they interact with the health system, and standardization of data management across borders, all have a role to play in health security (ADB 2016f). Investments need to go beyond traditional communicable diseases surveillance systems and need to build strong foundations for digitally enabled information systems, which appreciate the patient at the center.

---

[8]   WHO. *Health Security and Health Systems Strengthening—An Integrated Approach.* http://www.who.int/csr/disease/ebola/health-systems-recovery/health-security.pdf?ua=1.

Access Innovative Financing

As many DMCs begin to grapple with what is looming in the post-donor funding environment and are compelled to look more to their own resources, development partners have a role to assist countries to tap into innovative financing mechanisms, such as blended loan products, bonds, risk transfer products, and public–private collaboration, to mobilize funding for health security.

Box 12.3: International and Regional Global Health Security Initiatives

International Health Regulations (2005)

IHR (2005) is a legally binding set of regulations designed to "prevent, protect against, control and provide a public health response to the international spread of disease in ways that are commensurate with and restricted to public health risks, and which avoid unnecessary interference with international traffic and trade." They came into effect on 15 June 2007, and 196 countries agreed to abide by the regulations that require events of public health significance (including zoonotic diseases) to be reported to the World Health Organization (WHO). The regulations include specific measures at ports, airports, and ground crossings to limit the spread of health risks to neighboring countries.[a]

Asia Pacific Strategy for Emerging Diseases and Public Health Emergencies

The newly updated Third Asia Pacific Strategy for Emerging Diseases (APSED)[b] provides a common framework for action for the region to implement and strengthen the core capacities required under the 2005 IHR. The 2017 version, APSED-III, contributes to health systems strengthening and universal health coverage by focusing on eight essential public health functional areas necessary for public health emergency preparedness, risk mitigation, and response operation.

Sendai Framework for Disaster Risk Reduction 2015–2030

The Sendai Framework for Disaster Risk Reduction[c] was adopted by United Nations (UN) member states in March 2015 at the UN World Conference on Disaster Risk Reduction in Sendai, Japan and endorsed by the UN General Assembly in June 2015. Health is treated as a key element of the framework. The framework's goal is to prevent new disaster risks and reduce existing ones through the implementation of integrated cross-sector measures that prevent and reduce hazard exposure and vulnerability to disaster, increase preparedness for response and recovery, and thus strengthen resilience. Four of the seven Sendai Framework global targets are health-related: sustainably reduce disaster mortality, number of affected people, infrastructure damage, and service disruption; and sustainably increase the number of countries with disaster risk reduction strategies. The Sendai Framework also emphasizes resilient health systems by integrating disaster risk management into government policies.

continued on next page

Box 12.3: *continued*

One Health

One Health is a UN initiative to forge close collaboration between human and animal health to address the risk from zoonoses. It is an approach to designing and implementing programs, policies, legislation, and research so that different sectors can connect and collaborate. Taking a One Health approach is especially powerful when tackling issues of food safety, antimicrobial resistance, and the control of zoonoses.[d]

Global Health Security Agenda

Launched in February 2014, the Global Health Security Agenda (GHSA)[e] is a growing partnership of 64 countries, international organizations, and nongovernment stakeholders to help build countries' capacity to help create a world safe and secure from infectious disease threats, and elevate global health security as a national and global priority.

GHSA takes a multilateral and multisector approach to strengthening both global and national capacity to prevent, detect, and respond to human and animal infectious disease threats. It facilitates collaborative efforts to achieve specific and measurable targets around biological threats. It also supports the achievement of the requirements for global health security, including the IHR (2005) and the Organization of Animal Health's Performance of Veterinary Services Pathway, and other relevant frameworks. In addition to individual countries, advisory partners include WHO, Food and Agriculture Organization of the United Nations, World Organisation for Animal Health, Interpol, Economic Community of West African States, UN Office for Disaster Risk Reduction, and European Union.

[a] WHO. 2005. *International Health Regulations*. Third Edition. Geneva: WHO.

[b] WHO. 2016. *Asia Pacific Strategy for Emerging Diseases and Public Health Emergencies (APSED-III): Advancing Implementation of International Health Regulations beyond 2016*. Geneva: WHO.

[c] WHO. 2015. *Sendai Framework for Disaster Risk Reduction*. Geneva: WHO.

[d] WHO. 2017. *One Health*. Geneva: WHO.

[e] *Global Health Security Agenda*. https://www.ghsagenda.org/.

Source: Compiled by authors.

References

Adiga, A., S. Chu, S. Eubank, C. J. Kuhlman, B. Lewis, A. Marathe, M. Marathe, E. K. Nordnerg, S. Swarup, A. Vullikanti, and M. L. Wilson. 2018. Disparities in Spread and Control of Influenza in Slums of Delhi: Findings from an Agent-based Modelling Study. *BMJ Open.* 8 (1): e017353. https://doi.org/10.1136/bmjopen-2017-017353.

Andersen, G., A. Rambault, W. I. Lipkin, E. C. Holmes, and R. F. Garry. 2020. The Proximal Origin of SARS-CoV-2. *Nature Medicine.* 26. pp. 450–452. https://www.nature.com/articles/s41591-020-0820-9.

Asian Development Bank (ADB). 2015a. *Game Changers, Success Stories, Lessons Learned: The ADB Cooperation Fund for Fighting HIV/AIDS in Asia and the Pacific.* Manila. https://www.adb.org/publications/game-changers-success-stories-lessons-learned-fighting-hiv-aids.

_____. 2015b. *Malaria Elimination: An Entry Point for Strengthening Health Systems and Regional Health Security, and a Public Health Best-Buy.* Manila. https://www.adb.org/sites/default/files/publication/178203/malaria-elimination.pdf.

_____. 2015c. *Universal Health Coverage by Design: ICT-enabled Solutions are the Future of Equitable, Quality Health Care and Resilient Health Systems.* Manila. https://www.adb.org/publications/universal-health-coverage-by-design.

_____. 2016a. *Strong Supply Chains Transform Public Health.* Manila. https://www.adb.org/sites/default/files/publication/214036/strong-supply-chains.pdf.

_____. 2016b. *The Geography of Universal Health Coverage.* Manila. https://www.adb.org/sites/default/files/publication/183422/geography-uhc.pdf.

_____. 2016c. *Monitoring Universal Health Coverage in the Western Pacific: Framework, Indicators, and Dashboard.* Manila. https://www.adb.org/sites/default/files/publication/203926/uhc-western-pacific.pdf.

_____. 2016d. *Greater Mekong Subregion Health Impact Assessment Project: Project Brief.* Manila. https://www.adb.org/sites/default/files/publication/186064/gms-hia-project.pdf.

_____. 2016e. *Digital Health Infrastructure: The Backbone of Surveillance for Malaria Elimination*. Manila. https://www.adb.org/publications/digital-health-infrastructure-malaria-elimination.

_____. 2016f. *On the Road to Universal Health Coverage: Every Person Matters*. Manila. https://www.adb.org/sites/default/files/publication/183512/uhc-every-person-matters.pdf.

_____. 2017. *CAREC 2030: Connecting the Region for Shared and Sustainable Development*. Manila. https://www.carecprogram.org/uploads/2017-CAREC-2030.pdf.

_____. 2018a. *Regional Malaria and Other Communicable Disease Threats Trust Fund: Final Report*. Manila. https://www.adb.org/sites/default/files/publication/471081/malaria-trust-fund-report.pdf.

_____. 2018b. *Strong Regulation of Medical Products: Cornerstone of Public Health and Regional Health Security*. Manila. https://www.adb.org/publications/strong-regulation-medical-products.

_____. 2018c. *Building Capacity for Geo-Enabling Health Information Systems: Supporting Equitable Health Services and Well-Being for All*. Manila. https://www.adb.org/sites/default/files/publication/401686/adb-brief-088-geo-enabling-health-information-systems.pdf.

_____. 2018d. *Unique Health Identifier Assessment Tool Kit*. Manila. https://www.adb.org/sites/default/files/institutional-document/421911/unique-health-identifier-assessment-tool-kit.pdf.

_____. 2018e. *Transforming Health Systems through Good Digital Health Governance*. Manila. https://www.adb.org/sites/default/files/publication/401976/sdwp-051-transforming-health-systems.pdf.

_____. 2018f. *Digital Health Convergence Meeting Tool Kit*. Manila. https://www.adb.org/sites/default/files/publication/424311/sdwp-052-guidance-investing-digital-health.pdf.

_____. 2018g. *Guidance for Investing in Digital Health*. Manila. https://www.adb.org/publications/guidance-investing-digital-health.

_____. 2018h. *Digital Health Impact Framework User Manual.* Manila. https://www.adb.org/sites/default/files/publication/465611/sdwp-057-digital-health-impact-framework-manual.pdf.

_____. 2018i. *Portable Screening Devices for Medicine Quality: Putting Power into the Hands of Regulators in Low-Resource Settings.* Manila. https://www.adb.org/sites/default/files/publication/461051/adb-brief-101-screening-devices-medicine-quality.pdf.

_____. 2018j. *Health Impact Assessment: A Good Practice Sourcebook.* Manila. https://www.adb.org/sites/default/files/institutional-document/452951/health-impact-assessment-sourcebook.pdf.

_____. 2018k. *A Health Impact Assessment Framework for Special Economic Zones in the Greater Mekong Subregion.* Manila. https://www.adb.org/sites/default/files/publication/426306/health-impact-assessment-framework-economic-zones-gms.pdf.

_____. 2019. International Migration in Asia and the Pacific: Determinants and Role of Economic Integration. *Economics Working Paper Series.* No. 592. Manila. https://www.adb.org/publications/migration-asia-pacific-role-economic-integration.

_____. 2020a. *An Updated Assessment of the Economic Impact of COVID-19.* Manila. https://www.adb.org/sites/default/files/publication/604206/adb-brief-133-updated-economic-impact-covid-19.pdf.

_____. 2020b. ADB Triples COVID-19 Response Package to $20 Billion. Press release, Manila, 13 April. https://www.adb.org/news/adb-triples-covid-19-response-package-20-billion.

Association of Southeast Asian Nations (ASEAN). 2020a. Joint Statement of the Special ASEAN Plus Three Summit on Coronavirus Disease 2019 (COVID-19). 14 April. https://asean.org/storage/2020/04/Final-Joint-Statement-of-the-Special-APT-Summit-on-COVID-19.pdf.

_____. 2020b. Risk Assessment for International Dissemination of COVID-19 to the ASEAN Region. ASEAN Biodiaspora Virtual Center, 15 May. https://asean.org/storage/2020/02/COVID-19_Report-of-ASEAN-BioDiaspora-Regional-Virtual-Center_15May2020.pdf.

Bhatia, R. and J. P. Narain. 2010. The Growing Challenge of Antimicrobial Resistance in the South-East Asia Region—Are We Losing the Battle? *Indian Journal of Medical Research*. 132 (5). pp. 482–86.

Bismonte, C. 2020. The Disproportionate Effect of COVID-19 on Migrant Workers in ASEAN. *The Diplomat*. 22 May. https://thediplomat.com/2020/05/the-disproportionate-effect-of-covid-19-on-migrant-workers-in-asean/.

Doshi, S., B. Silk, D. Dutt, M. Ahmed, A. Cohen, T. Taylor, W. A. Brooks, D. Goswami, S. P. Luby, A. M. Fry, and P. K. Ram. 2015. Household-level Risk Factors for Influenza Among Young Children in Dhaka, Bangladesh: A Case–control Study. *Tropical Medicine and International Health*. 20 (6). pp. 719–29. https://doi.org/10.1111/tmi.12475.

Duke-NUS Medical School Centre of Regulatory Excellence. 2020. CoRE Webinar Series: Global Regulatory Coordination to Facilitate Access to COVID-19 Diagnostics and Therapies. https://www.duke-nus.edu.sg/core/events/past-events/detail/index/2020-core-webinar-series-covid-19-Global-Regulatory-Coordination-to-Facilitate-COVID-19-Diagnostics-and-Therapies-Access.

Fields, R. 2020. Immunization in the Time of COVID-19 and Beyond. *Medium*. 8 May. https://medium.com/@JSIhealth/immunization-in-the-time-of-covid-19-and-beyond-374bb55aae7d.

Global Health Security Agenda. https://www.ghsagenda.org/.

Green, A. 2019. The Activists Trying to 'Decolonize' Global Health. *Devex*. 21 May. https://www.devex.com/news/the-activists-trying-to-decolonize-global-health-94904.

Gronvall, G. K. 2020. The Scientific Response to COVID-19 and Lessons for Security. *Survival*. 62 (3). pp. 77–92. https://doi.org/10.1080/00396338.2020.1763613.

Gupta, V., J. D. Kramer, R. Katz, A. Jha, V. Kerry, J. Sane, J. Ollgren, and L. O. Salminen. 2018. Analysis of Results from the Joint External Evaluation: Examining its Strength and Assessing for Trends Among Participating Countries. *Journal of Global Health*. 8 (2). 020416. https://doi.org/10.7189/jogh.08.020416.

Horby, P., D. Pfeiffer, and H. Oshitani. 2013. Prospects for Emerging Infections in East and Southeast Asia 10 Years after Severe Acute Respiratory Syndrome. *Emerging Infectious Diseases.* 19 (6). pp. 853–60. https://dx.doi.org/10.3201/eid1906.121783.

Irfan, S. D., M. O. Faruque, M. U. Islam, S. S. Sanjoy, D. Afrin, and A. Hossain. 2017. Socio-demographic Determinants of Adult Tuberculosis: A Matched Case-control Study in Bangladesh. *American Journal of Infectious Diseases.* 13 (3). pp. 32–7. https://thescipub.com/PDF/ajidsp.2017.32.37.pdf.

Joint United Nations Programme on HIV/AIDS. 2020. The Cost of Inaction: COVID-19-related Service Disruptions Could Cause Hundreds of Thousands of Extra Deaths From HIV. 11 May. https://www.unaids.org/en/resources/presscentre/pressreleaseandstatementarchive/2020/may/20200511_PR_HIV_modelling.

Jones, K. E., N. G. Patel, M. A. Levy, A. Storeygard, D. Balk, J. L. Gittleman, and P. Daszak. 2008. Global Trends in Emerging Infectious Diseases. *Nature.* 451 (7181). pp. 990–93. https://www.nature.com/articles/nature06536.

Keusch, G. T., M. Pappaioanou, M. C. Gonzalez, K. A. Scott, and P. Tsai, eds. 2009. *Sustaining Global Surveillance and Response to Emerging Zoonotic Diseases.* National Research Council (US) Committee on Achieving Sustainable Global Capacity for Surveillance and Response to Emerging Diseases of Zoonotic Origin. Washington, DC: National Academies Press. https://www.nap.edu/catalog/12625/sustaining-global-surveillance-and-response-to-emerging-zoonotic-diseases.

Lee, J. W. and W. J. McKibbin. 2004. Estimating the Global Economic Costs of SARS. In S. Knobler, A. Mahmoud, S. Lemon, A. Mack, L. Sivitz, and K. Oberholtzer, eds. *Institute of Medicine (US) Forum on Microbial Threats. Learning from SARS: Preparing for the Next Disease Outbreak: Workshop.* Washington, DC: National Academies Press. https://www.ncbi.nlm.nih.gov/books/NBK92473/.

Morris, D. E., D. W. Cleary, and S. C. Clarke. 2017. Secondary Bacterial Infections Associated with Influenza Pandemics. *Frontiers in Microbiology.* 8 (1041). pp. 1–17. https://www.frontiersin.org/articles/10.3389/fmicb.2017.01041/full.

National Advisory Committee on SARS and Public Health. 2003. *Learning from SARS: Renewal of Public Health in Canada: A Report of the National Advisory Committee on SARS and Public Health.* Ottawa: Health Canada. https://www.canada.ca/en/public-health/services/reports-publications/learning-sars-renewal-public-health-canada.html.

Oliver Wyman. n.d. Report to ADB on Private Sector Market Opportunities for Health.

Persad, G., and E. J. Emanuel. 2020. The Ethics of COVID-19 Immunity-Based Licenses ("Immunity Passports"). *Journal of the American Medical Association.* 323 (22). pp. 2241–2242. doi:10.1001/jama.2020.8102.

Phelan, A. L. 2020. COVID-19 Immunity Passports and Vaccination Certificates: Scientific, Equitable, and Legal Challenges. *The Lancet.* 395 (10237). pp. 1595–1598. https://www.thelancet.com/pdfs/journals/lancet/PIIS0140-6736(20)31034-5.pdf.

Riley, L. W., E. Raphael, and R. Snyder. 2020. A Billion People Live in Slums. Can They Survive the Virus? *New York Times.* 8 April. https://www.nytimes.com/2020/04/08/opinion/coronavirus-slums.html.

Roos, R. 2012. CDC Estimate of Global H1N1 Pandemic Deaths: 284,000. University of Minnesota Center for Infectious Disease Research and Policy. 27 June. https://www.cidrap.umn.edu/news-perspective/2012/06/cdc-estimate-global-h1n1-pandemic-deaths-284000.

Smith, R. D. 2003. Global Public Goods and Health. *Bulletin of the World Health Organization.* 81 (7). pp. 473–550.

Song, J. 2015. *Antimicrobial Resistance Control in Asia.* London: Global Health Dynamics. http://www.globalhealthdynamics.co.uk/wp-content/uploads/2015/05/06_Song.pdf.

South Asian Association for Regional Cooperation (SAARC). 2020. "The Leaders of the Member States of the SAARC held a Video Conference on 15 March 2020 to discuss measures to contain the spread of COVID-19 in the region." http://saarc-sec.org/news/detail_front/pres-release-the-leaders-of-the-member-states-of-the-south-asian-association-for-regional-cooperation-saarc-held-a-video-conference-on-15-march-2020-to-discuss-measures-to-contain-the-spread-of-covid-19-in-the-region.

Stewart-Weeks, M. 2020. Can We Declare a Covid Dividend? *Public Purpose.* 3 April. https://publicpurpose.com.au/can-we-declare-a-covid-dividend/.

United Nations. 2006. *World Urbanization Prospects: The 2005 Revised Population Data.* New York: United Nations. http://www.un.org/esa/population/publications/WUP2005/2005WUPHighlights_Final_Report.pdf.

United Nations Department of Economic and Social Affairs. 2020. *World Economic Situation and Prospects as of mid-2020.* Economic Analysis, 13 May. https://www.un.org/development/desa/dpad/publication/world-economic-situation-and-prospects-as-of-mid-2020/.

United Nations Development Programme (UNDP) Eurasia. 2020. *Rethinking Development after Coronavirus.* New York: UNDP. https://medium.com/innovation-in-the-age-of-the-sustainable-developme/rethinking-development-after-coronavirus-6ba4db362ba6.

United Nations Economic and Social Commission for Asia and the Pacific (ESCAP). 2020. *Combating COVID-19 in Asia and the Pacific: Measures, Lessons and the Way Forward.* Bangkok: ESCAP. https://www.unescap.org/sites/default/files/xPB112_Combating%20COVID-19%20in%20Asia%20and%20the%20Pacific.pdf.

_____. 2017a. Leave No One Behind: Disaster Resilience for Sustainable Development. *Asia-Pacific Disaster Report.* Bangkok: ESCAP. http://www.unescap.org/sites/default/files/publications/0_Disaster%20Report%202017%20High%20res.pdf.

_____. 2017b. Disaster Resilience for Sustainable Development. *Asia-Pacific Disaster Report.* Bangkok: ESCAP. http://www.unescap.org/sites/default/files/1_Disaster%20Report%202017%20Low%20res.pdf.

United Nations International Organization for Migration (IOM). 2020a. *Migration Report 2020.* Geneva. https://www.un.org/sites/un2.un.org/files/wmr_2020.pdf.

_____. 2020b. *Labour Migration.* Thailand. https://thailand.iom.int/labour-migration.

United Nations Human Settlements Programme and ESCAP. 2015. *The State of Asian and Pacific Cities*. Bangkok: ESCAP. http://www.unescap. org/sites/default/files/The%20State%20of%20Asian%20and%20 Pacific%20Cities%202015.pdf.

World Bank. 2012. People, Pathogens, and Our Planet. In *The Economics of One Health*. Volume 2. Washington, DC: World Bank.

World Health Organization (WHO). 2005. *International Health Regulations*. Third Edition. Geneva: WHO. https://apps.who.int/iris/bitstream/han dle/10665/246107/9789241580496-eng.pdf;jsessionid=8B2324876E200 7CDDC869968F6E92113?sequence=1.

_____. 2015. *Sendai Framework for Disaster Risk Reduction*. Geneva: WHO.

_____. 2016. *Asia Pacific Strategy for Emerging Diseases and Public Health Emergencies (APSED-III): Advancing Implementation of International Health Regulations beyond 2016*. Geneva: WHO.

_____. 2017. *One Health*. Geneva: WHO.

_____. 2020a. *Coronavirus disease 2019 (COVID-19) Situation Report – 52*. Geneva. https://www.who.int/docs/default-source/coronaviruse/ situation-reports/20200312-sitrep-52-covid-19.pdf?sfvrsn=e2bfc9c0_4.

_____. 2020b. *Coronavirus Disease (COVID-19) Situation Report—117*. Geneva. https://www.who.int/docs/default-source/coronaviruse/situation-reports/20200516-covid-19-sitrep-117.pdf?sfvrsn=8f562cc_2.

_____. 2020c. Guiding Principles for Immunization Activities During the COVID-19 Pandemic. Interim Guidance. 26 March. https://apps. who.int/iris/bitstream/handle/10665/331590/WHO-2019-nCoV-immunization_services-2020.1-eng.pdf?sequence=1&isAllowed=y.

_____. 2020d. Q&A: Malaria and COVID-19. 1 May. https://www.who.int/ emergencies/diseases/novel-coronavirus-2019/question-and-answers-hub/q-a-detail/malaria-and-the-covid-19-pandemic.

WHO Regional Office for the Western Pacific. 2016. *Regional Framework for Urban Health in the Western Pacific 2016–2020: Healthy and Resilient Cities*. Manila: WHO. Regional Office for the Western Pacific. http://iris. wpro.who.int/handle/10665.1/13047.

———. 2010. *Asia Pacific Strategies for Emerging Diseases*. Manila: World Health Organization Regional Office for the Western Pacific. http://www.wpro.who.int/emerging_diseases/APSED2010/en/#.

World Livestock (FAO). 2013. *Changing Disease Landscapes*. Rome: United Nations Food and Agriculture Organization.

WHO/UN-HABITAT. 2016. *Global Report on Urban Health: Equities, Wealthier Cities for Sustainable Development*. Geneva: WHO. http://www.who.int/kobe_centre/measuring/urban-global-report/ugr_full_report.pdf.

Zhou, F., T. Yu, R-H. Du, G-H. Fan, Y. Liu, and Z. Liu. 2020. Clinical Course and Risk Factors for Mortality of Adult Patients with COVID-19 in Wuhan, China: A Retrospective Cohort Study. *The Lancet*. 395 (10229). pp. 1054–62. https://www.thelancet.com/journals/lancet/article/PIIS0140-6736(20)30566-3/fulltext#tbl2.

Zhu, Y., J. Xie, F. Huang, and L. Cao. 2020. Association Between Short-term Exposure to Air Pollution and COVID-19 Infection: Evidence from China. *Science of The Total Environment*. 727 (13870). https://www.sciencedirect.com/science/article/pii/S004896972032221X.

Carbon Market Cooperation to Build a Low-Carbon Future

13

Virender Kumar Duggal

Introduction

A stable climate is a global public good that is shared by all countries and regions. Although Asia and the Pacific has become a driver of global economic growth, the region is also the biggest contributor to the greenhouse gas emissions that are causing climate change.

In 2018, Asia and the Pacific generated about 51% of global carbon dioxide (CO_2) emissions (Figure 13.1). Of this, the region's developing countries accounted for about 43% (Global Carbon Atlas 2019). In 2018, the People's Republic of China (PRC) was responsible for 28% and India was responsible for 8% of global CO_2 emissions (Global Carbon Atlas 2019). Much lower emissions in the rest of the region reflect the significant divergence[1] in the size and structure of its economies.

Although the average annual growth rate of global greenhouse gas emissions slowed to 2.5% in 2010–2018, from 6.3% in the previous decade (Figure 13.2), the regional share is expected to continue to grow as a result of increasing urbanization and economic growth grounded in heavy dependency on fossil fuels and inefficient energy use. Across the 10 countries of the Association of Southeast Asian Nations (ASEAN) alone, energy-related emissions are expected to almost double by 2040 compared at present (Paltsev et al. 2017) as fossil fuel consumption is projected to increase by two-thirds (International Energy Agency 2019).

---

[1]   The Asia and the Pacific comprises a diverse group of countries which are classified as least-developed countries, landlocked developing countries, small island developing states, middle-income countries, and high-income economies. See United Nations Industrial Development Organization (2015).

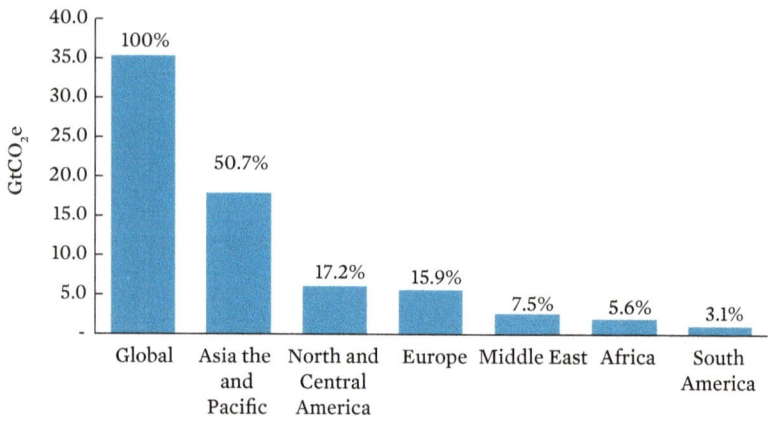

Figure 13.1: Total Carbon Dioxide Emissions from Fossil Fuel Combustion, 2018

$GtCO_2e$ = gigatons of carbon dioxide equivalent.
Source: Global Carbon Atlas. 2019. CO_2 Emissions. http://www.globalcarbonatlas.org/en/CO2-emissions (accessed 9 December 2019).

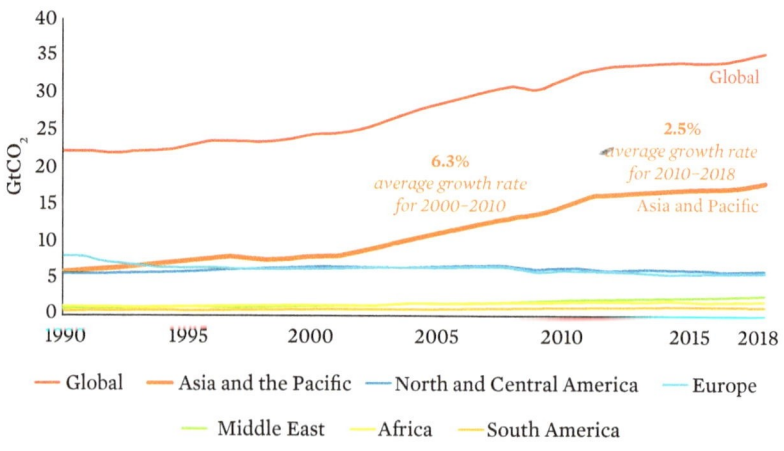

Figure 13.2: Regional Carbon Dioxide Emissions from Fossil Fuel Combustion, 1990–2018

$GtCO_2$ = gigatons of carbon dioxide.
Source: Global Carbon Atlas. 2019. CO_2 Emissions. http://www.globalcarbonatlas.org/en/CO2-emissions (accessed 9 December 2019).

Countries in Asia and the Pacific can play a vital role in the transformation needed to avoid catastrophic climate change. This can be done by working together to recognize and exploit inherent synergies between existing and emerging opportunities for collaboration on climate change mitigation. Regional cooperation and integration can help countries in the region change course from driving the problem to being drivers of the solution. This would equally help regional economic growth to become more socially and environmentally sustainable.

International cooperation and integration can take place at global, regional, and subregional levels, and most countries of Asia and the Pacific participate in this. International carbon markets are central to such cooperation. As platforms for monetizing and trading emission credits, carbon markets aim to achieve more cost-effective mitigation.

This chapter focuses on how, by taking part in carbon markets, countries of the region can raise the efficacy of their participation in global cooperation and integration on climate change. It also looks at other forms of subregional cooperation and integration, given that the "region as a frame for action on climate policy and GHG [greenhouse gas] mitigation has not as yet been given a lot of attention in the literature related to development, energy and climate change" (Uddin and Nylander 2018).

The Paris Agreement

The fight against climate change has gained momentum since the signing of the historic Paris Agreement under the UN Framework Convention on Climate Change (UNFCCC) in 2015. The new global framework is anchored on bottom-up mitigation commitments specified in progressively more ambitious nationally determined contributions (NDCs) from 2020 onward (UNFCCC 2015). NDCs are to be updated every 5 years. Among the 197 Parties[2] to the Convention, the 189 Parties that have so far ratified the Paris Agreement are economies at every level of development. The bottom-up approach gives countries the autonomy to reflect their national priorities, circumstances, and capabilities.

---

[2]   The 197 countries that have ratified the UNFCCC are called Parties to the Convention.

As of August 2020, 186 Parties, including most of ADB's DMCs, had communicated their first NDCs. This kind of broad support indicates a willingness of all signatories to do their part in achieving the goal of limiting the rise in surface global temperature to well below 2°C by 2100 and pursuing more ambitious efforts to limit this rise to 1.5°C above preindustrial temperatures. To achieve this, a balance between anthropogenic emissions by sources and removal of greenhouse gas sinks is to be reached. This balance is commonly referred to as net-zero emissions, or carbon neutrality (Art. 4.1, Paris Agreement). The goal is to achieve net-zero emissions by 2050 to meet the 1.5°C target, or by 2070 for the 2°C target.

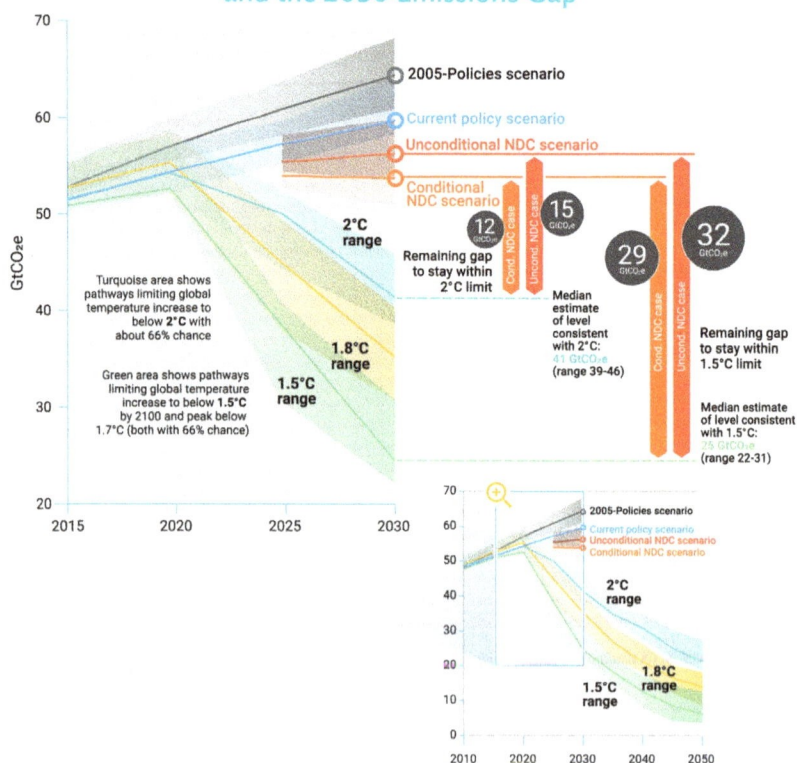

Figure 13.3: Emissions Across Scenarios and the 2030 Emissions Gap

$GtCO_2e$ = gigatons of carbon dioxide equivalent, NDC = nationally determined contribution.

Note: Based on median estimate and the 10th and 90th percentile range.

Source: United Nations Environment Programme. 2019. *Emissions Gap Report 2019*. Nairobi. https://www.unenvironment.org/resources/emissions-gap-report-2019.

However, the collective ambition expressed by the sum of NDCs is largely insufficient to meet the Paris Agreement goals, and all countries need to raise their aspirations (UN Environment Programme [UNEP] 2019). If all the submitted NDCs were achieved in full, further reductions would still be needed to achieve Paris Agreement goals. These, as shown in Figure 13.3, are of about 12 $GtCO_2e$ (gigatons of equivalent carbon dioxide) by 2030 to reach the 2°C target, and 29 $GtCO_2e$ to meet the 1.5°C target. UNEP further emphasizes that countries must increase their NDC ambitions threefold to achieve the 2°C goal, or fivefold to achieve the 1.5°C goal.

Entering 2021–2030, countries have the enormous challenge of ramping up climate action. A wide range of approaches, instruments, and forms of support—including bilateral, multilateral, and international cooperation—will be necessary.

Carbon markets are critical for building confidence in a country's ability to achieve a self-imposed contribution goal by reducing mitigation costs through cooperation with other countries, and, later, in increasing its ambitions.

Carbon Markets in the Climate Policy Toolbox

Carbon markets aim to reduce emissions cost-effectively by either setting limits on emissions and enabling the trading of units ("cap and trade") or specifying a baseline and reducing emissions below it ("baseline and credit"). Cap-and-trade systems transact emissions allowances, while baseline-and-credit systems generate tradeable emissions credits.

By putting a price on carbon emissions, carbon markets help to internalize the environmental and social costs of carbon pollution, and so incentivize a low-carbon pathway (UN Development Programme [UNDP] 2020). Carbon markets offer two fundamental opportunities for spurring cooperation between countries with vastly different economic conditions, and the acceptance of targets/caps among them. The first opportunity is to reduce the cost of climate change mitigation, while the second is to access new revenue flows to finance it.

Carbon markets are climate policy instruments created through policy decisions and implemented through regulations. At their core, they are economic instruments that largely rely on differences in marginal abatement costs between countries and sectors. A marginal abatement cost, in general,

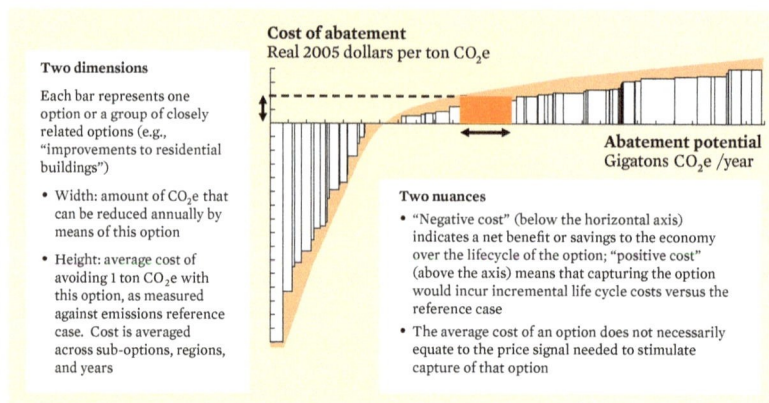

Figure 13.4: How to Read a Marginal Abatement Cost Curve

Cost of abatement
Real 2005 dollars per ton CO_2e

Two dimensions

Each bar represents one
option or a group of closely
related options (e.g.,
"improvements to residential
buildings")

Abatement potential
Gigatons CO_2e /year

- Width: amount of CO_2e that
  can be reduced annually by
  means of this option

- Height: average cost of
  avoiding 1 ton CO_2e with
  this option, as measured
  against emissions reference
  case. Cost is averaged
  across sub-options, regions,
  and years

Two nuances

- "Negative cost" (below the horizontal axis)
  indicates a net benefit or savings to the economy
  over the lifecycle of the option; "positive cost"
  (above the axis) means that capturing the option
  would incur incremental life cycle costs versus the
  reference case

- The average cost of an option does not necessarily
  equate to the price signal needed to stimulate
  capture of that option

CO_2e = carbon dioxide equivalent.
Source: Creyts, J., A. Derkach, S. Nyquist, K. Ostrowski, and J. Stephenson. 2007.
Reducing US Greenhouse Gas Emissions: How Much at What Cost. McKinsey & Company.
https://www.mckinsey.com/business-functions/sustainability/our-insights/reducing-us-greenhouse-gas-emissions.

measures the cost of reducing one more unit of greenhouse gas emission, typically, of a ton of CO_2e. A simple illustration of how to read a marginal abatement cost curve is shown in Figure 13.4.

With regard to international carbon markets, heterogeneities across countries suggest each market has different marginal abatement costs. It is this that creates an opportunity to achieve carbon emission reductions at minimum cost through the transfer of emission credits or allowances (Li and Zhang 2018). For example, a market with a higher marginal abatement cost can benefit from purchasing relatively inexpensive allowances from other markets, leading to a mitigation at a lower cost. The trading of carbon credits between two companies in a domestic carbon market can also take place because carbon markets "equalize marginal abatement costs across individual emitters while giving them continuing incentives to search for cheaper abatement options through both existing and new technologies" (Dellink et al. 2014).

Cap-and-trade systems and baseline-and-credit mechanisms function differently and are established distinctly from each other but can also interact.

Cap-and-trade systems, which are also known as emissions trading systems (ETS), set a mandatory limit or a cap on emissions on a predefined set of sources (UNDP 2020). Covered entities need to surrender sufficient allowances to cover their emissions. They now have the choice to undertake emissions reduction measures in their facilities or acquire allowances from other entities. If the price is sufficiently attractive, they can reduce emissions way below the level of the cap and sell the difference. The critical issue for ETS is the stringency of the cap; allowance prices may remain low if the cap is set leniently and go up if the cap is rather stringent.

As will be seen, ETS can be implemented at subnational, national, and regional levels, and can help a jurisdiction ensure it meets a predetermined part of its NDC target. Some also allow the use of emissions credits generated through baseline-and-credit systems and purchased from entities outside the ETS boundary.[3]

Under baseline-and-credit mechanisms, entities can invest in mitigation actions and demonstrate that the mitigation actions resulted in less emissions than what would most likely have occurred if action had not been taken. When they do so, they are issued emissions credits, or offsets. Credits can be used instead of allowances or as offset against carbon tax obligations.

Many baseline-and-credit mechanisms are governed by international organizations that are responsible for ensuring emissions reductions generated through mitigation actions are real, measurable, and verifiable, and for issuing emission credits. In this way, internationally fungible offsets are generated and then can be traded to meet the demand for offsets that arises from cap-and-trade systems or carbon taxes. The largest and most internationally far-reaching baseline-and-credit mechanism is the Clean Development Mechanism (CDM), which is governed by the UNFCCC. The mechanism was designed to provide offsets usable for complying with industrialized country emission targets under the Kyoto Protocol (UNFCCC 2012). Voluntary carbon markets also exist to serve demand from consumers and the private sector to offset the emissions they produce. Organizations that issue voluntary emission reductions include Gold Standard, Verra, and Climate Action Reserve.

---

[3] For example, under Phase II of the Republic of Korea's ETS, regulated facilities are allowed to use carbon credits generated outside of the country under the Clean Development Mechanism (CDM) for up to 5% of their compliance obligation, provided that the CDM projects are developed by companies based in the Republic of Korea (ADB 2018c).

Article 6 of the Paris Agreement: The Foundation for Post-2020 Carbon Markets

Article 6 of the Paris Agreement is referred to as the "markets article." While Article 6 has garnered support, it has also attracted criticism (ADB 2018a). Labeling Article 6 as a market article is somewhat simplistic and does not do it justice, as it is actually much more than that (ADB 2018a). Article 6 provides a framework for general cooperation in implementation of the Paris Agreement and NDCs. Once precise provisions are agreed, they provide a means to create an international carbon market. This leads to a convergence of domestic carbon pricing approaches—both the cap-and-trade and baseline-and-credit systems.

Article 6 established the basis for using international carbon markets to achieve Paris Agreement objectives, specifically through Article 6.2, which covers cooperative approaches to international transfers of mitigation outcomes, and Article 6.4, which provides for a centrally overseen mechanism like the CDM, under the Kyoto Protocol.

However, the framework must be sufficiently attractive to mobilize Parties and be translated into mitigation actions, and its internationally transferred mitigation outcomes (ITMOs) must represent credible emission reduction activities or be part of ETS with a real scarcity of emissions allowances.

Article 6 has great potential to meet these needs because Parties can use it strategically to complement domestic climate policies and reach and improve their mitigation policy objectives. Given the Paris Agreement's bottom–up approach, Parties can use Article 6 in very different ways, matching national factors that include the domestic climate policy landscape. Article 6 can also be used for identifying and bridging policy gaps, and for mobilizing private finance to identify cost-effective mitigation opportunities. It could also help Parties to further align their mitigation actions with other sustainable development priorities.

Although Article 6.2 neither defines cooperative approaches nor restricts what they should look like, it requires that they respect the principles of environmental integrity and transparency. Moreover, robust accounting ensures the avoidance of double counting. Principally, Article 6.2 makes it possible to trade emissions between states, link ETS bilaterally or multilaterally, and create baseline-and-credit mechanisms.

Article 6.2's broad degrees of flexibility and freedom, and support for decentralized governance of mitigation, can enable the transformative decoupling of economic growth and rising emissions. It provides huge flexibility and opens the door to creativity. It reflects the understanding that no one-size-fits-all solution to international cooperation on carbon markets can achieve sufficient mitigation to reach the Paris Agreement's ambitious targets, while providing a greater level of flexibility. Under Article 6.2, cooperation can be bilateral or multilateral and involve actors from the public and private sectors and civil society, or any such combination. It can stimulate project, program, and policy actions, and therefore go much further than CDM ever could. It can involve attempts to stimulate innovation, finance concrete investments, regulate emissions at source, or transform entire sectors of an economy. In this sense, Article 6.2 is a cry for a paradigm shift[4] in how we think about climate change mitigation—not least a paradigm shift in the way we think about carbon markets—and the formation of partnerships to achieve it.

Article 6.2 does not offer centralized governance structures for operationalizing cooperation. These must be defined and provided by the participating countries. Neither does Article 6.2 provide the institutional infrastructure to operationalize cooperation—other than a UNFCCC Secretariat-run registry for ITMOs, which countries can use to avoid the expense of setting up their own registries. Examples of needed institutional infrastructure include: systems for approving cooperative mitigation actions for generating ITMOs; systems for monitoring, reporting, and verifying emission reductions that result from cooperative mitigation actions and the issuance of ITMOs; accounting systems for attributing mitigation outcomes to legal entities (be they public or private); and registries that track ITMOs intended to achieve NDC targets and ensure that they are not claimed by more than one Party to the Paris Agreement (i.e., avoiding double counting). These too must be provided by the participating countries.

Finally, the expectation that carbon markets will facilitate access to new revenue streams for funding climate change mitigation means that participation will be *competitive*. There is only so much revenue available. Competitiveness in attracting foreign direct investment demands that investors regard conditions in which mitigation actions are pursued as providing sufficient capacity and

---

[4] A paradigm shift is a fundamental change in approach or underlying assumptions. See Hermwille (2016) for a discussion on paradigm shifts and transformation in climate policy.

stability. Developing countries in particular need to demonstrate they are competitive enough to influence the flow of foreign direct investments.

Clearly, the cooperation and scaling up of mitigation actions envisioned in the ethos of Article 6.2 require new forms and scales of coordinated effort. Although commonly perceived as a platform for cooperation between developed and developing countries, Article 6.2 also creates an intrinsic mechanism for nurturing regional and subregional cooperation between developing countries. The Intergovernmental Panel on Climate Change (IPCC) has recognized that coordinated actions of countries in regions can play an important role in making the implementation of mitigation actions more efficient, and so that regional cooperation may provide opportunities to further achieve global mitigation objectives (IPCC 2014). The regional dimension of development is recognized as critical for an effective and coordinated response to an ever-growing number of development challenges (UN Regional Commissions 2011). In fact, attempting to scale up mitigation action to the levels required by the Paris Agreement may be "more sensible"[5] at regional than at broader international levels, because regional actors are better positioned to utilize and coordinate physical, institutional, and political resources to deliver on shared goals to provide public goods such as: decent work and economic growth (UN Sustainable Development Goal [SDG] 8), access to affordable and clean energy (SDG 7), good health and well-being (SDG 3), sustainable cities and communities (SDG 11), and poverty alleviation (SDG 1). Regional actors are also motivated by the necessity of making frugal use of public resources to join forces to provide the governance and institutional structures and capacities required to participate.

The Landscape of Emissions Trading Systems

The share of global emissions covered by ETS has doubled to around 9% since the European Union started its ETS in 2005 (International Carbon Action Partnership [ICAP] 2020a). Although this trend was expected to continue in 2020 as sectors and systems were added, restrictions due to the COVID-19 pandemic are testing the resilience of ETS worldwide.[6] Prices in some established ETS have fallen, while some jurisdictions have

---

[5]   In Chapter 1, Scott Barrett argues that "the supply of regional public goods can be a more sensible response than pursuit only of national goals."

[6]   ICAP (2020a) estimates that by 2021, 14% of global emissions will come under ETS as more systems come online, including from the PRC.

delayed strengthening their carbon pricing instruments and extended their compliance deadlines (World Bank 2020). But by the third quarter of 2020, most had recouped their losses.

Through 2020, the number of carbon pricing initiatives and ETS around the world increased. According to the ICAP, 21 ETS were in force, 8 were under development, and 16 under consideration as of 23 June 2020 (ICAP 2020a). These included subnational systems such as the Regional Greenhouse Gas Initiative in the United States (US) and an array of provincial ETS in the PRC. The largest and most established example is the European Union Emissions Trading System (EU ETS), but that is expected to be soon overtaken by a nationwide ETS in the PRC.[7] Nonetheless, the EU has outlined the importance of a revised and strengthened ETS as a key instrument for delivering carbon neutrality and supporting the European Green Deal (ICAP 2020a).

ETS developed for distinct jurisdictions can also be linked, as doing so can improve liquidity, efficiency, and stability (Li and Zhang 2018). Examples include the Western Climate Initiative, which links ETS of the American state of California with that of the Canadian province of Quebec, and the linking of the EU ETS and Swiss ETS (ICAP 2020a). The United Kingdom (UK) is considering implementing its own ETS and linking it with the EU ETS following its departure from the EU. In the northeastern US, New Jersey and Virginia are recent entrants to the Regional Greenhouse Gas Initiative, while Pennsylvania is set to join. Similarly, 10 northeastern states are moving forward with a cap-and trade program for the transportation sector (ICAP 2020a).

By the end of 2019, ETS worldwide had raised over $78 billion through auctioning revenue (ICAP 2020a). This revenue can be utilized in various ways, but jurisdictions have tended to fund climate programs (including energy efficiency and renewable energy programs), compensate disadvantaged groups, and use it to help finance the general budget (ICAP 2020a). In terms of jurisdictions, the Regional Greenhouse Gas Initiative dedicates more than half of its revenue to energy efficiency projects such as retrofitting and insulation programs, while Quebec allocates the largest share of its auction revenue to promoting clean transport (ICAP 2020a). The global ETS landscape in June 2020 is shown in Figure 13.5.

---

[7] The subnational ETS in the PRC has been developed as functional pilots, with the aim of linking them together as a national system.

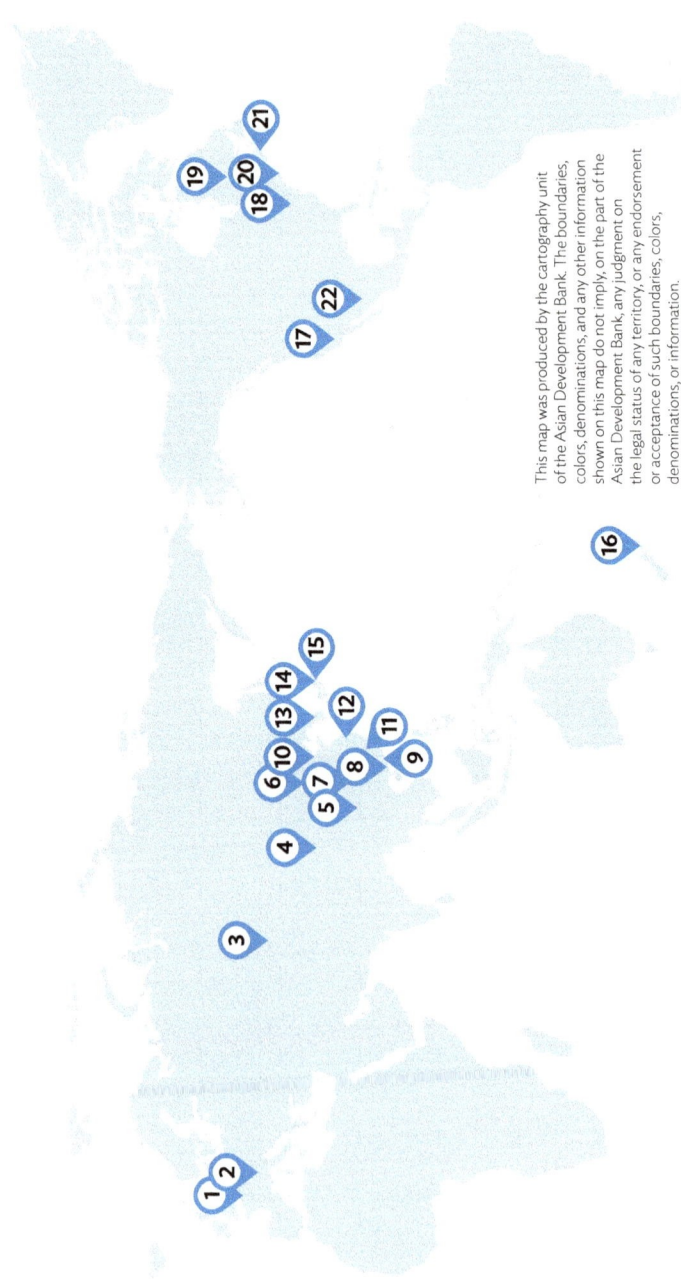

Figure 13.5: Existing and Schedules Emissions Trading Systems around the World

continued on next page

Figure 13.5: *continued*

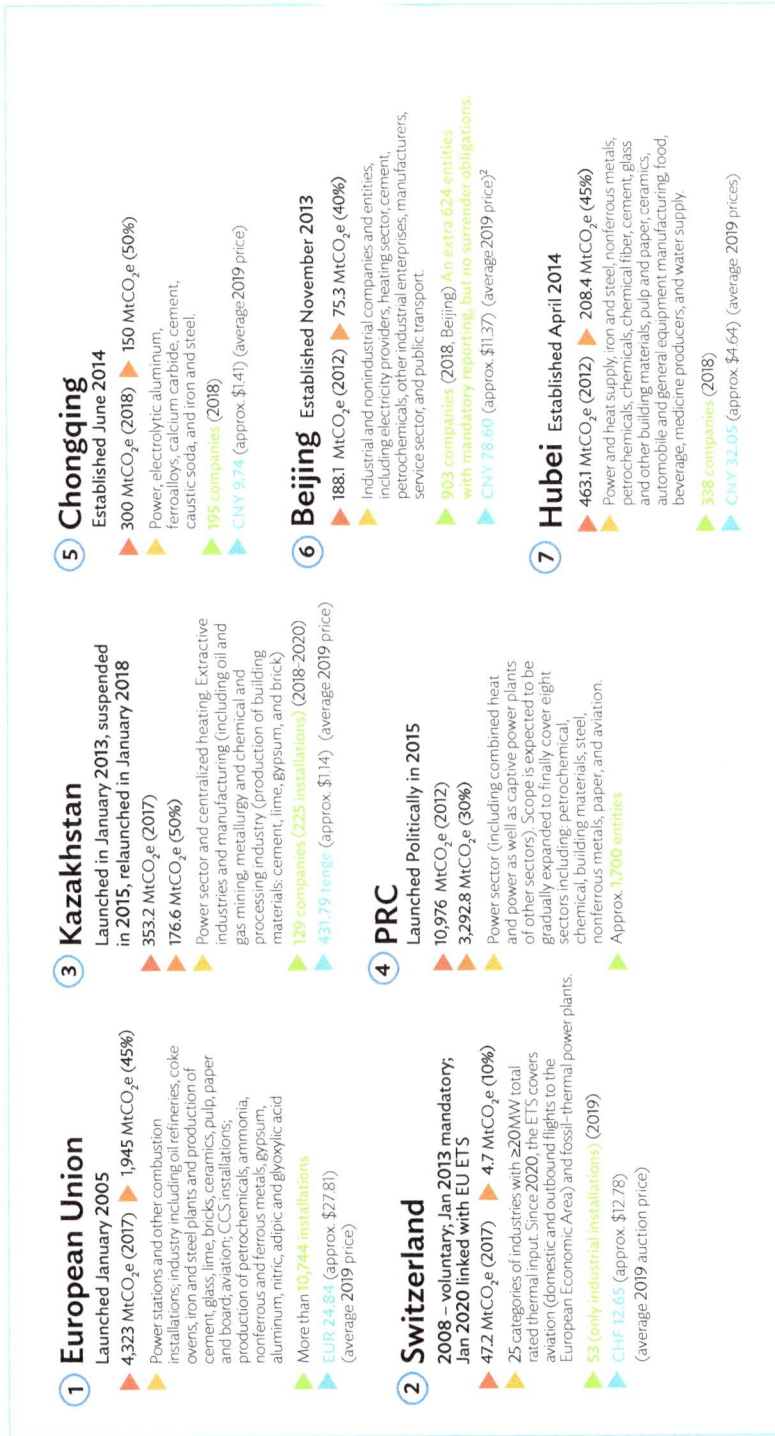

(1) European Union
Launched January 2005

▲ 4,323 MtCO$_2$e (2017) ▲ 1,945 MtCO$_2$e (45%)

▲ Power stations and other combustion installations; industry including oil refineries, coke ovens, iron and steel plants and production of cement, glass, lime, bricks, ceramics, pulp, paper and board; aviation; CCS installations; production of petrochemicals, ammonia, nonferrous and ferrous metals, gypsum, aluminum, nitric, adipic and glyoxylic acid

▲ More than 10,744 installations

▲ EUR 24.84 (approx. $27.81) (average 2019 price)

(2) Switzerland
2008 – voluntary; Jan 2013 mandatory; Jan 2020 linked with EU ETS

▲ 47.2 MtCO$_2$e (2017) ▲ 4.7 MtCO$_2$e (10%)

▲ 25 categories of industries with ≥20MW total rated thermal input. Since 2020, the ETS covers aviation (domestic and outbound flights to the European Economic Area) and fossil-thermal power plants.

▲ 53 (only industrial installations) (2019)

▲ ChF 12.65 (approx $12.78) (average 2019 auction price)

(3) Kazakhstan
Launched in January 2013, suspended in 2015, relaunched in January 2018

▲ 353.2 MtCO$_2$e (2017)
▲ 176.6 MtCO$_2$e (50%)

▲ Power sector and centralized heating. Extractive industries and manufacturing (including oil and gas mining, metallurgy and chemical and processing industry (production of building materials: cement, lime, gypsum, and brick)

▲ 129 companies (225 installations) (2018–2020)

▲ 431.79 tenge (approx $1.14) (average 2019 price)

(4) PRC
Launched Politically in 2015

▲ 10,976 MtCO$_2$e (2012)
▲ 3,292.8 MtCO$_2$e (30%)

▲ Power sector (including combined heat and power as well as captive power plants of other sectors). Scope is expected to be gradually expanded to finally cover eight sectors including: petrochemical, chemical, building materials, steel, nonferrous metals, paper, and aviation.

▲ Approx. 1,700 entities

(5) Chongqing
Established June 2014

▲ 300 MtCO$_2$e (2018) ▲ 150 MtCO$_2$e (50%)

▲ Power, electrolytic aluminum, ferroalloys, calcium carbide, cement, caustic soda, and iron and steel.

▲ 195 companies (2018)

▲ CNY 9.74 (approx. $1.41) (average 2019 price)

(6) Beijing Established November 2013

▲ 188.1 MtCO$_2$e (2012) ▲ 75.3 MtCO$_2$e (40%)

▲ Industrial and nonindustrial companies and entities, including electricity providers, heating sector, cement, petrochemicals, other industrial enterprises, manufacturers, service sector, and public transport.

▲ 903 companies (2018, Beijing) An extra 624 entities with mandatory reporting, but no surrender obligations.

▲ CNY 78.60 (approx. $11.37) (average 2019 price)[2]

(7) Hubei Established April 2014

▲ 463.1 MtCO$_2$e (2012) ▲ 208.4 MtCO$_2$e (45%)

▲ Power and heat supply, iron and steel, nonferrous metals, petrochemicals, chemicals, chemical fiber, cement, glass and other building materials, pulp and paper, ceramics, automobile and general equipment manufacturing, food, beverage, medicine producers, and water supply.

▲ 338 companies (2018)

▲ CNY 32.05 (approx $4.64) (average 2019 prices)

continued on next page

Figure 13.5: continued

continued on next page

8 Guangdong Established December 2013
▲ 610.5 MtCO₂e (2012) ▲ 366.3 MtCO₂e (60%)
▲ Power, iron and steel, cement, papermaking, aviation, and petrochemicals.
▲ 279 companies (2019)
▲ CNY 23.20 (approx. $3.36) (average 2019 prices)

9 Shenzhen Established June 2013
▲ 83.45 MtCO₂e (2010) ▲ 33.38 MtCO₂e (40%)
▲ Power, water, gas, manufacturing sectors, buildings, port and subway sectors, public buses, and other non-transport sectors.
▲ 794 companies (2017)
▲ CNY 13.70 (approx. $1.98) (average 2019 prices)

10 Tianjin Established December 2013
▲ 215 MtCO₂e (2012) ▲ 118.25 MtCO₂e (55%)
▲ Heat and electricity production, iron and steel, petrochemicals, chemicals, and exploration of oil and gas. Papermaking, aviation, and building materials from 2019.
▲ 113 companies (2019)
▲ CNY13.69 (approx. $1.98) (2019)

11 Fujian Established September 2016
▲ 240 MtCO₂e (2016) ▲ 144 MtCO₂e (60%)
▲ Electricity, petrochemical, chemical, building materials, iron and steel, nonferrous metals, paper, aviation, and ceramics.
▲ 255 installations (2018)
▲ CNY16.25 (approx. $2.35) (2019)

12 Shanghai Established November 2013
▲ 297.7 MtCO₂e (2012) ▲ 170 MtCO₂e (57%)
▲ Airports, aviation, chemical fiber, chemicals, commercial, power and heat, water suppliers, hotels, financial, iron and steel, petrochemicals, ports, shipping, nonferrous metals, building materials, paper, railways, rubber, and textiles with various inclusion thresholds.
▲ 298 companies (2018)
▲ CNY 40.46 (approx. $5.86) (2019)

13 Republic of Korea Established January 2015
▲ 709.1 MtCO₂e (2017) ▲ 496.40 MtCO₂e (70%)
▲ 64 subsectors from heat and power, industry, building transportation, waste sector, and public (2018–2020). The same sectors are expected for third phase (2021–2025).
▲ 610 entities
▲ KRW 29,821 (approx. $25.59) (average 2019 price)

14 Saitama Established April 2011
▲ 36.60 MtCO₂e (2016) ▲ 6.6 MtCO₂e (18%)
▲ Consumption of fuels, heat, and electricity in commercial and industrial buildings.
▲ 600 facilities (February 2018)

15 Tokyo
Established April 2010
▲ 64.8 MtCO₂e (2017) ▲ 12.9 MtCO₂e (20%)
▲ Consumption of fuels, heat, and electricity in commercial and industrial buildings.
▲ Approx. 1,123 liable entities
▲ JPY 600 (approx $5.50) (estimated standard price 2019)

16 New Zealand
Established 2008, further reformed in 2019
▲ 81.0 MtCO₂e (2017) ▲ 41.3 MtCO₂e (51%)
▲ Forestry (mandatory: deforesting pre-1990 forest land, voluntary: post-1989 forest land), stationary energy, industrial processing, liquid fossil fuels, waste, and synthetic greenhouse gases.
▲ 2,409 entities while 2,134 entities with voluntary reporting (2019)
▲ NZD 24.82 (approx. $16.33) (average 2019 prices)

17 California Initiated in 2012, obligations began January 2013
▲ 424 MtCO₂e (2017) ▲ 339.2 MtCO₂e (80%)
▲ Large industrial facilities, electricity generation, electricity imports, other stationary combustion and CO₂ suppliers, suppliers of natural gas, reformulated blend stock for oxygenate blending (RBOB) and distillate fuel oil, liquid petroleum gas, and liquefied natural gas.
▲ Approx. 500 entities (2015–2017)
▲ $16.84 (average price 2019)

Figure 13.5: *continued*

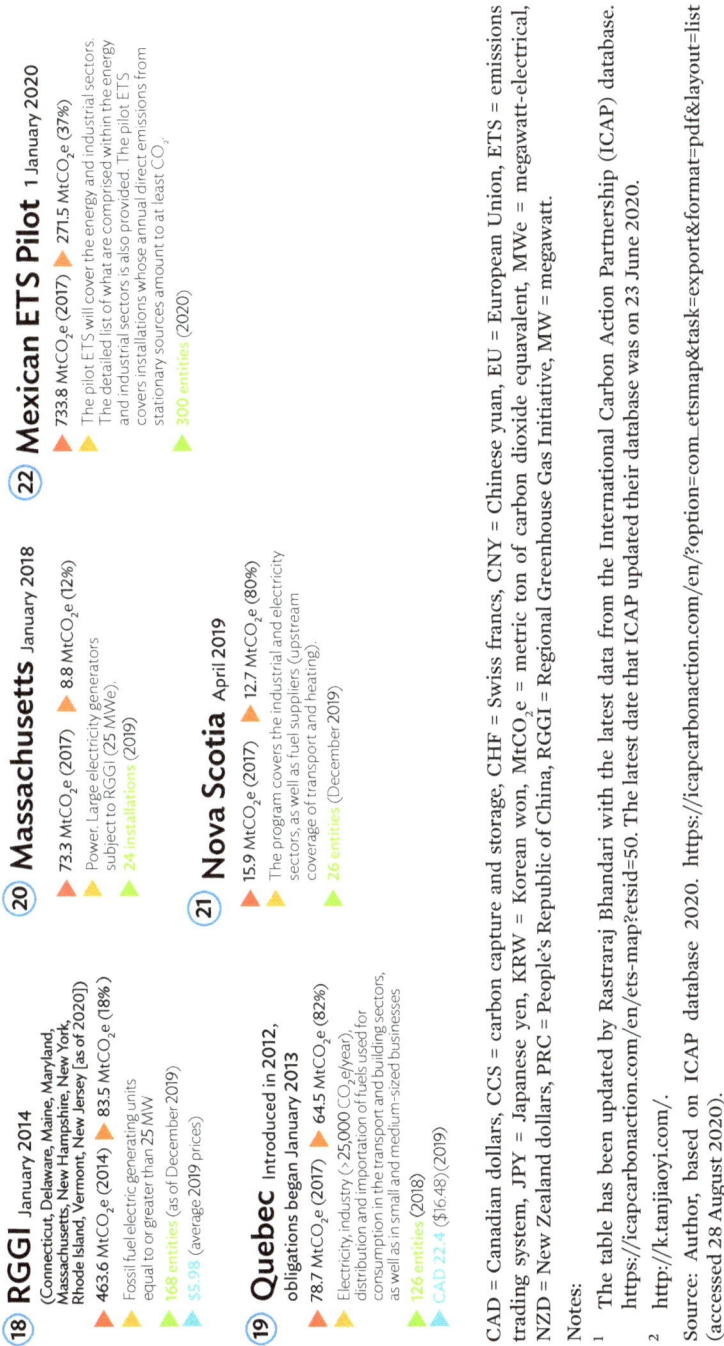

(18) RGGI January 2014

(Connecticut, Delaware, Maine, Maryland, Massachusetts, New Hampshire, New York, Rhode Island, Vermont, New Jersey [as of 2020])

▲ 463.6 MtCO$_2$e (2014) ▲ 83.5 MtCO$_2$e (18%)

▲ Fossil fuel electric generating units equal to or greater than 25 MW

▲ 168 entities (as of December 2019)

▲ $5.98 (average 2019 prices)

(19) Quebec Introduced in 2012, obligations began January 2013

▲ 78.7 MtCO$_2$e (2017) ▲ 64.5 MtCO$_2$e (82%)

▲ Electricity, industry (>25,000 CO$_2$e/year), distribution and importation of fuels used for consumption in the transport and building sectors, as well as in small and medium-sized businesses

▲ 126 entities (2018)

▲ CAD 22.4 ($16.48) (2019)

(20) Massachusetts January 2018

▲ 73.3 MtCO$_2$e (2017) ▲ 8.8 MtCO$_2$e (12%)

▲ Power. Large electricity generators subject to RGGI (25 MWe).

▲ 24 installations (2019)

(21) Nova Scotia April 2019

▲ 15.9 MtCO$_2$e (2017) ▲ 12.7 MtCO$_2$e (80%)

▲ The program covers the industrial and electricity sectors, as well as fuel suppliers (upstream coverage of transport and heating).

▲ 26 entities (December 2019)

(22) Mexican ETS Pilot 1 January 2020

▲ 733.8 MtCO$_2$e (2017) ▲ 271.5 MtCO$_2$e (37%)

▲ The pilot ETS will cover the energy and industrial sectors. The detailed list of what are comprised within the energy and industrial sectors is also provided. The pilot ETS covers installations whose annual direct emissions from stationary sources amount to at least CO$_2$.

▲ 300 entities (2020)

CAD = Canadian dollars, CCS = carbon capture and storage, CHF = Swiss francs, CNY = Chinese yuan, EU = European Union, ETS = emissions trading system, JPY = Japanese yen, KRW = Korean won, MtCO$_2$e = metric ton of carbon dioxide equivalent, MWe = megawatt-electrical, NZD = New Zealand dollars, PRC = People's Republic of China, RGGI = Regional Greenhouse Gas Initiative, MW = megawatt.

Notes:

[1] The table has been updated by Rastraraj Bhandari with the latest data from the International Carbon Action Partnership (ICAP) database. https://icapcarbonaction.com/en/ets-map?etsid=50. The latest date that ICAP updated their database was on 23 June 2020.

[2] http://k.tanjiaoyi.com/.

Source: Author, based on ICAP database 2020. https://icapcarbonaction.com/en/?option=com_etsmap&task=export&format=pdf&layout=list (accessed 28 August 2020).

Emissions Trading Systems in Asia and the Pacific

Although the growth of ETS in the Americas has led the way in 2019, countries in Asia and the Pacific continue to make significant progress. The PRC is preparing for the full launch of its national ETS and the Republic of Korea held its first regular auction of allowances in 2019 (ICAP 2020a). In the Philippines, the House of Representatives Committee on Climate Change conditionally approved a cap-and-trade bill in February 2020 (ICAP 2020a), while in June, New Zealand passed the Climate Change Response (Emissions Trading Reform) Amendment Act (ICAP 2020j). Among the broad array of reforms, there are provisions to phase down free allocation to emissions-intensive and trade-exposed industries, while introducing an emissions cap under New Zealand's ETS that aligns with emission budgets and long-term targets (ICAP 2020j).

The section below outlines some key developments in the design and implementation of ETS for a number of countries.

People's Republic of China: Presently, eight ETS pilots continue to increase their activity. Although launched politically in 2017, the wider national ETS is still under development (ICAP 2020b). In 2019, progress was made, although responsibilities were transferred from the National Development and Reform Commission (NDRC) to the newly created Ministry for Ecology and Environment (MEE) (ICAP 2020b). The MEE has since worked on capacity building, improving plans for a national registry and trading system, and the development of direct greenhouse gas reporting system for national enterprises alongside progress toward passing laws for ETS implementation by publishing a draft of the Interim Regulation on Carbon Emission Trading for public consultation (ICAP 2020b). The official operation of the ETS, which includes allowances spot trading for compliance purposes, is expected to commence in late 2020. The PRC, in its NDC under the Paris Agreement, has explicitly defined the goal of implementing a national ETS, but it has not said anything about linking the domestic ETS to international markets (Amarjargal et al. 2020), even though there were a lot of discussions on the linkage of PRC ETS to international market.

Republic of Korea: The Korean Emissions Trading Scheme was launched in 2015 and is currently the second-largest carbon market after the EU ETS, covering 610 of the Republic of Korea's largest emitters, which account for about 70% of national greenhouse gas emissions (ICAP 2020e). The second phase (2018–2020) saw the first regular auction of allowances

(3% auctioned with 97% free allowances) in comparison to almost all allowances being freely allocated in the first phase; an expansion of benchmark-based allocation; new banking rules; and, from 2019, increased use of international credits (ICAP 2020e). The Korea Development Bank and the Industrial Bank of Korea were named as market makers to enhance liquidity in the same year. Finally, reforms for phase 3 (2021–2025) were also released in 2019. Key developments for the third phase include: (i) a to-be-determined stricter emissions cap, (ii) an increasing share of auctioning for nonenergy-intensive and trade-exposed (EITE) entities to at least 10%, and (iii) increasing use of sector-specific benchmarking to 70% (ICAP 2020e). Moreover, access to international credits will be expanded.

Japan: The two ETS in force in Japan include the Tokyo ETS launched in 2010 and the Saitama ETS, which was established in 2011 (ICAP 2020h; ICAP 2020f). Both are linked to each other. The Tokyo system is special as it focuses on large commercial buildings not covered in other ETS (ICAP 2020h). During the first compliance period, 15 credit transfers took place between the Saitama Prefecture and Tokyo (9 cases from Tokyo to Saitama, and 6 cases from Saitama to Tokyo). In 2019, both Tokyo and Saitama announced targets for the third compliance period (fiscal years 2020–2024). Over that time, the facilities will be required to reduce emissions by 25% or 27% in Tokyo and by 20% or 22% in Saitama, depending on their category (ICAP 2020h; ICAP 2020f).

Kazakhstan: Kazakhstan launched its ETS (referred to as Kazakh ETS or KAZ ETS) in January 2013 as the first cap-and-trade system in Asia that resembles EU ETS in its design (ICAP 2020d). The system never generated transactions and was formally suspended in 2016–2017 to improve the monitoring, reporting, and verification (MRV) system and emissions regulations. KAZ ETS restarted on 1 January 2018 with new trading procedures, but activity seems minimal (Amarjargal et al. 2020). It is not clear if the national ETS will be linked with the international carbon market, though the NDC said Kazakhstan "will consider adequately discounting international units for compliance to ensure a contribution to net global emissions reduction" (Amarjargal et al. 2020). KAZ ETS saw its first exchange of allowances at the end of 2019 (ICAP 2020d).

Thailand: Thailand is operating a voluntary ETS (Thailand V-ETS) and a mandatory one is under consideration (ICAP 2020g). In its NDC, Thailand also specified interest in exploring the potential of bilateral, regional, and international market mechanisms, and said it is developing a legal framework and road map for ETS (Government of Thailand 2015). The second pilot phase (2018–2020) has tested the MRV, the registry, and the trading platform for an additional five industrial sectors, including petroleum refinery, glass, plastic, food and feed, and ceramics (ICAP 2020g). Furthermore, MRV for another three industrial sectors were being developed in 2020. Thailand is also developing draft laws for emissions reporting and establishment of the ETS (ICAP 2020g).

Viet Nam: Viet Nam is considering an ETS for the steel sector and market-based instruments for the waste sector. It is working on options for carbon pricing approaches and developing pilot crediting programs for the steel and waste sectors that may start after 2020 (Amarjargal et al. 2020). Implementation of sector-focused instruments will draw on experiences from the planned MRV system and previously developed plan for Nationally Appropriate Mitigation Actions (ICAP 2020i).

Indonesia: The Ministry of Environment and Forestry drafts regulations for a pilot ETS (ICAP 2020c). This follows adoption of the Government Regulation on Environmental Economic Instruments in 2017, which set a mandate for an emissions and/or waste permit trading system to be implemented by 2024 (ICAP 2020c).

Synergies between Regional Cooperation and Integration and Carbon Markets

The international focus during the late 1990s on developing a single global market for trading emission credits resulted in the design of the Kyoto Protocol as a cap-and-trade system that committed governments to achieving emissions reductions through domestic action or by trading credits. This was supplemented with project-based flexibility mechanisms, including the Clean Development Mechanism (CDM) and Joint Implementation.[8] The Kyoto global carbon market thrived in the 2000s, but suffered increasing mistrust after the global financial crisis of 2008 and the failure of the Copenhagen conference in 2009, which caused demand for CDM offsets to

---

[8] Joint Implementation is one of three flexibility mechanisms defined in Article 6 of the Kyoto Protocol. It allows a country with an emission reduction or limitation commitment under the Kyoto Protocol (Annex B Party) to earn emission reduction units (ERUs) from an emission reduction or emission removal project in another Annex B Party, to meet its own Kyoto target.

shrink at the same time that the number of CDM projects was increasing. This led to a fragmentation into national, bilateral, and regional approaches to utilizing carbon markets, which reduced the scope of cost-effective mitigation. Regional cooperation and integration[9] can help overcome this fragmentation and widen the scope of carbon markets, thereby increasing efficiency gains. Although no clear unidirectional causality exists between regional carbon market cooperation and other forms of regional cooperation and integration,[10] existing regional cooperation—particularly when aimed at achieving integration—creates fertile ground for the development of regional carbon markets. Equally important, however, is the role that regional carbon markets play in supporting and enhancing regional cooperation. Broader regional cooperation and integration efforts can help to pave the way for carbon markets to take the same approach.

The synergies between regional cooperation and integration, and carbon markets, can be leveraged to improve efforts to mitigate climate change. As noted in the Executive Summary of this book, "Strong policy coordination through sharing knowledge and experience could promote best practices and maximize policy impacts by creating synergies and reducing duplication." This is certainly true for carbon markets, where cooperation can lead to knowledge sharing that reduces duplication of effort, enables shared learning, and reduces the cost of implementing mitigation actions.

Links between carbon markets and efforts to integrate them within the region (and beyond) draw rationale from the overall increase of efficiency of broader markets as a climate policy tool to reduce greenhouse gas emissions. When carbon markets are linked or integrated in the region, a wide range of administrative, economic, and political benefits opens up. Regional economies, being different in size and structure and, more significantly, in their experience of and readiness for using carbon market instruments, have much to benefit from adapting the best practices of their regional neighbors

---

[9] Promoting regional cooperation and integration is one of the seven operational priorities of ADB's Strategy 2030 (ADB 2018b). The operational plan for achieving ADB's goals for regional cooperation and integration includes support in the following areas that are of direct relevance to carbon markets: collective actions to mitigate cross-border risks such as climate change, energy security, enhancing financial sector cooperation, and subregional initiatives for greater market integration (ADB 2019b).

[10] In the context of this chapter, most of the immediate opportunities for regional cooperation and integration and for the development of regional carbon markets are subregional. In the remaining text, the term regional is intended to encompass and, in most cases, relate primarily to such subregional efforts. Cooperation and integration can be achieved through both high-level political agreements and low-level cross-border initiatives.

in framing their own policies and devising regulations. Alignment of policies and practices can only assure quicker and closer integration and achieving gains from lower administrative and compliance costs.

From an economic standpoint, integrated carbon markets can increase efficiencies by expanding the pool of abatement options, and so improve market liquidity and reduce competition distortions. The extent of efficiency gains depends on the heterogeneity of the available abatement options. A more diverse system is likely to have a broader set of mitigation options, and very different abatement costs between each option. Integration of various domestic systems allows these cost differentials to be harnessed: the larger the difference, the higher the gains from trade. Integration of domestic systems with similar characteristics and abatement costs will likely produce limited efficiency gains. And although linked or integrated domestic emissions systems are likely to be economically efficient, the expanded size of the market also contributes to the liquidity. Greater liquidity allows the market to be driven by fundamentals, not speculation. This reduces market volatility and, most importantly, opportunities for market manipulation.

Areas of opportunity to harness synergies between regional cooperation and integration initiatives and carbon markets include cooperative efforts to:

- Increase regional competitiveness for accessing international climate and carbon finance; promote innovation and regional market competitiveness through research and development on renewable energy and energy-efficient technologies.
- Ensure equal treatment across investments in renewable energy and energy-efficient technologies and processes by putting a price on carbon.
- Adopt regionally harmonized approaches to expressing national climate mitigation targets; sharing experiences and harmonizing approaches to establishing governance and policy structures that are required to trade in carbon markets under the Paris Agreement.
- Apply a common MRV system.
- Create the shared institutional infrastructure required for participating in carbon markets under the Paris Agreement.
- Gain experience with, and link, domestic ETS.

Examples include efforts to promote regional cooperation and integration in climate, energy, and development policies; efforts to support research and development in renewable energy and energy-efficient technologies; coordinated MRV; and encouragement for advanced low-carbon technologies.

Regional carbon markets can also strengthen cooperation and integration in their underlying economic sectors. Examples include promoting bilateral and/or regional trade in electricity and the supply of other regional public goods mentioned elsewhere in this book.

Opportunities for Carbon Markets to Improve Climate Change Mitigation

Reducing the Costs of Climate Action and Achieving Nationally Determined Contribution Targets

The most prominent economic arguments for regional or linked carbon markets is their ability to achieve emission reductions at the lowest possible cost to the economy. As cost is the most significant impediment to ambitious climate mitigation targets, any climate policy that can reduce the cost of reducing emissions should lessen the political resistance to climate ambitions.

Such carbon markets provide an economic instrument to shift abatement actions from one country to another by allowing installations in the first country to count the emission reductions they facilitate in the second country toward meeting their own obligations.

Strong support for international cooperation stems from the belief that working together can bring multiple benefits. The first among these is the expectation that international collaboration will help Parties to the Paris Agreement meet their NDC targets cost-effectively and, as a result, help them to become more ambitious. International market-based cooperation is commonly viewed as key to increasing the cost-effectiveness and flexibility of mitigation actions.

Recent analysis from the International Emissions Trading Association, indicates that cooperation through Article 6 could reduce costs by more than 60%, saving about $249 billion a year by 2030; and then by approximately 40%, or $345 billion a year, to 2050; and thereafter by about 30%, or $988 billion a year, by 2100 (Edmonds et al. 2019). While this does not account for transaction costs and assumes a simple general equilibrium, it gives a glimpse into the magnitude of possible efficiency gains.

As mentioned, regional and international linking of domestic ETS expands the coverage of each national system, including adding participants with a greater range of mitigation options across systems. The EU ETS was launched to enable the EU to reach climate mitigation targets. With its 27 member states and the participation of Iceland, Liechtenstein, Norway, and Switzerland, it is the clearest example of a regional effort to achieve cost-effective emission reductions. Bilateral linking of domestic ETS in a region can also lower climate change mitigation costs. For example, one study estimates that Quebec's link with the ETS of California, would reduce compliance costs in the province by 52% to 57%, saving from $387 million to $532 million by 2020 (Purdon et al. 2014).

Carbon Markets as a Tool to Foster Regional Trade

Linking, and in the process harmonizing, public-driven systems can support deeper economic integration. Experience gained through establishing standardized and harmonized approaches to regional carbon markets and the financial incentives that emerge from regional attempts to reduce emissions, can pave the way for regional integration to foster trade of goods and services. In recent decades, many countries in Asia and the Pacific have become leading manufacturers of low-carbon technologies (such as wind turbines, solar cells, and biomass gasifiers). India, for example, has established strong capability for making wind power generators, while other countries in the region, such as Sri Lanka and Bangladesh, have good potential for harnessing wind energy. Regional cooperation for supplying technical equipment and services can develop this and improve the region's energy security. Carbon finance mobilized through any of the bilateral, regional, or international carbon markets can alleviate financial barriers and promote trade of such technologies (and associated services) within the region.

In the Greater Mekong Subregion (GMS), impressive economic growth in recent years has been accompanied by increasing electrification and a growing demand for electricity. Interest in deepening connections between GMS power systems to better facilitate cross-border electricity trading has been growing. This in turn makes large-scale renewable generation options such as hydropower plants, solar photovoltaic farms, and offshore wind more viable, given that dispatch will become easier and an interconnected grid experiences lower intermittency of supply than when renewable electricity is generated from national sources alone. Upscaling will enable further cost reductions and so create a "virtuous circle."

Article 6 of the Paris Agreement provides for both technology transfer and subregional power markets-type of cooperation, which are well-suited for baseline-and-credit approaches to using carbon markets, and to linking of domestic ETSs. Such linking both requires and creates opportunities for more extensive policy harmonization and integration in Asia and the Pacific than currently available.

Emerging opportunities that exist for creating subregional power markets in Asia and the Pacific are exemplified by Bhutan and India. Cross-border electricity trade is a win-win solution for both countries with respect to generating substantial benefits from trade, while addressing the commitments to tackle climate change.[11] Besides direct positive impacts on emissions from this type of trade, the introduction of new hydropower generation can enable India to eliminate its fossil fuel-fired baseload and backup capacity from its grid, while increasing the quantity of intermittent power sources (wind and solar) in its electricity supply mix. Potential emission reductions from these transformational systemic spin-off effects are substantial. Scaling up this type of mutually beneficial cooperation can facilitate an increased share of renewables in the regional supply mix due to the improved ability to deal with intermittent power sources (Bahar and Sauvage 2013). Box 13.1 offers more detail.

Regional Cooperation Promotes Stability

Regional cooperation under Article 6 can contribute to increasing the stability of carbon markets by dampening price fluctuations that can result from the short-term supply and demand imbalances that often characterize smaller market systems. For countries that have established domestic carbon markets, linking to others in the region can promote stability by increasing and diversifying the range of participating buyers and sellers.

This is particularly important for smaller cap-and-trade systems. Largely for this reason, nearly all small domestic cap-and-trade systems have taken steps

---

[11] An umbrella intergovernmental agreement was signed between Bhutan and India in 2006. Details can be found at https://www.mea.gov.in/bilateral-documents.htm?dtl/6279/Agreements_signed_between_India_and_Bhutan. There is also a cross-border power trade project involving India and Bhutan under the CDM. Bhutan's NDC emphasizes expanding this type of cooperation as a key strategy in its NDC. India's NDC emphasizes promoting greater use of renewables in the energy mix. For the CDM project, see UNFCCC CDM Project 9210: Punatsangchhu-I Hydroelectric Project, Bhutan. Bhutan's and India's NDCs: Royal Government of Bhutan, September 2015; and Government of India, October 2016.

Box 13.1: Dagachhu Hydropower Project, Bhutan

Dagachhu Hydropower Project is a 126-megawatt run-of-the-river hydropower project on the Dagachhu River in Dagana *dzongkhag* (district) in the southwestern part of Bhutan. The project is the first public–private partnership venture for hydropower in Bhutan. Developed by the Dagachhu Hydro Power Corporation Limited (DHPC), other partners include Druk Green Power Corporation, Tata Power Company Limited (India), and National Pension and Provident Fund of Bhutan. The power generated is exported to the national grid of India, making the project the first cross-border project activity registered under the Clean Development Mechanism of the Kyoto Protocol on climate change. The export of 392 gigawatt-hours of renewable electricity to India results in a reduction of about 382,000 equivalent tons of carbon dioxide a year compared to the baseline of the Indian electricity grid.

As well as contributing to Bhutan's economy through sale of power to India and reducing greenhouse gas emissions, the project delivers a host of other benefits and contributes to sustainable development in the region, including giving local communities better access to stable and low-cost power, providing employment opportunities (during construction as well as operation of the project), and improving incomes for local residents through increased economic activities in the region. Health benefits are associated with the reduction in air pollution through shifting from firewood to electrical appliances for cooking and heating, while upgrading infrastructure for mobile and internet has increased communications, as well as the road network built to smooth the construction and operations of the project. The project also provided budgetary support to improve facilities in local schools.

The Asian Development Bank (ADB) has provided support to Dagachhu Hydropower Project, first through providing a sovereign loan and then upfront carbon finance, with ADB's Future Carbon Fund pre-purchasing carbon credits generated by the project. In addition, the Technical Support Facility under ADB's Carbon Market Program supported the project in securing registration under the Clean Development Mechanism.

Source: Asian Development Bank. 2010. *Dagachhu Hydro Power Project-First Cross-Border Clean Development Mechanism Initiative.* Manila. https://www.adb.org/publications/dagachhu-hydro-power-project-first-cross-border-clean-development-mechanism-initiative.

to link with other carbon markets. For example, Norway created a one-way link with the EU ETS in 2005, and joined it in 2008. New Zealand's ETS had established a one-way link to the CDM before 2015, and the link between the Swiss ETS and EU ETS came into force on 1 January 2020 (European Commission 2019).

Reducing the Risks and Cost of Participation

Participating in carbon markets under the Paris Agreement—because of its innovative character—involves inherent costs, a large share of which is fixed and therefore not linked to market size. Each country wanting to participate in carbon markets has to figure out the best way of implementing it and a strategy to ensure cooperation is affordable and fair. That there is safety in numbers certainly applies. For countries with limited experience in cap-and-trade and new forms of cooperation that will emerge from Article 6.2 (including sector- and policy-based approaches), the cost of "getting it right" can become a burden and the perceived risk of "getting it wrong" a deterrent to taking part. A regional approach enables countries to share intellectual resources and their relevant experience, as well as sharing expenses, especially those that are fixed. This can reduce both the risk and cost of participation, and it can enable early engagement in opportunities to reap the benefits that carbon markets represent.

Carbon Leakage and Perverse Incentives to Constrain Ambition

Carbon leakage refers to the situation that would occur if businesses in certain industry sectors or subsectors, for reasons of costs related to climate policies, were to transfer production to countries with less stringent emission constraints, increasing their total emissions. Carbon leakage happens where competing firms face different carbon emission costs—and so is often closely related to cost competitiveness. It could present policy makers with a combination of undesirable environmental, economic, and political outcomes (Partnership for Market Readiness 2015). The risk of carbon leakage may be large in certain energy-intensive industries.

Regional cooperation on carbon markets may encourage conditions for fair competition and integrated investment among participating countries. Regional linking of carbon markets reduces the risk of carbon leakage where emissions-intensive production shifts from a system with a stringent emission cap (therefore, higher cost of compliance) to one with a more lenient cap. Similarly, regional cooperation avoids the risk of carbon leakage between countries that have adopted cap-and-trade and others that have not.

Further, regional cooperation and integration can avoid regional imbalances in efforts to adopt carbon market systems that, left unchecked, would discourage some countries from making their NDCs more ambitious. For example, a country with potential to replace fossil fuels with renewable resources in its domestic energy mix has a perverse incentive to export its renewable energy instead if doing so can both bring in carbon market revenues from exporting internationally transferred mitigation outcomes (ITMOs) and create new jobs. Regional cooperation can eliminate this risk.

Deploying Advanced Low-Carbon Technologies

Many countries in Asia and the Pacific are centers for technological innovation in advanced low-carbon technologies. Regional cooperation and integration within the region may be accentuated through transfers of such cutting-edge technologies. Being much more expensive than prevailing technologies, advanced low-carbon technologies are usually inaccessible to developing countries. Carbon markets can provide upfront financing required to overcome financial hurdles to implementation.

Baseline-and-credit mechanisms can support the transfer and diffusion of advanced low-carbon technologies by generating revenues that improve the financial viability of mitigation actions. The Japanese government's Joint Crediting Mechanism (JCM) featured in Box 13.2 is a good example of a carbon market mechanism that promotes regional cooperation to achieve emissions mitigation through diffusion of advanced low-carbon technologies in developing countries (ADB 2019a).

Box 13.2: Joint Crediting Mechanism

The Joint Crediting Mechanism (JCM) is a project-based bilateral offset crediting mechanism initiated by the Government of Japan in 2010. It aims to facilitate the diffusion of leading low-carbon technologies that contribute to greenhouse gas mitigation and can ultimately contribute to sustainable development in participating countries. Since 2013, JCM-related financing schemes have supported 178 projects in 17 countries. Of these, 64 have been registered as JCM projects, with 35 already having issued JCM credits.

Asia and the Pacific has the largest presence in the JCM as the Japanese government has entered bilateral agreements with 11 developing member countries of the Asian Development Bank (ADB) and supported 160 projects, 59 of which have been registered. The financial support includes one of ADB's trust funds, the Japan Fund for the Joint Crediting Mechanism (JFJCM), which has provided six ADB-financed projects with additional grants. These projects employ low-carbon technologies, services, systems, and infrastructure in sectors such as renewable energy, energy efficiency, waste handling and disposal, transport, biomass utilization, fluorocarbons recovery and destruction, and forestry to meet the varying interests and development needs of the developing member countries and contribute to reducing emissions. JFJCM financed advanced battery energy storage in Maldives as part of a hybrid renewable energy system of solar photovoltaics, energy storage, and energy-efficient diesel generators. The first-of-its-kind technology provides high-speed charge and discharge characteristics that deepen renewable energy penetration and reduce the system's diesel consumption. Having upfront finance for the project was critical to overcoming the cost barrier of the advanced battery and enabling the required high initial investment.

continued on next page

Box 13.2: *continued*

The JCM was developed as an innovative approach for the post-Kyoto Protocol climate regime and is a good fit for cooperative approaches under Article 6.2 of the Paris Agreement. The JCM is expected to be subject to Article 6.2 guidance because Japan and the participating countries intend the emission reductions or removals they achieve will be used toward meeting their respective goals for nationally defined contributions under the Paris Agreement. Furthermore, the JCM was designed to provide robust methodologies, transparency, conservative baselines, and environmental integrity, while contributing to sustainable development and maintaining simplicity and practicality.

The JCM has created opportunities for the private sector in developing and developed countries. Furthermore, regular dialogue between participating developing member countries and Japan has improved cooperation among the governments in addressing climate change, while increasing the capacity of developing member countries to engage in new project-based bilateral cooperation guided by Article 6.

Whereas several initiatives up to 2020 have tested new types of carbon market collaboration under the Paris Agreement, the JCM is the only example of a project-based international cooperative approach applicable under Article 6.2 and the most-developed example of bilateral collaboration. The JCM is a frontrunner for the bilateral cooperative approaches under Article 6 and a source of valuable lessons as the Article 6 rule book is finalized in ongoing negotiations.

Source: ADB. 2019. *Article 6 of the Paris Agreement: Drawing Lessons from the Joint Crediting Mechanism.* Manila. https://www.adb.org/publications/article-6-paris-agreement-lessons-jcm.

Carbon Financing

Regional cooperation in carbon markets can lead finance to flow from countries with higher abatement costs to countries with lower abatement costs. As mentioned, cost-effectiveness is a primary reason for promoting carbon markets as a tool for achieving the Paris Agreement goals. According to UNFCCC (2012), by the end of 2011, the CDM was used to transfer more than 750 million carbon credits. Sale of these credits, or Certified Emission Reductions, generated $9.5 billion to $13.5 billion for host countries (UNFCCC 2012).[12] This revenue had contributed to stimulating $215.4 billion in investments in CDM projects by June 2012, of which $21.5 to $43 billion was in foreign direct investment (UNFCCC 2012). The CDM experience has demonstrated that significant carbon finance can be generated through global baseline-and-credit mechanisms provided that demand is sufficiently

---

[12] One Certified Emission Reduction represents the avoidance of 1 ton of carbon dioxide equivalent (CO_2e) being emitted to the atmosphere.

high. Similar regional approaches could also generate substantial investment flows.

Challenges in Maximizing Regional Cooperation and Carbon Market Synergies

Asia and the Pacific's Carbon Market Evolution

ETS links are not likely to emerge in Asia and the Pacific in the near term. Many have a long way to go to achieve the kind of liberalized competitive electricity markets that make ETS implementation easier. And, for an ETS to be lined, such systems must exist in the first place.

EU ETS and California/Quebec ETS links illustrate two important aspects of the preconditions for linking: early consideration for linking to help align system design, and strong political will supported by close trading relations between regions to be linked (ADB 2015). A difference with the EU is that in Asia it is difficult to set up a regional-level regulatory system that helps to strengthen and smooth the functioning of an ETS and its administrative operation. Although some countries in the region have implemented ETS, there is no harmonized system. It would be useful to cooperate toward adopting a more harmonized (and potentially integrated) regulatory approach for Asia and the Pacific, which could help link different systems (Shi et al. 2019).

Contextual Differences

Significant opportunities exist in the region to capture benefits from carbon markets, but there are also many challenges. Two of the most prominent are differences in economic systems and the politics relating to bilateral and multilateral cooperation. Differences in economic systems and political realities are reflected in significant variations in NDCs across countries. Lack of uniformity in NDC target types, sectoral priorities, and units of measurement presents a challenge to the regional linking of carbon markets and for establishing other forms of cooperation on climate change mitigation. They may also reflect deeper differences in perspective that could make finding common ground difficult when attempting to initiate cooperative efforts. The 5-year review cycle for updating national commitments in NDCs (the 2020 and 2025 updates, in particular) could be used to harmonize NDCs and promote regional convergence on matters that are important for linking carbon markets. Regional cooperation on the review and revision of NDCs could contribute valuably to harmonizing NDCs in ways that increase the potential to take part in emerging carbon market initiatives under Article 6.2.

Political, Policy, and Legislative Challenges

Achieving regional cooperation related to climate change on a significant scale, such as by linking ETS, can be difficult politically and requires extensive effort to harmonize policies.[13] This can be challenging in regions where countries do not share a common policy and political platform. This is particularly true if potential cooperation partners have concerns regarding sovereign control over the design and implementation of cooperative mechanisms, as doing so inevitably requires compromising domestic priorities and needs to some extent.

The general lack of readiness for operationalizing carbon markets under Article 6 is exacerbated by political, policy, and legislative challenges for achieving regional cooperation and integration in climate and energy policies. As with finance, effective cooperation in carbon markets will not occur in the absence of appropriate legal and institutional frameworks, which in Asia and the Pacific are yet to be developed nationally, let alone regionally. This situation represents both a challenge to the emergence of carbon markets and an opportunity to strengthen regional cooperation and integration at the political, policy, and legislative levels, so that the ideas and solutions needed to develop governance, policy, and institutional components of national frameworks for operationalizing Article 6 can be shared.

Conflicting Interest in Making Mitigation Outcomes Count toward Nationally Determined Contributions

The fact that all Parties to the Paris Agreement have NDCs creates tensions between those countries interested in counting imported mitigation outcomes toward their NDC targets, and those that export them to generate revenue. This also influences the conditions for regional carbon market

---

[13] In Chapter 10, Park, Rosenkranz, and Tayag argue that, "Without an appropriate legal and institutional framework, effective finance will not develop."

collaboration among developing countries: collaborative efforts may require negotiation over sharing the mitigation outcomes that result. This may or may not result in cross-border trade, as in some cases the exporting country may be satisfied with the revenue generated from the underlying investment and have less interest in generating and selling carbon credits or in using them toward their own NDCs.

The example of cross-border electricity trade between countries is a case in point. The country that imports lower emission-intensive electricity may expect to claim ownership of mitigation outcomes associated with the imports. This would run against the approach in the Bhutan–India CDM collaboration described in Box 13.1. International baseline rules for low-emissions power exports support this expectation. Given Article 6.2's far-reaching freedoms to negotiate the sharing of mitigation outcomes, countries are free to negotiate any percentages they deem appropriate.

Institutional and Infrastructural Capacity for Cooperation under Article 6.2

Robust monitoring, reporting, and verification (MRV) systems are the backbone for the success of carbon markets. The capacity to carry out MRV systems, and their quality, is limited in many countries in Asia and the Pacific. Transfers of mitigation outcomes across borders will be challenging without a universal linking mechanism (Michaelowa et al. 2019). While Article 6.2 provides an accounting framework for linking emissions trading transactions and ITMOs, it does not specify or regulate how such linking and transfers can or should be done. This is another area where regional cooperation can lead the way. Countries participating in regional cooperation efforts, particularly under Article 6.2, would benefit from designing their MRV systems together. This would create standardization and harmonization from the outset and could also build opportunities for reducing costs by sharing infrastructure such as a common registry system.

Article 6 Rulebook Delays

Continued failure to reach agreement over guidance and rules for Article 6 has created uncertainty over when rules for international carbon markets under the Paris Agreement will be set and what implications this will have for some key decisions about international cooperation.[14] The bottom-up architecture of the Paris Agreement brings further complexity to international market-based cooperative approaches. The decentralized approach under Article 6.2 offers flexibility and choice around countries' approaches. However, issues about consistency and the integrity of mitigation action are obvious and reflected in the complexity and the slow pace of Article 6 negotiations. As a result, many countries have hesitated to take the action needed to prepare for entering new and emerging carbon markets. It is still possible to initiate actions before formal adoption of the Article 6 rule book since the design and regulatory frameworks will largely be governed by participating countries. For example, the JCM highlighted in Box 13.2 is operating with the view to being one of the mechanisms under Article 6.2 mechanism, and it has produced tangible reductions in emissions.

Conclusions

Asia and the Pacific has been the main contributor to global greenhouse gas emissions for almost 2 decades. Although the COVID-19 pandemic has resulted in a decline, the region's emissions will likely rebound unless governments make strong interventions. This trend is likely to continue if appropriate measures are not taken immediately. Considering this, all countries need to look beyond stimulating short-term economic recovery and carve a path of long-term climate-resilient recovery with green fiscal recovery packages.

Countries outlined their climate ambitions with the adoption of the Paris Agreement in 2015. However, the first round of NDCs does not demonstrate sufficient ambition to reach the agreement's goals. Besides a call to action to raise ambition, there is an immediate need to help countries overcome associated barriers. Among others, access to finance and clean technology are key obstacles to adoption of ambitious climate change mitigation strategies for many countries in Asia and the Pacific. A combination of high existing fiscal deficits and risk of inflation pressure in the aftermath of the COVID-19 pandemic is another impediment to countries undertaking green recovery strategies.

With this in mind, carbon markets are an important economic instrument for reducing emissions cost-efficiently and for incentivizing revenue transfers

---

[14] Attempts to reach a decision on the Rulebook for Article 6 failed at both the 24th Conference of the Parties (COP24) in Katowice (2018) and at COP25 in Madrid (2019).

and technology diffusion. International carbon market mechanisms have potential to channel finance to governments and private sectors in developing countries for multiple uses. Domestic carbon markets that are eventually linked internationally can be a key source of government revenue, raising billions of dollars through the auction of allowances.

Overall, cooperation and integration can help Asia and the Pacific lead the world in climate change mitigation. Inherent synergies between voluntary strategic regional cooperation and integration, and carbon markets, can be harnessed to promote other subregional cooperation and integration efforts, while the use of carbon markets helps countries reach Paris Agreement goals. Regional and subregional cooperation and integration focused on participation in carbon markets is key to unlocking the region's full potential for climate change mitigation.

Countries in the region have demonstrated a successful track record in utilizing carbon market instruments through initiatives such as the CDM and the JCM. About 80% of CDM projects and 90% of JCM projects are hosted by Asia and the Pacific (Amarjargal et al. 2020). Interest within the region on the continued use market mechanisms is also very high. Out of ADB's 41 developing member countries from Asia and the Pacific, 20 have, are considering, or intend to use market mechanisms in their NDCs.[15] In terms of ETS in Asia and the Pacific, 21 are either in force, under development, or under consideration at national or subnational levels (ICAP 2020a).

The time is now right to build on the existing interest, institutions, and expertise in Asia and the Pacific, while identifying what works best in different country settings. The region is quite vast and its economies are diverse in both size and structure, with all parts of the development spectrum represented. Further, the diversity of NDCs across the region presents challenges and opportunities for cooperation and integration in developing carbon markets.

There is also a growing interest across the region in engaging with market mechanisms under Article 6 of the Paris Agreement. Article 6 provides flexibility for countries to cooperate in achieving climate targets and paving the way for raising ambitions. Article 6.2 requires new forms, and new

---

[15] Sixteen developing member countries did not state specifically or were not clear in their nationally determined contributions (NDCs) whether they would be using or considering market mechanisms. Five said they had no intention to use market mechanisms in their NDCs.

scales, of coordinated effort. Article 6.2 also creates an intrinsic platform for nurturing regional and subregional cooperation between developing countries. Indeed, immediate attempts to scale up mitigation action to meet Paris Agreement requirements may make more sense carried out in regions rather that in the international level, given the regional opportunities to harness and coordinate the use of physical, institutional, and political resources, and to deliver on shared goals to provide public goods.

Cooperation can lead to knowledge sharing that reduces duplication of effort, enables shared learning, and cuts the cost of mitigation actions. Regional cooperation can also decrease the costs and risks associated with participating in cooperative approaches under Article 6.2 *per se*. However, there are also challenges. Two of the most prominent are the differences in economic systems and politics relating to bilateral and multilateral cooperation. Ironically, these serve as primary motivators for getting started, because attempts to find common ground, and the building of relationships and trust that occur in that search, are important for bridging differences.

A pertinent question is how to initiate regional cooperation for utilizing carbon market instruments. Opportunities under Article 6.2 can be prioritized. They include the promotion of innovation and regional market competitiveness and collective effort to organize regional instruments for cross-border trade in electricity, the dissemination of waste-to-energy systems, and the development of domestic and regionally linked ETS. Regional cooperation and integration should also directly facilitate participation in carbon markets under Article 6.2 by increasing readiness. This can be encouraged through sharing experiences and harmonizing approaches to developing the governance, policy, and institutional frameworks necessary for participating in emerging carbon markets. Harmonizing NDCs and developing shared infrastructure such as systems for monitoring, reporting, and verifying mitigation actions, will also help, as will putting in place accounting mechanisms and a shared registry.

By reaping the benefits of regional cooperation and integration and promoting the use of carbon markets, Asia and the Pacific can become a driver of the solution to the climate change problem, and help make sure that economic growth in the region is socially and environmentally sustainable.

References

Amarjargal, B., H. Ebro, J. Nylander, and V. K. Duggal. 2020. *Achieving Nationally Determined Contributions through Market Mechanisms in Asia and the Pacific*. Asian Development Bank. Manila. https://doi.org/10.22617/WPS200088-2.

Asian Development Bank (ADB). 2010. *Dagachhu Hydro Power Project-First Cross-Border Clean Development Mechanism Initiative*. Manila. https://www.adb.org/publications/dagachhu-hydro-power-project-first-cross-border-clean-development-mechanism-initiative.

——. 2015. *Emissions Trading Schemes and Their Linking: Challenges and Opportunities in Asia and the Pacific*. Manila. https://www.adb.org/sites/default/files/ publication/182501/emissions-trading-schemes.pdf.

——. 2018a. *Decoding Article 6 of the Paris Agreement*. Manila. https://www.adb.org/publications/ decoding-article-6-paris-agreement.

——. 2018b. *Strategy 2030—Achieving a Prosperous, Inclusive Resilient and Sustainable Asia and the Pacific*. Manila. https://www.adb.org/documents/strategy-2030-prosperous-inclusive-resilient-sustainable-asia-pacific.

——. 2018c. *The Korea Emissions Trading Scheme—Challenges and Emerging Opportunities*. Manila. https://www.adb.org/publications/korea-emissions-trading-scheme.

——. 2019a. *Article 6 of the Paris Agreement: Drawing Lessons from the Joint Crediting Mechanism*. https://www.adb.org/publications/article-6-paris-agreement-lessons-jcm.

——. 2019b. *Strategy 2030 Operational Plan for Priority 7—Fostering Regional Cooperation and Integration 2019–2024*. Manila. https://www.adb.org/documents/strategy-2030-op7-regional-cooperation-integration.

Bahar, H. and J. Sauvage. 2013. "Cross-Border Trade in Electricity and the Development of Renewables-Based Electric Power: Lessons from Europe." *OECD Trade and Environment Working Papers* No. 2013/02. OECD Publishing, Paris. https://doi.org/10.1787/5k4869cdwnzr-en.

Creyts, J., A. Derkach, S. Nyquist, K. Ostrowski, and J. Stephenson. 2007. *Reducing US Greenhouse Gas Emissions: How Much at What Cost.* McKinsey & Company. https://www.mckinsey.com/business-functions/ sustainability/our-insights/reducing-us-greenhouse-gas-emissions.

Dellink, R., S. Jamet, J. Chateau, and R. Duval. 2014. Towards Global Carbon Pricing: Direct and Indirect Linking of Carbon Markets. *OECD Journal: Economic Studies* 2013/1. https://doi.org/10.1787/eco_studies-2013-5k421kk9j3vb.

Edmonds, J., D. Forrister, L. Clarke, S. de Clara, and C. Munnings. 2019. *The Economic Potential of Article 6 of the Paris Agreement and Implementation Challenges.* Washington, DC: IETA, University of Maryland and CPLC. https://www.ieta.org/resources/International_WG/Article6/CLPC_A6%20report_no%20crops.pdf.

European Commission. 2019. Agreement on Linking the Emissions Trading Systems of the EU and Switzerland. Press release. 9 December. https:// ec.europa.eu/commission/presscorner/detail/en/IP_19_6708.

Global Carbon Atlas. 2019. CO_2 *Emissions.* http://www.globalcarbonatlas. org/en/CO2-emissions (accessed 9 December 2019).

Government of Bhutan. 2015. Kingdom of Bhutan: Intended Nationally Determined Contribution. Thimphu. https://www4.unfccc. int/sites/ndcstaging/PublishedDocuments/Bhutan%20First/ BhutanINDC-20150930.pdf.

Government of India. 2016. India's Intended Nationally Determined Contribution: Working Towards Climate Justice. New Delhi. https:// www4.unfccc.int/sites/ndcstaging/PublishedDocuments/India%20 First/INDIA%20INDC%20TO%20UNFCCC.pdf.

Government of Thailand. 2015. Submission by Thailand: Intended Nationally Determined Contribution and Relevant Information. Bangkok. https://www4.unfccc.int/sites/ndcstaging/PublishedDocuments/ Thailand%20First/Thailand_INDC.pdf.

Hermwille, L. 2016. Climate Change as a Transformation Challenge. A New Climate Policy Paradigm? GAIA 25/1(2016): 19–22. https://epub.

wupperinst.org/frontdoor/deliver/index/docId/6276/file/6276_
Hermwille.pdf.

International Carbon Action Partnership (ICAP). 2020a. *Emissions Trading Worldwide: Status Report 2020*. Berlin. https://icapcarbonaction.com/en/icap-status-report-2020.

——. 2020b. *ETS Detailed Information: China* (Update as of 23 June 2020). https://icapcarbonaction.com/en/?option=com_etsmap&task=export&format=pdf&layout=list&systems[]=55.

——. 2020c. *ETS Detailed Information: Indonesia* (Update as of 23 June 2020). https://icapcarbonaction.com/en/?option=com_etsmap&task=export&format=pdf&layout=list&systems[]=104.

——. 2020d. *ETS Detailed Information: Kazakhstan* (Update as of 23 June 2020). https://icapcarbonaction.com/en/?option=com_etsmap&task=export&format=pdf&layout=list&systems[]=46.

——. 2020e. *ETS Detailed Information: Republic of Korea* (Update as of 23 June 2020). https://icapcarbonaction.com/en/?option=com_etsmap&task=export&format=pdf&layout=list&systems[]=47.

——. 2020f. *ETS Detailed Information: Saitama, Japan* (Update as of 23 June 2020). https://icapcarbonaction.com/en/?option=com_etsmap&task=export&format=pdf&layout=list&systems[]=84.

——. 2020g. *ETS Detailed Information: Thailand* (Update as of 23 June 2020). https://icapcarbonaction.com/en/?option=com_etsmap&task=export&format=pdf&layout=list&systems[]=81.

——. 2020h. *ETS Detailed Information: Tokyo, Japan* (Update as of 23 June 2020). https://icapcarbonaction.com/en/?option=com_etsmap&task=export&format=pdf&layout=list&systems[]=51.

——. 2020i. *ETS Detailed Information: Vietnam* (Update as of 23 June 2020). https://icapcarbonaction.com/en/?option=com_etsmap&task=export&format=pdf&layout=list&systems[]=83.

———. 2020j. "New Zealand Passes Legislation Finalizing ETS Reforms." Blog. https://icapcarbonaction.com/en/news-archive/715-new-zealand-passes-legislation-finalizing-ets-reforms.

Intergovernmental Panel on Climate Change (IPCC). 2014. *Climate Change 2014, Mitigation of Climate Change—Working Group III Contribution to the Fifth Assessment Report of the Intergovernmental Panel on Climate Change.* Edited by E. Ottmar, R. Pichs-Madruga, Y. Sokona, K. Seyboth, P. Matschoss, S. Kadner, et al. Cambridge, UK: Cambridge University Press. https://www.ipcc.ch/report/ar5/wg3/.

International Energy Agency (IEA). 2019. *Southeast Asia Energy Outlook 2019.* Paris. https://webstore.iea.org/southeast-asia-energy-outlook-2019.

Li, J. and J. Zhang. 2018. Regional Cooperation on Carbon Markets in East Asia. *Asian Development Review* 35 (2): 153–179.

Michaelowa, A., I. Shishlov, and D. Brescia. 2019. Evolution of International Carbon Markets: Lessons for the Paris Agreement. *Wiley Interdisciplinary Reviews: Climate Change* 10 (6): e613.

Olivier, J. and J. Peters. 2019. Trends in Global CO_2 and Total Greenhouse Gas Emissions. *PBL Netherlands Environmental Assessment Agency 5.* https://www.pbl.nl/sites/default/files/downloads/pbl-2020-trends-in-global-co2-and-total-greenhouse-gas-emissions-2019-report_4068.pdf.

Paltsev, S., M. Mehling, N. Winchester, J. Morris, and K. Ledvina. 2017. *Pathways to Paris: ASEAN—Technology and Policy Options to Reduce GHG Emissions.* Cambridge: Massachusetts Institute of Technology.

Partnership for Market Readiness (PMR). 2015. Carbon Leakage: Theory, Evidence, and Policy. *PMR Technical Note 11.* World Bank. Washington, DC.

Purdon, M., D. Houle, and E. Lachapelle. 2014: *The Political Economy of California and Quebec's Cap-and-Trade Systems.* Ottawa: Sustainable Prosperity (University of Ottawa).

Shi, Y., S. R. Paramati, and X. Ren. 2019. *The Growth of Carbon Markets in Asia: The Potential Challenges for Future Development.* Tokyo: Asian Development Bank Institute.

Uddin, N., and J. Nylander. 2018. Upscaled Climate Change Mitigation Efforts: The Role of Regional Cooperation in Southeast Asia. In *Handbook of Southeast Asian Development*, edited by A. McGregor and F. Miller. Routledge.

United Nations Development Programme (UNDP). 2020. *About Carbon Markets at UNDP SDG Finance.* New York. https://www.sdfinance. undp.org/content/sdfinance/en/home/solutions/carbon-markets.html.

United Nations Environment Programme (UNEP). 2019. *Emissions Gap Report 2019.* Nairobi. https://www.unenvironment.org/resources/ emissions-gap-report-2019.

United Nations Framework Convention on Climate Change (UNFCCC). 2012. *Benefits of the Clean Development Mechanism.* Rio de Janeiro. http://cdm.unfccc.int/about/dev_ben/index.html.

———. 2015. *Paris Agreement to the United Nations Framework Convention on Climate Change.* FCCC/CP/2015/10/Add.1. https://unfccc.int/sites/ default/files/english_paris_agreement.pdf.

United Nations Industrial Development Organization (UNIDO). 2015. *Inclusive and Sustainable Industrial Development in Asia and the Pacific.* Vienna. https://www.unido.org/sites/default/files/2015-07/ UNIDO_in_ASP_Region_0.pdf.

UN Regional Commissions. 2011. *The Regional Dimension of Development and the UN System.* New York. http://www.regionalcommissions.org/ PrintRegionalDimensionStudy.pdf.

World Bank. 2020. *State and Trends of Carbon Pricing 2020.* Washington, DC. https://openknowledge.worldbank.org/handle/10986/33809.

Regional Cooperation and Integration for Ocean Health and a Sustainable Blue Economy

14

Lisa Kircher Pagkalinawan, Anna Oposa, and Eva McGovern[1]

Introduction

From the earliest records, fishers, merchants, traders, and explorers in Asia and the Pacific viewed the oceans as common property (Schrijver 2016). As civilizations evolved, coastal populations gained cultural identity and well-being from the oceans, and benefited from shipping, coastal and marine tourism, and natural resources such as fish and seaweed. These shared benefits helped build current Asia and Pacific societies and economies. However, the ocean is not a limitless resource. Transboundary threats such as climate change, pollution, overfishing, and unsustainable development have pushed marine ecosystems to the brink of collapse. Overexploitation of resources has been especially rampant because of Asia and the Pacific's vast areas of international waters, maritime territorial disputes, weak enforcement of regulations, and lack of a regional security organization (Anwar 2006).

Solving these transboundary challenges to ocean health and productivity requires coordinated implementation of best practices, good governance, and enforcement of international agreements among governments, international organizations, and other partners. This can be accomplished through regional cooperation, which can develop shared goals and priorities, create clear and consistent standards, and build mechanisms to attract capital. Regional cooperation can also help bring down the cost of political, climate, and project risk insurance, which are often essential to making projects financially viable. It is also critical to achieving the Sustainable Development Goals (SDGs) because their multisector nature requires collaborative approaches involving many stakeholders. This is especially true for SDG 14, "Life Below Water," since oceans are public goods that provide benefits beyond a single country's jurisdiction.

[1] The authors wish to thank Arunkumar Abraham and Melissa Walsh for their valuable contributions, and the ADB staff and partner organization staff who provided critical inputs.

Oceans provide livelihoods for millions of people. The monetary value of the "blue economy" is estimated at $3 trillion to $6 trillion globally (OECD 2016).[2] In contrast to conventional exploitation of marine resources, the strength of the blue economy is defined by the environmental, social, and economic sustainability of sectors that impact and/or derive benefits from the ocean (Figure 14.1). In ocean-dependent communities across Asia and the Pacific, investments in ecosystem and natural resource management, pollution control, and resilient infrastructure improve resilience, create jobs, and stimulate sustainable economic growth. Regional cooperation and integration helps the blue economy expand when it builds robust institutions, supports trade, and forges financial links. In addition, reducing or removing barriers at borders increases trade in goods and services, cross-border investment, labor mobility, and technology transfers that together help create a larger, regionally integrated market and more efficient supply chains across economies that rely on the ocean.[3] Over the past 20 years or so, trade and financial linkages in Asia and the Pacific have increased markedly and driven economic growth, even with the slowdown following the 2008 global financial crisis (ADB 2018) and significant disruptions from coronavirus disease (COVID-19) lockdowns.

Multilateral developments banks, such as the Asian Development Bank (ADB), facilitate regional cooperation and integration by providing knowledge support and financing for ocean health initiatives. ADB has supported regional cooperation and integration in Asia and the Pacific for more than 50 years, and has increased its work on ocean health issues. In May 2019, ADB launched an Action Plan for Healthy Oceans and Sustainable Blue Economies to scale up investments and technical assistance to $5 billion over 5 years. To achieve this, ADB will use its convening power to share knowledge, facilitate regional dialogue and partnerships, and generate capital.

This chapter reviews the progress and prospects of regional cooperation and integration in Asia and the Pacific to improve ocean health and stimulate the blue economy. This is approached through a synthesis of issues, experiences, case studies, lessons learned, and recommendations based on research and publications from many institutions and scientists around the world. Their work is acknowledged accordingly.

---

[2] United Nations Conference on Trade and Development (UNCTAD). *Oceans Economy and Fisheries.* https://unctad.org/en/Pages/DITC/Trade-and-Environment/Oceans-Economy. aspx.

[3] ADB. *ADB's Work in Regional Cooperation and Integration.* https://www.adb.org/themes/ regional-cooperation/overview.

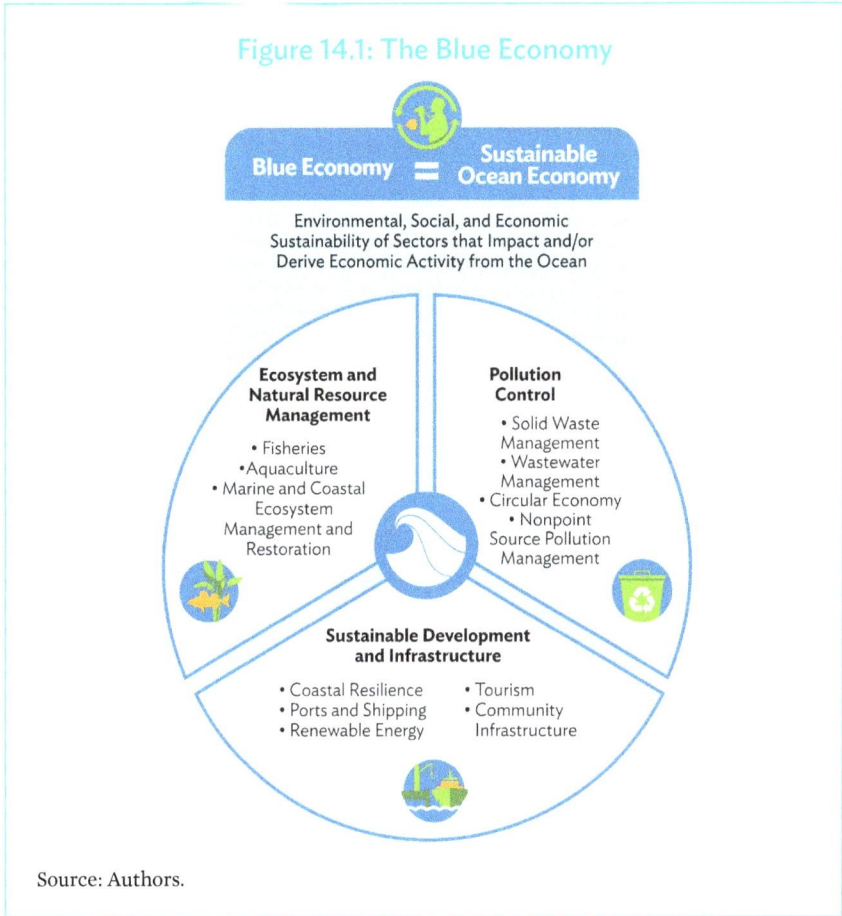

Figure 14.1: The Blue Economy

Blue Economy = Sustainable Ocean Economy

Environmental, Social, and Economic
Sustainability of Sectors that Impact and/or
Derive Economic Activity from the Ocean

Ecosystem and Natural Resource Management
• Fisheries
• Aquaculture
• Marine and Coastal Ecosystem Management and Restoration

Pollution Control
• Solid Waste Management
• Wastewater Management
• Circular Economy
• Nonpoint Source Pollution Management

Sustainable Development and Infrastructure
• Coastal Resilience
• Ports and Shipping
• Renewable Energy
• Tourism
• Community Infrastructure

Source: Authors.

The Ocean as a Regional Public Good

The entire ocean is a public good because its services and benefits are available to everyone. At the same time, anything that damages the ocean affects the entire planet. The UN Convention on the Law of the Sea (UNCLOS), which was developed from 1973 to 1982, states that "the problems of ocean space are closely interrelated and need to be considered as a whole" and that the high seas or area beyond national jurisdiction is a "common heritage of mankind" wherein its "exploration and exploitation ... shall be carried out for the benefit of mankind as a whole" (UN 1982). The Rio Declaration on Environment and Development in 1992 further emphasized that the marine environment "forms an integrated whole that is an essential component of the global life-support system" (UN 1992).

Managing the ocean is a complex matter. Utilization, management, and conservation of coastal and marine resources are the responsibility of national governments within the boundaries of national ocean territories and exclusive economic zones. However, governance is ambiguous over large areas: nearly two-thirds of ocean areas lie in the high seas, where no single state has authority (Pew Charitable Trusts 2016). Complementing international oceans governance frameworks and national laws, regional cooperation and integration has been increasingly used to manage shared seas and oceans. In Asia and the Pacific, seas and oceans are now treated as regional public goods or public goods whose benefits extend beyond a single nation's territory to a well-defined region (Sandler 2003). According to ADB, "The case for regional public goods embodies the need to harness the opportunities of regional cooperation and integration and to take collective action to tackle challenges shared by neighboring economies" (ADB 2018). Regional cooperation and integration can drive economic growth in the shipping, fisheries, and tourism sectors. It can also be effective in dealing with challenges caused by increasing economic interdependence, such as the spread of contagious diseases and marine plastic pollution.

Asia and the Pacific Shared Oceans Benefits: Ecosystem Services and the Blue Economy

The oceans as regional public goods provide vital goods and services that support Asia and the Pacific. Oceans produce more than half of the oxygen in the atmosphere. They regulate climate and provide energy sources (oil, gas, wave, tidal, and thermal) and pharmaceutical resources. It has been projected that ocean energy (mainly wave energy and tidal streams) can generate 20,000–80,000 terawatt-hours of electricity, which represents as much as four times the global demand for electricity (Boshell 2020). By 2016, seven marine-derived pharmaceuticals were approved for clinical use, including four anticancer drugs (Jaspars et al. 2016). A protein from ocean algae and horseshoe crab blood is also being explored for the coronavirus disease (COVID-19) vaccine (Arnold 2020; Degnarain 2020). The oceans provide cultural services (recreational, aesthetic, and spiritual) and support economies and livelihoods in fisheries, shipping, and tourism (Marine Biology Conservation Society 2020). Many migratory marine species, such as whales, dolphins, seabirds, turtles, and sharks, figure prominently in the regional tourism industry and culture.

Oceans are climate regulators, having absorbed 93% of the Earth's additional heat since the 1970s. Coastal marine habitats (mangrove forests, coral reefs, and seagrass beds) not only act as natural buffers from extreme weather events, but also absorb up to seven times more carbon per unit area than tropical rainforests.[4] The region is home to three-quarters of all coral reefs and more than half of all remaining mangrove areas. Without oceans functioning as the world's largest active carbon sink, climate change impacts would be more intense.

Asia and the Pacific plays a vital role in global food and nutritional security as the world's primary source of seafood. The top six producers (inland capture plus aquaculture) are all in Asia and accounted for 57% of total inland water catches in 2018 (Food and Agriculture Organization of the United Nations [FAO] 2020). The Coral Triangle (Box 14.1, p. 552), is a geographic biodiversity hot spot that covers six countries in Asia and the Pacific. It is a nursery and spawning ground for tuna, supporting the multibillion-dollar tuna industry and supplying more than 30% of the global market.[5] Demand for tuna and tuna-like species such as bonitos, Spanish and king mackerels, and butterfly kingfish continues to grow (Majkowski 2007), hitting the highest catch on record in 2018 at over 7.9 million tons (FAO 2020).

The fisheries and aquaculture sectors provide direct employment to about 59.5 million people, with 85% in Asia and the Pacific, 9% in Africa, and 6% in the rest of the world. When those employed in post-harvest operations and marketing are added, women account for half of all workers in the sector. Fish, as a source of protein, healthy fats, and essential nutrients, is an integral part of the diet in much of the region. Fish provides more than half of the intake of animal protein in several countries, including Cambodia, Indonesia, Sri Lanka, and several small island developing states.[6] Fish also provide important micronutrients, such as iodine, omega-3 fatty acids, and iron, for pregnant women and infants.[7]

---

[4] International Union for Conservation of Nature (IUCN). *Issues Brief: Ocean and Climate Change*. https://www.iucn.org/resources/issues-briefs/ocean-and-climate-change.

[5] Worldwide Fund for Nature (WWF). *Coral Triangle: Facts*. https://wwf.panda.org/knowledge_hub/where_we_work/coraltriangle/coraltrianglefacts/.

[6] IUCN. *Issues Brief: Ocean and Climate Change*. https://www.iucn.org/resources/issues-briefs/ocean-and-climate-change.

[7] FAO. *Fish and Human Nutrition*. http://www.fao.org/fileadmin/user_upload/newsroom/docs/BlueGrowthNutritionRev2.pdf.

In Asia and the Pacific, oceans contribute significantly to the gross domestic product (GDP) of many developing countries—including as much as 13% in Indonesia and 19% in Viet Nam. The combined annual economic value of Melanesia's oceans is estimated at $5.4 billion. Tourism, fisheries, and shipping industries are at the heart of the region's blue economy. In Asia and the Pacific, international tourism receipts were valued at about $443 billion in 2019 (UN World Tourism Organization [UNWTO] 2020), and it was the world's fastest-growing travel and tourism region (World Economic Forum 2019). Receipts accounted for a 30% share of international tourism, second only to Europe (UNWTO 2020). The small island developing states—many in the Pacific region—rely heavily on tourism and fishing licenses. Tourism accounts for about 20% of GDP for two-thirds of them (OECD 2018), while fees from fishing licenses account for more than half of government revenue for countries such as Kiribati, the Marshall Islands, and Tuvalu (Gillett and Ikatonga Tauati 2018). Therefore, the health of ecosystems is particularly important. It has been estimated that 80% of all tourism is concentrated in coastal areas, particularly beaches and coral reefs.[8] Reef-dependent tourism alone accounts for 43% of GDP in Maldives (Spalding et al. 2017).

Improved maritime transport links in Asia and the Pacific have been fundamental to global economic growth. Connections between and among countries in the region have widened the market of local producers, created employment, and generated income. Seaweed is an industry that has benefited from improved connectivity. Global production doubled from 2005 to 2015 and 8 out of the 10 biggest seaweed producers are Asian. The trade for edible seaweed is also almost exclusively in Asia. The industry provides employment for women in the fisheries sector because seaweed farms are located along the coast which is more accessible for women and children. The industry in Asia and the Pacific is expected to grow at 2% to 3% a year (FAO 2018).

Asia is also home to the three largest shipbuilding economies in the world, with the People's Republic of China (PRC), Japan, and the Republic of Korea building 80% of the world's ships (in terms of compensated gross tons) and dominating the global market for bulkers, tankers, and containerships (Gourdon and Steidl 2019). In 2017, the Republic of the Marshall Islands became the world's second-largest ship registry after Panama. Ship registration is important for healthy oceans, as registered ships must be

---

[8] WWF. *Marine Problems: Coastal and Tourism Development.* https://wwf.panda.org/our_work/our_focus/oceans_practice/problems/tourism/.

inspected regularly to ensure that they follow legal standards for safety and pollution prevention, among others (International Registries, Inc. 2017). Maritime transport continues to be the main mode of globalized trade and manufacturing supply chains, with more than 80% of the world's merchandise trade by volume carried by sea. Trade routes in Asia are especially crucial: 41% of the total goods loaded in 2018 originated in Asia, and 61% of total goods were received in Asia (UNCTAD 2019).

Asia and the Pacific Shared Ocean Threats and Impacts

While Asia and the Pacific oceans benefit billions of people as a regional public good, they also exemplify the tragedy of the commons.[9] Challenges and threats to ocean health such as marine pollution, overfishing, habitat loss, species loss, and climate change in one country can have a negative ripple effect across the whole region.

Marine pollution, caused by nonpoint source pollution, solid waste and untreated wastewater, shipping, and urban activities, follows no borders. Nonpoint source pollution comes from many diffuse sources, such as excess fertilizers, insecticides, oil, grease, sediment, and toxic chemicals from agricultural, urban, and residential areas.[10] Because of them, ocean "dead zones" (areas where there is so little oxygen that almost nothing can survive) have quadrupled since 1950 (Breitburg et al. 2018). Plastic waste and pollution are an urgent issue for Asia because 8 of the 10 rivers that transport 88%–95% of the global load of plastics into the sea are in the region (Schmidt, Krauth, and Wagner 2017). The mismanagement of waste in the region is caused mainly by unsustainable production and consumption patterns, poor or insufficient waste management systems and infrastructure, and the global waste trade—where waste produced in developed countries is often exported to and disposed of in developing countries (Leung 2019). Huge volumes of plastic waste have become an eyesore along beaches and created the Great Pacific Garbage Patch, an area in the North Pacific where marine debris has accumulated. Plastic debris is known to harm more than

---

[9]   The tragedy of the commons is a situation where individuals, acting independently and according to their own self-interest, consume a shared resource for personal gain at the expense of other individuals. It leads to overexploitation, overconsumption, and the depletion of natural resources.

[10] United States Environmental Protection Agency. *Basic Information about Nonpoint Source (NPS) Pollution.* https://www.epa.gov/nps/basic-information-about-nonpoint-source-nps-pollution.

260 species of marine life through ingestion, entanglement, and absorption of toxic substances leached from plastic fragments (Lascelles 2014) and accelerate coral reef disease (Lamb 2018). A quarter of all fish caught now contain microplastic in their guts (National Oceanic and Atmospheric Administration 2014). While the impact of microplastic on human health remains unknown, ingestion has been proven across the world (Schwabl et al. 2019).

Oil spills can also have catastrophic impacts. About 49% come from operational discharges from ships or land-based sources and accidental spills from ships, while other sources are from natural seepage and oil extraction (National Oceanic and Atmospheric Administration 2015). Numerous oil spills in the Straits of Singapore and Malacca have killed fish and crustaceans, damaged shorelines and beaches, and destroyed mangrove forests and coral reefs (International Tanker Owners Pollution Federation 2000; Kiong and Saparudin 2010). Recognizing the need for regional cooperation, a memorandum of understanding between the governments of Indonesia, Malaysia, and Singapore, and nongovernment associations in Japan was signed in 1981 (Ibarhim 1995).

Besides the effects of pollution, Asia and the Pacific is losing its marine ecosystems at an alarming rate due to overexploitation and increasing coastal populations and development. In the region, mangrove forests are lost at a rate of nearly double the global average (Strong and Minnemeyer 2015). From 1980 until 2009, seagrass cover reportedly decreased at about 7% globally, and losses may be more severe in Southeast Asia (Fortes et al. 2018). Rising temperatures and sea levels are projected to cause the death of 70% to 90% of coral reefs by 2052 (Intergovernmental Panel on Climate Change 2018). Degradation of these ecosystems mean that coastal protection is weakened, fish stocks are damaged, and massive amounts of greenhouse gases are released into the atmosphere and ocean. Since oceans and coastal marine habitats of Asia and the Pacific are essential for global climate regulation and seafood sources, habitat loss and climate change will have cascading impacts.

There are many other threats to marine wildlife. In particular, at least 21% of migratory marine species are considered threatened with extinction because of hazards encountered during their movements (Lascelles et al. 2014). Besides pollution, they are threatened with overfishing, ship strikes, bycatch, and poaching. One example is the whale shark, a species where 75% of the global population live in the Indo-Pacific. Whale sharks tagged in the

Philippines have been sighted in Indonesia, Malaysia, and Taipei,China. Due to the many threats along its migratory routes, populations in the Indo-Pacific have fallen by as much as 92%, contributing to the overall global decline of 63% over 75 years. In 2016, the International Union for the Conservation of Nature declared the whale shark as endangered—just two categories away from extinction (Wongruang 2018). More countries must implement conservation measures for whale sharks and other migratory marine species, otherwise survival rates will continue to be bleak if overexploitation and/or habitat loss persist across their migratory routes.

Another serious but underacknowledged threat to the region's oceans is the introduction of alien invasive species (AIS). If unmanaged, they can do significant damage to fisheries, aquaculture, human health, and infrastructure. For example, although the Northern Pacific sea star (*Asterias amurensis*) is native to Japan, the PRC, the Korean peninsula, and the far North Pacific, it was unintentionally introduced to Tasmania, Australia as larvae, most likely through ballast water or as fouling on ships from Japan. In 1995, the Northern Pacific sea star became the dominant invertebrate predator in Tasmania's Derwent Estuary and a threat to native sea star populations and aquaculture industry (De Poorter, Darby, and MacKay 2009). Oceanic islands are particularly vulnerable due to the low in-built resistance of local ecosystems. Recent extinctions of many plant and animal species in oceanic islands have been linked to AIS (SPREP 2016). AIS can be introduced intentionally (e.g., as live bait or gourmet food) or unintentionally (such as through ship ballast water,[11] on a ship's hull, escapees from aquariums). Eradication of AIS is costly, time-consuming, and much more difficult in marine environments. As shipping activity increases and trade routes expand, so does the risk of AIS (De Poorter, Darby, and MacKay 2009).

Overfishing, or fishing beyond the biological limits of fish stocks, is a major and persistent threat driven by the global demand for fish and the increasing intensity of fishing. In Southeast Asia, 64% of fisheries' resource base is at medium to high risk from overfishing (De Riddler and Nindang 2018). In 2018, the Pacific bluefin tuna was reported to be severely overfished, with its population at just 3.3% of what it likely would be if unfished (Nickson 2018).

Illegal unreported and unregulated (IUU) fishing and fisheries subsidies are major contributors to overfishing. IUU fishing, in particular, has a major impact on food security and the recovery of marine ecosystems because its extent is

---

[11] The accumulation of various organisms on ships' hulls.

unknown.[12] Its link to human rights abuses also requires critical attention (FAO 2019; FAO, ILO, and International Organization for Migration 2019). At least 17,000 fishers are estimated to be working and living below acceptable standards in Southeast Asia's seas alone (Rose 2018). IUU fishing in the high seas is even murkier. Monitoring and surveillance remain a challenge because roles and responsibilities between and among countries are unclear. Two-thirds of fish stocks in the high seas are estimated to be fished beyond sustainable limits.

For decades, governments have been subsidizing the cost of vessel fuel and upgrades, port renovations, and other expenses that help industrial fishing fleets to drop nets farther from shore at longer periods and with greater capacity. Studies show that without government subsidies, which amount to about $22.2 billion a year, as much as 54% of fishing in the high seas would be unprofitable (Jarret 2020). As early as 1999, fishery subsidies were already a concern for the Association of Southeast Asian Nations (ASEAN). In 2001, one of the major recommendations from a regional meeting of ASEAN member countries was to "[r]emove subsidies which are clearly shown to contribute to unsustainable fisheries practices, especially those encouraging expansion of fishing capacity for fully exploited resources" (Asia-Pacific Economic Cooperation [APEC] 2001).

Though maritime shipping has improved connectivity and supported the economy, the industry comes with issues in safety and security. In 2018, Asia and the Pacific accounted for 45% of the vessels that were sunken, submerged, wrecked, or stranded globally. These were caused by inclement weather, collisions, or fires (Lee 2019). Maritime terrorism and piracy, and the illegal trade of weapons, drugs, and humans on ships, have substantial economic and human costs. Global trade routes used by traffickers overlap with known pirate and terrorist hot spots—and with the world's major transit routes for the legitimate commodities trade. In the late 1990s up until 2006, pirate attacks were concentrated in Southeast Asian waters.[13] In these attacks, seafarers are hijacked, held hostage, injured, or killed (Nincic 2013). In 2006, the governments of Indonesia, Malaysia, Singapore, and Thailand officially launched the Malacca Straits Patrol, a set of cooperative measures for better security and intelligence exchange. This led to a drop in piracy incidents in subsequent years (World Politics Review 2018; Ramani 2019).

[12] Each government has its own standard procedures and requirements for registering and licensing fishers.

[13] International Maritime Organization. *Maritime Security and Piracy.* http://www.imo.org/en/OurWork/Security/Pages/MaritimeSecurity.aspx.

However, piracy continues to be a problem in Southeast Asia, which had the world's highest rate of piracy in 2017 (World Politics Review 2018).

The oceans of Asia and the Pacific have not escaped the impacts of COVID-19. While reports show some short-term environmental benefits from lockdowns and economic slowdowns, such as reduced pressures from tourism, fishing, and shipping, the larger implications of the pandemic are alarming (UN News 2020; Kassem 2020). IUU fishing has risen as governments focus on pandemic concerns instead of enforcement (Solano and Torchia 2020). International tourism, shipping, fisheries, offshore renewables, and aquaculture have been significantly damaged. ADB's *Asian Development Outlook 2020* report estimates that 3 months of pandemic-induced interruptions in tourism will shrink the tourism-based economies of Palau, the Cook Islands, Samoa, and Vanuatu (ADB 2020). Decreased demand for seafood from hotels and restaurants reeling from a drop in international tourism (22% in the first quarter of 2020) has reduced fishing activity in the region, while temporary closure of seaports has cut off access to markets (Bennett et al. 2020). Fish and seafood exports could drop by a third, while cargo trade could dip by 10% (Hudson 2020). However, the full impact of COVID-19 on oceans will not be fully understood for years since data collection and monitoring in many locations has been suspended as the global community prioritizes containing the pandemic.

Finally, the ocean bears the brunt of climate change. Increasing emissions of carbon dioxide and other greenhouse gases from human activities have been major contributors to ocean acidification and deoxygenation, increased ocean temperatures, increased frequency and severity of extreme weather events, and sea level rise. In the Pacific island region, sea level rise greater than 1 meter is likely within the 21st century and 2 meters by 2100 is plausible (Garner et al. 2018). This will have major impacts on many coastal communities and small island developing states. As the ocean absorbs more carbon dioxide, waters become more acidic, making it more difficult for mollusks (such as oysters, clams, mussels) and corals to build hard shells and skeletons.[14] Warming waters have caused massive death of marine life and shifted species distribution (Sanford et al. 2019). The impacts of climate change threaten ocean-dependent livelihoods and at-risk communities. Coastal communities in Asia and the Pacific are especially vulnerable: 9 out of the 10 most populous cities exposed to extreme events and

---

[14] National Oceanic Atmospheric and Administration-US Department of Commerce. *Ocean Acidification.* https://www.noaa.gov/education/resource-collections/ocean-coasts/ocean-acidification.

coastal flooding are in Asia, itself a region that experiences average daily losses of $200 million because of disasters caused by natural hazards. The small island developing states collectively contribute to less than 1% of global greenhouse gases, yet are disproportionately affected (UN Office of the High Representative for the Least Developed Countries 2015). Sea level rise threatens the existence of up to 97% of the people in Pacific island states (Andrew et al. 2019).

If the region's oceans continue to decline, the enormous potential of its blue economy will be lost, disrupting food security, livelihoods, public health, and disaster resilience. Given the interconnectedness of coastal and marine environments, dealing with issues that affect the oceans requires an approach integrated at the national, regional, and global levels.

Frameworks and Instruments for Ocean Governance

The interconnectedness of the oceans creates complex management and governance issues, as benefits and burdens do not recognize borders. Various frameworks and instruments have been created to address international and regional issues. The overarching legal framework for ocean governance is UNCLOS. Described as the "constitution of the oceans," UNCLOS establishes regulations for maritime activities such as fishing, shipping, mining, and pollution. The UN Fish Stock Agreement lays out principles for the conservation and management of straddling and highly migratory fish stocks (UN 1995). The 1995 FAO Code of Conduct for Responsible Fisheries set international standards of behavior for responsible practices to ensure effective conservation, management, and development of marine and aquatic resources, while accounting for the impact of fishing on the ecosystems and biodiversity.[15] The International Convention for the Prevention of Pollution from Ships (MARPOL) tackles transboundary pollution from ships, such as oil, sewage, and garbage (International Maritime Organization 1973). In 2016, the Agreement on Port State Measures to Prevent, Deter and Eliminate IUU Fishing entered into force as the world's first binding international agreement to prevent vessels engaged in IUU fishing from using ports and landing catches (FAO 2016).

Other international treaties for the environment consider marine species and ecosystems. The UN Framework Convention on Climate Change (UNFCCC) identifies oceans and coastal ecosystems as a priority area (UNFCCC 2018).

---

[15] FAO. *IUU Fishing. Code of Conduct for Responsible Fisheries.* http://www.fao.org/iuu-fishing/international-framework/code-of-conduct-for-responsible-fisheries/en/.

In 2010, the Convention on Biological Diversity aimed for 10% of the world's oceans to be protected by 2020 (Convention on Biological Diversity 2010). The Convention on Migratory Species (CMS) of Wild Animals and the Convention on International Trade in Endangered Species have growing lists to ensure protection of marine wildlife, including seabirds (CITES 2020; CMS 2020). In 2015, the UN identified "Life Below Water" as one of its 17 SDGs under the 2030 Agenda for Sustainable Development, highlighting the need for urgent attention and cooperation for oceans (UN 2015).

Though many legal frameworks and conventions address ocean issues, significant gaps remain. Discussions are ongoing for a multilateral, legally binding agreement to eliminate marine plastic pollution (Simon et al. 2018). Negotiations are also taking place for creation of a new international instrument under UNCLOS to help better manage and monitor the high seas.

Regional Cooperation and Integration Initiatives

Numerous intergovernmental organizations, agreements, programs, and initiatives have been created to improve regional cooperation and integration on ocean-related transboundary issues in national and international waters. This section features 18 of them as a diverse sample of regional cooperation mechanisms and governance structures, including programs with specific focus on ocean health and fisheries issues, and selected initiatives with regional importance that can play increasing roles in tackling ocean health and blue economy issues. The 18 entities include regional fisheries management organizations (RFMOs); regional fisheries bodies; UN Environment Programme (UNEP) Regional Seas Programmes; and large marine ecosystem mechanisms in East Asia, Pacific, South Asia, and Southeast Asia. Space here limits the selection to three to four entities per subregion (with some highlighted in Boxes 14.1, 14.2, and 14.3), yet many other interesting entities are relevant to this discussion.[16]. This is especially true in the Pacific due to the importance of the ocean for the people living there, the existential threat of climate change, the large number of small island developing states, and the challenges they face communicating and coordinating over large distances.

---

[16] UNEP. 2016. *Regional Oceans Governance: Making Regional Seas Programmes, Regional Fishery Bodies and Large Marine Ecosystem Mechanisms Work Better Together.* Nairobi. https://www.cbd.int/doc/meetings/mar/soiom-2016-01/other/soiom-2016-01-unep-06-en.pdf.

Of the 18 selected regional cooperation and integration initiatives, 15 are presented in the form of a rapid survey and 3 as more detailed case studies. Information is a synthesis of desk research. Each description includes basic details of the entity and—to the extent available—information about its achievements, challenges, lessons learned, and opportunities, with a focus on cooperation and integration. A summary analysis is included in the next section, and is intended to guide the development or improvement of similar regional entities and initiatives.

Regional Fisheries Management Organizations

RFMOs are made up of countries that share a practical and/or financial interest in managing and conserving fish stocks in a particular area. Some member countries are coastal states whose exclusive economic zone is covered by the RFMO, while others are members because they are fishing entities, or have distant water fishing fleets (Pew Charitable Trusts 2012). Although RFMOs are important in facilitating cooperation between fishing countries, historically they have not been able to reduce overfishing and improve fish stocks. This is mainly because many are not structured to limit fishing because they were established when ocean resources were considered virtually unlimited (Pew Charitable Trusts 2012). There are 17 RFMOs worldwide; 4 of the most relevant to Asia and the Pacific are summarized in Table 14.1.

Regional—Asia and the Pacific

Asia-Pacific Economic Cooperation

APEC's Oceans and Fisheries Working Group (OFWG) reports to the Senior Officials Steering Committee on Economic and Technical Cooperation. It was formed in 2011 to facilitate free trade and promote aquaculture and the sustainable use of fisheries, marine ecosystem resources, and related goods and services. The OFWG does this by encouraging cooperation among governments, academia, private industry, and regional and international organizations (APEC 2020). The 2019 APEC Roadmap on Marine Debris Management and the 2019 Roadmap on Combatting Illegal Unreported and Unregulated Fishing are currently being developed. OFWG compiles the APEC *Marine Sustainable Development Report* to identify gaps and challenges and increase collaboration among APEC economies on sustainable development. The APEC *Marine Sustainable Development Report 2* focuses

Table 14.1: Regional Fisheries Management Organizations in Asia and the Pacific

RFMO	Objective	Successes	Challenges
Western and Central Pacific Fisheries Commission (WCPFC) *Entered into force in 2004.* *Twenty-six members. Asia and the Pacific members: Australia; the People's Republic of China (PRC); the Cook Islands; the Federated States of Micronesia; Fiji; Indonesia; Japan; Kiribati; the Republic of Korea; the Marshall Islands; Nauru; New Zealand; Niue; Palau; Papua New Guinea; the Philippines; Samoa; Solomon Islands; Taipei,China; Tonga; Tuvalu; and Vanuatu.*	Global fisheries agreement focusing on the conservation and sustainable management of highly migratory fish stocks such as tunas, billfish, and marlin.	Conducted stock assessments for skipjack tuna, Southeast Pacific striped marlin, oceanic white tip shark, and North Pacific striped marlin. Expected to undertake negotiations to develop a new tropical tuna measure by 2021.	Overfishing: four key commercial tuna stocks: bigeye, skipjack, South Pacific albacore, and yellowfin assessed as managed above sustainable limits. Difficulties in reporting its accomplishments in absence of a strategic or corporate plan.
Indian Tuna Ocean Commission (IOTC) *Entered into force in 1998.* *Thirty-four members. Asia and the Pacific members: Australia, Bangladesh, the PRC, India, Indonesia, Japan, the Republic of Korea, Malaysia, Maldives, Mauritius, Pakistan, the Philippines, Sri Lanka, and Thailand.*	Intergovernmental organization mandated to conserve, manage tuna and tuna-like species such as blue marlin, swordfish, and mackerels in the Indian Ocean and adjacent seas for sustainable development of fisheries.	Reduced the impact of FADs on marine ecosystems.[a] Non-entangling FADs will be required in 2020, and biodegradable FADs in 2022. Reduced the number of active FADs per vessel, and scaled down each vessel's total, active and inactive FAD count. Took steps to standardize FAD marking, tracking, and retrieval procedures.	Noncompliance issues in data collection, sharing requirements, and capacity building by certain parties. Limitations in capacity management, catch limitations and allocations, monitoring, control, and surveillance, and for following up on infringements.

continued on next page

Table 14.1: continued

RFMO	Objective	Successes	Challenges
Commission for the Conservation of Southern Bluefin Tuna (CCSBT) *Established in 1994.* *Eight members. Asia and the Pacific members: Australia, Bangladesh, the PRC, India, Indonesia, Japan, the Republic of Korea, Malaysia, Maldives, Mauritius, Pakistan, the Philippines, Sri Lanka, and Thailand.*	Intergovernmental organization that aims to conserve and manage the optimum utilization of southern bluefin tuna throughout its geographic distribution.	Reduced operating costs through decentralized operations with members undertaking their own science, administration, and monitoring. Applied certain rules of other RFMOs and harmonized some of its decisions (e.g., for transshipments) with those of other tuna RFMOs as well.	Need for clear roles, responsibilities, and performance standards have yet to be set. Systems and processes need to ensure the rights and responsibilities of all members, and encourage cooperation from nonmembers, and considers the special requirements and capacity-building needs of developing members and cooperating nonmembers in terms of compliance with the commission's obligations.
South Pacific Regional Fisheries Management Organisation (SPRFMO) *Established in 2009.* *Fifteen members from Asia, Europe, the Americas, and Oceania. Asia and the Pacific members: the PRC; the Cook Islands; the Republic of Korea; New Zealand; Taipei,China; and Vanuatu.*	Intergovernmental organization focused on the long-term conservation and sustainable use of the fishery resources of the South Pacific Ocean.	Progressive recovery of the jack mackerel stock in the eastern Pacific Ocean. Reliable stock assessments undertaken, especially of jack mackerel. Provided good quality scientific advice, even in the absence of adequate data.	Need to expand to other stocks within its purview, particularly jumbo flying squid, and update measures for bottom fishing (usually involves dropping a weighted hook near the ocean floor to catch fish that congregate around structures such as rocks or reefs) More effective use of collected data needed.

continued on next page

Table 14.1: *continued*

RFMO	Objective	Successes	Challenges
		Adopted conservation and management measures concerning monitoring, control, and surveillance, drawing on the best practices of other RFMOs.	Overall, needs to adopt a more comprehensive ecosystem approach to fisheries management.

FAD = fishing aggregating device, PRC = People's Republic of China, RFMO = regional fisheries management organization.

a A FAD is an object, such as a buoy attached to something on the ocean floor with a rope, that fishers put in the ocean to attract fish, most commonly pelagic fish such as tuna. The fishers then harvest the fish that congregate near the FAD.

Sources: WCPFC Secretariat. 2019. *2019 Annual Report of the Executive Director*. Federated States of Micronesia https://www.wcpfc.int/node/44211; WCPFC. *About WCPFC*. https://www.wcpfc.int/about-wcpfc; IOTC. 2016. *Report of the 2nd IOTC Performance Review*. Seychelles. https://www.iotc.org/documents/report-2nd-iotc-performance-review; IOTC. *Structure of the Commission*. https://www.iotc.org/about-iotc/structure-commission; CCSBT. 2015. *Strategic Plan for the Commission for the Conservation of Southern Bluefin Tuna 2015–2020*. Canberra. https://www.ccsbt.org/en/system/files/resource/en/4e0d6cf52db2b/EC_Info01-AdoptedStrategicPlan.pdf; CCSBT. *Origins of the Convention*. https://www.ccsbt.org/en/content/origins-convention; P. Ridings et al. 2018. *Report of the South Pacific Regional Fisheries Management Organisation Performance Review Panel*. Wellington, New Zealand. https://www.sprfmo.int/assets/Basic-Documents/Convention-and-Final-Act/2018-SPRFMO-Performance-Review/2018-12-01-REPORT-SPRFMO-PERFORMANCE-REVIEW-FINAL.pdf.

on how APEC can advance regional economic integration and collaboration and mobilize resources. The report notes that many APEC economies have started to implement SDG 14 and have developed the following good practices: (i) having mutually reinforcing objectives to achieve environmental, economic, and social results; (ii) encouraging participation of local communities, the general public, producers, and consumers; and (iii) effectively using information, data, scientific knowledge, and technology to design and implement effective solutions (APEC Ocean and Fisheries Working Group 2019).

Box 14.1: Coral Triangle Initiative on Coral Reefs, Fisheries, and Food Security

Description. The Coral Triangle, often called the "Amazon of the Seas," is located along the equator where the Western Pacific and Indian Oceans meet. Its valuable assets include the greatest extent of mangrove forests in the world, and spawning and juvenile growth areas for the world's largest and most valuable tuna fishery.[a] It is considered the global center of marine biodiversity, with more than 76% of the known coral species, 6 out of the 7 known marine turtle species, and about 3,000 species of reef fish—more than twice the number found on reefs elsewhere (ADB 2010). The Coral Triangle Initiative on Coral Reefs, Fisheries, and Food Security (CTI-CFF) was launched in 2007 and established in 2009 as a formal intergovernmental partnership, recognized by the leaders of six countries: three in Southeast Asia (Indonesia, Malaysia, and the Philippines) and three in the Pacific (Papua New Guinea, Solomon Islands, and Timor-Leste) to protect the region's valuable economic and environmental assets through regional cooperation (Figure 14.1.1).

Figure 14.1.1: Coral Triangle Initiative Implementation Area

Note: Based on original map from Coral Geographic, this map was produced by the ADB cartography unit.

continued on next page

Box 14.1: *continued*

The CTI-CFF has benefited from significant external financing and technical assistance provided by a range of multilateral and bilateral donors, nongovernment and community-based organizations, and private foundations. These include the governments of Australia, Germany, and the United States (US), as well as the European Union. The Asian Development Bank (ADB), with cofinancing from the Global Environment Facility, has supported two regional technical assistance projects and two national loan projects (Indonesia and the Philippines). Other multilateral donors include Food and Agriculture Organization, United Nations Development Programme, United Nations Environment Programme, and World Bank. Other funding and important technical assistance has been provided by a range of organizations, notably, World Wildlife Fund for Nature, Conservation International, The Nature Conservancy, Coral Triangle Center, Wildlife Conservation Society, Southeast Asia Fisheries Development Center, and a host of national counterparts.

The CTI-CFF features a Regional Plan of Action that provides an overarching framework for national plans of action—all of which set goals and technical targets in areas related to: (i) Marine Protected Areas, (ii) an ecosystem-based approach to fisheries management, (iii) managing large seascapes, (iv) climate change adaptation, and (v) threatened species. The Regional Secretariat's operations and related programs are funded by "assessed contributions" from each country and are an important indicator of their ownership and commitment.

The CTI-CFF has made significant progress in facilitating information exchange, building institutional capacity, and strengthening regional policy dialogue.

Successes, according to Abraham (2015), have included creating:

- A system of governance guiding interaction between member states, and a functional regional secretariat to coordinate efforts.
- A CTI brand identity that has given stakeholders a sense of belonging and realization of the importance of the initiative for managing coastal and marine resources, and food security.
- A suite of capacity development tools, instruments, and approaches that were developed, tested, and are being scaled up, especially to strengthen Marine Protected Areas and manage large seascapes.
- A strong coalition of multilateral and bilateral institutions, willing to continue investing in sustainable development of the Coral Triangle region.
- A group of nongovernment and community-based organizations that have leveraged their networks of partners, dedicated resources, and formed powerful working relationships among themselves and within the communities where they work.
- Increased engagement by national and local institutions, with domestic financial resources committed to localized projects and programs, in addition to sustaining the Regional Secretariat.

Challenges

- Initial phases mainly supported by external actors, which slowed down buy-in by member countries.
- Coordination of region-wide actions were constrained by geographic distance between the Pacific and Southeast Asia.

continued on next page

Box 14.1: *continued*

- Uneven technical and financial capacity across the member countries made it difficult to internalize tools and instruments, e.g., for assessing the management of protected areas.
- Limited ability to engage the highest levels of government, mainly because the CTI-CFF was viewed as a fisheries and conservation initiative without linkages to economic development and job creation.
- Difficulties in getting a professionally staffed Regional Secretariat in place and functioning well, supplemented by a process-intensive bureaucracy.
- Mixed success across technical areas with some moving forward faster than others.

Lessons learned

- Need to fill in financing gaps by employing a more systematic, coordinated approach to resource mobilization; defining the role of the Regional Secretariat more clearly; and using the regional and national plans of action to attract, guide, and shape investments.
- Balancing national and regional interests and priorities are important, as is achieving a common understanding of how benefits from regional public goods are gained and shared.
- Alleviating poverty among fisher and coastal communities across the region, especially in view of the coronavirus disease (COVID-19) pandemic, continues to be a priority.

[a] CTI-CFF. 2009. *Regional Plan of Action: Coral Triangle Initiative on Coral Reefs, Fisheries and Food Security (CTI-CFF)*. Jakarta: Coral Triangle Initiative on Coral Reefs, Fisheries and Food Security (CTI-CFF) Interim Regional Secretariat.

Sources: A. Abraham 2015. *Stock-Take of CTI-CFF Programs and Projects: Strategic Review of Progress and Future Directions*. Jakarta: Coral Triangle Initiative on Coral Reefs, Fisheries and Food Security (CTI-CFF) Interim Regional Secretariat; ADB. 2010. *Coral Triangle Initiative Brochure*. Manila.

East Asia

Coordinating Body on the Seas of East Asia

Coordinating Body on the Seas of East Asia (COBSEA) is an intergovernmental organization that supports Cambodia, the PRC, Indonesia, the Republic of Korea, Malaysia, the Philippines, Singapore, Thailand, and Viet Nam in the development and protection of the marine environment and coastal areas of East Asian Seas. COBSEA is one of UNEP's Regional Seas Programmes. It oversees implementation of the Action Plan for the Protection and Development of the Marine Environment and Coastal Areas of the East Asian Seas Region (East Asian Seas Action Plan), which was adopted in April 1981 and revised in 1994. Activities support the COBSEA Strategic Directions 2018–2022, and include: establishing Marine Protected Areas, restoring marine and coastal habitats, and developing a pollution management plan and waste management policies.

The COBSEA Regional Action Plan on Marine Litter has played an important role in identifying common priorities and providing a framework for regional cooperation. COBSEA is considering developing regional activity centers to improve implementation and has gathered lessons learned about such centers from other organizations. These include the need to ensure they serve the interests of participating countries and that sustainable institutional and financing arrangements are put in place. Indonesia has established the Regional Capacity Centre for Clean Seas to leverage multi-stakeholder collaboration and institutional strengthening to assist countries in developing national capacities to implement the East Asian Seas Action Plan and its Strategic Directions (UNEP 2019).

Northwest Pacific Action Plan

The Action Plan for the Protection, Management and Development of the Marine and Coastal Environment of the Northwest Pacific Region (the Northwest Pacific Action Plan or NOWPAP) is an intergovernmental organization adopted by the PRC, Japan, the Republic of Korea, and the Russian Federation in 1994 as one of UNEP's Regional Seas Programmes. The goal of NOWPAP is the wise use, development, and management of the coastal and marine environment to provide long-term benefits for people, while protecting human health and the environment.[17] In 2018, member states agreed to develop a Regional Action Plan on Marine and Coastal Biodiversity Conservation to coordinate activities of each of the four regional activity centers and more effectively guide marine biodiversity conservation efforts. The Marine Environmental Emergency Preparedness and Response Regional Activity Centre leads cooperation on dealing with oil, hazardous and noxious substances, and marine pollution using many different communication channels and capacities for practical responses. However, member states have suggested that the center develop a mid- or long-term strategy and address budgetary limitations (UNEP 2020).

---

[17] UNEP. *About NOWPAP Environment.* https://www.unenvironment.org/nowpap/who-we-are/about-nowpap-environment.

Partnerships in Environmental Management for the Seas of East Asia

Partnerships in Environmental Management for the Seas of East Asia (PEMSEA) is an intergovernmental organization that fosters and sustains healthy and resilient coasts and oceans, communities, and economies across the seas of East Asia. It does this through integrated management solutions and partnerships. PEMSEA was established as a regional governance mechanism in 2009, following a series of projects beginning in 1994 supported by UNDP, Global Environment Facility, and other organizations. It has 11 country partners: Cambodia, the PRC, Indonesia, Japan, the Democratic People's Republic of Korea, the Republic of Korea, the Lao People's Democratic Republic, the Philippines, Singapore, Timor-Leste, and Viet Nam.

PEMSEA is the regional coordinating mechanism for the Sustainable Development Strategy for the Seas of East Asia, a regional framework for governments and other stakeholders to implement commitments under existing international agreements.[18] For the past 25 years, PEMSEA's facilitation of multisector cooperation and partnerships through integrated coastal management has helped improve coastal and ocean governance and the successful implementation of many different management programs (PEMSEA 2019a). Financial stability is a key challenge for the organization since only four countries are currently making voluntary contributions to the PEMSEA Trust Fund (PEMSEA 2018a). Challenges also exist in regional cooperation, including that region-wide strategies for conserving biologically connected Marine Protected Areas and sustainable fishing have yet to be established, while there is a lack of a scientifically and systematically designated network for protected areas under a master plan and little technical capacity in assessing and evaluating the effectiveness of biodiversity conservation. Evidence-based measures to show changes in biodiversity status are also absent (PEMSEA 2018b).

Pacific

Parties to the Nauru Agreement

Parties to the Nauru Agreement (PNA) is a subregional fisheries agreement enacted in 1982 between the Federated States of Micronesia, Kiribati, the Marshall Islands, Nauru, Palau, Papua New Guinea, Solomon Islands, and Tuvalu. The PNA has implemented many conservation measures that were

---

[18] PEMSEA. http://www.pemsea.org/.

the first of its kind, such as closing the high seas to fishing, controls on fish attracting devices, protection of whale sharks, and bycatch reduction initiatives to ensure that no dolphins are caught in PNA waters. In 2011, the Marine Stewardship Council, an independent nonprofit that sets standards for sustainable fishing, certified the PNA's skipjack tuna as sustainable. The PNA controls half the global supply of skipjack tuna (the species of tuna most commonly canned), making it the world's largest sustainable tuna purse seine fishery.[19] An ADB report on Pacific island economies recognized the PNA's Vessel Day Scheme, which limits fishing activity across participants' exclusive economic zones, as "an outstanding global example of coastal states taking control of a fishery based on highly migratory stocks" (ADB 2016). Being a successful case study poses challenges in sustaining the gains and increasing meaningful participation among the parties (IUCN 2015). Another successful case study is explored in Box 14.2.

Box 14.2: The Micronesia Challenge

Description. Located in the northern part of the tropical Pacific, the more than 2,000 islands of Micronesia are home to a wide variety of habitats and biodiversity: more than 1,400 species of plants, 1,300 species of fish, and 535 kinds of corals, as well as hundreds of birds, amphibians, insects, reptiles, and mammals, many of which are found nowhere else in the world. Micronesia also provides habitats for migratory birds and fish, including much of the world's tuna.[a] The Micronesia Challenge is a commitment made in 2006 by five governments—the Federated States of Micronesia, the Republic of the Marshall Islands, Republic of Palau, the United States territory of Guam, and the Commonwealth of the Northern Mariana Islands—to preserve the natural resources that Pacific traditions, cultures, and livelihoods depend on.[b] The challenge has grown into a network supported by over 50 partners globally (Figure 14.2.1).[c]

The original goal was to conserve at least 30% of the near-shore marine resources and 20% of the terrestrial resources across Micronesia by 2020 to protect unique, locally and globally important island biodiversity, and sustain the livelihoods and cultures of Micronesian communities. This has been increased to manage at least 50% of near-shore resources and at least 30% of terrestrial resources across Micronesia by 2030 (Micronesia Conservation Trust 2020).

continued on next page

---

[19] PNA. 2011. 3 PNA Countries Close Their Waters to Foreign Tuna Fleets to Maintain Sustainable Fishing Limits. 21 November. https://pnatuna.com/node/76.

Box 14.2: *continued*

Figure 14.2.1: The Micronesia Challenge

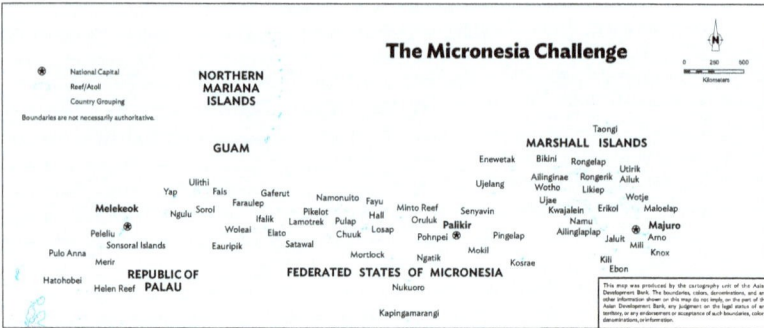

The UN Environment-Global Environment Facility project Micronesia Challenge: Sustainable Finance Systems for Island Protected Area Management was implemented from 2011 to 2015. The project financed the establishment of a Micronesia Challenge Endowment Fund (MCEF) that was managed by the nonprofit Micronesian Conservation Trust. Financial, and technical support has been provided by many other organizations, including: the United States Department of the Interior, the National Oceanographic and Atmospheric Administration, Germany's Federal Ministry for the Environment, the Nature Conservation and Nuclear Safety, the Nature Conservancy, and Conservation International.

Successes. A recent evaluation found tremendous effort have been undertaken across the region to make progress on coordinating and sharing information, increasing financial and technical resources for conservation, developing capacity for effective resource management, and supporting conservation and management actions with communities (Gombos 2020). Specifically, Micronesia Challenge has leveraged $82 million for conservation efforts, including about $20 million for the regional endowment fund. This important contribution to the establishment, operation, and diversification of financing systems in the region can provide long-term resources for conservation. Other successes noted by the International Union for Conservation of Nature (2015) include:

- More than 70 marine areas placed under conservation across all jurisdictions.
- Improved science-to-management decision-making enabled 20 new fisheries management policies based on marine data and standardized monitoring protocols and region-wide databases.
- Doubling of capacity and increasing the pace of progress toward Micronesia Challenge goals, including integrating the Marine Protected Area Management Effectiveness Tool into management procedures.
- Support for the completion of 96 college certificates, degrees, and internships for youth and staff.
- Inspiring similar regional commitments, including the Caribbean Challenge Initiative, the Aloha+ Challenge, and the Coral Triangle Initiative.
- The Global Environment Facility (GEF) project succeeded in attracting and utilizing champions for raising funds and the profiles of the project and the wider Micronesia Challenge.
- The GEF project built on lessons from related initiatives in Micronesia and global experience of sustainable financing for biodiversity conservation. The project made good use of Micronesia Challenge agreement and partnerships; these brought valuable expertise and knowledge to the project and helped build on existing institutional structures and capacity.

continued on next page

Box 14.2: *continued*

Challenges. An unclear framework and inadequate political and financial investments in governance mechanisms, resulting from insufficient regional coordination and communication, caused most of the challenges during the first phase (to 2020). Significant financial resources were needed for conservation schemes to succeed since the Micronesian Conservation Trust began with very limited resources and had to use an incremental approach to raising funds (Gastelumendi et al. 2012). Since the endowment fund has invested in stocks and bonds, whose performance depends on world markets, there was some concern about investment risks being too high. There was also a degree of political risk due to changes in government, with individuals in some countries advocating for independent endowment funds (UN Environment Programme 2017).

Lessons learned. The Micronesian Conservation Trust started small and built up success over time to generate a substantial amount of sustainable financing and invested the funds in an endowment. This process created a strong sense of empowerment among stakeholders (Gastelumendi et al. 2012). The financial success elevated the importance of conservation in the eyes of local politicians and citizens, and encouraged politicians to publicly support and prioritize conservation, which gave the Micronesia Challenge political influence (Sustainable Hawaii Initiative and Micronesia Challenge). Other lessons learned include:

- A more bottom-up planning approach is needed to better align with local priorities and engage more stakeholders.
- Engaging legislators and other decision makers in field trips increased their awareness and understanding of natural resources, threats, and impacts.
- Healthy competition can be created among communities to achieve the best-managed Marine Protected Areas and have the highest fish biomass.
- Other financing sources can diversify financing and lower risk, such as tourism taxes, debt swaps/conversions and conservation easements, revenues from fishing licenses, and climate change funds.
- The GEF financing was critical for capitalizing the MCEF, by encouraging other donors and the participating governments to contribute. At the regional level, additional donor money was leveraged for related projects.

[a] Micronesia Challenge. *We Are One: Business Plan and Conservation Campaign.* http://www.glispa.org/images/MC-BusinessPlan_LowRes.pdf.
[b] Micronesia Challenge. http://www.micronesiachallenge.org/.
[c] A list of the 50 partners can be found at http://www.micronesiachallenge.org.

Sources: Gastelumendi, J, S. Irawan, L. Schindler, W. Kostka, K. Petrini, and A. Heikens. 2012. Case Study Report: Micronesian Conservation Trust. A joint Nature Conservancy; United Nations Development Programme; Micronesian Conservation Trust Working Paper; Gombos, M. 2020. *Micronesia Challenge Evaluation: A Stakeholder-Based Review of a Pioneering Regional Conservation Initiative.* Denver, Colorado: Sea Change Consulting. Micronesia Conservation Trust. 2020. The Federated States of Micronesia Sixth National Report to the Convention on Biological Diversity. February; International Union for Conservation of Nature. 2015. Parties to the Nauru Agreement (PNA). Interview with Maurice Brownjon. 2 June; Sustainable Hawaii Initiative and Micronesia Challenge (MC). Learning Exchange (LEX) Report. Unpublished; United Nations Environment Programme. 2017. *Terminal evaluation of the UN Environment GEF Project "Micronesia Challenge: Sustainable Finance Systems for Island Protected Area Management."* Nairobi.

Office of the Pacific Ocean Commissioner

The Office of the Pacific Ocean Commissioner (OPOC) was established within the Pacific Islands Forum Secretariat in 2014. It is the highest regional Pacific entity mandated to lead on ocean matters. OPOC provides high-level advocacy and attention to Pacific Ocean priorities, decisions, and processes at national, regional, and international levels, and is an influential supporter of improved cooperation, coordination, and collaboration in the region.[20] Key OPOC efforts to date include the establishment of the Pacific Ocean Alliance, which brings together all stakeholders on an equal footing to create dialogue around emerging, cross-cutting ocean issues, in a variety of forums (Vince et al. 2017). OPOC is responsible for the development of key messages and the promotion of regional ocean policy and regional ocean interests, in coordination with relevant Council of Regional Organisations of the Pacific[21] agencies. They also maintain a register of Pacific Ocean initiatives and projects, to monitor progress and address gaps as well as support countries, including Pacific Permanent Missions to the UN, with coordinated advice on cross-sector ocean issues, such as biodiversity, in areas beyond national jurisdiction and marine spatial planning. OPOC also supports regional preparatory processes to review and develop ocean policy, identify emerging issues, and report progress under SDG14 (OPOC).

Secretariat of the Pacific Regional Environment Programme

The Secretariat of the Pacific Regional Environment Programme (SPREP) is a regional organization with 21 Pacific island member countries and territories[22] and five developed country members.[23] With a mandate to promote cooperation for environmental protection and sustainable development, an annual budget of approximately $30 million, and

---

[20] OPOC. https://opocbluepacific.net/office-of-pacific-ocean-commissioner/.

[21] The Council of Regional Organisations of the Pacific or CROP is made up of the heads of intergovernmental regional organizations in the Pacific and functions as a coordination mechanism and a high-level policy advisory body.

[22] American Samoa, the Cook Islands, the Federated States of Micronesia, Fiji, French Polynesia, Guam, Kiribati, the Marshall Islands, Nauru, New Caledonia, Niue, the Commonwealth of the Northern Mariana Islands, Palau, Papua New Guinea, Samoa, Solomon Islands, Territory of the Wallis and Futuna Islands, Tokelau, Tonga, Tuvalu, and Vanuatu.

[23] The five developed member countries of SPREP are Australia, France, New Zealand, the United Kingdom, and the United States.

more than 90 full-time staff, SPREP is well positioned to spur regional coordination.

Current focus areas include climate change resilience, island and ocean ecosystems, effective waste management and pollution control, and environmental governance. Since its establishment in 1993, SPREP has effectively coalesced its membership around key ocean issues such as protecting whales, the Pacific Year of the Coral Reef thematic campaign, invasive species, and ocean pollution. SPREP's four information portals are widely used throughout the region.[24] In 2019, in partnership with Japan and Samoa, SPREP officially opened the Pacific Climate Change Centre to improve regional coordination and share climate change information, traditional knowledge, and solutions.

South Asia

South Asia Co-operative Environment Programme

The South Asia Cooperative Environment Programme (SACEP) is an intergovernmental organization established in 1982 by Afghanistan, Bangladesh, Bhutan, India, Maldives, Nepal, Pakistan, and Sri Lanka to promote and support the protection, management, and improvement of the environment and sustainable development of the region. SACEP also acts as the secretariat of the South Asian Seas Programme, which is supported by UNEP. The South Asian Seas Programme is a regional platform for protection and sustainable management of the marine environment, including preparation of regional action plans and policies. It works on coral reef issues, capacity development, and awareness raising and sharing experience among member countries (SACEP 2018).

Noteworthy activities include the Plastic Free Rivers and Seas for South Asia Project, launched in 2020, the 2018 Regional Marine Litter Action Plan, and the 2014 Regional Marine and Coastal Biodiversity Strategy for the South Asian Seas Region. Despite SACEP's funding and human resource constraints, it has good potential to improve resource-based cooperation (Swain 2002) through the planned Inter-Regional Organization Dialogue Committee, which will bring South Asia regional organizations together

---

[24] SPREP. Information Portals. https://www.sprep.org/information-portals.

as part of the Plastic Free Rivers and Seas for South Asia Project. SACEP has also been active in regional cooperation and integration on adaptation to climate change, specifically in advancing the Nationally Determined Contributions of its member states under the Paris Agreement.

Box 14.3: Bay of Bengal Programme Inter-Governmental Organisation

Description. The Bay of Bengal is the largest bay in the world. It comprises 31% of the world's coastal fishers and provides food, livelihood, and social benefits for over 400 million people. The Bay of Bengal Large Marine Ecosystem (BOBLME) covers 6.2 million square kilometers—about 66% is within the exclusive economic zones of eight countries (Bangladesh, India, Indonesia, Malaysia, Maldives, Myanmar, Sri Lanka, and Thailand), and, as shown in Figure 14.3.1, the rest is made up of the high seas (The Economist 2013; Bay of Bengal Large Marine Ecosystem Project). The BOBLME is an area of high biodiversity and critical habitats such as mangroves (12% of world mangrove resources); coral reefs (8% of the world's coral reefs) and extensive seagrass beds.[a]

Figure 14.3.1: Bay of Bengal Large Marine Ecosystem

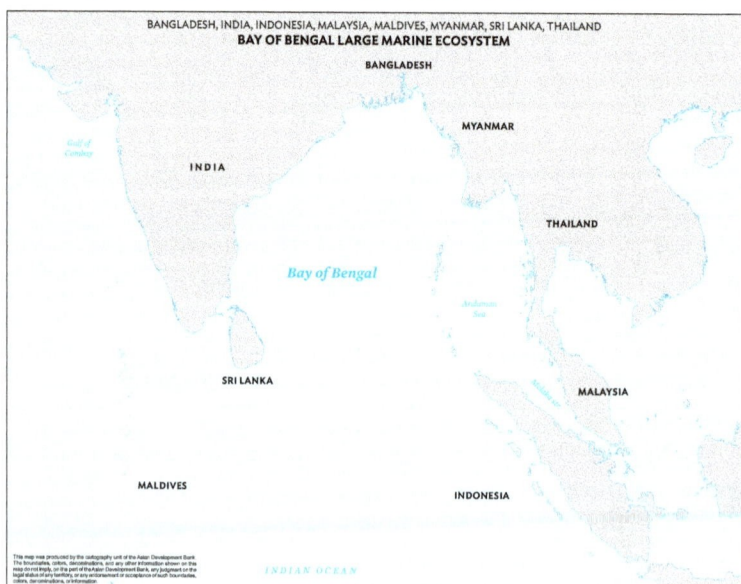

BANGLADESH, INDIA, INDONESIA, MALAYSIA, MALDIVES, MYANMAR, SRI LANKA, THAILAND
BAY OF BENGAL LARGE MARINE ECOSYSTEM

BANGLADESH

MYANMAR

Gulf of Cambay

INDIA

THAILAND

Bay of Bengal

Andaman Sea

SRI LANKA

MALAYSIA

MALDIVES

INDONESIA

INDIAN OCEAN

Note: Boundaries as identified by the BOBLME Programme.
Source: Adapted by the Asian Development Bank with permission from the BOBLME Programme.

continued on next page

Box 14.3: *continued*

The Bay of Bengal Programme Inter-Governmental Organization on coastal fisheries (BOBP-IGO) was established in 2003 as a regional fishery body with four member states: Bangladesh, India, Maldives, and Sri Lanka. Its mandate is to improve cooperation among member countries and other countries and organizations in the region and provide technical and management advisory services for sustainable coastal fisheries development and management in the Bay of Bengal.

In 2009, an eight-country Transboundary Diagnostic Analysis supported by the Global Environment Facility (GEF), in partnership with the Food and Agriculture Organization (FAO), identified priority environmental issues and root causes. At the regional level, the main institutional barrier was the absence of an appropriate forum for region-wide multinational dialogue, planning, monitoring, and reporting on the progress of sustainable development. The diagnostic analyses led to the development of a Strategy Action Programme for the BOBLME, signed by all eight countries in 2017. Action has been supported by the GEF, and led by FAO in coordination with Asian Development Bank (ADB), United Nations (UN) Environment Programme, International Union for Conservation of Nature (IUCN) and UN Industrial Development Organization as well as focal agencies in each country.

The strategy implementation program promoted an integrated approach to tackling the drivers of environmental degradation in the BOBLME. However, there is no centralized regional body with legal personality, such as the CTI-CFF Regional Secretariat. Instead, the BOBP-IGO follows a network coordination model involving focal national agencies in the eight countries and international technical assistance agencies, while FAO provides secretariat services. This model is being reviewed and adapted in the context of a new, second phase called Sustainable Management of BOBLME Programme implemented jointly by FAO and ADB, with support from GEF.

Successes. Phase 1 successfully established mechanisms for cooperation and collaboration between member states, built trust and a shared vision among the eight states, and made good progress on biodiversity and sustainable fishing. Other successes included:

- Improved knowledge of location and status of Marine Protected Areas in the BOBLME through the online MPA Atlas with the WorldFish Center and hosted on the ReefBase website.
- Production of a training manual for the ecosystem-based approach to fisheries management, which has been adopted by the Coral Triangle Initiative on Coral Reefs, Fisheries, and Food Security, and other regional organizations.
- Regional Integrated Coastal Management postgraduate certificate course initiated (which integrates the BOBLME ecosystem-based approach to fisheries management training as a component) in collaboration with Asian Institute for Technology and IUCN.
- Sustainable fisheries management implemented for hilsa and Indian mackerel.
- Regional fisheries and mangrove development programs implemented to support local livelihoods.
- National baseline pollution reports produced to develop sewage management approaches.
- Numerous cross-sector and multidisciplinary stakeholders and partners convened to address key issues under the SAP.

continued on next page

Box 14.3: *continued*

Challenges. Phase 1 concentrated heavily on fisheries and coastal management, with less focus on other key themes, particularly land- and sea-based sources of pollution, integrating integrated coastal management with sustainable land management, and supporting sustainable livelihoods development at scale. While there have been pockets of success, in general there has been limited impact on policy, institutional arrangements, planning and management approaches within the BOBLME (FAO 216).

Lessons Learned.[b] Given the decentralized nature of the approach, national governments have taken limited ownership of the BOBLME Strategic Action Plan. Phase 2 explores and refines a more durable coordination mechanism.

- Countries need to see demonstrable benefits from the strategic plan, in particular a flow of investment to support priority actions. These are addressed in the context of Phase 2, and participation of national governments, other multilateral and bilateral agencies, and nongovernment organizations.
- Dealing with local and national issues should be the priority, with other benefits coming from collaboration between countries as a secondary step.
- Knowledge products and science-based initiatives can take too much time and be too complicated. Instead, the focus should be on what is needed to make management decisions. Improved management systems should be put in place as soon as possible even if not fully developed.

[a] Bay of Bengal Large Marine Ecosystem Project. https://www.boblme.org/About_BOBLME_Brochure_2011.pdf.
[b] FAO (2016).

Sources: The Bay of Bengal Large Marine Ecosystem Project; *The Economist*. 2013. The Bay of Bengal: New Bay Dawning. 27 April; FAO. 2016. *Final Evaluation of Sustainable Management of the Bay of Bengal Large Marine Ecosystem (BOBLME) Project*. Rome.

South Asian Association for Regional Cooperation

The South Asian Association for Regional Cooperation (SAARC) is an intergovernmental organization founded in 1985 dedicated to economic, technological, social, and cultural development, with an emphasis on the collective self-reliance development strategy. It has eight members: Afghanistan, Bangladesh, Bhutan, India, Maldives, Nepal, Pakistan, and Sri Lanka. Although environment is an area of cooperation, there has not been significant focus on the marine environment beyond the 2014 Kathmandu Declaration, in which member states affirmed their commitment to promote the blue economy and the need for collaboration and partnership in this area.

The SAARC environment ministers have not met since September 2011.[25] ADB and SAARC have had a partnership since 2004 to cooperate through consultations and knowledge sharing, and SAARC is involved in two of ADB's regional platforms: South Asia Subregional Economic Cooperation and Central Asia Regional Economic Cooperation (ADB 2019).

Southeast Asia

Indonesia–Malaysia–Thailand Growth Triangle

The Indonesia-Malaysia-Thailand Growth Triangle (IMT-GT) is a subregional framework established in 1993 to accelerate economic cooperation and integration among states and provinces in the three countries. ADB has been involved in the IMT-GT program since its inception and has been a Regional Development Partner since 2007.[26] IMT-GT promotes private sector-led economic growth and the development of the subregion by focusing on agriculture and agro-based industry, tourism, halal products, and services.[27] Priorities related to healthy oceans are tourism and pollution control. IMT-GT's promotion of cross-border tourism has the goal of making the subregion a single tourism destination that is sustainable, inclusive, and competitive. For pollution control, IMT-GT's Green Cities Initiative has assisted five cities—Melaka, Songkhla, Hat Yai, Medan, and Batam—to develop Green City Action Plans with significant private sector investment. All these cities are coastal. The initiative will be expanded to create an extensive network of green cities across the subregion (ASEAN 2017).

In September 2019, ministers expressed interest in developing ocean health initiatives. ADB suggested several areas of focus, including regional cooperation and integration, marine conservation, sustainable tourism, and fisheries management. IMT-GT has adopted a project-based approach to regional integration focused on projects that are scalable, replicable, and sustainable; particularly encouraging projects that include small and medium-sized enterprises as partners and are applicable to

---

[25] SAARC. Area of Cooperation. http://globalsummitryproject.com.s197331.gridserver.com/archive/saarc/saarc-sec.org/areaofcooperation/cat-detail1a12.html?cat_id=54.

[26] ADB. Indonesia-Malaysia-Thailand Growth Triangle (IMT-GT). https://www.adb.org/countries/subregional-programs/imt-gt.

[27] IMT-GT. About IMT-GT. https://imtgt.org/about-imt-gt/.

ocean health and blue economy investments. Having a secretariat as the central point of coordination has enabled IMT-GT to manage its project approach successfully. Effective stakeholder engagement has created a common subregional-focused purpose for all three countries across a range of sectors. It has been especially important for local governments to participate in strategy development and implementation, and to provide a working understanding of subregional issues and policy implementation. Including the private sector as an equal partner has also been important to the initiative's success in fostering economic growth (Centre for IMT-GT Subregional Cooperation 2017).

Brunei Darussalam–Indonesia–Malaysia–Philippines East ASEAN Growth Area

The Brunei Darussalam–Indonesia–Malaysia–Philippines East ASEAN Growth Area (BIMP-EAGA) is a cooperation initiative established in 1994 to accelerate the socioeconomic development of less-developed, marginalized, and geographically remote areas within these four countries. ADB, as the Regional Development Advisor, provides technical and strategic guidance, knowledge- and capacity-building support, and infrastructure project financing for greater connectivity.[28] The BIMP-EAGA Vision for 2025 has three target outcomes: (i) competitive and green manufacturing; (ii) sustainable, competitive and climate-resilient agro-industry and fisheries; and (iii) sustainable tourism. Target outputs relevant to ocean health are: inter-connected ferry services and seaport facilities; sustainable, competitive, and climate-resilient fisheries; and sustainable ecotourism and fishing practices.[29] BIMP-EAGA has had significant achievements over its 26 years. Growing networks of roads, bridges, ports, power interconnections, and telecommunications have enhanced trade and investment across the subregion by reducing the cost of doing business and providing greater opportunities for small and medium-sized enterprises. Collaboration in agro-industries and fisheries, environment, and tourism have helped address shared development challenges.

The BIMP-EAGA Green Cities Initiative includes many coastal cities—such as Kendari in Indonesia and Kota Kinabalu in Malaysia—that have identified pollution management projects, including solid waste management,

---

[28] ADB. Brunei Darussalam–Indonesia–Malaysia–Philippines East ASEAN Growth Area (BIMP-EAGA). https://www.adb.org/countries/subregional-programs/bimp-eaga.

[29] BIMP-EAGA https://www.bimp-eaga.asia/index.php/.

wastewater treatment, and sanitation, that will reduce land-based pollution of the ocean. Lessons that have shaped BIMP-EAGA cooperation include the importance of national governments to fill infrastructure gaps, provide a sound regulatory environment, and resolve issues such as cross-border trade. Activities should support local government priorities and communities' aspirations and encourage local executives to create a conducive local business environment. A strong secretariat, the BIMP-EAGA Facilitation Center, has provided a wide range of coordinative functions across various subregional institutions. Sharing BIMP-EAGA's experiences has improved ASEAN-wide implementation of tested agreements and protocols.[30]

ASEAN Working Group on Coastal and Marine Environments

The ASEAN Working Group on Coastal and Marine Environments, which first convened in 1999, aims to ensure that ASEAN's coastal and marine environments are sustainably managed; that its unique ecosystems, pristine areas, and species are protected; and that its economic activities are sustainably managed. It has also helped instill public awareness of the coastal and marine environment. The working group is a consultative forum to promote coordination and collaboration among ASEAN and other regional marine-related initiatives to ensure a well-coordinated and integrated approach to the conservation and sustainable management of coastal and marine environment.[31] ADB and the ASEAN Secretariat have a memorandum of understanding in place to collaborate on accelerating ASEAN processes in Asia. The ASEAN Heritage Parks Programme serves as a regional network of national protected areas of high conservation importance. Currently, 9 out of 49 declared heritage parks have marine components. However, lack of public awareness about them has led to illegal harvesting of plants and animals, unsustainable tourism, and human–wildlife conflict. To address this, the ASEAN Centre for Biodiversity, as the secretariat, implemented a capacity development project in 2015 to develop and improve Heritage Parks Programme staff capabilities in data curation and management, and raised awareness through a communication, education, and public awareness strategy and action plan (Japan–ASEAN Integration Fund Management Team 2020).

---

[30] BIMP-EAGA. 2017. *BIMP-EAGA Vision 2025*. Manila.

[31] ASEAN. ASEAN Cooperation on Coastal and Marine Environment. https://environment. asean.org/awgcme/.

Summary Analysis

Although the 18 regional cooperation and integration initiatives and case studies described above are quite diverse, some common themes emerged when reviewing their successes and lessons learned in addition to individual experiences that may be useful for others to follow. The main recurring success areas centered around two areas: (i) governance, and (ii) knowledge and capacity building. Lessons learned have been organized according to regional and national governance, knowledge and capacity building, and finance (Table 14.2).

Governance

- Established mechanisms for cooperation and collaboration between member states fostered trust and a shared vision, and made good progress through dialogue, research, increasing knowledge, and transboundary demonstrations.
- Created synergy through multisector cooperation and partnerships to improve governance and implement management programs.
- Identified common priorities and provided a regional framework for cooperation.
- Contributed to subregional economic integration that accelerated economic growth.
- Brought together relevant stakeholders on an equal footing to create dialogue around emerging, cross-cutting ocean issues.
- Inspired similar regional island commitments.

Knowledge and Capacity Building

- Built on lessons from related initiatives in the subregion, global experience, and existing institutional structures and capacity, and used partnerships to bring in expertise and knowledge.
- "Oceans Champions" provided high-level advocacy and attention to ocean priorities, decisions, and processes at national, regional, and international levels; and improved cooperation, coordination, and collaboration.
- Facilitated information exchange, built institutional capacity, and strengthened regional policy dialogue.
- Raised awareness through a communication, education, and public information strategy and action plan.

Table 14.2: Regional Cooperation for Ocean Health, the Blue Economy: Lessons Learned

Regional Governance	National and Local Governance	Knowledge and Capacity Building	Finance
Need multiple and mutually reinforcing objectives addressing environmental, economic, and social dimensions of sustainability.	Focus should be on addressing local and national issues, with regional collaboration as a secondary step.	Knowledge and lessons learned should be shared nationally and across the region, with solutions adapted to local conditions.	Mobilizing financial resources (in the form of donations, endowments, and other mechanisms) raised the profile of conservation to politicians and citizens. This encouraged politicians to prioritize and publicly support the conservation initiative.
Need a strong secretariat to provide a central point of coordination.	Integrate regional priorities with national priorities in as many sectors as possible.	Given the urgency of the issues being faced, improved management systems should be put in place as soon as possible even if they are not fully developed.	
A decentralized structure, although a low-cost and flexible approach, can result in unclear allocation of costs and difficulties in getting members to agree on regional undertakings.	Strengthen national government systems and ownership so they can assume an effective role in project implementation and sustainability.	Bring legislators and other decision makers on field trips to increase understanding and motivation to act.	Diversify financing sources to lower risk, such as tourism taxes, debt swaps/conversions and conservation easements, revenues from fishing licenses, and climate change funds.
Need clear roles, responsibilities, and performance standards to be set among the member countries and secretariat.	National governments' role should fill infrastructure gaps, provide an enabling policy and regulatory environment, and resolve issues such as cross-border trade.		
Need to establish protocols for process management (i.e., conduct of meetings and dispute resolution) to ensure continuity of leadership and participation of key stakeholders.	Local governments should participate in strategy development to ensure that new activities align with their priorities and local communities' aspirations, and provide a working understanding of the subregional context, issues, and policy implementation.		Partner financing is critical to capitalize funds by encouraging other major donors and governments to contribute.
Governance must be strengthened through increased transparency, accountability, and public participation.	Local governments can provide incentives and information on potential markets to create a conducive business environment, scale up good practices, provide technical support and advice, leverage financing, and act as a bridge to national government agencies.		
Stakeholder engagement is crucial for creating a common purpose at a subregional level, across a range of sectors.			

Source: Compiled by authors.

- Improved science-to-management decision-making, such as new fisheries management policies and standardized monitoring protocols and databases.

Regional Prospects: Recommendations and Opportunities

As this brief survey of regional cooperation and integration initiatives shows, a great deal of effort has gone into building and maintaining many different initiatives to facilitate multilateral and multi-stakeholder actions to counter the destruction and overexploitation of marine ecosystems and resources. There are many examples of successful approaches, impactful achievements, and useful lessons learned. However, the key problems facing the oceans remain as pressing as when these initiatives started. Land-based pollution and overexploitation of high-value species—often due to fishing overcapacity,[32] subsidies, illegal unreported and unregulated (IUU), and transboundary industrial-scale fishing—are among the most serious challenges. These are more difficult to address than many land-based problems, mainly because it is very difficult to enforce regulations across huge areas of open ocean and the ocean environment and humans' interaction with it has not been well studied. Also, management of international waters requires strong cooperation mechanisms. Therefore, multi-stakeholder dialogues, partnerships, and intergovernmental agreements and organizations are essential to align currently fragmented actions into substantial, sustainable impacts (ESCAP 2020). A broad range of recommendations to accomplish this are presented below, organized into four key areas: ocean governance, blue economy, knowledge management, and green recovery.

Ocean Governance

Regional cooperation and integration initiatives have strengthened regional oceans governance mainly by improving coordination and collaboration among international, national, and community level stakeholders; generating scientific data; and building capacity. However, they must deal with many governance challenges. The following are some recommendations to make the existing system more effective and efficient. These need to be done

---

[32] Fishing overcapacity occurs when fishing fleets in a given area are capable of harvesting more fish than can be replaced through reproduction.

within existing funding and time constraints or additional resources need to be identified for implementation.

Promote implementation and enforcement of multilateral agreements through regional cooperation and integration. Initiatives are improved by multilateral agreements such as international conventions and agreements, as mentioned in the Oceans Governance and Frameworks section. However, weak implementation and enforcement of their provisions have hampered efforts to address pressing transboundary issues. Regional organizations should strengthen the implementation, monitoring, and enforcement of multilateral agreements by providing a more effective enabling environment, technical assistance, and support for action at the national and regional level. Regional cooperation and integration is needed to build capacity for enforcement where it is most needed within a given jurisdiction or area of coverage, and international agreements need to be translated into local and national laws to enable enforcement on the ground (ESCAP 2020).

Improve institutional capacity. Regional cooperation and integration initiatives and mechanisms tend to have inadequate capacity and financial and human resources to effectively implement their mandates, and often operate using slow and bureaucratic management systems. The need for well-run institutions and governance mechanisms is a challenge that also faces many countries in the region, which have vastly different levels of expertise. To overcome these challenges, better management systems should be put in place to optimize the use of human, financial, and technical resources (UNEP 2016).

Strengthen and institutionalize coordination mechanisms. Another key challenge is the organizational complexity of regional oceans governance, which is especially high in the Pacific and East Asian subregions. Creating new initiatives may add costs in time, effort, and resources that outweigh their usefulness given existing organizations that cover overlapping geographic areas. Although there is currently no overarching framework for cooperation, regional oceans governance mechanisms have facilitated coordination and collaboration. For example, UNEP Regional Seas Programmes and regional fisheries bodies have formalized partnerships through memoranda of understanding and other instruments. These efforts should be strengthened. This can be done by clarifying the roles and responsibilities of the various organizations and encouraging the sharing of data among organizations that protect the same species or have overlapping geographic areas. Organizations can attend each other's meetings, define specific areas of cooperation, and institutionalize mechanisms that work well.

Enhance transparency and strengthen relationships with stakeholders. Regional cooperation and integration initiatives should increase stakeholders' inputs into decision-making by improving working relationships with stakeholder organizations and formal observers who attend their official meetings. At a minimum, stakeholders should be given access to concise, readable meeting reports in a timely manner. Meaningful private sector participation helps promote investment and economic growth in the subregional area. Relationships with countries that are not formal members of regional intergovernmental organizations can be improved by developing clear mechanisms to grant them cooperating status so these countries can enjoy benefits of participation equal to their compliance with specific agreements. For example, a noncontracting party can implement restrictions on IUU vessels that is comparable to the obligations of formal member countries.

Blue Economy

Private sector investments have made a strong impact on achieving the SDGs in the region's coastal and marine environments (PEMSEA 2019b), but governments need to create a stronger enabling environment to grow the blue economy. This must support fiscal policies, including taxes and subsidies, that promote more environmentally and socially sustainable business models and products for sectors that impact the ocean. About 40% of government support to fisheries pays for input subsidies that often contribute to unsustainable fishing—while also benefiting large producers over small fishers. The World Trade Organization is currently negotiating rules on harmful fisheries subsidies, which is an important step toward meeting the SDGs. In the meantime, governments should reform their support policies by redirecting support away from damaging and destructive economic activities and tax harmful activities in the oceans. To support these reforms, the Organisation for Economic Co-operation and Development (OECD) has launched the Sustainable Ocean for All Initiative. It examines the policy frameworks and economic instruments (including taxes, fees, and charges) adopted by developing countries in the ocean economy and assesses how countries can improve the sustainability of their ocean economies (Gurría 2020).

Promote inclusive and resilient value chains to enable economic recovery. Inclusive and resilient international and regional trade is vital to overcome the immediate consequences of the COVID-19 downturn and tackle longer-term challenges to international trade such as in fisheries and shipping. Regional cooperation and integration initiatives described in this chapter can enable this by supporting international and regional trade agreements, including new ones such as for digital services. They can support more inclusive and resilient value chains to spur economic growth by encouraging their member countries to develop clear and consistent standards and procedures for international trade. Initiatives can make interventions when necessary, such as to resolve cross-border trade issues. This should be done with a focus on small and medium-sized enterprises and vulnerable populations, and on collaborations to address critical waste management and natural resource management issues to improve ocean health and strengthen the blue economy.

Strengthen the shipping industry's environmental standards. The shipping industry is critical to the blue economy in Asia and the Pacific. However, rapid growth in trade and connectivity creates concerns over the industry's environmental impacts, safety, and efficiency. There is growing demand to reduce marine-related accidents and optimize operations. In addition, the Pacific island countries remain isolated from global and regional maritime trade. Regional dialogue among governments and the global and regional shipping industry is essential to develop tangible solutions for increasing marine connectivity for the Pacific island countries and making it more inclusive, safe, and efficient. The sustainability of the maritime transport sector also depends on addressing the environmental impacts of shipping on the oceans, including carbon dioxide emissions, pollution, and the transportation of invasive species. These reforms can be supported by regional cooperation and integration and the following international agreements: the International Convention for the Prevention of Pollution from Ships, the International Convention for the Control and Management of Ships' Ballast Water and Sediments, and the International Convention for the Safety of Life at Sea. All three were developed by the International Maritime Organization (ESCAP 2020).

Coordinate action and circular economy approaches to dramatically reduce marine plastic pollution. Plastic waste costs $13 billion in annual damage to marine ecosystems, and the overall natural capital cost of plastic use in consumer goods alone is $75 billion (UNEP 2014). The total cost to society of the production of plastic consumer goods is much higher. Other major societal costs come from air pollution from incinerating plastics, and greenhouse gas emissions from extracting and processing raw materials (Carr 2019). In addition, marine plastic pollution has reduced marine ecosystem service delivery by roughly 1% to 5%, for an annual loss to society of $500 billion to $2.5 trillion (Beaumont et al. 2019). To reduce these huge losses, effective national policies and frameworks need to be developed and enforced.

Several countries in the region, such as Indonesia, the Philippines, and Thailand, have or are developing national plans of action on waste management, circular economy, and marine debris. The Global Plastic Action Partnership, launched in 2018, is a multi-stakeholder platform that aims to translate political commitments into action. It has already partnered with the governments of Indonesia and Viet Nam for their respective National Plastic Action Partnerships.[33] Indonesia's efforts include a multi-agency Financing Task Force, co-chaired by ADB, to develop a financing road map to reach Indonesia's plastic leakage reduction targets and circular economy ambitions.

Regional and international dialogues and partnerships are needed to share and scale up innovative national policies and scientific and technological advancements to reduce plastic waste in the marine environment (ESCAP 2020). International conventions and multilateral agreements on marine pollution also need to be enforced. These include the Basel Convention on the Control of Transboundary Movements of Hazardous Wastes and Their Disposal, the ASEAN Framework of Action on Marine Debris (ESCAP 2020), and the Pacific Regional Action Plan for Marine Litter 2018–2025 (SPREP 2018).

Knowledge Sharing

Currently, the world has better maps of Mars and Venus than the ocean floor (Pierceall 2017). There are considerable data gaps in ocean governance and resource use, and existing data are usually fragmented, siloed, or difficult to access. This deficiency limits our understanding of coastal and marine issues and how one country's decisions and actions impact others.

---

[33] Global Plastic Action Partnership. GPAP: About. https://globalplasticaction.org/about/.

Regional data-sharing systems are needed to track SDG progress and improve management of ocean resources. Considering the limited data available, the region will not achieve SDG 14 by 2030. Significant information gaps exist in the areas of ocean acidification, sea level rise, fisheries and fishing-related activities, and economic benefits for small island developing states and the least-developed countries. Transboundary industrial-scale fisheries generally collect a large amount of data but face restrictions in sharing it, while small coastal fisheries do not have enough information. Limited data sharing reduces the opportunity for integrated analysis of fisheries needed to improve management (ESCAP 2020). Accordingly, more open systems for sharing and harmonizing data are needed across national statistical systems, as well as improved collection and management of data by countries (ESCAP 2020). Better data collection and sharing will also support innovations in marine science and technology. There is demand for innovation in oil spill tracking, circular economy, and underwater drones, to name a few (Mill 2018).

Campaigns raise awareness and promote cooperation. The UN Decade of Ocean Science for Sustainable Development (2021–2030) is an opportunity to raise public awareness and accelerate cooperation among ocean stakeholders to use ocean science to help countries improve conditions for sustainable development ocean resources. Regional events, such as the Asia Pacific Day for the Ocean, are another opportunity for exchange of information, good practices, data, and statistics to accelerate progress toward achieving SDG 14 (ESCAP 2020). International events such as the UN World Ocean Conference and Our Ocean also provide a venue for leaders to discuss and make further commitments to ocean health.

COVID-19: A Blue Lens for Green Recovery

COVID-19 lockdowns have had a devastating effect on economies worldwide, creating an urgent need to create jobs and livelihood opportunities that meet new economic realities and ways of working, especially for those in the informal sector. This is perhaps a once-in-a-generation opportunity to make transformative investments in much more resilient and sustainable systems to improve the overall well-being and quality of life for everyone. The PRC and Republic of Korea are taking bold steps to invest stimulus funds in environmentally sound investments and green jobs (Sambhi 2020). But for less-developed countries in Asia and the Pacific, achieving transformational change through a green recovery will require cooperation and collaboration with other countries, international organizations, and a wide range of partners. And given the importance of the blue economy in Asia and the Pacific, green recovery in the region must also apply a "blue lens" and integrate support for ocean-related industries (Kemper 2020).

As described by the One Health approach, public health is dependent on well-functioning, healthy ecosystems (Settele et al. 2020). Therefore, restoring and sustaining marine ecosystems can help countries recover from the COVID-19 crisis, both in terms of health and economic recovery. By providing livelihoods, food security, and disaster resiliency, healthy oceans can prevent millions of people in the Asia and Pacific region from sliding into poverty as a result of the economic crisis prompted by the pandemic. For example, investments in nature-based solutions such as coral reef and mangrove restoration can substantially increase fish stocks in coastal areas. Regional cooperation must support these endeavors.

Conclusion

This chapter has presented a broad range of regional cooperation and integration initiatives that have developed collaborative approaches to managing ocean resources and addressing issues inherent to regional public goods, such as transboundary pollution. In general, these entities have been useful for bringing countries together for cooperative action by providing a structure and venue for dialogue and decision-making. Dialogues were also more successful when nongovernment organizations and the private sector were included and given relatively equal standing with government. As a result, decision-making was more transparent and information was shared widely. However, most entities struggled with financial sustainability of their operations, integration with national-level priorities and actions, and developing a structure with a good balance between a strong secretariat and semiautonomous subregional or national nodes.

Key recommendations and actions based on these observations are to (i) further strengthen the institutional capacity of regional coordination entities while raising their profile and support from key national decision makers, (ii) mobilize sufficient funds and establish financing structures to ensure financial sustainability, and (iii) improve impact and sustainable investment through job creation for communities dependent on ocean resources and ecosystems—especially those who have lost livelihoods because of COVID-19. In addition, regional cooperation and integration to improve ocean health and achieve SDG 14: Life Below Water should be strengthened by institutionalizing consistent measures for sharing experiences and lessons learned and coordinate efforts among the many initiatives working for common goals in the region. This is critical to increase synergy and alignment of priorities and avoid overlap, duplication, and working at cross purposes.

ADB and other multilateral development institutions can facilitate greater regional cooperation and the development of regional public goods by providing more knowledge support and financing for ocean health initiatives and by playing the role of an honest broker and coordinator to increase trust and help regional economies take collective action to deal with transnational challenges. Multilateral developments banks can also add value by bringing different sectors together to develop holistic solutions, with a focus on collaboration toward achieving SDG 14 and other cross-cutting SDGs.

Asia and the Pacific has greatly benefited from regional cooperation and integration through strengthened economies, stronger country connections, and the establishment of shared goals and priorities, whether economic, environmental, or social. The COVID-19 pandemic now calls for even greater collaborative efforts and presents an opportunity for countries, regions, and subregions to redesign their economies for recovery toward a sustainable green and blue future. Addressing ocean health as well as the climate crisis is vital to prevent or mitigate future crises and protect the most vulnerable in our interconnected world.

References

Abraham, A. 2015. *Stock-Take of CTI-CFF Programs and Projects: Strategic Review of Progress and Future Directions.* Jakarta: Coral Triangle Initiative on Coral Reefs, Fisheries and Food Security (CTI-CFF) Interim Regional Secretariat.

Andrew, N. et al. 2019. Coastal Proximity of Populations in 22 Pacific Island Countries and Territories. PLoS ONE 14 (9). e0223249.

Anwar, D. F. 2006. Resource Issues and Ocean Governance in Asia Pacific: An Indonesian Perspective. *Contemporary Southeast Asia.* 28 (3). pp. 466–489.

Arnold, C. 2020. Horseshoe Crab Blood is key to Making a COVID-19 Vaccine—but the Ecosystem may Suffer. *National Geographic.* 2 July.

Asian Development Bank (ADB). 2010. *Coral Triangle Initiative Brochure.* Manila.

——. 2016. *Pacific Economic Monitor.* Manila.

——. 2018. *Asian Economic Integration Report 2018: Toward Optimal Provision of Regional Public Goods in Asia and the Pacific.* Manila.

——. 2019. *13th Informal Meeting of the South Asian Association for Regional Cooperation (SAARC) Finance Ministers—Shixin Chen.* Manila.

——. 2020. *Asian Development Outlook 2020.* Manila.

——. *ADB's Work in Regional Cooperation and Integration.* https://www.adb.org/themes/regional-cooperation/overview.

Asia-Pacific Economic Cooperation (APEC) Ocean and Fisheries Working Group. 2019. *Marine Sustainable Development Report 2: Supporting Implementation of Sustainable Development Goal 14 and Related Goals in APEC.* Singapore.

——. 2020. *Ocean and Fisheries.* Manila.

Association of Southeast Asian Nations (ASEAN). 2017. *Joint Statement Tenth Indonesia-Malaysia-Thailand Growth Triangle Summit*. Jakarta.

———. *ASEAN Cooperation on Coastal and Marine Environment*. https://environment.asean.org/awgcme/.

Bay of Bengal Large Marine Ecosystem (BOBLME) Project. https://www.boblme.org/.

Beaumont, N. et al. 2019. Global Ecological, Social and Economic Impacts of Marine Plastic. *Marine Pollution Bulletin*. 142 (1). pp. 189–195.

Bennett, N. J. et al. 2020. The COVID-19 Pandemic, Small-Scale Fisheries and Coastal Fishing Communities. *Coastal Management*. 48 (4). pp. 336–347.

Boshell, F. et al. 2020. Unlocking the Potential of Ocean Energy: From Megawatts to Gigawatts. *Energy Post EU*. 3 June.

Breitburg, D. et al. 2018. Declining Oxygen in the Global Ocean and Coastal Waters. *Science*. 359 (6371).

Brunei Darussalam–Indonesia–Malaysia–Philippines East ASEAN Growth Area. 2017. *BIMP-EAGA Vision 2025*. Manila.

Carr, S. 2019. What is Marine Plastic Pollution Costing Us? The Impacts of Marine Plastic on the Blue Economy. *The Skimmer*. 12 (6). Woodinville, Washington: Open Communications for the Ocean.

Commission for the Conservation of Southern Bluefin Tuna (CCSBT). 2015. *Strategic Plan for the Commission for the Conservation of Southern Bluefin Tuna 2015–2020*. Canberra.

———. *Origins of the Convention*. https://www.ccsbt.org/en/content/origins-convention.

Coral Triangle Initiative on Coral Reefs, Fisheries and Food Security (CTI-CFF). 2009. *Regional Plan of Action*. Jakarta: Coral Triangle Initiative on Coral Reefs, Fisheries and Food Security (CTI-CFF) Interim Regional Secretariat. http://coraltriangleinitiative.org/rpoa.

Centre for Indonesia–Malaysia–Thailand Growth Triangle Subregional Cooperation. 2017. *IMT-GT Implementation Blueprint 2017–2021.* Putrajaya, Malaysia.

Convention on Biological Diversity. 2010. *Aichi Targets: Target 11.* Rio de Janeiro.

Convention on International Trade in Endangered Species of Wild Fauna and Flora (CITES). 2020. *The CITES Species.* Geneva. https://www. cites.org/eng/disc/species.php.

Convention on Migratory Species (CMS). 2020. *Marine Migratory Species.* Bonn. https://www.cms.int/en/document/marine-migratory-species.

De Poorter, M., C. Darby, and J. MacKay. 2009. *Marine Menace: Alien Invasive Species in the Marine Environment.* Geneva: IUCN.

De Riddler, K., and S. Nindang. 2018. "Southeast Asia's Fisheries Near Collapse from Overfishing." *The Asia Foundation.* 28 March.

Degnarain, N. 2020. Will Ocean Seabed Mining Delay the Discovery of Potential Coronavirus Vaccines? *Forbes.* 2 March.

Food and Agriculture Organization of the United Nations (FAO). 2002. *Report of the Second Ad Hoc Meeting of Intergovernmental Organizations on Work Programmes Related to Subsidies in Fisheries.* Rome: FAO.

——. 2016. *Agreement on Port State Measures to Prevent, Deter and Eliminate Illegal, Unreported and Unregulated Fishing.* Revised Edition. Rome.

——. 2016. Final Evaluation of Sustainable Management of the Bay of Bengal Large Marine Ecosystem (BOBLME) Project. Rome: FAO.

——. 2018. The Global Status of Seaweed Production, Trade, and Utilization. *Globefish Research Programme.* 124. Rome: FAO.

——. 2019. "Asia-Pacific Revenues and Livelihoods Threatened as Billions Lost Annually to Illegal, Unreported, Unregulated Fishing." Rome: FAO. 5 June.

——. 2020. *The State of World Fisheries and Aquaculture 2020. Sustainability in Action.* Rome: FAO.

———. *Fish and Human Nutrition*. Rome: FAO. http://www.fao.org/fileadmin/user_upload/newsroom/docs/BlueGrowthNutritionRev2.pdf.

———. *IUU Fishing. Code of Conduct for Responsible Fisheries*. Rome: FAO. http://www.fao.org/iuu-fishing/international-framework/code-of-conduct-for-responsible-fisheries/en/.

FAO, International Labour Organization (ILO), and International Organization for Migration (IOM). 2019. *Joint Statement on the International Day for the Fight against IUU Fishing*. Rome. 5 June.

Fortes, M. D. et al. 2018. Seagrass in Southeast Asia: A Review of Status and Knowledge Gaps, and a Road Map for Conservation. *Botanica Marina*. 61(3). pp. 268–88.

Garner, A. et al. 2018. Evolution of 21st Century Sea Level Rise Projections. *Earth's Future*. 6 (11). pp. 1603–1615.

Gastelumendi, J. et al. 2012. Case Study Report: Micronesian Conservation Trust. A joint Nature Conservancy; United Nations Development Programme; Micronesian Conservation Trust Working Paper.

Gillett, R., and M. Ikatonga Tauati. 2018. *Fisheries of the Pacific Islands Regional and national information*. Apia: FAO.

Global Plastic Action Partnership. *GPAP: About*. https://globalplasticaction.org/about/.

Gombos, M. 2020. *Micronesia Challenge Evaluation: A Stakeholder-Based Review of a Pioneering Regional Conservation Initiative*. Denver, Colorado: Sea Change Consulting.

Gourdon, K., and C. Steidl. 2019. Global Value Chains and the Shipbuilding Industry. *OECD Science, Technology and Industry Working Papers No. 2019/08*. Organisation for Economic Co-operation and Development, Paris.

Gurría, A. 2020. Virtual Ocean Dialogues on Finance and the Sustainable Blue Economy. 1 June. Paris: OECD. https://www.oecd.org/about/secretary-general/virtual-ocean-dialogues-on-finance-and-sustainable-blue-economy-june-2020.htm.

Hudson, A. 2020. The Ocean and COVID-19. United Nations Development Programme. 8 June. https://www.undp.org/content/undp/en/home/blog/2020/the-ocean-and-covid-19.html.

Ibarhim, R. 1995. International/Regional Cooperation to Oil Spill Response in the Straits of Malacca: An Overview. In *Oil Spill Symposium 1995: International Cooperation and the Current Set-up by the Oil Industry.* Tokyo. 23–24 March 1995.

International Maritime Organization. 1973. *The International Convention for the Prevention of Pollution from Ships.* London. http://www.imo.org/en/About/Conventions/ListOfConventions/Pages/International-Convention-for-the-Prevention-of-Pollution-from-Ships-(MARPOL).aspx.

——. *Maritime Security and Piracy.* http://www.imo.org/en/OurWork/Security/Pages/MaritimeSecurity.aspx.

International Registries, Inc. 2017. The Republic of the Marshall Islands Registry Now World's 2nd Largest. Reston: International Registries, Inc. https://www.register-iri.com/blog/the-republic-of-the-marshall-islands-registry-now-worlds-2nd-largest/.

Indian Ocean Tuna Commission (IOTC). 2016. *Report of the 2nd IOTC Performance Review.* Seychelles.

——. *Structure of the Commission.* https://www.iotc.org/about-iotc/structure-commission.

International Tanker Owners Pollution Federation. 2000. NATUNA SEA, Indonesia/Singapore/Malaysia. https://www.itopf.org/in-action/case-studies/case-study/natuna-sea-indonesiasingaporemalaysia-2000/.

International Union for Conservation of Nature (IUCN). 2015. Parties to the Nauru Agreement (PNA). Interview with Maurice Brownjon. 2 June. https://www.iucn.org/content/parties-nauru-agreement-pna-interview-maurice-brownjon.

——. *Issues Brief: Ocean and Climate Change.* https://www.iucn.org/resources/issues-briefs/ocean-and-climate-change.

Japan–ASEAN Integration Fund Management Team. 2020. *ASEAN Strengthens the ASEAN Heritage Parks Programme through Capacity Building and Information Development*. 29 June. https://environment. asean.org/asean-strengthens-the-asean-heritage-parks-programme-through-capacity-building-and-information-development/.

Jarret, I. 2020. Fisheries Subsidies Reform Could Reduce Overfishing and Illegal Fishing Case Studies Find. *Pew Charitable Trusts*. 22 July.

Jaspars, M. et al. 2016. The Marine Biodiscovery Pipeline and Ocean Medicines of Tomorrow. *Journal of the Marine Biological Association of the United Kingdom*. 96 (1). pp. 151–158.

Kassam, A. 2020. More Masks than Jellyfish: Coronavirus Waste Ends up in Ocean. *The Guardian*. 8 June.

Kemper, K. 2020. Why We Need a Blue Recovery. *World Bank Blogs*. 1 July.

Kiong, J. and K. Saparudin. 2010. Major Oil Spills in the Straits of Singapore. *Singapore Infopedia*. https://eresources.nlb.gov.sg/infopedia/articles/SIP_1101_2010-09-06.html.

Micronesia Conservation Trust. 2020. *The Federated States of Micronesia Sixth National Report to the Convention on Biological Diversity*. February.

Lamb, J. B. 2018. Plastic Waste Associated with Disease on Coral Reefs. *Science*. 359 (6374). pp. 460–462.

Lascelles, B. et al. 2014. Migratory Marine Species: Their Status, Threats and Conservation Management Needs. *Aquatic Conservation Marine and Freshwater Ecosystems* 24 (2). pp. 111–127.

Lee, H. L. 2019. Asia Pacific Remains Top Shipping Casualty Losses in 2018: Allianz. *Seatrade Maritime News*. 4 June.

Leung, H. 2019. Southeast Asia Doesn't Want to Be the World's Dumping Ground. Here's How Some Countries Are Pushing Back. *Time Magazine*. 3 June.

Majkowski, J. 2007. *Global Fishery Resources of Tuna and Tuna-Like Species*. Rome: Food and Agriculture Organization.

Marine Biology Conservation Society. 2020. *Marine Biodiversity*. https://marinebio.org/conservation/marine-conservation-biology/biodiversity/.

Masson-Delmotte, V. et al. 2018. *Global Warming of 1.5°C. An IPCC Special Report*. Geneva: Intergovernmental Panel on Climate Change.

Mill, P. 2018. Saving the Seas: New technologies to Protect the Ocean. *Singularity Hub*. 15 December. https://singularityhub.com/2018/12/15/saving-the-seas-new-technologies-to-protect-the-oceans/.

National Oceanic and Atmospheric Administration Marine Debris Program. 2014. *Ingestion: Occurrence and Health Effects of Anthropogenic Debris Ingested by Marine Organisms*. Silver Spring, Maryland. https://marinedebris.noaa.gov/file/2318/download?token=VQeHMU9J.

National Oceanic and Atmospheric Administration Office of Response and Restoration. 2015. How Does Oil Get into the Ocean?, Silver Spring, Maryland. https://response.restoration.noaa.gov/about/media/how-does-oil-get-ocean.html.

National Oceanic Atmospheric and Administration-US Department of Commerce. Ocean Acidification. https://www.noaa.gov/education/resource-collections/ocean-coasts/ocean-acidification.

Nickson, A. 2018. Pacific Bluefin Tuna Stock Remains Highly Depleted, New Science Shows. *The Pew Charitable Trusts*. 21 May. https://www.pewtrusts.org/en/research-and-analysis/articles/2018/05/21/pacific-bluefin-tuna-stock-remains-highly-depleted-new-science-shows.

Nincic, D. 2013. Maritime Security: Current Threats and Implications. *The Pacific Maritime Magazine*. 1 October. https://www.pacmar.com/story/2013/10/01/features/maritime-security-current-threats-and-implications/184.html.

Office of the Pacific Ocean Commissioner (OPOC). https://opocbluepacific.net/office-of-pacific-ocean-commissioner/.

Organisation for Economic Co-operation and Development (OECD). 2016. *The Ocean Economy in 2030*. Paris: OECD Publishing.

———. 2018. *Making Development Co-operation Work for Small Island Developing States.* Paris: OECD Publishing. https://www.oecd-ilibrary. org/development/making-development-co-operation-work-for-small-island-developing-states_9789264287648-en.

Partnerships in Environmental Management for the Seas of East Asia (PEMSEA). 2018a. *Scaling up the implementation of the Sustainable Development Strategy for the Seas of East Asia (SDS-SEA) Mid Term Review Final Report.* Quezon City, Philippines.

———. 2018b. *SDS-SEA Sustainable Development Strategy for the Seas of East Asia Implementation Plan 2018–2022.* Quezon City, Philippines: PEMSEA.

———. 2019a. *PEMSEA in Action: PEMSEA Annual Report 2018.* Quezon City, Philippines: PEMSEA.

———. 2019b. "11th Partnership Council Meeting Report on Agenda Item: 9.0 (Technical Session): PEMSEA Post-2020 Futures Strategy and Report". Quezon City, Philippines: PEMSEA.

———. http://www.pemsea.org/.

Parties to the Nauru Agreement (PNA). 2011. 3 PNA Countries Close Their Waters to Foreign Tuna Fleets to Maintain Sustainable Fishing Limits. 21 November. https://pnatuna.com/node/76.

———. About Us. www.pnatuna.com.

The Pew Charitable Trusts. 2012. FAQ: What is a Regional Fishery Management Organization? *Fact Sheet.* 23 February.

Pew Charitable Trusts. 2016. *Protecting Ocean Life in the High Seas.* Washington, DC.

Pierceall, K. 2017. We Have Better Maps of Mars than of the Ocean Floor. Drones Could Change That. *The Virginian-Pilot.* 25 April.

Ramani, V. 2019. Troubled Waters: Piracy and Maritime Security in Southeast Asia. *Kontinentalist.* 22 August. https://kontinentalist.com/stories/troubled-waters-piracy-and-maritime-security-in-southeast-asia.

Rana, K.J., R. Grainger, and A. Crispoldi-Hotta. 1998. *Current Methods and Constraints for Monitoring Production from Inland Capture Fisheries and Aquaculture*. Rome: Food and Agriculture Organization.

Ridings, P. et al. 2018. *Report of the South Pacific Regional Fisheries Management Organisation Performance Review Panel*. Wellington, New Zealand.

Rose, J. 2018. Caught in the Net: Slavery on Southeast Asian Seas. *The Interpreter*. 31 October. https://www.lowyinstitute.org/the-interpreter/caught-net-slavery-southeast-asian-seas.

Sambhi, S. 2020. How Green are Asia's Post-Covid Economic Recovery Plans? *Eco-Business*. 26 June. https://www.eco-business.com/news/how-green-are-asias-post-covid-economic-recovery-plans/?sw-signup=true.

Sandler, T. 2003. Assessing the Optimal Provision of Public Goods: In Search of the Holy Grail. In *Providing Global Public Goods: Managing Globalization, edited by* I. Kaul, P. Conceicao, K. Le Goulven, and R. U. Mendoza. New York: Oxford University Press.

Sanford, E., J. Sones, M. García-Reyes, J. Goddard, and J. Largier. 2019. "Widespread Shifts in the Coastal Biota of Northern California during the 2014–2016 Marine Heatwaves." *Scientific Reports* 9 (4216). https://www.nature.com/articles/s41598-019-40784-3.

Schmidt, C., T. Krauth, and S. Wagner. 2017. Export of Plastic Debris by Rivers into the Sea. *Environmental Science & Technology* 51 (21): 12246–53. https://www.gwern.net/docs/economics/2017-schmidt.pdf.

Schrijver, N. 2016. Managing the Global Commons: Common Good or Common Sink? *Third World Quarterly* 37 (7): 1252–67. https://www.tandfonline.com/doi/full/10.1080/01436597.2016.1154441.

Schwabl, P., S. Köppel, P Königschofer, T. Bucsics, M. Trauner, T. Reiberger, et al. 2019. Detection of Various Microplastics in Human Stool. *Annals of Internal Medicine* 171 (7): 453–57. https://www.acpjournals.org/doi/abs/10.7326/M19-0618.

Secretariat of the Pacific Regional Environment Programme (SPREP). 2016. Battling Invasive Species in the Pacific: Outcomes of the Regional GEF-

PAS IAS Project. In *Prevention, Control and Management of Invasive Species in the Pacific Islands 2011–2016*. Apia, Samoa: SPREP. https://www.sprep.org/attachments/Publications/BEM/battling-invasive-species-pacific.pdf.

———. 2018. *Pacific Regional Action Plan for Marine Litter 2018–2025*. https://www.sprep.org/attachments/Circulars/prap_marine_litter.pdf.

———. https://www.sprep.org/information-portals.

Settele, J., S. Diaz, E. Brondizio, and P. Daszak. 2020. IPBES Guest Article: COVID-19 Stimulus Measures Must Save Lives, Protect Livelihoods, and Safeguard Nature to Reduce the Risk of Future Pandemics. *Intergovernmental Science-Policy Platform on Biodiversity and Ecosystem Services*. 27 April. https://ipbes.net/covid19stimulus.

Simon, N. et al. 2018. *No More Plastics in the Ocean: Gaps in Global Plastic Governance and Options for a Legally Binding Agreement to Eliminate Marine Plastic Pollution*. Berlin: Adelphi.

Solano, G. and C. Torchia. 2020. 260 Chinese Boats Fish Near Galapagos: Ecuador on Alert. *The Washington Post*. 31 July.

South Asia Co-operative Environment Programme (SACEP). 2018. *Towards Litter Free Indian Ocean: Summary of the Regional Marine Litter Action Plan for SAS Region*. Colombo: SACEP.

Spalding, M. et al. 2017. Mapping the Global Value and Distribution of Coral Reef Tourism. *Marine Policy*. 82 (1). pp. 104–113.

Strong, A. and S. Minnemeyer. 2015. Satellite Data Reveals State of the World's Mangroves. *World Resources Institute*. 20 February. https://www.wri.org/blog/2015/02/satellite-data-reveals-state-world-s-mangrove-forests.

Sustainable Hawaii Initiative and Micronesia Challenge (MC). *Learning Exchange (LEX) Report*. Unpublished. https://data.nodc.noaa.gov/coris/library/NOAA/CRCP/NMFS/PIRO/Projects/30041/PIMPAC2018_Learning_Exchange_Sustainable_Hawaii_Initiative_Micronesia_Challenge.pdf.

Swain, A. 2002. "Southern Africa Through Green Lenses." In *Theory, Change and Southern Africa's Future*, edited by P. Vale, L. Swatuk, and B. Oden. Houndmills: Palgrave.

The Economist. 2013. The Bay of Bengal: New Bay Dawning. 27 April. https://www.economist.com/asia/2013/04/27/new-bay-dawning.

United Nations (UN). 1995. *UN Conference on Straddling Fish Stocks and Highly Migratory Fish Stocks: Overview*. New York. https://www.un.org/Depts/los/convention_agreements/convention_overview_fish_stocks.htm.

———. 2015. *About the Sustainable Development Goals*. https://www.un.org/sustainabledevelopment/sustainable-development-goals/.

UN Conference on Trade and Development (UNCTAD). 2019. *Review of Maritime Transport*. New York.

———. Oceans Economy and Fisheries. https://unctad.org/en/Pages/DITC/Trade-and-Environment/Oceans-Economy.aspx.

UN Conference on Environment and Development. *Agenda 21: Programme of Action for Sustainable Development*. 1992. New York: UN Department of Public Information.

UN Division for Ocean Affairs and the Law of the Sea. 1982. *United Nations Convention on the Law of the Seas: Overview and Full Text*. New York: UN General Assembly.

UN Economic and Social Commission for Asia and the Pacific (ESCAP). 2020. *Changing Sails: Accelerating Regional Actions for Sustainable Oceans in Asia and the Pacific*. Bangkok.

UN Environment Programme (UNEP). 2014. *Valuing Plastics: The Business Case for Measuring, Managing and Disclosing Plastic Use in the Consumer Goods Industry*. Nairobi.

———. 2016. *Regional Oceans Governance: Making Regional Seas Programmes, Regional Fishery Bodies and Large Marine Ecosystem Mechanisms Work Better Together*. Nairobi.

———. 2017. *Terminal Evaluation of the UN Environment GEF Project Micronesia Challenge: Sustainable Finance Systems for Island Protected Area Management*. Nairobi.

———. 2019. *Report of the 24th Intergovernmental Meeting of the Coordinating Body on the Seas of East Asia*. Nairobi.

———. 2020. *Report of the Executive Director of the United Nations Environment Programme on the Progress in the Implementation of the Northwest Pacific Action Plan in 2018–2019*. Nairobi.

———. *About NOWPAP Environment*. https://www.unenvironment.org/nowpap/who-we-are/about-nowpap-environment.

UN Framework Convention on Climate Change (UNFCCC). 2018. Oceans, Coastal Areas and Ecosystems. New York. https://www4.unfccc.int/sites/NWPStaging/Pages/oceans-page.aspx.

UN News. 2020. COVID-19 Could Help Turn the Tide on Ocean Health in Asia-Pacific. 13 May. https://news.un.org/en/story/2020/05/1063832.

UN Office of the High Representative for the Least Developed Countries, Landlocked Developing Countries and Small Island Developing States (UN-OHRLLS). 2015. *SIDS in Numbers: Climate Change Edition*. New York.

UN Environmental Protection Agency. *Basic Information about Nonpoint Source (NPS) Pollution*. https://www.epa.gov/nps/basic-information-about-nonpoint-source-nps-pollution.

Vince, J. et al. 2017. Ocean Governance in the South Pacific Region: Progress and Plans for Action. *Marine Policy* 79 (1). pp. 40-45.

Western and Central Pacific Fisheries Commission (WCPFC) Secretariat. 2019. *2019 Annual Report of the Executive Director*. Federated States of Micronesia.

———. *About WCPFC*. https://www.wcpfc.int/about-wcpfc.

World Tourism Organization (UNWTO). *International Tourism Receipts*. https://www.unwto.org/global-and-regional-tourism-performance.

Wongruang, P. 2018. Special Report: Whale Sharks Threatened with Extinction. *The Nation, Thailand.* 26 May.

World Economic Forum. 2019. The Travel and Tourism Competitiveness Report 2019.

World Politics Review. 2018. *Why Southeast Asia Remains a Hotbed for Piracy.* 8 February.

Worldwide Fund for Nature (WWF). *Coral Triangle: Facts.*

———. *Marine Problems: Coastal and Tourism Development.*

Index

Boxes, figures, notes, and tables are indicated by b, f, n, and t following the page number.

www.ingramcontent.com/pod-product-compliance
Lightning Source LLC
Chambersburg PA
CBHW040931050426
42334CB00060B/3133